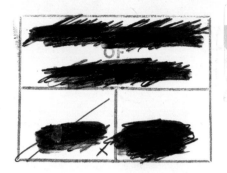

A SECOND TREASURY
OF KNITTING PATTERNS

also by Barbara G. Walker
A TREASURY OF KNITTING PATTERNS

A Second Treasury
of Knitting Patterns

 BARBARA G. WALKER

Photography by William J. Williams

CHARLES SCRIBNER'S SONS · NEW YORK

Macmillan Publishing Company
866 Third Avenue, New York, NY 10022
Collier Macmillan Canada, Inc.

Library of Congress Catalog Card Number 75-102725

ISBN 0-684-16938-x

Macmillan books are available at special discounts for
bulk purchases for sales promotions, premiums, fund
raising, or educational use. For details, contact:

Special Sales Director
Macmillan Publishing Company
866 Third Avenue
New York, NY 10022

10   9   8

Printed in the United States of America

TO THE FURTHER ENRICHMENT
OF A BELOVED CRAFT
THIS BOOK IS HOPEFULLY DEDICATED

ACKNOWLEDGEMENTS

Many have contributed to the making of this book. I am grateful for the encouragement and patience of my husband, Gordon N. Walker, and for the taste and judgment of my editor, Elinor Parker. My photographer, William J. Williams, has worked with the same great skill and craftsmanship that distinguished his illustrations in my previous book. My proofreader, Beverly Tharp, has given tireless devotion and care to what is surely the least inspiring aspect of any publication, and surely the most demanding aspect of a book full of knitting directions.

I am deeply indebted to Mrs. John W. Campbell, whose magnificent library gave me many of my sources. Mrs. Edward W. Jones, Mrs. D. W. Hallstein, Miss A. Rosander and Mrs. Guy A. Gifford also contributed source materials. My thanks go to all the readers of *A Treasury of Knitting Patterns* who sent patterns for me to add to this new collection, with a special thank-you to Hildegard M. Elsner, whose splendid collection of European patterns gave me so much material.

Yarns used in making swatches came from the Spinnerin Yarn Company. I am indebted also to Liz Blackwell, Spinnerin's fashion director, and Elizabeth Zimmermann, television's "Busy Knitter", for their continuing interest in this book; and to Pat Trexler for her enthusiastic recommendation of my work to the readers of her knitting column.

B. G. W.

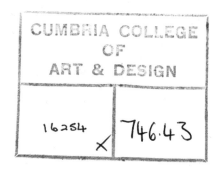
CONTENTS

Chapter Two
SLIP-STITCH PATTERNS 20

Chapter Three
SLIP-STITCH COLOR PATTERNS 35

Chapter Four
MOSAIC PATTERNS 60

Chapter Five

FANCY COLOR PATTERNS 88

Chapter Six
FANCY TEXTURE PATTERNS 121

Chapter Seven
TWIST-STITCH PATTERNS 143

Chapter Eight
CABLES 165

Chapter Nine
CABLE-STITCH PATTERNS 199

Chapter Thirteen
LACE PANELS AND INSERTIONS 300

Chapter Fourteen
BORDERS   327

Chapter Fifteen
EDGINGS   352

Introduction

My previous book, *A Treasury of Knitting Patterns,* was a collection of more than five hundred and fifty patterns—which seemed like a good many. But since the publication of that book, hundreds more have been added to my collection. These additional patterns are unusual and exciting, well worth sharing with my readers. In fact, many of them have come to me through the kindness of my readers themselves. My thanks go out to all the generous, industrious, and creative knitters whose contributions appear in these pages.

Some of the patterns in this book are contemporary originals, representing the constant and continuous flow of creative ideas in knitting. There is literally no end to this flow; it goes on forever because new ideas are always possible. Other patterns are traditional, representing the best efforts of past centuries. There are many lovely patterns that were popular a hundred years ago, and have since fallen into disuse because modern knitters do not know them. I have resurrected these from old, forgotten books, and translated them into modern terminology so that they can be used again, lending their beauty to new works as to old. Still other patterns have come from other areas of the world—from Europe, South America, and the Orient. Like music, knitting truly is a universal language.

This book is not just for the experienced knitter. It is for the beginner as well. There are many simple patterns here, which can be worked as easily as stockinette stitch and still give the novice knitter a feeling of having accomplished something original. The beginner usually makes a "first garment" in stockinette stitch—knit on the right side, purl on the wrong side—and if it comes out not *too* many sizes too big or too small, and *does* possess two sleeves more or less the same length and width, she gains the impression that she has learned to knit. Alas, she has not—not yet. She has *begun* to learn to knit.

Stockinette stitch is the *canvas* of the knitting artist. Upon either one of its two surfaces, knit or purl, the creative knitter arranges and displays her designs. Like canvas, it is a universal background for the play of line, shape, color and texture.

Though it may appear in large areas of a garment, it should not be used unrelieved for the entire garment. All-over plain stockinette stitch is dull to look at and boring to work, even for the beginner. Though it may be done entirely by hand, it lacks the inimitable flavor of hand-knitting. A machine can make it very nicely, but the hand-knitter is not a machine and should not try to imitate one.

This being so, there is no reason to spend the time and care of hand-knitting on a garment of stockinette stitch. It is a waste of both. The finished garment, which ought to display the knitter's taste and skill, displays nothing but poverty of invention. There are hundreds of easy pattern stitches with which the beginner can put that essential touch of originality into her garments. The beginner should learn to use some of them right away; this is the only route to real mastery of the subject of knitting. It doesn't take much—just a simple pattern or two, either all over the garment or in panel formation. With just a few lines, provided they are well-chosen and well-placed, the plain canvas becomes a work of art.

Another good reason for learning to use patterns properly is that today's yarns really deserve it. Modern fiber technology has resulted in a quality explosion in both natural and synthetic yarns. Manufacturers present the knitter with a limitless choice of excellent material, spun with a perfection that most knitters of past centuries could only dream about. Yet those knitters created patterns and designs of soaring beauty, even when they had nothing to work with but coarse homespun wool. How much more admirable our workmanship ought to be, with such superb material at our disposal! Having spent good money (often quite a lot of it) on the high-quality product that is a modern yarn, we should never insult and degrade it by using it badly. Rather let it lend its intrinsic beauty to a well-planned and well-executed design with the aristocratic air of real hand-knitting.

With the help of this book, even a "first garment" can be an original. Put a bit of texture, a band, or a panel of pattern into that drearily unadorned first sweater. The knitting will be far less tedious, and the result far more satisfying.

How to do it? Work from stitch gauge and stitch multiples. First of all, make a practice swatch of the pattern you would like to use, being sure that the yarn and needles are the same as those to be used in the garment. Block the swatch and take its *gauge*: so many stitches to the inch. If the gauge is the same as that of a commercial garment pattern you'd like to use, then you can go ahead and make the garment by following that pattern. If the gauge is *almost* the same, adjust it by changing needle sizes. Sometimes, a radical change in gauge is not feasible because it spoils the pattern. You would not want to work a lace pattern, for instance, with needles so small that the knitting will become tight and close up the holes in the lace. In such a case, determine the right needle size for the pattern stitch and then knit to your own measurements by multiplying your gauge by the number of inches desired. This is the best way to insure a perfect fit. The proportions of a commercial garment pattern may not suit *your* figure; so although you use such a pattern as a guide, you should not follow it slavishly if it does not match the measurements that *you* require. Women who sew know that no two figures are exactly alike, therefore dress patterns sometimes need to be altered to the individual taste; it is the same with knitting. It isn't hard to create your own garment pattern, simply by measuring a garment that does fit you well, then multiplying your stitch gauge to those measurements. (See the Stitch-Count Guide at the end of this introductory section for a general idea of how this is done.)

Having ascertained the number of stitches needed for the width of your garment, then figure the number of pattern repeats, or multiples, that will go into it. Let's assume that your gauge is 5 stitches to the inch, and you require 20 inches, or 100 stitches. The pattern you want to use has a multiple of 10 stitches plus 5. This will give 95 stitches in pattern, 5 stitches are left over, an uneven number. In order to center the pattern, you should cast on either one more or one less stitch (101 or 99), then work 3 (in the first case) or 2 (in the second case) stitches plain at each side edge. If the multiple is too large to fit comfortably into the number of stitches you require, then work on your practice swatch until you learn the pattern well enough to omit *part* of a repeat and still keep the pattern correct. You have to do this when shaping the garment anyway, so it is just as well to learn it from the beginning. Some knitters do not think in terms of the number of *stitches* required, but rather in terms of the number of *pattern repeats* required; this is a good system too. If you know that one repeat of the pattern is 2 inches wide, then you know that 10 repeats will make 20 inches.

With some patterns it is possible to ignore the multiples—just cast on the required number of stitches and work across until you run out of stitches, stopping the pattern wherever it happens to be. Mosaic patterns lend themselves to this sort of treatment, as do knit-purl combinations where the wrong-side rows copy the right-side rows ("knit all knit sts and purl all purl sts") and other patterns where wrong-side rows are purled plain and the stitch count remains the same on every row. It is even possible to work lace patterns this way—those that are purled plain on the wrong-side rows—but in this case you must be sure that the last yarn-overs have corresponding decreases, so that the number of stitches remains the same. Of course if you work this way the pattern will not be "centered" on the fabric—the right-hand edge will have a whole repeat and the left-hand edge a partial one. But there *are* patterns in which this is not a crucial matter.

A very easy way to insert stitch-pattern interest into a garment is to use some of the many vertical-panel or insertion patterns. A panel can be worked between two markers on the needle, so there is no question about where to begin and end it. Narrow vertical patterns can be worked at the center of a front or a back or a sleeve, placed next to the borders of a cardigan, or spaced between the shaping lines of a skirt. When working with vertical panels, you can place them out of range of the shaping decreases (or increases) and have no worry about keeping the pattern correct in shaping. Horizontal pattern changes, or "bands", are easily and effectively placed on yokes, skirt hems, sleeve cuffs, or straight across the body of the garment. Slip-stitch color patterns used in one or two repeats of the pattern rows make fancy horizontal stripes of contrasting color, and add a lot of sparkle to an otherwise plain garment. You can also use several different color patterns in several different colors against a plain background: a few repeats of Pattern 1, a few rows of background color, a few repeats of Pattern 2, a few more rows of background color, and so on.

There are many ways in which a beginner can use patterns without any commercial design to follow. Just an enlarged practice swatch can become a lovely stole, scarf, baby blanket, shawl, table mat, luncheon cloth or apron. Anyone can make a plain knitted rectangle (varying the length-to-width proportions) for any of these items. Even children can knit little samples of the more dense pattern stitches to make hot-dish mats and potholders, or of simple lace to make a doll's skirt, evening wrap or head scarf. Lace curtains, decorative hangings, and pillow covers can also be made as flat pieces, with no shaping at all. Edges can be finished with fringe, crochet, seed stitch, garter stitch, strips of a different pattern, or any one of the Edgings from the last chapter—there are many of them, ranging from very simple to very fancy. The beginner can make things like afghans and bedspreads out of pattern "strips", perfectly straight, even *before* she has learned anything about shaping! But every new pattern stitch you try has something to teach you, so no one could look upon this kind of knitting as "non-learning". On the contrary, it does much to increase the beginner's confidence and skill in handling the needles. The great thing about learning a large number of patterns is that it actually increases the learner's imaginative capacity. Each pattern seems to suggest possible uses for itself as the worker tries it out and watches it develop.

Try it out—those are the most important words in any system of developing knitting skills. Don't just look at these patterns; don't just read about them. *Try* them. Any experienced knitter knows that *her fingers understand* what her eyes and her mind sometimes fail to grasp. An unfamiliar technique sounds puzzling when you read it; but when you *try* it—it works! Knitting is a tactile experience, in which ideas come from the hands through the intellect, and not from the intellect alone. The novice knitter should make swatches and swatches and more swatches, trying all sorts of patterns and always watching carefully what her hands are doing. This is the only way to effect the unique union of hand and mind that turns a novice into a master craftsman. Besides, this kind of learning is wonderful fun!

Even the accomplished knitter, who already knows most of the things mentioned in the preceding paragraphs, can still learn much by trying out unfamiliar patterns. Patterns can be altered, divided, enlarged or reduced—played with, in short, until the knitter achieves a totally new effect that satisfies her own creative instinct. No matter how many different patterns you know, there are always more to be learned; and no matter how many you have learned, there are always new ways to use them. The larger your vocabulary of patterns, the more freely you can select and combine them in novel ways to suit any purpose. To knit creatively, you have only to let your imagination go. Combine cables, lace panels and textures in the same garment—why not? Combine a dozen different color patterns in a dozen different bands of color! Put lace patterns together, as many as can fit into your stitches! Enjoy yourself, and while doing so you can become a true artist of the needle, creating magnificent one-of-a-kinds that do justice to your skill. Remember that you are a hand knitter, with a brain that no knitting machine can ever imitate.

Handicrafts of all kinds hold a deep, unspoken philosophy, which contributes to the satisfaction of their practitioners even though the latter may not be conscious of it. Thousands of years of history have passed over human civilization, and during all that time human beings have fought, killed, plundered, and wronged each other in every possible way. Of such stuff history is made. But also during all that time, *other* human beings have quietly and patiently persevered in the development of arts, crafts, inventions and ideas. From these millions of creative workers, most of them unnoticed and unknown in the upheavals of history, have come the good and lasting things in the sum total of human culture. The builders, the weavers, the artisans, the carvers and smiths, the poets and musicians, the inventors of new techniques in all fields—these were, and are, the *makers* of civilization. The eternal calm figure of the needleworker looms large among them, for the arts of thread and yarn have been with us since the beginning.

When you embroider, crochet, or knit, there are centuries in your hands. You are a *maker*, doing the same thing that others have done for several thousand years. Their ideas created the techniques you now use. Who knows what pair of hands first cabled some stitches across some other stitches? Who knows where and when the first yarn-over strand was put on a needle to make an opening? All that matters is that these things *were* done, somewhere, by someone. Now they are a part of the very ancient craft called knitting. This craft has endured, for the same reason that all such crafts endure: because people have loved it.

Right now, in the twentieth century, handicrafts in general and needlework in particular are flourishing in a new Golden Age of popularity. Perhaps the hectic pace of modern life leads people to seek moments of peaceful satisfaction in the ancient disciplines of *making*. Perhaps today's more cultivated tastes prize the inimitable beauty of hand work above the lesser charms of machine-made goods. Perhaps new techniques and ideas have given impetus to needlework as a highly versatile medium of self-expression. Perhaps the labor of the needle seems more attractive to more people because it is now a luxury rather than a necessity—for luxuries always outshine their poor plain sisters the necessities.

For any or all of these reasons, the fact remains that the age-old pleasures of knitting are being enthusiastically re-discovered all over the civilized world. The modern discoverers are not all women, either. Men too are finding enjoyment in following the footsteps of their predecessors, the millions of male knitters whose skill contributed so much to the past growth of this unique craft. Anyone who loves knitting—or any other form of needlework—should feel glad to be alive in this time, which rivals or even surpasses previous "great periods" of creativity in the field. The traditions produced in such periods are still with us. The patterns that grew out of them are still available; many are here, in this book. Use these patterns to refine and embellish your own ideas, and you become one of the *makers* of the world. Your hands too can hold and transmit the legacy of one of civilization's most beloved arts.

ABOUT NOMENCLATURE

Knitting pattern names are a collector's nightmare. Different localities know the same pattern by different names, or different patterns by the same name; though some of the oldest patterns do have definite titles that have stuck to them through their wanderings. The majority of contempory patterns are nameless. The author of this book has retained names that appear to be widely known, or that contributors have given to their own patterns, and freely invented names for the others. This collection also includes many patterns that are the author's own originals. These, of course, bear names that were devised for them at the time of their creation.

Barbara G. Walker

Mount Kemble Lake
Morristown, New Jersey
1969

Glossary of Terms and Abbreviations

I. BASICS

K—Knit.

P—Purl.

St—Stitch. Sts—Stitches.

B—Work through the back loop of the stitch. "K1-b" means: knit one stitch through its back loop, inserting the needle into the stitch from the right-hand side. "P1-b" means: purl one stitch through its back loop, placing the right-hand needle point behind the stitch as if to insert the needle between the first and second stitches from the back, then inserting it, instead, into the *back* loop of the first stitch from the left-hand side, and wrapping the yarn around the needle point in front to complete the purl stitch as usual.

Sl—Slip. To pass a stitch or stitches from the left-hand needle to the right-hand needle without working them. The right-hand needle is always inserted into a stitch that is to be slipped *as if to purl* (i.e., from the right-hand side), unless directions specify "as if to knit" or "knitwise" (i.e., from the left-hand side).

Sl-st—Slip-stitch. A stitch that has been slipped.

Wyib—With yarn in back. Used with slip-stitches, it means that the yarn is carried across *behind* the stitch, on the side of the fabric that is *away from* the knitter. Whether this is a right or wrong side makes no difference.

Wyif—With yarn in front. When a stitch is slipped, the yarn is carried across in *front* of the stitch, on the side that is *facing* the knitter.

Rep—Repeat.

Rep from *—Repeat all material that comes after the *, in the same order.

( ) Parentheses—Indicates a repeat of material within the parentheses (or brackets) as many times as specified immediately after them; i.e., "(k2 tog, k1) 3 times" means: k2 tog, k1, k2 tog, k1, k2 tog, k1.

II. DECREASES

K2 tog—Knit two stitches together as one stitch.

P2 tog—Purl two stitches together as one stitch.

K2 tog-b—Insert the needle from the right into the back loops of two stitches at once, and knit them together as one stitch.

P2 tog-b—Turn the work over slightly and insert the needle from the left into the back loops of the second and first stitches, in that order, then wrap yarn around needle in front to complete the purl stitch. Same action as "p1-b" performed on two stitches at once. NOTE: In some circumstances, and for some knitters, "p2 tog-b" is awkward to work. The same effect can be obtained if desired by working the two stitches in the following manner: p1, sl the resulting st back to left-hand needle, then with point of right-hand needle lift the *next* stitch over the purled st and off the left-hand needle; then sl the same st back to right-hand needle and proceed. This is like a "psso" in reverse.

Sl 1, k1, psso—Slip 1 st wyib, knit 1 st, and pass the slipped stitch over; that is, insert the point of left-hand needle into the slipped stitch and draw it over the knit stitch and off the right-hand needle.

Ssk—Slip, slip, knit. This abbreviation is used almost always throughout this book, *instead of* the more usual "sl 1, k1, psso", because it is shorter, less easily confused with "sl 1, k2 tog, psso", and when done as directed makes a neater-looking decrease. Work "ssk" as follows: slip the first and second stitches *knitwise,* one at a time, then insert the tip of the left-hand needle into the *fronts* of these two stitches from the left, and knit them together from this position. (If, after trying this, the knitter still prefers to use "sl 1, k1, psso" for every "ssk", it is quite permissible to do so.)

Double decreases—These are k3 tog, p3 tog, k3 tog-b, sl 1—k2 tog—psso, all of which are self-explanatory; and p3 tog-b, which can be worked as described above under "p2 tog-b", by purling two stitches together, returning the resulting stitch to the left-hand needle, and passing the next stitch over. A double decrease makes 1 stitch out of 3.

NOTE: To work "k3 tog" so that it is the *exact opposite* of "sl 1—k2 tog—psso", do it this way: ssk, then sl the resulting st back to left-hand needle; then with point of right-hand needle pass the *next* stitch over the "ssk" stitch and off left-hand needle; then sl the st back to right-hand needle. This makes a double decrease slanting to the right, which will precisely match the left-slanting "sl 1—k2 tog—psso". It is a valuable trick especially for bisymmetrical lace patterns, where the decreases should always match.

Sl 2—k1—p2sso—This is a double decrease that is used when it is desirable to have the central stitch prominent. It is worked as follows: insert the needle into the fronts of the second and first stitches on the left-hand needle, as if to k2 tog; do not knit these stitches together, but *slip* them, both at once, from this position. Knit the next stitch on left-hand needle, then insert left-hand needle point into *both* slipped stitches at once and draw them *together* over the knit stitch and off right-hand needle, just as in "psso".

Sl 2—p1—p2sso—This double decrease is worked from the wrong side of the fabric, and is the corresponding opposite of "sl 2—k1—p2sso", likewise producing a dominant central stitch on the right side. Though it is not widely known, it should be in every knitter's repertoire of techniques because it is the only way to obtain this effect from the wrong side. Work "sl 2—p1—p2sso" as follows: turn the work over slightly, keeping yarn in front, and insert the needle from the left into the back loops of the second and first stitches, in that order, as if to p2 tog-b; do not purl these stitches together, but *slip* them, both at once, from this position. Purl the next stitch on left-hand needle, then insert left-hand needle point into *both* slipped stitches at once and draw them *together* over the purled stitch and off right-hand needle. The "p2sso" is just the same as when the decrease is worked from the right side.

III. INCREASES

Inc—Make two stitches out of one, by knitting into the front and back of the same stitch. This also may be done purlwise, by purling into the front and back of the same stitch, or it may be worked by (k1, p1) into one stitch, or (p1, k1) into one stitch.

M1—Make One. A method of adding a new stitch without leaving a hole or bump. Unless otherwise specified, it is done as follows: insert needle from behind under the *running thread* (which is the strand running from the base of the stitch just worked to the base of the next stitch) and lift this thread onto the left-hand needle; then knit one stitch into the *back* of it. "M1" can also be done purlwise, by purling into the back of the running thread, or by other methods which are explained in the patterns where they occur.

Knit next st in the row below—This is an increase *only* when followed by "then knit the st on needle". To knit in the row below, instead of working the loop that is *on* the needle, work into the loop that is immediately *under* the needle—i.e., the same loop that was on the needle in the preceding row. "Purl next st in the row below" is done the same way.

Yo—Yarn over. Take the yarn over the top of the needle once before making the next stitch. If the next stitch is to be knitted, then the yarn is simply taken over the top of the needle to the back, where it is in position to knit. If the next stitch is to be purled, then the yarn is taken over the needle to the back, then under the needle to the front, where it is in position to purl. (Note: English knitting directions distinguish between these by calling a yo before a knit switch "wf"—wool forward—and a yo before a purl stitch "wrn"—wool round needle.) A yo also may be worked in reverse: i.e., under the needle to the back, then over the needle to the front. This reverse yo is sometimes used on purl rows.

(Yo) twice, yo2, or 00—All these mean the same thing: a double yarn-over. The yarn passes over the needle to the back, under the needle to the front, and over the needle to the back again before making the next stitch, so that there are *two* extra strands on the needle. A double yarn-over is usually worked as two new stitches on the return row, by working (k1, p1) or (p1, k1) into the long loop.

(K1, yo, k1) in next st, (k1, p1, k1) in next st, (k1, yo, k1, yo, k1) in next st—these are various ways of making three or more stitches out of a single stitch. All material within the parentheses is to be worked in the *same* stitch before passing on to the next one.

IV. SPECIAL KNITTING ACTIONS

RT—Right Twist. K2 tog, leaving sts on left-hand needle; then insert right-hand needle from the front *between* the two sts just knitted together, and knit the first st again; then slip both sts from needle together. (For alternative method, see the introduction to chapter on Twist-Stitch Patterns.)

LT—Left Twist. With right-hand needle behind left-hand needle, skip one st and knit the second st in *back* loop; then insert right-hand needle into the backs of both sts (the skipped st and the second st) and k2 tog-b. (For alternative method, see the introduction to chapter on Twist-Stitch Patterns.)

FC—Front Cross. In cabling, the double-pointed needle carrying a stitch or stitches is held in *front* of the work (toward the knitter) while other stitches are being worked behind it. This produces a cable cross to the left.

BC—Back Cross. In cabling, the double-pointed needle carrying a stitch or stitches is held in *back* of the work (away from the knitter) while other stitches are being worked in front. This produces a cable cross to the right.

FKC, BKC, SFC, SBC, FPC, BPC, etc.—These are arbitrary abbreviations given with cable patterns when there are a number of different types of crossings in the same pattern, to distinguish one from another. Explanations are given in the individual pattern notes.

MB—Make Bobble. Usually done by increasing in one stitch, then working back and forth on the increased stitches for a specified number of short rows. Methods vary according to pattern.

V. GENERAL

Turn—This means that the work is turned around in the knitter's hands at some point *before* the end of a row, in order to work backward over the most recent stitches for a specified distance.

Short row—This is the knitting that is done after a turn. It may involve only a few stitches, or many—according to pattern—but in all cases the number of stitches in a short row is less than the total number of stitches on the needles.

Drop stitch—A stitch dropped off the needles. In some patterns it is picked up again after some other stitches have been worked; in other patterns it is unraveled downward for a certain number of rows and then picked up; in still other patterns it is simply left off the needles and ignored.

Dip stitch—A new stitch created by knitting into the fabric a certain number of rows below the stitches on the needle. The dip-stitch loop is drawn by the right-hand needle point through to the front and up, to be slipped on to the left-hand needle. Usually it is worked together with the next stitch on the needle.

Dpn—Double-pointed needle or cable needle.

Motif—The dominant figure or design unit in a pattern.

Panel—A portion of the knitting that develops a narrow vertical pattern, such as a cable, or an insertion in lace. For panel patterns directions are given in the number of stitches required to make the width of a single panel, rather than in multiples of stitches.

Spot-pattern or allover pattern—An arrangement of motifs all over the fabric, alternating at even intervals both vertically and horizontally.

Half-drop—A method of converting a panel pattern into a spot-pattern, by working the first half of the pattern rows in one panel along with the second half of the pattern rows in the adjoining panel.

MC—Main Color. The predominating color in a pattern of two or more colors.

CC—Contrasting Color. The "accent" color that is played against the main color.

Stockinette Stitch—"plain knitting". Knit right-side rows, purl wrong-side rows. For circular knitting, knit all rounds.

Reverse Stockinette Stitch—"purl fabric". Purl right-side rows, knit wrong-side rows. For circular knitting, purl all rounds.

Garter Stitch—knit all rows, both right and wrong sides. For circular knitting, knit one round, purl one round.

Adapting Patterns for Circular Knitting

Directions for pattern stitches almost always are given in terms of straight knitting—that is, for working back and forth on single-pointed needles. But if you want to use any particular pattern stitch for an article knitted in rounds—such as a sock, a skirt, a seamless sweater or a tubular dress—it is an easy matter to convert the pattern rows into rounds. There are only two major steps to this process.

The first step is to omit the edge stitches. Most patterns have extra stitches at the beginning and end of each row, for finishing off the sides of a straight-knit piece. These are the "plus" stitches in "Multiple of ____ plus ____". In circular knitting, you do not want to interrupt the continuous spiral of rounds with extra stitches that contribute nothing to the development of the pattern. So the number of stitches in a round should be the multiple required for the pattern only—plus none. For example, if a pattern takes a multiple of 10 stitches plus 3, you cast on a multiple of 10 stitches and forget the extra 3. Pattern rounds are worked from the directions given *after* the asterisk, ignoring what comes before it. Likewise, the ending material, if any, that follows "rep from * " is ignored. This is a simple matter when the pattern has the same number of edge stitches on every row.

But what if the edge stitches vary in number? Perhaps you want to use a pattern in which you see "k2" before the asterisk in one right-side row, and "k7" before the asterisk in the next right-side row. Clearly, it will throw your pattern out of kilter if you omit the 5 extra stitches and begin your next "right-side" round at the asterisk. So you must subtract the same "k2" as before, and begin your round with "k5"—i.e., the stitches left over after the same 2 edge stitches are removed. If you are in doubt about where the actual pattern starts and finishes, you can chart one or two repeats of the pattern on graph paper, including both edges, then draw a vertical line down each side of the actual pattern repeat to slice off stitches that are not needed. In this way it is easy to see just where to begin and end each round. Of course if you are working on a series of panels, this problem will not exist because there are no edge stitches to worry about.

The second step is to convert wrong-side rows into right-side rows. You are always on the right side of the fabric in circular knitting, so the wrong-side rows must be worked inside-out. There are different ways of doing this, depending on the type of pattern you are using.

In the first place, all wrong-side *knit* stitches must be worked as *purl* stitches, and vice versa. Since a purl stitch is only a backward knit stitch, it follows that the purl side of the stitch must be on the *outside* of the fabric if the wrong side is knit. Conversely, the knit side of the stitch must show if the wrong side is purled.

When using slip-stitch patterns, the wrong-side "with yarn in front" and "with yarn in back" must be reversed. If a wrong-side row calls for a stitch to be slipped with yarn in front, then that strand of yarn is to cross the stitch on the wrong side, where it will not show. Obviously this means slipping the same stitch with yarn in *back* when you are working in rounds. If a wrong-side stitch should be slipped with yarn in back in flat knitting, then in circular knitting it must be slipped with yarn in front.

The easiest kind of pattern to convert is a bisymmetrical one: that is, a pattern in which the right-hand edge of the row is the same as the left-hand edge, but in reverse. When rows become rounds, they all go from right to left, with none returning from left to right. So in a bisymmetrical pattern, you can read the wrong-side rows just as they are given, from the beginning to the end, reversing knits and purls and other pattern operations as required. But if the pattern is *not* bisymmetrical, instead going off-center in some way, then all wrong-side rows must be read *backward*, from the end to the beginning. Remember that a wrong-side row in flat knitting works from left to right (looking at it from the right side of the fabric), whereas your "wrong-side" *round* progresses from right to left. Unless you are very experienced, or the pattern is very simple, it is not advisable to try reading these rows straight off from the end of the row to the beginning. It is too easy to miss things when you are reading this way. A better method is to re-write the pattern for yourself on a separate piece of paper, turning the wrong-side rows around as you write them. Then you can work from this revised set of directions with much less likelihood of mistakes.

Most patterns are very easily converted to circular knitting. A cable pattern in which the wrong-side rows call for "knit all knit sts and purl all purl sts" is very simple; you still do exactly that on every alternate round. A lace pattern in which all wrong-side rows are purled is very easy, too; you just knit (instead of purl) the alternate rounds. Those laces that have yarn-overs and decreases on *both* sides of the fabric are even easier; most of them were intended for circular knitting in the first place. "P2 tog", being a right-slanting decrease on the right side, is the same thing as "k2 tog", and is so worked. "P2 tog-b" similarly converts to "ssk"—a left-slanting decrease. In conformity with the rule of reading wrong-side rows backward, the yarn-over-decrease unit that reads "yo, p2 tog" on the wrong side is worked in a *round* as "k2 tog, yo". In the same way, "p2 tog-b, yo" becomes "yo, ssk".

In circular knitting you will have some kind of a marker on the needle to tell you where you finish one round and begin the next one. This can be a commercial ring marker, a safety pin, or a little hoop of sewing thread. It is carried right along with the knitting, being slipped from the left needle point to the right needle point each time you come around to it again and begin the next round. Sometimes the novice knitter will be using a pattern that travels diagonally, and will be working cheerfully along until she comes to the point where the diagonal pattern line *crosses* the marker; then she will panic. Here are two stitches that must be knitted *together*, and the marker is squarely in between them! What to do? And to which round does the decrease belong—the round just finished, or the round just starting?

What to do is easy. Slip one or the other of the two stitches temporarily in order to release the marker, take it off the needle, and replace it one stitch over to the left or to the right so the two stitches can be worked together as required. If the working unit is "k2 tog, yo", for instance, and the marker is between the two stitches, you take it off, knit two together, put it back, then work the yo. This replaces the marker in exactly the same spot where it was before. If the two stitches are to be twisted or cabled, then you remove the marker one stitch away from its place, work the twist or cross, and continue with the next round, not forgetting to move the marker *back again* to its original place the next time you come around to it. Once a diagonal pattern has crossed the marker, it belongs to the round *where it is now,* even though the action of crossing it may have taken place on the other side of the marker.

Slip-stitch color patterns adapt very well to circular knitting. The strands are changed at the point where the rounds start and finish, unused strands being simply dropped there and left hanging, to be picked up when they are needed again. When changing colors, always pick up the new strand on the *same* side where you picked up all the others—to the left or to the right of the old strand, either way. Then the loose strands will be neatly twisted around each other as they spiral upward from round to round. Pattern stripes will not meet precisely at the point where the rounds change, so it is a good idea to place your marker where a slight jog in the pattern will not be obvious—at a "side seam", for instance, or the underarm line on a sleeve.

One rather intriguing problem in circular knitting is presented by the seamless skirt, which tapers toward the waist and grows wider toward the hem. This cannot be made like a straight tube, with pattern repeats in the same order all along the way. There will be decreases if the skirt is being worked from the bottom up, or increases if it is being worked from the top down. These shaping units must be kept in a strict vertical line, and the pattern must be altered evenly on either side of them, just as the grain lines in a sewn skirt are matched across a dart or seam. There may be 8 or 10 decreases (or increases) evenly spaced around a decrease (or increase) round. If you really understand how your pattern stitch works, you can incorporate these shaping units without difficulty, keeping the pattern correct on either side. But if you are not sure of yourself on this point, you can restrict your pattern to 8 or 10 *panels* around the skirt, each panel having and keeping the same number of stitches, while the shaping units are worked between the panels as very long and very skinny triangles of purl, stockinette stitch, garter stitch, or some other simple texture. Some pretty ribbed effects can be obtained by this means. For example, a pattern made primarily of knit stitches, like a lace or eyelet pattern, can be shaped with purled panels: these will "retreat" around the lower edge and give the appearance of pleats. Cable and twist panels make beautiful ribbed skirts that will keep their shape and resist "sit-out bulge".

The easiest way to make a skirt like this is to begin at the waist and work down. Cast on the multiple required for the waist measurement, work the waistband straight in ribbing or whatever, then start the pattern panels and add one more stitch *between* these panels with each increase round. The pattern panels are kept intact on the same number of stitches, but they spread apart from each other as new stitches are added. Commercial garment patterns seldom give directions for a skirt worked from the waist down. Usually, they go from the bottom up. But there are definite advantages to working in the other direction. A skirt worked from the top down can be tried on and checked for fit and length while the work is still in progress. It isn't even necessary to take it off the circular needle in order to try it on. Just slip half of the stitches onto *another* circular needle temporarily, so the skirt can be spread out around the hips. Furthermore, if the bound-off edge is at the bottom, the skirt can be much more easily shortened or lengthened according to fashion's changing hemlines. Knitting can be unraveled quickly from the bound-off edge to pull out a few inches or add more inches. But to unravel from the cast-on edge is tricky work, nearly impossible for the novice to accomplish successfully.

Another kind of circular knitting is called "medallion knitting". It is used for making flat, decorative articles such as doilies, table centerpieces, mats or shawls in circular, octagonal, pentagonal or square shapes. Usually it is begun at the center, by casting on just one or two stitches to each needle in a set of double-pointed needles. The medallion grows outward from the center, like a spider web, by working increases in every round or every other round. The increases are yo's if the medallion is made of lace. Medallion knitting can become exceedingly intricate. Some of the world's finest examples of "art knitting" are done in the medallion form. In the last century, exquisite articles were created in fine lace medallion knitting, to serve as the ever-popular doilies, antimacassars, bonnet caps and table dressings. This delicate art is not so widely practiced today, but it is by no means dead. There are still people who love to do fine medallion knitting, and use it to create heirloom tablecloths and bedspreads as well as single-medallion pieces. Simpler medallion work, too, is within the grasp of any knitter. Small medallions in heavy yarn make excellent potholders, hot-dish mats, or round cushion covers. Any sort of pattern can be worked into the segments of the knitted medallion as it grows, using the same principles that apply to other kinds of circular knitting. New repeats of the same pattern, or panels of different patterns, can be added as the segments enlarge. *En passant,* here's a small hint for devotees of medallion knitting in fine lace, who may have noticed that their double-pointed needles tend to fall out of the few beginning stitches. Don't use needles—use toothpicks.

The vast majority of patterns are very easy to adapt to circular knitting, so don't be afraid to try it. You can make socks, tubular scarves and ties, seamless skirts, sweaters and dresses in any pattern that you find appealing. The important thing is to *know your pattern.* Always make your practice swatch and study it as you go, thinking in terms of omitting the edge stitches later and working the wrong-side rows from the right side instead. If you know exactly how any pattern is formed, you should be able to make it flat, round, backward, forward, or upside down. You can make any pattern in any shape, size, or type of article. One of the most fascinating qualities of knitting is its infinite flexibility with regard to shape. To acquire the skill to manipulate this flexibility as you wish, all you have to do is—try!

STITCH-COUNT GUIDE

Garment size	8	10	12	14	16	18
Chest measurement (garment)	34″	36″	38″	40″	42″	44″
Width of back or front of garment .	17″	18″	19″	20″	21″	22″
Width of sleeve at underarm	13″	13½″	14″	14½″	15″	15½″

Stitch gauges:

5 sts to 1 inch (average gauge for knitting worsted)

	8	10	12	14	16	18
Number of sts on back or front of garment at chest	85	90	95	100	105	110
Number of sts on sleeve at underarm	65	68	70	73	75	78

6 sts to 1 inch (average gauge for sport yarn)

	8	10	12	14	16	18
Number of sts on back or front of garment at chest	102	108	114	120	126	132
Number of sts on sleeve at underarm	78	81	84	87	90	93

7 sts to 1 inch (average gauge for fingering yarn)

	8	10	12	14	16	18
Number of sts on back or front of garment at chest	119	126	133	140	147	154
Number of sts on sleeve at underarm	91	95	98	102	105	109

NOTE: These figures can be used only as a *rough* guide. They are based on the *average* knitter's *average* gauge in stockinette stitch. If you normally knit to a different gauge, or if you use a pattern stitch that is tighter or looser than stockinette stitch, then you must make up your own stitch count by multiplying the desired number of inches by *your* gauge. This is not difficult to do; a few minutes' study of this chart will show how it is done. The size measurements given above are also approximate; for best results, take your *own* measurements and adjust the stitch count accordingly. Measure a sweater or dress that fits you well, then use these measurements to design your knitwear originals.

A NOTE ON CONTINENTAL-STYLE KNITTING

A number of people who knit in the continental style (i.e., with the yarn held in the left hand, wrapped over the left forefinger) have written to me, asking how to convert pattern stitches to this style. In all cases their confusion arises from a misunderstanding of their own way of knitting. Since this misunderstanding seems to be widespread, it should be pointed out that there is no method of "converting" from American style to continental style because *it makes no difference* which style is used, as far as the finished result is concerned. Every swatch in this book was knitted continental-style, because the author happens to use that style by preference.

The misunderstanding lies in the manner of making purl stitches. In continental-style knitting it is very easy to wrap the yarn the wrong way around the needle when making a purl stitch—that is, under the needle instead of over it. When stitches are purled in this way, they are turned on the needle, so that on the following knit row it is necessary to knit all stitches through the back loops in order to straighten them out again. It is possible to make perfectly good knitted articles in this manner as long as they are worked in plain stockinette stitch. But when pattern stitches are attempted, it becomes clear that this way of knitting is an error.

If you are a continental-style knitter who thinks it "makes a difference", try this simple test. Purl one row of a stockinette-stitch fabric in your usual way. Then turn the work and knit the next row in your usual way *half way across,* and stop. Look at the stitches on the right-hand needle. Each stitch will have the *right*-hand side of its loop on the front of the needle, toward you. This is the correct position. Then look at the stitches on the left-hand needle. If these stitches have the *left*-hand side of their loops on the front of the needle, then you have been purling the wrong way. Every stitch should have the right-hand loop on the front of the needle, both knit and purl rows; and stitches are never knitted in the back unless the pattern specifically calls for this action.

The right way to purl, in either style, is to pass the yarn from the front *over* the needle and down behind it. In continental-style knitting the yarn is pushed down *between* the needle points by the left forefinger (around which the yarn is wrapped) each time a purl stitch is made. If you are one of the continental-style knitters who purl with the yarn passing under the needle and up, it is necessary for you to learn to wrap the yarn in the other direction. Then you can work all knit stitches in the *front* loops in the correct manner.

A SECOND TREASURY
OF KNITTING PATTERNS

CHAPTER ONE

Knit-Purl Combinations

Of all types of knitting patterns, knit-purl combinations are the simplest in technique—though not necessarily naive or crude in design. On the contrary, many knit-purl patterns are highly sophisticated. The fancier ones require just as much care and patience on the part of the knitter as do the intricate figures in lace or cable stitches.

However, because of the simplicity of technique, most knit-purl patterns work very quickly. The new knitter will find them useful as an introduction to pattern work in general; even though she may know nothing more than "knit" and "purl", she can still create handsomely designed fabrics and in so doing, gain practice in stitch-counting and shaping. Nor does the experienced knitter ever consider herself above using simple knit-purl combinations, because many of them give beautiful effects that cannot be obtained by any other method.

Any fabric with a knit-purl design should be firm and solid, in order to show the design to best advantage. This means that the needles should not be too large in proportion to the weight of the yarn. Oversized needles make a loose, limp, sloppy piece of knitting, perhaps with small holes at the points of change from purl to knit or from knit to purl stitches. So there is an upper limit on needle size. If you are trying to adjust your gauge to that of a commercial garment design, and require larger needles than the recommended size, be careful. Should your knitting become too loose, keep the smaller needles and cast on an extra inch or two of stitches to make the necessary width measurement in *your* gauge.

Colors should be solid, too, to do justice to a knit-purl pattern. Stripes of contrasting color usually detract from the motifs, which are subtle rather than bold. Variegated or ombre yarns also can "kill" the pattern. Heavy or bulky yarns, however, do quite well in knit-purl combinations, which can give bulky knits just the right amount of texture interest when a bolder pattern might be excessive.

Knit-purl combinations fall roughly into three categories: rib, welt, and scatter patterns. Rib patterns are those in which the motifs are mostly vertical, in knit stitches displayed against a background of purl. Welt patterns are those in which the motifs are mostly horizontal, in purl stitches on a background of knit stitches. In scatter patterns, the two types of stitches are more or less evenly distributed, so that the fabric will incline to lie flat. Some patterns combine these types, like the "basketweave" patterns in which welts predominate for a few rows, then ribs in the next few rows.

These patterns make wonderful sweaters, jackets, coats, dresses, cushions, afghans, baby clothes—anything. Try out as many as you like, and use them where you will. Why make your first sweater a plain, featureless, around-the-house garment, when with just a tiny extra effort you can work it in one of these patterns and make it an "original" that you would be proud to wear anywhere? Why learn to knit on a plain ribbed or garter-stitch scarf, when you could make it of a beautiful pattern stitch in the same amount of time? With knit-purl combinations, pattern knitting comes easily, does not bore the knitter, and yields results so satisfying that the beginner is encouraged to move on and try different techniques later.

Sailor's Rib Pattern

Sailor's Rib Pattern

Like Double Seed Stitch, which it resembles in part, this pattern demonstrates the fact that a design so simple that any child can make it still looks interesting and effective. This attractive rib texture is good for sweaters, coats, scarves—almost anything. It also looks well in panels, combined with cables or other patterns.

Multiple of 5 sts plus 1.

Row 1 (Right side)—K1-b, * p1, k2, p1, k1-b; rep from *.
Row 2—P1, * k1, p2, k1, p1; rep from *.
Row 3—K1-b, * p4, k1-b; rep from *.
Row 4—P1, * k4, p1; rep from *.

Repeat Rows 1–4.

Twin Rib

The interesting thing about this simple knit-purl fabric is that it looks exactly the same on both sides, even though the two sides are differently worked. It is not sufficiently elastic to be used as a true ribbing, but a beginner could use it as an attractive allover texture for sweaters, jackets, scarves, or baby blankets. It has no curl, and therefore serves well as a border pattern wherever the springiness of a true ribbing is undesirable, such as on button bands, pockets, and coat cuffs.

Multiple of 6 sts.

Row 1—* K3, p3; rep from *.
Row 2—* K1, p1; rep from *.

Repeat Rows 1 and 2.

Twin Rib

Steep Diagonal Rib

Left unpressed, this pattern gives an attractive texture of deep rounded ribs running diagonally. This, or variations of it, is often used to make heelless socks such as bed socks, which will adapt to the shape of the foot and ankle without any shaping of the knitting itself.

Odd-numbered rows used on the right side will make diagonal ribs running upward to the right. Even-numbered rows used on the right side will make the ribs run upward to the left.

Steep Diagonal Rib

Multiple of 6 sts.

Row 1—* P3, k3; rep from *.
Row 2 and all other even-numbered rows—Knit all knit sts and
  purl all purl sts.
Row 3—P2, * k3, p3; rep from *, end k3, p1.
Row 5—P1, * k3, p3; rep from *, end k3, p2.
Row 7—* K3, p3; rep from *.
Row 9—K2, * p3, k3; rep from *, end p3, k1.
Row 11—K1, * p3, k3; rep from *, end p3, k2.
Row 12—See Row 2.

Repeat Rows 1–12.

Fluted Rib

This pattern looks the same on both sides, and when left unpressed it makes a fabric that is very gently fluted or "rippled" into wide, soft ribs. It is excellent for straight, gathered skirts, because the flutings will gather themselves nicely at the upper edge and can be drawn together as tightly or loosely as desired. Fluted Rib is good too for scarves, baby blankets, afghans and throws, and it is easy for the novice knitter to work.

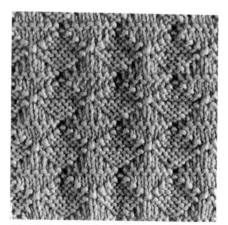

Fluted Rib

Multiple of 8 sts plus 1.

Rows 1, 2, and 3—P1, * k7, p1; rep from *.
Row 4—K2, * p5, k3; rep from *, end p5, k2.
Row 5—P3, * k3, p5; rep from *, end k3, p3.
Rows 6, 7, and 8—K4, * p1, k7; rep from *, end p1, k4.
Row 9—Repeat Row 5.
Row 10—Repeat Row 4.

Repeat Rows 1–10.

Shadow Rib

Shadow Rib

Just the very simplest kind of knitting makes this neatly ribbed fabric for all kinds of sweaters, skirts, coats and dresses. It will not "draw in" like a true ribbing, and it gives the general appearance of a purl fabric ornamented with slim vertical bars.

Multiple of 3 sts plus 2.

Row 1 (Wrong side)—Knit.
Row 2—P2, * k1-b, p2; rep from *.

Repeat Rows 1 and 2.

Belt Welt

Easy enough for the rawest beginner to work, yet attractive enough for the expert to choose on occasion, this pattern gives a pleasing texture to sweaters, scarves, and baby things. The wrong side is interesting, too. Belt Welt is also one of the best patterns in the world for garments that are worked sideways—from the right side seam to the left side seam or vice versa.

Multiple of 6 sts plus 2.

Rows 1 and 3 (Right side)—Knit.
Rows 2 and 4—Purl.
Rows 5 and 7—K2, * p4, k2; rep from *.
Rows 6 and 8—P2, * k4, p2; rep from *.

Repeat Rows 1–8.

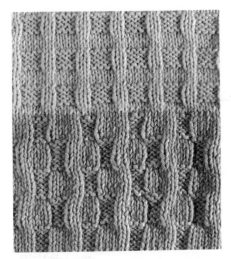

ABOVE: *Belt Welt*
BELOW: *Broken Block Pattern*

Broken Block Pattern

This simple pattern makes wavy ribs without any effort at all. Left unpressed, it takes on quite a deep texture that looks as though it might have been created by some much more intricate knitting.

Multiple of 8 sts.

Rows 1, 3, and 5 (Right side)—* P3, k5; rep from *.
Rows 2, 4, and 6—* P5, k3; rep from *.
Rows 7, 9, and 11—* K5, p3; rep from *.
Rows 8, 10, and 12—* K3, p5; rep from *.

Repeat Rows 1–12.

Seeded Rib Check

Here is an easy texture pattern that is very handsome in sport sweaters, jackets, and casual dresses. The Variation, below, gives a softly ribbed fabric similar to Mistake-Stitch Ribbing, not elastic enough for a true ribbing but very attractive for an entire garment. Both patterns are reversible.

Multiple of 4 sts plus 3.

Row 1—K3, * p1, k3; rep from *.
Row 2—K1, * p1, k3; rep from *, end p1, k1.
Rows 3 and 5—Repeat Row 1.
Rows 4 and 6—Repeat Row 2.
Rows 7, 9, and 11—Repeat Row 2.
Rows 8, 10, and 12—Repeat Row 1.

Repeat Rows 1–12.

ABOVE: *Seeded Rib Check*
BELOW: *Seeded Rib Pattern*

VARIATION: *SEEDED RIB PATTERN*

Contributed by Ruth Berry, Cleveland, Ohio

Repeat Rows 1 and 2 only of Seeded Rib Check, above.

Square Lattice

This charming rectilinear design is very simply constructed of knit ribs, purl welts, and seed stitch blocks. It will make beautifully tailored suits, coats, and jackets, or easy afghan squares and baby blankets.

Multiple of 14 sts plus 2.

Row 1 (Right side)—Knit.
Rows 2, 4, and 6—P2, * (k1, p1) twice, k1, p2; rep from *.
Rows 3, 5, and 7—K3, * p1, k1, p1, k4; rep from *, end last repeat k3.
Row 8—P2, * k12, p2; rep from *.
Row 9—K2, * p12, k2; rep from *.
Row 10—Purl.
Rows 11, 13, and 15—K2, * (p1, k1) twice, p1, k2; rep from *.
Rows 12, 14, and 16—P3, * k1, p1, k1, p4; rep from *, end last repeat p3.
Row 17—P7, * k2, p12; rep from *, end k2, p7.
Row 18—K7, * p2, k12; rep from *, end p2, k7.

Repeat Rows 1–18.

Square Lattice

Seed-Pearl Block Stitch

Definitely a pattern, yet definitely understated, this subtle arrangement of tiny purl dots can be worked by any person capable of counting up to 8. It is appropriate for almost any kind of knitwear. It can also be worked crosswise, as in a garment that is knitted in the length from one side to the other. If desired, a strand of contrasting color can be threaded through the purl stitches in the vertical rows and through the knit stitches in the horizontal rows, to make a plaid effect.

Multiple of 8 sts plus 1.

Row 1 (Wrong side) and all other wrong-side rows—Purl.
Row 2—P1, * k1, p1; rep from *.
Rows 4, 8, and 12—Knit.
Rows 6 and 10—P1, * k7, p1; rep from *.

Repeat Rows 1–12.

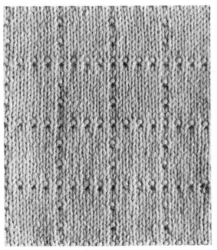

Seed-Pearl Block Stitch

Ripple Stripe Pattern

Contributed by Hildegard M. Elsner, Aldan, Pennsylvania

This is a very pretty and very simple variation on Ripple Stitch, excellent for "easy-knit" but attractive sweaters, skirts, and dresses.

Multiple of 8 sts plus 1.

Row 1 (Right side)—K4, * p1, k7; rep from *, end p1, k4.
Row 2—P3, * k3, p5; rep from *, end k3, p3.
Row 3—K2, * p2, k1, p2, k3; rep from *, end last repeat k2.
Row 4—P1, * k2, p3, k2, p1; rep from *.
Row 5—K1, * p1, k5, p1, k1; rep from *.
Row 6—Purl.

Repeat Rows 1–6.

Ripple Stripe Pattern

Little Pyramid

Here is a handsome little texture pattern that is really a six-row development of Double Seed Stitch. The "little pyramids" are wide, short triangles of knit and purl stitches. If the odd-numbered rows are used on the *right* side, then the knit triangles will point upward and the purl triangles will point downward (Knit Pyramid). If the odd-numbered rows are used on the *wrong* side, then the effect is reversed (Purl Pyramid). The forward-and-backward alternation of the same three rows to form the pattern is interesting. The fabric is flat, firm, and shapely, requiring little or no blocking.

Multiple of 6 sts plus 5.

Row 1—K5, * p1, k5; rep from *.
Row 2—K1, * p3, k3; rep from *, end p3, k1.
Row 3—P2, * k1, p5; rep from *, end k1, p2.
Row 4—Repeat Row 3.
Row 5—Repeat Row 2.
Row 6—Repeat Row 1.

Repeat Rows 1–6.

Little Pyramid
ABOVE: *Knit Pyramid*
BELOW: *Purl Pyramid*

Rib and Welt Diagonals

The interesting thing about this fabric is that it is entirely reversible—the same on both sides—except that the diagonals run in opposite directions. If odd-numbered rows are used as right-side rows, the diagonals slant to the right. If even-numbered rows are used as right-side rows, the diagonals slant to the left.

This pattern is perfect for a simple scarf, such as a beginner might make as soon as she has learned to knit and purl. Such a scarf shows the same attractive texture any way it is turned, and looks very "professional" despite the simplicity of the pattern.

Multiple of 8 sts.

Row 1—* K1, p1, k1, p5; rep from *.
Row 2 and all other even-numbered rows—Knit all knit sts and purl all purl sts.
Row 3—K1, p1, * k5, p1, k1, p1; rep from *, end k5, p1.
Row 5—K1, * p5, k1, p1, k1; rep from *, end p5, k1, p1.
Row 7—* K5, p1, k1, p1; rep from *.
Row 9—P4, * k1, p1, k1, p5; rep from *, end (k1, p1) twice.
Row 11—K3, * p1, k1, p1, k5; rep from *, end p1, k1, p1, k2.
Row 13—P2, * k1, p1, k1, p5; rep from *, end k1, p1, k1, p3.
Row 15—K1, * p1, k1, p1, k5; rep from *, end p1, k1, p1, k4.
Row 16—See Row 2.

Repeat Rows 1–16.

ABOVE: *Rib and Welt Diagonals*
BELOW: *Four Winds Check*

KNIT-PURL COMBINATIONS   9

Four Winds Check

Simple yet handsome, this pattern makes dramatic coats, suits, and sweaters. Since the stitch gauge is approximately the same as stockinette stitch, the novice knitter can substitute this pattern for a "plain" garment with satisfying results.

Multiple of 14 sts plus 2.

Rows 1 and 3 (Right side)—K1, * (p1, k1-b) twice, k10; rep from *, end k1.
Rows 2 and 4—P1, * p7, k3, (p1-b, k1) twice; rep from *, end p1.
Row 5—Knit.
Rows 6 and 8—P8, * (k1, p1-b) twice, p10; rep from *, end last repeat p4.
Rows 7 and 9—K1, * p3, (k1-b, p1) twice, k7; rep from *, end k1.
Rows 10 and 12—P1, * (k1, p1-b) twice, p10; rep from *, end p1.
Rows 11 and 13—K1, * k7, p3, (k1-b, p1) twice; rep from *, end k1.
Row 14—Purl.
Rows 15 and 17—K8, * (p1, k1-b) twice, k10; rep from *, end last repeat k4.
Rows 16 and 18—P1, * k3, (p1-b, k1) twice, p7; rep from *, end p1.

Repeat Rows 1–18.

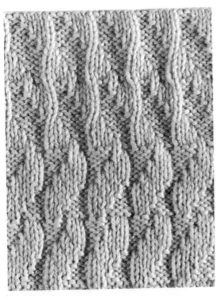

Seaweed
ABOVE: *Even-numbered rows on right side*
BELOW: *Odd-numbered rows on right side*

Seaweed

This pattern makes two quite different designs, depending on whether the odd-numbered or even-numbered rows are shown. With the even-numbered rows on the right side, it looks more "seaweedy", with off-center ribs waving gracefully to the left. With odd-numbered rows on the right side, the motifs become gently curved knit blocks tending upward to the right.

Multiple of 6 sts.

Row 1—* P4, k2; rep from *.
Row 2 and all other even-numbered rows—Knit all knit sts and purl all purl sts.
Row 3—* P3, k3; rep from *.
Row 5—* P2, k4; rep from *.
Row 7—P1, * k4, p2; rep from *, end k4, p1.
Row 9—P1, * k3, p3; rep from *, end k3, p2.
Row 11—P1, * k2, p4; rep from *, end k2, p3.
Row 12—See Row 2.

Repeat Rows 1–12.

Block Quilting

This handsome pattern has been turning up in many sweater designs in recent years. It is very simple to work, yet lends a distinctive touch to a plain garment.

Multiple of 14 sts.

Rows 1, 3, and 5 (Wrong side)—K3, * p8, k6; rep from *, end p8, k3.
Rows 2 and 4—Knit.
Row 6—K2, * p2, k6, p2, k4; rep from *, end last repeat k2.
Row 7—P3, * k2, p4, k2, p6; rep from *, end last repeat p3.
Row 8—K4, * p2, k2, p2, k8; rep from *, end last repeat k4.
Row 9—P5, * k4, p10; rep from *, end k4, p5.
Rows 10, 11, and 12—Repeat Rows 8, 7, and 6.

Repeat Rows 1–12.

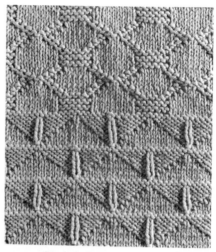

ABOVE: *Block Quilting*
BELOW: *Thunderbird Pattern*

Thunderbird Pattern

The "thunderbirds" are shallow purled triangles with a knit rib in the center. Arranged in this way, they make a horizontal type of pleating that is pretty when worked from the top down, because the pleats then roll under slightly at the bottom, as if the fabric were tucked horizontally. The thunderbird motifs also can be worked at a distance from each other, spaced apart on a stockinette fabric.

Multiple of 14 sts plus 1.

Rows 1 and 2—Knit.
Row 3 (Wrong side)—K1, * p13, k1; rep from *.
Row 4—K1, * p1, k11, p1, k1; rep from *.
Row 5—P1, * k2, p9, k2, p1; rep from *.
Row 6—K1, * p3, k7, p3, k1; rep from *.
Row 7—P1, * k4, p5, k4, p1; rep from *.
Row 8—K1, * p5, k3, p5, k1; rep from *.
Row 9—P1, * k6, p1; rep from *.
Rows 10 and 11—Purl.
Row 12—K7, * p1, k13; rep from *, end p1, k7.
Row 13—P6, * k1, p1, k1, p11; rep from *, end last repeat p6.
Row 14—K5, * p2, k1, p2, k9; rep from *, end last repeat k5.
Row 15—P4, * k3, p1, k3, p7; rep from *, end last repeat p4.
Row 16—K3, * p4, k1, p4, k5; rep from *, end last repeat k3.
Row 17—P2, * k5, p1, k5, p3; rep from *, end last repeat p2.
Row 18—K1, * p6, k1; rep from *.

Repeat Rows 1–18.

Imitation Aran Pattern

This pattern is a real "cheat". With only simple knit and purl stitches it endeavors to capture the flavor of the classic Aran Diamonds with Moss Stitch. The Moss Stitch is there; but since there is no cabling, the knit borders of the diamonds lack the highly embossed beauty of the real thing. However, the pattern is not unattractive, and could be well used in a sweater that is not as fancy as a true Aran knit but where a little texture interest is desired.

Panel of 17 sts.

Row 1 (Right side)—K1, p6, k3, p6, k1.
Row 2 and all other wrong-side rows—Knit all knit sts and purl all purl sts.
Row 3—K1, p5, k5, p5, k1.
Row 5—K1, p4, k3, p1, k3, p4, k1.
Row 7—K1, p3, k3, p1, k1, p1, k3, p3, k1.
Row 9—K1, p2, k3, (p1, k1) twice, p1, k3, p2, k1.
Row 11—K1, p1, k3, (p1, k1) 3 times, p1, k3, p1, k1.
Row 13—K4, (p1, k1) 4 times, p1, k4.
Rows 15 and 16—Repeat Rows 11 and 12.
Rows 17 and 18—Repeat Rows 9 and 10.
Rows 19 and 20—Repeat Rows 7 and 8.
Rows 21 and 22—Repeat Rows 5 and 6.
Rows 23 and 24—Repeat Rows 3 and 4.

Repeat Rows 1–24.

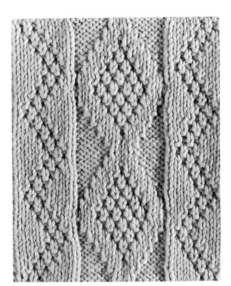

CENTER PANEL: *Imitation Aran Pattern*
SIDE PANELS: *Moss Stitch Zigzag*

Moss Stitch Zigzag

Here is a simple texture panel that can be used in combination with fancier panels or continuously all the way across a fabric. When two panels of Moss Stitch Zigzag are worked on either side of a common center, one of them should be started on Row 1 and the other on Row 9 so that the design will balance.

Panel of 7 sts.

Row 1 (Right side)—P1, k1, p1, k4.
Row 2 and all other wrong-side rows—Knit all knit sts and purl all purl sts.
Row 3—(K1, p1) twice, k3.
Row 5—K2, p1, k1, p1, k2.
Row 7—K3, (p1, k1) twice.
Row 9—K4, p1, k1, p1.
Rows 11 and 12—Repeat Rows 7 and 8.
Rows 13 and 14—Repeat Rows 5 and 6.
Rows 15 and 16—Repeat Rows 3 and 4.

Repeat Rows 1–16.

Moss and Rib Block Stitch

Two versions of the block stitch are given—two different patterns, actually, but both having moss and ribbing elements. Both can be shown either way round. The odd-numbered and even-numbered sides of the fabric are different, but equally attractive. Beginners may enjoy either version; the pattern rows are easy to remember and plain to see, but changeable enough to prevent boredom while knitting.

VERSION I

Multiple of 12 sts plus 7.

Row 1—K3, p1, k3, * p2, k1, p2, k3, p1, k3; rep from *.

Row 2 and all other even-numbered rows—Knit all knit sts and purl all purl sts.

Row 3—K2, p1, k1, p1, k2, * p2, k1, p2, k2, p1, k1, p1, k2; rep from *.

Row 5—(K1, p1) 3 times, k1, * p2, k1, p2, (k1, p1) 3 times, k1; rep from *.

Rows 7 and 9—Repeat Rows 3 and 1.

Row 11—(K1, p2) twice, * k3, p1, k3, p2, k1, p2; rep from *, end k1.

Row 13—(K1, p2) twice, * k2, p1, k1, p1, k2, p2, k1, p2; rep from *, end k1.

Row 15—(K1, p2) twice, * (k1, p1) 3 times, (k1, p2) twice; rep from *, end k1.

Rows 17 and 19—Repeat Rows 13 and 11.

Row 20—See Row 2.

Repeat Rows 1–20.

Moss and Rib Block Stitch
ABOVE, LEFT: *Version I,*
  showing odd-numbered rows
BELOW, LEFT: *Version I,*
  showing even-numbered rows
ABOVE, RIGHT: *Version II,*
  showing odd-numbered rows
BELOW, RIGHT: *Version II,*
  showing even-numbered rows

VERSION II

Multiple of 12 sts plus 7.

Row 1—(P1, k1) 3 times, * p2, k1, p1, k1, p2, (k1, p1) twice, k1; rep from *, end p1.

Row 2 and all other even-numbered rows—Knit all knit sts and purl all purl sts.

Row 3—P1, * k1, p1; rep from *.

Row 5—Repeat Row 1.

Row 7—(K1, p1) twice, k1, * p2, (k1, p1) twice, k1, p2, k1, p1, k1; rep from *, end p1, k1.

Row 9—Repeat Row 3.

Row 11—Repeat Row 7.

Row 12—See Row 2.

Repeat Rows 1–12.

Rib and Chevron

Rib and Chevron

This is a wonderful pattern for sport sweaters. It gives a general impression of a broad ribbing, but has far more texture interest.

Multiple of 14 sts.

Row 1 (Right side)—* K1, p4, k4, p4, k1; rep from *.
Row 2 and all other wrong-side rows—Knit all knit sts and purl all purl sts.
Row 3—* K1, p3, k6, p3, k1; rep from *.
Row 5—* K1, p2, (k2, p1) twice, k2, p2, k1; rep from *.
Row 7—* K1, p1, (k2, p2) twice, k2, p1, k1; rep from *.
Row 9—* K3, p3, k2, p3, k3; rep from *.
Row 11—* K2, (p4, k2) twice; rep from *.
Row 13—K1, * p5, k2; rep from *, end p5, k1.
Row 14—See Row 2.

Repeat Rows 1–14.

Garter Stitch Diamonds and Ribbing Diamonds

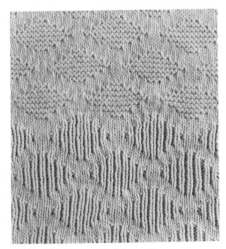

ABOVE: *Garter Stitch Diamonds*
BELOW: *Ribbing Diamonds*

A comparison of these two patterns is instructive in the matter of vertical and horizontal motifs. Although both patterns are arranged so as to have the same number of rows and stitches, yet their shapes differ. The Ribbing Diamonds appear larger and higher, and—naturally, since they are composed of ribbing—they draw the fabric together more. The Ribbing Diamonds fabric has a very beautiful wrong side consisting of diamonds outlined by purl, which could serve as well as the right side in many cases. But the wrong side of Garter Stitch Diamonds is not particularly interesting, since purl and garter stitch do not offer much contrast to each other.

Both patterns can be rearranged in a multitude of ways. They can be made bigger or smaller, taller or wider, or even combined—ribbed motifs can alternate with garter stitch motifs either vertically, horizontally, or diagonally.

I. GARTER STITCH DIAMONDS

Multiple of 18 sts plus 1.

Row 1 (Right side) and all other right-side rows—Knit.
Row 2—K2, * p6, k3; rep from *, end last repeat k2.
Row 4—P6, * k7, p11; rep from *, end last repeat p6.
Row 6—P4, * k11, p7; rep from *, end last repeat p4.
Row 8—P2, * k15, p3; rep from *, end last repeat p2.

Rows 10, 12, and 14—Repeat Rows 6, 4, and 2.
Row 16—K4, * p11, k7; rep from *, end last repeat k4.
Row 18—K6, * p7, k11; rep from *, end last repeat k6.
Row 20—K8, * p3, k15; rep from *, end last repeat k8.
Row 22—Repeat Row 18.
Row 24—Repeat Row 16.

Repeat Rows 1–24.

II. RIBBING DIAMONDS

Multiple of 18 sts plus 1.

Row 1 (Right side)—* K2, (p1, k1) 8 times; rep from *, end k1.
Row 2 and all other wrong-side rows—Knit all knit sts and purl all purl sts.
Row 3—* K4, (p1, k1) 6 times, k2; rep from *, end k1.
Row 5—* K6, (p1, k1) 4 times, k4; rep from *, end k1.
Row 7—* K1, p1, k6, p1, k1, p1, k6, p1; rep from *, end k1.
Row 9—* (K1, p1) twice, k11, p1, k1, p1; rep from *, end k1.
Row 11—* (K1, p1) 3 times, k7, (p1, k1) twice, p1; rep from *, end k1.
Row 13—* (K1, p1) 4 times, k3, (p1, k1) 3 times, p1; rep from *, end k1.
Rows 15, 17, 19, 21, and 23—Repeat Rows 11, 9, 7, 5, and 3.
Row 24—See Row 2.

Repeat Rows 1–24.

Pythagorean Pattern

A handsomely-textured arrangement of—what else?—right-angled triangles, this pattern is complicated to look at, but not to make. Both sides are alike.

Multiple of 12 sts.

Rows 1 and 2—* P6, k6; rep from *.
Rows 3 and 4—* K1, p5, k5, p1; rep from *.
Rows 5 and 6—* K2, p4, k4, p2; rep from *.
Rows 7 and 8—* K3, p3; rep from *.
Rows 9 and 10—* K4, p2, k2, p4; rep from *.
Rows 11 and 12—* K5, p1, k1, p5; rep from *.
Rows 13 and 14—* K6, p6; rep from *.
Rows 15 and 16—* P6, k6; rep from *.
Rows 17 and 18—* P5, k1, p1, k5; rep from *.
Rows 19 and 20—* P4, k2, p2, k4; rep from *.
Rows 21 and 22—* P3, k3; rep from *.
Rows 23 and 24—* P2, k4, p4, k2; rep from *.
Rows 25 and 26—* P1, k5, p5, k1; rep from *.
Rows 27 and 28—* K6, p6; rep from *.

Repeat Rows 1–28.

Pythagorean Pattern

Two Double Pennant Patterns

Both of these patterns consist of vertical ribs with pointed "pennant" motifs branching off from each side alternately; and both have extremely attractive designs on the "wrong" side of the fabric, so the knitter can use either pattern either way round.

DOUBLE PENNANT I

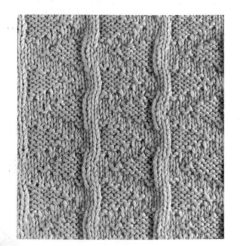

Double Pennant I

Multiple of 12 sts plus 2.

Row 1 (Wrong side)—P2, * k2, p6, k2, p2; rep from *.
Row 2—K2, * p4, k8; rep from *.
Row 3—* P6, k6; rep from *, end p2.
Row 4—K2, * p8, k4; rep from *.
Rows 5, 6, and 7—Repeat Rows 3, 2, and 1.
Row 8—* K8, p4; rep from *, end k2.
Row 9—P2, * k6, p6; rep from *.
Row 10—* K4, p8; rep from *, end k2.
Rows 11 and 12—Repeat Rows 9 and 8.

Repeat Rows 1–12.

DOUBLE PENNANT II

Double Pennant II

Multiple of 10 sts plus 1.

Row 1 (Right side)—K1, * p7, k3; rep from *.
Row 2—* P4, k6; rep from *, end p1.
Row 3—K1, * p5, k5; rep from *.
Row 4—* P6, k4; rep from *, end p1.
Row 5—K1, * p3, k7; rep from *.
Row 6—* P8, k2; rep from *, end p1.
Row 7—K1, * p1, k9; rep from *.
Rows 8, 9, 10, 11, 12, and 13—Repeat Rows 6, 5, 4, 3, 2, and 1.
Row 14—P2, * k7, p3; rep from *, end k7, p2.
Row 15—* K3, p7; rep from *, end k1.
Row 16—P1, * k6, p4; rep from *.
Row 17—* K5, p5; rep from *, end k1.
Row 18—P1, * k4, p6; rep from *.
Row 19—* K7, p3; rep from *, end k1.
Row 20—P1, * k2, p8; rep from *.
Row 21—* K9, p1; rep from *, end k1.
Rows 22, 23, 24, 25, 26, 27, and 28—Repeat Rows 20, 19, 18, 17, 16, 15, and 14.

Repeat Rows 1–28.

Fancy Lozenge Pattern

In this handsome pattern are flattened diamonds decorated with alternating diagonals. The wrong side is very attractive. Fancy Lozenge Pattern serves nicely for afghan strips, sweaters, skirts, and baby blankets.

Fancy Lozenge Pattern

Multiple of 18 sts plus 2.

Row 1 (Right side)—P2, * k4, p4, k2, p2, k4, p2; rep from *.

Row 2—K3, * p4, k2, p2, k2, p4, k4; rep from *, end last repeat k3.

Row 3—K2, * p2, k4, p4, k4, p2, k2; rep from *.

Row 4—P1, * k4, (p4, k2) twice, p2; rep from *, end k1.

Row 5—P2, * k2, p2, k8, p2, k2, p2; rep from *.

Row 6—K1, * p2, k4, p6, k2, p2, k2; rep from *, end p1.

Row 7—K2, * p2, k2, p2, k4, (p2, k2) twice; rep from *.

Row 8—P1, * k2, p2, k2, p6, k4, p2; rep from *, end k1.

Rows 9, 11, and 12—Repeat Rows 5, 3, and 2.

Row 10—K1, * p2, (k2, p4) twice, k4; rep from *, end p1.

Row 13—P2, * k4, p2, k2, p4, k4, p2; rep from *.

Row 14—P5, * (k2, p2) twice, k2, p8; rep from *, end last repeat p5.

Row 15—K4, * (p2, k2) twice, p4, k6; rep from *, end last repeat k4.

Row 16—P3, * (k2, p2) 3 times, k2, p4; rep from *, end last repeat p3.

Row 17—K4, * p4, (k2, p2) twice, k6; rep from *, end last repeat k4.

Row 18—Repeat Row 14.

Repeat Rows 1–18.

Moss Diamond and Lozenge Pattern

Contributed by Hildegard M. Elsner, Aldan, Pennsylvania

This pattern is ideal for scarves, because it is exactly alike on both sides. It is a rather ingenious arrangement of Moss Stitch "diamonds"—which aren't true diamonds, as they are off-center by one stitch—with lozenges of knit and purl. A smaller version, which splits the lozenges across the middle and places the diamonds in vertical alignment, can be had in either of two ways: by working Rows 1—24 only, or Rows 25—44 only. In either case, the back and front are still identical.

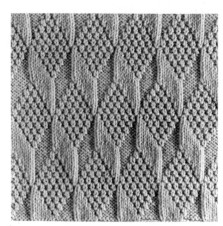
Moss Diamond and Lozenge Pattern

Rows 1 and 2—* K6, p6; rep from *.

Rows 3 and 4—* P1, k5, p5, k1; rep from *.

Rows 5 and 6—* K1, p1, k4, p4, k1, p1; rep from *.

Rows 7 and 8—* P1, k1, p1, k3, p3, k1, p1, k1; rep from *.

Rows 9 and 10—* (K1, p1) twice, k2, p2, (k1, p1) twice; rep from *.

Rows 11 and 12—* P1, k1; rep from *.

Rows 13 and 14—* K1, p1; rep from *.

Rows 15 and 16—* (P1, k1) twice, p2, k2, (p1, k1) twice; rep from *.

Rows 17 and 18—* K1, p1, k1, p3, k3, p1, k1, p1; rep from *.

Rows 19 and 20—* P1, k1, p4, k4, p1, k1; rep from *.

Rows 21 and 22—* K1, p5, k5, p1; rep from *.

Rows 23 and 24—* P6, k6; rep from *.

Rows 25 and 26—* P5, k1, p1, k5; rep from *.

Rows 27 and 28—* P4, (k1, p1) twice, k4; rep from *.

Rows 29 and 30—* P3, (k1, p1) 3 times, k3; rep from *.

Rows 31 and 32—* P2, (k1, p1) 4 times, k2; rep from *.

Rows 33 and 34—* P1, k1; rep from *.

Rows 35 and 36—* K1, p1; rep from *.

Rows 37 and 38—* K2, (p1, k1) 4 times, p2; rep from *.

Rows 39 and 40—* K3, (p1, k1) 3 times, p3; rep from *.

Rows 41 and 42—* K4, (p1, k1) twice, p4; rep from *.

Rows 43 and 44—* K5, p1, k1, p5; rep from *.

Repeat Rows 1–44.

Pavilion Pattern

Contributed by Hildegard M. Elsner, Aldan, Pennsylvania

Both sides of this pattern are interesting, although the odd-numbered rows are shown here as the right side. Many knitters may prefer to use the even-numbered rows as the right side instead.

Multiple of 18 sts.

Row 1—* K2, p1, k5, p7, k3; rep from *.

Row 2 and all other even-numbered rows—Knit all knit sts and purl all purl sts.

Row 3—* (K1, p1) twice, k5, p5, k4; rep from *.

Row 5—* P1, k3, p1, k5, p3, k5; rep from *.

Row 7—* K5, p1, k5, p7; rep from *.

Row 9—* (P1, k5) twice, p5, k1; rep from *.

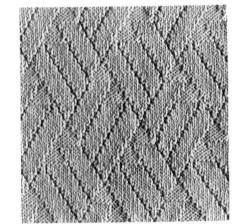

Pavilion Pattern

Row 11—* K1, (p1, k5) twice, p3, k2; rep from *.
Row 13—K2, * p1, k5; rep from *, end last repeat k3.
Row 15—* K3, p1, k5, p1, k3, p1, k1, p1, k2; rep from *.
Row 17—* K4, p1, k5, p1, k1, p1, k3, p1, k1; rep from *.
Row 19—* K5, p7, k5, p1; rep from *.
Row 21—* P1, k5, p5, k5, p1, k1; rep from *.
Row 23—* K1, p1, k5, p3, k5, p1, k2; rep from *.
Row 25—* K2, p7, k5, p1, k3; rep from *.
Row 27—* K1, p1, k1, p5, k5, p1, k4; rep from *.
Row 29—* P1, k3, p3, k5, p1, k5; rep from *.
Row 31—* K5, p1; rep from *.
Row 33—* K4, p1, k1, p1, k3, p1, k5, p1, k1; rep from *.
Row 35—* (K3, p1) twice, k1, p1, k5, p1, k2; rep from *.
Row 36—See Row 2.

Repeat Rows 1–36.

CHAPTER TWO

Slip-Stitch Patterns

Slip-stitch knitting is easy, fast, and fascinating. Many beautiful effects can be created with slip-stitches, either in a solid color or in combinations of two or more colors. Patterns for the former will be found in this chapter; patterns for the latter will be found in the following chapters.

Two special terms—wyif and wyib—have been coined by the author to clear up a certain ambiguity previously associated with slip-stitch patterns. The plain, bald "sl 1" so often encountered in other knitting directions usually implies with yarn in *back* (wyib) on a right-side row, and with yarn in *front* (wyif) on a wrong-side row. But quite a few patterns require a reversal of this procedure. Therefore the directions in these chapters have no reference to the right or wrong side of the fabric at all. "Front" is the side that is *facing* the knitter at the moment when the stitch is slipped, whichever side it may be; "back" is the side that is *away from* the knitter. With this distinction clearly in mind, you should have no difficulty in working a large variety of delightful slip-stitch patterns.

Most of these patterns make dense, firm fabrics. Slip-stitches tend to draw the rows more tightly together than plain knitting, and so in most cases more rows will be required to reach a given length. Some patterns do all sorts of fancy things with the slipped stitches, to create intricate designs; others are exceedingly simple. Any knitter can find a slip-stitch pattern to suit her own level of ability and her own taste. It is interesting, too, to try these patterns in different types of yarns and different needle sizes. Sometimes several completely different effects can be obtained from the same pattern under these circumstances. Thus the reader is advised *not* to accept every photographed swatch as an invariable picture of the pattern. Follow directions carefully, but do it *your* way, with *your* yarn; and don't be surprised if the pattern comes out with a new and unusual appearance.

Rank and File Stitch

This is a nice little texture pattern with a soldierly arrangement of slip-stitches marching in disciplined formation across the fabric. Use it in chunky sweaters, hats, jackets, coats or slippers.

Even number of sts.

Row 1 (Right side)—Knit.
Row 2—K1, * sl 2 wyif, put yarn to back, sl the same 2 sts back to left-hand needle and knit them; rep from *, end k1.
Row 3—K1, * p1, sl 1 wyib; rep from *, end k1.
Row 4—K1, * sl 1 wyif, k1; rep from *, end k1.

Repeat Rows 1–4.

Rank and File Stitch

Cartridge-Belt Rib

Although this is not a ribbing, in the sense of possessing horizontal elasticity, it does make vertical flutings that are gently rounded out from the fabric. It is close, firm, non-curling, and looks the same on both sides. The pattern makes simple but beautiful borders, well-mannered sportswear, and easy-to-knit afghans.

Multiple of 4 sts plus 3.

Row 1—K3, * sl 1 wyif, k3; rep from *.
Row 2—K1, * sl 1 wyif, k3; rep from *, end sl 1, k1.

Repeat Rows 1 and 2.

Cartridge-Belt Rib

Swag Stitch, or Scallop Stitch

This is an easy pattern showing embossed horizontal strands. It enjoyed considerable popularity in the U.S. during the 1940's. It is attractive in blouses (especially yokes), baby wear, collars, pockets, and other accent areas.

Multiple of 5 sts plus 2.

Row 1 (Wrong side) and all other wrong-side rows—Purl.
Row 2—Knit.
Rows 4 and 6—P2, * sl 3 wyif, p2; rep from *.

Repeat Rows 1–6.

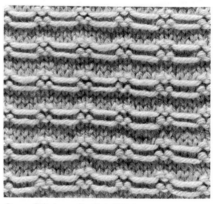

Swag Stitch, or Scallop Stitch

Slipped Rib Check

Multiple of 4 sts plus 3.

Row 1 (Wrong side)—Purl.
Rows 2, 4, and 6—P1, * sl 1 wyib, p3; rep from *, end sl 1, p1.
Rows 3 and 5—K1, * p1, k3; rep from *, end p1, k1.
Row 7—Purl.
Rows 8, 10, and 12—P3, * sl 1 wyib, p3; rep from *.
Rows 9 and 11—K3, * p1, k3; rep from *.

Repeat Rows 1–12.

VARIATION: BASKETWEAVE CHECK

Multiple of 6 sts plus 2.

Row 1 (Wrong side)—Purl.
Rows 2, 4, and 6—K1, * p2, sl 2 wyib, p2; rep from *, end k1.
Rows 3 and 5—K3, * p2, k4; rep from *, end last repeat k3.
Row 7—Purl.
Rows 8, 10 and 12—K1, sl 1 wyib, * p4, sl 2 wyib; rep from *, end p4, sl 1 wyib, k1.
Rows 9 and 11—K1, p1, * k4, p2; rep from *, end k4, p1, k1.

Repeat Rows 1–12.

ABOVE: *Slipped Rib Check*
BELOW: *Basketweave Check*

Slip-Stitch Weave

Contributed by Toshiko Sugiyama, Oakland, California

This simple pattern gives a flat, shapely fabric that is slightly nubby in texture, very nice for suits, coats and dresses. The two-color version, below, is a small-patterned tweed.

Odd number of sts.

Rows 1 and 3 (Wrong side)—Purl.
Row 2—P1, * sl 1 wyib, p1; rep from *.
Row 4—P2, * sl 1 wyib, p1; rep from *, end p1.

Repeat Rows 1–4.

TWO-COLOR VARIATION

Work Rows 1 and 2 in Color A, Rows 3 and 4 in Color B.

ABOVE: *Slip-Stitch Weave*
BELOW: *Two-Color Variation*

Fluted Fabric Stitch

This version of Fabric Stitch (*A Treasury of Knitting Patterns*, p. 99) is really different. It gives softly-rounded little columns of woven strands, very beautiful in coats, suits, and jackets. The wrong side resembles a ribbing on a seed-stitch background. The pattern is pretty in one, two, or three colors. Simply repeat the same two pattern rows for each color, when working with more than one—changing strands at the beginning of each right-side row.

ABOVE: *Fluted Fabric Stitch*
BELOW: *Fluted Fabric Stitch in two colors*

Multiple of 4 sts plus 1.

Row 1 (Right side)—P1, * k1, sl 1 wyif, k1, p1; rep from *.
Row 2—K1, * sl 1 wyib, p1, sl 1 wyib, k1; rep from *.

Repeat Rows 1 and 2.

Jacquard Stitch

This handsome, well-bred "weave" can be varied in many ways. Its lines need not zigzag; they can be worked as continuous diagonals simply by repeating the first six rows only (for a left diagonal) or the last six rows only (for a right diagonal). Or, the zigzag pattern can be made larger, by continuing the diagonals for a greater distance before turning (i.e., work the first six rows twice, then the last six rows twice, making 24 rows to a repeat). The pattern can be worked also on different multiples, with 3, 5, or 6 plain knit stitches between the slipped stitches; or the woven strands can span 3 stitches instead of 2. Any version is good for making a quietly elegant fabric that will enhance suits, coats, tailored dresses, classic sweaters, cushions, gloves, etc.

Jacquard Stitch

Multiple of 6 sts plus 4.

Row 1 (Right side)—K1, * sl 2 wyif, k4; rep from *, end sl 2, k1.
Row 2—P1, sl 1 wyib, * p4, sl 2 wyib; rep from *, end p2.
Row 3—K3, * sl 2 wyif, k4; rep from *, end k1.
Row 4—P4, * sl 2 wyib, p4; rep from *.
Row 5—K5, * sl 2 wyif, k4; rep from *, end sl 2, k3.
Row 6—P2, * sl 2 wyib, p4; rep from *, end sl 1, p1.
Row 7—Repeat Row 1.
Rows 8, 9, 10, 11, and 12—Repeat Rows 6, 5, 4, 3, and 2.

Repeat Rows 1–12.

Jacquard Diamonds

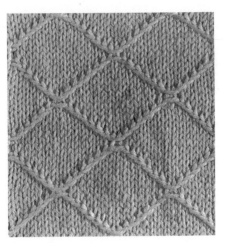

Jacquard Diamonds

These are not "real" diamonds. They are adjoining chevrons, worked horizontally, alternating so as to touch at each crest. If a plain horizontal-wave effect is wanted, Rows 1–10 will give the single chevron pattern.

Multiple of 16 sts plus 1.

Row 1 (Right side)—K1, * k15, sl 1 wyif; rep from *, end k16.
Row 2—P1, sl 1 wyib, * p13, sl 3 wyib; rep from *, end last repeat sl 1, p1 instead of sl 3.
Row 3—K1, * sl 2 wyif, k11, sl 2 wyif, k1; rep from *.
Row 4—P2, * sl 2 wyib, p9, sl 2 wyib, p3; rep from *, end last repeat p2.
Row 5—K3, * sl 2 wyif, k7, sl 2 wyif, k5; rep from *, end last repeat k3.
Row 6—P4, * sl 2 wyib, p5, sl 2 wyib, p7; rep from *, end last repeat p4.
Row 7—K5, * sl 2 wyif, k3, sl 2 wyif, k9; rep from *, end last repeat k5.
Row 8—P6, * sl 2 wyib, p1, sl 2 wyib, p11; rep from *, end last repeat p6.
Row 9—K7, * sl 3 wyif, k13; rep from *, end last repeat k7.
Row 10—P8, * sl 1 wyib, p15; rep from *, end last repeat p8.
Rows 11, 12, 13, 14, 15, 16, 17, and 18—Repeat Rows 9, 8, 7, 6, 5, 4, 3, and 2.

Repeat Rows 1–18.

Double Knit Fabric

Double Knit Fabric

Contributed by Eugen K. Beugler, Dexter, Oregon

This pattern resembles ribbing on the right side, and a purl fabric on the wrong side. Actually, it is neither. It is a very soft, thick, cosy fabric for warm winter sweaters and really cuddly afghans. This is not the same thing as Double Knitting, which has two separate sides to it (See *A Treasury of Knitting Patterns*, p. 99).

Odd number of sts.

Row 1 (Right side)—K1, * sl 1 wyib, k1; rep from *.
Row 2—K1, * p1, k1; rep from *.

Repeat Rows 1 and 2.

Vandyke Swag Stitch

The Swag Stitch technique is used here to make a beautifully "tailored" fabric for suits, jackets, and coats. It is very easy to work, and so even a beginner can use it to make clothes with a trim fashion look.

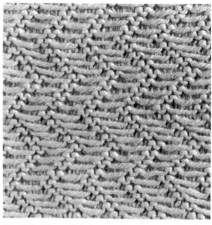

Vandyke Swag Stitch

Multiple of 5 sts plus 2.

Row 1 (Wrong side) and all other wrong-side rows—K1, purl to last st, k1.

Row 2—K1, * sl 3 wyif, p2; rep from *, end k1.

Row 4—K1, p1, * sl 3 wyif, p2; rep from *, end sl 3, p1, k1.

Row 6—K1, * p2, sl 3 wyif; rep from *, end k1.

Row 8—K1, sl 1 wyif, * p2, sl 3 wyif; rep from *, end p2, sl 2, k1.

Row 10—K1, sl 2 wyif, * p2, sl 3 wyif; rep from *, end p2, sl 1, k1.

Rows 12, 14, and 16—Repeat Rows 8, 6, and 4.

Repeat Rows 1–16.

Dimple Stitch

Slipped strands, caught up 4 rows later, are used to pull this bold, puffy fabric together. The wrong side, which might serve just as well as a right side, shows a deep honeycomb formation in purl stitches.

ABOVE: *Dimple Stitch, right side*
BELOW: *Dimple Stitch, wrong side*

Multiple of 6 sts plus 5.

Row 1 (Right side)—Knit.

Rows 2 and 4—K1, * sl 3 wyif, p3; rep from *, end sl 3, k1.

Row 3—K1, * sl 3 wyib, k3; rep from *, end sl 3, k1.

Rows 5 and 7—Knit.

Row 6—Purl.

Row 8—K1, p1, * insert needle from below under the 3 loose strands of Rows 2, 3, and 4, and knit next st, bringing st out under strands; p5; rep from *, end last repeat p1, k1 instead of p5.

Row 9—Knit.

Rows 10 and 12—K1, * p3, sl 3 wyif; rep from *, end p3, k1.

Row 11—K4, * sl 3 wyib, k3; rep from *, end k1.

Rows 13 and 15—Knit.

Row 14—Purl.

Row 16—K1, p4, * knit next st under 3 loose strands of Rows 10, 11, and 12; p5; rep from *, end last repeat p4, k1.

Repeat Rows 1–16.

Blind Buttonhole Stitch

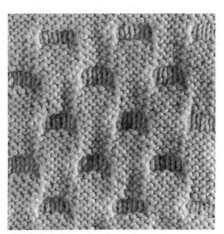

Blind Buttonhole Stitch

Deeply sunk in a heavy purl fabric, these buttonless "buttonholes" make winter sweaters and sportswear with plenty of texture. The wrong side is a surprise bonus—an attractive design of horizontal welts formed of slipped strands and purl stitches.

Multiple of 10 sts plus 2.

Rows 1, 3, and 5 (Wrong side)—Knit.
Rows 2 and 4—Purl.
Rows 6, 8, and 10—K6, * sl 5 wyib, k5; rep from *, end sl 5, k1.
Rows 7 and 9—K1, * sl 5 wyif, p5; rep from *, end k1.
Rows 11 through 15—Repeat Rows 1 through 5.
Rows 16, 18, and 20—K1, * sl 5 wyib, k5; rep from *, end k1.
Rows 17 and 19—K1, * p5, sl 5 wyif; rep from *, end k1.

Repeat Rows 1–20.

Blocks and Bars

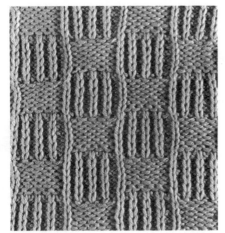

Blocks and Bars

This fabric must be felt to be appreciated. It is so dense and cosy as to seem almost like a double-knit. With its attractive checkerboard design, it makes wonderful coats, lap robes, cushions, and heavy outdoor sweaters. The wrong side looks like stockinette stitch, with tighter and looser stitches arranged in blocks between purled scallops.

Multiple of 24 sts plus 3.

Row 1 (Wrong side)—Purl.
Row 2—K1, sl 1 wyib, * (p1, sl 1 wyif) 5 times, p1, (sl 1 wyib, p2) 4 times, sl 1 wyib; rep from *, end k1.
Row 3—K1, * (p1, k2) 4 times, p1, (sl 1 wyib, k1) 5 times, sl 1 wyib; rep from *, end p1, k1.
Rows 4 through 12—Repeat Rows 2 and 3, 4 times more; then repeat Row 2 again.
Row 13—Purl.
Row 14—K1, * (sl 1 wyib, p2) 4 times, sl 1 wyib, (p1, sl 1 wyif) 5 times, p1; rep from *, end sl 1 wyib, k1.
Row 15—K1, p1, * (sl 1 wyib, k1) 5 times, sl 1 wyib, (p1, k2) 4 times, p1; rep from *, end k1.
Rows 16 through 24—Repeat Rows 14 and 15, 4 times more; then repeat Row 14 again.

Repeat Rows 1–24.

Jewel Cross-Rib

This is a beautiful old pattern derived from a simple Block Stitch, making a very sophisticated texture that resembles small cables enclosing ovals of garter stitch. Its curved and interwoven lines draw the eye into intricate designs, but the pattern is very simple to work.

Jewel Cross-Rib

Multiple of 7 sts plus 1.

Rows 1, 3, and 5 (Wrong side)—P3, * k2, p5; rep from *, end k2, p3.

Rows 2, 4, and 6—Knit.

Rows 7 and 9—K2, * sl 1 wyif, k2, sl 1 wyif, k3; rep from *, end last repeat k2.

Row 8—K2, * sl 1 wyib, k2, sl 1 wyib, k3; rep from *, end last repeat k2.

Row 10—K2, * drop first sl-st off needle to front of work, sl next 2 sts to right-hand needle, drop second sl-st off needle to front of work; then pick up the first dropped st onto left-hand needle, sl the same 2 sts back to left-hand needle, then with point of right-hand needle pick up the second dropped st and replace it on left-hand needle; k7; rep from *, end last repeat k6.

Repeat Rows 1–10.

Slip-Stitch Smocking

Contributed by Hildegard M. Elsner, Aldan, Pennsylvania

Multiple of 8 sts plus 7.

Row 1 (Right side)—K1, * sl 1 wyib, k4, pass sl-st over the 4 knit sts, p3; rep from *, end last repeat k1 instead of p3.

Row 2—K1, p1, * k1, knit 1 st under running thread between the st just worked and the next st, k1, p5; rep from *, end last repeat p1, k1 instead of p5.

Row 3—K2, * p3, k5; rep from *, end p3, k2.

Row 4—K1, p1, * k3, p5; rep from *, end k3, p1, k1.

Row 5—K2, * p3, sl 1 wyib, k4, pass sl-st over the 4 knit sts; rep from *, end p3, k2.

Row 6—K1, * p5, k1, knit 1 st under running thread, k1; rep from *, end p5, k1.

Row 7—K1, * k5, p3; rep from *, end k6.

Row 8—K1, * p5, k3; rep from *, end p5, k1.

Slip-Stitch Smocking

Repeat Rows 1–8.

Twice-Turned Stitch

ABOVE: *Twice-Turned Stitch*
BELOW: *Twice-Turned Ribbing*

This attractive, deep-textured fabric has stitches that are turned once as slipped, and a second time as they are knitted through the back. (See Twice-Turned Check.) The variation, below, is even deeper in texture and has the appearance of a ribbing, though not much elasticity. Either version is nice for thick, cosy jackets, coats, and blankets.

Odd Number of sts.

Row 1 (Wrong side)—Purl.
Row 2—K1, * keeping yarn in back, insert needle from the *left* into *back* loop of next st, as if to p1-b, and *slip* the st from this position; k1; rep from *.
Row 3—P1, * sl 1 wyif, p1; rep from *.
Row 4—K1, * k1-b, k1; rep from *.

Repeat Rows 1–4.

VARIATION: *TWICE-TURNED RIBBING*

Odd number of sts.

Row 1 (Wrong side)—K1, * p1, k1; rep from *.
Row 2—P1, * slip next st from back as in Row 2 above; p1; rep from *.
Row 3—K1, * sl 1 wyif, k1; rep from *.
Row 4—P1, * k1-b, p1; rep from *.

Repeat Rows 1–4.

Slip-Cross Open Cable

CENTER PANEL: *Slip-Cross Open Cable*
SIDE PANELS: *Slip-Cross Coin Cable*

NOTE: On right-side (even-numbered) rows sl all sl-sts wyib. On wrong-side (odd-numbered) rows sl all sl-sts wyif.

Panel of 10 sts.

Row 1 (Wrong side)—K3, p1, k2, p1, k3.
Row 2—P3, sl 1, p2, sl 1, p3.
Row 3—K3, sl 1, k2, sl 1, k3.
Row 4—P1, sl the next 2 purl sts, drop next st off needle to front of work, sl the same 2 purl sts back to left-hand needle, pick up dropped st and knit it, p4, drop next st off needle to front of work, p2, pick up dropped st and knit it, p1.
Rows 5 and 7—K1, p1, k6, p1, k1.
Row 6—P1, k1, p6, k1, p1.
Row 8—P1, sl 1, p6, sl 1, p1.
Row 9—K1, sl 1, k6, sl 1, k1.

Row 10—P1, drop next st off needle to front of work, p2, pick up dropped st and knit it; p2, sl the next 2 purl sts, drop next st off needle to front of work, sl the same 2 purl sts back to left-hand needle, pick up dropped st and knit it, p3.

Rows 11, 12, and 13—Repeat Rows 1, 2, and 3.

Row 14—P3, drop next st off needle to front of work, sl the 2 purl sts, drop next st off needle to front; then holding the 2 purl sts on right-hand needle, pick up the first dropped st onto left-hand needle, then sl the 2 purl sts back to left-hand needle; then pick up the second dropped st and return it to left-hand needle; then k1, p2, k1 across these 4 sts; p3.

Repeat Rows 1–14.

Slip-Cross Coin Cable

Panel of 9 sts.

Rows 1 and 3 (Wrong side)—K2, p5, k2.

Row 2—P2, k5, p2.

Row 4—P2, sl 1 wyib, k3, sl 1 wyib, p2.

Row 5—K2, sl 1 wyif, p3, sl 1 wyif, k2.

Row 6—P2, drop first sl-st off needle to front of work, sl next 3 sts, drop second sl-st off needle to front; then holding the 3 knit sts on right-hand needle pick up the first dropped st onto left-hand needle; then sl the 3 knit sts back to left-hand needle; then with point of right-hand needle pick up the second dropped st and place it on left-hand needle; then k5, p2.

Rows 7 and 8—Repeat Rows 1 and 2.

Repeat Rows 1–8.

Slip-Cross Double Cables

These are pretty cables, easy to work, and done without any actual cabling. Other arrangements of slipped and slip-crossed stitches in the cable form are possible, but these three will serve as a demonstration. If desired, the twist row may be omitted from Versions I and II, by working Row 2 in these versions the same as Row 2 of Version III.

All three versions: Panel of 12 sts.

NOTES: Right Slip-Cross (RSC), worked on 4 sts: drop 1st sl-st off needle to front of work, sl the next 2 purl sts, drop 2nd sl-st off needle to front of work; then with left-hand needle pick up the 1st dropped st, then sl the same 2 purl sts back to left-hand needle, then with right-hand needle pick up 2nd dropped st and place it on left-hand needle; then k1, p2, k1 across the 4 sts.

Left Slip-Cross (LSC), worked on 4 sts: drop 1st sl-st off needle to front of work, sl the next 2 purl sts, drop 2nd sl-st off needle to front of work; then sl the 2 purl sts back to left-hand needle, pick up the 2nd dropped st and knit it, p2, then pick up the 1st dropped st and knit it.

Slip-Cross Double Cables
LEFT: *Version I,*
  "Opening" Cable with Left Twist
RIGHT: *Version II,*
  "Closing" Cable with Right Twist
CENTER: *Version III,*
  Medallion Cable with Purl Twist

VERSION I:
"OPENING" CABLE WITH LEFT TWIST

Row 1 (Wrong side)—K2, p1, k2, p2, k2, p1, k2.

Row 2—P2, k1, p2, skip next st and knit in back of 2nd st, then knit in front of skipped st, then sl both sts from needle together; p2, k1, p2.

Row 3—Repeat Row 1.

Row 4—P2, sl 1 wyib, p2, sl 2 wyib, p2, sl 1 wyib, p2.

Row 5—K2, sl 1 wyif, k2, sl 2 wyif, k2, sl 1 wyif, k2.

Row 6—P2, RSC, LSC, p2.

Repeat Rows 1–6.

VERSION II:
"CLOSING" CABLE WITH RIGHT TWIST

Work the same as Version I, with the following exceptions:

Row 2—P2, k1, p2, skip next st and knit in front of 2nd st, then knit in front of skipped st, then sl both sts from needle together; p2, k1, p2.

Row 6—P2, LSC, RSC, p2.

VERSION III:
MEDALLION CABLE WITH PURL TWIST

Row 1 (Wrong side)—K2, p1, k2, p2, k2, p1, k2.

Row 2—P2, k1, p2, k2, p2, k1, p2.

Row 3—K2, p1, k2, skip next st and purl the 2nd st, then purl the skipped st and sl both sts from needle together; k2, p1, k2.

Row 4—Repeat Row 2.

Row 5—Repeat Row 1.

Row 6—P2, sl 1 wyib, p2, sl 2 wyib, p2, sl 1 wyib, p2.

Row 7—K2, sl 1 wyif, k2, sl 2 wyif, k2, sl 1 wyif, k2.

Row 8—P2, LSC, RSC, p2.

Row 9—Repeat Row 1.

Row 10—Repeat Row 2.

Row 11—Repeat Row 1.

Rows 12 and 13—Repeat Rows 6 and 7.

Row 14—P2, RSC, LSC, p2.

Repeat Rows 1–14.

Bud Stitch

In both Bud Stitch and Cornflower Pattern, each motif consists of five "made" stitches, like a bobble; but these increased stitches are differently handled. In Bud Stitch they are drawn all together to make a clump, five rows later. In Cornflower Pattern they are fanned out to each side. Both patterns make a novel and intriguing texture, the Bud Stitch being a little more highly embossed.

NOTE: The 3 stitches slipped knitwise in Rows 6 and 12 of this pattern are slipped all together, *not* one at a time. Insert needle into 3rd, 2nd, and 1st stitch in that order, and slip them off.

ABOVE: *Bud Stitch*
BELOW: *Cornflower Pattern*

Multiple of 10 sts plus 2.

Row 1 (Wrong side)—Purl.
Row 2—K8, * (k1, yo, k1, yo, k1) in next st, k9; rep from *, end last repeat k3.
Row 3—P3, * purl the 5 new sts wrapping yarn twice for each st, p9; rep from *, end last repeat p8.
Row 4—K8, * sl 5 wyib dropping extra wraps, k9; rep from *, end last repeat k3.
Row 5—P3, * sl 5 wyif, p9; rep from *, end last repeat p8.
Row 6—K8, * sl 3 knitwise—k2 tog—p3sso, k9; rep from *, end last repeat k3.
Row 7—Purl.
Row 8—K3, * (k1, yo, k1, yo, k1) in next st, k9; rep from *, end last repeat k8.
Row 9—P8, * purl the 5 new sts wrapping yarn twice for each st, p9; rep from *, end last repeat p3.
Row 10—K3, * sl 5 wyib dropping extra wraps, k9; rep from *, end last repeat k8.
Row 11—P8, * sl 5 wyif, p9; rep from *, end last repeat p3.
Row 12—K3, * sl 3 knitwise—k2 tog—p3sso, k9; rep from *, end last repeat k8.

Repeat Rows 1–12.

Cornflower Pattern

See Bud Stitch.

Multiple of 18 sts plus 2.

Row 1 (Right side)—K5, * (k1, yo, k1, yo, k1) in next st, k17; rep from *, end last repeat k14.
Row 2—P14, * purl the 5 new sts wrapping yarn twice for each st, p17; rep from *, end last repeat p5.
Row 3—K1, * sl 4 wyib, drop first elongated st off needle to front of work, sl the same 4 sts back to left-hand needle, pick up dropped st knitwise and sl it onto left-hand needle; then k2 tog-b (the elongated st and the next st); k3, sl 3 wyib dropping extra wraps, drop last elongated st off needle to front, sl 4 wyib, pick up dropped st onto left-hand needle, sl the same 4 sts back to left-hand needle; k3, k2 tog (the last of the 4 sts and the elongated st); k9; rep from *, end k1.

Row 4—P14, * sl 3 wyif, p17; rep from *, end last repeat p5.

Row 5—K2, * sl 3 wyib, drop next elongated st off needle to front, sl the same 3 sts back to left-hand needle, pick up dropped st knitwise and sl it onto left-hand needle; then k2 tog-b; k2, sl 1 wyib, drop next elongated st off needle to front, sl 3 wyib, pick up dropped st onto left-hand needle, sl the same 3 sts back to left-hand needle; k2, k2 tog, k11; rep from *.

Row 6—Purl.

Row 7—K14, * (k1, yo, k1, yo, k1) in next st, k17; rep from *, end last repeat k5.

Row 8—P5, * purl the 5 new sts wrapping yarn twice for each st, p17; rep from *, end last repeat p14.

Row 9—K10, rep from * of Row 3; end last repeat k1 instead of k9.

Row 10—P5, * sl 3 wyif, p17; rep from *, end last repeat p14.

Row 11—K11, rep from * of Row 5; end last repeat k2 instead of k11.

Row 12—Purl.

Repeat Rows 1–12.

Sprig Pattern

Sprig Pattern

Here is an ingenious texture stitch to place all over your pastel spring sweater or your little girl's party dress. The directions are long, but the pattern is very easy to learn in one repeat.

Multiple of 16 sts plus 5.

NOTES: Right Cross (RC)—sl 1 purl st wyib, drop next (slipped) st off needle to front of work, sl the same purl st back to left-hand needle, pick up dropped st and knit it, p1.

Left Cross (LC)—drop (slipped) st off needle to front of work, p1, then pick up dropped st and knit it.

Inc 5—(k1, yo, k1, yo, k1) in the same st. All slip-stitches on wrong-side rows are slipped with yarn in *front*.

Row 1 (Right side)—P2, * inc 5, p3, k1, p3; rep from *, end p3.

Row 2—K3, * k3, sl 1, k3, p5; rep from *, end k2.

Row 3—P2, * k5, p3, inc 5, p3, k5, p3, k1, p3; rep from *, end p3.

Row 4—K3, * k3, sl 1, k3, p1, p3 tog, p1, k3, p5, k3, p1, p3 tog, p1; rep from *, end k2.

Row 5—P2, * sl 1—k2 tog—psso, p3, k5, p3, sl 1—k2 tog—psso, p3, k1, p3; rep from *, end p3.

Row 6—K6, * sl 1, k7, p1, p3 tog, p1, k7; rep from *, end last repeat k6.

Row 7—P6, * sl 1—k2 tog—psso, p5, p2 tog, (k1, yo, k1) in next st, p2 tog, p5; rep from *, end last repeat p4.

Row 8—K5, * sl 1, p1, sl 1, k13; rep from *.

Row 9—P12, * RC, k1, LC, p11; rep from *, end last repeat p4.

Row 10—K4, * (sl 1, k1) twice, sl 1, k11; rep from *, end k1.

Row 11—P11, * RC, p1, k1, p1, LC, p9; rep from *, end last repeat p3.

Row 12—K3, * (sl 1, k2) twice, sl 1, k9; rep from *, end k2.

Row 13—P10, * RC, p2, k1, p2, LC, p7; rep from *, end last repeat p2.

Row 14—K2, * (sl 1, k3) twice, sl 1, k7; rep from *, end k3.

Row 15—P3, * p3, k1, p3, inc 5; rep from *, end p2.

Row 16—K2, * p5, k3, sl 1, k3; rep from *, end k3.

Row 17—P3, * p3, k1, p3, k5, p3, inc 5, p3, k5; rep from *, end p2.

Row 18—K2, * p1, p3 tog, p1, k3, p5, k3, p1, p3 tog, p1, k3, sl 1, k3; rep from *, end k3.

Row 19—P3, * p3, k1, p3, sl 1—k2 tog—psso, p3, k5, p3, sl 1—k2 tog—psso; rep from *, end p2.

Row 20—K6, * p1, p3 tog, p1, k7, sl 1, k7; rep from *, end last repeat k6.

Row 21—P4, * p2 tog, (k1, yo, k1) in next st, p2 tog, p5, sl 1—k2 tog—psso, p5; rep from *, end p1.

Row 22—* K13, sl 1, p1, sl 1; rep from *, end k5.

Row 23—P4, * RC, k1, LC, p11; rep from *, end p1.

Row 24—K12, * (sl 1, k1) twice, sl 1, k11; rep from *, end last repeat k4.

Row 25—P3, * RC, p1, k1, p1, LC, p9; rep from *, end p2.

Row 26—K11, * (sl 1, k2) twice, sl 1, k9; rep from *, end last repeat k3.

Row 27—P2, * RC, p2, k1, p2, LC, p7; rep from *, end p3.

Row 28—K10, * (sl 1, k3) twice, sl 1, k7; rep from *, end last repeat k2.

Repeat Rows 1–28.

Saracen's Crown

This beautiful pattern makes a unique panel decoration for any sweater. Though the directions may seem complicated, it is simple to work. After making just one Crown, the knitter can easily see just how to make the next, without any further reading of the directions. Saracen's Crown can be arranged as a spot-pattern, as well as a panel.

Panel of 17 sts.

NOTES: K1-2w—K1 wrapping yarn twice around needle.

Dw—drop wrap; that is, drop extra wrappings off needle as the stitch is slipped.

RSC (Right Slip-Cross)—sl 2 purl sts, drop next (elongated) st off needle to front of work, sl the same 2 purl sts back to left-hand needle, pick up dropped st and place it on left-hand needle, then k1, p2 across these 3 sts.

LSC (Left Slip-Cross)—drop the elongated st off needle to front of work, sl next 2 purl sts, pick up dropped st and place on left-hand needle, sl the same 2 purl sts back to left-hand needle, then p2, k1 across these 3 sts.

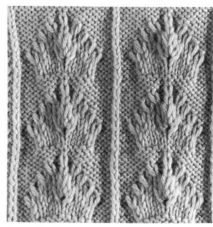

Saracen's Crown

Row 1 (Right side)—P4, k9, p4.

Row 2—K4, p9, k4.

Row 3—P4, k1-2w, k3, (k1, yo, k1, yo, k1) in next st, k3, k1-2w, p4.

Row 4—K4, sl 1 wyif dw, p3, p5 wrapping yarn twice for each st, p3, sl 1 wyif dw, k4.

Row 5—P2, RSC, k1-2w, k2, sl 5 wyib dw, k2, k1-2w, LSC, p2.

Row 6—K5, sl 1 wyif dw, p2, sl 5 wyif, p2, sl 1 wyif dw, k5.

Row 7—P3, RSC, k1-2w, k2 tog, sl 3 wyib, ssk, k1-2w, LSC, p3.

Row 8—K6, sl 1 wyif dw, p1, sl 3 wyif, p1, sl 1 wyif dw, k6.

Row 9—P4, RSC, k1-2w, sl 2 knitwise—k1—p2sso, k1-2w, LSC, p4.

Row 10—K7, sl 1 wyif dw, p1, sl 1 wyif dw, k7.

Row 11—P5, RSC, sl 1 wyib, LSC, p5.

Row 12—K8, sl 1 wyif, k8.

Row 13—P8, k1, p8.

Row 14—Knit.

Repeat Rows 1–14.

CHAPTER THREE

Slip-Stitch Color Patterns

Many knitters like to use the "Fair Isle" method of forming designs in color, changing the colors as required for each stitch, and stranding the unused colors across the back of the fabric. But there are no patterns for "Fair Isle" knitting in this book. "Fair Isle" knitting is plain stockinette stitch, with no texture interest; the designs are made only by alternating colors.

Slip-stitch color knitting, on the other hand, presents true stitch patterns which are embellished and enhanced by contrasting colors. It is easier for the novice to master, because it does not require careful regulation of tension. It does not even require two yarns of the same weight and thickness. Exciting effects can be obtained by combining not only different colors, but also different textures of yarn: a heavy-weight with a lightweight, a wool with a cotton, or a standard yarn with a ribbon. Metallic yarns, too, can be combined with the non-glittering kind to make delightfully dressy fabrics. These patterns are to *create* with. Modern knitting yarns offer a wide variety of colors, textures, and fiber types to work with; and slip-stitch color patterns offer an equally wide variety of wonderful ways to put them together.

Even if you have never tried patterns of this type before, you will have no difficulty in understanding them and using them. There is nothing to remember about the knitting technique except the distinction between "wyif" and "wyib". *Front* is always the side of the knitting that *faces* you as you knit, and *back* is always the side that faces away from you. It does not matter whether you are looking at the right or wrong side. Colors are changed at the end of a row, simply by dropping the strand that was just used and picking up a different strand from below. Thus, no strands ever have to be cut or broken. It is a good idea to drop the old strand in *front* (i.e., toward the knitter) of the new one, so that all will be woven neatly around the side edge of the finished knitting.

No black-and-white picture can do justice to a pattern that is intended to be worked in color. So it is particularly important in color work to take up yarn and needles, and actually try the patterns. You will like the rapidity and ease with which most of them can be worked, and you will enjoy seeing the design as it should look—that is, colorful!

Ridge Check Pattern

Ridge Check Pattern

Slipped-stitch ridges, translated into two colors, make this beautiful easy-to-work check that goes well in any sweater, jacket, skirt, or dress. The long slipped stitches carry each color upward against a stripe of contrasting color.

Multiple of 4 sts plus 3. Colors A and B.

Row 1 (Wrong side)—With A, purl.
Rows 2 and 4—With B, k3, * sl 1 wyib, k3; rep from *.
Row 3—With B, p3, * sl 1 wyif, p3; rep from *.
Row 5—With B, purl.
Rows 6, 7, and 8—With A, repeat Rows 2, 3, and 4.

Repeat Rows 1–8.

Blended Stripes

Blended Stripes

The unusual touch here is the working of slip-stitches on the purl side of the fabric, which imparts enough tension to prevent curling, and makes a nice firm knit piece. Since the purled colors alternate on every row, the stripes are blended together at the edges. This is a "beginner's pattern", useful for almost any kind of garment.

Multiple of 4 sts plus 3. Colors A and B.

Cast on with Color A and knit one row.

Row 1 (Right side)—With B, k1, * sl 1 wyib, p3; rep from *, end sl 1, k1.
Row 2—With B, k1, * sl 1 wyif, k3; rep from *, end sl 1, k1.
Row 3—With A, p3, * sl 1 wyib, p3; rep from *.
Row 4—With A, k3, * sl 1 wyif, k3; rep from *.

Repeat Rows 1–4.

Long-Slip Stripes

Contributed by Hildegard M. Elsner, Aldan, Pennsylvania

This pattern looks nicest when worked in many colors, using the same 4 rows for each color in turn. Because of the long slip-stitches, the fabric will curl while the work is in progress; but it can be pressed flat when finished.

Odd number of sts. Colors A and B.

Cast on with Color A and purl one row.

Rows 1 and 3 (Right side)—With B, k1, * sl 1 wyib, k1; rep from *.

Row 2—With B, p1, * sl 1 wyif, p1; rep from *.

Row 4—With B, purl.

Rows 5, 6, 7, and 8—With A, repeat Rows 1, 2, 3, and 4.

Repeat Rows 1–8.

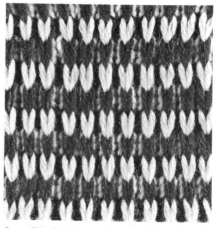

Long-Slip Stripes

Bean-Sprout Pattern

This is a simple and pretty little "dot" design with some of the dots elongated and others not. To reinforce the suggested springlike theme of young shoots, work it in green and yellow, or in two shades of green.

Multiple of 6 sts plus 5. Colors A and B.

Row 1 (Right side)—With A, knit.

Row 2—With A, purl.

Row 3—With B, k2, * sl 1 wyib, k1; rep from *, end k1.

Row 4—With B, k1, * (k1, sl 1 wyif) twice, p1, sl 1 wyif; rep from *, end k1, sl 1, k2.

Rows 5 and 7—With A, k5, * sl 1 wyib, k5; rep from *.

Rows 6 and 8—With A, p5, * sl 1 wyif, p5; rep from *.

Rows 9 and 10—With A, repeat Rows 1 and 2.

Row 11—With B, k1, * sl 1 wyib, k1; rep from *.

Row 12—With B, k1, * sl 1 wyif, p1, (sl 1 wyif, k1) twice; rep from *, end sl 1, p1, sl 1, k1.

Rows 13 and 15—With A, k2, * sl 1 wyib, k5; rep from *, end sl 1, k2.

Rows 14 and 16—With A, p2, * sl 1 wyif, p5; rep from *, end sl 1, p2.

Repeat Rows 1–16.

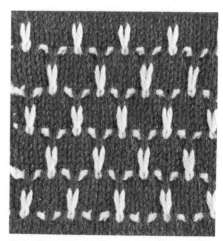

Bean-Sprout Pattern

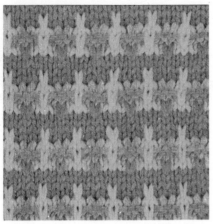

Black Forest Pattern

Black Forest Pattern

This three-color variation on the endlessly-variable Three-and-One theme comes from southern Germany and Austria. It makes charming sport sweaters, caps and mittens for children or adults, and is so easy to work that it might well serve as the beginner's first attempt at a three-color garment.

Multiple of 4 sts plus 3. Colors A, B, and C.

Row 1 (Right side)—With A, knit.
Row 2—With A, purl.
Row 3—With B, k3, * sl 1 wyib, k3; rep from *.
Row 4—With B, p3, * sl 1 wyif, p3; rep from *.
Row 5—With C, k1, * sl 1 wyib, k3; rep from *, end sl 1, k1.
Row 6—With C, k1, * sl 1 wyif, k3; rep from *, end sl 1, k1.
Rows 7 and 8—With B, repeat Rows 3 and 4.
Row 9—With A, repeat Row 5.
Row 10—With A, p1, * sl 1 wyif, p3; rep from *, end sl 1, p1.

Repeat Rows 1–10.

Carrousel Check

Here is a very attractive three-color pattern that is easy to work, novel, and striking. It makes a firm, non-curling fabric that is suitable for almost any type of garment. It is gay enough for children's wear, yet sophisticated enough for high-fashion clothing.

Multiple of 8 sts plus 5. Colors A, B, and C.

Cast on with Color C and purl one row.

Row 1 (Right side)—With A, k5, * sl 1 wyib, sl 1 wyif, sl 1 wyib, k5; rep from *.
Row 2—With A, k1, p3, k1, * sl 1 wyif, sl 1 wyib, sl 1 wyif, k1, p3, k1; rep from *.
Row 3—With B, k1, * sl 1 wyib, sl 1 wyif, sl 1 wyib, k5; rep from *, end last repeat k1 instead of k5.
Row 4—With B, k1, * sl 1 wyif, sl 1 wyib, sl 1 wyif, k1, p3, k1; rep from *, end sl 1 wyif, sl 1 wyib, sl 1 wyif, k1.
Rows 5 and 6—With C, repeat Rows 1 and 2.
Rows 7 and 8—With A, repeat Rows 3 and 4.
Rows 9 and 10—With B, repeat Rows 1 and 2.
Rows 11 and 12—With C, repeat Rows 3 and 4.

Repeat Rows 1–12.

Carrousel Check

American Beauty Tweed

This pattern is the opposite of English Rose Tweed, although it alternates colors in the same way. Instead of a loose fabric, the American Beauty makes a tight, dense one, suitable for coats and other outdoor garments. It is cheerful and gay when worked in three bright, strongly contrasting colors; subtle when worked in three different shades of the same color.

Multiple of 4 sts. Colors A, B, and C.

Cast on with Color A and purl one row.

Row 1 (Right side)—With B, k1, * sl 2 wyib, k2; rep from *, end sl 2, k1.

Row 2—With B, k1, * sl 1 wyib, sl 1 wyif, p2; rep from *, end sl 1 wyib, sl 1 wyif, k1.

Row 3—With C, k3, * sl 2 wyib, k2; rep from *, end k1.

Row 4—With C, k1, * p2, sl 1 wyib, sl 1 wyif; rep from *, end p2, k1.

Rows 5 and 6—With A, repeat Rows 1 and 2.

Rows 7 and 8—With B, repeat Rows 3 and 4.

Rows 9 and 10—With C, repeat Rows 1 and 2.

Rows 11 and 12—With A, repeat Rows 3 and 4.

Repeat Rows 1–12.

American Beauty Tweed

Color-Seeded Pattern

Basically Seed Stitch, this pattern shows the novel use of purled stitches on the right side, to make a scattering of color spots. The exceedingly simple technique gives a flat, firm, non-curling fabric.

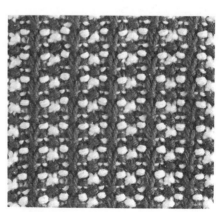

Multiple of 4 sts plus 3. Colors A and B.

Row 1 (Right side)—With A, p1, * k1, p1; rep from *.

Row 2—With A, repeat Row 1.

Row 3—With B, p1, k1, p1, * sl 1 wyib, p1, k1, p1; rep from *.

Row 4—With B, p1, k1, p1, * sl 1 wyif, p1, k1, p1; rep from *.

Repeat Rows 1–4.

Color-Seeded Pattern

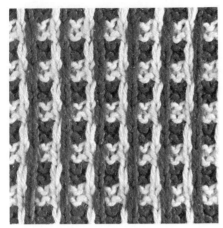

Dovetail Stripes

Multiple of 4 sts. Colors A and B.

Cast on with Color A.

Rows 1 and 3 (Right side)—With B, k2, * sl 1 wyib, k3; rep from *, end sl 1, k1.

Rows 2 and 4—With B, k1, * sl 1 wyif, p1, k2; rep from *, end sl 1, p1, k1.

Rows 5 and 7—With A, k1, * sl 1 wyib, k3; rep from *, end sl 1, k2.

Rows 6 and 8—With A, k1, * p1, sl 1 wyif, k2; rep from *, end p1, sl 1, k1.

Repeat Rows 1–8.

Dovetail Stripes

Two-Tone Lattice

Contributed by Hildegard M. Elsner, Aldan, Pennsylvania

Here an ordinary check pattern is transformed into a superbly graceful latticework design by the simple expedient of straining stitches—that is, by stretching the same pairs of slip-stitches over 4 rows instead of the usual 2. As is always the case when stitches are so treated, the fabric is very dense and sturdy. Use this pattern to make a beautiful pair of mittens, or a sofa cushion in your choice of decorator colors. A third color can be introduced, if desired, on Rows 5 and 6.

Multiple of 6 sts plus 2. Colors A and B.

Cast on with Color A and knit one row.

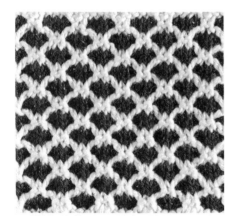

Row 1 (Right side)—With B, k1, sl 1 wyib, * k4, sl 2 wyib; rep from *, end k4, sl 1, k1.

Row 2—With B, p1, sl 1 wyif, * p4, sl 2 wyif; rep from *, end p4, sl 1, p1.

Row 3—With A, repeat Row 1.

Row 4—With A, k1, sl 1 wyif, * k4, sl 2 wyif; rep from *, end k4, sl 1, k1.

Row 5—With B, k3, * sl 2 wyib, k4; rep from *, end sl 2, k3.

Row 6—With B, p3, * sl 2 wyif, p4; rep from *, end sl 2, p3.

Row 7—With A, repeat Row 5.

Row 8—With A, k3, * sl 2 wyif, k4; rep from *, end sl 2, k3.

Repeat Rows 1–8.

Two-Tone Lattice

Twice-Turned Check

This easy-to-work pattern makes a firm, flat, close fabric for suits, coats, cushions, casual dresses and sweaters. The slipped stitches are the ones that are "twice-turned"—the first time by the way in which they are twisted when slipped, the second time by being knitted through the back loops. As a result the pattern takes on an appearance of small cross-hatched diagonals, though in fact there are no such diagonals because the slip-stitches really go straight up.

Twice-Turned Check

Odd number of sts. Colors A and B.

Row 1 (Wrong side)—With A, knit.
Row 2—With B, k1, * keeping yarn in back, insert needle from the *left* into the *back* loop of next st, as if to p1-b; *slip* the st from this position; k1; rep from *.
Row 3—With B, k1, * sl 1 wyif, k1; rep from *.
Row 4—With A, k1, * k1-b, k1; rep from *.
Row 5—With A, knit.
Row 6—With B, k2, rep from * of Row 2; end k1.
Row 7—With B, k2, * sl 1 wyif, k1; rep from *, end k1.
Row 8—With A, k2, * k1-b, k1; rep from *, end k1.

Repeat Rows 1–8.

Ribbon Bow

This is a charming, easy-to-work pattern for little girls' dresses, baby sweaters, and dainty blouses. The Color B yarn resembles a ribbon woven vertically through the fabric and tied at intervals. Rows 1 and 2 can be worked with real ribbon, instead of yarn, for an especially pretty effect.

Ribbon Bow

Multiple of 4 sts plus 3. Colors A and B.

Cast on with Color A and purl one row.

Row 1 (Right side)—With B, k1, * sl 1 wyib, k3; rep from *, end sl 1, k1.
Row 2—With B, k1, * sl 1 wyif, k1, k1 wrapping yarn 3 times, k1; rep from *, end sl 1, k1.
Row 3—With A, k3, * sl 1 wyib dropping extra wraps, k3; rep from *.
Row 4—With A, p3, * sl 1 wyib, p3; rep from *.
Row 5—With A, k3, * sl 1 wyib, k3; rep from *.
Rows 6, 7, and 8—With A, repeat Rows 4 and 5, then Row 4 again.

Repeat Rows 1–8.

SLIP-STITCH COLOR PATTERNS   41

Pearl Tweed

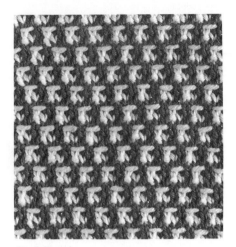

Pearl Tweed

Here is a very novel tweed pattern with a gentle diagonal line and a horizontal accent formed by the strands woven across the front of the fabric. It is an excellent pattern for coats, suits, sweaters, and skirts.

Multiple of 3 sts plus 2. Colors A and B.

Cast on with A and purl one row. —

Row 1 (Right side)—With B, k1, * sl 2 wyif, k1; rep from *, end k1.

Row 2—With B, p1, * k1, p1, sl 1 wyif; rep from *, end p1.

Row 3—With A, k3, * sl 1 wyib, k2; rep from *, end sl 1, k1.

Row 4—With A, purl.

Row 5—With B, k2, * sl 2 wyif, k1; rep from *.

Row 6—With B, p2, * sl 1 wyif, k1, p1; rep from *.

Row 7—With A, k1, * sl 1 wyib, k2; rep from *, end k1.

Row 8—With A, purl.

Row 9—With B, k1, sl 1 wyif, * k1, sl 2 wyif; rep from *, end k1, sl 1 wyif, k1.

Row 10—With B, p1, * sl 1 wyif, k1, p1; rep from *, end p1.

Row 11—With A, k2, * sl 1 wyib, k2; rep from *.

Row 12—With A, purl.

Repeat Rows 1–12.

French Weave, Plain and Fancy

ABOVE: *French Weave, Plain*
BELOW: *French Weave, Fancy*

Here are two patterns that incorporate the same two-color motif; a small diamond-shaped figure with a short woven strand of contrasting color in the center. In the Plain version, a lattice-like design, this motif is clearly seen. In the Fancy version the pattern goes off-center, to make an intricate and interesting series of diagonal lines; but the little diamonds are still there. Both versions are easy to work.

I. FRENCH WEAVE, PLAIN

Multiple of 4 sts plus 3. Colors A and B.

Row 1 (Wrong side)—With A, purl.

Row 2—With B, k1, sl 1 wyif, k1, * sl 1 wyib, k1, sl 1 wyif, k1; rep from *.

Row 3—With B, p3, * sl 1 wyif, p3; rep from *.

Row 4—With A, k1, * sl 1 wyib, k3; rep from *, end sl 1, k1.
Row 5—With A, purl.
Row 6—With B, k1, sl 1 wyib, k1, * sl 1 wyif, k1, sl 1 wyib, k1; rep from *.
Row 7—With B, p1, * sl 1 wyif, p3; rep from *, end sl 1, p1.
Row 8—With A, k3, * sl 1 wyib, k3; rep from *.

Repeat Rows 1–8.

II. FRENCH WEAVE, FANCY

Multiple of 5 sts plus 4. Colors A and B.

Row 1 (Wrong side)—With A, purl.
Row 2—With B, k1, sl 1 wyib, * k1, sl 1 wyif, k1, sl 2 wyib; rep from *, end k2.
Row 3—With B, k1, p1, * sl 1 wyif, sl 1 wyib, p3; rep from *, end sl 1 wyif, k1.
Row 4—With A, k3, * sl 1 wyib, k4; rep from *, end k1.
Row 5—With A, purl.
Row 6—With B, k2, * sl 2 wyib, k1, sl 1 wyif, k1; rep from *, end sl 1 wyib, k1.
Row 7—With B, k1, sl 1 wyib, * p3, sl 1 wyif, sl 1 wyib; rep from *, end p1, k1.
Row 8—With A, k5, * sl 1 wyib, k4; rep from *, end last repeat k3.

Repeat Rows 1–8.

Woven Block Stitch

This is a very easy-to-work pattern that is particularly attractive in coats or jackets. It can be worked in three colors: the first 14 rows with A and B, the second 14 rows with A and C—and so on, alternating colors in the woven bands.

Multiple of 9 sts plus 4. Colors A and B.

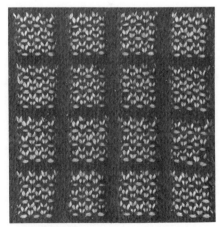

Row 1 (Right side)—With A, knit.
Row 2—With A, purl.
Row 3—With B, k1, * sl 2 wyib, k1, (sl 1 wyif, k1) 3 times; rep from *, end sl 2 wyib, k1.
Row 4—With B, k1, * sl 2 wyif, p7; rep from *, end sl 2 wyif, k1.
Row 5—With A, k3, * sl 1 wyif, (k1, sl 1 wyif) 3 times, k2; rep from *, end k1.
Row 6—With A, purl.
Rows 7 through 14—Repeat Rows 3 through 6 twice more.

Repeat Rows 1–14.

Woven Block Stitch

Wave and Box Stitch

Wave and Box Stitch

This pattern and the ones that follow it are "double-ended" patterns, which means that they are not always turned at the end of a row, but sometimes there will be two consecutive rows on the right side or two consecutive rows on the wrong side. To accomplish this, it is necessary to do the knitting on *a circular needle or a pair of double-pointed needles* when working back and forth across the piece. In round knitting, of course, there is no necessity to worry about which strand is dropped on which end of the row, because at the end of a round the knitter can choose either strand to continue.

In Wave and Box Stitch, the stitches are slipped to the other end of the needle after every even-numbered or B row, so that the A strand always *follows* the B strand.

Multiple of 10 sts plus 5. Colors A and B.

Row 1 (Wrong side)—With A, purl.
Row 2—With B, knit. Sl sts to other end of needle.
Row 3—With A, knit.
Row 4—With B, p1, * sl 3 wyif, p7; rep from *, end sl 3, p1.
 Sl sts to other end of needle.
Row 5—With A, purl.
Row 6—With B, k1, * sl 3 wyib, k7; rep from *, end sl 3, k1. Sl sts to other end of needle.
Row 7—With A, knit.
Row 8—With B, repeat Row 4. Sl sts to other end of needle.
Rows 9, 10, and 11—Repeat Rows 1, 2, and 3.
Row 12—With B, p6, * sl 3 wyif, p7; rep from *, end sl 3, p6. Sl sts to other end of needle.
Row 13—With A, purl.
Row 14—With B, k6, * sl 3 wyib, k7; rep from *, end sl 3, k6. Sl sts to other end of needle.
Row 15—With A, knit.
Row 16—With B, repeat Row 12. Sl sts to other end of needle.

Repeat Rows 1–16.

Stripe and Rib Pattern

Like all color patterns worked back and forth on double-pointed needles, this one is very easy to do in round knitting. Color B rounds are always worked like Row 2; Color A rounds are always knitted plain. The pattern geometry here is clear, formal, and sharply rectilinear, like a bold plaid.

Multiple of 4 sts plus 3. Colors A and B.

SPECIAL NOTE: This pattern must be worked back and forth on a circular needle or a pair of double-pointed needles.

Row 1 (Right side)—With A, knit.
Row 2—Sl sts to other end of needle, right side still facing, and with B, k1, * sl 1 wyib, k3; rep from *, end sl 1, k1.
Row 3—With A, purl.
Row 4—Sl sts to other end of needle, wrong side still facing, and with B, p1, * sl 1 wyif, p3; rep from *, end sl 1, p1.
Rows 5, 6, 7, and 8—Repeat Rows 1, 2, 3, and 1 again.
Row 9—With B, p1, * sl 1 wyif, p3; rep from *, end sl 1, p1.
Row 10—Sl sts to other end of needle, wrong side still facing, and with A, purl.
Row 11—With B, k1, * sl 1 wyib, k3; rep from *, end sl 1, k1.
Row 12—Sl sts to other end of needle, right side still facing, and with A, knit.
Rows 13 and 14—Repeat Rows 9 and 10.

Repeat Rows 1–14.

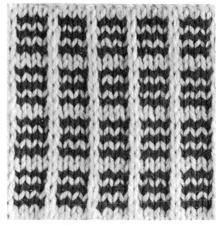

Stripe and Rib Pattern

Reversible Two-Tone Pattern

Contributed by Bernice Haedike, Oak Park, Illinois

This fascinating little knitting trick is a form of Double Knitting (*A Treasury of Knitting Patterns,* p. 99), and gives two separate layers of soft stockinette stitch, connected at the edges but entirely open throughout the center like the two sides of a pocket. The difference here is that these two back-to-back layers are worked in different colors, one side in Color A, the other in Color B—and both are worked at the same time. Each color is therefore a "lining" for the other. All kinds of reversible articles can be made with this pattern; jackets, coats, scarves, baby blankets, belts.

The knitting is simple, but watch out for just two points where errors are easy to make. These points are the ends of Rows 2 and 4, when both strands are together at the same edge. Be sure always to take up the *B* strand at these two points. Color A always *follows* Color B across the rows, after the stitches are slipped to the other end of the needle. When changing colors, be sure to pick up the new strand from *under* the old one, so the two will be twisted together at the edges without leaving any holes.

Reversible Two-Tone Pattern

The double fabric may be closed at the top by binding off all stitches in the usual way, or it may be left open, forming a pouch, by slipping all the A stitches onto one needle and all the B stitches onto another, and binding off each separately. Be generous when casting on; naturally a double-thick fabric comes out about half the width of a single thickness.

Even number of sts. Colors A and B.

NOTE: This pattern must be worked on a circular needle or a pair of double-pointed needles.

Cast on with Color A, then join Color B.

Row 1—With B, * k1, sl 1 wyif; rep from *. Sl sts to other end of needle and take up A strand.

Row 2—With A, * sl 1 wyib, p1; rep from *. Turn work and take up B strand.

Row 3—With B, * sl 1 wyib, p1; rep from *. Sl sts to other end of needle and take up A strand.

Row 4—With A, * k1, sl 1 wyif; rep from *. Turn work and take up B strand.

Repeat Rows 1–4.

Woven Plaid

Woven Plaid

A 36-row repeat is rather long for a color pattern; but in fact there are only 8 pattern rows here. On the second half (Rows 19–36) the same rows are worked on opposite sides of the fabric. The directions at the end of each row—either "turn" or "sl sts to other end of needle"—are to be considered *part of that row*. Follow these directions as soon as the row is completed, so you will not lose track of which side of the fabric you are working on. Keep the wrong-side strands *loose* when slipping each 5-stitch group.

Multiple of 10 sts plus 2. Colors A and B.

Cast on with Color A and purl one row.

SPECIAL NOTE: This pattern must be worked back and forth on a circular needle or a pair of double-pointed needles.

Row 1 (Right side)—With B, k1, * (sl 1 wyif, sl 1 wyib) twice, sl 1 wyif, k5; rep from *, end k1. Sl sts to other end of needle.

Row 2—With A, k1, * k5, sl 5 wyib; rep from *, end k1. Turn.

Row 3—With B, k1, * p5, (sl 1 wyif, sl 1 wyib) twice, sl 1 wyif; rep from *, end k1. Sl sts to other end of needle.

Row 4—With A, k1, * sl 5 wyif, p5; rep from *, end k1. Turn.

Rows 5, 6, 7, 8, and 9—Repeat Rows 1, 2, 3, 4, and Row 1 again.

Row 10—With A, k1, * k5, (sl 1 wyif, sl 1 wyib) twice, sl 1 wyif; rep from *, end k1. Turn.

Row 11—With B, k1, * p5, sl 5 wyif; rep from *, end k1. Sl sts to other end of needle.

Row 12—With A, k1, * (sl 1 wyif, sl 1 wyib) twice, sl 1 wyif, p5; rep from *, end k1. Turn.

Row 13—With B, k1, * sl 5 wyib, k5; rep from *, end k1. Sl sts to other end of needle.

Rows 14, 15, 16, 17, and 18—Repeat Rows 10, 11, 12, 13, and Row 10 again.

Row 19—With B, k1, * p5, (sl 1 wyib, sl 1 wyif) twice, sl 1 wyib; rep from *, end k1. Sl sts to other end of needle.

Row 20—With A, k1, * sl 5 wyif, p5; rep from *, end k1. Turn. (I.e., same as Row 4.)

Row 21—With B, k1, * (sl 1 wyib, sl 1 wyif) twice, sl 1 wyib, k5; rep from *, end k1. Sl sts to other end of needle.

Row 22—With A, k1, * k5, sl 5 wyib; rep from *, end k1. Turn. (I.e., same as Row 2.)

Rows 23, 24, 25, 26, and 27—Repeat Rows 19, 20, 21, 22, and Row 19 again.

Row 28—With A, k1, * (sl 1 wyib, sl 1 wyif) twice, sl 1 wyib, p5; rep from *, end k1. Turn.

Row 29—With B, k1, * sl 5 wyib, k5; rep from *, end k1. Sl sts to other end of needle. (I.e., same as Row 13.)

Row 30—With A, k1, * k5, (sl 1 wyib, sl 1 wyif) twice, sl 1 wyib; rep from *, end k1. Turn.

Row 31—With B, k1, * p5, sl 5 wyif; rep from *, end k1. Sl sts to other end of needle. (I.e., same as Row 11.)

Rows 32, 33, 34, 35, and 36—Repeat Rows 28, 29, 30, 31, and Row 28 again.

Repeat Rows 1–36.

Tiny Check

The little checks in this pattern are made of a single Color B stitch apiece, which means that in flat knitting the pattern must be worked back and forth on a circular needle or a pair of double-pointed needles, as given. For round knitting, as in socks, seamless sweaters, skirts, or other tubular articles, the pattern may be adapted very easily by knitting instead of purling Rows 1 and 4, and slipping sts wyib instead of wyif in Row 4. The "sl sts to other end of needle" direction can be ignored, since at the end of a round either strand may be picked up at will.

Odd number of sts. Colors A and B.

SPECIAL NOTE: This pattern must be worked back and forth on a circular needle or a pair of double-pointed needles.

Row 1 (Wrong side)—With A, purl.
Row 2—With B, k1, * sl 1 wyib, k1; rep from *.
Row 3—Sl all sts to other end of needle and with A, knit.
Row 4—With B, p2, * sl 1 wyif, p1; rep from *, end p1. Sl all sts to other end of needle.

Repeat Rows 1–4.

Tiny Check

Woven Polka Dot Pattern

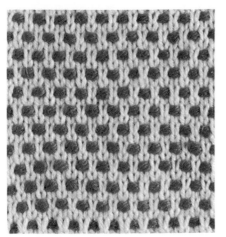

Woven Polka Dot Pattern

This is an "easy" version of Swedish Weave; it is simplified because the yarns are handled one at a time, instead of both together. The principle remains the same, however; Color B is never worked, only woven: in this case, twice for each "dot", so that there is a double strand showing instead of a single one. The single purl stitch at the beginning of Rows 4 and 8 anchors Color B at the left-hand edge. On the right-hand edge it is automatically caught as the strands are twisted up the side. With this pattern it is especially important always to pick up a new strand from *behind* the old one when changing colors.

A three-color version of the pattern might be worked with a Color C introduced in Rows 7 and 8.

Odd number of sts. Colors A and B.

Row 1 (Right side)—With A, knit.

Row 2—With A, k1, purl to last st, k1.

Row 3—With B, * sl 1 wyib, sl 1 wyif; rep from *, end sl 1 wyib. (No sts are knitted in Color B; the strand is simply woven through the Color A sts.)

Row 4—With B, p1, * sl 1 wyib, sl 1 wyif; rep from *.

Rows 5 and 6—With A, repeat Rows 1 and 2.

Row 7—With B, * sl 1 wyif, sl 1 wyib; rep from *, end sl 1 wyif.

Row 8—With B, carry yarn around side edge of work and p1, * sl 1 wyif, sl 1 wyib; rep from *.

Repeat Rows 1–8.

Two-Color Bind Stitch

ABOVE: *Two-Color Bind Stitch*
BELOW: *Swedish Dot Pattern*

Work this pattern with a light hand, being careful not to bind the stitches too tightly. "Squeezing" will spoil its appearance. The wrapped strands should be soft and reasonably loose, though not slack. The pattern is pretty, too, in three colors. Simply alternate the three colors continuously, giving 4 rows to each in turn.

Multiple of 4 sts plus 2. Colors A and B.

Cast on with Color A and purl one row.

Row 1 (Right side)—With B, k1, * sl 2 wyif, put yarn to back and sl the same 2 sts back to left–hand needle, bring yarn to front and sl the same 2 sts wyif again, put yarn to back and k2; rep from *, end k1.

Row 2—With B, p3, * sl 2 wyif, p2; rep from *, end sl 2, p1.

Row 3—With B, k3, * p2, k2; rep from *, end p2, k1.

Row 4—With B, purl.

Row 5—With A, k3, rep from * of Row 1; end last repeat k1
   instead of k2.
Row 6—With A, p1, * sl 2 wyif, p2; rep from *, end p1.
Row 7—With A, k1, * p2, k2; rep from *, end k1.
Row 8—With A, purl.

Repeat Rows 1–8.

Swedish Dot Pattern

This charming and simple little pattern is easy to knit in color-
reversal stripes, as follows: work Rows 1 through 10 as given. Then
work Rows 1 through 4 in Color B, Rows 11 and 12 in Color
A, and Rows 1 through 4 in Color B; then begin again at Row
1 with A. This will give dark stripes with light dots, alternating
with light stripes with dark dots.

Multiple of 4 sts plus 2. Colors A and B.

Rows 1 and 3 (Right side)—With A, knit.
Rows 2 and 4—With A, purl.
Row 5—With B, k3, * sl 2 wyif, k2; rep from *, end sl 2, k1.
Row 6—With B, k1, * sl 2 wyif, k2; rep from *, end k1.
Rows 7, 8, 9, and 10—With A, repeat Rows 1, 2, 3, and 4.
Row 11—With B, repeat Row 6.
Row 12—With B, repeat Row 5.

Repeat Rows 1–12.

Salt and Pepper Tweed

This attractive variation on a two-color Fabric Stitch can be
used either way round. The right side is a tweedy mixture; the
wrong side shows a series of narrow horizontal stripes. This pattern
closes up into a thick, dense fabric, and should be worked with
large needles. More than two colors can be used, if desired; simply
repeat the same two pattern rows for each color.

Even number of sts. Colors A and B.

Cast on with Color A.

Row 1 (Right side)—With B, * k1, sl 1 wyib; rep from *.
Row 2—With B, * k1, sl 1 wyif; rep from *.
Rows 3 and 4—With A, repeat Rows 1 and 2.

Repeat Rows 1–4.

Salt and Pepper Tweed
ABOVE: *right side*
BELOW: *wrong side*

Four-Color Mix

Four-Color Mix

This pattern is a real mixture. Single stitches of each of the four colors chase each other all over the fabric in rich profusion. All sorts of subtle heathery or tweedy effects are possible with this pattern, depending on how your chosen colors blend or contrast with each other.

Multiple of 4 sts plus 3. Colors A, B, C, and D.

Cast on with Color A and purl one row.

Row 1 (Right side)—With B, k1, * sl 1 wyib, k3; rep from *, end sl 1, k1.
Row 2—With C, p3, * sl 1 wyif, p3; rep from *.
Row 3—With D, repeat Row 1.
Row 4—With B, repeat Row 2.
Row 5—With A, repeat Row 1.
Row 6—With D, repeat Row 2.
Row 7—With C, repeat Row 1.
Row 8—With A, repeat Row 2.

Repeat Rows 1–8.

Sherwood Pattern

Sherwood Pattern

This is a simple three-and-one pattern having only eight rows in fact; but in the alternation of colors these 8 rows are repeated 3 times. This makes a fabric with a very pleasing and subtle design that seems more complicated than it really is.

Multiple of 4 sts plus 3. Colors A, B, and C.

Row 1 (Right side)—With A, knit.
Row 2—With A, purl.
Row 3—With B, k3, * sl 1 wyib, k3; rep from *.
Row 4—With B, k3, * sl 1 wyif, k3; rep from *.
Row 5—With C, k1, * sl 1 wyib, k3; rep from *, end sl 1, k1.
Row 6—With C, k1, * sl 1 wyif, k3; rep from *, end sl 1, k1.
Row 7—With A, repeat Row 3.
Row 8—With A, p1, k1, p1, * sl 1 wyif, p1, k1, p1; rep from *.
Rows 9 and 10—With B, repeat Rows 1 and 2.
Rows 11 and 12—With C, repeat Rows 3 and 4.
Rows 13 and 14—With A, repeat Rows 5 and 6.
Rows 15 and 16—With B, repeat Rows 7 and 8.
Rows 17 and 18—With C, repeat Rows 1 and 2.
Rows 19 and 20—With A, repeat Rows 3 and 4.
Rows 21 and 22—With B, repeat Rows 5 and 6.
Rows 23 and 24—With C, repeat Rows 7 and 8.

Repeat Rows 1–24.

Dice Check

Like most of the really ingenious patterns in knitting, this one is created by a small—almost insignificant—change in a commonly known technique. Here, an ordinary two-stitch check is transformed by the simple expedient of carrying a third color back and forth, one row at a time. This enables the knitter to work an elegant, tidy three-color check without breaking any of the three strands. The pattern is so easy to work that a beginner may use it to make a beautiful coat, casual dress, sweater, mittens or baby clothes.

Multiple of 4 sts plus 2. Colors A, B, and C.

Row 1 (Wrong side)—With A, purl.
Row 2—With B, k1, sl 1 wyib, * k2, sl 2 wyib; rep from *, end k2, sl 1, k1.
Row 3—With B, p1, sl 1 wyif, * p2, sl 2 wyif; rep from *, end p2, sl 1, p1.
Row 4—With A, knit.
Row 5—With C, p2, * sl 2 wyif, p2; rep from *.
Row 6—With C, k2, * sl 2 wyib, k2; rep from *.

Repeat Rows 1–6.

Dice Check

Syncopated Tweed

This beautiful tweed is so simple as to be well within the reach of any beginner; yet the finished fabric seems to be quite a complex arrangement of color spots. It is a dense fabric that tends to curl forward, because of the pull of the long slip-stitches, and so it requires pressing.

Multiple of 3 sts plus 2. Colors A, B, and C.

Row 1 (Right side)—With A, knit.
Row 2—With A, k1, * sl 1 wyif, p2; rep from *, end k1.
Row 3—With B, k3, * sl 1 wyib, k2; rep from *, end sl 1, k1.
Row 4—With B, repeat Row 2.
Row 5—With C, knit.
Row 6—With C, k1, p1, * sl 1 wyif, p2; rep from *, end sl 1, p1, k1.
Row 7—With A, k2, * sl 1 wyib, k2; rep from *.
Row 8—With A, repeat Row 6.
Row 9—With B, knit.
Row 10—With B, k1, * p2, sl 1 wyif; rep from *, end k1.
Row 11—With C, k1, * sl 1 wyib, k2; rep from *, end k1.
Row 12—With C, repeat Row 10.

Repeat Rows 1–12.

Syncopated Tweed

Barred Stripes

Barred Stripes

Here is a simple and attractive pattern of the "ladder" type, making a nice firm fabric for ski sweaters and other outdoor wear. The wrong side shows the same pattern in purl stitches.

Multiple of 4 sts plus 2. Colors A and B.

Cast on with A and purl one row.

Row 1 (Right side)—With B, k1, * sl 2 wyif, k2; rep from *, end k1.

Row 2—With B, k1, * p2, sl 2 wyif; rep from *, end k1.

Row 3—With A, k3, * sl 2 wyif, k2; rep from *, end sl 2 wyif, k1.

Row 4—With A, k1, * sl 2 wyif, p2; rep from *, end k1.

Repeat Rows 1–4.

Bold Check Pattern

This is a big, striking check suitable for sport coats, sweaters and blankets.

Multiple of 10 sts plus 2. Colors A and B.

Row 1 (Right side)—With A, knit.

Row 2—With A, (k1, p1) twice, k1, * p2, k1, p1, k1; rep from *, end p2, (k1, p1) twice, k1.

Row 3—With B, k1, * k5, (sl 1 wyib, k1) twice, sl 1 wyib; rep from *, end k1.

Row 4—With B, k1, * (sl 1 wyif, k1) twice, sl 1 wyif, k5; rep from *, end k1.

Row 5—With A, k2, * sl 1 wyib, k1, sl 1 wyib, k7; rep from *.

Row 6—With A, * (k1, p1) 3 times, (k1, sl 1 wyif) twice; rep from *, end k2.

Rows 7, 8, 9, 10, 11, and 12—Repeat Rows 3, 4, 5, and 6, then Rows 3 and 4 again.

Rows 13 and 14—With A, repeat Rows 1 and 2.

Row 15—With B, k1, * (sl 1 wyib, k1) twice, sl 1 wyib, k5; rep from *, end k1.

ABOVE: *Bold Check Pattern*
BELOW: *Garter-Stitch Stripe Version*

Row 16—With B, k1, * k5, (sl 1 wyif, k1) twice, sl 1 wyif; rep from *, end k1.

Row 17—With A, * k7, sl 1 wyib, k1, sl 1 wyib; rep from *, end k2.

Row 18—With A, k2, * (sl 1 wyif, k1) twice, (p1, k1) 3 times; rep from *.

Rows 19, 20, 21, 22, 23, and 24—Repeat Rows 15, 16, 17, and 18, then Rows 15 and 16 again.

Repeat Rows 1–24.

VARIATION:
GARTER-STITCH STRIPE VERSION

Work the same as Bold Check Pattern above, with the following exceptions:

Rows 5, 9, 17, and 21—With A, knit.

Rows 6 and 10—With A, k1, * (p1, k1) twice, p1, k5; rep from *, end k1.

Rows 18 and 22—With A, k1, * k5, (p1, k1) twice, p1; rep from *, end k1.

Tuscan Pattern

Here is a delightful pattern of big checks in contrasting garter-stitch and woven-stitch textures, for beautiful tweedy coats and jackets.

Tuscan Pattern

Multiple of 10 sts plus 9. Colors A and B.

Cast on with Color A and purl one row.

Row 1 (Right side)—With B, k2, * (sl 1 wyif, k1) twice, sl 1 wyif, k5; rep from *, end last repeat k2.

Row 2—With B, repeat Row 1.

Row 3—With A, k1, * (sl 1 wyif, k1) 3 times, sl 1 wyif, k3; rep from *, end last repeat k1.

Row 4—With A, k1, * (sl 1 wyif, p1) 3 times, sl 1 wyif, k3; rep from *, end last repeat k1.

Rows 5 through 14—Repeat Rows 1 through 4 twice more, then Rows 1 and 2 again.

Row 15—With A, k3, * sl 1 wyif, k1, sl 1 wyif, k7; rep from *, end last repeat k3.

Row 16—With A, p3, * sl 1 wyif, p1, sl 1 wyif, p7; rep from *, end last repeat p3.

Rows 17 and 18—With B, k1, sl 1 wyif, * k5, (sl 1 wyif, k1) twice, sl 1 wyif; rep from *, end k5, sl 1 wyif, k1.

Row 19—With A, k2, sl 1 wyif, * k3, (sl 1 wyif, k1) 3 times, sl 1 wyif; rep from *, end k3, sl 1 wyif, k2.

Row 20—With A, k1, p1, sl 1 wyif, * k3, (sl 1 wyif, p1) 3 times, sl 1 wyif; rep from *, end k3, sl 1 wyif, p1, k1.

Rows 21 through 30—Repeat Rows 17 through 20 twice more, then Rows 17 and 18 again.

Row 31—With A, k8, * sl 1 wyif, k1, sl 1 wyif, k7; rep from *, end k1.

Row 32—With A, p8, * sl 1 wyif, p1, sl 1 wyif, p7; rep from *, end p1.

Repeat Rows 1–32.

Sandwich Stitch

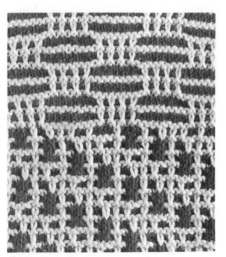

ABOVE: *Sandwich Stitch*
BELOW: *Watergate Pattern*

A simple variation on a garter-stitch stripe is seen here, which makes a sporty check for children's sweaters, jackets and coats. Recommended for beginning knitters.

Multiple of 16 sts plus 9. Colors A and B.

NOTE: Odd-numbered rows are right-side rows.

Rows 1, 2, 5, 6, 9, 10, 13, and 14—With A, knit.
Rows 3 and 7—With B, (k1, sl 1 wyib) 4 times, * k9, (sl 1 wyib, k1) 3 times, sl 1 wyib; rep from *, end k1.
Rows 4 and 8—With B, (k1, sl 1 wyif) 4 times, * p9, (sl 1 wyif, k1) 3 times, sl 1 wyif; rep from *, end k1.
Rows 11 and 15—With B, k9, * (sl 1 wyib, k1) 3 times, sl 1 wyib, k9; rep from *.
Rows 12 and 16—With B, p9, * (sl 1 wyif, k1) 3 times, sl 1 wyif, p9; rep from *.

Repeat Rows 1–16.

Watergate Pattern

Like Sandwich Stitch, this pattern has a garter-stitch-stripe basis, but is a little more complicated. Certain background stitches are carried up over the stripes to make motifs that "travel" on a shallow diagonal.

Multiple of 20 sts plus 3. Colors A and B.

NOTE: On all odd-numbered (right-side) rows, sl all sl-sts wyib. On all even-numbered (wrong-side) rows, sl all sl-sts wyif. Cast on with A and knit one row.

Row 1 (Right side)—With B, k1, * sl 1, k2, (sl 1, k1) twice, sl 1, k2, (sl 1, k4) twice; rep from *, end sl 1, k1.
Rows 2, 6, 10, and 14—With B, purl all the sts knitted on previous row, slipping all sl-sts wyif.
Row 3—With A, * k13, sl 2, k3, sl 2; rep from *, end k3.
Row 4—With A, k3, * sl 2, k3, p2, k13; rep from *.
Row 5—With B, k1, * sl 1, k4, sl 1, k2, (sl 1, k1) twice, sl 1, k2, sl 1, k4; rep from *, end sl 1, k1.
Row 7—With A, k3, * sl 2, k13, sl 2, k3; rep from*.
Row 8—With A, k3, * p2, k13, sl 2, k3; rep from * .
Row 9—With B, k1, * (sl 1, k4) twice, sl 1, k2, (sl 1, k1) twice, sl 1, k2; rep from *, end sl 1, k1.
Row 11—With A, k3, * sl 2, k3, sl 2, k13; rep from *.
Row 12—With A, * k13, sl 2, k3, p2; rep from *, end k3.

Row 13—With B, * (k1, sl 1) twice, k2, sl 1, (k4, sl 1) twice, k2, sl 1; rep from *, end k1, sl 1, k1.

Row 15—With A, k8, * sl 2, k3, sl 2, k13; rep from *, end last repeat k8.

Row 16—With A, k8, * sl 2, k3, p2, k13; rep from *, end last repeat k8.

Repeat Rows 1–16.

Winged Wave Pattern

This charming fabric is thick, warm, non-curling, and beautiful in all types of sportswear. The pattern is easy to work, although the main pattern row (Row 6) seems complicated in the directions; but the technique is soon learned, and is worked in much less time than it takes to tell about it.

Multiple of 8 sts plus 2. Colors A and B.

PREPARATION ROWS:

Row 1 (Wrong side)—With A, k4, * p2 wrapping yarn twice for each st, k6; rep from *, end last repeat k4.

Row 2—With B, k4, * sl 2 wyib dropping extra wraps, k6; rep from *, end last repeat k4.

End of Preparation Rows.

Row 3—With B, k4, * sl 2 wyif, k6; rep from *, end last repeat k4.

Row 4—With B, k4, * sl 2 wyib, k6; rep from *, end last repeat k4.

Row 5—With B, k3, * p1 wrapping yarn twice, sl 2 wyif, p1 wrapping yarn twice, k4; rep from *, end last repeat k3.

Row 6—With A, k1, * sl 3 wyib dropping extra wrap from 3rd st; drop first elongated Color A st off needle to front of work, sl the same 3 sts back to left-hand needle, pick up dropped st and knit it; then k2, sl 1 wyib, drop second elongated Color A st off needle to front of work, sl 3 wyib dropping extra wrap from 1st st, pick up dropped st and place it on left-hand needle, then sl *two* (the 2nd and 3rd) of the 3 slipped sts back to left-hand needle, then k3; rep from *, end k1.

Rows 7, 8, 9, and 10—Repeat Rows 3, 4, 5, and 6, reversing colors (i.e., A, A, A, B).

Omit Rows 1 and 2, repeat Rows 3–10.

Winged Wave Pattern

Holiday Stripes

Holiday Stripes

A drop-stitch technique is used in this stripe pattern, which combines all the best elements of pattern knitting. It is highly ingenious in concept and execution; it is strikingly novel in effect; and it is exceedingly simple to work. If you look carefully, you will see little slip-stitch "cables" embedded in the fabric. These can be brought out, if desired, by working in a single solid color with purl stitches, instead of knit stitches, inserted between them (i.e., on right-side rows purl the first stitch and every 4th stitch thereafter). But in two-color knitting, the "cables" form the rick-rack-like stripes and thus do not exist as vertical patterns.

Multiple of 4 sts plus 2. Colors A and B.

Row 1 (Wrong side)—With A, purl.
Row 2—With B, * k1, sl 1 wyib; rep from *, end k2.
Row 3—With B, p4, * sl 1 wyif, p3; rep from *, end sl 1, p1.
Row 4—With B, * k1, drop sl-st off needle to front of work, k2, pick up dropped st and knit it ; rep from *, end k2.
Row 5—With B, purl.
Rows 6, 7, and 8—With A, repeat Rows 2, 3, and 4.

Repeat Rows 1–8.

Petal Quilting

Petal Quilting

Multiple of 8 sts plus 1. Colors A and B.

Row 1 (Right side)—With A, knit.
Row 2—With A, k1, * p1 wrapping yarn twice, k5, p1 wrapping yarn twice, k1; rep from *.
Row 3—With B, k1, * sl 1 wyib dropping extra wrap, k5, sl 1 wyib dropping extra wrap, k1; rep from *.
Rows 4 and 6—With B, p1, * sl 1 wyif, p5, sl 1 wyif, p1; rep from *.
Row 5—With B, k1, * sl 1 wyib, k5, sl 1 wyib, k1; rep from *.
Row 7—With A, k1, * drop Color A sl-st off needle to front of work, k2, pick up dropped st and knit it; k1, sl 2 wyib, drop next Color A sl-st off needle, sl the same 2 sts back to left-hand needle, pick up dropped st and knit it; k2, sl 1 wyib; rep from *, end last repeat k1 instead of sl 1.

Row 8—With A, k3, * p1, k1, p1, k2, sl 1 wyif, k2; rep from *, end p1, k1, p1, k3.

Row 9—With A, knit.

Row 10—With A, k3, * p1 wrapping yarn twice, k1, p1 wrapping yarn twice, k5; rep from *, end last repeat k3.

Row 11—With B, k3, * sl 1 wyib dropping extra wrap, k1, sl 1 wyib dropping extra wrap, k5; rep from *, end last repeat k3.

Rows 12 and 14—With B, p3, * sl 1 wyif, p1, sl 1 wyif, p5; rep from *, end last repeat p3.

Row 13—With B, k3, * sl 1 wyib, k1, sl 1 wyib, k5; rep from *, end last repeat k3.

Row 15—With A, k1, * sl 2 wyib, drop Color A sl-st off needle to front of work, sl the same 2 sts back to left-hand needle, pick up dropped st and knit it; k2, sl 1 wyib, drop next Color A sl-st off needle, k2, pick up dropped st and knit it, k1; rep from *.

Row 16—With A, k1, * p1, k2, sl 1 wyif, k2, p1, k1; rep from *.

Repeat Rows 1–16.

Surprise Pattern in three colors

Surprise Pattern

The "surprise" is the way this pattern looks when it is worked in only two colors instead of three. The shapes are entirely different. For the two-color version, simply alternate colors every other row, as follows: Rows 1, 4, 5, 8, 9, and 12 in Color A; Rows 2, 3, 6, 7, 10, and 11 in Color B.

Multiple of 4 sts plus 1. Colors A, B, and C.

Row 1 (Wrong side)—With A, purl.

Row 2—With B, k2, * sl 1 wyib, k3; rep from *, end sl 1, k2.

Row 3—With B, p2, * sl 1 wyif, p3; rep from *, end sl 1, p2.

Row 4—With C, k4, * sl 1 wyib, k3; rep from *, end k1.

Row 5—With C, p4, * sl 1 wyif, p3; rep from *, end p1.

Row 6—With A, k1, * sl 1 wyib, k1; rep from *.

Row 7—With A, purl.

Row 8—With B, k2, * sl 1 wyib, k1; rep from *, end k1.

Row 9—With B, p4, * sl 1 wyif, p3; rep from *, end p1.

Row 10—With C, k2, * sl 1 wyib, k3; rep from *, end sl 1, k2.

Row 11—With C, purl.

Row 12—With A, k1, * sl 1 wyib, k1; rep from *.

Repeat Rows 1–12.

Surprise Pattern in two colors

Outlined Check Pattern

Outlined Check Pattern

This pretty four-color design is worked from both edges at once. Color A is always left at the right-hand edge, Colors C and D are always left at the left-hand edge, and Color B travels back and forth to connect them.

Multiple of 10 sts plus 4.

Colors A, B, C, and D.

Row 1 (Right side)—With A, knit.
Row 2—With A, purl.
Row 3—With B, k1, * sl 2 wyib, k8; rep from *, end sl 2, k1.
Row 4—With C, p1, sl 3 wyif, * p6, sl 4 wyif; rep from *, end p6, sl 3, p1.
Row 5—With C, k1, sl 3 wyib, * k6, sl 4 wyib; rep from *, end k6, sl 3, k1.
Row 6—With B, p1, * sl 2 wyif, p8; rep from *, end sl 2, p1.
Rows 7 and 8—With A, repeat Rows 1 and 2.
Row 9—With B, k6, * sl 2 wyib, k8; rep from *, end sl 2, k6.
Row 10—With D, p5, * sl 4 wyif, p6; rep from *, end sl 4, p5.
Row 11—With D, k5, * sl 4 wyib, k6; rep from *, end sl 4, k5.
Row 12—With B, p6, * sl 2 wyib, p8; rep from *, end sl 2, p6.

Repeat Rows 1–12.

Haystack Stripe

Haystack Stripe

This is a gay and interesting pattern of only eight rows, which are repeated three times in order to alternate the colors. At first glance it appears to be a design of horizontal stripes, which are elongated upward and downward at intervals. But look more closely, and you will see that it is really a pattern of slip-cross cables, worked continuously across the fabric with a half-drop. This true design immediately becomes apparent if the pattern is worked in one solid color, using the basic eight rows only.

Multiple of 6 sts plus 2. Colors A, B, and C.

Cast on with Color A and knit one row.

Row 1 (Wrong side)—With A, k1, * p1 wrapping yarn twice, p1, p1 wrapping yarn twice, p3; rep from *, end k1.
Row 2—With B, k4, * sl 1 wyib dropping extra wrap, k1, sl 1 wyib dropping extra wrap, k3; rep from *, end last repeat k1 instead of k3.
Row 3—With B, k1, * sl 1 wyif, p1, sl 1 wyif, p3; rep from *, end k1.
Row 4—With B, k4, * drop next st off needle to front of work, sl 1 wyib, drop next st off needle to front of work; then with left-hand needle pick up *first* dropped st,

sl the same center st from right-hand needle back to left-hand needle, then pick up *second* dropped st and replace it on left-hand needle; then k6 (the 3 sts just crossed, and the following 3); rep from *, end last repeat k4 instead of k6.

Row 5—With B, k1, * p3, p1 wrapping yarn twice, p1, p1 wrapping yarn twice; rep from *, end k1.

Row 6—With C, k1, * sl 1 wyib dropping extra wrap, k1, sl 1 wyib dropping extra wrap, k3; rep from *, end k1.

Row 7—With C, k1, * p3, sl 1 wyif, p1, sl 1 wyif; rep from *, end k1.

Row 8—With C, k1, rep from * of Row 4 across to last st, end k1.

Row 9—With C, repeat Row 1.

Rows 10, 11, 12, and 13—With A, repeat Rows 2, 3, 4, and 5.

Rows 14, 15, 16, and 17—With B, repeat Rows 6, 7, 8, and 1.

Rows 18, 19, 20, and 21—With C, repeat Rows 2, 3, 4, and 5.

Rows 22, 23, and 24—With A, repeat Rows 6, 7, and 8.

Repeat Rows 1–24.

Four-Color Progressive Tweed

This pattern is so named because it "progresses" from right to left; each succeeding spot of the same color is moved two stitches over from its previous position. Try it in four gently-shading colors, such as cream, beige, gold and brown; or try it in four wildly contrasting ones—white, orange, emerald and black, for instance. The effect is very pleasing either way.

Multiple of 6 sts plus 2. Colors A, B, C, and D.

Cast on with Color A and purl one row.

Row 1 (Right side)—With B, k1, * sl 2 wyib, k4; rep from *, end k1.

Row 2—With B, k1, * k2, p2, sl 2 wyif; rep from *, end k1.

Row 3—With C, k3, * sl 2 wyib, k4; rep from *, end sl 2, k3.

Row 4—With C, k1, * p2, sl 2 wyif, k2; rep from *, end k1.

Row 5—With D, k1, * k4, sl 2 wyib; rep from *, end k1.

Row 6—With D, k1, * sl 2 wyif, k2, p2; rep from *, end k1.

Rows 7 and 8—With A, repeat Rows 1 and 2.

Rows 9 and 10—With B, repeat Rows 3 and 4.

Rows 11 and 12—With C, repeat Rows 5 and 6.

Rows 13 and 14—With D, repeat Rows 1 and 2.

Rows 15 and 16—With A, repeat Rows 3 and 4.

Rows 17 and 18—With B, repeat Rows 5 and 6.

Rows 19 and 20—With C, repeat Rows 1 and 2.

Rows 21 and 22—With D, repeat Rows 3 and 4.

Rows 23 and 24—With A, repeat Rows 5 and 6.

Repeat Rows 1–24.

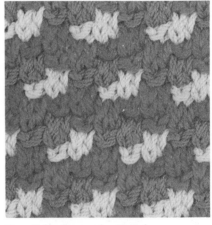

Four-Color Progressive Tweed

CHAPTER FOUR

Mosaic Patterns

Mosaic patterns are sophisticated designs in slip-stitch color knitting. The patterns themselves are complicated, but the knitting technique is not. Here, the most straightforward principle of slip-stitch color knitting is applied to a number of complex geometrical shapes, illustrating the enormous variety and flexibility of one simple knitting method. The basic principle is this: portions of each row are hidden behind slipped stitches carried up from a different-colored row below. This means that (1) every slip-stitch is slipped with yarn in *back* on right-side rows, and the same stitch is slipped again, but with yarn in *front,* on wrong-side rows. (2) Colors are alternated every two rows, and (3) each slip-stitch spans two rows and is caught again with its own color on the third row.

Most of these patterns call for *knitting* wrong-side rows, which gives the fabric a nubby garter-stitch texture. But *purling* can be substituted at will, if a smooth stockinette-type texture is desired. Some patterns look better one way, some the other; it depends upon the taste of the individual knitter, and upon the individual way of knitting. Remember, though, that if a pattern is shown in garter stitch, a stockinette version of the same pattern will look slightly elongated vertically. Conversely, a stockinette-type pattern will broaden and shorten a little when worked in garter stitch.

There is, then, nothing special about the method of making mosaics. It is a way of using colors which precludes having to change yarns in mid-row and strand across the back, as in "Fair Isle" knitting. Thus there are no bobbins, and no thickening of the fabric due to unused strands lying on the back. The method is superior to "Fair Isle" knitting except for one limitation: each area of "solid" color must contain dots of the opposite color. The reason for this is that the yarn must be caught and knitted at least every third stitch, lest the intervening slip-stitches be unattractively squeezed together.

Although the knitting technique is simple and easy, the pattern directions, in most cases, tend to be long. Therefore they must be read carefully as the work progresses. This diversity of rows, however, produces fanciful and charming designs with an intricate interplay of color. The variety of designs that can be made in this way is incredible; it is literally endless.

Now here is the most fascinating fact about mosaic patterns in general: *they can be worked on any number of stitches at all!* There is no need for the knitter to figure the closest multiple for a given size, or to juggle the pattern so as to work half a repeat or a third of a repeat for the sake of an extra inch. All that is necessary is to cast on the number of stitches that you want, then begin each pattern row at the right-hand edge according to the directions, and work across until you run out of stitches. If the row comes to an end in the middle of a repeat, it makes no difference! The return row is worked by knitting (or purling) and slipping the same stitches that were worked on the preceding row—so the beginning of the wrong-side row is not critical, and there are no special directions for it. All you have to do is look at the work to see which stitches were used in the preceding row, and which were not. You can "center" the pattern by using the recommended multiple of stitches if it is possible. But if, for reasons of size, this is not possible—you can forget it!

The patterns given here do not represent a really thorough exploration of all possible designs in mosaic knitting. On the contrary, they are just a beginning. Once the easy technique of mosaic knitting is clearly understood, any number of new and original patterns can be devised. In knitting as in most other creative crafts, simplicity means versatility. Mosaic knitting features a technique of the utmost simplicity and an application as broad as human ingenuity itself.

Two "Beginner's Mosaics"— Macedonian Stitch and Russian Stitch

I. MACEDONIAN STITCH

Multiple of 4 sts plus 3. Colors A and B.

Row 1 (Right side)—With A, knit.
Row 2—With A, purl.
Row 3—With B, k3, * sl 1 wyib, k3; rep from *.
Row 4—With B, k3, * sl 1 wyif, k3; rep from *.
Row 5—With A, k2, * sl 1 wyib, k1; rep from *, end k1.
Row 6—With A, p2, * sl 1 wyif, p1; rep from *, end p1.
Row 7—With B, k1, * sl 1 wyib, k3; rep from *, end sl 1, k1.
Row 8—With B, k1, * sl 1 wyif, k3; rep from *, end sl 1, k1.
Rows 9 and 10—With A, repeat Rows 1 and 2.
Rows 11 and 12—With B, repeat Rows 7 and 8.
Rows 13 and 14—With A, repeat Rows 5 and 6.
Rows 15 and 16—With B, repeat Rows 3 and 4.

Repeat Rows 1–16.

ABOVE: *Macedonian Stitch*
BELOW: *Russian Stitch*

II. RUSSIAN STITCH

Multiple of 5 sts plus 1. Colors A and B.

Cast on with Color A and knit one row.

Row 1 (Right side)—With B, * k4, sl 1 wyib; rep from *, end k1.
Row 2—With B, p1, * sl 1 wyif, p4; rep from *.
Row 3—With A, k5, * sl 1 wyib, k4; rep from *, end k1.
Row 4—With A, k5, * sl 1 wyif, k4; rep from *, end k1.
Row 5—With B, k1, * sl 1 wyib, k4; rep from *.
Row 6—With B, * p4, sl 1 wyif; rep from *, end p1.
Rows 7 and 8—With A, repeat Rows 3 and 4.

Repeat Rows 1–8.

Sliding Bricks

Multiple of 15 sts plus 2. Colors A and B.

Cast on with Color A and purl one row.

NOTE: On all right-side (odd-numbered) rows, sl all sl-sts with yarn in *back*. All wrong-side rows use the same color as the preceding right-side row.

Sliding Bricks

Row 1 (Right side)—With B, k1, * (k1, sl 1) twice, k10, sl 1; rep from *, end k1.
Row 2 and all other wrong-side rows using Color B—*Knit* all sts knitted on previous row; sl all the same sl-sts with yarn in *front*.
Row 3—With A, k5, * sl 1, k4, sl 1, k9; rep from *, end last repeat k6.
Row 4 and all other wrong-side rows using Color A—*Purl* all sts knitted on previous row; sl all the same sl-sts with yarn in *front*.
Row 5—With B, k1, * k10, (sl 1, k1) twice, sl 1; rep from *, end k1.
Row 7—With A, k1, * sl 1, k4, sl 1, k9; rep from *, end k1.
Row 9—With B, k7, * (sl 1, k1) twice, sl 1, k10; rep from *, end last repeat k5.
Row 11—With A, k2, * sl 1, k9, sl 1, k4; rep from *.
Rows 13 and 14—With B, repeat Rows 9 and 10.
Rows 15 and 16—With A, repeat Rows 7 and 8.
Rows 17 and 18—With B, repeat Rows 5 and 6.
Rows 19 and 20—With A, repeat Rows 3 and 4.
Rows 21 and 22—With B, repeat Rows 1 and 2.
Row 23—With A, * k9, sl 1, k4, sl 1; rep from *, end k2.
Row 24—See Row 4.

Repeat Rows 1–24.

Three-and-One Mosaic

Multiple of 4 sts plus 3. Colors A and B.

Row 1 (Right side)—With A, knit.
Row 2—With A, knit.
Row 3—With B, k3, * sl 1 wyib, k3; rep from *.
Row 4—With B, k3, * sl 1 wyif, k3; rep from *.
Row 5—With A, k1, * sl 1 wyib, k3; rep from *, end sl 1, k1.
Row 6—With A, k1, * sl 1 wyif, k3; rep from *, end sl 1, k1.
Row 7—With B, k2, * sl 1 wyib, k1; rep from *, end k1.
Row 8—With B, k2, * sl 1 wyif, k1; rep from *, end k1.
Rows 9 and 10—With A, repeat Rows 3 and 4.
Rows 11 and 12—With B, repeat Rows 5 and 6.
Rows 13 and 14—With A, knit.
Rows 15 and 16—Repeat Rows 11 and 12.
Rows 17 and 18—Repeat Rows 9 and 10.
Rows 19 and 20—Repeat Rows 7 and 8.
Rows 21 and 22—Repeat Rows 5 and 6.
Rows 23 and 24—Repeat Rows 3 and 4.

Repeat Rows 1–24.

Three-and-One Mosaic

Chessboard

Multiple of 14 sts plus 2. Colors A and B.

NOTE: On all right-side rows, sl all sl-sts with yarn in *back*.

Rows 1 and 2—With A, knit.
Rows 3, 7, 11, and 15 (Right side)—With B, k1, * k7, (sl 1, k1) 3 times, sl 1; rep from *, end k1.
Row 4 and all other wrong-side rows—Knit the same sts worked on previous row, with the same color; sl all the same sl-sts with yarn in *front*.
Rows 5, 9, and 13—With A, k1, * (sl 1, k1) 3 times, sl 1, k7; rep from *, end k1.
Rows 17 and 18—With A, knit.
Rows 19, 23, 27, and 31—With B, k1, * (sl 1, k1) 3 times, sl 1, k7; rep from *, end k1.
Rows 21, 25, and 29—With A, k1, * k7, (sl 1, k1) 3 times, sl 1; rep from *, end k1.
Row 32—See Row 4.

Repeat Rows 1–32.

Chessboard

Wave

Multiple of 5 sts plus 2. Colors A and B.

Cast on with A and knit one row.

NOTE: On all right-side rows sl all sl-sts with yarn in *back*.

Row 1 (Right side)—With B, k5, * sl 1, k4; rep from *, end sl 1, k1.

Row 2 and all other wrong-side rows—Knit (or purl) the same sts worked on previous row, with the same color; sl all the same sl-sts with yarn in *front*.

Row 3—With A, k1, * sl 1, k4; rep from *, end k1.

Row 5—With B, k2, * sl 1, k4; rep from *.

Row 7—With A, k3, * sl 1, k4; rep from *, end sl 1, k3.

Row 9—With B, * k4, sl 1; rep from *, end k2.

Row 11—With A, repeat Row 1.

Row 13—With B, repeat Row 3.

Row 15—With A, repeat Row 5.

Row 17—With B, repeat Row 7.

Rows 19, 21, 23, 25, 27, 29, and 31—Repeat Rows 15, 13, 11, 9, 7, 5, and 3.

Row 32—See Row 2.

Repeat Rows 1–32.

LEFT: *Wave*
RIGHT: *Dotted Wave*

Dotted Wave

Multiple of 6 sts plus 2. Colors A and B.

Cast on with B and knit one row.

NOTE: On all right-side rows, sl all sl-sts with yarn in *back*.

Row 1 (Right side)—With A, * k5, sl 1; rep from *, end k2.

Row 2 and all other wrong-side rows—Knit (or purl) the same sts worked on previous row, with the same color; sl all the same sl-sts with yarn in *front*.

Row 3—With B, k2, * sl 1, k3, sl 1, k1; rep from *.

Row 5—With A, k3, * sl 1, k5; rep from *, end sl 1, k4.

Row 7—With B, k4, * sl 1, k1, sl 1, k3; rep from *, end (sl 1, k1) twice.

Row 9—With A, k1, * sl 1, k5; rep from *, end k1.

Row 11—With B, k2, * sl 1, k1, sl 1, k3; rep from *.

Rows 13, 15, 17, 19, and 21—Repeat Rows 1, 3, 5, 7, and 9.

Rows 23, 25, 27, and 29—Repeat Rows 7, 5, 3, and 1.

Rows 31, 33, 35, 37, and 39—Repeat Rows 11, 9, 7, 5, and 3.

Row 40—See Row 2.

Repeat Rows 1–40.

Three Reversible-Texture Mosaics: Little Castle, Sliding Block Pattern, and Cage Pattern

All three of these patterns combine knit and purl stitches on the wrong-side rows to make varying texture effects. These effects can be reversed, by reading "knit" for "purl" and vice versa *on the wrong-side* rows only. Or, a straight stockinette or garter-stitch type of fabric can be achieved by purling all the wrong-side stitches, in the first case, or knitting them, in the second.

ABOVE: *Little Castle*
BELOW, LEFT: *Sliding Block Pattern*
BELOW, RIGHT: *Cage Pattern*

I. LITTLE CASTLE

Multiple of 8 sts plus 5. Colors A and B.

Cast on with Color A and purl one row.

Row 1 (Right side)—With B, k4, * sl 1 wyib, k3; rep from *, end k1.
Row 2—With B, k4, * sl 1 wyif, k3; rep from *, end k1.
Row 3—With A, k1, * sl 1 wyib, k1; rep from *.
Row 4—With A, p1, * sl 1 wyif, k1, sl 1 wyif, p1; rep from *.
Row 5—With B, k2, * sl 1 wyib, k7; rep from *, end sl 1, k2.
Row 6—With B, k2, * sl 1 wyif, k7; rep from *, end sl 1, k2.
Row 7—With A, k1, * sl 1 wyib, k1, sl 1 wyib, k5; rep from *, end last repeat k1.
Row 8—With A, p1, * sl 1 wyif, k1, sl 1 wyif, p5; rep from *, end last repeat p1.
Rows 9, 10, 11, and 12—Repeat Rows 1, 2, 3, and 4.
Row 13—With B, k6, * sl 1 wyib, k7; rep from *, end last repeat k6.
Row 14—With B, k6, * sl 1 wyif, k7; rep from *, end last repeat k6.
Row 15—With A, k5, * sl 1 wyib, k1, sl 1 wyib, k5; rep from *.
Row 16—With A, p5, * sl 1 wyif, k1, sl 1 wyif, p5; rep from *.

Repeat Rows 1–16.

II. SLIDING BLOCK PATTERN

Multiple of 6 sts plus 3. Colors A and B.

Cast on with Color A and knit one row.

Row 1 (Right side)—With B, * k5, sl 1 wyib; rep from *, end k3.
Row 2—With B, p3, * sl 1 wyif, p5; rep from *.
Row 3—With A, k1, * sl 1 wyib, k5; rep from *, end sl 1, k1.
Row 4—With A, k1, * sl 1 wyif, k5; rep from *, end sl 1, k1.
Row 5—With B, k3, * sl 1 wyib, k5; rep from *.
Row 6—With B, * p5, sl 1 wyif; rep from *, end p3.
Rows 7 and 8—With A, repeat Rows 3 and 4.

Repeat Rows 1–8.

III. CAGE PATTERN

Multiple of 6 sts. Colors A and B.

Cast on with Color A and purl one row.

Row 1 (Right side)—With B, k5, * sl 2 wyib, k4; rep from *, end k1.

Row 2—With B, k5, * sl 2 wyif, k4; rep from *, end k1.

Row 3—With A, k1, * sl 1 wyib, k2; rep from *, end sl 1, k1.

Row 4—With A, p1, * sl 1 wyif, p2; rep from *, end sl 1, p1.

Row 5—With B, k2, * sl 2 wyib, k4; rep from *, end sl 2, k2.

Row 6—With B, k2, * sl 2 wyif, k4; rep from *, end sl 2, k2.

Rows 7 and 8—With A, repeat Rows 3 and 4.

Repeat Rows 1–8.

Vertical Chain

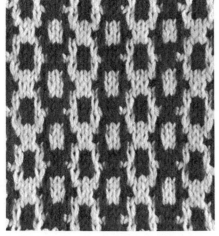

Vertical Chain

There are really two chains, interlocked with each other, in this pattern—a dark one on a light background, and a light one on a dark background. Thus the pattern is nothing but a simple variation on slipped vertical stripes.

Multiple of 8 sts plus 2. Colors A and B.

Cast on with Color A and purl one row.

NOTE: On all right-side (odd-numbered) rows, slip all sl-sts with yarn in *back*.

Row 1 (Right side)—With B, k3, * sl 1, k2, sl 1, k4; rep from *, end last repeat k3.

Row 2 and all other wrong-side rows—Purl (or knit) the same sts worked on previous row, with the same color; sl all the same sl-sts with yarn in *front*.

Row 3—With A, k1, sl 1, * k2, sl 2; rep from *, end k2, sl 1, k1.

Row 5—With B, repeat Row 1.

Row 7—With A, k2, * sl 1, k4, sl 1, k2; rep from *.

Row 9—With B, repeat Row 3.

Row 11—With A, repeat Row 7.

Row 12—See Row 2.

Repeat Rows 1–12.

Fretted Mosaic

Multiple of 6 sts plus 2. Colors A and B.

NOTE: On all right-side rows, sl all sl-sts with yarn in *back*.

Rows 1 and 2—With A, knit.

Row 3 (Right side)—With B, k1, * sl 1 wyib, k5; rep from *, end k1.

Row 4 and all other wrong-side rows—Knit the same sts worked on previous row, with the same color; sl all the same sl-sts with yarn in *front*.

Row 5—With A, k2, * sl 1, k3, sl 1, k1; rep from *.

Row 7—With B, k1, * sl 1, k3, sl 1, k1; rep from *, end k1.

Row 9—With A, k6, * sl 1, k5; rep from *, end sl 1, k1.

Rows 11 and 12—With B, knit.

Row 13—With A, k4, * sl 1, k5; rep from *, end sl 1, k3.

Row 15—With B, * k3, sl 1, k1, sl 1; rep from *, end k2.

Row 17—With A, k2, * sl 1, k1, sl 1, k3; rep from *.

Row 19—With B, k3, * sl 1, k5; rep from *, end sl 1, k4.

Row 20—See Row 4.

Repeat Rows 1–20.

Fretted Mosaic

Fretted Band Pattern

Multiple of 6 sts plus 2. Colors A and B.

NOTE: On all right-side rows, sl all sl-sts with yarn in *back*.

VERSION I: BASIC FRETTED BAND

Rows 1 and 2—With B, knit.

Row 3 (Right side)—With A, k6, * sl 1, k5; rep from *, end sl 1, k1.

Row 4 and all subsequent wrong-side rows—Knit the same sts worked on previous row, with the same color; sl all the same sl-sts with yarn in *front*.

Row 5—With B, k1, sl 1, * k3, sl 1, k1, sl 1; rep from *, end last repeat k2 instead of k1, sl 1.

Row 7—With A, k4, * sl 1, k1, sl 1, k3; rep from *, end last repeat k1.

Row 9—With B, k3, * sl 1, k1, sl 1, k3; rep from *, end last repeat k2.

Row 11—With A, k4, * sl 1, k5; rep from *, end sl 1, k3.

Row 12—See Row 4.

Repeat Rows 1–12.

Fretted Band Pattern, Version I
(Basic Fretted Band)

Fretted Band Pattern, Version II
(Alternating Fretted Band)

VERSION II: ALTERNATING FRETTED BAND

Rows 1 and 2—With A, knit.

Row 3 (Right side)—With B, k3, * sl 1, k5; rep from *, end sl 1, k4.

Row 4 and all subsequent wrong-side rows—See Row 4, above.

Rows 5 through 14—Repeat Rows 3 through 12 of Version I, above.

Row 15—With B, k1, * sl 1, k5; rep from *, end k1.

Rows 17 and 18—With A, knit.

Rows 19 through 36—Repeat Rows 1 through 18, reversing colors.

Repeat Rows 1–36.

Pin Box Pattern

Pin Box Pattern

To see how this clever pattern is constructed, plot it on graph paper. Put all the slip-stitches in their proper positions, and lo and behold, a diamond appears! Yet the motifs are quite evidently square—or nearly so.

Pin Box Pattern is actually made with pin stripes in a diamond formation. The diamond shapes *can* be seen on the wrong side. The pattern can be varied by knitting, instead of purling, the wrong-side rows; then the "boxes" will come out a little shorter and squarer, and the surface of the fabric will be rough and nubby.

Multiple of 12 sts plus 3. Colors A and B.

NOTE: On all odd-numbered (right-side) rows, sl all sl-sts with yarn in *back*.

Row 1 (Right side)—With A, knit.

Row 2—With A, purl.

Row 3—With B, k1, * sl 1, k11; rep from *, end sl 1, k1.

Row 4 and all subsequent wrong-side rows—Purl all sts knitted on previous row, with same color; sl all the same sl-sts with yarn in *front*.

Row 5—With A, k2, * sl 1, k9, sl 1, k1; rep from *, end k1.

Row 7—With B, (k1, sl 1) twice, * k7, (sl 1, k1) twice, sl 1; rep from *, end k7, (sl 1, k1) twice.

Row 9—With A, k2, sl 1, k1, sl 1, * k5, (sl 1, k1) 3 times, sl 1; rep from *, end k5, sl 1, k1, sl 1, k2.

Row 11—With B, (k1, sl 1) 3 times, * k3, (sl 1, k1) 4 times, sl 1; rep from *, end k3, (sl 1, k1) 3 times.

Row 13—With A, k2, * sl 1, k1; rep from *, end k1.
Rows 15, 17, 19, 21, 23, and 25—Repeat Rows 11, 9, 7, 5, 3, and 1.
Row 27—With B, k7, * sl 1, k11; rep from *, end last repeat k7.
Row 29—With A, k6, * sl 1, k1, sl 1, k9; rep from *, end last repeat k6.
Row 31—With B, k5, * (sl 1, k1) twice, sl 1, k7; rep from *, end last repeat k5.
Row 33—With A, k4, * (sl 1, k1) 3 times, sl 1, k5; rep from *, end last repeat k4.
Row 35—With B, k3, * (sl 1, k1) 4 times, sl 1, k3; rep from *.
Row 37—With A, repeat Row 13.
Rows 39, 41, 43, 45, and 47—Repeat Rows 35, 33, 31, 29, and 27.
Row 48—See Row 4.

Repeat Rows 1–48.

Maze Pattern

Here is a fascinating arrangement of color stripes for a definitely unusual sweater or coat. It is surprisingly easy to knit.

Multiple of 14 sts plus 2. Colors A and B.

Cast on with Color A and purl one row.

NOTE: On all right-side (odd-numbered) rows, sl all sl-sts with yarn in *back*.

Row 1 (Right side)—With B, k1, * k7, (sl 1, k1) 3 times, sl 1; rep from *, end k1.

Row 2 and all other wrong-side rows—Purl all sts worked on previous row, with the same color; sl all the same sl-sts with yarn in *front*.

Row 3—With A, k1, * sl 1, k7, (sl 1, k1) 3 times; rep from *, end k1.

Row 5—With B, k2, * sl 1, k7, (sl 1, k1) 3 times; rep from *.

Row 7—With A, * (k1, sl 1) twice, k7, sl 1, k1, sl 1; rep from *, end k2.

Row 9—With B, k2, * sl 1, k1, sl 1, k7, (sl 1, k1) twice; rep from *.

Row 11—With A, * (k1, sl 1) 3 times, k7, sl 1; rep from *, end k2.

Row 13—With B, k1, * (k1, sl 1) 3 times, k7, sl 1; rep from *, end k1.

Row 15—With A, k1, * (sl 1, k1) 3 times, sl 1, k7; rep from *, end k1.

Row 17—With B, repeat Row 1.

Row 19—With A, * k7, (sl 1, k1) 3 times, sl 1; rep from *, end k2.

Row 21—With B, k6, * (sl 1, k1) 3 times, sl 1, k7; rep from *, end last repeat k3.

Row 23—With A, k5, * (sl 1, k1) 3 times, sl 1, k7; rep from *, end last repeat k4.

Row 25—With B, k4, * (sl 1, k1) 3 times, sl 1, k7; rep from *, end last repeat k5.

Row 27—With A, k3, * (sl 1, k1) 3 times, sl 1, k7; rep from *, end last repeat k6.

Row 29—With B, k2, * (sl 1, k1) 3 times, sl 1, k7; rep from *.

Row 31—With A, repeat Row 15.

Row 32—See Row 2.

Repeat Rows 1–32.

Maze Pattern

Assyrian Stripe Pattern

As Mosaics go, this one is simple to work because the directions are neither long nor complex—just repetitive. Yet it is a stunning pattern for any ski sweater, border, child's jacket, or hat.

Multiple of 16 sts plus 1. Colors A and B.

NOTE: On all right-side (odd-numbered) rows, sl all sl-sts with yarn in *back*.

Rows 1 and 2—With A, knit.
Row 3 (Right side)—With B, k1, * sl 1, k1; rep from *.
Row 4 and all other wrong-side rows—Knit (or purl) all the same sts worked on previous row, with the same color; sl all the same sl-sts with yarn in *front*.
Row 5—With A, k8, * sl 1, k15; rep from *, end sl 1, k8.
Row 7—With B, k2, * (sl 1, k1) twice, sl 1, k3; rep from *, end last repeat k2.
Row 9—With A, k7, * sl 3, k13; rep from *, end sl 3, k7.
Row 11—With B, k4, * sl 1, k7; rep from *, end sl 1, k4.
Row 13—With A, k5, * sl 1, k1, sl 3, k1, sl 1, k9; rep from *, end last repeat k5.
Rows 15, 17, 19, 21, 23 and 25—Repeat Rows 11, 9, 7, 5, 3, and 1.
Rows 27 through 51—Repeat Rows 1 through 25, reversing colors.
Row 52—With B, knit.

Repeat Rows 1–52.

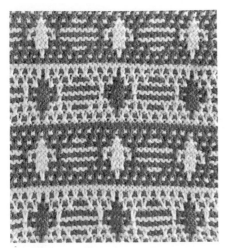

Assyrian Stripe Pattern

Stripes and Diamonds

Dotted diamonds appear to be embossed on a striped fabric in this pattern, which can be used to make a very handsome two-color garment. Various rearrangements of knits and purls can be applied to make different texture effects.

Multiple of 10 sts plus 1. Colors A and B.

Cast on with Color A and knit one row.

NOTE: On all right-side (odd-numbered) rows, sl all sl-sts wyib; on all wrong-side (even-numbered) rows, sl all sl-sts wyif.

Row 1 (Right side)—With B, k5, * sl 1, k9; rep from *, end sl 1, k5.
Row 2—With B, p5, * sl 1, p9; rep from *, end sl 1, p5.
Row 3—With A, knit.
Row 4—With A, k4, * p3, k7; rep from *, end p3, k4.
Row 5—With B, k4, * sl 1, k1, sl 1, k7; rep from *, end last repeat k4.
Row 6—With B, p4, * sl 1, k1, sl 1, p7; rep from *, end last repeat p4.

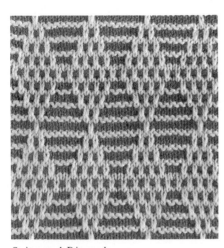

Stripes and Diamonds

Row 7—With A, knit.
Row 8—With A, k3, * p5, k5; rep from *, end p5, k3.
Row 9—With B, k3, * (sl 1, k1) twice, sl 1, k5; rep from *, end last repeat k3.
Row 10—With B, p3, * (sl 1, k1) twice, sl 1, p5; rep from *, end last repeat p3.
Row 11—With A, knit.
Row 12—With A, k2, * p7, k3; rep from *, end p7, k2.
Row 13—With B, k2, * (sl 1, k1) 3 times, sl 1, k3; rep from *, end last repeat k2.
Row 14—With B, p2, * (sl 1, k1) 3 times, sl 1, p3; rep from *, end last repeat p2.
Row 15—With A, knit.
Row 16—With A, purl.
Rows 17 and 18—With B, k1, * sl 1, k1; rep from *.
Rows 19 and 20—With A, repeat Rows 15 and 16.
Rows 21 and 22—With B, repeat Rows 13 and 14.
Rows 23 and 24—With A, repeat Rows 11 and 12.
Rows 25 and 26—With B, repeat Rows 9 and 10.
Rows 27 and 28—With A, repeat Rows 7 and 8.
Rows 29 and 30—With B, repeat Rows 5 and 6.
Rows 31 and 32—With A, repeat Rows 3 and 4.

Repeat Rows 1–32.

City Lights

Multiple of 6 sts plus 3. Colors A and B.

Cast on with Color A and purl one row.

NOTE: On all right-side (odd-numbered) rows, sl all sl-sts with yarn in *back*.

On all wrong-side (even-numbered) rows, sl all sl-sts with yarn in *front*.

Rows 1 and 2—With B, knit.
Row 3 (Right side)—With A, k2, * sl 1, k1; rep from *, end k1.
Row 4—With A, k2, * (sl 1, p1) twice, sl 1, k1; rep from *, end k1.
Row 5—With B, k3, * sl 1, k1, sl 1, k3; rep from *.
Row 6—With B, k3, * sl 1, p1, sl 1, k3; rep from *.
Row 7—With A, k4, * sl 1, k5; rep from *, end sl 1, k4.
Row 8—With A, p4, * sl 1, p5; rep from *, end sl 1, p4.
Row 9—With B, k1, * sl 1, k5; rep from *, end sl 1, k1.
Row 10—With B, k1, * sl 1, k2, p1, k2; rep from *, end sl 1, k1.
Row 11—With A, repeat Row 3.
Row 12—With A, p2, * (sl 1, k1) twice, sl 1, p1; rep from *, end p1.
Rows 13 and 14—With B, repeat Rows 9 and 10.
Rows 15 and 16—With A, repeat Rows 7 and 8.
Rows 17 and 18—With B, repeat Rows 5 and 6.
Rows 19 and 20—With A, repeat Rows 3 and 4.

Repeat Rows 1–20.

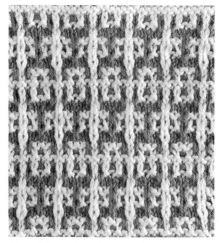

City Lights

Four "Flying Cross" Mosaics: Illusion Stripe, Dogtooth Cross, Diagonal Chain, and Egyptian Cross

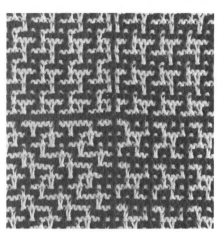

ABOVE, LEFT: *Illusion Stripe*
ABOVE, RIGHT: *Dogtooth Cross*
BELOW, LEFT: *Diagonal Chain*
BELOW, RIGHT: *Egyptian Cross*

The flying cross or four-armed cross (of which the swastika is one example) is an ancient and recurrent theme in geometric patterns the world over. Here it can be traced in four fascinating mosaic designs. In each, the basic motif is a small three-stitch square with a dot of contrasting color in the center and four "arms" proceeding from the corners. But this motif is very differently handled in each of the four.

The first two, Illusion Stripe and Dogtooth Cross, are similar but illustrate a small change that makes a big difference. Look at the light-colored shapes against the background of dark-colored ones, then at the dark-colored shapes against the background of the light-colored ones. In Illusion Stripe, both are alike—hence the "illusion". But in Dogtooth Cross the two colors form very different designs. The contrast between "dark" shapes and "light" shapes is even greater in the third and fourth patterns. Exchange the positions of dark and light rows, and these patterns will alter radically in their appearance. The last pattern, Egyptian Cross, begins and ends with plain knit rows and thus will make a very interesting border design as well as an allover pattern.

NOTES FOR ALL FOUR PATTERNS: On all right-side (odd-numbered) rows, slip all sl-sts with yarn in *back*. On all wrong-side (even-numbered) rows, knit (or purl) the same sts worked on previous row, with the same color; sl all the same sl-sts with yarn in *front*.

I. ILLUSION STRIPE

Multiple of 6 sts plus 2. Colors A and B.

Cast on with Color A and knit one row.

Row 1 (Right side)—With B, k1, * k5, sl 1; rep from *, end k1.
Row 3—With A, k1, * sl 1, k1, sl 1, k3; rep from *, end k1.
Row 5—With B, k4, * sl 1, k5; rep from *, end last repeat k3.
Row 7—With A, k3, * sl 1, k5; rep from *, end last repeat k4.
Row 9—With B, k4, * sl 1, k1, sl 1, k3; rep from *, end last repeat k1.
Row 11—With A, k1, * sl 1, k5; rep from *, end k1.
Row 12—See Notes.

Repeat Rows 1–12.

II. DOGTOOTH CROSS

Multiple of 6 sts plus 2. Colors A and B.

Cast on with Color A and knit one row.

Row 1 (Right side)—With B, * k5, sl 1; rep from *, end k2.
Row 3—With A, k2, * sl 1, k3, sl 1, k1; rep from *.
Row 5—With B, k3, * sl 1, k5; rep from *, end last repeat k4.
Row 7—With A, k2, * sl 1, k5; rep from *.
Row 9—With B, k1, * sl 1, k1; rep from *, end k1.
Row 11—With A, k1, * k5, sl 1; rep from *, end k1.
Row 12—See Notes.

Repeat Rows 1–12.

III. DIAGONAL CHAIN

Multiple of 8 sts plus 1. Colors A and B.

Cast on with Color A and knit one row.

Row 1 (Right side)—With B, * k7, sl 1; rep from *, end k1.
Row 3—With A, k2, * sl 1, k3; rep from *, end last repeat k2.
Row 5—With B, k1, * sl 1, k1, sl 1, k5; rep from *.
Row 7—With A, k4, * sl 1, k1, sl 1, k5; rep from *, end last repeat k2.
Row 9—With B, * k1, sl 1, k5, sl 1; rep from *, end k1.
Row 11—With A, k4, * sl 1, k3; rep from *, end k1.
Row 13—With B, k3, * sl 1, k7; rep from *, end last repeat k5.
Row 15—With A, k2, * sl 1, k5, sl 1, k1; rep from *, end sl 1, k6.
Row 16—See Notes.

Repeat Rows 1–16.

IV. EGYPTIAN CROSS

Multiple of 8 sts plus 3. Colors A and B.

Cast on with Color A and knit one row.

Row 1 (Right side)—With B, k1, * sl 1, k3, (sl 1, k1) twice; rep from *, end sl 1, k1.
Row 3—With A, k4, * sl 1, k3; rep from *, end last repeat k2.
Row 5—With B, k1, * sl 1, k1, sl 1, k5; rep from *, end sl 1, k1.
Row 7—With A, k4, * sl 1, k1, sl 1, k5; rep from *, end last repeat k4.
Row 9—With B, k1, * sl 1, k5, sl 1, k1; rep from *, end sl 1, k1.
Row 11—With A, k2, * sl 1, k3; rep from *, end k1.
Row 13—With B, k1, * (sl 1, k1) twice, sl 1, k3; rep from *, end sl 1, k1.
Rows 15 and 16—With A, knit.

Repeat Rows 1–16.

ABOVE: *Miniature Mosaic*
BELOW: *Pyramid*

Miniature Mosaic

Multiple of 8 sts plus 3. Colors A and B.

Cast on with A and knit one row.

NOTE: On all right-side rows, sl all sl-sts with yarn in *back*.

Row 1 (Right side)—With B, k1, * sl 1, k7; rep from *, end sl 1, k1.

Row 2 and all other wrong-side rows—Knit (or purl) the same sts worked on previous row, with the same color; sl all the same sl-sts with yarn in *front*.

Row 3—With A, k4, * sl 1, k1, sl 1, k5; rep from *, end last repeat k4.

Row 5—With B, k3, * sl 1, k3; rep from *.

Row 7—With A, k2, * sl 1, k5, sl 1, k1; rep from *, end k1.

Row 9—With B, k5, * sl 1, k7; rep from *, end last repeat k5.

Rows 11 and 12—With A, repeat Rows 7 and 8.

Rows 13 and 14—With B, repeat Rows 5 and 6.

Rows 15 and 16—With A, repeat Rows 3 and 4.

Repeat Rows 1–16.

Pyramid

Multiple of 14 sts plus 3. Colors A and B.

Cast on with A and knit one row.

NOTE: On all right-side rows, sl all sl-sts with yarn in *back*.

Row 1 (Right side)—With B, k8, * sl 1, k13; rep from *, end last repeat k8.

Row 2 and all other wrong-side rows—Knit (or purl) the same sts worked on previous row, with the same color; sl all the same sl-sts with yarn in *front*.

Row 3—With A, k2, * (sl 1, k1) twice, sl 1, k3, (sl 1, k1) 3 times; rep from *, end k1.

Row 5—With B, k7, * sl 1, k1, sl 1, k11; rep from *, end last repeat k7.

Row 7—With A, k2, * sl 1, k1, sl 1, k7, (sl 1, k1) twice; rep from *, end k1.

Row 9—With B, k5, * (sl 1, k1) 3 times, sl 1, k7; rep from *, end last repeat k5.

Row 11—With A, k2, * sl 1, k11, sl 1, k1; rep from *, end k1.

Row 13—With B, k3, * (sl 1, k1) 5 times, sl 1, k3; rep from *.

Row 15—With A, k1, * sl 1, k13; rep from *, end sl 1, k1.

Row 16—See Row 2.

Repeat Rows 1–16.

Lattice

Multiple of 12 sts plus 3. Colors A and B.

Cast on with A and knit one row.

NOTE: On all right-side rows sl all sl-sts with yarn in *back*.

Row 1 (Right side)—With B, k1, * sl 1, k11; rep from *, end sl 1, k1.

Row 2 and all other wrong-side rows—Knit (or purl) the same sts worked on previous row, with the same color; sl all the same sl-sts with yarn in *front*.

Row 3—With A, k4, * (sl 1, k1) 3 times, sl 1, k5; rep from *, end last repeat k4.

Row 5—With B, k3, * sl 1, k7, sl 1, k3; rep from *.

Row 7—With A, k2, * sl 1, k3, sl 1, k1; rep from *, end k1.

Row 9—With B, k5, * sl 1, k3, sl 1, k7; rep from *, end last repeat k5.

Row 11—With A, k2, * sl 1, k1, sl 1, k5, (sl 1, k1) twice; rep from *, end k1.

Row 13—With B, k7, * sl 1, k11; rep from *, end last repeat k7.

Rows 15 and 16—With A, repeat Rows 11 and 12.

Rows 17 and 18—With B, repeat Rows 9 and 10.

Rows 19 and 20—With A, repeat Rows 7 and 8.

Rows 21 and 22—With B, repeat Rows 5 and 6.

Rows 23 and 24—With A, repeat Rows 3 and 4.

Repeat Rows 1–24.

Lattice

Fancy Lattice

Multiple of 14 sts plus 3. Colors A and B.

Cast on with A and knit one row.

NOTE: On all right-side rows sl all sl-sts with yarn in *back*.

Row 1 (Right side)—With B, k2, * (sl 1, k1) 3 times, k2, (sl 1, k1) 3 times; rep from *, end k1.

Row 2 and all other wrong-side rows—Knit (or purl) the same sts worked on previous row, with the same color; sl all the same sl-sts with yarn in *front*.

Row 3—With A, k7, * sl 1, k1, sl 1, k11; rep from *, end last repeat k7.

Row 5—With B, k1, sl 1, k1, * (sl 1, k4) twice, (sl 1, k1) twice; rep from *.

Row 7—With A, k4, * sl 1, k7, sl 1, k5; rep from *, end last repeat k4.

Row 9—With B, k5, * (sl 1, k1) 3 times, sl 1, k7; rep from *, end last repeat k5.

Row 11—With A, k1, * sl 1, k13; rep from *, end sl 1, k1.

Rows 13 and 14—With B, repeat Rows 9 and 10.

Rows 15 and 16—With A, repeat Rows 7 and 8.

Rows 17 and 18—With B, repeat Rows 5 and 6.

Rows 19 and 20—With A, repeat Rows 3 and 4.

Repeat Rows 1–20.

Fancy Lattice

Greek Cross Medallion

Greek Cross Medallion

Multiple of 14 sts plus 3. Colors A and B.

Cast on with A and knit one row.

NOTE: On all right-side rows, sl all sl-sts with yarn in *back*.

Row 1 (Right side)—With B, k2, * sl 1, k1, (sl 1, k3) twice, (sl 1, k1) twice; rep from *, end k1.

Row 2 and all other wrong-side rows—Knit (or purl) the same sts worked on previous row, with the same color; sl all the same sl-sts with yarn in *front*.

Row 3—With A, k5, * sl 1, k5, sl 1, k7; rep from *, end last repeat k5.

Row 5—With B, k2, * (sl 1, k3) 3 times, sl 1, k1; rep from *, end k1.

Row 7—With A, k3, * sl 1, k3, sl 1, k1, (sl 1, k3) twice; rep from *.

Row 9—With B, k4, * sl 1, k7, sl 1, k5; rep from *, end last repeat k4.

Row 11—With A, k1, * sl 1, k3, (sl 1, k1) 3 times, sl 1, k3; rep from *, end sl 1, k1.

Rows 13 and 14—With B, repeat Rows 9 and 10.

Rows 15 and 16—With A, repeat Rows 7 and 8.

Rows 17 and 18—With B, repeat Rows 5 and 6.

Rows 19 and 20—With A, repeat Rows 3 and 4.

Repeat Rows 1–20.

Key and Basket Pattern

Key and Basket Pattern

Multiple of 16 sts plus 3. Colors A and B.

Cast on with A and knit one row.

NOTE: On all right-side rows, sl all sl-sts with yarn in *back*.

Row 1 (Right side)—With B, k1, * (k1, sl 1, k3, sl 1) twice, k3, sl 1; rep from *, end k2.

Row 2 and all other wrong-side rows—Knit (or purl) the same sts worked on previous row, with the same color; sl all the same sl-sts with yarn in *front*.

Row 3—With A, k1, * sl 1, k3; rep from *, end sl 1, k1.

Row 5—With B, k4, * sl 1, k1, (sl 1, k3) twice, sl 1, k5; rep from *, end last repeat k4.

Row 7—With A, k2, * sl 2, k3, (sl 1, k3) twice, sl 2, k1; rep from *, end k1.

Row 9—With B, k4, * (sl 1, k3) twice, sl 1, k1, sl 1, k5; rep from *, end last repeat k4.

Row 11—With A, repeat Row 3.

Row 13—With B, k2, * (sl 1, k3) twice, sl 1, k1, sl 1, k3, sl 1, k1; rep from *, end k1.

Row 15—With A, k3, * sl 1, k3; rep from *.

Row 17—With B, k2, * (sl 1, k1, sl 1, k3) twice, sl 1, k3; rep from *, end k1.

Row 19—With A, repeat Row 3.

Row 21—With B, k4, * sl 1, k1, sl 1, k5, (sl 1, k3) twice; rep from *, end last repeat k2.

Row 23—With A, k3, * sl 1, k3, sl 2, k1, sl 2, k3, sl 1, k3; rep from *.

Row 25—With B, k2, * sl 1, k3, sl 1, k5, sl 1, k1, sl 1, k3; rep from *, end k1.

Row 27—With A, repeat Row 3.

Row 29—With B, k4, * (sl 1, k3, sl 1, k1) twice, sl 1, k3; rep from *, end last repeat k2.

Row 31—With A, repeat Row 15.

Row 32—See Row 2.

Repeat Rows 1–32.

Oblong Medallion

Multiple of 24 sts plus 3. Colors A and B.

Cast on with A and knit one row.

Note: On all right-side rows, sl all sl-sts with yarn in *back*.

Oblong Medallion

Row 1 (Right side)—With B, k5, * sl 1, k4, sl 1, k5, sl 1, k4, sl 1, k7; rep from *, end last repeat k5.

Row 2 and all other wrong-side rows—Knit (or purl) the same sts worked on previous row, with the same color; sl all the same sl-sts with yarn in *front*.

Row 3—With A, k6, * sl 1, k4, sl 1, k3, sl 1, k4, sl 1, k9; rep from *, end last repeat k6.

Row 5—With B, k2, * (sl 1, k4) twice, sl 1, k1, sl 1, (k4, sl 1) twice, k1; rep from *, end k1.

Row 7—With A, k3, * sl 1, k4, sl 1, k9, sl 1, k4, sl 1, k3; rep from *.

Row 9—With B, k4, * sl 1, k4, sl 1, k7, sl 1, k4, sl 1, k5; rep from *, end last repeat k4.

Row 11—With A, k1, * sl 1, k3, sl 1, k4, (sl 1, k1) 3 times, sl 1, k4, sl 1, k3; rep from *, end sl 1, k1.

Rows 13 and 14—With B, repeat Rows 9 and 10.

Rows 15 and 16—With A, repeat Rows 7 and 8.

Rows 17 and 18—With B, repeat Rows 5 and 6.

Rows 19 and 20—With A, repeat Rows 3 and 4.

Rows 21 and 22—With B, repeat Rows 1 and 2.

Row 23—With A, k2, sl 1, k1, * sl 1, k4, (sl 1, k3) twice, sl 1, k4, (sl 1, k1) 3 times; rep from *, end sl 1, k4, (sl 1, k3) twice, sl 1, k4, sl 1, k1, sl 1, k2.

Row 24—See Row 2.

Repeat Rows 1–24.

Double Medallion

Double Medallion

Multiple of 22 sts plus 3. Colors A and B.

Cast on with A and knit one row.

NOTE: On all right-side rows, sl all sl-sts with yarn in *back*.

Row 1 (Right side)—With B, k3, * (sl 1, k8) twice, sl 1, k3; rep from *.

Row 2 and all other wrong-side rows—Knit (or purl) the same sts worked on previous row, with the same color; sl all the same sl-sts with yarn in *front*.

Row 3—With A, k4, * (sl 1, k1) 3 times, k6, (sl 1, k1) 3 times, k4; rep from *, end last repeat k3.

Row 5—With B, k9, * sl 1, k5, sl 1, k15; rep from *, end last repeat k9.

Row 7—With A, (k1, sl 1) 3 times, * k4, sl 1, k3, sl 1, k4, (sl 1, k1) 4 times, sl 1; rep from *, end k4, sl 1, k3, sl 1, k4, (sl 1, k1) 3 times.

Row 9—With B, k6, * sl 1, k4, sl 1, k1, sl 1, k4, sl 1, k9; rep from *, end last repeat k6.

Row 11—With A, k2, * sl 1, k4, sl 1, k9, sl 1, k4, sl 1, k1; rep from *, end k1.

Row 13—With B, k3, * sl 1, k4, (sl 1, k1) 4 times, sl 1, k4, sl 1, k3; rep from *.

Row 15—With A, k4, * sl 1, k15, sl 1, k5; rep from *, end last repeat k4.

Rows 17 and 18—With B, repeat Rows 13 and 14.

Rows 19 and 20—With A, repeat Rows 11 and 12.

Rows 21 and 22—With B, repeat Rows 9 and 10.

Rows 23 and 24—With A, repeat Rows 7 and 8.

Rows 25 and 26—With B, repeat Rows 5 and 6.

Rows 27 and 28—With A, repeat Rows 3 and 4.

Repeat Rows 1–28.

Fancy Parallelogram

Fancy Parallelogram

Multiple of 16 sts plus 2. Colors A and B.

Cast on with A and knit one row.

NOTE: On all right-side rows, sl all sl-sts with yarn in *back*.

Row 1 (Right side)—With B, k1, * k4, sl 1, k11; rep from *, end k1.

Row 2 and all other wrong-side rows—Knit (or purl) the same sts worked on previous row, with the same color; sl all the same sl-sts with yarn in *front*.

Row 3—With A, k1, * (k3, sl 1) twice, (k1, sl 1) 3 times, k2; rep from *, end k1.
Row 5—With B, k1, * k2, sl 1, k3, sl 1, k7, sl 1, k1; rep from *, end k1.
Row 7—With A, k1, * k1, (sl 1, k3) twice, sl 1, k1, sl 1, k3, sl 1; rep from *, end k1.
Row 9—With B, k1, * k4, (sl 1, k3) 3 times; rep from *, end k1.
Row 11—With A, k1, * (k3, sl 1) 3 times, k4; rep from *, end k1.
Row 13—With B, k1, * sl 1, k3, sl 1, k1, (sl 1, k3) twice, sl 1, k1; rep from *, end k1.
Row 15—With A, k1, * k1, sl 1, k7, sl 1, k3, sl 1, k2; rep from *, end k1.
Row 17—With B, k1, * k2, (sl 1, k1) 3 times, (sl 1, k3) twice; rep from *, end k1.
Row 19—With A, k1, * k11, sl 1, k4; rep from *, end k1.
Row 20—See Row 2.

Repeat Rows 1–20.

Crown Chevron

Multiple of 18 sts plus 3. Colors A and B.

Cast on with Color A and purl one row.

Note: On all right-side (odd-numbered) rows, sl all sl-sts with yarn in *back*.

Row 1 (Right side)—With B, k2, * sl 1, k2, (sl 1, k4) twice, sl 1, k2, sl 1, k1; rep from *, end k1.
Row 2 and all other wrong-side rows—Purl (or knit) the same sts worked on previous row, with the same color; sl all the same sl-sts with yarn in *front*.
Row 3—With A, k1, * sl 1, k4, sl 1, k1, sl 1, k3, sl 1, k1, sl 1, k4; rep from *, end sl 1, k1.
Row 5—With B, k3, * sl 1, k5, sl 1, k1, sl 1, k5, sl 1, k3; rep from *.
Row 7—With A, k2, * (sl 1, k1) twice, sl 1, k7, (sl 1, k1) 3 times; rep from *, end k1.
Row 9—With B, k7, * (sl 1, k1) 3 times, sl 1, k11; rep from *, end last repeat k7.
Row 11—With A, k2, * sl 1, k1, (sl 1, k5) twice, (sl 1, k1) twice; rep from *, end k1.
Row 13—With B, k5, * sl 2, k7; rep from *, end last repeat k5.
Row 15—With A, k1, * sl 1, k5, (sl 1, k1) 3 times, sl 1, k5; rep from *, end sl 1, k1.
Row 17—With B, k2, * sl 1, k1, sl 1, k11, (sl 1, k1) twice; rep from *, end k1.
Row 19—With A, k5, * (sl 1, k1) 5 times, sl 1, k7; rep from *, end last repeat k5.
Row 21—With B, k2, * sl 1, k5, sl 1, k3, sl 1, k5, sl 1, k1; rep from *, end k1.
Row 23—With A, k3, * sl 1, k1, (sl 1, k4) twice, sl 1, k1, sl 1, k3; rep from *.
Row 25—With B, k1, * sl 1, k4, sl 1, k2, sl 1, k1, sl 1, k2, sl 1, k4; rep from *, end sl 1, k1.
Row 27—With A, knit.
Row 28—With A, purl (or knit).

Repeat Rows 1–28.

Crown Chevron

Yang and Yin, or Endless Branch

Yang and Yin, or Endless Branch

Multiple of 20 sts plus 2. Colors A and B.

Cast on with A and purl one row.

Note: On all right-side rows, sl all sl-sts with yarn in *back*.

Row 1 (Right side)—With B, k1, * k2, sl 2, k6, sl 2, k8; rep from *, end k1.

Row 2 and all other wrong-side rows—Purl the same sts worked on previous row, with the same color; sl all the same sl-sts with yarn in *front*.

Row 3—With A, k1, * k4, (sl 2, k6) twice; rep from *, end k1.

Row 5—With B, k1, * sl 2, k4, sl 2, k2; rep from *, end k1.

Row 7—With A, k1, * k2, (sl 2, k4) 3 times; rep from *, end k1.

Row 9—With B, k1, * k4, sl 2, k6, sl 2, k4, sl 2; rep from *, end k1.

Row 11—With A, k1, * sl 2, k4, sl 2, k2; rep from *, end k1.

Row 13—With B, k1, * k2, sl 2, k10, sl 2, k4; rep from *, end k1.

Row 15—With A, k1, * sl 2, k10, sl 2, k6; rep from *, end k1.

Row 17—With B, k1, * k4, sl 2, k2, sl 2; rep from *, end k1.

Row 19—With A, k1, * k2, sl 2, k6, sl 2, k4, sl 2, k2; rep from *, end k1.

Row 21—With B, k1, * (sl 2, k4) twice, sl 2, k6; rep from *, end k1.

Row 23—With A, k1, * k4, sl 2, k2, sl 2; rep from *, end k1.

Row 24—See Row 2.

Repeat Rows 1–24.

Fancy Chevron

Fancy Chevron

Multiple of 26 sts plus 3. Colors A and B.

Cast on with A and purl one row.

Note: On all right-side rows, sl all sl-sts with yarn in *back*. On all wrong-side rows, sl all sl-sts with yarn in *front*.

Row 1 (Right side)—With B, k9, * sl 2, k7, sl 2, k15; rep from *, end last repeat k9.

Row 2—With B, k9, * sl 2, p7, sl 2, k15; rep from *, end last repeat k9.

Row 3—With A, k2, * (sl 1, k1) twice, sl 1, k4, sl 2, k3, sl 2, k4, (sl 1, k1) 3 times; rep from *, end k1.

Row 4—With A, k2, * (sl 1, k1) twice, sl 1, p4, sl 2, k3, sl 2, p4, (sl 1, k1) 3 times; rep from *, end k1.

Row 5—With B, k7, * sl 2, k4, sl 1, k1, sl 1, k4, sl 2, k11; rep from *, end last repeat k7.

Row 6—With B, k7, * sl 2, p4, sl 1, k1, sl 1, p4, sl 2, k11; rep from *, end last repeat k7.

Row 7—With A, k2, * sl 1, k1, sl 1, k4, sl 2, k7, sl 2, k4, (sl 1, k1) twice; rep from *, end k1.

Row 8—With A, k2, * sl 1, k1, sl 1, p4, sl 2, k7, sl 2, p4, (sl 1, k1) twice; rep from *, end k1.

Row 9—With B, k5, * sl 2, k4, (sl 1, k1) 3 times, sl 1, k4, sl 2, k7; rep from *, end last repeat k5.

Row 10—With B, k5, * sl 2, p4, (sl 1, k1) 3 times, sl 1, p4, sl 2, k7; rep from *, end last repeat k5.

Row 11—With A, k2, * sl 1, k4, sl 2, k11, sl 2, k4, sl 1, k1; rep from *, end k1.

Row 12—With A, k2, * sl 1, p4, sl 2, k11, sl 2, p4, sl 1, k1; rep from *, end k1.

Row 13—With B, k3, * sl 2, k4, (sl 1, k1) 5 times, sl 1, k4, sl 2, k3; rep from *.

Row 14—With B, k3, * sl 2, p4, (sl 1, k1) 5 times, sl 1, p4, sl 2, k3; rep from *.

Row 15—With A, k5, * sl 2, k15, sl 2, k7; rep from *, end last repeat k5.

Row 16—With A, p5, * sl 2, k15, sl 2, p7; rep from *, end last repeat p5.

Row 17—With B, k2, * sl 1, k8, sl 2, k3, sl 2, k8, sl 1, k1; rep from *, end k1.

Row 18—With B, k2, * sl 1, p8, sl 2, p3, sl 2, p8, sl 1, k1; rep from *, end k1.

Row 19—With A, k3, * sl 2, k8, sl 1, k1, sl 1, k8, sl 2, k3; rep from *.

Row 20—With A, p3, * sl 2, p8, sl 1, k1, sl 1, p8, sl 2, p3; rep from *.

Repeat Rows 1–20.

Divided Diamond

Multiple of 22 sts plus 2. Colors A and B.

Cast on with A and knit one row.

Note: On all right-side rows, sl all sl-sts with yarn in *back*.

Row 1 (Right side)—With B, k1, * k10, sl 1, k3, sl 1, k7; rep from *, end k1.

Row 2 and all other wrong-side rows—Knit (or purl) the same sts worked on previous row, with the same color; sl all the same sl-sts with yarn in *front*.

Row 3—With A, k1, * (k1, sl 1) 4 times, k3, sl 1, k1, sl 1, k3, (sl 1, k1) twice, sl 1; rep from *, end k1.

Row 5—With B, k1, * k8, (sl 1, k3) twice, sl 1, k5; rep from *, end k1.

Row 7—With A, k1, * (k1, sl 1) 3 times, k3, sl 1, k5, sl 1, k3, sl 1, k1, sl 1; rep from *, end k1.

Row 9—With B, k1, * k6, sl 1, k3, (sl 1, k1) twice, (sl 1, k3) twice; rep from *, end k1.

Row 11—With A, k1, * (k1, sl 1) twice, k3, sl 1, k9, sl 1, k3, sl 1; rep from *, end k1.

Divided Diamond

Row 13—With B, k1, * k4, sl 1, k3, (sl 1, k1) 4 times, sl 1, k3,
sl 1, k1; rep from *, end k1.

Row 15—With A, k1, * k1, sl 1, k3, sl 1, k13, sl 1, k2; rep from *, end k1.

Row 17—With B, k1, * sl 1, k1, sl 1, k3, (sl 1, k1) 6 times, sl 1, k3; rep from *,
end k1.

Row 19—With A, k1, * k3, sl 1, k17, sl 1; rep from *, end k1.

Row 21—With B, k1, * k2, sl 1, k17, sl 1, k1; rep from *, end k1.

Row 23—With A, k1, * k1, sl 1, k3, (sl 1, k1) 6 times, sl 1, k3, sl 1; rep from *,
end k1.

Row 25—With B, k1, * sl 1, k3, sl 1, k13, sl 1, k3; rep from *, end k1.

Row 27—With A, k1, * (k3, sl 1) twice, (k1, sl 1) 4 times, k3, sl 1, k2; rep from
*, end k1.

Row 29—With B, k1, * sl 1, k1, sl 1, k3, sl 1, k9, sl 1, k3, sl 1, k1; rep from *, end
k1.

Row 31—With A, k1, * k5, sl 1, k3, (sl 1, k1) twice, sl 1, k3, sl 1, k4; rep from *,
end k1.

Row 33—With B, k1, * (sl 1, k1) twice, sl 1, k3, sl 1, k5, sl 1, k3, (sl 1, k1) twice;
rep from *, end k1.

Row 35—With A, k1, * k7, (sl 1, k3) twice, sl 1, k6; rep from *, end k1.

Row 37—With B, k1, * (sl 1, k1) 3 times, sl 1, k3, sl 1, k1, sl 1, k3, (sl 1, k1) 3 times;
rep from *, end k1.

Row 39—With A, k1, * k9, sl 1, k3, sl 1, k8; rep from *, end k1.

Row 40—See Row 2.

Repeat Rows 1–40.

Trellis Diamond

Trellis Diamond

Multiple of 30 sts plus 3. Colors A and B.

Cast on with A and knit one row.

NOTE: On all right-side rows, sl all sl-sts with yarn in *back*.

Row 1 (Right side)—With B, k8, * (sl 1, k3) 4 times, sl 1, k13;
rep from *, end last repeat k8.

Row 2 and all other wrong-side rows—Knit (or purl) the same
sts worked on previous row, with the same color; sl all the same
sl-sts with yarn in *front*.

Row 3—With A, k1, * (sl 1, k3) 3 times, sl 1, k1, (sl 1, k3) 4 times;
rep from *, end sl 1, k1.

Row 5—With B, k6, * (sl 1, k3) 5 times, sl 1, k9; rep from *,
end last repeat k6.

Row 7—With A, k1, sl 1, k1, * (sl 1, k3) 3 times, sl 1, k1, (sl 1,
k3) 3 times, (sl 1, k1) twice; rep from *.

Row 9—With B, k4, * (sl 1, k3) 6 times, sl 1, k5; rep from *,
end last repeat k4.

Row 11—With A, k1, * (sl 1, k3) 3 times, sl 1, k5, (sl 1, k3) 3 times; rep from *, end sl 1, k1.

Row 13—With B, k2, * (sl 1, k3) 3 times, (sl 1, k1) twice, (sl 1, k3) 3 times, sl 1, k1; rep from *, end k1.

Row 15—With A, k3, * (sl 1, k3) twice, sl 1, k9, (sl 1, k3) 3 times; rep from *.

Row 17—With B, k2, * sl 1, k1, (sl 1, k3) 7 times; rep from *, end k1.

Row 19—With A, k1, * (sl 1, k3) twice, sl 1, k13, (sl 1, k3) twice; rep from *, end sl 1, k1.

Row 21—With B, k4, * (sl 1, k3) 6 times, sl 1, k1, sl 1, k3; rep from *, end last repeat k2.

Rows 23 and 24—With A, repeat Rows 15 and 16.

Rows 25 and 26—With B, repeat Rows 13 and 14.

Rows 27 and 28—With A, repeat Rows 11 and 12.

Rows 29 and 30—With B, repeat Rows 9 and 10.

Rows 31 and 32—With A, repeat Rows 7 and 8.

Rows 33 and 34—With B, repeat Rows 5 and 6.

Row 35—With A, k1, * (sl 1, k3) 4 times, sl 1, k1, (sl 1, k3) 3 times; rep from *, end sl 1, k1.

Row 36—See Row 2.

Repeat Rows 1–36.

Arabic Block

This is a slip-stitch adaptation of an ancient Arabic design. The method here has a touch of novelty; in order that the same strand of yarn can be used all the way across each row, the left-hand half of the pattern is always two rows behind the right-hand half. Thus a positive-and-negative checkered effect is achieved, and the blocks of color can be alternated without picking up new strands of yarn in mid-row.

Multiple of 54 sts plus 2. Colors A and B.

Cast on with A and knit one row.

NOTE: On all right-side rows, sl all sl-sts with yarn in *back*.

Row 1 (Right side)—With B, k1, * [(sl 1, k1) 10 times, sl 1, k3, sl 1, k1, sl 1], k23, (sl 1, k1) twice; rep from *, end k1.

Row 2 and all other wrong-side rows—Knit (or purl) the same sts worked on previous row, with the same color; sl all the same sl-sts with yarn in *front*.

Row 3—With A, k1, * [k7, sl 1, k13, sl 1, k3, sl 1, k1], rep [to] of Row 1; rep from *, end k1.

Row 5—With B, k1, * [(sl 1, k1) twice, sl 1, k5, (sl 1, k1) 4 times, (sl 1, k3) twice, sl 1], rep [to] of Row 3; rep from *, end k1.

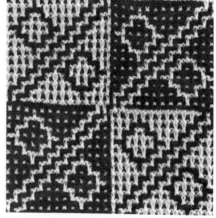

Arabic Block

Row 7—With A, k1, * [k5, sl 1, k3, sl 1, k9, (sl 1, k3) twice], rep [to] of Row 5; rep from *, end k1.

Row 9—With B, k1, * [(sl 1, k1, sl 1, k3) twice, (sl 1, k1) twice, (sl 1, k3) twice, sl 1, k1, sl 1], rep [to] of Row 7; rep from *, end k1.

Row 11—With A, k1, * [k3, sl 1, k7, sl 1, k5, sl 1, k3, sl 1, k5], rep [to] of Row 9; rep from *, end k1.

Row 13—With B, k1, * [sl 1, k3, (sl 1, k1) 3 times, (sl 1, k3) 3 times, (sl 1, k1) twice, sl 1], rep [to] of Row 11; rep from *, end k1.

Row 15—With A, k1, * [k3, sl 1, k7, (sl 1, k3) twice, sl 1, k7], rep [to] of Row 13; rep from *, end k1.

Row 17—With B, k1, * [(sl 1, k1, sl 1, k3) twice, (sl 1, k3) twice, (sl 1, k1) 3 times, sl 1], rep [to] of Row 15; rep from *, end k1.

Row 19—With A, k1, * [k5, (sl 1, k3) 3 times, sl 1, k9], rep [to] of Row 17; rep from *, end k1.

Row 21—With B, k1, * [(sl 1, k1) twice, sl 1, k5, (sl 1, k3) twice, (sl 1, k1) 4 times, sl 1], rep [to] of Row 19; rep from *, end k1.

Row 23—With A, k1, * [k7, (sl 1, k3) 3 times, sl 1, k7], rep [to] of Row 21; rep from *, end k1.

Row 25—With B, k1, * [(sl 1, k1) 4 times, (sl 1, k3) twice, sl 1, k5, (sl 1, k1) twice, sl 1], rep [to] of Row 23; rep from *, end k1.

Row 27—With A, k1, * [k9, (sl 1, k3) 3 times, sl 1, k5], rep [to] of Row 25; rep from *, end k1.

Row 29—With B, k1, * [(sl 1, k1) 3 times, (sl 1, k3) 3 times, sl 1, k1, sl 1, k3, sl 1, k1, sl 1], rep [to] of Row 27; rep from *, end k1.

Row 31—With A, k1, * [k7, (sl 1, k3) twice, sl 1, k7, sl 1, k3], rep [to] of Row 29; rep from *, end k1.

Row 33—With B, k1, * [(sl 1, k1) twice, (sl 1, k3) 3 times, (sl 1, k1) 3 times, sl 1, k3, sl 1], rep [to] of Row 31; rep from *, end k1.

Row 35—With A, k1, * [k5, sl 1, k3, sl 1, k5, sl 1, k7, sl 1, k3], rep [to] of Row 33; rep from *, end k1.

Row 37—With B, k1, * [sl 1, k1, (sl 1, k3) twice, (sl 1, k1) twice, sl 1, (k3, sl 1, k1, sl 1) twice], rep [to] of Row 35; rep from *, end k1.

Row 39—With A, k1, * [(k3, sl 1) twice, k9, sl 1, k3, sl 1, k5], rep [to] of Row 37; rep from *, end k1.

Row 41—With B, k1, * [(sl 1, k3) twice, (sl 1, k1) 4 times, sl 1, k5, (sl 1, k1) twice, sl 1], rep [to] of Row 39; rep from *, end k1.

Row 43—With A, k1, * [k1, sl 1, k3, sl 1, k13, sl 1, k7], rep [to] of Row 41; rep from *, end k1.

Row 45—With B, k1, * [sl 1, k1, sl 1, k3, (sl 1, k1) 10 times, sl 1], rep [to] of Row 43; rep from *, end k1.

Row 47—With A, k1, * [(k1, sl 1) twice, k23], rep [to] of Row 45; rep from *, end k1.

Row 49—With B, k1, * k23, (sl 1, k1) twice, rep [to] of Row 47; rep from *, end k1.

Row 50—See Row 2.

Rows 51 through 100—Repeat Rows 1 through 50, reversing colors; Color A for 51 and 52, Color B for 53 and 54, etc.

Repeat Rows 1–100.

Flare

Multiple of 55 sts plus 2. Colors A and B.

NOTE: On all right-side rows, sl all sl-sts with yarn in *back*.

Flare

Row 1 (Right side)—With A, knit.

Row 2—With A, knit.

Row 3—With B, k1, * k18, sl 1, k3, sl 1, k2, (sl 1, k1) twice, sl 1, k2, sl 1, k3, sl 1, k18; rep from *, end k1.

Row 4 and all other wrong-side rows—Knit (or purl) the same sts worked on previous row, with the same color; sl all the same sl-sts with yarn in *front*.

Row 5—With A, k1, * (sl 1, k1) 7 times, sl 1, k4, sl 1, k3, sl 1, k2, sl 1, k1, sl 1, k2, sl 1, k3, sl 1, k4, (sl 1, k1) 7 times, sl 1; rep from *, end k1.

Row 7—With B, k1, * k15, sl 1, k4, sl 1, k3, (sl 1, k2) twice, sl 1, k3, sl 1, k4, sl 1, k15; rep from *, end k1.

Row 9—With A, k1, * (k1, sl 1) 6 times, k4, sl 2, k3, sl 2, k2, sl 2, k1, sl 2, k2, sl 2, k3, sl 2, k4, (sl 1, k1) 6 times; rep from *, end k1.

Row 11—With B, k1, * k12, sl 1, k5, sl 1, k4, sl 1, (k3, sl 1) twice, k4, sl 1, k5, sl 1, k12; rep from *, end k1.

Row 13—With A, k1, * (sl 1, k1) 4 times, sl 1, k4, sl 1, k1, sl 1, k3, sl 1, k1, sl 1, k2, (sl 1, k1) 3 times, sl 1, k2, sl 1, k1, sl 1, k3, sl 1, k1, sl 1, k4, (sl 1, k1) 4 times, sl 1; rep from *, end k1.

Row 15—With B, k1, * k9, sl 1, k6, sl 1, k5, sl 1, (k4, sl 1) twice, k5, sl 1, k6, sl 1, k9; rep from *, end k1.

Row 17—With A, k1, * (k1, sl 1) 3 times, k4, sl 1, k1, sl 2, k3, sl 1, k1, sl 2, k2, sl 1, (k1, sl 2) twice, k1, sl 1, k2, sl 2, k1, sl 1, k3, sl 2, k1, sl 1, k4, (sl 1, k1) 3 times; rep from *, end k1.

Row 19—With B, k1, * k6, sl 1, k7, sl 1, k6, sl 1, (k5, sl 1) twice, k6, sl 1, k7, sl 1, k6; rep from *, end k1.

Row 21—With A, k1, * sl 1, k1, sl 1, k4, (sl 1, k1) twice, sl 1, k3, (sl 1, k1) twice, sl 1, k2, (sl 1, k1) 5 times, sl 1, k2, (sl 1, k1) twice, sl 1, k3, (sl 1, k1) twice, sl 1, k4, sl 1, k1, sl 1; rep from *, end k1.

Row 23—With B, k1, * k3, sl 1, k8, sl 1, k7, sl 1, (k6, sl 1) twice, k7, sl 1, k8, sl 1, k3; rep from *, end k1.

Row 25—With A, k1, * k4, (sl 1, k1) twice, sl 2, k3, (sl 1, k1) twice, sl 2, k2, (sl 1, k1) twice, sl 2, k1, sl 2, (k1, sl 1) twice, k2, sl 2, (k1, sl 1) twice, k3, sl 2, (k1, sl 1) twice, k4; rep from *, end k1.

Row 27—With B, k1, * sl 1, k9, sl 1, k8, (sl 1, k7) twice, sl 1, k8, sl 1, k9, sl 1; rep from *, end k1.

Rows 29 and 30—With A, knit.

Rows 31 and 32—With B, knit.

Rows 33–58—Repeat Rows 3–28, reversing colors.

Rows 59 and 60—With B, knit.

Repeat Rows 1–60.

Odin's Eagles

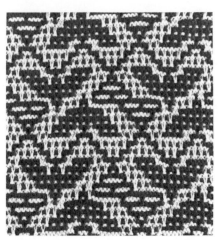

Odin's Eagles

As its name implies, this pattern is derived from traditional Scandinavian designs. A kinship can be seen between the "eagle" motifs and those of the Crown Chevron. Odin's Eagles make a splendid border design when the pattern rows 1 through 42 are worked once, with Rows 43 and 44 knit plain with Color A. This pattern also makes beautiful cushions and handbags; articles like these can be worked with the required large multiple of stitches without any adjustment of the pattern to a given size. However, the knitter should remember that a mosaic pattern *can* be worked on any number of stitches, even if the final repeats end somewhere in the middle of the directions—so large multiples present no problem in patterns of this type.

Multiple of 32 sts plus 3. Colors A and B.

Cast on with Color A and knit one row.

NOTE: On all right-side (odd-numbered) rows, slip all sl-sts with yarn in *back*.

Row 1 (Right side)—With B, k2, * (sl 1, k1, sl 1, k3) twice, (sl 1, k1) 3 times, (sl 1, k3, sl 1, k1) twice, sl 1, k1; rep from *, end k1.

Row 2 and all other wrong-side rows—Knit (or purl) the same sts worked on previous row, with the same color; sl all the same sl-sts with yarn in *front*.

Row 3—With A, k7, * sl 1, k3, sl 1, k11; rep from *, end last repeat k7.

Row 5—With B, k5, * sl 2, k5, sl 2, k6, sl 1, k1, sl 1, k5, sl 1, k1, sl 1, k6; rep from *, end last repeat k4.

Row 7—With A, k2, * sl 1, k1, (sl 1, k4) twice, (sl 1, k1) twice, (sl 1, k6) twice, sl 1, k1; rep from *, end k1.

Row 9—With B, * k7, sl 1, k3, sl 1, k7, (sl 1, k1) twice, sl 1, k3, (sl 1, k1) twice, sl 1; rep from *, end k3.

Row 11—With A, k2, * (sl 1, k1) 7 times, sl 1, k7, sl 1, k1, sl 1, k7; rep from *, end k1.

Row 13—With B, k1, * sl 1, k15, (sl 1, k1) twice, sl 1, k7, (sl 1, k1) twice; rep from *, end sl 1, k1.

Row 15—With A, k4, * (sl 1, k1) 5 times, sl 1, k7, sl 1, k5, sl 1, k7; rep from *, end last repeat k6.

Row 17—With B, k1, * sl 1, k1, sl 1, k11, sl 2, k1, sl 2, k11, sl 1, k1; rep from *, end sl 1, k1.

Row 19—With A, k8, * sl 1, k1, sl 1, k6, sl 1, k2, (sl 1, k4) twice, sl 1, k9; rep from *, end last repeat k4.

Row 21—With B, k7, * sl 1, k3, (sl 1, k1) twice, sl 1, k3, sl 1, k19; rep from *, end last repeat k15.

Row 23—With A, k1, * sl 1, k4, sl 1, k2, sl 1, k6, sl 1, k1, sl 1, k9, sl 1, k4; rep from *, end sl 1, k1.

Row 25—With B, k7, * sl 2, k1, sl 2, k11, (sl 1, k1) twice, sl 1, k11; rep from *, end last repeat k7.

Row 27—With A, k4, * sl 1, k7, (sl 1, k1) 5 times, sl 1, k7, sl 1, k5; rep from *, end last repeat k4.

Row 29—With B, k5, * (sl 1, k1) twice, sl 1, k15, (sl 1, k1) twice, sl 1, k7; rep from *, end last repeat k5.

Row 31—With A, k2, * sl 1, k7, (sl 1, k1) 7 times, sl 1, k7, sl 1, k1; rep from *, end k1.

Row 33—With B, k3, * (sl 1, k1) twice, sl 1, k7, sl 1, k3, sl 1, k7, (sl 1, k1) twice, sl 1, k3; rep from *.

Row 35—With A, k1, * sl 1, k6, (sl 1, k1) twice, (sl 1, k4) twice, (sl 1, k1) twice, sl 1, k6; rep from *, end sl 1, k1.

Row 37—With B, k4, * sl 1, k1, sl 1, k6, sl 2, k5, sl 2, k6, sl 1, k1, sl 1, k5; rep from *, end last repeat k4.

Row 39—With A, k3, * sl 1, k11, sl 1, k3; rep from *.

Row 41—With B, k2, * sl 1, k3, (sl 1, k1) 3 times, sl 1, k3, sl 1, k1; rep from *, end k1.

Row 43—With A, k5, * sl 1, k7; rep from *, end last repeat k5.

Row 44—See Row 2.

Repeat Rows 1–44.

CHAPTER FIVE

Fancy Color Patterns

This is a group of truly fascinating patterns. Some of them employ slip-stitches, but other knitting techniques are used as well: yarn-overs, short rows, bobbles, dip stitches, passed stitches—almost anything. These are Fancy Texture Patterns in color.

This section constitutes a demonstration of the enormous number of things that can be done with strands of two or three different colors and assorted knitting techniques. There are beautiful and unusual shapes here, which are enhanced by the interplay of light and dark, bright and subtle shades. Color work often seems to bring out the best of the pattern designer's ingenuity. Much variety is possible, too, in the use of color within the same pattern; this is for *you* to discover. If Color A happens to be a light color, and Color B a dark one, reverse them and see how different the pattern looks! Or try the same pattern, first with two strongly contrasting colors and then with two subtle ones, or with two shades of the same color.

You can do a lot of exciting things with these patterns, and use up a lot of old odds and ends of leftover yarn in trying them out. And when you have collected a large number of "test swatches" in all the colors of the rainbow and then some, sew them all together. The result will be the most glorious afghan you ever saw! You don't have to worry about working to a specific gauge in your test swatches, either. If they come out in several different sizes, just make a paper square the size of the smallest, place the square on each of the larger swatches, mark around its edge, and machine-stitch on the marks, twice around. Then you can cut off the excess from the larger squares without fear of raveling the knitting, and when they are sewn together (which is easily done, now that all are uniform in size and shape) the machine-stitching is concealed.

So—take out that old box of odd ounces and half-ounces of this and that—pick up your needles—and have fun.

Checked Rose Fabric

Like Rose Fabric, from which it is derived, this pattern makes a soft, deep texture with a good deal of lateral spread. Cast on and bind off very loosely, measure carefully, and beware of starting with too many stitches.

SPECIAL NOTE: This pattern must be worked back and forth on a circular needle or a pair of double-pointed needles.

Odd number of sts. Colors A and B.

Cast on with B and knit one row.

Row 1 (Wrong side)—With A, k1, * knit next st in the row below, k1; rep from *.

Row 2—With A, knit first st in the row below, * k1, knit next st in the row below; rep from *.

Row 3—With B, repeat Row 1.

Row 4—Sl all sts to other end of needle and with A, repeat Row 2.

Row 5—With A, repeat Row 1.

Row 6—Sl all sts to other end of needle and with B, repeat Row 2.

Repeat Rows 1–6.

Checked Rose Fabric

Rickrack Stripe

Contributed by Hildegard M. Elsner, Aldan, Pennsylvania

Either version of this pattern is beautiful in three colors. Continue to alternate the three colors, allotting 2 pattern rows to each color. The wrong side of this fabric is very interesting also.

Even number of sts. Colors A and B.

Cast on with Color A and purl one row.

Row 1 (Right side)—With B, k1, * skip 1 st and insert needle from front into the st *in the row below* the 2nd st on left-hand needle; draw through a loop, sl the loop onto left-hand needle and knit it together with the skipped st through *back* loops; k1; rep from *, end k1.

Row 2—With B, purl.

Rows 3 and 4—With A, repeat Rows 1 and 2.

Repeat Rows 1–4.

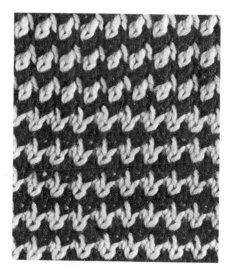

ABOVE: *Rickrack Stripe*
BELOW: *Alternating Rickrack Stripe*

VARIATION: *ALTERNATING RICKRACK STRIPE*

Work the same as above, with the following exception:

Row 3—With A, k2, rep from * of Row 1, end k2.

Leaning Stripe Pattern

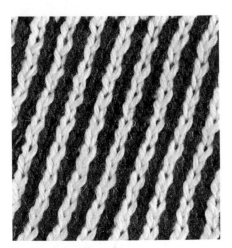

Leaning Stripe Pattern

Multiple of 3 sts. Colors A and B.

Cast on with Color A.

NOTE: Right Twist (RT)—Skip 1 st and knit into 2nd st, then knit the skipped st, then sl both sts from needle together.

Preparation Row (Right side)—With B, * k2, sl 1 wyib; rep from *, end k3.

Row 1—With B, p3, * sl 1 wyif, p2; rep from *.

Row 2—With A, k1, * RT, sl 1 wyib; rep from *, end k2.

Row 3—With A, * p2, sl 1 wyif; rep from *, end p3.

Row 4—With B, k1, * sl 1 wyib, RT; rep from *, end sl 1, k1.

Row 5—With B, p1, * sl 1 wyif, p2; rep from *, end sl 1, p1.

Row 6—With A, * RT, sl 1 wyib; rep from *, end RT, k1.

Rows 7 through 12—Repeat Rows 1 through 6, reversing colors.

Repeat Rows 1–12.

Swedish Weave

Swedish Weave
ABOVE: *knit side*
BELOW: *purl side*

In this pattern Color B is never worked, only passed back and forth between the needles as the knitting is done with Color A. The Color B strand need not be held in the fingers at all, but simply pushed from front to back as required. In this way the strand is kept quite loose, which gives the best results. The fabric has an unusually beautiful purl side.

Odd number of sts. Colors A and B.

Cast on with Color A and purl one row. Join Color B.

Row 1 (Right side)—k1 Color A st, passing Color B strand across st at front of work; * pass Color B strand to back between needles and knit next Color A st with B in back; pass Color B strand to front between needles and knit next Color A st with B in front; rep from *.

Row 2—P1 Color A st and bring Color B strand around edge to pass in front (i.e., on the wrong side of work) of purl st; * pass Color B strand to back between needles and purl next Color A st with B in back; pass Color B strand to front between needles and purl next Color A st with B in front; rep from *.

Repeat Rows 1 and 2.

Two "Turning" Patterns: String of Purls and Short-Row Pattern

Both of these unusual patterns are made by turning the work around and working back over the most recent stitches, after the manner of a bobble. The String of Purls is akin to the Bubble Bobble, although the extra or "turned" stitches do not protrude so much. The Short-Row Pattern picks up two extra stitches at each end of a "turned" row, so that the motif spreads out into a sort of upside-down pyramid.

I. STRING OF PURLS

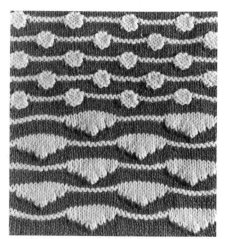

Multiple of 12 sts. Colors A and B.

Rows 1 and 3 (Wrong side)—With A, purl.

Row 2—With A, knit.

Row 4—With B, k11, * turn; sl 1 wyif, k3, turn; p4, k12; rep from *, end last repeat k1 instead of k12.

Row 5—With B, k5, * turn; p4, turn; k3, sl 1 wyif, k12; rep from *, end last repeat k7 instead of k12.

Row 6—With A, k8, * sl 2 wyib, k10; rep from *, end last repeat k2 instead of k10.

Rows 7, 8, and 9—With A, repeat Rows 1, 2, and 3.

Row 10—With B, k5, * turn; sl 1 wyif, k3, turn; p4, k12; rep from *, end last repeat k7 instead of k12.

Row 11—With B, k11, * turn; p4, turn; k3, sl 1 wyif, k12; rep from *, end last repeat k1 instead of k12.

Row 12—With A, k2, * sl 2 wyib, k10; rep from *, end last repeat k8 instead of k10.

Repeat Rows 1–12.

ABOVE: *String of Purls*
BELOW: *Short-Row Pattern*

II. SHORT-ROW PATTERN

Multiple of 22 sts plus 4. Colors A and B.

Rows 1 and 3 (Right side)—With A, knit.

Rows 2 and 4—With A, purl.

Row 5—With B, k2, * k7, turn; sl 1 wyif, p2, turn; sl 1 wyib, k4, turn; sl 1 wyif, p6, turn; sl 1 wyib, k8, turn; sl 1 wyif, p10, turn; sl 1 wyib, k21; rep from *, end k2.

Row 6—With B, k2, * k11, p11; rep from *, end k2.

Rows 7 through 10—With A, repeat Rows 1 through 4.

Row 11—With B, k13, rep from * of Row 5, end last repeat k12 instead of k21.

Row 12—With B, k2, * p11, k11; rep from *, end k2.

Repeat Rows 1–12.

Fancy Shingle Pattern

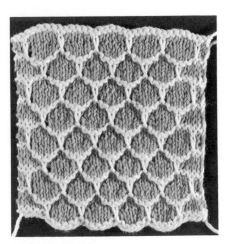

Fancy Shingle Pattern

This pattern produces overlapping "shingles" that are raised at the lower edges and decorated with scalloped borders of Color A. The method of avoiding holes on the turning rows is the same as that used by knowledgeable knitters in garment shaping, such as the short rows on shoulders or collars: i.e., "hooking" the yarn around an unworked stitch before turning the work. By trying the pattern both with and without this little trick, the novice knitter can prove its advantages for herself.

Multiple of 6 sts plus 3. Colors A and B.

Row 1 (Wrong side)—With A, knit.
Row 2—With B, k4, * sl 1 wyib, k5; turn; sl 1 wyif, p4; turn; sl 1 wyib, k4; turn; sl 1 wyif, p4; then sl the next (Color A) st wyif, sl the following st wyib; bring yarn through to front (i.e., wrong side of work), then sl the last 2 sts back again to left-hand needle; turn; sl 1 wyib, k4; rep from *, end sl 1 wyib, k4.
Row 3—With B, p4, * sl 1 wyif, p5; rep from *, end sl 1, p4.
Row 4—With A, k4, * k1-b, k5; rep from *, end k1-b, k4.
Row 5—With A, knit.
Row 6—With B, k1, rep from * of Row 2; end sl 1 wyib, k1.
Row 7—With B, p1, * sl 1 wyif, p5; rep from *, end sl 1, p1.
Row 8—With A, k1, * k1-b, k5; rep from *, end k1-b, k1.

Repeat Rows 1–8.

Two-Color Star Stitch

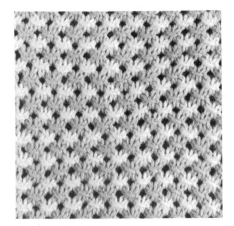

Two-Color Star Stitch

This is a remarkably beautiful openwork pattern used for fancy baby clothes, yokes, dress sleeves, evening purses, cushions, place mats, and the like. It may be lined with a fabric matching one of the colors or with a contrasting color. It also looks well when done in ribbon, or a combination of ribbon and yarn.

Multiple of 3 sts. Colors A and B.

Row 1 (Wrong side)—With A, purl.
Row 2—With A, k2, * yo, k3, pass first of the 3 knit sts over the 2nd and 3rd sts; rep from * , end k1.
Row 3—With B, purl.
Row 4—With B, k1, * k3, pass first of the 3 knit sts over the 2nd and 3rd sts, yo; rep from *, end k2.

Repeat Rows 1–4.

Closed Star Stitch

Though the technique here is basically the same as the Two-Color Star Stitch, the yarn-over is replaced by a lifted increase from the wrong side, which makes a tighter fabric, more suitable to work in medium-weight and heavy yarns. This version is good for suits, jackets, and afghans.

Multiple of 3 sts plus 2. Colors A and B.

Cast on with A and purl one row.

Row 1 (Right side)—With A, k1, * k3, pass first of the 3 knit sts over the 2nd and 3rd sts; rep from *, end k1.

Row 2—With B, p1, * insert needle from behind under running thread between the st just worked and the next st, and purl this thread; p2; rep from *, end p1.

Row 3—With B, k2, rep from * of Row 1 across.

Row 4—With A, p2, rep from * of Row 2 across.

Repeat Rows 1–4.

Closed Star Stitch

Butterfly Quilting

It is particularly important in this pattern to keep the Color B strands *loose* as they are carried across the front of the fabric. The pattern will be spoiled if these strands are taut.

Multiple of 6 sts plus 3. Colors A and B.

Cast on with Color A and purl one row.

Row 1 (Right side)—With B, k2, * sl 5 wyif, k1; rep from *, end k1.

Row 2—With B, p2, * sl 5 wyib, p1; rep from *, end p1.

Row 3—With A, knit.

Row 4—With A, purl.

Row 5—With A, k4, * insert needle under the loose Color B strands and knit next st, catching both strands behind st as it is knitted; k5; rep from *, end last repeat k4.

Row 6—With A, purl.

Row 7—With B, k1, sl 3 wyif, * k1, sl 5 wyif; rep from *, end k1, sl 3 wyif, k1.

Row 8—With B, p1, sl 3 wyib, * p1, sl 5 wyib; rep from *, end p1, sl 3 wyib, p1.

Rows 9 and 10—With A, repeat Rows 3 and 4.

Row 11—With A, k1, * insert needle under the loose Color B strands and knit next st, k5; rep from *, end last repeat k1.

Row 12—With A, purl.

Repeat Rows 1–12.

Butterfly Quilting

Fireflowers

Fireflowers

This is a 20-row pattern, with the extra rows serving only to alternate colors. It may be worked in three colors only—one for the background, two for the pattern stripes—by repeating just Rows 1-20. Or it may be worked in two colors, using B for Rows 11 and 12 as well as 1 and 2. In this four-color version, it is best to break the strands of B, C, and D after the second and twelfth rows, rather than carrying them up the side of the piece, because it is a long stretch before these colors are repeated.

The "ssk" (which involves one long stitch and one background stitch) at the left-hand sides of the flowers must be worked correctly for best results. Be sure you slip both stitches *knitwise* before knitting them together; for if the long stitch is slipped purlwise it will be twisted, and will spoil the shape of the flower. The strands should be quite loose.

This pattern may be used in one, two, or three repeats as a pretty border design.

Multiple of 4 sts plus 1. Colors A, B, C, and D.

Cast on with Color A and knit two rows.

Row 1 (Right side)—With B, k2, * sl 1 wyib, k1, (k1, yo, k1, yo, k1) in next st, k1; rep from *, end sl 1 wyib, k2.

Row 2—With B, k2, * sl 1 wyif, k1, p5 wrapping yarn twice for each st, k1; rep from *, end sl 1 wyif, k2.

Row 3—With A, k4, * sl 5 wyib dropping extra wraps, k3; rep from *, end k1.

Row 4—With A, k4, * sl 5 wyif, k3; rep from *, end k1.

Row 5—With A, k3, * k2 tog, sl 3 wyib, ssk, k1; rep from *, end k2.

Row 6—With A, k3, * p1, sl 3 wyif, p1, k1; rep from *, end k2.

Row 7—With A, k3, * k2 tog, sl 1 wyib, ssk, k1; rep from *, end k2.

Row 8—With A, k3, * p1, sl 1 wyif, p1, k1; rep from *, end k2.

Row 9—With A, k4, * k1-b, k3; rep from *, end k1.

Row 10—With A, k4, * p1-b, k3; rep from *, end k1.

Row 11—With C, k2, * (k1, yo, k1, yo, k1) in next st, k1, sl 1 wyib, k1; rep from *, end (k1, yo, k1, yo, k1) in next st, k2.

Row 12—With C, k2, * p5 wrapping yarn twice for each st, k1, sl 1 wyif, k1; rep from *, end p5 wrapping yarn twice for each st, k2.

Row 13—With A, k2, * sl 5 wyib dropping extra wraps, k3; rep from *, end last repeat k2.

Row 14—With A, k2, * sl 5 wyif, k3; rep from *, end last repeat k2.

Row 15—With A, k1, * k2 tog, sl 3 wyib, ssk, k1; rep from *.

Row 16—With A, k1, * p1, sl 3 wyif, p1, k1; rep from *.

Row 17—With A, k1, * k2 tog, sl 1 wyib, ssk, k1; rep from *.

Row 18—With A, k1, * p1, sl 1 wyif, p1, k1; rep from *.

Row 19—With A, k2, * k1-b, k3; rep from *, end last repeat k2.

Row 20—With A, k2, * p1-b, k3; rep from *, end last repeat k2.

Rows 21 and 22—With D, repeat Rows 1 and 2.

Rows 23 through 30—With A, repeat Rows 3 through 10.

Rows 31 and 32—With B, repeat Rows 11 and 12.
Rows 33 through 40—With A, repeat Rows 13 through 20.
Rows 41 and 42—With C, repeat Rows 1 and 2.
Rows 43 through 50—With A, repeat Rows 3 through 10.
Rows 51 and 52—With D, repeat Rows 11 and 12.
Rows 53 through 60—With A, repeat Rows 13 through 20.

Repeat Rows 1–60.

Scrap-Yarn Afghan Stitch

Here is an excellent solution to every knitter's perennial problem: what to do with leftover yarn scraps. This easy-to-work pattern, knitted in strips of 63 or 75 stitches each, will produce a beautiful afghan that uses every little yarn-end in your scrap box—the more colors, the better. Strips can be sewn or crocheted together at the sides, either across the width or along the length of the afghan, as desired. The cast-on and bound-off edges of each strip will form a handsomely scalloped self-border.

Colors are worked two at a time and changed at will at the beginning of any right-side row. The illustration shows three stripes of each color, but you need not stick to this or any other system; random alternation of colors is effective too. This pattern is as flexible as your imagination. You may use all kinds of yarn in the same piece; single strands of the heavier ones, double or triple strands of the thinner ones.

When used with the same two or three colors throughout, the pattern makes a delightful scarf, lap robe, or baby blanket. A stockinette-stitch variation, given below, will make lovely sweaters and jackets with scalloped edges.

Scrap-Yarn Afghan Stitch

Multiple of 12 sts plus 3. Colors A and B.

Cast on with Color A and knit one row.

Row 1 (Right side)—With B, k1, ssk, * k9, sl 2—k1—p2sso; rep from *, end k9, k2 tog, k1.
Row 2—With B, k1, * p1, k4, (k1, yo, k1) in next st, k4; rep from *, end p1, k1.
Rows 3 and 4—With A, repeat Rows 1 and 2.

Repeat Rows 1–4.

STOCKINETTE-STITCH VARIATION
(*not illustrated*)

Rows 1 and 3—Same as above.
Rows 2 and 4—P6, * (p1, yo, p1) in next st, p9; rep from *, end last repeat p6.

Quilted Check

Multiple of 6 sts plus 2. Colors A and B.

Cast on with Color A and knit one row.

Row 1 (Wrong side)—With A, p1, * sl 3 wyib, p3; rep from *, end p1.

Row 2—With B, * k5, sl 1 wyif; rep from *, end k2.

Row 3—With B, p2, * sl 1 wyib, p5; rep from *.

Row 4—With A, * k5, insert left-hand needle down behind loose Color A strand of Row 1; lift this strand over point of left-hand needle and k2 tog-b (i.e., the Color A strand and the 1st Color B st on needle); rep from *, end k2.

Row 5—With A, p4, * sl 3 wyib, p3; rep from *, end sl 3, p1.

Row 6—With B, k2, * sl 1 wyif, k5; rep from *.

Row 7—With B, * p5, sl 1 wyib; rep from *, end p2.

Row 8—With A, k2, * insert left-hand needle under Color A strand of Row 5, and k2 tog-b, as in Row 4; k5; rep from *.

Repeat Rows 1–8.

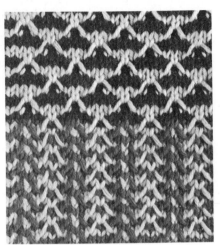

ABOVE: *Quilted Check*
BELOW: *Interlaced Stripe*

Interlaced Stripe

Contributed by Hildegard M. Elsner, Aldan, Pennsylvania

Multiple of 6 sts plus 2. Colors A and B.

PREPARATION ROWS

Row 1 (Right side)—With A, knit.

Row 2—With A, p1, * sl 3 wyib, p3; rep from *, end p1.

Row 3—With B, knit.

End of preparation rows.

Row 4—With B, p4, * sl 3 wyib, p3; rep from *, end sl 3, p1.

Row 5—With A, * k5, insert left-hand needle down behind loose Color A strand of Row 2; lift this strand over point of left-hand needle and k2 tog-b (i.e., the Color A strand and the 1st Color B st on needle); rep from *, end k2.

Row 6—With A, p1, * sl 3 wyib, p3; rep from *, end p1.

Row 7—With B, k2, * insert left-hand needle down behind loose Color B strand of Row 4, lift up and k2 tog-b, as in Row 5; k5; rep from *.

Omitting preparation rows, repeat Rows 4–7.

Plaited Diagonal Stripe

Each right-side row decreases one stitch in each pattern repeat, and each wrong-side row restores it by a yo. Since the fabric is quite dense laterally, it is a good idea to bind off on the wrong side *without* restoring the subtracted stitches; this will prevent the bind-off row from showing an unattractive "spread".

Plaited Diagonal Stripe

Multiple of 4 sts plus 2. Colors A and B.

Cast on with A and purl one row.

Row 1 (Right side)—With B, k1, * sl 1 wyib, k2, psso the 2 knit sts, sl 1 wyib; rep from *, end k1.
Row 2—With B, * p1, sl 1 wyif, p1, yo; rep from *, end p2.
Row 3—With A, k3, * sl 2 wyib, k2, pass the *second* sl-st over the 2 subsequent knit sts; rep from *, end sl 1, k2.
Row 4—With A, p2, * sl 1 wyif, p1, yo, p1; rep from * to last 4 sts, end sl 1, p3.
Row 5—With B, k2, * sl 2 wyib, k2, pass the *second* sl-st over the 2 subsequent knit sts; rep from * to last 4 sts, end sl 1, k3.
Row 6—With B, p3, * sl 1 wyif, p1, yo, p1; rep from *, end sl 1, p2.
Row 7—With A, k1, * sl 2 wyib, k2, pass the *second* sl-st over the 2 subsequent knit sts; rep from *, end k1.
Row 8—With A, p2, * yo, p1, sl 1 wyif, p1; rep from *.

Repeat Rows 1–8.

Thorn Pattern

This pattern is simple to work, and creates a really beautiful fabric. The technique is ingenious and unusual, but no "acrobatic" knitting is required to accomplish it; on the contrary, it goes very quickly. The fabric is firm enough for suits and coats, though not truly heavy.

Thorn Pattern

Multiple of 4 sts plus 1. Colors A and B.

Row 1 (Right side)—With A, k2, * (k1, yo, k1) in next st, k3; rep from *, end last repeat k2.
Row 2—With B, p2, * sl 3 wyif, p3; rep from *, end last repeat p2.
Row 3—With B, k1, * k2 tog, sl 1 wyib, ssk, k1; rep from *.
Row 4—With A, p4, * sl 1 wyif, p3; rep from *, end p1.
Row 5—With A, k4, * (k1, yo, k1) in next st, k3; rep from *, end k1.
Row 6—With B, p4, * sl 3 wyif, p3; rep from *, end p1.
Row 7—With B, k3, * k2 tog, sl 1 wyib, ssk, k1; rep from *, end k2.
Row 8—With A, p2, * sl 1 wyif, p3; rep from *, end last repeat p2.

Repeat Rows 1–8.

Dip-and-Slip Tweed

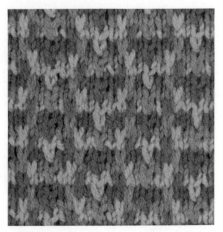

Dip-and-Slip Tweed
ABOVE: *Version I*
BELOW: *Version II*

Either version of this pattern makes a subtle and beautiful tweed that is easy to work. In Version I there are 5 consecutive stitches of the same color above each dip stitch; in Version II these lines of color are broken by slip-stitches so that the pattern seems smaller.

NOTE: Dip stitch (both versions)—insert needle into the front of st in the 3rd row below the first st on left-hand needle; draw up a loop, slip this loop onto left-hand needle and k2 tog-b (i.e., the loop and the first st), completing dip stitch.

VERSION I

Multiple of 10 sts plus 7. Colors A, B, and C.

Cast on with Color A and purl one row.

Row 1 (Preparation row, right side)—With B, knit.
Row 2 (Preparation row)—With B, purl.
Row 3—With C, k3, * dip st, k2, sl 1 wyib, k3, sl 1 wyib, k2; rep from *, end dip st, k3.
Row 4—With C, k1, * p5, sl 1 wyif, p3, sl 1 wyif; rep from *, end p5, k1.
Row 5—With A, k1, * sl 1 wyib, k3, sl 1 wyib, k2, dip st, k2; rep from *, end sl 1, k3, sl 1, k1.
Row 6—With A, k1, * sl 1 wyif, p3, sl 1 wyif, p5; rep from *, end sl 1, p3, sl 1, k1.
Rows 7 and 8—With B, repeat Rows 3 and 4.
Rows 9 and 10—With C, repeat Rows 5 and 6.
Rows 11 and 12—With A, repeat Rows 3 and 4.
Rows 13 and 14—With B, repeat Rows 5 and 6.

Omitting preparation rows, repeat Rows 3–14.

VERSION II

Multiple of 10 sts plus 7. Colors A, B, and C.

Cast on with Color A and purl one row.

Row 1 (Preparation row, right side)—With B, k6, * sl 1 wyib, k3, sl 1 wyib, k5; rep from *, end k1.
Row 2 (Preparation row)—With B, k1, * p5, sl 1 wyif, p3, sl 1 wyif; rep from *, end p5, k1.
Row 3—With C, k1, * sl 1 wyib, k1, dip st, k1, sl 1 wyib, k5; rep from *, end last repeat k1 instead of k5.
Row 4—With C, k1, * sl 1 wyif, p3, sl 1 wyif, p5; rep from *, end last repeat k1 instead of p5.
Row 5—With A, k6, * sl 1 wyib, k1, dip st, k1, sl 1 wyib, k5; rep from *, end k1.

Row 6—With A, k1, * p5, sl 1 wyif, p3, sl 1 wyif; rep from *, end p5, k1.
Rows 7 and 8—With B, repeat Rows 3 and 4.
Rows 9 and 10—With C, repeat Rows 5 and 6.
Rows 11 and 12—With A, repeat Rows 3 and 4.
Rows 13 and 14—With B, repeat Rows 5 and 6.

Omitting preparation rows, repeat Rows 3–14.

North Star Pattern

Dip-stitches are used in this pretty design to make small cross-shaped or star-shaped motifs against a continuous background of Color A. Keep the yarn *loose* behind each group of three slipped stitches in Rows 5, 7, 11, and 13.

Multiple of 6 sts plus 5. Colors A, B, and C.

PREPARATION ROWS

Rows 1 and 3 (Right side)—With A, knit.
Rows 2 and 4—With A, purl.

End of preparation rows.

Row 5—With B, k1, * sl 3 wyib, k1, make dip st as follows: insert needle into front of st in the 3rd row below the next st on left-hand needle, and draw through a loose loop; sl loop onto left-hand needle and k2 tog-b (the loop and the next st)—dip st completed—k1; rep from *, end sl 3 wyib, k1.
Row 6—With B, p2, * sl 1 wyif, p5; rep from *, end sl 1, p2.
Row 7—With A, k4, * sl 3 wyib, k3; rep from *, end k1.
Row 8—With A, p5, * sl 1 wyif, p5; rep from *.
Row 9—With A, k5, * sl 1 wyib, k5; rep from *.
Row 10—With A, purl.
Row 11—With C, k2, * make dip st as in Row 5, k1, sl 3 wyib, k1; rep from *, end: make dip st, k2.
Row 12—With C, repeat Row 8.
Row 13—With A, k1, * sl 3 wyib, k3; rep from *, end sl 3, k1.
Row 14—With A, repeat Row 6.
Row 15—With A, k2, * sl 1 wyib, k5; rep from *, end sl 1, k2.
Row 16—With A, purl.

Omitting preparation rows, repeat Rows 5–16.

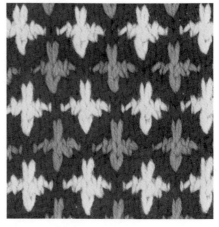

North Star Pattern

Chain of Triangles

Stitches are increased on the Color B rows in this pattern, and reduced to the original number again on the Color A rows. The variation, below, is a pretty "rib" design. Both versions are easy to work.

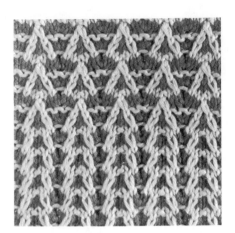

ABOVE: *Chain of Triangles*
BELOW: *Variation*

Multiple of 6 sts plus 3. Colors A and B.

Row 1 (Wrong side)—With A, k2, * p2, k1; rep from *, end k1.
Row 2—With B, k1, inc in next st, * sl 1 wyib, k3, sl 1 wyib, (k1, p1, k1) in next st; rep from *, end sl 1, k3, sl 1, inc in next st, k1.
Row 3—With B, p3, * sl 1 wyif, p3; rep from *.
Row 4—With A, k3, * ssk, sl 1 wyib, k2 tog, k3; rep from *.
Row 5—With A, k3, * p1, sl 1 wyif, p1, k3; rep from *.
Row 6—With B, k2, inc in next st, * (sl 1 wyib, k1) twice, (k1, p1, k1) in next st, k1; rep from *, end sl 1, k1, sl 1, inc in next st, k2.
Row 7—With B, p4, * sl 1 wyif, p1, sl 1 wyif, p5; rep from *, end last repeat p4.
Row 8—With A, k4, * sl 1—k2 tog—psso, k5; rep from *, end last repeat k4.

Repeat Rows 1–8.

VARIATION

Rows 1, 2, and 3—Same as rows 1, 2, and 3 above.
Row 4—With A, k3, * ssk, k1, k2 tog, k3; rep from *.

Repeat Rows 1–4.

Two-Color Plaited Basketweave

On a purely physical basis, this pattern is not an easy one to work. It is *extremely* dense (a large number of stitches makes a surprisingly small piece) and should be worked with large needles. The dropped stitch may shorten so much that it is difficult to retrieve, especially in Row 2. But this awkwardness can be overcome by putting the stitch on a cable needle instead of simply dropping it. Some knitters will find one of these methods preferable, some the other. Notice that the third, or "extra" stitch in each pattern repeat is lost in the background as the fabric pulls together. This gives additional depth and thickness to the knitting, making a fabric so tough and durable that it would even serve as a rug.

Two-Color Plaited Basketweave

Multiple of 3 sts. Colors A and B.

Cast on with Color A and knit one row.

Row 1 (Wrong side)—With B, p3, * sl 1 wyif, p2; rep from *.

Row 2—With B, k2, * drop next (Color A) st off needle to front of work, k2, then with point of left-hand needle pick up dropped st and slip it onto right-hand needle without working; rep from *, end k1.

Row 3—With A, * p2, sl 1 wyif; rep from *, end p3.

Row 4—With A, k1, * sl 2 wyib, drop next (Color B) st off needle to front of work, sl the same 2 sts back to left-hand needle, pick up dropped st onto right-hand needle without working, k2; rep from *, end k2.

Repeat Rows 1–4.

False Flame Stitch

Here is a knitted imitation of the Flame Stitch, or Bargello Pattern. It may be worked in three or four colors if desired, simply by repeating the 4 pattern rows for each stripe of color. It is very handsome in a progressive series of colors, such as: white, yellow, orange, red; or: white, light gray, dark gray, black. The 3 Preparation Rows are always worked in the last color to be used.

Multiple of 4 sts plus 1. Colors A and B.

<small>Preparation Rows:</small>

Row 1 (Wrong side)—With A, purl.

Row 2—With A, knit.

Row 3—With A, p2, * p1 wrapping yarn twice, p3; rep from *, end last repeat p2.

End of preparation rows.

False Flame Stitch

Row 4—With B, k2, * sl 1 wyib dropping extra wrap, k1, insert needle into next st 2 rows below and draw through a loop loosely; knit next st and pass the loop over the st just knitted; k1; rep from *, end sl 1 wyib, k2.

Row 5—With B, p2, * sl 1 wyif, p3; rep from *, end sl 1 wyif, p2.

Row 6—With B, knit.

Row 7—With B, p2, * p1 wrapping yarn twice, p3; rep from *, end last repeat p2.

Rows 8 through 11—With A, repeat Rows 4 through 7.

Omitting preparation rows, repeat Rows 4–11.

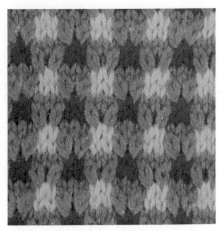

Double Twist Check

Double Twist Check

Multiple of 6 sts plus 3. Colors A, B, and C.

Row 1 (Wrong side)—With A, purl.
Row 2—With B, k1, * k4, sl 2 wyib; rep from *, end k2.
Row 3—With B, p2, * sl 2 wyif, p4; rep from *, end p1.
Row 4—With A, k2, * sl 2 wyib, RT, LT; rep from *, end k1.
Row 5—With A, purl.
Row 6—With C, k2, * sl 2 wyib, k4; rep from *, end k1.
Row 7—With C, p1, * p4, sl 2 wyif; rep from *, end p2.
Row 8—With A, k1, * RT, LT, sl 2 wyib; rep from *, end k2.

Repeat Rows 1–8.

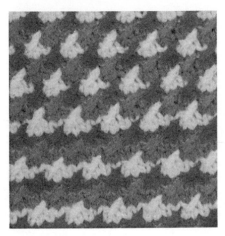

Fingertip Tweed
ABOVE: *Check Version*
BELOW: *Stripe Version*

Fingertip Tweed

In Version I of this pattern, the middle stitch of the 3 knit stitches (which is the slipped stitch of the previous row) presents the back loop, so it is somewhat easier to work it as a "k1-b" than as a plain knit stitch. This action produces a third variation, which is not shown; the knitter may try it, and see what it looks like. Knitting this middle stitch in its front loop, in spite of the way it is turned, makes the twisted diagonal point above each check; so be sure to do this if you want your sample to look like the illustration. This distinction does not exist, of course, in Version II.

Multiple of 4 sts plus 3. Colors A, B, and C.

Cast on with Color C.

I. CHECK VERSION

Row 1 (Right side)—With A, k3, * skip 1 st and insert needle purlwise into the front of 2nd st, then slip this st *over* skipped st onto right-hand needle (leaving skipped st in place); k3; rep from *.
Row 2—With A, p3, * sl 1 wyif, p3; rep from *.
Row 3—With B, k1, rep from * of Row 1; end last repeat k1 instead of k3.
Row 4—With B, p1, * sl 1 wyif, p3; rep from *, end sl 1, p1.
Rows 5 and 6—With C, repeat Rows 1 and 2.
Rows 7 and 8—With A, repeat Rows 3 and 4.
Rows 9 and 10—With B, repeat Rows 1 and 2.
Rows 11 and 12—With C, repeat Rows 3 and 4.

Repeat Rows 1–12.

II. STRIPE VERSION

Work the same as I, above, except: *purl* all sts on all wrong-side rows.

Cactus Flower

Though done with a technique similar to that of Counterpoint Quilting, this pattern has quite a different appearance. On Rows 2 and 8, the strand should be kept *loose* behind the three slipped stitches, as this is the strand that will be picked up later (Rows 5 and 11). Widely varying effects can be had from this pattern by alternating light and dark, bright and dull colors on different rows.

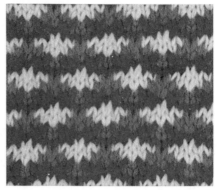

Cactus Flower

Multiple of 6 sts plus 5. Colors A, B, and C.

Cast on with Color A and purl one row.

Row 1 (Right side)—With B, k2, * sl 1 wyib, k5; rep from *, end sl 1, k2.

Row 2—With B, p4, * sl 3 wyib, p3; rep from *, end p1.

Row 3—With C, k1, * sl 1 wyib, k1, sl 1 wyib, k3; rep from *, end (sl 1, k1) twice.

Row 4—With C, purl.

Row 5—With A, k1, * sl 3 wyib, k1, insert needle under the loose Color B strand on front of fabric and knit next st, catching strand behind st; k1; rep from *, end sl 3, k1.

Row 6—With A, p2, * sl 1 wyif, p5; rep from *, end sl 1, p2.

Row 7—With B, k5, * sl 1 wyib, k5; rep from *.

Row 8—With B, p1, * sl 3 wyib, p3; rep from *, end sl 3, p1.

Row 9—With C, k4, * sl 1 wyib, k1, sl 1 wyib, k3; rep from *, end k1.

Row 10—With C, purl.

Row 11—With A, k2, * knit next st under loose Color B strand (as in Row 5), k1, sl 3 wyib, k1; rep from *, end knit next st under loose strand, k2.

Row 12—With A, p5, * sl 1 wyif, p5; rep from *.

Repeat Rows 1–12.

Counterpoint Quilting

Contributed by Hildegard M. Elsner, Aldan, Pennsylvania

Multiple of 6 sts plus 5. Colors A, B, and C.

Row 1 (Wrong side)—With A, p4, * sl 3 wyib, p3; rep from *, end p1.

Row 2—With B, knit.

Row 3—With B, repeat Row 1.

Rows 4 and 5—With C, repeat Rows 2 and 3.

Row 6—With A, k5, * insert needle from front under the 3 loose strands and upward to knit next st, catching all 3 strands behind st as it is knitted; k5; rep from *.

Row 7—With A, p1, * sl 3 wyib, p3; rep from *, end last repeat p1.

Row 8—With B, knit.

Row 9—With B, repeat Row 7.

Rows 10 and 11—With C, repeat Rows 8 and 9.

Row 12—With A, k2, rep from * of Row 6; end last repeat k2 instead of k5.

Counterpoint Quilting

Repeat Rows 1–12.

Fancy Diagonal Stripe

Fancy Diagonal Stripe

This pattern is an elaboration of Plaited Diagonal Stripe, done with a similar technique, and should be bound off in the same way (i.e., on the wrong side, omitting all yo's) for the same reason. Although the basis of the two patterns is the same, the general effect is quite different; this one is decidedly more complex, both in appearance and in construction. Note that in this pattern the slip-stitches are sometimes single, sometimes double; when they are double, it is always the *second* of the two slipped stitches that is passed over two subsequent knit stitches. The wrong side of this fabric shows a very interesting diagonal stripe in purl and slipped stitches. For a test swatch, cast on a *minimum* of 18 sts.

Multiple of 8 sts plus 2. Colors A and B.

Cast on with A and purl one row.

NOTE: On all right-side (odd-numbered) rows sl all sl-sts with yarn in back; on all wrong-side (even-numbered) rows sl all sl-sts with yarn in front.

Row 1 (Right side)—With B, k2, * sl 1, k2, psso the 2 knit sts, sl 2, k2, pass 2nd sl-st over the 2 knit sts, k1; rep from *.

Row 2—With B, p2, * yo, p1, sl 1, p1, yo, p3; rep from *.

Row 3—With A, k1, * sl 1, k2, psso the 2 knit sts, k1, sl 1, k2, psso the 2 knit sts, sl 1; rep from *, end k1.

Row 4—With A, p1, * sl 1, p1, yo, p3, yo, p1; rep from *, end p1.

Row 5—With B, k3, * sl 2, k2, pass 2nd sl-st over the 2 knit sts, k1, sl 1, k2, psso the 2 knit sts; rep from *, end sl 2, k2, pass 2nd sl-st over the 2 knit sts, k3.

Row 6—With B, p4, * yo, p1, sl 1, p1, yo, p3; rep from *, end yo, p1, sl 1, p3.

Row 7—With A, k3, * sl 1, k2, psso the 2 knit sts, sl 2, k2, pass 2nd sl-st over the 2 knit sts, k1; rep from *, omitting final "k1" from last repeat.

Row 8—With A, p1, * yo, p1, sl 1, p1, yo, p3; rep from *, end p1.

Row 9—With B, k1, * sl 2, k2, pass 2nd sl-st over the 2 knit sts, k1, sl 1, k2, psso the 2 knit sts; rep from *, end k1.

Row 10—With B, p2, * yo, p3, yo, p1, sl 1, p1; rep from *.

Row 11—With A, * k1, sl 1, k2, psso the 2 knit sts, sl 2, k2, pass 2nd sl-st over the 2 knit sts; rep from *, end k2.

Row 12—With A, * p3, yo, p1, sl 1, p1, yo; rep from *, end p2.

Row 13—With B, k4, * sl 1, k2, psso the 2 knit sts, sl 2, k2, pass 2nd sl-st over the 2 knit sts; k1; rep from *, end sl 1, k2, psso the 2 knit sts, sl 1, k2.

Row 14—With B, p2, * sl 1, p1, yo, p3, yo, p1; rep from *, end sl 1, p1, yo, p5.

Row 15—With A, k2, * sl 2, k2, pass 2nd sl-st over the 2 knit sts, k1, sl 1, k2, psso the 2 knit sts; rep from *.

Row 16—With A, * p1, yo, p3, yo, p1, sl 1; rep from *, end p2.

Repeat Rows 1-16.

Two-Color Dip Stitch

A dip stitch is made by the technique demonstrated here, of pulling a stitch through the fabric from several rows below. This pattern may be worked in solid color for an attractive texture; or, it may be shown on the wrong side. The rather unusual practice of showing "broken" color bands in the purl stitches gives this fabric a beaded effect.

Two-Color Dip Stitch

Multiple of 8 sts plus 3. Colors A and B.

Cast on with Color A and purl one row.

Rows 1 and 3 (Wrong side)—With B, purl.
Rows 2 and 4—With B, knit.
Row 5—With A, knit.
Row 6—With A, k1, * insert right-hand needle from front under purled loop of next st 6 rows below; knit an extra st in this st; then knit the next st on left-hand needle and pass the extra st over it (dip stitch made); k7; rep from *, end last repeat k1.
Rows 7 through 10—With B, repeat Rows 1 through 4.
Row 11—With A, knit.
Row 12—With A, k5, * make dip stitch as in Row 6, k7; rep from *, end last repeat k5.

Repeat Rows 1–12.

Dip-Stitch Check

Contributed by Toshiko Sugiyama, Oakland, California

Multiple of 4 sts plus 3. Colors A and B.

Dip-Stitch Check

Rows 1 and 3 (Wrong side)—With A, purl.
Row 2—With A, knit.
Row 4—With B, k3, * insert needle into front of the 3rd st below the next st on left-hand needle, and draw up a loop; then knit the next st on left-hand needle and pass the loop over the st just knitted; k3; rep from *.
Rows 5, 6, and 7—With B, repeat Rows 1, 2, and 3.
Row 8—With A, k1, rep from * of Row 4; end last repeat k1 instead of k3.

Repeat Rows 1–8.

Sunrise Shell Pattern

Sunrise Shell Pattern

This striking three-color design bears some resemblance to a crocheted Shell Stitch, and makes beautiful handbags, cushions, afghans, hats, coats, and sweaters. Drop-stitches and *wrong*-side twists are used to make the pattern. The wrong-side Left Twist (LT) only sounds difficult; it is easy to work once the idea is grasped. Turning the work over slightly, so as to see the right side, insert the needle from the left into the back loop of the second stitch, then bring the needle point *around* the skipped stitch to the front, or wrong, side (where the yarn is held, waiting to purl); wrap yarn and purl, letting the needle point "back out" of the stitch in the usual way. Then work the skipped stitch as directed.

Multiple of 6 sts plus 3. Colors A, B, and C.

Cast on with Color A and purl one row.

NOTES: Right Twist (RT)—skip 1 st and purl the 2nd st, then purl the skipped st, then sl both sts from needle together.

Left Twist (LT)—skip 1 st and purl the 2nd st in *back* loop, then purl the skipped st in the usual way, then sl both sts from needle together.

PREPARATION ROWS

Rows 1 and 3 (Right side)—With B, knit.
Row 2—With B, purl.
Row 4—With B, p2, * RT, p1, LT, p1; rep from *, end p1.

End of preparation rows.

Row 5—With C, k4, * drop next st off needle and unravel 4 rows down; insert needle from front into the st in 5th row below and knit, catching the 4 loose strands in st; k5; rep from *, end last repeat k4.
Row 6—With C, purl.
Row 7—With C, knit.
Row 8—With C, p2, * LT, p1, RT, p1; rep from *, end p1.
Row 9—With A, k1, rep from * of Row 5; end last repeat k1 instead of k5.
Row 10—With A, purl.
Row 11—With A, knit.
Row 12—With A, p2, * RT, p1, LT, p1; rep from *, end p1.
Rows 13 through 16—With B, repeat Rows 5 through 8.
Rows 17 through 20—With C, repeat Rows 9 through 12.
Rows 21 through 24—With A, repeat Rows 5 through 8.
Rows 25 through 28—With B, repeat Rows 9 through 12.

Omitting preparation rows, repeat Rows 5–28.

English Rose Tweed

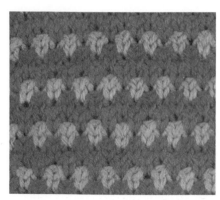

Here is a really lovely three-color pattern that is easy to work. It makes a flat, rather loose, and very wide fabric. Beware of casting on too many stitches, and be sure to bind off loosely.

This pattern will make charming sweaters, vests, jackets, coats, and children's wear. Try it in two or three different types of yarn—such as wool with ribbon, slubbed yarns with smooth, etc. The wrong side is beautiful, too.

English Rose Tweed

Even number of sts. Colors A, B, and C.

Cast on with Color C and knit one row.

Row 1 (Right side)—With A, k1, * p1, k1 in the row below; rep from *, end k1.
Row 2—With A, knit.
Row 3—With B, k1, * k1 in the row below, p1; rep from *, end k1.
Row 4—With B, knit.
Rows 5 and 6—With C, repeat Rows 1 and 2.
Rows 7 and 8—With A, repeat Rows 3 and 4.
Rows 9 and 10—With B, repeat Rows 1 and 2.
Rows 11 and 12—With C, repeat Rows 3 and 4.

Repeat Rows 1–12.

Three-Color Daisy Stitch

Sometimes this pattern is referred to as Star Stitch—which is fair enough, as it does form little star-like motifs—but then it is often confused with the *other* Star Stitch which is worked in quite a different way. Daisy Stitch is beautiful in one, two, three or four colors; the three-color version here will suffice to demonstrate. Note that on the "p3 tog, yo, p3 tog again" operation, the stitches are *not* removed from the left-hand needle until the whole operation is completed.

Three-Color Daisy Stitch

Multiple of 4 sts plus 1. Colors A, B, and C.

Row 1 (Right side)—With A, knit.
Row 2—With A, k1, * p3 tog, yo, purl the same 3 sts tog again, k1; rep from *.
Row 3—With B, knit.
Row 4—With B, k1, p1, k1, * p3 tog, yo, purl the same 3 sts tog again, k1; rep from *, end p1, k1.
Rows 5 and 6—With C, repeat Rows 1 and 2.
Rows 7 and 8—With A, repeat Rows 3 and 4.
Rows 9 and 10—With B, repeat Rows 1 and 2.
Rows 11 and 12—With C, repeat Rows 3 and 4.

Repeat Rows 1–12.

Fan Dip Stitch

There are several details to be considered, if this pattern is to be worked most successfully. The "dipped" strands should not be twisted as they are passed over the subsequent stitch; therefore they must be turned *knitwise* as they are placed on the right-hand needle. To accomplish this, after drawing up the loop insert the left-hand needle behind the *back* strand of the loop, and through the loop to the front, slipping the loop onto the left-hand needle in this way. Then slip the loop *purlwise* back onto the right-hand needle, and it will be in the correct position. This "juggling" of the loop also affords an opportunity to lengthen it and loosen it; the pattern can be spoiled by work that is too tight. Notice that all three loops are taken from the *same* purled stitch 5 rows below.

This pattern need not be worked in two colors. It is an exceedingly pretty texture pattern when done in the same color throughout.

Multiple of 10 sts plus 2. Colors A and B.

Cast on with Color A and knit one row.

Row 1 (Wrong side)—With A, p8, * k1, p9; rep from *, end last repeat p3.
Rows 2 and 4—With B, knit.
Rows 3 and 5—With B, purl.
Row 6—With A, * (k1, insert right-hand needle from the front under the purled Color A st 5 rows below, and draw up a loop; knit next st and pass the loop over the st just worked) 3 times, k4; rep from *, end k2.
Row 7—With A, p3, * k1, p9; rep from *, end last repeat p8.
Rows 8, 9, 10, and 11—With B, repeat Rows 2, 3, 4, and 5.
Row 12—With A, k5, rep from * of Row 6: end last repeat k1 instead of k4.

Repeat Rows 1–12.

ABOVE: *Fan Dip Stitch*
BELOW: *Shell Dip Stitch*

Shell Dip Stitch

This pattern is similar in principle to Fan Dip Stitch, but the technique is a little different. The shells can be made by "dipping" the right-hand needle, but the use of a crochet hook gives more control of the length of the six loops, which should be reasonably uniform. To find the right stitch from which to take the loops, count 3 stitches over on the left-hand needle and then 3 ridges down, beginning with the ridge immediately under the needle. Insert hook under the third ridge, just above the last Color A row.

In a single color, Shell Dip Stitch is a very pretty texture pattern.

Multiple of 14 sts plus 2. Colors A and B.

Cast on with Color A and knit one row.

Rows 1, 2, 3, 4, 5, and 6—With B, knit.

Row 7 (Right side)—With A, k9, * (insert crochet hook into the front of st 5 rows below the 3rd st on left-hand needle, and draw through a long loop; sl this loop on right-hand needle, then knit the next st) 6 times, taking all 6 loops from the same st below; k8; rep from *, end last repeat k1.

Row 8—With A, k1, * (p2 tog-b) 3 times, p1, (p2 tog) 3 times, k7; rep from *, end k1.

Rows 9, 10, 11, 12, 13, and 14—With B, knit.

Row 15—With A, k2, rep from * of Row 7 across.

Row 16—With A, k8, * (p2 tog-b) 3 times, p1, (p2 tog) 3 times, k7; rep from *, end last repeat k1.

Repeat Rows 1–16.

Florentine Frieze

The elements of this pattern are simple—a few woven bands, a little quilting—but the finished effect is one of intricate and amazing beauty. The caught-up strands make shapes reminiscent of the famous "garland" frieze in baroque decoration. The pattern makes a stunning yoke for a Scandinavian-type sweater, or fancy mittens, or decorative bands around skirts and sleeves. It is very good also for home accessories such as cushions and slipcovers.

Florentine Frieze

Multiple of 4 sts plus 1. Colors A and B.

Row 1 (Wrong side)—With A, purl.

Row 2—With B, k1, * sl 1 wyib, sl 1 wyif, sl 1 wyib, k1; rep from *.

Row 3—With B, p1, * sl 3 wyib, yo, p1; rep from *.

Row 4—With A, knit, dropping all yo's off needle to make long loose Color B strands across front of work.

Row 5—With A, purl.

Row 6—With B, k1, * sl 1 wyib, insert needle from front under the loose Color B strand and knit next st, bringing needle out under strand to catch strand behind st; sl 1 wyib, k1; rep from *.

Row 7—With B, k1, * sl 1 wyif, p1, sl 1 wyif, k1; rep from *.

Row 8—With A, knit.

Row 9—With A, purl.

Row 10—With B, k1, * sl 1 wyif, k1; rep from *.

Rows 11 through 20—Repeat Rows 1 through 10, reversing colors.

Repeat Rows 1–20.

Bonbon Pattern

Bonbon Pattern

Here is a pretty three-color pattern with one little twist stitch. If you do not know how to make a Left Twist (LT), see Glossary.

Multiple of 10 sts plus 4. Colors A, B, and C.

Row 1 (Wrong side)—With A, knit.
Row 2—With B, k6, * sl 2 wyib, k8; rep from *, end sl 2, k6.
Row 3—With B, p4, * sl 6 wyif, p4; rep from *.
Row 4—With B, k4, * sl 6 wyib, k4; rep from *.
Row 5—With B, p6, * sl 2 wyif, p8; rep from *, end sl 2, p6.
Row 6—With A, k6, * LT, k8; rep from *, end LT, k6.
Row 7—With A, knit.
Row 8—With C, k1, * sl 2 wyib, k8; rep from *, end sl 2, k1.
Row 9—With C, p1, sl 4 wyif, * p4, sl 6 wyif; rep from *, end p4, sl 4, p1.
Row 10—With C, k1, sl 4 wyib, * k4, sl 6 wyib; rep from *, end k4, sl 4, k1.
Row 11—With C, p1, * sl 2 wyif, p8; rep from *, end sl 2, p1.
Row 12—With A, k1, * LT, k8; rep from *, end LT, k1.

Repeat Rows 1–12.

Four-Color Blister Stitch

Four-Color Blister Stitch

This beautiful pattern is worked by the drop-stitch technique (see Drop-Stitch Honeycomb) and is a 12-row repetition; the additional rows serve to alternate colors. The surface of the fabric is very "bumpy", each little blister standing out in relief against the Color A background.

Multiple of 4 sts plus 3. Colors A, B, C, and D.

Cast on with Color A and purl one row.

Rows 1 and 3 (Right side)—With B, knit.
Rows 2 and 4—With B, purl.
Row 5—With A, k3, * drop next st off needle and unravel 4 rows down; insert needle from front into Color A st in 5th row below and knit, catching the 4 loose strands in st; k3; rep from *.
Row 6—With A, purl.
Rows 7 through 10—With C, repeat Rows 1–4.
Row 11—With A, k1, rep from * of Row 5; end last repeat k1 instead of k3.
Row 12—With A, purl.

Rows 13 through 16—With D, repeat Rows 1–4.
Rows 17 and 18—With A, repeat Rows 5 and 6.
Rows 19 through 22—With B, repeat Rows 1–4.
Rows 23 and 24—With A, repeat Rows 11 and 12.
Rows 25 through 28—With C, repeat Rows 1–4.
Rows 29 and 30—With A, repeat Rows 5 and 6.
Rows 31 through 34—With D, repeat Rows 1–4.
Rows 35 and 36—With A, repeat Rows 11 and 12.

Repeat Rows 1–36.

Three Flowers

Three Flowers

Here is a delightful pattern of knitted-in "embroidery", ideal for borders or accent bands (on a yoke, for instance). The pattern is shown in alternating bands of contrasting color, which is another pleasing idea for cushions, handbags, dirndls or Tyrolean vests. Multicolored odds and ends of yarn can be used up by making such articles in as many different-colored bands as desired.

Multiple of 10 sts plus 3. Colors A, B, and C.

Row 1 (Right side)—With A, knit.

Row 2—With A, purl.

Row 3—With B, knit.

Row 4—With B, k5, * k3 wrapping yarn 3 times for each st, k7; rep from *, end last repeat k5.

Row 5—With A, k1, * sl 1 wyib, k3, sl 3 wyib dropping extra wraps, k3; rep from *, end sl 1, k1.

Row 6—With A, p1, * sl 1 wyif, p3, sl 3 wyif, p3; rep from *, end sl 1, p1.

Row 7—With A, k5, * sl 3 wyib, k7; rep from *, end last repeat k5.

Row 8—With A, p5, * sl 3 wyif, p7; rep from *, end last repeat p5.

Row 9—With A, k3, * sl 2 wyib, drop next (1st Color B) st off needle to front of work, sl the same 2 sts back to left-hand needle, pick up dropped st and knit it; k3, drop next (3rd Color B) st off needle to front of work, k2, pick up dropped st and knit it; k3; rep from *.

Row 10—With C, p1, sl 2 wyif, * [(p1, k1, p1) in next st, sl 2 wyif] twice, (p1, k1, p1) in next st, sl 3 wyif; rep from *, end [(p1, k1, p1) in next st, sl 2 wyif] 3 times, p1.

Row 11—With C, k1, sl 2 wyib, * Make Bobble (MB) in next 3 (increased) sts as follows: p3, turn and k3, turn and sl 1—k2 tog—psso, completing bobble; (sl 2 wyib, MB) twice, sl 3 wyib; rep from *, end (MB, sl 2 wyib) 3 times, k1.

Row 12—With A, purl, purling into the *back* of each bobble st.

Rows 13 and 14—With A, repeat Rows 1 and 2.

Repeat Rows 1–14.

NOTE: Garter-stitch stripes of different colors may be inserted between repeats.

Paving Stones

Contributed by Hildegard M. Elsner, Aldan, Pennsylvania

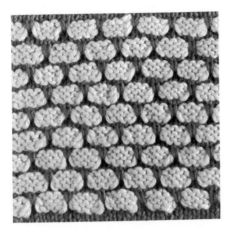

Paving Stones

Here is a drop-stitch pattern with purled rows on the right side, giving an impression of rough-hewn rectangular blocks set in a wall or pavement. The wrong side of the fabric is attractive, showing deeply indented Color B knit stitches outlined by purl in the manner of the Two-Color Dip Stitch. (See also Four-Color Blister Stitch.)

Multiple of 4 sts plus 1. Colors A and B.

Cast on with Color A and knit one row.

Row 1 (Wrong side)—With A, purl.
Rows 2 and 3—With B, knit.
Row 4—With B, purl.
Row 5—With B, knit.
Row 6—With A, k2, * drop next st off needle and unravel 4 rows down; insert needle into the front of Color A st in 5th row below and knit, catching the 4 loose strands in st; k3; rep from *, end last repeat k2.
Rows 7, 8, 9, 10, and 11—Repeat Rows 1, 2, 3, 4, and 5.
Row 12—With A, k4, rep from * of Row 6; end k1.

Repeat Rows 1–12.

Knitter's Choice

Knitter's Choice
ABOVE: *First decrease*
CENTER: *Second decrease*
BELOW: *Third decrease*

Choose one of three different types of decrease, here, to make the puffy Color B motifs the shape that you prefer. The first decrease, a simple k5 tog-b, swirls the long stitches to the left. The second makes a square shape with Color A stitches encroaching at the top. The third makes the central stitch prominent. Another idea is to work the pattern in more than two colors, using a different decrease in each different-colored row of puffs.

Multiple of 4 sts plus 1. Colors A and B.

Cast on with Color A and knit two rows.

NOTES: First decrease—k5 tog-b.
Second decrease—k2 tog-b, k3 tog, then pass the k2-tog-b st over the k3-tog st.
Third decrease—insert needle into first 3 sts as if to k3 tog, and *slip* the sts from this position; k2 tog, then pass the 3 slipped sts all together over the k2-tog st.

Row 1 (Right side)—With B, k2, * sl 1 wyib, k1, (k1, yo, k1, yo, k1) in next st, k1; rep from *, end sl 1 wyib, k2.

Row 2—With B, k2, * sl 1 wyif, k1, k5 wrapping yarn twice for each st, k1; rep from *, end sl 1 wyif, k2.

Row 3—With A, k4, * sl 5 wyib dropping extra wraps, k3; rep from *, end k1.

Rows 4 and 6—With A, k4, * sl 5 wyif, k3; rep from *, end k1.

Row 5—With A, k4, * sl 5 wyib, k3; rep from *, end k1.

Row 7—With A, k4, * work next 5 sts tog using first, second, or third decrease, k3; rep from *, end k1.

Row 8—With A, knit.

Row 9—With B, k2, * (k1, yo, k1, yo, k1) in next st, k1, sl 1 wyib, k1; rep from *, end (k1, yo, k1, yo, k1) in next st, k2.

Row 10—With B, k2, * k5 wrapping yarn twice for each st, k1, sl 1 wyif, k1; rep from *, end k5 wrapping yarn twice for each st, k2.

Row 11—With A, k2, * sl 5 wyib dropping extra wraps, k3; rep from *, end last repeat k2.

Rows 12 and 14—With A, k2, * sl 5 wyif, k3; rep from *, end last repeat k2.

Row 13—With A, k2, * sl 5 wyib, k3; rep from *, end last repeat k2.

Row 15—With A, k2, * work next 5 sts tog using first, second, or third decrease, k3; rep from *, end last repeat k2.

Row 16—With A, knit.

Repeat Rows 1–16.

Crazy Quilted Pattern

This pattern is a development of Mrs. Hunter's Pattern, done in two colors for greater contrast. The passing of the yo's over subsequent stitches is delayed 4 rows, so that the yo's are elongated into V-shaped quilting strands. The result is a novelty fabric with isolated openings and considerable texture interest.

Multiple of 3 sts plus 2. Colors A and B.

Cast on with A and knit one row.

Row 1 (Wrong side)—With A, k1, * p3, (yo) twice; rep from *, end k1.

Row 2—With B, k1, * sl the yo st wyib, dropping 2nd yo off needle; k3; rep from *, end k1.

Rows 3 and 5—With B, k1, * p3, sl 1 wyif; rep from *, end k1.

Row 4—With B, k1, * sl 1 wyib, k3; rep from *, end k1.

Row 6—With A, k1, * sl 1 wyib (this is the Color A yo st), k3, psso the 3 knit sts; rep from *, end k1.

Repeat Rows 1–6.

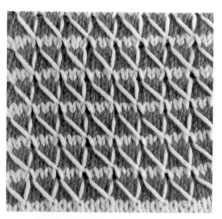

Crazy Quilted Pattern

Long Bobble Pattern

These bold pear-shaped bobbles are ingeniously constructed of a central increase, four turning rows, and two lateral decreases on the return row; then the entire assemblage is carried upward for 5 rows more by slipping the stitches. Packing these unusual bobbles close together, this pattern makes a very thick novelty fabric for hats, cushions, handbags, patch pockets, afghan squares, borders, etc. After having learned how to make this type of bobble, the knitter may use it also in other contexts.

Multiple of 6 sts plus 3. (15 sts minimum) Colors A and B.

Cast on with Color A and knit one row.

Row 1 (Right side)—With B, k1, * sl 1 wyib, k2, (k1, yo, k1) in next st, k1, (turn and p5, turn and k5) twice, k1; rep from *, end sl 1 wyib, k1.

Row 2—With B, k1, * sl 1 wyif, k1, p2 tog, p1, p2 tog-b, k1; rep from *, end sl 1 wyif, k1.

Rows 3, 5, and 7—With A, k3, * sl 3 wyib, k3; rep from *.

Rows 4 and 6—With A, k3, * sl 3 wyif, k3; rep from *.

Row 8—With A, k3, * p3, k3; rep from *.

Row 9—With B, k4, rep from * of Row 1: end sl 1 wyib, k4.

Row 10—With B, k4, rep from * of Row 2; end sl 1 wyif, k4.

Rows 11, 13, and 15—With A, k6, * sl 3 wyib, k3; rep from *, end k3.

Rows 12 and 14—With A, k6, * sl 3 wyif, k3; rep from *, end k3.

Row 16—With A, k6, * p3, k3; rep from *, end k3.

Repeat Rows 1–16.

Long Bobble Pattern

Puffball Plaid

A puffball is like a bobble—a knobby, knot-like formation made in a single stitch—but notice the difference here in the manner of working it. Each new loop is placed on the left-hand needle and then knitted, exactly as in the method of casting on that is called "knitting-on". Puffballs can also be used as spot-patterns on a plain solid-color stockinette fabric, or to replace bobbles or popcorns in any fancy pattern.

Multiple of 9 sts plus 4. Colors A and B.

Row 1 (Wrong side)—With A, purl.

Row 2—With A, knit.

Row 3—With A, k1, * p2, k7; rep from *, end p2, k1.

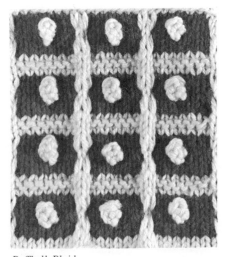

Puffball Plaid

Row 4—With A, k1, * k2 wrapping yarn twice for each st, k7; rep from *, end k2 wrapping yarn twice, k1.

Row 5—With B, k1, * sl 2 wyif dropping extra wraps, p7; rep from *, end sl 2, k1.

Row 6—With B, k1, * sl 2 wyib, k7; rep from *, end sl 2, k1.

Row 7—With B, k1, * sl 2 wyif, p7; rep from *, end sl 2, k1.

Row 8—Repeat Row 6.

Row 9—With A, k1, * p2, sl 3 wyif, p1, sl 3 wyif; rep from *, end p2, k1.

Row 10—With A, k1, * k2 wrapping yarn twice for each st, sl 3 wyib, make Puffball in next st as follows: insert needle in st as if to knit, draw through a loop and place this loop on left-hand needle; (insert needle into front of new loop and knit, then place next new loop on left-hand needle) 4 times, making 5 new loops in all; then k6 (the 5 new loops, plus the original st); then pass the 2nd, 3rd, 4th, 5th and 6th sts on right-hand needle one at a time over the 1st (original) st, completing Puffball; sl 3 wyib; rep from *, end k2 wrapping yarn twice, k1.

Rows 11 and 12—With B, repeat Rows 5 and 6.

Repeat Rows 1–12.

Cluster Quilting

This beautiful pattern is made by a fascinatingly unusual technique that is much less complicated than it seems at first glance. Novice knitters are likely to be frightened by the long lines of loose stitches dropped off the needle in Rows 4 and 10, looking as though they might disappear forever. But don't worry—they won't. The following rows pick them up again very neatly, one at a time. Since the dropped stitches are never crossed, there is no problem about knowing which one to pick up next; it is always the nearest one available.

Multiple of 8 sts plus 1. Colors A and B.

Preparation row, wrong side—With A, p1, * p1 wrapping yarn twice, p5, p1 wrapping yarn twice, p1; rep from *.

Row 1—With B, k1, * sl 1 wyib dropping extra wrap, k5, sl 1 wyib dropping extra wrap, k1; rep from *.

Row 2—With B, p1, * sl 1 wyif, p5, sl 1 wyif, p1; rep from *.

Row 3—With B, k1, * sl 1 wyib, k5, sl 1 wyib, k1; rep from *.

Cluster Quilting

Row 4—With B, purl, dropping all elongated Color A sl-sts off needle to back (i.e., to *right* side of fabric).

Row 5—With A, k1, sl 1 wyib, k1, * pick up first dropped st and knit it, k1, pick up next dropped st and knit it; then (with yarn in back sl the last 3 sts worked back to left-hand needle, pass yarn to front, sl the same 3 sts back again to right-hand needle, pass yarn to back) twice; k1, sl 3 wyib, k1; rep from *, end last repeat sl 1 wyib, k1 instead of sl 3 wyib, k1.

Row 6—With A, p1, sl 1 wyif, * (p1, p1 wrapping yarn twice) twice, p1, sl 3 wyif; rep from *, end last repeat sl 1 wyif, p1 instead of sl 3 wyif.

Row 7—With B, k3, * sl 1 wyib dropping extra wrap, k1, sl 1 wyib dropping extra wrap, k5; rep from *, end last repeat k3.

Row 8—With B, p3, * sl 1 wyif, p1, sl 1 wyif, p5; rep from *, end last repeat p3.

Row 9—With B, k3, * sl 1 wyib, k1, sl 1 wyib, k5; rep from *, end last repeat k3.

Row 10—With B, purl, dropping all elongated Color A sl-sts off needle to back.

Row 11—With A, k1, pick up first dropped st and knit it, k1, sl 3 wyib, k1; rep from * of Row 5; end pick up last dropped st and knit it, k1.

Row 12—With A, p1, * p1 wrapping yarn twice, p1, sl 3 wyif, p1, p1 wrapping yarn twice, p1; rep from *.

Omitting preparation row, repeat Rows 1–12.

Snowball Stitch

Snowball Stitch

Here is an unusual color-and-texture pattern with large purled clusters showing through a fabric of crossed elongated stitches. The effect is gay and informal, and the knitting firm and dense; so this pattern is ideal for warm ski sweaters, hats, and children's sportswear. It will also make cheerful cushion covers, extra-fancy sock tops, afghan squares, patch pockets and collars.

Multiple of 5 sts plus 1. Colors A and B.

Row 1 (Wrong side)—With A, purl.

Row 2—With A, knit.

Row 3—With A, p1, * p1 wrapping yarn twice around needle, p2, p1 wrapping yarn twice, p1; rep from *.

Row 4—With B, k1, * sl 1 wyib dropping extra wrap, k2, sl 1 wyib dropping extra wrap, (k1, yo, k1, yo, k1) in next st; rep from * across to last st, end last repeat with a plain k1.

Row 5—With B, k1, * sl 1 wyif, p2, sl 1 wyif, k5; rep from *, end sl 1, p2, sl 1, k1.

Row 6—With B, k1, * sl 1 wyib, k2, sl 1 wyib, p5; rep from *, end sl 1, k2, sl 1, k1.

Row 7—With B, k1, * sl 1 wyif, p2, sl 1 wyif, k2 tog, k3 tog, pass the k2-tog st over the k3-tog st; rep from *, end sl 1, p2, sl 1, k1.

Row 8—With A, k1, * drop first elongated st off needle to front of work, sl 2 wyib, drop next elongated st off needle to front; with left-hand needle pick up the first elongated st, sl the same 2 sts back to left-hand needle, then pick up the second elongated st onto left-hand needle, k5; rep from *.

Repeat Rows 1–8.

Picot Stripe

These decorative stripes have a lot of texture interest. The cleverly-constructed picot points are nubby, and stand out some-what from the background. This pattern makes excellent borders for collars, cuffs, and pockets, and is very attractive in ski sweaters.

Picot Stripe

Multiple of 10 sts. Colors A and B.

Row 1 (Wrong side)—With A, purl.

Row 2—With B, k2, *(k1, yo, k1, yo, k1, yo, k1) in next st, making seven sts from one; k9; rep from *, end last repeat k7.

Row 3—With B, knit.

Row 4—With A, k1, * k2 tog, k5, ssk, k7; rep from *, end last repeat k6.

Row 5—With A, p6, * p2 tog-b, p1, sl 1 wyif, p1, p2 tog, p7; rep from *, end last repeat p1.

Row 6—With A, k1, * k2 tog, sl 1 wyib, ssk, k7; rep from *, end last repeat k6.

Row 7—With A, purl.

Row 8—With B, k7, * (k1, yo, k1, yo, k1, yo, k1) in next st, k9; rep from *, end last repeat k2.

Row 9—With B, knit.

Row 10—With A, k6, * k2 tog, k5, ssk, k7; rep from *, end last repeat k1.

Row 11—With A, p1, * p2 tog-b, p1, sl 1 wyif, p1, p2 tog, p7; rep from *, end last repeat p6.

Row 12—With A, k6, * k2 tog, sl 1 wyib, ssk, k7; rep from *, end last repeat k1.

Repeat Rows 1–12.

Swallowtail Quilting

Swallowtail Quilting

This fancy design is an amalgam of three patterns. First, there is the simple stripe pattern of Rows 1–6; then there are two different half-drop patterns, one contained by Rows 1–6, 19–23, and 18; the other by Rows 13–17, 24 and 25, 2–5, and 12. Note that in these composite directions Row 1 does not appear again as Row 1 (it is replaced by Row 25), but it does reappear as Row 7.

"Knit the sl-st over" and "knit through the sl-st" are two actions with which the knitter may be unfamiliar, though they are not difficult to perform. To knit the sl-st over, pass the needle-point in front of the required number of skipped stitches (in this case, two), insert it into the front loop of the sl-st, then pass the needle-point back again in front of the same skipped stitches, catch the yarn to the right of the first stitch and knit, taking the sl-st off the left-hand needle but being careful not to let the two skipped stitches come off with it. To knit through the sl-st, insert the needle-point purlwise into the sl-st as if to slip it again, but do not slip it; knit the first stitch beyond it and bring this stitch back through the sl-st and off the left-hand needle, being careful not to let the sl-st come off too. This action can be repeated as many times as necessary—twice, in this pattern.

Multiple of 8 sts plus 1. Colors A and B.

Row 1 (Preparation—wrong side)—With A, k3, * p1, k1, p1, k5; rep from *, end last repeat k3.

Rows 2 and 4—With B, k3, * sl 1 wyib, k1, sl 1 wyib, k5; rep from *, end last repeat k3.

Rows 3 and 5—With B, p3, * sl 1 wyif, p1, sl 1 wyif, p5; rep from *, end last repeat p3.

Row 6—With A, k1, * skip 2 sts, knit Color A sl-st over the 2 skipped sts; k3, skip next Color A sl-st, knit next 2 sts through the sl-st, then knit the sl-st in back loop; k1; rep from *.

Rows 7 through 11—Repeat Rows 1 through 5.

Row 12—With A, k1, * skip 2 sts, knit Color A sl-st over the 2 skipped sts, k2, sl 1 wyib, skip next Color A sl-st, knit next 2 sts through the sl-st, then knit the sl-st in back loop; k1; rep from *.

Row 13—With A, k1, * p1, k2, sl 1 wyif, k2, p1, k1; rep from *.

Rows 14 and 16—With B, k1, * sl 1 wyib, k5, sl 1 wyib, k1; rep from *.

Rows 15 and 17—With B, p1, * sl 1 wyif, p5, sl 1 wyif, p1; rep from *.

Row 18—With A, k1, * skip Color A sl-st, knit next 2 sts through the sl-st, then knit the sl-st in back loop; k1, skip next 2 sts, knit next Color A sl-st over the 2 skipped sts, k3; rep from *.

Row 19—With A, k1, * p1, k5, p1, k1; rep from *.

Rows 20 through 23—Repeat Rows 14 through 17.

Row 24—With A, k1, * skip Color A sl-st, knit next 2 sts through the sl-st, then knit the sl-st in back loop; k1, skip next 2 sts, knit next Color A sl-st over the 2 skipped sts; k2, sl 1 wyib; rep from *, end last repeat k1 instead of sl 1.

Row 25—With A, k3, * p1, k1, p1, k2, sl 1 wyif, k2; rep from *, end p1, k1, p1, k3.

Omitting preparation row, repeat Rows 2–25.

House of Cards

Here is a fascinating pattern incorporating yarn-over stitches, slip-stitches, and contrasting colors. The stitch count varies; on Rows 2, 8, 14, and 20 the yarn-overs form increases; on Rows 6, 12, 18, and 24 the corresponding decreases are made to restore the original number of stitches. Each of these decreases includes a Color A slip-stitch carried from four rows below, and the Color B stitch adjoining it.

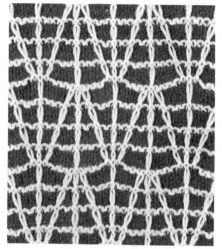

House of Cards

Multiple of 12 sts plus 3. Colors A and B.

NOTE: On right-side (even-numbered) rows, sl all sl-sts with yarn in back; on wrong-side (odd-numbered) rows, sl all sl-sts with yarn in front.

Row 1 (Wrong side)—With A, knit.

Row 2—With B, k1, * sl 1, k4, (sl 1, yo) twice, sl 1, k4; rep from *, end sl 1, k1. (On this row care must be taken to keep the 2 yo's strictly positioned between the 3 sl-sts. The central arrangement will be a double yo in Color B sts divided by a slipped Color A st.)

Row 3—With B, k1, * sl 1, p4, sl 1, purl the 1st yo, sl 1, knit the next yo, sl 1, p4; rep from *, end sl 1, k1. (On this row the same yo sts and sl-sts must be kept in strict order. Be sure the 1st Color A sl-st of the group is slipped onto right-hand needle *before* the following yo is worked. The same caution will apply to Rows 9, 15, and 21.)

Row 4—With B, k1, * sl 1, k4, (sl 1, k1) twice, sl 1, k4; rep from *, end sl 1, k1.

Row 5—With B, k1, * sl 1, p4, (sl 1, p1) twice, sl 1, p4; rep from *, end sl 1, k1.

Row 6—With A, k5, * k2 tog, k3, ssk, k7; rep from *, end last repeat k5.

Row 7—With A, knit.

Row 8—With B, k1, * sl 1, k3, sl 1, yo, k1, sl 1, k1, yo, sl 1, k3; rep from *, end sl 1, k1.

Row 9—With B, k1, * sl 1, p3, sl 1, p2, sl 1, p2, sl 1, p3; rep from *, end sl 1, k1.

Row 10—With B, k1, * sl 1, k3, sl 1, k2, sl 1, k2, sl 1, k3; rep from *, end sl 1, k1.

Row 11—With B, repeat Row 9.

Row 12—With A, k4, * k2 tog, k5, ssk, k5; rep from *, end last repeat k4.

Row 13—With A, knit.

Row 14—With B, k1, * sl 1, k2, sl 1, yo, k2, sl 1, k2, yo, sl 1, k2; rep from *, end sl 1, k1.

Row 15—With B, k1, * sl 1, p2, (sl 1, p3) twice, sl 1, p2; rep from *, end sl 1, k1.

Row 16—With B, k1, * sl 1, k2, (sl 1, k3) twice, sl 1, k2; rep from *, end sl 1, k1.

Row 17—With B, repeat Row 15.

Row 18—With A, k3, * k2 tog, k7, ssk, k3; rep from *.

Row 19—With A, knit.

Row 20—With B, k1, * sl 1, k1, sl 1, yo, k3, sl 1, k3, yo, sl 1, k1; rep from *, end sl 1, k1.

Row 21—With B, k1, * sl 1, p1, (sl 1, p4) twice, sl 1, p1; rep from *, end sl 1, k1.

Row 22—With B, k1, * sl 1, k1, (sl 1, k4) twice, sl 1, k1; rep from *, end sl 1, k1.

Row 23—With B, repeat Row 21.

Row 24—With A, k2, * k2 tog, k9, ssk, k1; rep from *, end k1.

Repeat Rows 1–24.

CHAPTER SIX

Fancy Texture Patterns

More unusual knitting techniques and arrangements of stitches will be found in this chapter than in any other. This is a miscellaneous assortment of patterns that will give various kinds of textured surface to your knitting, using methods that cannot be classified in any standard way because they are all different.

Even the highly experienced knitter will probably find among these patterns some ways of knitting that are unfamiliar. There are increase-and-decrease patterns, drop-stitch patterns, short-row patterns, elongated-stitch patterns, bobble and knot patterns, double-knit patterns, dip-stitch patterns, and others. Taken all together, they demonstrate the truly marvelous variety of things that can be done with knitting—a variety all the more remarkable when one considers the fact that knitting is basically the simplest operation imaginable: that of drawing a loop through another loop. How vast a structure of designs and skills has grown from that simple operation!

Fancy Texture Patterns are applicable, of course, to any and all kinds of knitting. What you do with them is up to you. Some might strike you as attractive patterns for a coat or a suit; some might seem just right for an afghan square; some might be appealing on a yoke for a sweater that you are making; some might serve for decorative panels on your dress, hat, or mittens. Each knitter will find a different set of favorites among these patterns, and use them in different ways. Extend your knitting skills by practicing those patterns that are new to your experience. There are great rewards for the knitter who does this; for she soon becomes mistress of an enormous, fascinating, and infinitely flexible "vocabulary" with which to express her own ideas.

Rambler Pattern

Most experienced knitters can tell at a glance how cable, lace, knit-purl and color patterns are worked; but many of the simple texture patterns are elusive, even to the discerning eye. Here is one of the simplest of these patterns; yet its mechanism may escape you, no matter how expert you are. Try to reproduce it *before* reading the directions!

This fabric is pleasingly fluffy, yet firm, and will not curl. It does spread, so be sure to cast on with an extra-large needle or with two needles held together. Bind off loosely. Use it for scarves, lightweight jackets, sweaters. The wrong side is interesting, too. The first two rows repeated alone will give a subtly ribbed appearance.

Rambler Pattern

Odd number of sts.

Rows 1, 3, 5, and 7 (Wrong side)—K2, * p1, k1; rep from *, end k1.

Rows 2, 4, 6, and 8—K1, * knit next st in the row below, p1; rep from *, end last repeat k1.

Rows 9, 11, 13, and 15—K1, * p1, k1; rep from *.

Rows 10, 12, 14, and 16—K1, p1, * knit next st in the row below, p1; rep from *, end k1.

Repeat Rows 1–16.

Small Quilted Cross-Stitch

Here is a truly charming fabric that is easy to work, firm, sturdy, luxuriously deep in texture, and perfectly flat, without any curl to it at all. It makes wonderful warm coats, suits and jackets which never require blocking and never sag out of shape. The fabric is dense because the pattern "draws in", and so requires a fairly large number of stitches to attain a given width; check gauge. This pattern can be used also for borders, collars, cuffs, patch pockets or pocket edges, and other details. Work it with a good firm yarn and small needles for a beautiful handbag to match your ensemble! Try it also in two colors, using Color A in Rows 1 and 2, Color B in Rows 3 and 4.

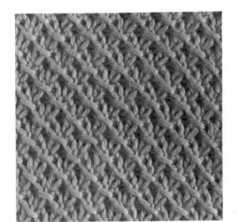

Small Quilted Cross-Stitch

Multiple of 4 sts plus 1.

Rows 1 and 3 (Wrong side)—K1, * p1, k1; rep from *.

Row 2—P1, * sl 1 knitwise wyib, knit into front and back of next st, k1, then pass sl-st over the last 3 sts made; p1; rep from *.

Row 4—P1, k1, p1, rep from * of Row 2; end k1, p1.

Repeat Rows 1–4.

Rosette Stitch

This simple stitch makes a beautiful fabric, very handsome in suits and coats. It is firm, close, and shows an unusual crochet-like surface.

Rosette Stitch

Even number of sts.

Rows 1 and 3 (Right side)—Knit.
Row 2—* P2 tog, leave on needle; knit same 2 sts tog and sl from needle together; rep from *.
Row 4—P1, rep from * of Row 2, end p1.

Repeat Rows 1-4.

Zigzag Ribbon Stitch

A handsome "flat" texture for tailored suits, skirts, cushions, bags, and dresses is made by this charming pattern, which depends upon simple stitch-lines for all its effect. It is interesting when a variegated yarn is used, or when worked in stripes of two or more colors.

Zigzag Ribbon Stitch

Multiple of 10 sts.

NOTES: Lifted Increase (LI): insert right-hand needle into the front of next st *in the row below,* and knit; then knit the st on needle.

Back Lifted Increase (BLI): insert right-hand needle into the back of next st *in the row below* (i. e., from the top down into the purled loop behind the st on needle), and knit; then knit the st on needle in the usual way.

Row 1 (Wrong side) and all other wrong-side rows—Purl.
Row 2—* LI, k2, ssk, k5; rep from *.
Row 4—K1, * LI, k2, ssk, k5; rep from *, end last repeat k4.
Row 6—K2, * LI, k2, ssk, k5; rep from *, end last repeat k3.
Row 8—K3, * LI, k2, ssk, k5; rep from *, end last repeat k2.
Row 10—K4, * LI, k2, ssk, k5; rep from *, end last repeat k1.
Row 12—* K5, LI, k2, ssk; rep from *.
Row 14—* K5, k2 tog, k2, BLI; rep from *.
Row 16—K4, * k2 tog, k2, BLI, k5; rep from *, end last repeat k1.
Row 18—K3, * k2 tog, k2, BLI, k5; rep from *, end last repeat k2.
Row 20—K2, * k2 tog, k2, BLI, k5; rep from *, end last repeat k3.
Row 22—K1, * k2 tog, k2, BLI, k5; rep from *, end last repeat k4.
Row 24—* K2 tog, k2, BLI, k5; rep from *.

Repeat Rows 1-24.

German Herringbone Rib

German Herringbone Rib

Contributed by Hildegard M. Elsner, Aldan, Pennsylvania

Beautiful ribbed and scalloped skirts can be made with this easy pattern, simply by starting at the bottom with 10 or 12 stitches to each purl rib instead of 2, and then decreasing in these purl ribs to narrow toward the waist. Matching sweaters or blouses can be made with the pattern as given.

Multiple of 15 sts plus 2.

Row 1 (Right side)—P2, * Make One (M1) by lifting running thread and knitting into the back of this thread, k3, p2, p3 tog, p2, k3, M1, p2; rep from *.
Row 2—K2, * p4, k5, p4, k2; rep from *.
Row 3—P2, * M1, k4, p1, p3 tog, p1, k4, M1, p2; rep from *.
Row 4—K2, * p5, k3, p5, k2; rep from *.
Row 5—P2, * M1, k5, p3 tog, k5, M1, p2; rep from *.
Row 6—K2, * p6, k1, p6, k2; rep from *.

Repeat Rows 1–6.

Boxed Bobble

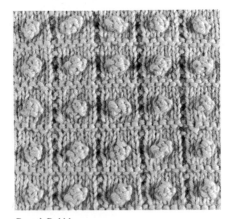

Boxed Bobble

This is a pretty arrangement of small bobbles in a knit-purl fabric of the utmost simplicity. It is a charming pattern for baby things, afghans, and fancy touches on garments such as pockets, panels, cuffs, and borders.

Multiple of 6 sts plus 1.

NOTE: Odd-numbered rows are wrong-side rows.

Rows 1, 2, and 3—Purl.
Row 4—P1, * k5, p1; rep from *.
Rows 5 and 7—Purl.
Row 6—P1, * k2, Make Bobble in next st as follows: knit into front, back, and front of same st; turn and k3, turn and p3, then pass 2nd and 3rd sts separately over the first st on right-hand needle, completing bobble; k2, p1; rep from *.
Row 8—Repeat Row 4.

Repeat Rows 1–8.

Tiny Bowknot

Contributed by Bernice Haedike, Oak Park, Illinois

This is a "little" texture pattern recommended for a beginner, since it is very easy and looks well when done with large needles.

Multiple of 6 sts.

Row 1 (Wrong side)—Purl.
Row 2—Knit.
Row 3—* P3, k3; rep from *.
Row 4—* P1, knit into next st in the row below, p1, k3; rep from *.
Rows 5 and 6—Repeat Rows 1 and 2.
Row 7—* K3, p3; rep from *.
Row 8—* K3, p1, knit into next st in the row below, p1; rep from *.

Repeat Rows 1–8.

Tiny Bowknot

Dot-Knot Stitch

Here is one of those little "hint-of-texture" patterns that relieve a plain stockinette fabric so nicely. It is attractive in almost any kind of yarn, but is not very successful in variegated colors. A plain color, however, points up the little knots quite well.

Multiple of 6 sts plus 1.

Rows 1 and 3 (Wrong side)—Purl.
Row 2—Knit.
Row 4—K3, * insert right-hand needle under running thread between 1st and 2nd sts on left-hand needle, and draw through a loop loosely; then insert right-hand needle between these same sts *above* running thread, and draw through another loop loosely; then bring yarn to front between needles and purl the 1st st on left-hand needle; then with point of left-hand needle pass the first *loop* over the 2nd loop and the purled st, and off needle; then pass the 2nd loop over the purled st and off needle; k5; rep from *, end last repeat k3.
Rows 5 and 7—Purl.
Row 6—Knit.
Row 8—K6, rep from * of Row 4, end k1.

Repeat Rows 1–8.

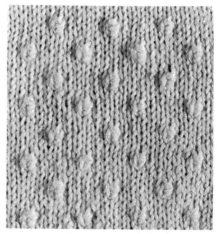

Dot-Knot Stitch

Irish Knot

Irish Knot

The Irish Knot is like a popcorn, except that it is completed all at once on a right-side row, by passing the increased stitches over the last stitch. This pattern gives a pleasing arrangement of Irish Knots within an embossed wave formation, very nice for a sweater or jacket with lots of texture interest.

Multiple of 14 sts plus 5.

Row 1 (Wrong side)—K6, * p2, k1, p1, k1, p2, k7; rep from *, end last repeat k6.

Row 2—P4, * p2 tog, k2, inc purlwise (by purling into the front and back of the next st), k1-b, inc purlwise, k2, p2 tog, p3; rep from *, end p1.

Row 3—K5, * p2, k2, p1, k2, p2, k5; rep from *.

Row 4—P3, * p2 tog, k2, inc purlwise, p1, k1-b, p1, inc purlwise, k2, p2 tog, p1; rep from *, end p2.

Row 5—K4, * p2, k3, p1, k3, p2, k3; rep from *, end k1.

Row 6—P2, k1-b, * p1, k2, p3, Make Knot (MK) as follows: (k1, p1, k1, p1, k1) loosely in next st, then with point of left-hand needle pass the 2nd, 3rd, 4th, and 5th sts on right-hand needle separately over the last st made, completing Knot; p3, k2, p1, k1-b; rep from *, end p2.

Row 7—K2, p1, * k1, p2, k7, p2, k1, p1; rep from *, end k2.

Row 8—P2, k1-b, * inc purlwise, k2, p2 tog, p3, p2 tog, k2, inc purlwise, k1-b; rep from *, end p2.

Row 9—K2, p1, * k2, p2, k5, p2, k2, p1; rep from *, end k2.

Row 10—P2, k1-b, * p1, inc purlwise, k2, p2 tog, p1, p2 tog, k2, inc purlwise, p1, k1-b; rep from *, end p2.

Row 11—K2, p1, * (k3, p2) twice, k3, p1; rep from *, end k2.

Row 12—P2, MK, * p3, k2, p1, k1-b, p1, k2, p3, MK; rep from *, end p2.

Repeat Rows 1–12.

Diagonal Knot Stitch

Diagonal Knot Stitch

This basic pattern can be rearranged in many ways. As given, the diagonals run upward to the left; they can be worked so as to run to the right instead, or arranged in chevrons or zigzags, or made wider by increasing in more than two stitches at a time. This kind of knot also can be worked as a spot-pattern on a stockinette fabric, distributed at regular intervals in clusters of two, three, or more "knot" stitches together. After learning how to make the basic knot, try several different arrangements of it for different effects.

Multiple of 6 sts.

NOTE: Increase (inc) as follows: (p1, k1, p1) into one stitch, making 3 sts from one. "(Inc) twice" means to increase thus in *each* of the next two sts, which results in a total of 6 sts.

Row 1 (Right side)—* (Inc) twice, k4; rep from *.
Row 2—* P4, (p3 tog) twice; rep from *.
Row 3—K1, * (inc) twice, k4; rep from *, end last repeat k3.
Row 4—P3, * (p3 tog) twice, p4; rep from *, end last repeat p1.
Row 5—K2, * (inc) twice, k4; rep from *, end last repeat k2.
Row 6—P2, * (p3 tog) twice, p4; rep from *, end last repeat p2.
Row 7—K3, * (inc) twice, k4; rep from *, end last repeat k1.
Row 8—P1, * (p3 tog) twice, p4; rep from *, end last repeat p3.
Row 9—* K4, (inc) twice; rep from *.
Row 10—* (P3 tog) twice, p4; rep from *.
Row 11—Inc, * k4, (inc) twice; rep from *, end k4, inc.
Row 12—P3 tog, * p4, (p3 tog) twice; rep from *, end p4, p3 tog.

Repeat Rows 1–12.

Diagonal Scallop Stitch

Here is a lovely, quick-knitting "little" texture pattern that is ideal for converting that dull stockinette sweater, dress, or coat into an interesting garment. It makes a nice firm fabric with hardly any curl to it, and so is easy to block. Naturally, because the passed-over strands pull the stitches together, the fabric is tighter than stockinette stitch and will require more stitches for any given measurement. Check your gauge, adjust the number of stitches accordingly, and then knit something really pretty, patterned all over with these attractive little diagonals.

Multiple of 4 sts plus 2.

Rows 1 and 3 (Wrong side)—Purl.
Row 2—K1, *insert needle from behind under the running thread between the st just worked and the next st, thus putting an extra strand on the needle; k2, then pass the extra strand over the 2 knit sts; k2; rep from *, end k1.
Row 4—K3, rep from * of Row 2; end last repeat k1 instead of k2.

Diagonal Scallop Stitch

Repeat Rows 1–4.

Three "Increase" Textures: Lambs' Tails, Clamshell, and Tear Drop

All three of these patterns are made by increasing, one way or another, in a single stitch. Therefore each of the three can be used in almost any kind of position, relative to the rest of the knitting. Here, all three are given as spot-patterns for the sake of simplicity.

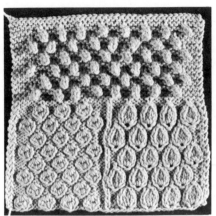

ABOVE: *Lambs' Tails*
BELOW, LEFT: *Clamshell*
BELOW, RIGHT: *Tear Drop*

I. LAMBS' TAILS

This is a highly original texture pattern consisting of small chains of knitted-on and bound-off stitches projecting from the fabric and hanging downward. As a spot-pattern in this demonstration, the little "tails" are scattered all over a garter-stitch background. But a Lamb's Tail can be worked into any single stitch, anywhere. A single row of them might decorate the edge of a collar or a sleeve; several rows could serve as a border at the bottom of a sweater, jacket, or coat. A longer "tail", made by casting on and binding off more stitches, can be used as a belt-carrier when tacked down at the lower end. The background need not be garter stitch; it can be anything. But it is a good idea always to purl into the stitch at the top of each "tail" on the return row.

As an allover pattern, Lambs' Tails is appropriate for hairy, nubby or tweedy yarns, when a very shaggy effect is desired. When used on a background of ribbing, it makes delightful "pullover" ski caps. Try it in stripes of different colors!

Multiple of 4 sts plus 1.

Rows 1 and 2—Knit.
Row 3 (Right side)—* K3, cast on 4 and bind off 4 in next st as follows: knit the st, place new loop on left-hand needle beside the original st; then knit the new loop and place next new loop on left-hand needle; repeat until there are 4 new loops on left-hand needle beside the original st. Then bind off 4 in the usual way, i.e., k2, pass first st over second, knit next st, pass second st over it, and so on until 4 sts have been bound off, the last one being passed over the original st, which is now on right-hand needle. Rep from *, end k1.
Row 4—K1, * p1, k3; rep from *.
Rows 5 and 6—Knit.
Row 7—K1, * cast on 4 and bind off 4 in next st, k3; rep from *.
Row 8—* K3, p1; rep from *, end k1.

Repeat Rows 1–8.

II. CLAMSHELL

Multiple of 4 sts plus 1.

Row 1 (Wrong side)—K2, * (p1, yo, p1, yo, p1) in next st, k3; rep from *, end last repeat k2.
Row 2—P2, * k5, p3; rep from *, end last repeat p2.
Row 3—K2, * p5, k3; rep from *, end last repeat k2.
Row 4—P2, * k5 tog-b, p3; rep from *, end last repeat p2.
Row 5—K4, * (p1, yo, p1, yo, p1) in next st, k3; rep from *, end k1.
Row 6—P4, * k5, p3; rep from *, end p1.
Row 7—K4, * p5, k3; rep from *, end k1.
Row 8—P4, * k5 tog-b, p3; rep from *, end p1.

Repeat Rows 1–8.

III. TEAR DROP

Contributed by Janida R. Bultman, Milwaukee, Wisconsin

Multiple of 4 sts plus 1.

NOTE: To bind off this pattern, end with Row 6 or Row 12, omitting the increases.

Preparation Row (Right side)—P1, * (k1, p1, k1, p1, k1) in next st, p3; rep from *.
Rows 1 and 3—* K3, p5; rep from *, end k1.
Row 2—P1, * k5, p3; rep from *.
Row 4—P1, * ssk, k1, k2 tog, p3; rep from *.
Row 5—* K3, p3; rep from *, end k1.
Row 6—P1, * sl 1—k2 tog—psso, p1, (k1, p1, k1, p1, k1) in next st, p1; rep from *.
Rows 7 and 9—K1, * p5, k3; rep from *.
Row 8—* P3, k5; rep from *, end p1.
Row 10—* P3, ssk, k1, k2 tog; rep from *, end p1.
Row 11—K1, * p3, k3; rep from *.
Row 12—P1, * (k1, p1, k1, p1, k1) in next st, p1, sl 1—k2 tog—psso, p1; rep from *.

Repeat Rows 1–12.

Two Drop-Stitch Patterns: Drop-Stitch Honeycomb and Parenthetical Rib

Patterns of this kind tend to scare the novice knitter, who often labors under an impression that a dropped stitch is a catastrophe. But a little practice with these patterns will demonstrate that it is a legitimate knitting technique that can be fun to use.

The usual fear is that the dropped stitch will unravel too far. Actually it is much less prone to do this than the beginner might think; but if it does, it is an easy matter to retrieve the stitch with a crochet hook or with the needles. Don't unravel by pulling the fabric apart laterally. Instead, use the right-hand needle point to pluck each strand out of the stitch above it.

Drop-stitches can be made on either side of the fabric, and can be either knitted or purled. These two patterns illustrate each case. Drop-Stitch Honeycomb is an interesting purl fabric, the knit side of which shows a variation of the classic Blister Check (*A Treasury of Knitting Patterns*, p. 69). Parenthetical Rib also has a very beautiful "wrong" side, which may appeal to the knitter so much that she is unable to decide which side to use. This dilemma can be solved by using Parenthetical Rib for a scarf, stole, or reversible sweater, so that both sides can be shown.

ABOVE: *Drop-Stitch Honeycomb*
BELOW: *Parenthetical Rib*

I. DROP-STITCH HONEYCOMB

Cast on a multiple of 4 sts plus 3, and purl one row.

Rows 1, 3, and 5 (Wrong side)—Knit.
Rows 2 and 4—Purl.
Row 6—P3, * drop next st off needle and unravel 5 rows down; then insert right-hand needle into the st from behind, lift the st and the 5 loose strands above it onto left-hand needle, and purl the st and the 5 loose strands all together; p3; rep from *.
Rows 7, 9, and 11—Knit.
Rows 8 and 10—Purl.
Row 12—P1, rep from * of Row 6; end last repeat p1 instead of p3.

Repeat Rows 1–12.

II. PARENTHETICAL RIB

Multiple of 12 sts plus 1.

Row 1 (Preparation row, right side)—P3, * k1-b, p5; rep from *, end k1-b, p3.
Row 2 (Preparation row)—K2, * p3, k4, p1, k4; rep from *, end last repeat k3.

End of preparation rows.

Rows 3, 5, and 7—* P3, k1-b, p3, k5; rep from *, end p1.
Rows 4 and 6—K1, * p5, k3, p1, k3; rep from *.
Row 8—K1, * p2, drop next st off needle and unravel 5 rows down; then insert needle into st from front and knit the st, catching the 5 loose strands behind the st as it is knitted; p2, k2, p3, k2; rep from *.
Rows 9, 11, and 13—P1, * k5, p3, k1-b, p3; rep from *.
Rows 10 and 12—* K3, p1, k3, p5; rep from *, end k1.
Row 14—* K2, p3, k2, p2, drop next st off needle, unravel 5 rows down, pick up and knit the st and the 5 strands as before; p2; rep from *, end k1.

Omitting preparation rows, repeat Rows 3–14.

Cocoon Stitch

A truly fascinating texture is presented by this increase-and-decrease pattern. Small purled "cocoons" are nested among waving knit ribs to make a beautifully bumpy fabric for your most interesting sweaters. The pattern knits up rapidly and requires little or no blocking.

Cocoon Stitch

Multiple of 8 sts plus 1.

Row 1 (Wrong side)—P1, * k1, p1, k5, p1; rep from *.
Row 2—K1, * p5, k1, p1, k1; rep from *.
Row 3—P1, * k1 under running thread between the st just worked and the next st, (k1, p1, k1) in next st, k1 under next running thread, p1, p5 tog, p1; rep from *.
Rows 4, 6, and 8—K1, * p1, k1, p5, k1; rep from *.
Rows 5 and 7—P1, * k5, p1, k1, p1; rep from *.
Row 9—P1, * p5 tog, p1, k1 under running thread, (k1, p1, k1) in next st, k1 under next running thread, p1; rep from *.
Rows 10, 11, and 12—Repeat Row 2, Row 1, and Row 2 again.

Repeat Rows 1–12.

Anemone Stitch

This beautiful stitch is ideal for afghan squares and cushions, as well as for garments. It looks very effective in two colors; simply work Rows 1 and 2 in one color, Rows 3 and 4 in the other. In the single-color version, the wrong side is also quite attractive.

Bind off on the wrong side, purling all sts. Or, if a right-side bind-off row is wanted, work one plain purl row and then bind off.

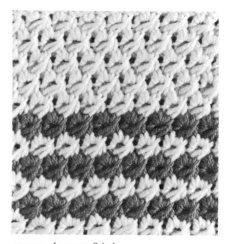

ABOVE: *Anemone Stitch*
BELOW: *Anemone Stitch in two colors*

Multiple of 4 sts.

Row 1 (Wrong side)—Purl, wrapping yarn twice for each st.
Row 2—* Sl 4 sts briefly in order to drop extra wraps, replace the 4 elongated sts on left-hand needle, then (k4 tog, p4 tog) twice into these same 4 sts; rep from *.
Row 3—P2, purl across wrapping yarn twice for each st, to the last 2 sts, end p2.
Row 4—K2, rep from * of Row 2 across to the last 2 sts, end k2.

Repeat Rows 1–4.

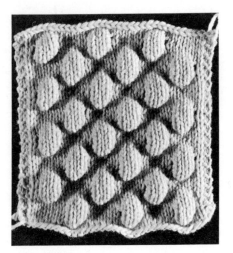

Bubble-Bobble

Bubble-Bobble

Contributed by Hildegard M. Elsner, Aldan, Pennsylvania

There are many ways of varying this unusual pattern, which comes from Czechoslovakia. Either the background stitches or the bobble stitches can be purled, instead of knitted, on the right side for texture contrast. The number of stitches to a repeat and the number of rows to the pattern can be changed to suit any proportions. The turning rows can be worked only twice, or can be worked 4 times or more to make the bobbles smaller or larger as desired. The sides of the bobbles are open, and so may be threaded with a contrasting ribbon that will run behind each bobble. With a double or single row of "Bubble-Bobbles" this can make an interesting border.

Multiple of 10 sts plus 2.

Rows 1 and 3 (Wrong side)—Purl.
Row 2—Knit.
Row 4—K1, * (k5, turn, p5, turn) 3 times, k10; rep from *, end k1.
Rows 5, 6, and 7—Repeat Rows 1, 2, and 3.
Row 8—K6, rep from * of Row 4; end last repeat k6 instead of k10.

Repeat Rows 1–8.

Dragonfly Check Pattern

In some cases, depending on the elasticity of the yarn and the individual technique of the knitter, the crochet hook may be dispensed with in working this pattern. Instead, the right-hand needle point can be taken *back* to the central decreased stitch to draw through the second loop in Rows 8 and 16. But if this is awkward to do or stretches the fabric too much, the crochet hook is recommended.

Multiple of 6 sts plus 3.

Rows 1, 3, and 5 (Wrong side)—K3, * p3, k3; rep from *.
Rows 2 and 4—P3, * k3, p3; rep from *.
Row 6—P3, * sl 2 knitwise—k1—p2sso, p3; rep from *. (The 3 sts brought together in this row—*not* the single st above them—make the "central decreased" st.)
Row 7—K3, * p1, k3; rep from *.

Dragonfly Check Pattern

Row 8—P2, * insert right-hand needle from the front into the central decreased st from Row 6 and draw through a loose loop onto right-hand needle; p3, insert a crochet hook into the front of same central decreased st, draw through a second loose loop, sl this loop onto right-hand needle; p1; rep from *, end p1.

Rows 9, 11, and 13—P3, * k3, p3; rep from *.

Rows 10 and 12—K3, * p3, k3; rep from *.

Row 14—K1, ssk, * p3, sl 2 knitwise—k1—p2sso; rep from *, end p3, k2 tog, k1.

Row 15—P2, * k3, p1; rep from *, end p1.

Row 16—P3, with crochet hook draw through a loop from the "ssk" st in Row 14 and sl this loop onto right-hand needle, p1, rep from * of Row 8 across to last 3 sts, with right-hand needle draw through a loop from the "k2 tog" st in Row 14, p3.

Repeat Rows 1–16.

Double Stockinette, or Miniature Herringbone

This is one of the "super-dense" fabrics. It has to be worked with needles that are fairly large, in proportion to the weight of the yarn. Even with large needles, the stitches will compress to a very small size. At first the technique may seem difficult, necessitating an extra push with an extra finger to get the first loop off the needle without allowing the second loop to follow. But this pattern is well worth taking a little trouble to learn. It makes a beautiful fabric that is luxuriously thick and cosy, perfect for extra-warm mittens, sturdy cushions, potholders, and comfortable, long-wearing slippers. Try it, too, in two colors. This is especially effective when the two colors are close together in shade, such as cream with fawn, rose with pink, blue with aqua, gold with rust, etc.

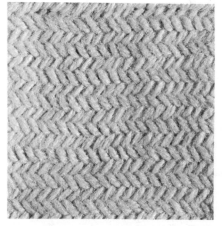

Double Stockinette, or Miniature Herringbone

Any number of sts.

Row 1 (Right side)—* K2 tog-b, but slip only the *first* of the two sts off needle; rep from *, knitting each second st together with the following st, until only one loop remains on the left-hand needle; end k1.

Row 2—* P2 tog, but slip only the *first* of the two sts off needle; rep from *, purling each second st together with the following st, until only one loop remains on the left-hand needle; end p1.

Repeat Rows 1 and 2.

Contributed by Bernice Haedike, Oak Park, Illinois

A very strong, thick fabric with all surface strands running upward from left to right (i.e., without the "herringbone" effect) is created by working "k2 tog" instead of "k2 tog-b" in Row 1. Worked in this way, the pattern resembles a heavy tapestry stitch such as petit point, gobelin or cross stitch. All pattern operations remain the same except that the right-side stitches are worked together in the front loops instead of the back loops.

Double Garter Stitch, or Back Stitch

Double Garter Stitch, or Back Stitch

Sometimes this fascinating pattern is called Double Knitting. The directions always say, "knit second loop of first stitch and first loop of next stitch together", which can easily confuse a newcomer to the pattern because it is hard to distinguish between the first and second loops. Either loop of each double-wrapped stitch can be presented first on the needle. So, to tell them apart, look at the double-wrapped stitch as you hold the work, and notice that it consists of one strand that runs down to the row below, and one strand that passes under the needle and up behind it. It is the *first* of these that is considered the "first loop". Thus, in working, catch the strand that communicates with the preceding row, and leave the loose strand on the needle to be knitted together with the next stitch. The "first loop" of the first stitch of each row is knitted plain; the last stitch of each row is knitted with a double wrap and both loops are taken off the needle.

Unlike Double Stockinette, this fabric is quite loose and elastic. It makes very beautiful scarves, baby blankets, afghans and throws. It is a one-row pattern, the Preparation Row not being repeated. To bind off, work the last row as usual but *without* the double wraps, then bind off the stitches loosely. The fabric is the same on both sides.

Any number of sts.

Preparation Row—Knit, wrapping yarn twice for each st.
Pattern Row—Knit first loop of first st only, leaving second loop on needle; * knit this second loop tog with first loop of next st, *wrapping yarn twice* and leaving second loop on needle; rep from *.

Repeat Pattern Row only.

Cording Stitch

This pattern makes firm, round, horizontal cords across the width of the fabric. The size of the cords can be varied, of course, depending on how many rows down the stitches are taken. This pattern is not suitable for vertical combination with other stitch patterns in the same piece, because the cords will pull the knitting up considerably, and cause puckering if there should be plain un-corded stitches alongside. It adapts nicely, however, to separate-piece accents such as patch pockets, button bands, cuffs, collars, and cushion covers. The cords may be worked in a contrasting color, allowing 4 rows of color for each cord in the pattern as given.

Any number of sts.

Rows 1, 3, 5, and 7 (Right side)—Knit.

Rows 2, 4, and 6—K1, purl across to last st, end k1.

Row 8 (Cording row)—K1, * with yarn in front, insert needle from the top down into the head of the purl st 4 rows below the next st on needle; pick up this loop, place it on left-hand needle and purl it together with next st; rep from * on every st across row to last st, end k1.

Repeat Rows 1–8.

Cording Stitch

Pillar and Web

This is a novelty pattern that has something of the quality of an openwork Ladder, except that there is no openwork involved in its making. Both sides of the fabric are very attractive, so the choice of sides is up to the knitter; here, the purl side is shown. In fine yarn this fabric makes a very pretty and unusual shell, stocking, or summer stole.

Multiple of 6 sts plus 2.

NOTE: 2 needle sizes are used—one needle 4 sizes larger than the other.

Row 1 (Wrong side)—With large needle, knit.

Row 2—With small needle, k1, * (skip 3 sts and purl the 4th st, drawing it off needle *over* the 3 skipped sts) 3 times, then purl the 3 skipped sts; rep from *, end k1.

Repeat Rows 1 and 2.

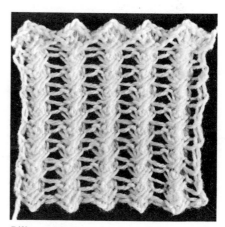

Pillar and Web

CENTER PANEL: *Ringlet Stitch Diamond*
SIDE PANELS: *Ringlet Stitch (vertical)*

Ringlet Stitch

A plain vertical Ringlet Stitch requires only two rows, as follows:

Even number of sts.

Row 1 (Wrong side)—Purl.
Row 2—K1, * Make Ringlet (MR) as follows on the next 2 sts: p2, then keeping yarn in front sl these 2 sts back to left-hand needle; take yarn around (passing in front of the 2 sts) to back, sl the sts back to right-hand needle; rep from *, end k1.

Repeat Rows 1 and 2.

VARIATION: *RINGLET STITCH DIAMOND*

It is easy to make Ringlet Stitch on the diagonal by adding 2 more rows, the 3rd row plain purl and the 4th row as Row 2, above, but beginning and ending with "k2". Other patterns can be worked in Ringlet Stitch against stockinette—bands, square checks, diagonal ribs, etc.

Panel of 14 sts.

Row 1 (Wrong side) and all other wrong-side rows—Purl.
Row 2—Knit.
Row 4—K6, MR on next 2 sts, k6.
Row 6—K5, (MR) twice on next 4 sts, k5.
Row 8—K4, (MR) 3 times on next 6 sts, k4.
Row 10—K3, (MR) 4 times on next 8 sts, k3.
Row 12—K2, (MR) 5 times on next 10 sts, k2.
Rows 14, 16, 18, and 20—Repeat Rows 10, 8, 6, and 4.

Repeat Rows 1–20.

Dragon Skin

Dragon Skin

Here is a fascinating variation on the many types of herringbone knitting, with more texture interest than most of the others. The shapes resemble overlapping scales, formed of very graceful curves and overlaid by straight ribs.

Multiple of 26 sts.

Row 1 (Wrong side) and all other wrong-side rows—Purl.
Row 2—* K1, Make One (M1) by lifting running thread and knitting into the back of this thread; ssk, k4, k2 tog, k3, M1, k2, M1, k3, ssk, k4, k2 tog, M1, k1; rep from *.

Row 4—* K1, M1, k1, ssk, k2, k2 tog, k4, M1, k2, M1, k4, ssk, k2, k2 tog, k1, M1, k1; rep from *.
Row 6—* K1, M1, k2, ssk, k2 tog, k5, M1, k2, M1, k5, ssk, k2 tog, k2, M1, k1; rep from *.
Row 8—* K1, M1, k3, ssk, k4, k2 tog, M1, k2, M1, ssk, k4, k2 tog, k3, M1, k1; rep from *.
Row 10—* K1, M1, k4, ssk, k2, k2 tog, k1, M1, k2, M1, k1, ssk, k2, k2 tog, k4, M1, k1; rep from *.
Row 12—* K1, M1, k5, ssk, k2 tog, k2, (M1, k2) twice, ssk, k2 tog, k5, M1, k1; rep from *.

Repeat Rows 1–12.

Hornets' Nest

The original stitch multiple given with this pattern doesn't last long—in fact it pertains only to the first preparation row. It may be restored before binding off, by omitting the last "Make 11" and "p3 tog" in the pattern rows, and decreasing the "nest" motifs that are already established.

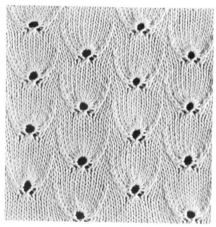

Hornets' Nest

Multiple of 20 sts plus 3.

NOTE: Make 11 as follows: *in the same stitch* (k1, yo) 5 times, and knit one more.

PREPARATION ROWS

Row 1 (Right side)—Knit.
Row 2—P15, * p3 tog, p17; rep from *, end last repeat p5.
Row 3—K5, * Make 11, k17; rep from *, end last repeat k15.
Row 4—Purl.
Row 5—K4, * k2 tog, k9, ssk, k15; rep from *, end last repeat k14.

End of Preparation Rows.

Row 6—Purl.
Row 7—K3, * k2 tog, k9, ssk, k13; rep from *.
Row 8—P5, * p3 tog, p21; rep from *, end last repeat p19.
Row 9—K2, * k2 tog, k9, ssk, k4, Make 11, k4; rep from *, end k1.
Rows 10 and 12—Purl.
Row 11—K1, * k2 tog, k9, ssk, k2; rep from *, end k2.
Row 13—* K13, k2 tog, k9, ssk; rep from *, end k3.
Row 14—P19, * p3 tog, p21; rep from *, end last repeat p5.
Row 15—K5, * Make 11, k4, k2 tog, k9, ssk, k4; rep from *, end last repeat k2.
Row 16—Purl.
Row 17—K4, * k2 tog, k9, ssk, k2; rep from *, end last repeat k1.

Omitting Preparation Rows, repeat Rows 6–17.

Wheat Sheaves

Wheat Sheaves

Here is a very old and very beautiful texture pattern that lends itself to any type of knitted garment, and any type of yarn. The directions appear complicated at first glance, but they are the repetitive sort that can be learned immediately, once the principle of the pattern is grasped. The "give" of the diamonds and the "take" of the ribs are developed by increasing in the former and clustering in the latter.

Multiple of 15 sts plus 14.

Row 1 (Right side)—(P2, k2) 3 times, p2, * Make One (M1) by lifting the running thread and knitting a stitch into the back of it, p1, M1, p2, (k2, p2) 3 times; rep from *.

Row 2—(K2, p2) 3 times, k2, * p1, k1, p1, k2, (p2, k2) 3 times; rep from *.

Row 3—(P2, k2) 3 times, p2, * M1, p1, k1, p1, M1, p2, (k2, p2) 3 times; rep from *.

Row 4—(K2, p2) 3 times, k2, * (p1, k1) twice, p1, k2, (p2, k2) 3 times; rep from *.

Row 5—(P2, k2) 3 times, p2, * M1, (p1, k1) twice, p1, M1, p2, (k2, p2) 3 times; rep from *.

Row 6—(K2, p2) 3 times, k2, * (p1, k1) 3 times, p1, k2, (p2, k2) 3 times; rep from *.

Row 7—(P2, k2) 3 times, p2, * M1, (p1, k1) 3 times, p1, M1, p2, (k2, p2) 3 times; rep from *.

Row 8—(K2, p2) 3 times, k2, * (p1, k1) 4 times, p1, k2, (p2, k2) 3 times; rep from *.

Row 9—(P2, k2) 3 times, p2, * M1, (p1, k1) 4 times, p1, M1, p2, (k2, p2) 3 times; rep from *.

Row 10—* K1, inc in next st, sl 10 wyib, pass the first of the 10 slipped sts over the other 9 sts; k2, (p1, k1) 5 times, p1; rep from *, end k1, inc in next st, sl 10, pass 1st sl-st over the other 9, k2.

Row 11—(P2, k2) 3 times, p2, * ssk, (p1, k1) 3 times, p1, k2 tog, p2, (k2, p2) 3 times; rep from *.

Row 12—(K2, p2) 3 times, k2, * (p1, k1) 4 times, p1, k2, (p2, k2) 3 times; rep from *.

Row 13—(P2, k2) 3 times, p2, * ssk, (p1, k1) twice, p1, k2 tog, p2, (k2, p2) 3 times; rep from *.

Row 14—(K2, p2) 3 times, k2, * (p1, k1) 3 times, p1, k2, (p2, k2) 3 times; rep from *.

Row 15—(P2, k2) 3 times, p2, * ssk, p1, k1, p1, k2 tog, p2, (k2, p2) 3 times; rep from *.

Row 16—(K2, p2) 3 times, k2, * (p1, k1) twice, p1, k2, (p2, k2) 3 times; rep from *.

Row 17—(P2, k2) 3 times, p2, * ssk, p1, k2 tog, p2, (k2, p2) 3 times; rep from *.

Row 18—(K2, p2) 3 times, k2, * p1, k1, p1, k2, (p2, k2) 3 times; rep from *.

Row 19—(P2, k2) 3 times, p2, * sl 1—k2 tog—psso, p2, (k2, p2) 3 times; rep from *.

Row 20—(K2, p2) 3 times, k2, * p1, k2, (p2, k2) 3 times; rep from *.

Repeat Rows 1–20.

Dura-Europos Patterns

Contributed by Virginia S. Gifford, Washington, D.C.

These two patterns come from the oldest known piece of knitting in existence. The city of Dura-Europos, on the bank of the Euphrates River in Syria, was founded in 300 B.C. and fell in 256 A.D. Archaeological explorations of this city by Yale University and the French Government uncovered samples of textiles made in the period between these two dates, among them a large fragment of undyed tan wool knitted in these patterns.

Tightly twisted stockinette stitch, made by knitting and purling into the backs of the stitches, is characteristic of the earliest knitting. It gives the authentic touch to the patterns, although they can be worked in plain knit and purl stitches also. Alternatively, the stitches may be "crossed" by working into the back loops on right-side rows only.

Knitter, let your hands reach back twenty centuries into the past and touch the hands of your unknown cultural ancestor who made that ancient fragment—never dreaming that he or she was making it for you!

NOTES: Increase (inc)—knit into the *back* of the st in the row below the next st on left-hand needle (inserting right-hand needle from the top down into the purled head of the st below the needle), then knit into the back of the st on left-hand needle.

Purl increase (purl inc)—purl into the front and back of the same stitch.

CENTER PANEL: *Dura-Europos Pattern I*
SIDE PANELS: *Dura-Europos Pattern II*

DURA-EUROPOS PATTERN I

Panel of 17 sts.

Row 1 (Right side)—P6, k5-b, p6.

Row 2—K6, p5-b, k6.

Row 3—P4, p2 tog, k1-b, inc, p1, inc, k1-b, p2 tog, p4.

Row 4—K5, (p1-b, k1) 3 times, p1-b, k5.

Row 5—P3, p2 tog, k1-b, (p1, inc) twice, p1, k1-b, p2 tog, p3.

Row 6—K4, p1-b, k1, (p2-b, k1) twice, p1-b, k4.

Row 7—P2, p2 tog, k1-b, p1, k1-b, inc, p1, inc, k1-b, p1, k1-b, p2 tog, p2.

Row 8—K3, (p1-b, k1) 5 times, p1-b, k3.

Row 9—P1, p2 tog, (k1-b, p1) twice, inc, p1, inc, (p1, k1-b) twice, p2 tog, p1.

Row 10—K2, (p1-b, k1) twice, p2-b, k1, p2-b, (k1, p1-b) twice, k2.

Row 11—P2 tog, (k1-b, p1) twice, k1-b, inc, p1, inc, k1-b, (p1, k1-b) twice, p2 tog.

Rows 12 and 14—K1, * p1-b, k1; rep from *.

Row 13—P1, * k1-b, p1; rep from *.

Row 15—Purl inc, (k1-b, p1) twice, k2 tog-b, k1-b, p1, k1-b, k2 tog, (p1, k1-b) twice, purl inc.

Rows 16, 18, 20, and 22—Repeat Rows 10, 8, 6, and 4.

FANCY TEXTURE PATTERNS 139

Row 17—P1, purl inc, (k1-b, p1) twice, k2 tog-b, p1, k2 tog, (p1, k1-b) twice, purl inc, p1.

Row 19—P2, purl inc, k1-b, p1, k2 tog-b, k1-b, p1, k1-b, k2 tog, p1, k1-b, purl inc, p2.

Row 21—P3, purl inc, k1-b, p1, k2 tog-b, p1, k2 tog, p1, k1-b, purl inc, p3.

Row 23—P4, purl inc, k1-b, k2 tog, k1-b, k2 tog-b, k1-b, purl inc, p4.

Row 24—Repeat Row 2.

Repeat Rows 1–24.

DURA-EUROPOS PATTERN II

Panel of 15 sts.

Rows 1 and 3 (Right side)—P1, purl inc, k3-b, k2 tog, k1-b, k2 tog-b, k3-b, purl inc, p1.

Row 2—K2, p11-b, k2.

Row 4—K1, p1-b, k1, p9-b, k1, p1-b, k1.

Row 5—P1, inc, p1, k2-b, k2 tog, k1-b, k2 tog-b, k2-b, p1, inc, p1.

Row 6—K1, p2-b, k1, p7-b, k1, p2-b, k1.

Row 7—P1, inc, k1-b, p1, k1-b, k2 tog, k1-b, k2 tog-b, k1-b, p1, k1-b, inc, p1.

Row 8—K1, p3-b, k1, p5-b, k1, p3-b, k1.

Row 9—P1, inc, k2-b, p1, k2 tog, k1-b, k2 tog-b, p1, k2-b, inc, p1.

Row 10—K1, p4-b, k1, p3-b, k1, p4-b, k1.

Repeat Rows 1–10.

Flower Garden

Flower Garden

Mary, Mary couldn't possibly be contrary, with a garden of these pretty posies blooming all over her sweater, or in a single horizontal band around the border of her skirt. Or, she could use a single flower motif in a vertical panel treatment, with a panel of 13 stitches—6 purl stitches each side of the flower. Although the motif requires 12 rows for completion, each flower, like a bobble, is made out of just one stitch.

Multiple of 12 sts plus 1.

Rows 1, 3, and 5 (Right side)—P12, * k1-b, p11; rep from *, end p1.

Rows 2, 4, 6, and 8—K12, * p1-b, k11; rep from *, end k1.

Row 7—P8, * insert a crochet hook (or point of right-hand needle) from front through the fabric at *right* of the twisted knit st in first row, catch yarn and draw through a long, loose loop; sl this loop onto right-hand needle, knit next st and pass the loop over st; p3, k1-b, p3, draw through another loop from *left* of same st in first row, sl the loop onto right-hand needle, knit next st and pass loop over it; p3; rep from *, end p5.

Row 9—P12, * (k1, yo) 3 times and k1, all in the same st, making 7 sts from one; p11; rep from *, end p1.

Row 10—K12, * p7, k11; rep from *, end k1.

Row 11—P12, * k2 tog-b, k3 tog-b, k2 tog, p11; rep from *, end p1.

Row 12—K12, * p3 tog, k11; rep from *, end k1.

Rows 13, 15, and 17—P6, * k1-b, p11; rep from *, end last repeat p6.

Rows 14, 16, 18, and 20—K6, * p1-b, k11; rep from *, end last repeat k6.

Row 19—P2, * draw through a long loop from *right* of twisted knit st in Row 13 and pass loop over next st as before; p3, k1-b, p3, draw through another loop from *left* of same st and pass loop over next st as before; p3; rep from *, end last repeat p2.

Row 21—P6, * make 7 sts from one as before, p11; rep from *, end last repeat p6.

Row 22—K6, * p7, k11; rep from *, end last repeat k6.

Row 23—P6, * k2 tog-b, k3 tog-b, k2 tog, p11; rep from *, end last repeat p6.

Row 24—K6, * p3 tog, k11; rep from *, end last repeat k6.

Repeat Rows 1–24.

Medallion with Cherries

Multiple of 18 sts plus 5. (41 sts minimum for pattern)

NOTE: In this pattern Make One (M1) as follows: insert needle from behind under the running thread between the st just worked and the next st, and *purl* this thread.

Row 1 (Right side)—K2, p1, * M1, k2-b, p2 tog, p1, (k1-b, p2) twice, k1-b, p1, p2 tog, k2-b, M1, p1; rep from *, end k2.

Row 2—K4, * p2, (k2, p1) 3 times, k2, p2, k3; rep from *, end k1.

Row 3—K2, p2, * M1, k2-b, p2, ssk, p1, k1-b, p1, k2 tog, p2, k2-b, M1, p3; rep from *, end last repeat p2, k2 instead of p3.

Row 4—K5, * p2, k2, (p1, k1) twice, p1, k2, p2, k5; rep from *.

Row 5—K2, (k1, yo, k1, yo, k1) in next st, * p2, M1, k2-b, p2, ssk, k1-b, k2 tog, p2, k2-b, M1, p2, (k1, yo, k1, yo, k1) in next st; rep from *, end k2.

Row 6—K2, p5, * k3, p2, k2, p3, k2, p2, k3, p5; rep from *, end k2.

Row 7—K7, * p3, M1, k2-b, p2, sl 1—k2 tog—psso, p2, k2-b, M1, p3, k5; rep from *, end k2.

Row 8—K2, p5, * k4, p2, k2, p1, k2, p2, k4, p5; rep from *, end k2.

Row 9—K2, ssk, k1, k2 tog, * p2, (k1, yo, k1, yo, k1) in next st, p1, M1, k2-b, p2 tog, k1-b, p2 tog, k2-b, M1, p1, (k1, yo, k1, yo, k1) in next st, p2, ssk, k1, k2 tog; rep from *, end k2.

Medallion with Cherries

Row 10—K2, p3 tog, * k2, p5, k2, p2, k1, p1, k1, p2, k2, p5, k2, p3 tog; rep from *, end k2.

Row 11—K2, k1-b, * p2, k5, p2, M1, k2-b, p3 tog, k2-b, M1, p2, k5, p2, k1-b; rep from *, end k2.

Row 12—K2, p1, * k2, p5, k3, p2, k1, p2, k3, p5, k2, p1; rep from *, end k2.

Row 13—K2, k1-b, * p2, ssk, k1, k2 tog, p3, k2-b, p1, k2-b, p3, ssk, k1, k2 tog, p2, k1-b; rep from *, end k2.

Row 14—K2, p1, * k2, p3 tog, k3, p2, k1, p2, k3, p3 tog, k2, p1; rep from *, end k2.

Row 15—K2, k1-b, * p2, k1-b, p1, p2 tog, k2-b, M1, p1, M1, k2-b, p2 tog, p1, k1-b, p2, k1-b; rep from *, end k2.

Row 16—K2, p1, * k2, p1, k2, p2, k3, p2, (k2, p1) twice; rep from *, end k2.

Row 17—K2, k1-b, * p1, k2 tog, p2, k2-b, M1, p3, M1, k2-b, p2, ssk, p1, k1-b; rep from *, end k2.

Row 18—K2, p1, * k1, p1, k2, p2, k5, p2, k2, p1, k1, p1; rep from *, end k2.

Row 19—K2, k1-b, * k2 tog, p2, k2-b, M1, p2, (k1, yo, k1, yo, k1) in next st, p2, M1, k2-b, p2, ssk, k1-b; rep from *, end k2.

Row 20—K2, p2, * k2, p2, k3, p5, k3, p2, k2, p3; rep from *, end last repeat p2, k2 instead of p3.

Row 21—K2, k2 tog, * p2, k2-b, M1, p3, k5, p3, M1, k2-b, p2, sl 1—k2 tog—psso; rep from *, end last repeat ssk, k2 instead of sl 1—k2 tog—psso.

Row 22—K2, p1, * k2, p2, k4, p5, k4, p2, k2, p1; rep from *, end k2.

Row 23—K2, k1-b, * p2 tog, k2-b, M1, p1, (k1, yo, k1, yo, k1) in next st, p2, ssk, k1, k2 tog, p2, (k1, yo, k1, yo, k1) in next st, p1, M1, k2-b, p2 tog, k1-b; rep from *, end k2.

Row 24—K2, p1, * k1, p2, k2, p5, k2, p3 tog, k2, p5, k2, p2, k1, p1; rep from *, end k2.

Row 25—K2, p2 tog, * k2-b, M1, p2, k5, p2, k1-b, p2, k5, p2, M1, k2-b, p3 tog; rep from *, end last repeat p2 tog, k2 instead of p3 tog.

Row 26—K3, * p2, k3, p5, k2, p1, k2, p5, k3, p2, k1; rep from *, end k2.

Row 27—K2, p1, * k2-b, p3, ssk, k1, k2 tog, p2, k1-b, p2, ssk, k1, k2 tog, p3, k2-b, p1; rep from *, end k2.

Row 28—K3, * p2, k3, p3 tog, k2, p1, k2, p3 tog, k3, p2, k1; rep from *, end k2.

Repeat Rows 1–28.

CHAPTER SEVEN

Twist-Stitch Patterns

The standard method of working a Right Twist is: skip 1 st, knit the second st, then knit the skipped st and sl both sts from needle together. The standard method of working a Left Twist is: skip 1 st and knit the second st in back loop, then knit the skipped st in front loop and sl both sts from needle together.

These methods, however, are not "standard" in this book. Both twists can be done in a better way—at least, in this author's opinion. Your opinion may differ; so if you prefer to stick to the standard methods, by all means do so. But first, do consult the Glossary of this book and try out the directions given for "RT" and "LT". If you like these newer methods, use them; if not, ignore them henceforth. For most knitters they *will* produce a somewhat neater result than the old standard methods, and are perhaps a little faster to work.

Some of the patterns in this section employ still other methods of twisting stitches, and in these cases the method is explained in the pattern notes. Even the old standard methods, as above, are explained wherever they are used. But where "RT" and "LT" occur in any pattern *without* specific twist directions, then the methods intended are the ones described in the Glossary.

Having settled all that, we can proceed to a discussion of twist patterns in general. Very interesting patterns they are, too. Twist stitches constitute an excellent way of making "traveling" diagonal lines and cable-like panels, without any fussing with a cable needle. Twist stitches therefore can be adapted to all sorts of designs and shapes and backgrounds. It is easy to invent original twist patterns for yourself, because the basic technique is simple and can be used to make diagonal lines go in any direction and for any distance. The patterns that are given here in the panel form are so close to cables that they can be used at will as substitutes for cables or in combination with them. You can even make an entire fisherman sweater without ever using a cable needle, simply by planning the sweater all in twist-stitch panels!

When you work with twist stitches, your gauge is likely to have more stitches to the inch than stockinette stitch in the same yarn on the same needles. Twists pull the fabric together laterally, so you must be sure to cast on enough stitches for the proper width. Twist patterns work well in any kind of yarn, from heavy to fine; but the needles must not be too large in proportion to the weight of the yarn, because a twist worked with over-large needles will "open up" the stitches and leave them looking limp and sloppy.

Twist-stitch patterns can be simple or complex, sporty or dressy, picturesque or elegant. They are not confined to any particular type of yarn or style of knitwear. You can use them in dress-up coats or sport jackets, ski sweaters or cocktail dresses, children's wear or afghans. Choose a few that you like, and try them. Put them together with other kinds of patterns for contrast. Little ideas that lead on to big ones abound in knitting patterns, and the twist stitch is certainly one of the best of these little ideas.

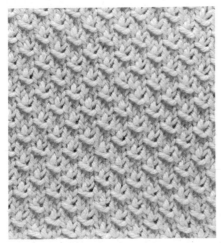

Purl-Twist Knot

Purl-Twist Knot

Contributed by Helen R. McShane, Brooklyn, New York

This is an easy pattern that gives a pretty, nubby allover texture for coats and suits, sweaters, dresses, etc. The wrong side is interesting too as a rough purl fabric with a hint of a design.

Multiple of 4 sts.

Rows 1 and 3 (Wrong side)—Purl.
Row 2—* K2, p2 tog and leave on needle; insert right-hand needle from back between the sts just purled tog, and purl the first st again; then sl both sts from needle together; rep from *.
Row 4—* P2 tog and purl first st again (as in Row 2), k2; rep from *.

Repeat Rows 1–4.

Little Wave

Little Wave

Contributed by Eugen K. Beugler, Dexter, Oregon

Multiple of 6 sts plus 1.

Row 1 (Right side)—Knit.
Row 2—P2, * k2, p4; rep from *, end k2, p3.
Row 3—K2, * LT, k4; rep from *, end LT, k3.
Row 4—P2, * k1, p1, k1, p3; rep from *, end last repeat p2.
Row 5—K3, * LT, k4; rep from *, end LT, k2.
Row 6—P3, * k2, p4; rep from *, end k2, p2.
Row 7—Knit.
Rows 8 and 10—Repeat Rows 6 and 4.
Row 9—K3, * RT, k4; rep from *, end RT, k2.
Row 11—K2, * RT, k4; rep from *, end RT, k3.
Row 12—Repeat Row 2.

Repeat Rows 1–12.

Grain of Wheat

Contributed by Hildegard M. Elsner, Aldan, Pennsylvania

Multiple of 4 sts.

Row 1 (Wrong side)—Purl.

Row 2—K1, p2, * skip 1 st and knit into the *back* of second st, then knit the skipped st, then sl both sts from needle together (Left Twist); p2; rep from *, end k1.

Row 3—K3, * p2, k2; rep from *, end k1.

Row 4—K3, * skip 1 st and knit into the *front* of second st, then knit the skipped st, then sl both sts from needle together (Right Twist); k2; rep from *, end k1.

Row 5—Purl.

Row 6—K1, * Left Twist, p2; rep from *, end Left Twist, k1.

Row 7—K1, p2, * k2, p2; rep from *, end k1.

Row 8—K1, * Right Twist, k2; rep from *, end Right Twist, k1.

Repeat Rows 1–8.

Grain of Wheat

Branching Rib Pattern

Multiple of 8 sts plus 4.

Rows 1, 3, and 5 (Wrong side)—K1, p3, * k5, p3; rep from *.

Row 2—* LT, k1, p5; rep from *, end LT, k1, p1.

Row 4—* K1, LT, p5; rep from *, end k1, LT, p1.

Row 6—P1, * k2, p4, RT; rep from *, end k2, p1.

Row 7—K1, * p2, k1, p1, k4; rep from *, end p2, k1.

Row 8—P1, * k2, p3, RT, p1; rep from *, end k2, p1.

Row 9—K1, * p2, k2, p1, k3; rep from *, end p2, k1.

Row 10—P1, * k2, p2, RT, p2; rep from *, end k2, p1.

Row 11—K1, * p2, k3, p1, k2; rep from *, end p2, k1.

Row 12—P1, * k2, p1, RT, p3; rep from *, end k2, p1.

Row 13—K1, * p2, k4, p1, k1; rep from *, end p2, k1.

Row 14—P1, * k2, RT, p4; rep from *, end k2, p1.

Rows 15, 17, and 19—* P3, k5; rep from *, end p3, k1.

Row 16—P1, * k1, RT, p5; rep from *, end k1, RT.

Row 18—P1, * RT, k1, p5; rep from *, end RT, k1.

Row 20—P1, * k2, LT, p4; rep from *, end k2, p1.

Rows 21, 23, 25, and 27—Repeat Rows 13, 11, 9, and 7.

Row 22—P1, * k2, p1, LT, p3; rep from *, end k2, p1.

Row 24—P1, * k2, p2, LT, p2; rep from *, end k2, p1.

Row 26—P1, * k2, p3, LT, p1; rep from *, end k2, p1.

Row 28—P1, * k2, p4, LT; rep from *, end k2, p1.

Repeat Rows 1–28.

Branching Rib Pattern

Austrian Block Pattern

Contributed by Hildegard M. Elsner, Aldan, Pennsylvania

Left unpressed, this simple but effective pattern closes up into deep ribs that are alternately broadened into leaf-like shapes and slimmed down to a single stitch. Because of this interesting texture, the pattern is good for bulky sweaters, and works beautifully in panels of 21 or 31 stitches.

Multiple of 10 sts plus 1.

Rows 1, 3, 5, 7, and 9 (Wrong side)—P1, * k2, p5, k2, p1; rep from *.

Rows 2, 4, 6, 8, and 10—K1-b, * p2, RT, k1, LT, p2, k1-b; rep from *.

Rows 11, 13, 15, 17, and 19—P3, * k2, p1, k2, p5; rep from *, end last repeat p3.

Rows 12, 14, 16, 18, and 20—K1, * LT, p2, k1-b, p2, RT, k1; rep from *.

Repeat Rows 1–20.

Austrian Block Pattern

Wickerwork Pattern

Contributed by Hildegard M. Elsner, Aldan, Pennsylvania

Multiple of 8 sts.

Row 1 (Wrong side)—P1, * k2, p2; rep from *, end k2, p1.
Row 2—* K1, p1, RT, LT, p1, k1; rep from *.
Row 3—* P1, k1, p1, k2, p1, k1, p1; rep from *.
Row 4—* K1, RT, p2, LT, k1; rep from *.
Row 5—P2, * k4, p4; rep from *, end k4, p2.
Row 6—Knit.
Row 7—Repeat Row 1.
Row 8—* LT, p1, k2, p1, RT; rep from *.
Row 9—* K1, p1, k1, p2, k1, p1, k1; rep from *.
Row 10—* P1, LT, k2, RT, p1; rep from *.
Row 11—K2, * p4, k4; rep from *, end p4, k2.
Row 12—Knit.

Repeat Rows 1–12.

Wickerwork Pattern

Twisted Diagonal Stripe

This neat and subtle fabric looks like the impossible accomplished—diagonal bands of ribbing on a knit-stitch background! Of course, it isn't real ribbing, just twisted stitches. The same pattern can be done equally well with right twists; but in this case, the diagonals must be moved one stitch to the *left* on every right-side row, instead of to the right as given.

Twisted Diagonal Stripe

Multiple of 9 sts plus 3.

Row 1 (Wrong side) and all other wrong-side rows—Purl.
Row 2—K3, * (LT) 3 times, k3; rep from *.
Row 4—K2, * (LT) 3 times, k3; rep from *, end k1.
Row 6—K1, * (LT) 3 times, k3; rep from *, end LT.
Row 8—* (LT) 3 times, k3; rep from *, end LT, k1.
Row 10—K1, (LT) twice, * k3, (LT) 3 times; rep from *, end k3, (LT) twice.
Row 12—(LT) twice, * k3, (LT) 3 times; rep from *, end k3, (LT) twice, k1.
Row 14—K1, LT, * k3, (LT) 3 times; rep from *.
Row 16—LT, * k3, (LT) 3 times; rep from *, end k1.
Row 18—K4, * (LT) 3 times, k3; rep from *, end last repeat k2.

Repeat Rows 1–18.

Twilled Stripe Pattern

Contributed by Suzanne Pryor, Wichita, Kansas

The slip-chain technique is used here to make a simple and beautiful ribbed fabric. It is particularly interesting when left unpressed, so that the ribs are allowed to close up together.

Twilled Stripe Pattern

Multiple of 7 sts plus 2.

NOTE: Left Twist (LT) as follows: skip 1 st and knit the second st in *back* loop, then slip the skipped st purlwise onto right-hand needle, then slip the knit st also.

Row 1 (Wrong side) and all other wrong-side rows—K2, * p5, k2; rep from *.
Row 2—P2, * LT, k3, p2; rep from *.
Row 4—P2, * k1, LT, k2, p2; rep from *.
Row 6—P2, * k2, LT, k1, p2; rep from *.
Row 8—P2, * k3, LT, p2; rep from *.

Repeat Rows 1–8.

Pier-Glass Pattern

Pier-Glass Pattern

Here is an attractive fancy-rib design for sweaters; its elements are simple, but its overall effect is very nice. Work it with smallish needles so that the twists, when purled on the right side, will not show too many or too large openings in the fabric.

Multiple of 13 sts plus 1.

Rows 1 and 3 (Wrong side)—P2, * k2, p1, k4, p1, k2, p3; rep from *, end last repeat p2.

Row 2—K2, * p2, k1, p4, k1, p2, k3; rep from *, end last repeat k2.

Row 4—K2, * p2, LT, p2, RT, p2, k3; rep from *, end last repeat k2.

Row 5—P2, * k3, p1, k2, p1, k3, p3; rep from *, end last repeat p2.

Row 6—K1, * LT, p2, LT, RT, p2, RT, k1; rep from *.

Row 7—P1, * k1, p1, k3, p2, k3, p1, k1, p1; rep from *.

Row 8—K1, * p1, LT, (p2, RT) twice, p1, k1; rep from *.

Row 9—P1, * k2, p1, k6, p1, k2, p1; rep from *.

Row 10—K1, * p2, LT, p4, RT, p2, k1; rep from *.

Rows 11 and 13—P1, * k3, p1, k4, p1, k3, p1; rep from *.

Row 12—K1, * p3, k1, p4, k1, p3, k1; rep from *.

Row 14—K1, * p2, RT, p4, LT, p2, k1; rep from *.

Row 15—P1, * k2, p1, k2, p2, (k2, p1) twice; rep from *.

Row 16—K1, * p1, (RT, p2) twice, LT, p1, k1; rep from *.

Rows 17 and 19—Repeat Rows 7 and 5.

Row 18—K1, * RT, p2, RT, LT, p2, LT, k1; rep from *.

Row 20—K2, *p2, RT, p2, LT, p2, k3; rep from *, end last repeat k2.

Repeat Rows 1–20.

Brocade Chevron

Brocade Chevron

Here is a beautiful pattern for sports wear, coats, yokes, or borders. The chevrons are done in Seed Stitch and set off by twisted edges. The fabric is firm and dense, and is best worked on smallish needles so that the stitches will lie close.

Multiple of 10 sts plus 4.

NOTES: Right Twist (RT)—skip 1 st and knit the 2nd st, then knit the skipped st, then sl both sts from needle together.

Left Twist (LT)—skip 1 st and knit the 2nd st in *back* loop, then knit the skipped st in *front* loop, then sl both sts from needle together.

All sl-sts are slipped with yarn in *front* (wrong side of fabric).

Row 1 (Wrong side)—Purl.
Row 2—K1, * RT, k8; rep from *, end RT, k1.
Row 3—P1, * sl 2, p8; rep from *, end sl 2, p1.
Row 4—K2, * LT, k6, RT; rep from *, end k2.
Row 5—K1, p1, * k1, sl 1, p6, sl 1, p1; rep from *, end k1, p1.
Row 6—P1, k1, * p1, LT, k4, RT, k1; rep from *, end p1, k1.
Row 7—(K1, p1) twice, * sl 1, p4, sl 1, (k1, p1) twice; rep from *.
Row 8—(P1, k1) twice, * LT, k2, RT, (p1, k1) twice; rep from *.
Row 9—K1, * (p1, k1) twice, sl 1, p2, sl 1, p1, k1; rep from *, end p1, k1, p1.
Row 10—P1, * (k1, p1) twice, LT, RT, k1, p1; rep from *, end k1, p1, k1.
Row 11—* (K1, p1) 3 times, sl 2, k1, p1; rep from *, end (k1, p1) twice.
Row 12—* (P1, k1) 3 times, RT, p1, k1; rep from *, end (p1, k1) twice.
Row 13—* K1, p1; rep from *.
Row 14—P1, * RT, (k1, p1) 4 times; rep from *, end RT, k1.
Row 15—K1, * sl 2, (p1, k1) 4 times; rep from *, end sl 2, k1.
Row 16—K2, * LT, (p1, k1) 3 times, RT; rep from *, end k2.
Row 17—P3, * sl 1, (k1, p1) 3 times, sl 1, p2; rep from *, end p1.
Row 18—K3, * LT, (k1, p1) twice, RT, k2; rep from *, end k1.
Row 19—P4, * sl 1, (p1, k1) twice, sl 1, p4; rep from *.
Row 20—K4, * LT, p1, k1, RT, k4; rep from *.
Row 21—P5, * sl 1, k1, p1, sl 1, p6; rep from *, end last repeat p5.
Row 22—K5, * LT, RT, k6; rep from *, end last repeat k5.
Row 23—P6, * sl 2, p8; rep from *, end last repeat p6.
Row 24—K6, * RT, k8; rep from *, end last repeat k6.

Repeat Rows 1–24.

Knit-Twist Lattice

This pattern makes a fine, sharp, clean lattice design on a knit-stitch ground. A single panel of 18 stitches is beautiful in fancy sweaters.

Multiple of 16 sts plus 2.

Row 1 (Wrong side) and all other wrong-side rows—Purl.
Row 2—K1, * LT, k4, RT; rep from *, end k1.
Row 4—K2, * LT, k2, RT, k2; rep from *.
Row 6—K3, * LT, RT, k4; rep from *, end last repeat k3.
Row 8—K4, * RT, k6; rep from *, end last repeat k4.
Row 10—K3, * RT, LT, k4; rep from *, end last repeat k3.
Row 12—K2, * RT, k2, LT, k2; rep from *.
Row 14—K1, * RT, k4, LT; rep from *, end k1.
Row 16—K8, * LT, k6; rep from *, end k2.

Repeat Rows 1–16.

Knit-Twist Lattice

Fractured Lattice

This pattern is simple to work and fascinating to look at. The twist-stitch lattice is broken, here, into overlapping chevrons made by diagonal lines. The herringbone effect makes it a good pattern for coats and suits.

Multiple of 8 sts.

Row 1 (Wrong side) and all other wrong-side rows—Purl.
Row 2—* LT, k2, LT, RT; rep from *.
Row 4—K1, * LT, k2, RT, k2; rep from *, end last repeat k1.
Row 6—* RT, LT, RT, k2; rep from *.
Row 8—K3, * LT, k2, RT, k2; rep from *, end LT, k3.

Repeat Rows 1–8.

Fractured Lattice

Carved Diamond Pattern

Multiple of 16 sts plus 1.

Row 1 (Wrong side) and all other wrong-side rows—Purl.
Row 2—K1, * (LT) 3 times, k3, (RT) 3 times, k1; rep from *.
Row 4—K2, * (LT) 3 times, k1, (RT) 3 times, k3; rep from *, end last repeat k2.
Rows 6 and 8—Repeat Rows 2 and 4.
Row 10—Knit.
Row 12—K2, * (RT) 3 times, k1, (LT) 3 times, k3; rep from *, end last repeat k2.
Row 14—K1, * (RT) 3 times, k3, (LT) 3 times, k1; rep from *.
Rows 16 and 18—Repeat Rows 12 and 14.
Row 20—Knit.

Repeat Rows 1–20.

Carved Diamond Pattern

Heraldic Pattern

Crossed swords and battle-flags hanging on a rough stone wall—does this design suggest such things to you? Even if it doesn't, it is still an exceedingly handsome pattern for a man's or a boy's sweater, and so easy to work that you can use it all over a garment for a *big* man whose sweaters take a lot of knitting.

Multiple of 12 sts.

Rows 1, 3, 5, and 7 (Wrong side)—K2, * p2, k4; rep from *, end p2, k2.
Row 2—K2, * RT, k4, LT, k4; rep from *, end last repeat k2.
Row 4—Knit.

Row 6—Repeat Row 2.
Row 8—K3, * LT, k2, RT, k6; rep from *, end last repeat k3.
Row 9—K2, * p3, k2, p3, k4; rep from *, end last repeat k2.
Row 10—K4, * LT, RT, k8; rep from *, end last repeat k4.
Row 11—K2, * p8, k4; rep from *, end last repeat k2.
Row 12—K5, * RT, k10; rep from *, end last repeat k5.
Rows 13 and 15—Repeat Rows 11 and 9.
Row 14—K4, * RT, LT, k8; rep from *, end last repeat k4.
Row 16—K3, * RT, k2, LT, k6; rep from *, end last repeat k3.
Rows 17, 19, 21, and 23—Repeat Rows 1, 3, 5, and 7.
Row 18—K2, * LT, k4, RT, k4; rep from *, end last repeat k2.
Row 20—Knit.
Row 22—Repeat Row 18.
Row 24—K9, rep from * of Row 8; end k3.
Row 25—K2, p2, * k4, p3, k2, p3; rep from *, end k4, p2, k2.
Row 26—K10, rep from * of Row 10; end k2.
Row 27—K2, p2, * k4, p8; rep from *, end k4, p2, k2.
Row 28—K11, * LT, k10; rep from *, end k1.
Rows 29 and 31—Repeat Rows 27 and 25.
Row 30—K10, rep from * of Row 14; end k2.
Row 32—K9, rep from * of Row 16; end k3.

Repeat Rows 1–32.

Heraldic Pattern

Ribbed Leaf Pattern

This beautiful twisted-all-over fabric is reminiscent of the shapes of fossilized fern leaves traced in rock. A single motif can be worked in cable fashion; see Ribbed Leaf Panel.

Multiple of 16 sts plus 1.

Row 1 (Wrong side) and all other wrong-side rows—Purl.
Row 2—K1, * LT, (RT) twice, k3, (LT) twice, RT, k1; rep from *.
Row 4—K2, * LT, (RT) twice, k1, (LT) twice, RT, k3; rep from *, end last repeat k2.
Row 6—K1, * (LT) twice, RT, k3, LT, (RT) twice, k1; rep from *.
Row 8—K2, * (LT) twice, RT, k1, LT, (RT) twice, k3; rep from *, end last repeat k2.
Row 10—K1, * (LT) 3 times, k3, (RT) 3 times, k1; rep from *.
Row 12—K2, * (LT) 3 times, k1, (RT) 3 times, k3; rep from *, end last repeat k2.
Rows 14, 16, 18, 20, and 22—Repeat Rows 10, 8, 6, 4, and 2.
Row 24—K2, * (RT) 3 times, k1, (LT) 3 times, k3; rep from *, end last repeat k2.
Row 26—K1, * (RT) 3 times, k3, (LT) 3 times, k1; rep from *.
Row 28—Repeat Row 24.

Repeat Rows 1–28.

Ribbed Leaf Pattern

Double Lattice

Double Lattice

Here is a pattern that will give the knitter plenty of practice in the use of twist stitches, since nearly all of them are twisted on the right-side rows. It also demonstrates how the twist-stitch technique can be a time-saver; imagine how long this handsome fabric would take to make, if all the stitches were cabled instead of twisted!

Multiple of 6 sts plus 4.

Row 1 (Wrong side) and all other wrong-side rows—Purl.
Row 2—* LT, (RT) twice; rep from *, end LT, RT.
Row 4—K1, LT, * RT, (LT) twice; rep from *, end k1.
Row 6—(LT) twice, * k2, (LT) twice; rep from *.
Row 8—K1, * (LT) twice, RT; rep from *, end LT, k1.
Row 10—RT, * LT, (RT) twice; rep from *, end LT.
Row 12—K3, * (RT) twice, k2; rep from *, end k1.

Repeat Rows 1–12.

Three Twist Patterns with Openwork: Diagonal Crepe Stitch, Deep Waffle Pattern, and Wide Waffle Pattern

All three of these patterns are deep in texture, thick but light and fluffy. Diagonal Crepe Stitch is a good thermal fabric; try it in a pair of "longjohns"! (Very handsome ones they will be, too.) Deep Waffle Pattern comes from Switzerland, and in fine yarn makes a delicate and lovely sweater or shell. Wide Waffle Pattern is an enlarged version with the pattern lines slanted more toward the horizontal.

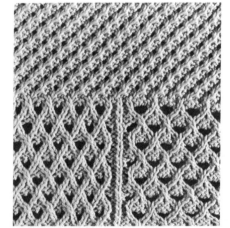

ABOVE: *Diagonal Crepe Stitch*
BELOW, LEFT: *Deep Waffle Pattern*
BELOW, RIGHT: *Wide Waffle Pattern*

I. DIAGONAL CREPE STITCH

Multiple of 4 sts plus 3.

Row 1 (Right side)—P1, RT, * p2, RT; rep from *.
Row 2—K1, * yo, p2 tog, k2; rep from *, end yo, p2 tog.
Row 3—K1, * p2, RT; rep from *, end p2.
Row 4—K3, * yo, p2 tog, k2; rep from *.

Repeat Rows 1–4.

II. DEEP WAFFLE PATTERN

Multiple of 4 sts plus 2.

Row 1 (Right side)—P2, * RT, p2; rep from *.
Row 2—K2, * p2, k2; rep from *.
Row 3—P1, * k2 tog, (yo) twice, ssk; rep from *, end p1.
Row 4—P2, * (k1, p1) into the double yo of previous row, p2; rep from *.
Row 5—K2, * p2, LT; rep from *, end p2, k2.
Row 6—P2, * k2, p2; rep from *.
Row 7—P1, yo, * ssk, k2 tog, (yo) twice; rep from *, end ssk, k2 tog, yo, p1.
Row 8—K2, * p2, (k1, p1) into the double yo of previous row; rep from *, end p2, k2.

Repeat Rows 1–8

III. WIDE WAFFLE PATTERN

Multiple of 6 sts plus 4.

Row 1 (Right side)—K2, p2, * LT, p4; rep from *, end LT, p2, k2.
Row 2—K4, * p2, k4; rep from *.
Row 3—K2, * k3 tog, yo, sl 1—k2 tog—psso; rep from *, end k2.
Row 4—K2, p1, * (k1, p1) twice in the yo of previous row, p2; rep from *, end last repeat p1, k2 instead of p2.
Row 5—K3, * p4, RT; rep from *, end p4, k3.
Row 6—K2, p1, * k4, p2; rep from *, end k4, p1, k2.
Row 7—K2, yo, * sl 1—k2 tog—psso, k3 tog, yo; rep from *, end k2.
Row 8—K2, (k1, p1) into the yo, * p2, (k1, p1) twice in the yo of previous row; rep from *, end p2, (k1, p1) into the yo, k2.

Repeat Rows 1–8.

Knit-Twist Lattice with Lace

This fabric looks beautiful and very fancy, although it is not at all difficult to work. *Notice* that in Rows 4 and 28 there is a double yo in the middle of each motif, although in the directions this double yo is split into two different sets of parentheses. Also, *notice* that another double yo is formed by the last and the first directions of Rows 10, 14, 18, and 22, when these pattern rows are repeated across. Always bear in mind that each double yo makes two new stitches on the needle, and is always worked (k1, p1) on the return row.

Knit-Twist Lattice With Lace

Multiple of 14 sts plus 2.

Row 1 (Wrong side) and all other wrong-side rows—Purl, working (k1, p1) into every double yo from a previous row.
Row 2—K4, * (yo, ssk) twice, (k2 tog, yo) twice, k2, RT, k2; rep from *, end last repeat k4 instead of k2, RT, k2.

Row 4—K1, * LT, k1, (k2 tog, yo) twice, (yo, ssk) twice, k1, RT; rep from *, end k1.
Row 6—K1, * k1, LT, k2, yo, ssk, k2 tog, yo, k2, RT, k1; rep from *, end k1.
Row 8—K1, * k2, LT, k1, k2 tog, (yo) twice, ssk, k1, RT, k2; rep from *, end k1.
Row 10—K1, * yo, ssk, k1, LT, k4, RT, k1, k2 tog, yo; rep from *, end k1.
Row 12—K1, * k2 tog, yo, k2, LT, k2, RT, k2, yo, ssk; rep from *, end k1.
Row 14—K1, * (yo, ssk) twice, k1, LT, RT, k1, (k2 tog, yo) twice; rep from *, end k1.
Row 16—K1, * (k2 tog, yo) twice, k2, LT, k2, (yo, ssk) twice; rep from *, end k1.
Row 18—K1, * (yo, ssk) twice, k1, RT, LT, k1, (k2 tog, yo) twice; rep from *, end k1.
Row 20—K1, * k2 tog, yo, k2, RT, k2, LT, k2, yo, ssk; rep from *, end k1.
Row 22—K1, * yo, ssk, k1, RT, k4, LT, k1, k2 tog, yo; rep from *, end k1.
Row 24—K3, * RT, k1, k2 tog, (yo) twice, ssk, k1, LT, k4; rep from *, end last repeat k3 instead of k4.
Row 26—K2, * RT, k2, yo, ssk, k2 tog, yo, k2, LT, k2; rep from *.
Row 28—K1, * RT, k1, (k2 tog, yo) twice, (yo, ssk) twice, k1, LT; rep from *, end k1.

Repeat Rows 1–28.

Gable Pattern

Gable Pattern

Little "windows" of faggoting add interest, here, to an allover pattern of twist-stitch chevrons. Notice that the decreases on either side of the openwork are worked in opposition to the slant of the stitches, to make sharp clear edges.

Multiple of 10 sts plus 2.

Row 1 (Right side)—K4, * RT, LT, k1, ssk, yo, k3; rep from *, end last repeat k1.
Row 2—P9, * p2 tog, yo, p8; rep from *, end p2 tog, yo, p1.
Row 3—K3, * RT, k2, LT, k4; rep from *, end last repeat k3.
Row 4—Purl.
Row 5—K2, * RT, k4, LT, k2; rep from *.
Row 6—P4, * p2 tog, yo, p8; rep from *, end p2 tog, yo, p6.
Row 7—K1, * RT, k1, ssk, yo, k3, LT; rep from *, end k1.
Rows 8, 10, 12, and 14—K2, * p2, p2 tog, yo, p4, k2; rep from *.
Rows 9, 11, and 13—P2, * k2, ssk, yo, k4, p2; rep from *.
Row 15—K1, * LT, k1, ssk, yo, k3, RT; rep from *, end k1.
Rows 16, 18, and 20—Repeat Rows 6, 4, and 2.
Row 17—K2, * LT, k4, RT, k2; rep from *.
Row 19—K3, * LT, k2, RT, k4; rep from *, end last repeat k3.
Row 21—K4, * LT, RT, k1, ssk, yo, k3; rep from *, end last repeat k1.
Rows 22, 24, 26, and 28—P5, * k2, p2, p2 tog, yo, p4; rep from *, end last repeat p1.
Rows 23, 25, and 27—K5, * p2, k2, ssk, yo, k4; rep from *, end last repeat k1.

Repeat Rows 1–28.

Three Knit-Twist Panels: V, Tent, and Heart

These are three fairly wide cable substitutes, all using the knit-twist method of crossing stitches. I and II, the "V" and the "Tent", are quite straightforward. Either could be used in a ribbed or panel-patterned skirt, as a minor design in a fisherman sweater, or as an allover pattern on a multiple of 12 stitches plus 2. These twisted diagonal stitches could also be arranged as zigzags, diamonds, braids, or plain diagonals running all to the right or all to the left—as when I or II is cut in half to make a panel 5 stitches wide with only the first or second half of each pattern rows being worked.

The "Heart" motif (III) is not often seen in knitting patterns, for the good reason that knitting, by its very nature, makes it difficult to form a rounded top to a design. The upper curves of any heart-shaped pattern, therefore, are usually made in some rather awkward way, by working 4 or 5 stitches together, for instance. This third panel suffers from the customary awkwardness but does manage to achieve a recognizable heart shape.

Knit-Twist Panels
LEFT: *"V" Panel*
CENTER: *Tent Panel*
RIGHT: *Heart Panel*

Each pattern: Panel of 14 sts.

Each pattern Row 1 (Wrong side) and every other wrong-side row—K2, p10, k2.

I. "V" PANEL

Row 2—P2, k3, RT, LT, k3, p2.
Row 4—P2, k2, RT, k2, LT, k2, p2.
Row 6—P2, k1, RT, k4, LT, k1, p2.
Row 8—P2, RT, k6, LT, p2.

Repeat Rows 1–8.

II. TENT PANEL

Row 2—P2, LT, k6, RT, p2.
Row 4—P2, k1, LT, k4, RT, k1, p2.
Row 6—P2, k2, LT, k2, RT, k2, p2.
Row 8—P2, k3, LT, RT, k3, p2.
Row 10—P2, k4, RT, k4, p2.

Repeat Rows 1–10.

TWIST-STITCH PATTERNS   155

III. HEART PANEL

Rows 2, 4, 6, and 8—Repeat Rows 2, 4, 6, and 8 of Pattern I.
Row 10—Repeat Row 2 again.
Row 12—P2, LT, RT, k2, LT, RT, p2.
Row 14—P2, k1, M1, k2 tog-b, k4, k2 tog, M1, k1, p2.
Row 16—P2, k10, p2.

Repeat Rows 1–16.

Tent Cable

CENTER PANEL: *Tent Cable*
SIDE PANELS: *Pigtail*

Repeated on a multiple of 14 sts instead of in a single panel, this pattern makes an attractive chevron.

Panel of 14 sts.

Row 1 (Right side)—(LT) twice, p6, (RT) twice.
Row 2—K1, p3, k6, p3, k1.
Row 3—P1, (LT) twice, p4, (RT) twice, p1.
Row 4—K2, p3, k4, p3, k2.
Row 5—P2, (LT) twice, p2, (RT) twice, p2.
Row 6—K3, p3, k2, p3, k3.
Row 7—P3, (LT) twice, (RT) twice, p3.
Row 8—K4, p6, k4.
Row 9—P4, LT, k2, RT, p4.
Row 10—K5, p4, k5.
Row 11—P5, LT, RT, p5.
Row 12—P3, k3, p2, k3, p3.

Repeat Rows 1–12.

Pigtail

Here is a very attractive small braided rib, which can be used as a single cable panel or worked as a fancy ribbing on a multiple of 5 stitches plus 2. When left unpressed, the Pigtail is very highly embossed, rounded and springy.

Panel of 7 sts.

Rows 1 and 3 (Wrong side)—K2, p3, k2.
Row 2—P2, RT, k1, p2.
Row 4—P2, k1, LT, p2.

Repeat Rows 1–4.

Twist-Rib Chevron

The outlines of this design happen to be filled in with twisted ribs—this is traditional—but they could be filled in with garter stitch, seed stitch, moss stitch, or plain stockinette. With any "filling" you like, this is a beautiful pattern for fancy sweaters, afghans, or dresses.

CENTER PANEL: *Twist-Rib Chevron*
SIDE PANELS: *Rapunzel's Braid*

Panel of 18 sts.

Row 1 (Wrong side)—K2, p1-b, k1, p1, k3, p2, k3, p1, k1, p1-b, k2.
Row 2—P2, k1-b, (RT, p3) twice, LT, k1-b, p2.
Row 3—K2, p2, (k4, p2) twice, k2.
Row 4—P2, RT, p3, RT, LT, p3, LT, p2.
Row 5—K7, p4, k7.
Row 6—P6, RT, k2-b, LT, p6.
Row 7—K6, p1, k1, p2-b, k1, p1, k6.
Row 8—P5, RT, p1, k2-b, p1, LT, p5.
Row 9—K5, p2, k1, p2-b, k1, p2, k5.
Row 10—P4, RT, k1-b, p1, k2-b, p1, k1-b, LT, p4.
Row 11—K4, p1, k1, p1-b, k1, p2-b, k1, p1-b, k1, p1, k4.
Row 12—P3, RT, p1, k1-b, p1, k2-b, p1, k1-b, p1, LT, p3.
Row 13—K3, (p2, k1, p1-b, k1) twice, p2, k3.
Row 14—P2, RT, k1-b, p1, k1-b, RT, LT, k1-b, p1, k1-b, LT, p2.
Row 15—K2, p1, k1, p1-b, k1, p6, k1, p1-b, k1, p1, k2.
Row 16—P2, (k1-b, p1) twice, RT, k2, LT, (p1, k1-b) twice, p2.
Row 17—K2, (p1-b, k1) twice, p1, k1, p2, k1, p1, (k1, p1-b) twice, k2.
Row 18—P2, k1-b, p1, k1-b, (RT, p1) twice, LT, k1-b, p1, k1-b, p2.
Row 19—K2, p1-b, k1, (p2, k2) twice, p2, k1, p1-b, k2.
Row 20—P2, k1-b, p1, RT, p2, k2, p2, LT, p1, k1-b, p2.

Repeat Rows 1–20.

Rapunzel's Braid

Try this beautiful little braid panel on each side of a V neckline, or flanking a wide cable. To make two braids twist in opposite directions, begin one of them with Row 1 and the other with Row 5.

Panel of 10 sts.

Rows 1 and 3 (Wrong side)—K3, p5, k2.
Row 2—P2, k3, RT, p3.
Row 4—P2, LT, RT, LT, p2.
Rows 5 and 7—K2, p5, k3.
Row 6—P3, LT, k3, p2.
Row 8—P2, RT, LT, RT, p2.

Repeat Rows 1–8.

TWIST-STITCH PATTERNS   157

Briar Rose

"Briar stems" gracefully entwined, and bobble-like "rosebuds", make this an exceptionally pretty panel to combine with lace, as well as with other twist patterns and with cables.

Panel of 13 sts.

Row 1 (Wrong side)—K3, p1, k1, p2, k2, p1, k3.
Row 2—P3, LT, p1, LT, RT, p3.
Row 3—K4, p2, k2, p1, k4.
Row 4—P2, (k1, yo, k1) in next st, turn and p3, turn and k3 wrapping yarn twice for each knit st; p1, LT, p1, RT, p4.
Row 5—K4, p2, k1, p1, k2, sl next 3 sts dropping extra wraps, sl the same 3 sts back to left-hand needle and p3 tog-b; k2.
Row 6—P2, LT, p1, k1-b, RT, LT, p3.
Row 7—K3, p1, k2, p2, k1, p1, k3.
Row 8—P3, LT, RT, p1, RT, p3.
Row 9—K4, p1, k2, p2, k4.
Row 10—P4, LT, p1, RT, p1, (k1, yo, k1) in next st, turn and p3, turn and k3 wrapping yarn twice for each knit st; p2.
Row 11—K2, sl next 3 sts dropping extra wraps, sl the same 3 sts back to left-hand needle and p3 tog; k2, p1, k1, p2, k4.
Row 12—P3, RT, LT, k1-b, p1, RT, p2.

Repeat Rows 1–12.

LEFT: *Briar Rose*
CENTER: *Teardrop Pendant on Seed Stitch*
RIGHT: *Square Knot*

Teardrop Pendant on Seed Stitch

Panel of 19 sts.

NOTES: Increase Right (inc R)—Insert right-hand needle downward into the *back* of the st *in the row below* the next st on left-hand needle (i.e., into the purled head of st on the back of the fabric), and knit; then knit the st on left-hand needle in the usual way.

Increase Left (inc L)—Knit (from front) into the st *in the row below* the next st on left-hand needle; then knit the st on left-hand needle in the usual way.

Row 1 (Wrong side)—K6, (p1, k1) 3 times, p1, k6.
Row 2—P5, RT, (k1, p1) twice, k1, LT, p5.
Row 3—K5, p2, (k1, p1) 3 times, p1, k5.
Row 4—P4, RT, (p1, k1) 3 times, p1, LT, p4.
Row 5—K4, (p1, k1) 5 times, p1, k4.
Row 6—P3, RT, (k1, p1) twice, (k1, p1, k1) in next st, (p1, k1) twice, LT, p3.

Row 7—K3, p2, k1, p1, k1, p5, k1, p1, k1, p2, k3.

Row 8—P2, RT, (p1, k1) twice, p1, inc R, k1, inc L, p1, (k1, p1) twice, LT, p2.

Row 9—K2, (p1, k1) 3 times, p7, (k1, p1) 3 times, k2.

Row 10—P2, k1-b, (k1, p1) 3 times, inc R, k3, inc L, (p1, k1) 3 times, k1-b, p2.

Row 11—K2, (p1, k1) 3 times, p9, (k1, p1) 3 times, k2.

Row 12—P2, k1-b, (k1, p1) 3 times, k2, sl 2—k1—p2sso, k2, (p1, k1) 3 times, k1-b, p2.

Row 13—Repeat Row 9.

Row 14—P2, k1-b, (k1, p1) 3 times, k1, sl 2—k1—p2sso, k1, (p1, k1) 3 times, k1-b, p2.

Row 15—K2, (p1, k1) 3 times, p5, (k1, p1) 3 times, k2.

Row 16—P2, k1-b, (k1, p1) 3 times, sl 2—k1—p2sso, (p1, k1) 3 times, k1-b, p2.

Row 17—K2, (p1, k1) 3 times, p3, (k1, p1) 3 times, k2.

Row 18—P2, LT, p1, k1, p1, RT, k1, LT, p1, k1, p1, RT, p2.

Row 19—K3, p2, k1, (p3, k1) twice, p2, k3.

Row 20—P3, LT, k1, RT, p1, k1, p1, LT, k1, RT, p3.

Repeat Rows 1–20.

Square Knot

The knit stitches in this simple panel follow exactly the course taken by the strands in an ordinary square knot. The pattern is excellent for sportswear of all kinds.

Panel of 12 sts.

Rows 1 and 3 (Wrong side)—K2, p1, k6, p1, k2.

Rows 2 and 4—P2, k1-b, p6, k1-b, p2.

Rows 5 and 7—K2, p1, k2, p2, k2, p1, k2.

Row 6—P2, k1-b, p2, RT, p2, k1-b, p2.

Row 8—P2, (LT, RT) twice, p2.

Rows 9 and 11—K3, p2, k2, p2, k3.

Row 10—P3, RT, p2, LT, p3.

Row 12—P3, k2, p2, k2, p3.

Rows 13 through 19—Repeat Rows 9 through 12, then Rows 9 through 11 again.

Row 20—P2, (RT, LT) twice, p2.

Rows 21 and 22—Repeat Rows 5 and 6.

Rows 23 through 26—Repeat Rows 1 through 4.

Repeat Rows 1–26.

Ribbed Leaf Panel

CENTER PANEL: *Ribbed Leaf Panel*
SIDE PANELS: *Grapevine Twist*

Panel of 19 sts.

Row 1 (Wrong side)—K8, p3, k8.
Row 2—P7, RT, k1, LT, p7.
Row 3—K7, p5, k7.
Row 4—P6, RT, k3, LT, p6.
Row 5—K6, p7, k6.
Row 6—P5, (RT) twice, k1, (LT) twice, p5.
Row 7—K5, p9, k5.
Row 8—P4, (RT) twice, k3, (LT) twice, p4.
Row 9—K4, p11, k4.
Row 10—P3, (RT) 3 times, k1, (LT) 3 times, p3.
Row 11—K3, p13, k3.
Row 12—P2, (RT) 3 times, k3, (LT) 3 times, p2.
Row 13—K2, p15, k2.
Row 14—P2, k1, (RT) 3 times, k1, (LT) 3 times, k1, p2.
Rows 15, 17, 19, 21, 23, and 25—Repeat Rows 13, 11, 9, 7, 5, and 3.
Row 16—P2, LT, (RT) twice, k3, (LT) twice, RT, p2.
Row 18—P3, LT, (RT) twice, k1, (LT) twice, RT, p3.
Row 20—P4, LT, RT, k3, LT, RT, p4.
Row 22—P5, LT, RT, k1, LT, RT, p5.
Row 24—P6, LT, k3, RT, p6.
Row 26—P7, LT, k1, RT, p7.

Repeat Rows 1–26.

Grapevine Twist

Panel of 13 sts.

NOTE: Make Bobble (MB) as follows—(k1, yo, k1, yo, k1) in one st, turn and k5, turn and p5, turn and k1, sl 1—k2 tog—psso, k1, turn and p3 tog, completing bobble.

Row 1 (Wrong side) and all other wrong-side rows—Purl.
Row 2—K2, LT, k2, RT, k5.
Row 4—K3, LT, RT, k6.
Row 6—K4, LT, k4, MB, k2.
Row 8—K5, LT, k2, RT, k2.
Row 10—K6, LT, RT, k3.
Row 12—K2, MB, k4, RT, k4.

Repeat Rows 1–12.

Sheepfold

Contributed by Elizabeth Zimmermann, Milwaukee, Wisconsin

This pattern was originally planned for circular knitting, so that all rows would be worked from the right side. To do it in this way, simply work all odd-numbered rows backward, substituting "knit" for "purl" and vice versa, and working plain RT and LT instead of RRT and RLT. When converted into back-and-forth knitting, the pattern calls for some twists made on the wrong side. (See Sunrise Shell Pattern for additional discussion of RLT.)

Notice that the usual right-side Left Twist is to be done by the classical method rather than the new method of working the two stitches together. The reason for this is that the two stitches together may become too tight for convenience in working the subsequent *wrong*-side twist. The Right Twist, on the other hand, can be worked either way (it is tidier when done by the new method) and so this is not described in the notes.

SIDE PANELS: *Sheepfold*
CENTER PANEL: *Medallion with Leaf*

Panel of 16 sts.

NOTES: Left Twist (LT)—skip 1 st and knit the 2nd st in *back* loop, then knit the skipped st in front loop in the usual way, and sl both sts from needle together.

Reverse Left Twist (RLT)—skip 1 st and purl the 2nd st in *back* loop, then purl the skipped st, then sl both sts from needle together.

Reverse Right Twist (RRT)—There are two methods of working this twist, the preferred one given first. (1) Skip 1 st and purl the 2nd st, then p2 tog (the skipped st and the 2nd st) and sl both sts from needle together. (2) Skip 1 st and purl the 2nd st, then purl the skipped st and sl both sts from needle together.

Row 1 (Wrong side)—K2, p12, k2.
Row 2—P2, LT, k8, RT, p2.
Row 3—K3, RRT, p6, RLT, p1, k2.
Row 4—P2, k2, LT, k4, RT, p4.
Row 5—K5, RRT, p2, RLT, p3, k2.
Row 6—P2, k4, LT, RT, p6.
Row 7—K7, RLT, p5, k2.
Row 8—P2, k6, LT, p6.
Row 9—K5, RLT, p7, k2.
Row 10—P2, k8, LT, p4.
Row 11—K3, RLT, p9, k2.
Row 12—P2, k10, LT, p2.
Rows 13 and 14—Repeat Rows 1 and 2.
Row 15—K2, p1, RRT, p6, RLT, k3.
Row 16—P4, LT, k4, RT, k2, p2.
Row 17—K2, p3, RRT, p2, RLT, k5.

Row 18—P6, LT, RT, k4, p2.
Row 19—K2, p5, RRT, k7.
Row 20—P6, RT, k6, p2.
Row 21—K2, p7, RRT, k5.
Row 22—P4, RT, k8, p2.
Row 23—K2, p9, RRT, k3.
Row 24—P2, RT, k10, p2.

Repeat Rows 1–24.

Medallion with Leaf

This pattern is attractive as a panel in fancy sweaters such as Aran knits. Or, it can be used to "dress up" afghans, coat sleeves, hats, mittens, or knee socks. There are, of course, many possible variations; the medallions can be larger or smaller, or filled in with purl, seed or moss stitch instead of garter stitch, or featuring some other motif instead of the embossed leaf in the center.

Panel of 19 sts.

NOTES: For RT and LT, RRT and RLT, see the Notes to Sheepfold.

Rows 1 and 3 (Wrong side)—K8, p3, k8.
Row 2—P8, skip 2 sts and knit into 3rd st, then into 1st and 2nd sts and sl all three together from needle (Twist 3); p8.
Row 4—P7, RT, k1-b, LT, p7.
Row 5—K6, RLT, k1, p1, k1, RRT, k6.
Row 6—P5, RT, k2, k1-b, k2, LT, p5.
Row 7—K5, (p1, k3) twice, p1, k5.
Row 8—P4, RT, k3, k1-b, k3, LT, p4.
Row 9—K4, (p1, k4) 3 times.
Row 10—P3, RT, k2, RT, k1-b, LT, k2, LT, p3.
Row 11—K3, p1, k2, RLT, k1, p1, k1, RRT, k2, p1, k3.
Row 12—P2, RT, k1, RT, p2, k1-b, p2, LT, k1, LT, p2.
Row 13—(K2, p1) twice, k3, p1, k3, (p1, k2) twice.
Row 14—P2, k4, p3, (k1, yo, k1, yo, k1) in next st, p3, k4, p2.
Rows 15 and 17—(K2, p1) twice, k3, p5, k3, (p1, k2) twice.
Row 16—P2, k4, p3, k5, p3, k4, p2.
Row 18—P2, k4, p3, ssk, k1, k2 tog, p3, k4, p2.
Row 19—(K2, p1) twice, k3, p3, k3, (p1, k2) twice.
Row 20—P2, k3, LT, p2, sl 1—k2 tog—psso, p2, RT, k3, p2.
Row 21—K2, p1, k3, p1, k5, p1, k3, p1, k2.
Row 22—P2, LT, k2, LT, p3, RT, k2, RT, p2.
Row 23—K3, (p1, k3) 4 times.
Row 24—P3, LT, k2, LT, p1, RT, k2, RT, p3.
Row 25—K4, p1, k3, p1, k1, p1, k3, p1, k4.

Row 26—P4, LT, k2, Twist 3, k2, RT, p4.
Row 27—K5, p1, k7, p1, k5.
Row 28—P5, LT, k5, RT, p5.
Row 29—K6, RRT, k3, RLT, k6.
Row 30—P7, LT, k1, RT, p7.

Repeat Rows 1–30.

Club Pattern

Here is a delightful combination of twists and bobbles, appropriate for all kinds of sportswear. Use it along with cables and other texture patterns.

Panel of 15 sts.

CENTER PANEL: *Club Pattern*
LEFT SIDE PANEL: *Right-Twist Ramp Pattern*
RIGHT SIDE PANEL: *Left-Twist Ramp Pattern*

Row 1 (Wrong side)—K4, (p1, k1) 4 times, k3.
Row 2—P3, (RT) twice, p1, (LT) twice, p3.
Row 3—K3, (p1, k1) twice, k2, (p1, k1) twice, k2.
Row 4—P2, (RT) twice, p3, (LT) twice, p2.
Row 5—K2, (p1, k1) twice, k4, (p1, k1) twice, k1.
Row 6—P1, (RT) twice, p5, (LT) twice, p1.
Row 7—(K1, p1) twice, k7, (p1, k1) twice.
Row 8—P1, Make Bobble (MB) as follows: (k1, yo, k1, yo, k1) in next st, turn and p5, turn and ssk, k3 tog, pass ssk st over the k3-tog st, completing Bobble; p1, LT, p5, RT, p1, MB, p1.
Row 9—K4, p1, k5, p1, k4.
Row 10—P4, LT, p3, RT, p4.
Row 11—K5, p1, k3, p1, k5.
Row 12—P5, MB, p3, MB, p5.

Repeat Rows 1–12.

Ramp Pattern

This design can slant upwards to the left or to the right, depending on how the knitter wishes to arrange it. Both versions are given. They can be worked separately, or placed together in combination.

I. LEFT-TWIST RAMP PATTERN

Row 1 (Wrong side)—K1, (p1, k1) 6 times.
Row 2—P1, (LT) 3 times, p6.
Row 3—K6, (p1, k1) 3 times, k1.
Row 4—P2, (LT) 3 times, p2, Make Bobble (MB) as follows: (k1, yo, k1, yo, k1) in next st, turn and p5, turn and k5, then pass the 4th, 3rd, 2nd and 1st of these 5 sts separately over the last st made, completing Bobble; p2.
Row 5—K5, (p1, k1) 3 times, k2.
Row 6—P3, (LT) 3 times, p4.
Row 7—K4, (p1, k1) 3 times, k3.
Row 8—P4, (LT) 3 times, p3.
Row 9—K3, (p1, k1) 3 times, k4.
Row 10—P2, MB, p2, (LT) 3 times, p2.
Row 11—K2, (p1, k1) 3 times, k5.
Row 12—P6, (LT) 3 times, p1.

Repeat Rows 1–12.

II. RIGHT-TWIST RAMP PATTERN

Row 1 (Wrong side)—K1, (p1, k1) 6 times.
Row 2—P6, (RT) 3 times, p1.
Row 3—K2, (p1, k1) 3 times, k5.
Row 4—P2, MB in next st same as above, p2, (RT) 3 times, p2.
Row 5—K3, (p1, k1) 3 times, k4.
Row 6—P4, (RT) 3 times, p3.
Row 7—K4, (p1, k1) 3 times, k3.
Row 8—P3, (RT) 3 times, p4.
Row 9—K5, (p1, k1) 3 times, k2.
Row 10—P2, (RT) 3 times, p2, MB, p2.
Row 11—K6, (p1, k1) 3 times, k1.
Row 12—P1, (RT) 3 times, p6.

Repeat Rows 1–12.

CHAPTER EIGHT

Cables

Not very many years ago, several kinds of sweaters peculiar to various coastal areas of the British Isles were suddenly discovered by the world of fashion. Their impact on that world was tremendous. Hardly ever before in history has any "peasant style" been so widely imitated, adapted, and adored. And hardly ever has so great an explosion of pattern ideas been derived from a single source.

For centuries, men and women in small fishing villages invented and developed prototypes of today's cable designs. Each family or clan had its own. When families were combined by intermarriage, family patterns also were combined into single garments. Combination of these patterns went on undisturbed for a long time, slowly developing a rich variety.

The Aran Isles, off the western coast of Ireland, are now famous as the source of the traditional fisherman sweater with its heavily embossed surface entirely covered by gorgeous cable combinations. But many other island and seaport localities contributed to the present abundance of cable designs. They come from Cornwall, Yorkshire, Guernsey, Jersey, and many other places. A special kind of fisherman sweater was known as the Bridal Shirt, traditionally knitted by the young fisherman or by his sweetheart, to be worn on his wedding day. The patterns in such garments were often inspired by things common to the daily work and life of the people: ropes, knots, chains, nets, waves, vines, berries, shellfish, driftwood.

It is a sad fact that when any particular branch of handicraft becomes wildly popular, it also becomes cheapened. In order to fill the world-wide demand for "Aran knits", knitwear manufacturers soon devised inexpensive ways to imitate them. Hand-knit sweaters, too, were made in hasty ways for the market, using bigger needles, fewer really intricate patterns, and hence less of the time and care necessitated by traditional methods.

But in the process of popularization, good things also happened to this type of knitting. Creative knitters everywhere began to build on the tradition, developing new and fascinating cable designs to be used along with the old ones. Therefore, many

CABLES   165

unusual contemporary cables will be found in this chapter, side by side with some of the classics. Today's hand knitter has no need to "make do" with the shoddy products that commercial fisherman sweaters all too often are. On the contrary, she can make cable-combination garments even more magnificent than the traditional ones, because she has more patterns to choose from than the old knitters ever had.

The great virtue of a cable-combination garment like a fisherman sweater is that it is—or should be—*one of a kind*. Cables can be put together according to the knitter's taste, and the result is something that no one else has ever done in just that way before. Anyone who has ever made *one* fisherman sweater will know how to make an original one by using different combinations. Patterns can be combined at will until the requisite number of stitches is achieved; then all that is necessary is to go ahead and knit them, keeping track of the row numbers in each one separately, so there is no confusion. Various panels can be packed closely together—the more the better—being set apart by no more than a single knit stitch. A rich profusion of embossed shapes is the mark of a truly fine Aran-style garment.

For the less ambitious knitter, there are many cables that can be worked all by themselves—just one or two panels—in an otherwise plain garment. Why leave a sleeve flat and unadorned, for instance, when an interesting cable panel can be run up the center of it? Why make a dull, plain cardigan for your husband, brother, father, son, or boy friend, when a pair of cables on each side of the front bands can make it look distinctively and handsomely masculine? It is so easy to designate the required number of stitches for your favorite cable, setting them off with markers if you like, and work the cable while the rest of the garment is being worked plain. It is a waste of your time and skill to hand-knit a garment all in stockinette stitch; a machine-made garment would serve just as well. Every garment you make should have a little bit of *you* in it, and this means a little bit of pattern that *you* have chosen for it. Cables are among the most adaptable patterns for this. They go anywhere, do anything, and always look in crisp, casual good taste.

LEFT: *Alternating Cable*
RIGHT: *Aran Braid*

Alternating Cable

This pattern is definitely "different". It is really a double cable, but worked alternately to the right and left so that the two sides do not correspond. The cable is simple to work.

Panel of 12 sts.

Row 1 (Wrong side) and all other wrong-side rows—K2, p8, k2.
Row 2—P2, k4, sl 2 sts to dpn and hold in front, k2, then k2 from dpn; p2.
Row 4—P2, k8, p2.
Row 6—Repeat Row 2.
Row 8—P2, sl 2 sts to dpn and hold in back, k2, then k2 from dpn; k4, p2.
Row 10—Repeat Row 4.
Row 12—Repeat Row 8.

Repeat Rows 1–12.

Aran Braid

With this easy pattern, even a beginner can make thick, fancy, intricate-looking cables to decorate hats, mittens, jackets, or outdoor sweaters. The pattern appears to be very carefully plaited, but in fact its four simple rows can be worked with a minimum of concentration.

Panel of 12 sts.

Rows 1 and 3 (Wrong side)—K2, p8, k2.
Row 2—P2, (sl 2 sts to dpn and hold in back, k2, then k2 from dpn) twice, p2.
Row 4—P2, k2, sl 2 sts to dpn and hold in front, k2, then k2 from dpn; k2, p2.

Repeat Rows 1–4.

Disc Cables

Contributed by Hildegard M. Elsner, Aldan, Pennsylvania

A circular shape is not common in knitting patterns, because knitting simply does not lend itself to the construction of such a shape. Knit and purl stitches, their angles and their methods of formation, are much better suited to vertical, horizontal, and diagonal designs. However, in these three cables—Banjo Cable, Dollar Cable, and Seed Wishbone—we see one of the few ways of making round shapes in knitting.

Disc Cables
LEFT: *Banjo Cable*
CENTER: *Dollar Cable*
RIGHT: *Seed Wishbone*

I. BANJO CABLE

Panel of 12 sts.

Row 1 (Wrong side)—K4, p4, k4.
Row 2—P4, k4, p4.
Row 3—K4, p1, sl 2 wyif, p1, k4.
Row 4—P2, sl next 3 sts to dpn and hold in back, k1, then p1, k1, p1 from dpn; sl next st to dpn and hold in front, k1, p1, k1, then k1 from dpn; p2.
Rows 5, 7, and 9—K2, (p1, k1) 3 times, p2, k2.
Rows 6, 8, and 10—P2, (k1, p1) 3 times, k2, p2.
Row 11—K2, sl 1 wyif, (k1, p1) 3 times, sl 1 wyif, k2.
Row 12—P2, sl next st to dpn and hold in front, p2, k1, then k1 from dpn; sl next 3 sts to dpn and hold in back, k1, then k1, p2 from dpn; p2.
Rows 13, 14, 15, and 16—Repeat Rows 1 and 2 twice.

Repeat Rows 1–16.

II. DOLLAR CABLE

Panel of 12 sts.

Row 1 (Wrong side)—K2, sl 1 wyif, p6, sl 1 wyif, k2.
Row 2—P2, sl next st to dpn and hold in front, p3, then k1 from dpn; sl next 3 sts to dpn and hold in back, k1, then p3 from dpn; p2.
Row 3—K5, p2, k5.
Row 4—P2, sl next 3 sts to dpn and hold in back, k1, then k3 from dpn; sl next st to dpn and hold in front, k3, then k1 from dpn; p2.
Rows 5, 7, and 9—K2, p8, k2.
Rows 6, 8, and 10—P2, k8, p2.

Repeat Rows 1–10.

III. SEED WISHBONE

Panel of 12 sts.

Row 1 (Right side)—P2, sl next 3 sts to dpn and hold in back, k1, then p1, k1, p1 from dpn; sl next st to dpn and hold in front, k1, p1, k1, then k1 from dpn; p2.
Rows 2, 4, and 6—K2, (p1, k1) 3 times, p2, k2.
Rows 3 and 5—P2, (k1, p1) 3 times, k2, p2.
Row 7—P2, k1, p1, k3, p1, k2, p2.
Row 8—K2, p1, k1, p3, k1, p2, k2.

Repeat Rows 1–8.

Five-Rib Braid Cables:
Tight, Loose, and Elongated

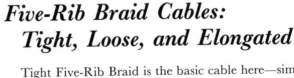

Tight Five-Rib Braid is the basic cable here—similar to Aran Braid, but with five interlocking ribs instead of four. The other two Five-Rib braids are variations. All three are beautiful cables, not difficult to work but interesting.

I. TIGHT FIVE-RIB BRAID

This little cable is very dense and firm, crossing two stitches over two every other row.

Panel of 14 sts.

Notes: Front Cross (FC)—sl 2 sts to dpn and hold in front, k2, then k2 from dpn.
Back Cross (BC)—sl 2 sts to dpn and hold in back, k2, then k2 from dpn.

LEFT: *Tight Five-Rib Braid*
CENTER: *Loose Five-Rib Braid*
RIGHT: *Elongated Five-Rib Braid*

Rows 1 and 3 (Wrong side)—K2, p10, k2.
Row 2—P2, k2, (FC) twice, p2.
Row 4—P2, (BC) twice, k2, p2.

Repeat Rows 1–4.

II. LOOSE FIVE-RIB BRAID

This cable has the same form as Tight Five-Rib Braid, but two plain right-side rows are inserted so that the pattern takes twice as many rows. Also, single purl stitches are placed between the ribs.

Panel of 18 sts.

NOTES: Front Cross (FC)—sl 3 sts to dpn and hold in front, k2, then sl the purl st from dpn back to left-hand needle and purl it, then k2 from dpn.

Back Cross (BC)—sl 3 sts to dpn and hold in back, k2, then sl the purl st from dpn back to left-hand needle and purl it, then k2 from dpn.

Row 1 (Wrong side) and all other wrong-side rows—K2, (p2, k1) 4 times, p2, k2.
Row 2—P2, (k2, p1) 4 times, k2, p2.
Row 4—P2, k2, (p1, FC) twice, p2.
Row 6—Repeat Row 2.
Row 8—P2, (BC, p1) twice, k2, p2.

Repeat Rows 1–8.

III. ELONGATED FIVE-RIB BRAID

One more plain row is included in this version, so that the pattern is elongated eccentrically, or half-way. Still another plain row could be inserted between Rows 6 and 8—making 12 rows in all—to form an even looser version. The wrong-side rows could be worked just like the wrong-side rows in the Loose Braid, but here they are purled, which makes a slight difference in the cabled crossings (see Notes).

Panel of 18 sts.

NOTES: FC and BC—same as for Loose Five-Rib Braid. The central stitch is not a purl stitch, since it is not knitted on the preceding row; nevertheless it is put back on the left-hand needle and purled in the same way.

Row 1 (Wrong side) and all other wrong-side rows—K2, p14, k2.
Rows 2, 4, 6, and 8—Same as Rows 2, 4, 6, and 8 of Loose Five-Rib Braid, above.
Row 10—Repeat Row 2.

Repeat Rows 1–10.

Rib and Purl Cable

Contributed by Marion C. Magnussen, Lake Mills, Wisconsin

Panel of 16 sts.

I. BACK CROSS VERSION

Rows 1, 3, and 5 (Right side)—K2, (p1, k1) 3 times, p6, k2.

Rows 2, 4, and 6—K8, (p1, k1) 3 times, k2.

Row 7—K2, sl next 7 sts to dpn and hold in back, p5, then (p1, k1) 3 times, p1 (the 7 sts from dpn); k2.

Rows 8, 10, 12, and 14—K3, (p1, k1) 3 times, k7.

Rows 9, 11, and 13—K2, p6, (k1, p1) 3 times, k2.

Row 15—K2, sl next 5 sts to dpn and hold in back, (p1, k1) 3 times, p1—the next 7 sts—then p5 from dpn; k2.

Row 16—Repeat Row 2.

Repeat Rows 1–16.

II. FRONT CROSS VERSION

Rows 1, 3, and 5 (Right side)—K2, p6, (k1, p1) 3 times, k2.

Rows 2, 4, and 6—K3, (p1, k1) 3 times, k7.

Row 7—K2, sl next 5 sts to dpn and hold in front, (p1, k1) 3 times, p1—the next 7 sts—then p5 from dpn; k2.

Rows 8, 10, 12, and 14—K8, (p1, k1) 3 times, k2.

Rows 9, 11, and 13—K2, (p1, k1) 3 times, p6, k2.

Row 15—K2, sl next 7 sts to dpn and hold in front, p5, then (p1, k1) 3 times, p1 (the 7 sts from dpn); k2.

Row 16—Repeat Row 2.

Repeat Rows 1–16.

Rib and Purl Cable
LEFT: *Back Cross Version*
RIGHT: *Front Cross Version*

Wrapped Rib Cable

This is nothing but a simple cable, broken at the sides by an encroachment, at intervals, of the purled background. The result is remarkably pretty and unusual. Recommended for beginners or near-beginners who are looking for an easy but "different" pattern.

Panel of 10 sts.

Rows 1, 3, and 5 (Right side)—P2, k6, p2.

Rows 2, 4, and 6—K2, p6, k2.

Row 7—P2, sl next 3 sts to dpn and hold in back, k3, then k3 from dpn; p2.

Rows 8, 10, and 12—Repeat Row 2.

Rows 9 and 11—Repeat Row 1.
Rows 13, 15, 17, and 19—P4, k2, p4.
Rows 14, 16, 18, and 20—K4, p2, k4.

Repeat Rows 1–20.

Crossed V Stitch

Contributed by Barbara N. Rankin, Cleveland Heights, Ohio

Panel of 15 sts.

LEFT: *Wrapped Rib Cable*
CENTER: *Crossed V Stitch*
RIGHT: *Gordian Knot*

NOTES: Front Cross (FC): sl 2 sts to dpn and hold in front, p1, then k2 from dpn.

Back Cross (BC): sl 1 st to dpn and hold in back, k2, then p1 from dpn.

Rows 1 and 3 (Wrong side)—K5, p2, k1, p2, k5.
Row 2—P5, sl next 3 sts to dpn and hold in back, k2, then sl the purl st from dpn back to left-hand needle and purl it, then k2 from dpn; p5.
Row 4—P4, BC, k1, FC, p4.
Row 5 and all subsequent wrong-side rows—Knit all knit sts and purl all purl sts.
Row 6—P3, BC, k1, p1, k1, FC, p3.
Row 8—P2, BC, (k1, p1) twice, k1, FC, p2.
Row 10—P1, BC, (k1, p1) 3 times, k1, FC, p1.
Row 12—BC, (k1, p1) 4 times, k1, FC.
Row 14—K2, p3, k2, p1, k2, p3, k2.

Repeat Rows 1–14.

Gordian Knot

In spite of its rather forbidding name, this pattern is easy to work. By a clever twist in the cabling technique, the central purl stitches are forced forward to make a tight little knot with the knit ribs crossed behind. The cable appears as a small chain with links tightly tied together.

Panel of 10 sts.

Row 1 (Right side)—(P2, k2) twice, p2.
Row 2—(K2, p2) twice, k2.
Row 3—P2, sl next 4 sts to dpn and hold in front, k2, then sl the 2 purl sts from dpn back to left-hand needle, then pass the dpn with 2 remaining knit sts to back of work; p2 from left-hand needle, then k2 from dpn; p2.
Rows 4, 6, and 8—Repeat Row 2.
Rows 5, 7, and 9—Repeat Row 1.
Row 10—Repeat Row 2.

Repeat Rows 1–10.

Four Cables with Openwork: Picot Eyelet Cable, Waves and Footprints, Highlight Cable, and Brisket Cable

All four of these cables are simple to work, and pretty either single or in combination. They are "idea" patterns, because the knitter can add touches of openwork to other types of cables as well. Only four out of a large number of possibilities are shown here.

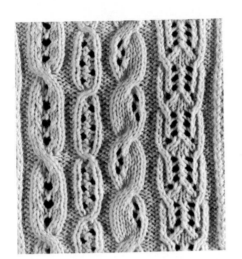

LEFT TO RIGHT:
1. *Picot Eyelet Cable*
2. *Waves and Footprints*
3. *Highlight Cable*
4. *Brisket Cable*

I. PICOT EYELET CABLE

Panel of 10 sts.

Row 1 (Wrong side)—K2, p6, k2.
Row 2—P2, k1, k2 tog, (yo) twice, ssk, k1, p2.
Row 3—K2, p2, (k1, p1) into the double yo of previous row, p2, k2.
Row 4—P2, k6, p2.
Row 5—Repeat Row 1.
Row 6—P2, sl next 4 sts to dpn and hold in front, k2, then sl the center 2 sts from dpn back to left-hand needle and knit them, then k2 from dpn; p2.
Rows 7 through 18—Repeat Rows 1 through 4, 3 times more.

Repeat Rows 1–18.

II. WAVES AND FOOTPRINTS

Panel of 8 sts.

Row 1 (Wrong side) and all other wrong-side rows—K2, (p1, k2) twice.
Rows 2, 6, and 10—P2, k1, yo, ssk, k1, p2.
Rows 4 and 8—P2, k1, k2 tog, yo, k1, p2.
Row 12—P2, k4, p2.
Row 14—P2, sl next 3 sts to dpn and hold in back, k1, then sl the center 2 sts from dpn back to left-hand needle and knit them, then k1 from dpn; p2.
Rows 16, 20, and 24—P2, k1, k2 tog, yo, k1, p2.
Rows 18 and 22—P2, k1, yo, ssk, k1, p2.
Row 26—Repeat Row 12.
Row 28—P2, sl next 3 sts to dpn and hold in front, k1, then sl the center 2 sts from dpn back to left-hand needle and knit them, then k1 from dpn; p2.

Repeat Rows 1–28.

III. HIGHLIGHT CABLE

Panel of 10 sts.

Row 1 (Wrong side) and all other wrong-side rows—K2, p6, k2.
Row 2—P2, k6, p2.
Row 4—P2, sl next 3 sts to dpn and hold in back, k3, then k3 from dpn; p2.
Row 6—Repeat Row 2.
Row 8—P2, k1, yo, k2 tog, k3, p2.
Row 10—P2, ssk, yo, k4, p2.
Row 12—Repeat Row 8.
Rows 14, 16, and 18—Repeat Rows 2, 4, and 6.
Row 20—P2, k3, ssk, yo, k1, p2.
Row 22—P2, k4, yo, k2 tog, p2.
Row 24—Repeat Row 20.

Repeat Rows 1–24.

IV. BRISKET CABLE

Panel of 13 sts.

Row 1 (Wrong side) and all other wrong-side rows—K2, p1, k1, p5, k1, p1, k2.
Rows 2, 4, and 6—P2, k1-b, p1, k1-b, yo, sl 1—k2 tog—psso, yo, k1-b, p1, k1-b, p2.
Row 8—P2, sl next 2 sts to dpn and hold in back, k1, then sl the purl st from dpn back to left-hand needle and purl it, then k1 from dpn; k1-b, k1, k1-b, sl next 2 sts to dpn and hold in front, k1, then sl the purl st from dpn back to left-hand needle and purl it, then k1 from dpn; p2.
Row 10—P2, k1-b, p1, yo, ssk, k1, k2 tog, yo, p1, k1-b, p2.

Repeat Rows 1–10.

CENTER PANEL: *Diamond with Chain*
SIDE PANELS: *Bobbled Cable*

Diamond with Chain

NOTES: Front Cross (FC): sl 2 sts to dpn and hold in front, p1, then k2 from dpn.

Back Cross (BC): sl 1 st to dpn and hold in back, k2, then p1 from dpn.

Single Front Cross (SFC): sl 1 st to dpn and hold in front, p1, then k1 from dpn.

Single Back Cross (SBC): sl 1 st to dpn and hold in back, k1, then p1 from dpn.

Single Knit Cross (SKC): Same as SBC, but *knit* both sts.

Panel of 16 sts.

Row 1 (Wrong side)—K6, p4, k6.
Row 2—P5, BC, FC, p5.
Row 3 and all subsequent wrong-side rows—Knit all knit sts and
   purl all purl sts.
Row 4—P4, BC, k2, FC, p4.
Row 6—P3, BC, p1, SKC, p1, FC, p3.
Row 8—P2, BC, p1, SBC, SFC, p1, FC, p2.
Row 10—P1, BC, p2, (k1, p2) twice, FC, p1.
Row 12—BC, p3, SFC, SBC, p3, FC.
Row 14—K2, p5, SKC, p5, k2.
Row 16—FC, p3, SBC, SFC, p3, BC.
Row 18—P1, FC, p2, (k1, p2) twice, BC, p1.
Row 20—P2, FC, p1, SFC, SBC, p1, BC, p2.
Row 22—P3, FC, p1, SKC, p1, BC, p3.
Row 24—P4, FC, p2, BC, p4.
Row 26—P5, FC, BC, p5.
Row 28—P6, sl next 2 sts to dpn and hold in back, k2, then k2
   from dpn; p6.

Repeat Rows 1–28.

Bobbled Cable

This is a simple eccentric cable with a purled bobble worked
into the broader portion. It is a basic demonstration only; bobbles
may be placed like this on any kind of cable, and in any quantity,
according to the taste of the knitter.

Panel of 11 sts.

Row 1 (Wrong side) and all other wrong-side rows—K2, p7, k2.
Row 2—For a right-twist cable, work Row 2 as follows: P2,
   sl 3 to dpn and hold in back, k4, then k3 from dpn; p2.
   For a left-twist cable, work Row 2 as follows: P2, sl 4 to dpn
   and hold in front, k3, then k4 from dpn; p2.
Row 4—P2, k7, p2.
Rows 6, 10, and 12—Repeat Row 4.
Row 8—Repeat Row 2.
Row 14—P2, k3, Make Bobble in center st as follows: (k1, yo,
   k1, yo, k1) in same st, making 5 sts from one; turn and k5,
   turn and p5, turn and ssk, k1, k2 tog, turn and p3 tog, com-
   pleting bobble; k3, p2.
Row 16—Repeat Row 4.

Repeat Rows 1–16.

Rope and Diamond

Here is a classic Aran diamond pattern enlivened by a simple 4-stitch cable up the middle. It is pleasing with vertical borders also made of 4-stitch cables on each side.

Panel of 18 sts.

NOTES: Front Cross (FC): sl 2 sts to dpn and hold in front, p1, then k2 from dpn.

Back Cross (BC): sl 1 st to dpn and hold in back, k2, then p1 from dpn.

Back Knit Cross (BKC): sl 2 sts to dpn and hold in back, k2, then k2 from dpn.

Row 1 (Wrong side)—K7, p4, k7.
Row 2—P6, BC *knitting all 3 sts,* FC *knitting all 3 sts,* p6.
Row 3 and all subsequent wrong-side rows—Knit all knit sts and purl all purl sts.
Row 4—P5, BC *knitting all 3 sts,* k2, FC *knitting all 3 sts,* p5.
Row 6—P4, BC, BKC, FC, p4.
Row 8—P3, BC, p1, k4, p1, FC, p3.
Row 10—P2, BC, p2, BKC, p2, FC, p2.
Row 12—P1, BC, p3, k4, p3, FC, p1.
Row 14—P1, k2, p4, BKC, p4, k2, p1.
Row 16—P1, FC, p3, k4, p3, BC, p1.
Row 18—P2, FC, p2, BKC, p2, BC, p2.
Row 20—P3, FC, p1, k4, p1, BC, p3.
Row 22—P4, FC, BKC, BC, p4.
Row 24—P5, FC, k2, BC, p5.
Row 26—P6, FC, BC, p6.
Row 28—P7, sl next 2 sts to dpn and hold in front, k2, then k2 from dpn, p7.

Repeat Rows 1–28.

LEFT: *Rope and Diamond*
CENTER: *Ripple and Rock*
RIGHT: *Raveled Braid*

Ripple and Rock

In this simple and pretty bobble cable, the bobble is unexpectedly placed in the *smaller* of the two diamond shapes, which gives a rather novel effect. The pattern is good in central sleeve panels. With a background worked in garter stitch instead of plain purl as shown, it makes a delightful buttonhole band for a cardigan—the buttonholes being placed in the middle of the larger diamonds.

Panel of 17 sts.

NOTES: Front Cross (FC) and Back Cross (BC): Same as for Rope and Diamond.

Row 1 (Wrong side)—K6, p2, k1, p2, k6.
Row 2—P5, BC, p1, FC, p5.
Row 3 and all subsequent wrong-side rows except Row 7—Knit all knit sts and purl all purl sts.
Row 4—P4, BC, p3, FC, p4.
Row 6—P4, k2, p2, Make Bobble in next st as follows: (k1, yo, k1, yo, k1) in same st, turn and p5, turn and k5, turn and p2 tog, p1, p2 tog, turn and sl 1—k2 tog—psso, completing Bobble; p2, k2, p4.
Row 7—K4, p2, k2, p1-b, k2, p2, k4.
Row 8—P4, FC, p3, BC, p4.
Row 10—P5, FC, p1, BC, p5.
Rows 12 and 14—Repeat Rows 2 and 4.
Row 16—P3, BC, p5, FC, p3.
Row 18—P2, BC, p7, FC, p2.
Row 20—P2, FC, p7, BC, p2.
Row 22—P3, FC, p5, BC, p3.
Rows 24 and 26—Repeat Rows 8 and 10.

Repeat Rows 1–26.

Raveled Braid

A plain plait cable is here "raveled out" at intervals to show its three component ribs. This cable combines well with wider and fancier ones.

Panel of 16 sts.

NOTES: Front Cross (FC), Back Cross (BC) and Back Knit Cross (BKC): Same as for Rope and Diamond.

Front Knit Cross (FKC): sl 2 sts to dpn and hold in front, k2, then k2 from dpn.

Row 1 (Wrong side) —K5, p6, k5.
Rows 2, 6, and 10—P5, k2, BKC, p5.
Row 3 and all subsequent wrong-side rows—Knit all knit sts and purl all purl sts.
Rows 4, 8, and 12—P5, FKC, k2, p5.
Row 14—P4, BC, k2, FC, p4.
Row 16—P3, BC, p1, k2, p1, FC, p3.
Row 18—P2, BC, p2, k2, p2, FC, p2.
Row 20—P2, FC, p2, k2, p2, BC, p2.
Row 22—P3, FC, p1, k2, p1, BC, p3.
Row 24—P4, FC, k2, BC, p4.

Repeat Rows 1–24.

Two Fancy Open Cables:
Open Cable with Waved Rib,
and Four-Rib Braid

I. OPEN CABLE WITH WAVED RIB

NOTES: Back Cross (BC): sl 1 st to dpn and hold in back, k2, then p1 from dpn.

Front Cross (FC): sl 2 sts to dpn and hold in front, p1, then k2 from dpn.

Single Back Cross (SBC): sl 1 st to dpn and hold in back, k1, then p1 from dpn.

Single Front Cross (SFC): sl 1 st to dpn and hold in front, p1, then k1 from dpn.

Fancy Open Cables
LEFT: *Open Cable with Waved Rib*
RIGHT: *Four-Rib Braid*

Panel of 15 sts.

Row 1 (Wrong side)—K2, p1, k2, p2, k1, p2, k2, p1, k2.

Row 2—P2, k1, p2, sl next 3 sts to dpn and hold in back, k2, then sl the purl st from dpn back to left-hand needle and purl it, then k2 from dpn; p2, k1, p2.

Row 3—Repeat Row 1.

Row 4—P2, SFC, BC, p1, FC, SBC, p2.

Rows 5 and 7—(K3, p3) twice, k3.

Row 6—P3, work BC but knit all 3 sts, p3, work FC but knit all 3 sts, p3.

Row 8—P2, BC, SFC, p1, SBC, FC, p2.

Rows 9 and 11—K2, p2, k2, p1, k1, p1, k2, p2, k2.

Row 10—P2, k2, p2, k1, p1, k1, p2, k2, p2.

Row 12—P2, FC, SBC, p1, SFC, BC, p2.

Rows 13 and 15—Repeat Rows 5 and 7.

Row 14—P3, work FC but knit all 3 sts, p3, work BC but knit all 3 sts, p3.

Row 16—P2, SBC, FC, p1, BC, SFC, p2.

Repeat Rows 1–16.

II. FOUR-RIB BRAID

NOTES: BC and FC—same as given for Open Cable with Waved Rib.

Panel of 17 sts.

Row 1 (Wrong side)—(K2, p2) twice, k1, (p2, k2) twice.

Row 2—P2, k2, p2, sl next 3 sts to dpn and hold in *back*, k2, sl the purl st from dpn back to left-hand needle and purl it, then k2 from dpn; p2, k2, p2.

Row 3—Repeat Row 1.

Row 4—P2, FC, BC, p1, FC, BC, p2.

Row 5—(K3, p4) twice, k3.

Row 6—P3, sl next 2 sts to dpn and hold in back, k2, then k2 from dpn; p3, sl next 2 sts to dpn and hold in front, k2, then k2 from dpn; p3.

Row 7—Repeat Row 5.

Row 8—P2, BC, FC, p1, BC, FC, p2.
Row 9—Repeat Row 1.
Row 10—P2, k2, p2, sl the next 3 sts to dpn and hold in *front*, k2, then sl the purl st from dpn back to left-hand needle and purl it, then k2 from dpn; p2, k2, p2.
Rows 11 through 16—Repeat Rows 3 through 8.

Repeat Rows 1–16.

Framed Cable

Try this graceful pattern instead of a simple cable in a tennis sweater or similar "classic" garment. The Framed Cable is remarkably elegant, too, as a border for a cardigan or a single sleeve panel. This is one of those why-didn't-*I*-think-of-that patterns, with exceedingly simple elements that happen to combine very successfully. (No, your author *didn't* think of it. It is an English pattern.)

Panel of 18 sts.

NOTES: Front Cross (FC): sl 3 sts to dpn and hold in front, k3, then k3 from dpn.

Single Front Cross (SFC): sl 1 st to dpn and hold in front, p1, then k1-b from dpn.

Single Back Cross (SBC): sl 1 st to dpn and hold in back, k1-b, then p1 from dpn.

Row 1 (Wrong side)—K5, p8, k5.
Row 2—P4, SBC, k6, SFC, p4.
Row 3 and all subsequent wrong-side rows—Knit all knit sts and purl all purl sts.
Row 4—P3, SBC, p1, k6, p1, SFC, p3.
Row 6—P2, SBC, p2, FC, p2, SFC, p2.
Row 8—P1, SBC, p3, k6, p3, SFC, p1.
Row 10—P1, SFC, p3, k6, p3, SBC, p1.
Row 12—P2, SFC, p2, FC, p2, SBC, p2.
Row 14—P3, SFC, p1, k6, p1, SBC, p3.
Row 16—P4, SFC, k6, SBC, p4.

Repeat Rows 1–16.

LEFT: *Framed Cable*
CENTER: *Ensign's Braid*
RIGHT: *Sausage Cable*

Ensign's Braid

This is an enlarged Four-Rib Braid with a different arrangement of the cabled crossings. There are two superimposed diamonds, the upper one crossing to the left and the lower to the right. The effect is intricate, although the working of the pattern is not.

Panel of 24 sts.

NOTES: Front Cross (FC): sl 3 sts to dpn and hold in front, k3, then k3 from dpn.

Back Cross (BC): sl 3 sts to dpn and hold in back, k3, then k3 from dpn.

Single Front Cross (SFC): sl 3 sts to dpn and hold in front, p1, then k3 from dpn.

Single Back Cross (SBC): sl 1 st to dpn and hold in back, k3, then p1 from dpn.

Row 1 (Wrong side)—K2, p3, k4, p6, k4, p3, k2.

Row 2—P2, k3, p4, BC, p4, k3, p2.

Row 3 and all subsequent wrong-side rows—Knit all knit sts and purl all purl sts.

Row 4—P2, (SFC, p2, SBC) twice, p2.

Row 6—P3, SFC, SBC, p2, SFC, SBC, p3.

Row 8—P4, FC, p4, BC, p4.

Row 10—P3, SBC, SFC, p2, SBC, SFC, p3.

Row 12—P2, (SBC, p2, SFC) twice, p2.

Row 14—P2, k3, p4, FC, p4, k3, p2.

Rows 16 and 18—Repeat Rows 4 and 6.

Row 20—P4, BC, p4, FC, p4.

Rows 22 and 24—Repeat Rows 10 and 12.

Repeat Rows 1–24.

Sausage Cable

This cable is made in long ovals with three little crossings in the center of each. The novel touch is seen in the method of decreasing and increasing between the "links".

Panel of 12 sts.

Rows 1, 3, 5, 7, 9, and 11 (Wrong side)—K2, p8, k2.

Row 2—P2, k2, sl next 2 sts to dpn and hold in front, k2, then k2 from dpn; k2, p2.

Rows 4 and 8—P2, k8, p2.

Rows 6 and 10—Repeat Row 2.

Row 12—P2, k2, k2 tog, ssk, k2, p2.

Row 13—K2, p6, k2.

Row 14—P2, k1, ssk, k2 tog, k1, p2.

Rows 15 and 17—K2, p4, k2.

Row 16—P2, sl next 2 sts to dpn and hold in back, k2, then k2 from dpn; p2.

Row 18—P2, k1, M1, k2, M1, k1, p2.

Row 19—Repeat Row 13.

Row 20—P2, (k2, M1) twice, k2, p2.

Repeat Rows 1–20.

Lobster Claw

Panel of 12 sts.

Row 1 (Wrong side)—Knit.
Row 2—P2, k1, p6, k1, p2.
Rows 3, 5, and 7—K2, p2, k4, p2, k2.
Rows 4 and 6—P2, k2, p4, k2, p2.
Row 8—P2, sl next 2 sts to dpn and hold in front, p2, yo, then k2 tog-b from dpn; sl next 2 sts to dpn and hold in back, k2 tog, yo, then p2 from dpn; p2.

Repeat Rows 1–8.

LEFT: *Lobster Claw*
CENTER: *Giant Embossed Plait*
RIGHT: *Elliptical Cable*

Giant Embossed Plait

Contributed by Grace E. Smith, LaVerne, California

This is a huge and heavy plait pattern made by a highly unusual method. Each of the plaited ribs is a series of short rows, and each one stands up a full quarter-inch, or more, from the background. If several of these giant plaits are being worked at once, then a separate cable needle will be required for each, because the stitches are left on the cable needle throughout an entire right-side row, and are not picked up again until the return row. (If you want to use a number of Giant Embossed Plaits but do not have a sufficient number of cable needles, round toothpicks will do nicely instead.)

Panel of 16 sts.

Preparation Row (Wrong side)—Purl.
Row 1—K10, (turn, p4, turn, k4) 3 times; then sl these 4 sts to dpn and leave at front of work. Pass yarn to back between needles, sl 4 sts from right-hand needle to left-hand needle, k10.
Row 2—P10, p4 from dpn, p2.
Row 3—K10, (turn, p4, turn, k4) 3 times; then sl these 4 sts to dpn and leave at front of work. Pass yarn to back between needles, sl 4 sts from left-hand needle to right-hand needle, k2.
Row 4—P2, p4 from dpn, p10.

Repeat Rows 1–4.

Elliptical Cable

Panel of 12 sts.

Row 1 (Wrong side) and all other wrong-side rows—K2, p2-b, p4, p2-b, k2.
Row 2—P2, k2-b, k4, k2-b, p2.

Row 4—P2, k2-b, sl next 2 sts to dpn and hold in back, k2, then k2 from dpn; k2-b, p2.

Rows 6 and 8—Repeat Row 2.

Row 10—P2, sl next 4 sts to dpn and hold in back, k2, then knit 1st 2 sts from dpn; bring dpn with remaining 2 sts through to front of work, k2, then k2 from dpn; p2.

Repeat Rows 1–10.

Nautical Twisted-Rope Cable

Contributed by Pauline Balbes, Hollywood, California

Big, bold, and bulky! This "giant" is wonderful for Aran-knit coats, jackets, sweaters and afghans. The panel includes the little four-stitch simple cables on each side, plus four more edge stitches.

Panel of 49 sts.

NOTES: Front Cross (FC): sl 2 sts to dpn and hold in front, k2, then k2 from dpn.

Back Cross (BC): sl 2 sts to dpn and hold in back, k2, then k2 from dpn.

Make One (M1): pick up running thread before next st and purl into the *back* of this thread.

CENTER PANEL: *Nautical Twisted-Rope Cable*
SIDE PANELS: *Dry Bones Cable*

Row 1 (Right side)—(P2, k4) 4 times, p1, (k4, p2) 4 times.

Rows 2, 4, 6, and 8—(K2, p4) 4 times, k1, (p4, k2) 4 times.

Row 3—(P2, FC, p2, k4) twice, p1, (k4, p2, BC, p2) twice.

Row 5—Repeat Row 1.

Row 7—P2, FC, p2, k4, p2, FC, p2, sl next 5 sts to dpn and hold in front, k4, then sl the purl st from dpn back to left-hand needle and purl it; then k4 from dpn; p2, BC, p2, k4, p2, BC, p2.

Row 9—P2, k4, p2, * M1, (k4, p2) twice, k4, M1 *, p1, repeat from * to *, p2, k4, p2.

Row 10—K2, p4, * k3, p4, (k2, p4) twice, rep from *, k3, p4, k2.

Row 11—P2, FC, p3, M1, k4, p2 tog, FC, p2 tog, k4, M1, p3, M1, k4, p2 tog, BC, p2 tog, k4, M1, p3, BC, p2.

Row 12—K2, p4, k4, * (p4, k1) twice, p4 *, k5, rep from * to *, k4, p4, k2.

Row 13—P2, k4, p4, * M1, k3, ssk, k4, k2 tog, k3, M1 *, p5, rep from * to *, p4, k4, p2.

Row 14—K2, p4, k5, p12, k7, p12, k5, p4, k2.

Row 15—P2, FC, p5, M1, k4, FC, k4, M1, p7, M1, k4, BC, k4, M1, p5, BC, p2.

Row 16—K2, p4, k6, p12, k9, p12, k6, p4, k2.

Row 17—P2, k4, p6, sl next 8 sts to dpn and hold in back, k4, then sl the 2nd 4 sts from dpn back to left-hand needle and knit them; then k4 from dpn; p9, sl next 8 sts to dpn and hold in front, k4, then sl the 2nd 4 sts from dpn back to left-hand needle and knit them; then k4 from dpn; p6, k4, p2.

Rows 18, 20, 22, and 24—Repeat Rows 16, 14, 12, and 10.

Row 19—P2, FC, p4, p2 tog, k4, FC, k4, p2 tog, p5, p2 tog, k4, BC, k4, p2 tog, p4, BC, p2.

Row 21—P2, k4, p3, * p2 tog, (k4, M1) twice, k4, p2 tog, p3, rep from *, k4, p2.

Row 23—P2, FC, p2, p2 tog, k4, M1, p1, FC, p1, M1, k4, p2 tog, p1, p2 tog, k4, M1, p1, BC, p1, M1, k4, p2 tog, p2, BC, p2.

Row 25—P2, k4, p1, p2 tog, * (k4, p2) twice, k4 *, p3 tog, rep from * to *, p2 tog, p1, k4, p2.

Row 26—Repeat Row 2.

Row 27—Repeat Row 7.

Row 28—Repeat Row 2.

Repeat Rows 1–28.

Dry Bones Cable

In strong contrast to the Nautical Twisted-Rope, this cable is about as skeletal and skinny as a cable can be. But its slender lines of single stitches suggest the wider motif that would result if these "bones" were fleshed out with seven knit stitches instead of the solitary one in the center.

Panel of 11 sts.

NOTES: Front Cross (FC): sl 1 st to dpn and hold in front, p1, then k1-b from dpn.

Back Cross (BC): sl 1 st to dpn and hold in back, k1-b, then p1 from dpn.

Rows 1 and 3 (Right side)—P5, k1-b, p5.

Row 2—K5, p1, k5.

Row 4—K2, (p1, k2) 3 times.

Row 5—P2, (k1-b, p2) 3 times.

Row 6—K2, p1, k5, p1, k2.

Row 7—P2, FC, p3, BC, p2.

Rows 8 and 10—K3, (p1, k3) twice.

Row 9—P3, sl next 4 sts to dpn and hold in front, drop next st off left-hand needle; sl the 3 purl sts from dpn back to left-hand needle, then with point of dpn pick up dropped st and place it on left-hand needle after the 3 purl sts; then k1, p3 from left-hand needle; then k1-b from dpn; p3.

Row 11—P2, BC, p3, FC, p2.

Rows 12, 13, 14, 15, and 16—Repeat Rows 6, 5, 4, 3, and 2.

Repeat Rows 1–16.

Hartshorn Cable

Panel of 28 sts.

NOTES: Front Cross (FC)—sl 2 sts to dpn and hold in front, p2, then k2 from dpn.

Front Knit Cross (FKC)—same as FC, but *knit* all 4 sts.

Back Cross (BC)—sl 2 sts to dpn and hold in back, k2, then p2 from dpn.

Back Knit Cross (BKC)—same as BC, but *knit* all 4 sts.

Single Front Cross (SFC)—sl 2 sts to dpn and hold in front, p1, then k2 from dpn.

Single Back Cross (SBC)—sl 1 st to dpn and hold in back, k2, then p1 from dpn.

Rows 1 and 3 (Wrong side)—K9, p10, k9.
Row 2—P9, BKC, k2, FKC, p9.
Row 4—P7, BC, k2, BKC, FC, p7.
Row 5 and all other wrong-side rows—Knit all knit sts and purl all purl sts.
Row 6—P5, BC, p1, SBC, k2, SFC, p1, FC, p5.
Row 8—P3, BC, p2, SBC, p1, k2, p1, SFC, p2, FC, p3.
Row 10—P3, k2, p3, SBC, p2, k2, p2, SFC, p3, k2, p3.
Row 12—P3, FC, SBC, p3, k2, p3, SFC, BC, p3.
Row 14—P5, BKC, p4, k2, p4, FKC, p5.
Row 16—P3, BC, FC, p2, k2, p2, BC, FC, p3.
Row 18—P3, k2, p4, FC, k2, BC, p4, k2, p3.
Row 20—P3, FC, p4, FKC, k2, p4, BC, p3.
Row 22—P5, FC, p2, k2, BKC, p2, BC, p5.
Row 24—P7, FC, FKC, k2, BC, p7.

Repeat Rows 1–24.

LEFT: *Hartshorn Cable*
RIGHT: *Double-Wrapped Braid*

Double-Wrapped Braid

Panel of 22 sts.

NOTES: FC, FKC, BC, and BKC—same as for Hartshorn Cable.

Rows 1 and 3 (Wrong side)—K5, p4, k8, p2, k3.
Row 2—P3, k2, p8, k4, p5.
Row 4—P3, FC, p6, FKC, p5.
Row 5 and all other wrong-side rows—Knit all knit sts and purl all purl sts.
Row 6—P5, FC, p2, BC, FC, p3.
Row 8—P7, k2, BC, p4, k2, p3.
Row 10—P7, BKC, p4, BC, p3.
Row 12—P5, BC, FC, BC, p5.
Row 14—P3, BC, p4, FKC, p7.

Row 16—P3, k2, p4, BC, k2, p7.
Row 18—P3, FC, BC, p2, FC, p5.
Row 20—P5, BKC, p6, FC, p3.
Row 22—P5, k4, p8, k2, p3.
Row 24—P5, BKC, p6, BC, p3.
Row 26—P3, BC, FC, p2, BC, p5.
Row 28—P3, k2, p4, FC, k2, p7.
Row 30—P3, FC, p4, FKC, p7.
Row 32—P5, FC, BC, FC, p5.
Row 34—P7, BKC, p4, FC, p3.
Row 36—P7, k2, FC, p4, k2, p3.
Row 38—P5, BC, p2, FC, BC, p3.
Row 40—P3, BC, p6, FKC, p5.

Repeat Rows 1–40.

Triplet Cable

CENTER PANEL: *Triplet Cable*
LEFT SIDE PANEL: *Cork Cable, Back Cross*
RIGHT SIDE PANEL: *Cork Cable, Front Cross*

In this beautiful design, three bobbles stand atop three ribs in the center of a fancy half-diamond, each motif opening out gracefully into the one above it. Notice the unusual use of cabled ribbing in the border, and of garter stitch for the central background.

Panel of 21 sts.

NOTES: Front Cross (FC): sl 3 sts to dpn and hold in front, k1, then k1-b, p1, k1-b from dpn.

Back Cross (BC): sl 1 st to dpn and hold in back, k1-b, p1, k1-b, then k1 from dpn.

Make Bobble (MB) as follows: (k1, yo, k1, yo, k1) in the same st, turn and p5, turn and k3, k2 tog, then pass the 3 knit sts one at a time over the last k2-tog st, completing bobble.

Row 1 (Wrong side)—K7, p1, k1, p3, k1, p1, k7.
Row 2—P6, BC, k1-b, FC, p6.
Row 3—K6, (p1, k1) 4 times, p1, k6.
Row 4—P5, BC, k1, k1-b, k1, FC, p5.
Row 5—K5, p1, k1, (p1, k2) twice, p1, k1, p1, k5.
Row 6—P4, BC, k2, k1-b, k2, FC, p4.
Row 7—K4, p1, k1, p2, k2, p1, k2, p2, k1, p1, k4.
Row 8—P3, BC, (k1-b, k2) twice, k1-b, FC, p3.
Row 9—K3, (p1, k1) twice, (p1, k2) twice, (p1, k1) twice, p1, k3.
Row 10—P2, BC, k1, (k1-b, k2) twice, k1-b, k1, FC, p2.

Row 11—K2, p1, k1, (p1, k2) 4 times, p1, k1, p1, k2.

Row 12—P1, BC, (k2, k1-b) 3 times, k2, FC, p1.

Row 13—(K1, p1) twice, k3, (p1, k2) twice, p1, k3, (p1, k1) twice.

Row 14—(P1, k1-b) twice, k3, (MB, k2) twice, MB, k3, (k1-b, p1) twice.

Row 15—(K1, p1) twice, k3, (p1-b, k2) twice, p1-b, k3, (p1, k1) twice.

Row 16—(P1, k1-b) twice, p3, k1-b, p1, k3-b, p1, k1-b, p3, (k1-b, p1) twice.

Repeat Rows 1–16.

Cork Cable

Here is a simple but interesting Irish cable design featuring three ribs crossing either to the left or to the right. The two types can be used to balance each other as shown. For a third variation, the cable can be worked in braided fashion by using the front cross (Version II, Row 6) on the sixth row and the back cross (Version I, Row 6) on the twelfth.

Panel of 14 sts.

VERSION I. BACK CROSS

Row 1 (Wrong side) and all other wrong-side rows—K2, (p2, k2) 3 times.

Rows 2, 4, 8, and 10—P2, (k2, p2) 3 times.

Row 6—P2, k2, p2, Back Cross the next 6 sts as follows: sl 4 sts to dpn and hold in back, k2, then sl the 2 purl sts back to left-hand needle and purl them; then k2 from dpn; p2.

Row 12—P2, Back Cross the next 6 sts as in Row 6; p2, k2, p2.

Repeat Rows 1–12.

VERSION II. FRONT CROSS

Work the same as I, above, with the following exceptions:

Row 6—P2, Front Cross the next 6 sts as follows: sl 4 sts to dpn and hold in front, k2, then sl the 2 purl sts back to left-hand needle and purl them; then k2 from dpn; p2, k2, p2.

Row 12—P2, k2, p2, Front Cross the next 6 sts as in Row 6; p2.

Repeat Rows 1–12.

Aran Diamond and Bobble

Panel of 17 sts.

NOTES: Front Cross (FC)—sl 2 sts to dpn and hold in front, p1, then k2 from dpn.

Back Cross (BC)—sl 1 st to dpn and hold in back, k2, then p1 from dpn.

Rows 1 and 3 (Wrong side)—K6, p2, k1, p2, k6.

Row 2—P6, sl next 3 sts to dpn and hold in back, k2, then sl the purl st from dpn back to left-hand needle and purl it, then k2 from dpn; p6.

Row 4—P5, BC, k1, FC, p5.

Row 5 and all subsequent wrong-side rows—Knit all knit sts and purl all purl sts.

Row 6—P4, BC, k1, p1, k1, FC, p4.

Row 8—P3, BC, (k1, p1) twice, k1, FC, p3.

Row 10—P2, BC, (k1, p1) 3 times, k1, FC, p2.

Row 12—P2, FC, (p1, k1) 3 times, p1, BC, p2.

Row 14—P3, FC, (p1, k1) twice, p1, BC, p3.

Row 16—P4, FC, p1, k1, p1, BC, p4.

Row 18—P5, FC, p1, BC, p5.

Row 20—Repeat Row 2.

Row 22—P5, BC, p1, FC, p5.

Row 24—P4, BC, p3, FC, p4.

Row 26—P4, k2, p2, Make Bobble as follows: (k1, yo, k1, yo, k1) in next st, turn and p5, turn and k5, turn and p2 tog, p1, p2 tog, turn and sl 1—k2 tog—psso, completing Bobble; p2, k2, p4.

Row 28—P4, FC, p3, BC, p4.

Row 30—Repeat Row 18.

Repeat Rows 1–30.

LEFT: *Aran Diamond and Bobble*
CENTER: *Clustered Braid*
RIGHT: *Cluster Cable*

Clustered Braid

Panel of 20 sts.

NOTES: FC and BC—same as for Aran Diamond and Bobble.

Back Knit Cross (BKC)—sl 2 sts to dpn and hold in back, k2, then k2 from dpn.

Rows 1 and 3 (Wrong side)—K4, (p4, k4) twice.

Row 2—P4, BKC, p4, sl next 2 sts to dpn and hold in front, k2, then k2 from dpn; p4.

Row 4—P3, BC, FC, p2, BC, FC, p3.

Row 5 and all subsequent wrong-side rows—Knit all knit sts and
   purl all purl sts.

Row 6—P2, (BC, p2, FC) twice, p2.

Row 8—P2, k2, p4, BKC, p4, k2, p2.

Row 10—P2, k2, p4, k4, p4, k2, p2.

Row 12—Repeat Row 8.

Row 14—P2, (FC, p2, BC) twice, p2.

Row 16—P3, FC, BC, p2, FC, BC, p3.

Rows 18 and 20—Repeat Rows 2 and 4.

Row 22—P3, (k2, p2) twice, k2; then sl the last 6 sts worked onto
   dpn and wrap yarn 4 times counterclockwise around these 6
   sts; then sl the 6 sts back to right-hand needle; p2, k2, p3.

Row 24—Repeat Row 16.

Repeat Rows 1–24.

Cluster Cable

Panel of 16 sts.

NOTES: FC, BC, and BKC—same as for Clustered Braid.

Single Front Cross (SFC)—sl 1 st to dpn and hold in front,
p1, then k1 from dpn.

Single Back Cross (SBC)—sl 1 st to dpn and hold in back, k1,
then p1 from dpn.

Rows 1 and 3 (Wrong side)—K6, p4, k6.

Row 2—P6, BKC, p6.

Row 4—P5, BC, FC, p5.

Row 5 and all subsequent wrong-side rows—Knit all knit sts and
   purl all purl sts.

Row 6—P4, BC, p2, FC, p4.

Row 8—P4, RT, p4, LT, p4.

Row 10—P3, SBC, SFC, p2, SBC, SFC, p3.

Row 12—P2, (SBC, p2, SFC) twice, p2.

Row 14—P2, k1, p4, k2; then sl the last 2 sts worked onto dpn
   and wrap yarn 6 times counterclockwise around these 2 sts; then
   sl the 2 sts back to right-hand needle; p4, k1, p2.

Row 16—P2, (SFC, p2, SBC) twice, p2.

Row 18—P3, SFC, SBC, p2, SFC, SBC, p3.

Row 20—P4, LT, p4, RT, p4.

Row 22—P4, FC, p2, BC, p4.

Row 24—P5, FC, BC, p5.

Repeat Rows 1–24.

Spanish Tile Cable

Contributed by Ruth S. Stein, Los Angeles, California

A diamond with a few novel touches, this large, commanding cable is ideal as a central motif in a fancy sweater or jacket. One repeat is handsome on the back of a mitten or glove. Note the small difference between the Front Cross and Back Cross versions.

Panel of 22 sts.

NOTES: Front Cross (FC): sl 3 sts to dpn and hold in front, k3, then k3 from dpn.

Back Cross (BC): sl 3 sts to dpn and hold in back, k3, then k3 from dpn.

Front Purl Cross (FPC): sl 3 sts to dpn and hold in front, p3, then k3 from dpn.

Back Purl Cross (BPC): sl 3 sts to dpn and hold in back, k3, then p3 from dpn.

Rows 1, 3, and 5 (Wrong side)—K8, p6, k8.
Rows 2 and 4—P8, k6, p8.
Row 6—P5, k3, FC, (or BC), k3, p5.
Rows 7, 9, and 11—K5, p12, k5.
Rows 8 and 10—P5, k12, p5.
Row 12—P2, k3, BPC, FPC, k3, p2.
Rows 13, 15, and 17—K2, p6, k6, p6, k2.
Rows 14 and 16—P2, k6, p6, k6, p2.
Row 18—P2, BPC, p6, FPC, p2.
Rows 19, 21, and 23—K2, p3, k12, p3, k2.
Rows 20 and 22—P2, k3, p12, k3, p2.
Row 24—P2, FC, p6, BC, p2.
Rows 25 through 29—Repeat Rows 13 through 17.
Row 30—P5, FC, BC, p5.
Rows 31 through 35—Repeat Rows 7 through 11.
Row 36—P8, FC (or BC), p8.

Repeat Rows 1–36.

Spanish Tile Cable
LEFT: *Front Cross*
RIGHT: *Back Cross*

CENTER PANEL: *Counter-Twisted Oval*
SIDE PANELS: *Twin Waves*

Counter-Twisted Oval

This graceful design develops from a small simple cable, which is twisted right, left, and right in the center.

Panel of 26 sts.

NOTES: Front Cross (FC)—sl 2 sts to dpn and hold in front, p2, then k2 from dpn.

Front Knit Cross (FKC)—Same as Front Cross, but *knit* all sts.

Single Front Cross (SFC)—sl 2 sts to dpn and hold in front, p1, then k2 from dpn.

Back Cross (BC)—sl 2 sts to dpn and hold in back, k2, then p2 from dpn.

Back Knit Cross (BKC)—Same as Back Cross, but *knit* all sts.

Single Back Cross (SBC)—sl 1 st to dpn and hold in back, k2, then p1 from dpn.

Rows 1 and 3 (Wrong side)—K11, p4, k11.
Row 2—P11, BKC, p11.
Row 4—P9, BKC, FKC, p9.
Row 5 and all subsequent wrong-side rows—Knit all knit sts and purl all purl sts.
Row 6—P7, BC, FKC, FC, p7.
Row 8—P5, BC, p2, k4, p2, FC, p5.
Row 10—P4, SBC, p4, FKC, p4, SFC, p4.
Row 12—P3, SBC, p3, BKC, FKC, p3, SFC, p3.
Row 14—P2, SBC, p2, BC, k4, FC, p2, SFC, p2.
Row 16—P2, k2, p1, BC, p2, BKC, p2, FC, p1, k2, p2.
Row 18—P2, k2, p1, k2, p4, k4, p4, k2, p1, k2, p2.
Row 20—P2, k2, p1, FC, p2, BKC, p2, BC, p1, k2, p2.
Row 22—P2, SFC, p2, FC, k4, BC, p2, SBC, p2.
Row 24—P3, SFC, p3, FC, BC, p3, SBC, p3.
Row 26—P4, SFC, p4, FKC, p4, SBC, p4.
Row 28—P5, FC, p2, k4, p2, BC, p5.
Row 30—P7, FC, FKC, BC, p7.
Row 32—P9, FC, BC, p9.

Repeat Rows 1–32.

Twin Waves

To arrange this cable in opposition panels as shown, in *one* of the panels work FKC instead of BKC in Rows 2 and 12. Begin one cable with Row 1, the other with Row 11.

Panel of 15 sts.

NOTES: FC, FKC, SFC, BC, BKC, and SBC—Same as for Counter-Twisted Oval.

Rows 1 and 3 (Wrong side)—K3, p4, k4, p2, k2.
Row 2—P2, k2, p4, BKC, p3.
Row 4—P2, FC, BC, k2, p3.
Row 5 and all subsequent wrong-side rows—Knit all knit sts and purl all purl sts.
Row 6—P4, BC, p1, SBC, p3.
Row 8—P3, SBC, p1, BKC, p4.
Row 10—P3, k2, BC, FC, p2.
Row 12—P3, BKC, p4, k2, p2.
Row 14—P3, k2, FC, BC, p2.
Row 16—P3, SFC, p1, FC, p4.
Row 18—P4, FKC, p1, SFC, p3.
Row 20—P2, BC, FC, k2, p3.

Repeat Rows 1–20.

Cam Cable

Here is a marvelously unusual cable for your most "original" fisherman sweaters. The big five-stitch rib is shredded into five separate ribs, in a diagonal ladder-like design. Notice that there is no actual crossing (5 over 5) of the large ribs, as this would squeeze the pattern too much. Instead, an illusion of a cable twist is cleverly achieved by means of increases and decreases.

CENTER PANEL: *Cam Cable*
SIDE PANELS: *Slack Line, or Drunken-Sailor Cable*

Panel of 20 sts.

NOTES: Front Cross (FC): sl 1 st to dpn and hold in front, p1, then k1 from dpn.

Double Front Cross (2FC): sl 2 sts to dpn and hold in front, p1, then k2 from dpn.

Triple Front Cross (3FC): sl 3 sts to dpn and hold in front, p1, then k3 from dpn.

Back Cross (BC): sl 1 st to dpn and hold in back, k1, then p1 from dpn.

Increase (inc): purl into the front and back of the same st.

Rows 1 and 3 (Wrong side)—K4, p5, k2, p5, k4.
Row 2—P4, k5, p2, k5, p4.
Row 4—P3, inc, k4, ssk, k2 tog, k4, inc, p3.
Row 5—K5, p10, k5.
Row 6—P4, BC, * sl next 4 sts to dpn and hold in front, p1, then k4 from dpn; k2 tog *, k2, inc, p4.
Row 7—K6, p7, k2, p1, k4.
Row 8—P3, BC, p2, rep from * to * of Row 6, inc, p5.
Row 9—K7, p5, k4, p1, k3.
Row 10—P2, BC, p3, BC, 3FC, p7.
Row 11—K7, p3, k2, p1, k4, p1, k2.
Row 12—P2, FC, p2, BC, p2, 3FC, p6.
Row 13—K6, p3, k4, p1, k2, p1, k3.
Row 14—P3, FC, BC, p3, BC, 2FC, p5.
Row 15—K5, p2, k2, p1, k4, p2, k4.
Row 16—P4, 2FC, p2, BC, p2, 2FC, p4.
Row 17—K4, p2, k4, p1, k2, p2, k5.
Row 18—P5, 2FC, BC, p3, BC, FC, p3.
Row 19—K3, p1, k2, p1, k4, p3, k6.
Row 20—P6, 3FC, p2, BC, p2, FC, p2.
Row 21—K2, p1, k4, p1, k2, p3, k7.
Row 22—P7, work 3FC but *knit* all sts, BC, p3, BC, p2.
Row 23—K3, p1, k4, p5, k7.
Row 24—P5, p2 tog, k1, * sl next 4 sts to dpn and hold in front, knit into front and back of next st, then k4 from dpn *, p2, BC, p3.
Row 25—K4, p1, k2, p7, k6.
Row 26—P4, p2 tog, k3, rep from * to * of Row 24, BC, p4.
Row 27—Repeat Row 5.

Row 28—P3, p2 tog, k5, purl into front and back of the running thread between the st just worked and the next st; k5, p2 tog, p3.

Repeat Rows 1–28.

Slack Line, or
Drunken-Sailor Cable

This pattern is fun, easy to work, and mysterious—everyone wonders how the cable is made to slither gently from side to side! It is done with increases and decreases on every 4th row. Notice that the cable is twisted to the right when traveling to the left, and to the left when traveling to the right. This makes it seem about to untwist itself, and adds to the "precarious" effect.

Panel of 12 sts.

NOTES: Front Cross (FC): sl 2 sts to dpn and hold in front, k2, then k2 from dpn.

Back Cross (BC): sl 2 sts to dpn and hold in back, k2, then k2 from dpn.

Increase (inc): Purl into the front and back of the same st.

Rows 1, 3, and 5 (Wrong side)—K2, p4, k6.
Row 2—P6, k4, p2.
Row 4—P6, FC, p2.
Row 6—P4, p2 tog, k4, inc, p1.
Row 7 and all subsequent wrong-side rows—Knit all knit and increase sts, purl all purl sts.
Row 8—P5, FC, p3.
Row 10—P3, p2 tog, k4, inc, p2.
Row 12—P4, FC, p4.
Row 14—P2, p2 tog, k4, inc, p3.
Row 16—P3, FC, p5.
Row 18—P1, p2 tog, k4, inc, p4.
Row 20—P2, FC, p6.
Row 22—P2, k4, p6.
Row 24—P2, BC, p6.
Row 26—P1, inc, k4, p2 tog, p4.
Row 28—P3, BC, p5.
Row 30—P2, inc, k4, p2 tog, p3.
Row 32—P4, BC, p4.
Row 34—P3, inc, k4, p2 tog, p2.
Row 36—P5, BC, p3.
Row 38—P4, inc, k4, p2 tog, p1.
Row 40—P6, BC, p2.

Repeat Rows 1–40.

Homes of Donegal

In the classic Aran tradition, this pattern clusters four greatly enlarged popcorn motifs—which really become bell motifs as a result—inside an embossed diamond. The same idea is often seen in an expanded form with larger diamonds containing five, seven or nine motifs.

LEFT: *Homes of Donegal*
RIGHT: *Spearhead and Chain*

Panel of 19 sts.

NOTES: BC (Back Cross): sl 1 st to dpn and hold in back, k2, then p1 from dpn.

FC (Front Cross): sl 2 sts to dpn and hold in front, p1, then k2 from dpn.

Rows 1 and 3 (Wrong side)—K7, p2, k1, p2, k7.

Row 2—P7, sl next 3 sts to dpn and hold in back, k2, sl the purl st from dpn back to left-hand needle and purl it, then k2 from dpn; p7.

Row 4—P6, BC, p1, FC, p6.

Row 5—K6, p2, k3, p2, k6.

Row 6—P5, BC, p1, (k1, yo, k1, yo, k1) in next st, p1, FC, p5.

Row 7—K5, p2, k2, p5, k2, p2, k5.

Row 8—P4, BC, p2, k5, p2, FC, p4.

Row 9—K4, p2, k3, p5, k3, p2, k4.

Row 10—P3, BC, p3, ssk, k1, k2 tog, p3, FC, p3.

Row 11—K3, p2, k4, p3, k4, p2, k3.

Row 12—P2, BC, p1, (k1, yo, k1, yo, k1) in next st, p2, sl 1—k2 tog—psso, p2, (k1, yo, k1, yo, k1) in next st, p1, FC, p2.

Row 13—K2, p2, k2, p5, k2, p1, k2, p5, k2, p2, k2.

Row 14—P1, BC, p2, k5, p5, k5, p2, FC, p1.

Row 15—K1, p2, k3, p5, k5, p5, k3, p2, k1.

Row 16—P1, FC, p2, ssk, k1, k2 tog, p5, ssk, k1, k2 tog, p2, BC, p1.

Row 17—K2, p2, k2, p3, k5, p3, k2, p2, k2.

Row 18—P2, FC, p1, sl 1—k2 tog—psso, p2, (k1, yo, k1, yo, k1) in next st, p2, sl 1—k2 tog—psso, p1, BC, p2.

Row 19—K3, p2, k1, p1, k2, p5, k2, p1, k1, p2, k3.

Row 20—P3, FC, p3, k5, p3, BC, p3.

Row 21—K4, p2, k3, p5, k3, p2, k4.

Row 22—P4, FC, p2, ssk, k1, k2 tog, p2, BC, p4.

Row 23—K5, p2, k2, p3, k2, p2, k5.

Row 24—P5, FC, p1, sl 1—k2 tog—psso, p1, BC, p5.

Row 25—K6, p2, k1, p1, k1, p2, k6.

Row 26—P6, FC, p1, BC, p6.

Repeat Rows 1–26.

Spearhead and Chain

The salty Aran Isles breathed a true flavor of the sea into this cable, inspired by the harpoon with attached chain or twisted rope. Slight variations on the stylized design create the more gentle Valentine Cable (*A Treasury of Knitting Patterns,* p. 253).

Panel of 26 sts.

NOTES: BC (Back Cross): sl 1 st to dpn and hold in back, k2, then p1 from dpn.

BKC (Back Knit Cross): sl 2 sts to dpn and hold in back, k2, then k2 from dpn.

FC (Front Cross): sl 2 sts to dpn and hold in front, p1, then k2 from dpn.

SBC (Single Back Cross): sl 1 st to dpn and hold in back, k1, then p1 from dpn.

SBKC (Single Back Knit Cross): Same as SBC, but knit both sts.

SFC (Single Front Cross): sl 1 st to dpn and hold in front, p1, then k1 from dpn.

SFKC (Single Front Knit Cross): Same as SFC, but knit both sts.

Row 1 (Wrong side)—(K2, p1) twice, k5, p4, k5, (p1, k2) twice.
Row 2—P2, SFC, SBC, p5, BKC, p5, SFC, SBC, p2.
Row 3—K3, p2, k6, p4, k6, p2, k3.
Row 4—P3, SBKC, p5, BC, FC, p5, SFKC, p3.
Row 5—K3, p2, k5, p2, k2, p2, k5, p2, k3.
Row 6—P2, SBC, SFC, p3, BC, p2, FC, p3, SBC, SFC, p2.
Row 7—(K2, p1) twice, k3, (p2, k1) twice, p2, k3, (p1, k2) twice.
Row 8—(P2, k1) twice, p2, BC, k4, FC, p2, (k1, p2) twice.
Row 9—(K2, p1) twice, k2, p2, k1, p4, k1, p2, k2, (p1, k2) twice.
Row 10—P2, SFC, SBC, p1, BC, p1, BKC, p1, FC, p1, SFC, SBC, p2.
Row 11—K3, (p2, k2) twice, p4, (k2, p2) twice, k3.
Row 12—P3, SBKC, (p1, BC) twice, (FC, p1) twice, SFKC, p3.
Row 13—K6, (p2, k2) 3 times, p2, k6.
Row 14—P5, (BC, p1) twice, (p1, FC) twice, p5.
Row 15—K5, p2, k2, p2, k4, p2, k2, p2, k5.
Row 16—P4, BC, p1, BC, p4, FC, p1, FC, p4.
Row 17—K4, p2, k2, p2, k6, p2, k2, p2, k4.
Row 18—P3, BC, p2, FC, p4, BC, p2, FC, p3.
Row 19—K3, (p2, k4) 3 times, p2, k3.
Row 20—P2, SBC, SFC, p3, FC, p2, BC, p3, SBC, SFC, p2.
Row 21—(K2, p1) twice, k4, p2, k2, p2, k4, (p1, k2) twice.
Row 22—(P2, k1) twice, p4, FC, BC, p4, (k1, p2) twice.

Repeat Rows 1–22.

Latticed Diamond

CENTER PANEL: *Latticed Diamond*
SIDE PANELS: *Riptide Wave*

In this beautiful cable, the three stitches forming the diamond borders are separated from each other, one at a time, to form the interior design of single knit stitches; then they re-join each other in the upper half of the diamond. Therefore there are three types of front cross and three types of back cross involved in working the pattern, but they differ only in the number of knit stitches used.

Panel of 22 sts.

NOTES: Single Front Cross (1FC)—sl 1 st to dpn and hold in front, p1, then k1 from dpn.

Double Front Cross (2FC)—sl 2 sts to dpn and hold in front, p1, then k2 from dpn.

Triple Front Cross (3FC)—sl 3 sts to dpn and hold in front, p1, then k3 from dpn.

Single Back Cross (1BC)—sl 1 st to dpn and hold in back, k1, then p1 from dpn.

Double Back Cross (2BC)—sl 1 st to dpn and hold in back, k2, then p1 from dpn.

Triple Back Cross (3BC)—sl 1 st to dpn and hold in back, k3, then p1 from dpn.

Rows 1 and 3 (Wrong side)—K8, p6, k8.

Row 2—P8, sl next 3 sts to dpn and hold in back, k3, then k3 from dpn, p8.

Row 4—P7, 3BC, 3FC, p7.

Row 5 and all subsequent wrong-side rows *except* Rows 13, 17, and 21—Knit all knit sts and purl all purl sts.

Row 6—P6, 3BC, p2, 3FC, p6.

Row 8—P5, 2BC, k1, p4, k1, 2FC, p5.

Row 10—P4, 2BC, p1, 1FC, p2, 1BC, p1, 2FC, p4.

Row 12—P3, 1BC, k1, p3, 1FC, 1BC, p3, k1, 1FC, p3.

Row 13—K3, p1, k1, p1, k4, sl next st to dpn and hold in front, p1, then p1 from dpn; k4, p1, k1, p1, k3.

Row 14—P2, 1BC, p1, 1FC, p2, 1BC, 1FC, p2, 1BC, p1, 1FC, p2.

Row 16—P2, k1, p3, 1FC, 1BC, p2, 1FC, 1BC, p3, k1, p2.

Row 17—K2, p1, (k4, sl next st to dpn and hold in back, p1, then p1 from dpn) twice, k4, p1, k2.

Row 18—P2, k1, p3, 1BC, 1FC, p2, 1BC, 1FC, p3, k1, p2.

Row 20—P2, 1FC, p1, 1BC, p2, 1FC, 1BC, p2, 1FC, p1, 1BC, p2.

Row 21—Repeat Row 13.

Row 22—P3, 1FC, k1, p3, 1BC, 1FC, p3, k1, 1BC, p3.

Row 24—P4, 2FC, p1, 1BC, p2, 1FC, p1, 2BC, p4.

Row 26—P5, 2FC, k1, p4, k1, 2BC, p5.

Row 28—P6, 3FC, p2, 3BC, p6.

Row 30—P7, 3FC, 3BC, p7.

Repeat Rows 1–30.

Riptide Wave

Panel of 12 sts.

Notes: 1FC, 2FC, 3FC, 1BC, 2BC, and 3BC—Same as for Latticed Diamond.

Row 1 (Wrong side)—K4, p3, k5.
Row 2—P4, 3BC, p4.
Row 3 and all subsequent wrong-side rows—Knit all knit sts and purl all purl sts.
Row 4—P3, 2BC, 1FC, p4.
Row 6—P2, 2BC, p2, 1FC, p3.
Row 8—P1, 2BC, p4, 1FC, p2.
Row 10—P1, 2FC, p4, 1BC, p2.
Row 12—P2, 2FC, p2, 1BC, p3.
Row 14—P3, 2FC, 1BC, p4.
Row 16—P4, 3FC, p4.
Row 18—P4, 1BC, 2FC, p3.
Row 20—P3, 1BC, p2, 2FC, p2.
Row 22—P2, 1BC, p4, 2FC, p1.
Row 24—P2, 1FC, p4, 2BC, p1.
Row 26—P3, 1FC, p2, 2BC, p2.
Row 28—P4, 1FC, 2BC, p3.

Repeat Rows 1–28.

Three Cables with Irish Knots: Hollow Oak, Crazy Maypole, and Lorgnette Cable

Though these three cables are quite diverse in appearance, all three are decorated with Irish Knots, single or in clusters. Hollow Oak and Lorgnette Cable are fairly straightforward patterns, with no tricks about them except their own special brand of novelty. But the knitter who uses Crazy Maypole must watch what she is doing. It is an off-center, free-swinging sort of pattern incorporating knots, twists, and an "inside-out" cable cross in which one knit stitch is crossed in front of two purl stitches—the reverse of the usual system. In spite of its apparent eccentricity, the Maypole is a highly disciplined design, consistent with its own internal symmetry; the second half of the pattern is the exact opposite, in every detail, of the first half.

LEFT: *Hollow Oak*
CENTER: *Crazy Maypole*
RIGHT: *Lorgnette Cable*

NOTE FOR ALL THREE PATTERNS: Make Knot (MK) as follows—
(k1, p1, k1, p1, k1, p1, k1) in one stitch, making 7 sts from 1;
then with point of left-hand needle pass the 2nd, 3rd, 4th, 5th,
6th, and 7th sts on right-hand needle separately over the last st
made, completing Knot.

I. HOLLOW OAK

Panel of 15 sts.

NOTES: Front Cross (FC)—sl 2 sts to dpn and hold in front,
p1, then k2 from dpn.

Back Cross (BC)—sl 1 st to dpn and hold in back, k2, then
p1 from dpn.

Rows 1, 3, 5, and 7 (Wrong side)—K5, p5, k5.
Row 2—P5, k2, MK, k2, p5.
Row 4—P5, MK, k3, MK, p5.
Row 6—Repeat Row 2.
Row 8—P4, BC, p1, FC, p4.
Row 9—K4, p2, k1, p1, k1, p2, k4.
Row 10—P3, BC, k1, p1, k1, FC, p3.
Row 11—K3, p3, k1, p1, k1, p3, k3.
Row 12—P2, BC, (p1, k1) twice, p1, FC, p2.
Row 13—K2, p2, (k1, p1) 3 times, k1, p2, k2.
Row 14—P2, k3, (p1, k1) twice, p1, k3, p2.
Rows 15, 17, and 19—Repeat Rows 13, 11, and 9.
Row 16—P2, FC, (p1, k1) twice, p1, BC, p2.
Row 18—P3, FC, k1, p1, k1, BC, p3.
Row 20—P4, FC, p1, BC, p4.

Repeat Rows 1–20.

II. CRAZY MAYPOLE

Panel of 18 sts.

NOTES: Front Cross (FC)—sl 1 st to dpn and hold in front,
p2, then k1 from dpn.

Back Cross (BC)—sl 2 sts to dpn and hold in back, k1, then
p2 from dpn.

Row 1 (Wrong side)—K9, p1, k2, p1, k5.
Row 2—P5, k1-b, p2, k1-b, p3, MK, p5.
Row 3—K5, p1, k3, p1, k2, p1, k5.
Row 4—P2, MK, p2, LT, p1, k1-b, p3, k1-b, p5.
Row 5—K5, p1, k3, p1, k1, p1, k3, p1, k2.
Row 6—P2, FC, p1, LT, k1-b, p1, BC, p2, MK, p2.
Row 7—K2, p1, k4, p1, k1, p2, k2, p1, k4.

Row 8—P4, FC, LT, RT, p2, BC, p2.
Row 9—K4, p1, k3, p2, k1, p1, k6.
Row 10—P6, LT, RT, p1, BC, p4.
Row 11—K6, p1, k2, p2, k7.
Row 12—P7, LT, BC, p6.
Row 13—K8, p3, k7.
Row 14—P7, FC, p2, MK, p5.
Row 15—K5, p1, k2, p1, k9.
Row 16—P5, MK, p3, k1-b, p2, k1-b, p5.
Row 17—K5, p1, k2, p1, k3, p1, k5.
Row 18—P5, k1-b, p3, k1-b, p1, RT, p2, MK, p2.
Row 19—K2, p1, k3, p1, k1, p1, k3, p1, k5.
Row 20—P2, MK, p2, FC, p1, k1-b, RT, p1, BC, p2.
Row 21—K4, p1, k2, p2, k1, p1, k4, p1, k2.
Row 22—P2, FC, p2, LT, RT, BC, p4.
Row 23—K6, p1, k1, p2, k3, p1, k4.
Row 24—P4, FC, p1, LT, RT, p6.
Row 25—K7, p2, k2, p1, k6.
Row 26—P6, FC, RT, p7.
Row 27—K7, p3, k8.
Row 28—P5, MK, p2, BC, p7.

Repeat Rows 1–28.

III. LORGNETTE CABLE

Panel of 12 sts.

NOTES: Front Cross (FC)—sl 2 sts to dpn and hold in front, p2, then k2 from dpn.

Back Cross (BC)—sl 2 sts to dpn and hold in back, k2, then p2 from dpn.

Single Front Cross (SFC)—sl 2 sts to dpn and hold in front, p1, then k2 from dpn.

Single Back Cross (SBC)—sl 1 st to dpn and hold in back, k2, then p1 from dpn.

Rows 1 and 3 (Wrong side)—K2, p2, k4, p2, k2.
Row 2—P2, k2, p4, k2, p2.
Row 4—P2, FC, BC, p2.
Row 5—K4, p4, k4.
Row 6—P4, FC, p4.
Row 7—K4, p2, k6.
Row 8—P6, SFC, p3.
Row 9—K3, p2, k7.
Row 10—P7, SFC, p2.
Row 11—K2, p2, k8.
Row 12—P3, MK, p4, k2, p2.

Rows 13, 15, 17, and 19—Repeat Rows 11, 9, 7, and 5.
Row 14—P7, SBC, p2.
Row 16—P6, SBC, p3.
Row 18—P4, work BC but *knit* all 4 sts; p4.
Row 20—P2, BC, FC, p2.
Rows 21, 22, 23, 24, and 25—Repeat Rows 1, 2, 3, 4, and 5.
Row 26—P4, BC, p4.
Row 27—K6, p2, k4.
Row 28—P3, SBC, p6.
Row 29—K7, p2, k3.
Row 30—P2, SBC, p7.
Row 31—K8, p2, k2.
Row 32—P2, k2, p4, MK, p3.
Rows 33, 35, 37, and 39—Repeat Rows 31, 29, 27, and 5.
Row 34—P2, SFC, p7.
Row 36—P3, SFC, p6.
Row 38—P4, work FC but *knit* all 4 sts; p4.
Row 40—Repeat Row 20.

Repeat Rows 1–40.

CHAPTER NINE

Cable-Stitch Patterns

The patterns in this section are distinguished from cables (although they are likewise worked with the aid of a cable needle) because they are intended primarily for use all over a fabric, rather than for use in isolated panels. However, there is nothing to prevent you from using these patterns in panels of one or two repeats if you wish. Use the given multiple of stitches, plus the edge stitches if any. For example, if a cable-stitch pattern is worked on a multiple of 10 stitches plus 5, you could work a single-repeat panel on 15 stitches, or a double-repeat panel on 25 stitches, etc.

Cable-stitch patterns make attractive fabrics, which in most cases have a great deal of depth and dimension to them. Take care, however, with your gauge. These patterns are practically *never* interchangeable with stockinette stitch, because the cabling action pulls the stitches together laterally and gives you quite a few *more* stitches to the inch than you would have in plain knitting. To make a garment wide enough to fit you, it is necessary to cast on more than your "standard" number of stitches. Therefore it is important to make test swatches and check the number of stitches—or pattern repeats, if you prefer to figure it that way—in any desired width measurement. Length measurements, however, will remain approximately average; the row gauge changes very little, if at all.

Cable-stitch patterns are frequently worked in medium to heavy yarn, to make firm, thick fabrics for sweaters, jackets, afghans, and coats. But they can be worked in fine yarn, too. There is no reason why a dress or baby sweater, in thin fingering yarn, cannot be worked in a cable-stitch pattern. Remember to use a cable needle *thinner* than the needles being used for the rest of the knitting, so the stitches will not be over-stretched in cabling (this is always a good idea for any kind of cabled pattern).

These patterns can be combined, too. One pattern might be used as a central panel, another for the remainder of the garment. Or perhaps you would like to make a set of "matching" cushions, each one in a different cable-stitch pattern. The possibilities, as usual, are endless.

Wave Lattice

Wave Lattice

This is a graceful "basketweave" pattern in which the left and right crosses alternate, which gives a wavy effect. On every other right-side row one set of ribs is "skipped" while the other set is being cabled.

Multiple of 6 sts plus 2.

Rows 1 and 3 (Wrong side)—K1, * k2, p4; rep from *, end k1.
Row 2—K1, * sl next 2 sts to dpn and hold in front, k2, then k2 from dpn; p2; rep from *, end k1.
Row 4—K1, p2, * k2, sl next 2 sts to dpn and hold in back, k2, then p2 from dpn; rep from *, end k5.
Rows 5 and 7—K1, * p4, k2; rep from *, end k1.
Row 6—K1, * p2, sl next 2 sts to dpn and hold in back, k2, then k2 from dpn; rep from *, end k1.
Row 8—K5, * sl next 2 sts to dpn and hold in front, p2, then k2 from dpn; k2; rep from *, end p2, k1.

Repeat Rows 1–8.

Two Variations on the Aran Honeycomb: Rings and Telescope Lattice

Both of these patterns contain portions of the classic Aran Honeycomb. Rings is a honeycomb with every other cell omitted; Telescope Lattice makes an allover pattern of the upper portions of the cells. Both make beautiful texture effects.

NOTES: FC (Front Cross): Sl 2 sts to dpn and hold in front, k2, then k2 from dpn.

BC (Back Cross): Sl 2 sts to dpn and hold in back, k2, then k2 from dpn.

I. RINGS

Aran Honeycomb Variation I: Rings

Multiple of 16 sts plus 2.

Row 1 (Wrong side) and all other wrong-side rows—Purl.
Rows 2, 6, 10, and 14—Knit.
Row 4—K1, * k8, FC, BC; rep from *, end k1.
Row 8—K1, * BC, FC, k8; rep from *, end k1.
Row 12—K1, * FC, BC, k8; rep from *, end k1.
Row 16—K1, * k8, BC, FC; rep from *, end k1.

Repeat Rows 1–16.

II. TELESCOPE LATTICE

Multiple of 12 sts plus 2.

Row 1 (Wrong side) and all other wrong-side rows—Purl.
Rows 2 and 6—Knit.
Row 4—K1, * BC, k4, FC; rep from *, end k1.
Row 8—K1, * k2, FC, BC, k2; rep from *, end k1.

Repeat Rows 1–8.

Rib and Braid Pattern

Tired of that dreary old "k2, p2" in a ribbed pullover? Try this beautiful contemporary German pattern instead! You'll have a much more interesting sweater, and enjoy working it.

Multiple of 18 sts plus 3.

NOTES: FC (Front Cross): sl 1 st to dpn and hold in front, p1, then k1 from dpn.
FKC (Front Knit Cross): same as FC, but knit both sts.
BC (Back Cross): sl 1 st to dpn and hold in back, k1, then p1 from dpn.
BKC (Back Knit Cross): same as BC, but knit both sts.

Rows 1 and 3 (Wrong side)—K3, * p2, k2, p2, k3; rep from *.
Row 2—P3, * BKC, p2, BKC, p3; rep from *.
Row 4—* P2, (BC, FC) twice, (p2, k2) twice; rep from *, end p3.
Rows 5 and 7—K3, * (p2, k2) twice, p1, k2, p2, k2, p1, k2; rep from *.
Row 6—* P2, k1, p2, FKC, p2, k1, (p2, k2) twice; rep from *, end p3.
Row 8—* P2, (FC, BC) twice, (p2, k2) twice; rep from *, end p3.
Row 9—Repeat first row.
Row 10—P3, * BKC, p2, BKC, p3, k2, p2, k2, p3; rep from *.
Rows 11 through 19—Repeat Rows 3 through 9, then repeat Rows 2 and 3 again.
Row 20—P3, * (k2, p2) twice, (BC, FC) twice, p2; rep from *.
Rows 21 and 23—* K2, p1, k2, p2, k2, p1, (k2, p2) twice; rep from *, end k3.
Row 22—P3, *(k2, p2) twice, k1, p2, FKC, p2, k1, p2; rep from *.
Row 24—P3, * (k2, p2) twice, (FC, BC) twice, p2; rep from *.
Rows 25 and 27—Repeat first row.
Row 26—P3, * k2, p2, k2, p3, BKC, p2, BKC, p3; rep from *.
Rows 28 through 32—Repeat Rows 20 through 24.

Repeat Rows 1–32.

Aran Honeycomb Variation II: Telescope Lattice

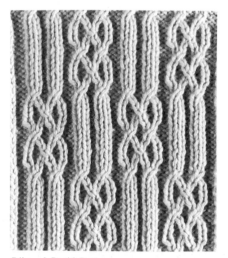

Rib and Braid Pattern

Arcade Pattern

Arcade Pattern

Contributed by Bernice Haedike, Oak Park, Illinois

This can be worked in a single panel of 15 stitches, in which case it looks more like a type of double cable with bobbles than an "arcade" of pillars and arches. It is unusual and pretty, and makes a fascinating allover design rich with texture interest.

Multiple of 13 sts plus 2.

NOTES: Front Cross (FC): sl 2 sts to dpn and hold in front, p1, then k2 from dpn.

Back Cross (BC): sl 1 st to dpn and hold in back, k2, then p1 from dpn.

Row 1 (Wrong side)—Knit.

Row 2—K3, * p3, (k1, yo, k1, yo, k1) in next st, p1, (k1, yo, k1, yo, k1) in next st, p3, k4; rep from *, end last repeat k3.

Row 3—P3, * k3, p5, k1, p5, k3, p4; rep from *, end last repeat p3.

Row 4—K3, * p3, ssk, k1, k2 tog, p1, ssk, k1, k2 tog, p3, k4; rep from *, end last repeat k3.

Row 5—P3, * k3, p3 tog, k1, p3 tog, k3, p4; rep from *, end last repeat p3.

Row 6—K3, * p4, (k1, yo, k1, yo, k1) in next st, p4, k4; rep from *, end last repeat k3.

Row 7—P3, * k4, p5, k4, p4; rep from *, end last repeat p3.

Row 8—K1, * FC, p3, ssk, k1, k2 tog, p3, BC; rep from *, end k1.

Row 9—K2, * p2, k3, p3 tog, k3, p2, k2; rep from *.

Row 10—P2, * FC, p5, BC, p2; rep from *.

Row 11—K3, * p2, k5, p2, k4; rep from *, end last repeat k3.

Row 12—P3, * FC, p3, BC, p4; rep from *, end last repeat p3.

Row 13—K4, * p2, k3, p2, k6; rep from *, end last repeat k4.

Row 14—P4, * FC, p1, BC, p6; rep from *, end last repeat p4.

Row 15—K5, * p2, k1, p2, k8; rep from *, end last repeat k5.

Row 16—P5, * sl next 3 sts to dpn and hold in back, k2, then sl the purl st from dpn back to left-hand needle and purl it; then k2 from dpn; p8; rep from *, end last repeat p5.

Repeat Rows 1-16.

Sunburst Check Pattern

Contributed by Hildegard M. Elsner, Aldan, Pennsylvania

This beautiful pattern comes from Austria, and lends itself to a multitude of uses. It is informal enough for ski sweaters, yet disciplined enough for fascinatingly embossed coatings. It will also make delightful afghans and baby blankets.

Multiple of 12 sts plus 2.

NOTES: Front Cross (FC)—sl 1 st to dpn and hold in front, p3, then k1 from dpn.

Back Cross (BC)—sl 3 sts to dpn and hold in back, k1, then p3 from dpn.

Row 1 (Right side)—K4, * p6, k6; rep from *, end p6, k4.
Row 2—P4, * k6, p6; rep from *, end k6, p4.
Row 3—K3, * FC, BC, k4; rep from *, end last repeat k3.
Row 4—P3, * k3, p2, k3, p4; rep from *, end last repeat p3.
Row 5—K2, * FC, k2, BC, k2; rep from *.
Row 6—P2, * k3, p4, k3, p2; rep from *.
Row 7—K1, * FC, k4, BC; rep from *, end k1.
Rows 8, 10, and 12—Repeat Row 1.
Rows 9 and 11—Repeat Row 2.
Row 13—K1, * BC, k4, FC; rep from *, end k1.
Rows 14, 16, and 18—Repeat Rows 6, 4, and 2.
Row 15—K2, * BC, k2, FC, k2; rep from *.
Row 17—K3, * BC, FC, k4; rep from *, end last repeat k3.
Rows 19 and 20—Repeat Rows 1 and 2.

Repeat Rows 1–20.

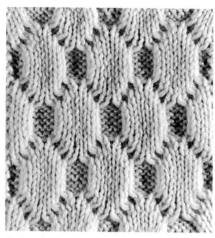

Sunburst Check Pattern

Two Cable-and-Texture Patterns: Sidecurl Pattern and Marrowbone Pattern

I. SIDECURL PATTERN

Simple cables are repeated across this fabric; the novel touch is given by small purled blocks which appear to continue the curve of the cable off to one side. This is an easy-to work pattern that makes a firm, thick fabric.

Multiple of 6 sts plus 2.

Rows 1 and 3 (Wrong side)—Purl.
Rows 2 and 4—Knit.
Row 5—K2, * p4, k2; rep from *.
Row 6—P2, * sl next 2 sts to dpn and hold in front, k2, then k2 from dpn; p2; rep from *.

Repeat Rows 1–6.

ABOVE: *Sidecurl Pattern*
BELOW: *Marrowbone Pattern*

II. MARROWBONE PATTERN

A beautiful variation on the cabled honeycomb is made here by stitches cabled in one direction only, while the other diagonals are formed of garter stitch. This pattern makes fine, sturdy afghans and sweaters in a non-curling fabric.

Multiple of 12 sts plus 4.

NOTE: Front Cross (FC): sl 3 sts to dpn and hold in front, k3, then k3 from dpn.

Rows 1 and 3 (Right side)—Knit.
Row 2—* P6, k6; rep from *, end p4.
Row 4—K2, * p6, k6; rep from *, end p2.
Row 5—K2, * k6, FC; rep from *, end k2.
Row 6—K4, * p6, k6; rep from *.
Rows 7 and 9—Knit.
Row 8—* K6, p6; rep from *, end k4.
Row 10—P2, * k6, p6; rep from *, end k2.
Row 11—K2, * FC, k6; rep from *, end k2.
Row 12—P4, * k6, p6; rep from *.

Repeat Rows 1–12.

Mutton-Chop Cables

Mutton-Chop Cables

Contributed by Hildegard M. Elsner, Aldan, Pennsylvania

These cables are Tyrolean, seen in ski sweaters. They are handsome in a single panel of 22 stitches, or as an allover pattern as given.

Multiple of 20 sts plus 2.

Rows 1 and 3 (Wrong side)—K2, * p8, k2; rep from *.
Row 2—K10, * p2, k18; rep from *, end last repeat k10.
Row 4—K2, * sl next 4 sts to dpn and hold in back, p4, then k4 from dpn; p2, sl next 4 sts to dpn and hold in front, k4, then p4 from dpn; k2; rep from *.
Rows 5 and 7—K6, * p4, k2, p4, k10; rep from *, end last repeat k6.
Row 6—K2, * p4, k4, p2, k4, p4, k2; rep from *.
Row 8—Repeat Row 2.
Row 9—Repeat Row 1.
Row 10—Repeat Row 2.

Repeat Rows 1–10.

Fancy Cable Check

In this pattern, small simple cables are placed to good advantage in a textured knit-purl fabric. Many slightly different arrangements are possible, but this one is typical. It makes excellent sport sweaters, blankets, throws, etc.

Multiple of 18 sts plus 1.

NOTE: Back Cross (BC): sl 3 sts to dpn and hold in back, k3, then k3 from dpn.

Row 1 (Right side)—K1, * p8, k1, p1, k6, p1, k1; rep from *.
Row 2—P1, * k1, p6, k1, p1, k8, p1; rep from *.
Row 3—K2, * p6, k2, p1, BC, p1, k2; rep from *, end last repeat k1.
Row 4—P1, * k1, p6, k1, p2, k6, p2; rep from *.
Row 5—K3, * p4, k3, p1, k6, p1, k3; rep from *, end last repeat k1.
Row 6—P1, * k1, p6, k1, p3, k4, p3; rep from *.
Row 7—K4, * p2, k4, p1, k6, p1, k4; rep from *, end last repeat k1.
Row 8—P1, * k1, p6, k1, p4, k2, p4; rep from *.
Row 9— * K10, p1, BC, p1; rep from *, end k1.
Rows 10 through 17—Repeat Rows 8, 7, 6, 5, 4, 3, 2, and 1.
Row 18—P1, * k1, p6, k1, p1; rep from *.
Row 19—K1, * p1, k6, p1, k1, p8, k1; rep from *.
Row 20—P1, * k8, p1, k1, p6, k1, p1; rep from *.
Row 21—K1, * p1, BC, p1, k2, p6, k2; rep from *.
Row 22—P2, * k6, p2, k1, p6, k1, p2; rep from *, end last repeat p1.
Row 23—K1, * p1, k6, p1, k3, p4, k3; rep from *.
Row 24—P3, * k4, p3, k1, p6, k1, p3; rep from *, end last repeat p1.
Row 25—K1, * p1, k6, p1, k4, p2, k4; rep from *.
Row 26—P4, * k2, p4, k1, p6, k1, p4; rep from *, end last repeat p1.
Row 27—K1, * p1, BC, p1, k10; rep from *.
Rows 28 through 36—Repeat Rows 26, 25, 24, 23, 22, 21, 20, 19, and 18.

Repeat Rows 1–36.

Fancy Cable Check

Cable and Ladder

Multiple of 14 sts plus 1.

Row 1 (Wrong side) and all other wrong-side rows—K1, * p2 tog, yo, p11, k1; rep from *.
Row 2—K1, * ssk, yo, sl next 3 sts to dpn and hold in back, k3, then k3 from dpn; k6; rep from *.
Row 4—K1, * ssk, yo, k12; rep from *.
Row 6—K1, * ssk, yo, k3, sl next 3 sts to dpn and hold in front, k3, then k3 from dpn; k3; rep from *.
Row 8—Repeat Row 4.

Repeat Rows 1–8.

Cable and Ladder

Knotted Lattice

Knotted Lattice

This handsome allover pattern has two-stitch ribs twisted, interlaced, curled around each other, and "traveled" diagonally across the fabric. It can be used in a panel of 20 stitches, but appears more intricate and interesting with more repeats.

Multiple of 12 sts plus 8.

NOTES: Front Cross (FC): sl 2 sts to dpn and hold in front, k2, then k2 from dpn.

Back Cross (BC): sl 2 sts to dpn and hold in back, k2, then k2 from dpn.

Single Front Cross (SFC): sl 2 sts to dpn and hold in front, p1, then k2 from dpn.

Single Back Cross (SBC): sl 1 st to dpn and hold in back, k2, then p1 from dpn.

Rows 1, 3, 5, 7, 9, and 11 (Wrong side)—K1, * p6, k2, p2, k2; rep from *, end p6, k1.

Row 2—K1, * BC, (k2, p2) twice; rep from *, end BC, k3.

Row 4—K3, * FC, p2, RT, p2, k2; rep from *, end FC, k1.

Row 6—K7, * p2, k2, p2, k6; rep from *, end k1.

Row 8—K1, * BC, k2, p2, RT, p2; rep from *, end BC, k3.

Row 10—K3, * FC, (p2, k2) twice; rep from *, end FC, k1.

Row 12—K1, p2, * k2, SFC, p1, RT, p1, SBC; rep from *, end k2, p2, k1.

Row 13—K3, * p2, k1; rep from *, end k2.

Row 14—K1, p2, * RT, p1, SFC, k2, SBC, p1; rep from *, end RT, p2, k1.

Rows 15, 17, 19, 21, 23, and 25—K3, * p2, k2, p6, k2; rep from *, end p2, k3.

Row 16—K1, p2, k2, p2, * BC, (k2, p2) twice; rep from *, end k1.

Row 18—K1, * p2, RT, p2, k2, FC; rep from *, end p2, RT, p2, k1.

Row 20—K1, * p2, k2, p2, k6; rep from *, end p2, k2, p2, k1.

Row 22—K1, * p2, RT, p2, BC, k2; rep from *, end p2, RT, p2, k1.

Row 24—K1, * (p2, k2) twice, FC; rep from *, end p2, k2, p2, k1.

Row 26—K1, p2, * RT, p1, SBC, k2, SFC, p1; rep from *, end RT, p2, k1.

Row 27—Repeat Row 13.

Row 28—K1, p2, * k2, SBC, p1, RT, p1, SFC; rep from *, end k2, p2, k1.

Repeat Rows 1–28.

Double-Knotted Lattice

This beautiful design will make the best "bold-and-bulky" sweater you ever saw! One of the finest of the heavy-lattice patterns, it has an aura of foursquare solidity. A single panel, 30 stitches wide, also makes an excellent cable.

Notice that although the four-stitch clusters made in Rows 14 and 28 can't be seen, they do serve a purpose. The stitches gathered together by these clusters form a tight base for the double knots worked in subsequent rows.

Double-Knotted Lattice

Multiple of 16 sts plus 14.

NOTES: FC, BC, SFC, and SBC—same as for Knotted Lattice.

Cluster 4 as follows (worked from wrong side): sl 4 wyib, pass yarn to front, sl the same 4 sts back to left-hand needle, pass yarn to back, sl 4 wyib again.

Row 1 (Right side)—P3, * FC, BC, p8; rep from *, end last repeat p3.

Rows 2 and 4—K3, * p8, k8; rep from *, end last repeat k3.

Row 3—P3, * k8, p8; rep from *, end last repeat p3.

Rows 5, 6, 7, 8, and 9—Repeat Rows 1 through 4, then Row 1 again.

Row 10—K3, * p2, Cluster 4, p2, k8; rep from *, end last repeat k3.

Row 11—P2, * SBC, p4, SFC, p6; rep from *, end last repeat p2.

Row 12—K2, * p2, k6; rep from *, end last repeat k2.

Row 13—P1, * SBC, p6, SFC, p4; rep from *, end last repeat p1.

Row 14—K1, p2, * k8, p2, Cluster 4, p2; rep from *, end k8, p2, k1.

Row 15—P1, k2, * p8, FC, BC; rep from *, end p8, k2, p1.

Rows 16 and 18—K1, p2, * k8, p8; rep from *, end k8, p2, k1.

Row 17—P1, k2, * p8, k8; rep from *, end p8, k2, p1.

Rows 19, 20, 21, 22, and 23—Repeat Rows 15 through 18, then Row 15 again.

Row 24—Repeat Row 14.

Row 25—P1, * SFC, p6, SBC, p4; rep from *, end last repeat p1.

Row 26—Repeat Row 12.

Row 27—P2, * SFC, p4, SBC, p6; rep from *, end last repeat p2.

Row 28—Repeat Row 10.

Repeat Rows 1–28.

Tudor Grillwork

Tudor Grillwork

A clever trick enables this lovely pattern to maintain the same fabric width throughout both the straight rib rows and the cabled rows. Ordinarily the latter would "draw in" more; but the increases made invisibly in Row 8 allow greater leeway for crossing the stitches. Another clever trick, that of twisting the straight ribs on every right-side row, gives a uniform depth and roundness to all the pattern lines, both vertical and diagonal.

Tudor Grillwork also makes a beautiful cable when used in a panel of 22 or 32 stitches.

Multiple of 10 sts plus 2.

NOTES: Front Cross (FC)—sl 2 sts to dpn and hold in front, p2, then k2 from dpn.

Back Cross (BC)—sl 2 sts to dpn and hold in back, k2, then p2 from dpn.

Back Knit Cross (BKC)—sl 2 sts to dpn and hold in back, k2, then k2 from dpn.

Rows 1, 3, 5, and 7 (Right side)—P5, * RT, p8; rep from *, end RT, p5.

Rows 2, 4, and 6—K5, * p2, k8; rep from *, end p2, k5.

Row 8—K5, * purl into the front and back of each of the next 2 sts, k8; rep from *, end last repeat k5.

Row 9—P5, * BKC, p8; rep from *, end last repeat p5.

Row 10—K5, * p4, k8; rep from *, end p4, k5.

Row 11—P3, * BC, FC, p4; rep from *, end last repeat p3.

Row 12—K3, * p2, k4; rep from *, end p2, k3.

Row 13—P1, * BC, p4, FC; rep from *, end p1.

Row 14—K1, p2, * k8, p4; rep from *, end k8, p2, k1.

Row 15—P1, k2, * p8, BKC; rep from *, end p8, k2, p1.

Rows 16 and 18—Repeat Rows 14 and 12.

Row 17—P1, * FC, p4, BC; rep from *, end p1.

Row 19—P3, * FC, BC, p4; rep from *, end last repeat p3.

Row 20—K5, * (p2 tog) twice, k8; rep from *, end last repeat k5.

Repeat Rows 1–20.

Cherry Tree

Cherry Tree

This is a handsome allover pattern of cabling and openwork, which could be used in a single panel of 19 stitches. It makes a very attractive fine-yarn sweater, a baby's dress, or a stole.

Multiple of 18 sts plus 1.

NOTES: Front Cross (FC): sl 1 st to dpn and hold in front, p2, then k1 from dpn.

Back Cross (BC): sl 2 sts to dpn and hold in back, k1, then p2 from dpn.

Row 1 (Wrong side)—K1, * p6, k5, p6, k1; rep from *.

Row 2—P1, * k3, BC, p5, FC, k3, p1; rep from *.

Row 3—K1, * p4, k9, p4, k1; rep from *.

Row 4—P1, * FC, k1, p1, (yo, p2 tog) 4 times, k1, BC, p1; rep from *.

Row 5—K3, * p6, k1, p6, k5; rep from *, end last repeat k3.

Row 6—P3, * FC, k3, p1, k3, BC, p5; rep from *, end last repeat p3.

Row 7—K5, * p4, k1, p4, k9; rep from *, end last repeat k5.

Row 8—P1, * (yo, p2 tog) twice, k1, BC, p1, FC, k1, p1, (yo, p2 tog) twice; rep from *.

Repeat Rows 1–8.

Exchange Cables

Planning to make a sweater with little cables all over? Use this charming pattern instead of all those endless rows of plain cables—you'll be glad you did. Each cable exchanges ribs with its neighbor at intervals, thus creating a far more interesting design.

And here's another sort of exchange, to work a variation that you can discover for yourself. Throughout the pattern, exchange the positions of "FC" and "BC"—working "FC" in place of every "BC", and vice versa—leaving all other directions the same. The result will surprise you!

For a test swatch, cast on a minimum of 32 sts.

Exchange Cables

Multiple of 16 sts.

NOTES: Front Cross (FC)—sl 2 sts to dpn and hold in front, k2, then k2 from dpn.

Front Purl Cross (FPC)—sl 2 sts to dpn and hold in front, p2, then k2 from dpn.

Single Front Cross (SFC)—sl 2 sts to dpn and hold in front, p1, then k2 from dpn.

Back Cross (BC)—sl 2 sts to dpn and hold in back, k2, then k2 from dpn.

Back Purl Cross (BPC)—sl 2 sts to dpn and hold in back, k2, then p2 from dpn.

Single Back Cross (SBC)—sl 1 st to dpn and hold in back, k2, then p1 from dpn.

Rows 1, 3, 5, 7, 9, and 11 (Wrong side)—K2, * p4, k4; rep from *, end p4, k2.

Rows 2, 6, and 10—P2, * FC, p4, BC, p4; rep from *, end last repeat p2.

Rows 4 and 8—P2, * k4, p4; rep from *, end k4, p2.

Row 12—P1, * SBC, FPC, BPC, SFC, p2; rep from *, end last repeat p1.

Rows 13 and 15—K1, * p2, k3, p4, k3, p2, k2; rep from *, end last repeat k1.

Row 14—P1, * k2, p3, BC, p3, k2, p2; rep from *, end last repeat p1.

Row 16—P1, * SFC, BPC, FPC, SBC, p2; rep from *, end last repeat p1.

Rows 17, 19, 21, 23, 25, and 27—Repeat odd-numbered rows 1 through 11.

Rows 18, 22, and 26—P2, * BC, p4, FC, p4; rep from *, end last repeat p2.

Rows 20 and 24—Repeat Rows 4 and 8.

Row 28—P1, SBC, SFC, * p2, SBC, FPC, BPC, SFC; rep from *, end p2, SBC, SFC, p1.

Rows 29 and 31—K1, (p2, k2) twice, * p2, k3, p4, k3, p2, k2; rep from *, end p2, k2, p2, k1.

Row 30—P1, (k2, p2) twice, * k2, p3, FC, p3, k2, p2; rep from *, end k2, p2, k2, p1.

Row 32—P1, SFC, SBC, * p2, SFC, BPC, FPC, SBC; rep from *, end p2, SFC, SBC, p1.

Repeat Rows 1–32.

Tilting Ladder Pattern

Tilting Ladder Pattern

In this utterly delightful fabric, a very clever use is made of the natural bias tendency of a lace trellis. The "ladders" seem to career at dangerous angles all through the pattern, but they are in fact quite well disciplined as far as knitting technique is concerned. Tilting Ladder Pattern is gay and fascinating in any kind of yarn, for any kind of garment.

Multiple of 13 sts plus 2.

Row 1 (Wrong side)—K2, * p5, k1, p5, k2; rep from *.
Row 2—P2, * k1, (yo, k2 tog) twice, p1, k5, p2; rep from *.
Rows 3 and 5—K2, * p4, k2, p5, k2; rep from *.
Row 4—P2, * k1, (yo, k2 tog) twice, p2, k4, p2; rep from *.
Row 6—P2, * k1, (yo, k2 tog) twice, p2, sl next 2 sts to dpn and hold in back, k2, then k2 from dpn, p2; rep from *.
Rows 7, 8, 9, 10, 11, and 12—Repeat Rows 3, 4, 5, and 6, then Rows 3 and 4 again.
Row 13—Repeat Row 1.
Row 14—P2, * k5, p1, (ssk, yo) twice, k1, p2; rep from *.
Rows 15 and 17—K2, * p5, k2, p4, k2; rep from *.
Row 16—P2, * k4, p2, (ssk, yo) twice, k1, p2; rep from *.
Row 18—P2, * sl next 2 sts to dpn and hold in front, k2, then k2 from dpn; p2, (ssk, yo) twice, k1, p2; rep from *.
Rows 19, 20, 21, 22, 23, and 24—Repeat Rows 15, 16, 17, and 18, then Rows 15 and 16 again.

Repeat Rows 1–24.

Crossed Banners

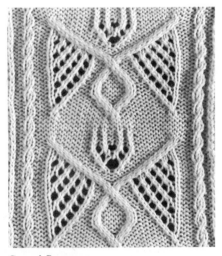

Crossed Banners

Two lacework flags topped by a small crown make an exceedingly elegant design for panel-, band-, or spot-pattern treatment. The small mock cables at the sides may be omitted, along with the edge stitches beyond them; this would leave a panel of 32 stitches. To conclude a single pattern used only once, work Rows 1 through 32 and then Rows 1, 2, and 3 again.

Panel of 40 sts.

NOTES: Front Cross (FC)—sl 2 sts to dpn and hold in front, p2, then k2 from dpn.

Back Cross (BC)—sl 2 sts to dpn and hold in back, k2, then p2 from dpn.

Front Knit Cross (FKC)—same as Front Cross, but *knit* all 4 sts.

Row 1 (Right side)—P2, k2, p32, k2, p2.

Row 2—K2, p2, k32, p2, k2.

Row 3—P2, RT, p32, RT, p2.

Rows 4 and 6—K2, p2, k3, p2, k9, p4, k9, p2, k3, p2, k2.

Row 5—P2, k2, p3, LT, p9, FKC, p9, RT, p3, k2, p2.

Row 7—P2, RT, p3, k1, yo, ssk, p6, BC, FC, p6, k2 tog, yo, k1, p3, RT, p2.

Rows 8, 10, 12, 14, 16, 18, and 20—Knit all knit sts, purl all purl and yo sts.

Row 9—P2, k2, p3, k2, yo, ssk, p3, BC, p4, FC, p3, k2 tog, yo, k2, p3, k2, p2.

Row 11—P2, RT, p3, k1, (yo, ssk) twice, p2, k2, p8, k2, p2, (k2 tog, yo) twice, k1, p3, RT, p2.

Row 13—P2, k2, p3, k2, (yo, ssk) twice, p1, FC, p4, BC, p1, (k2 tog, yo) twice, k2, p3, k2, p2.

Row 15—P2, RT, p3, k1, (yo, ssk) 3 times, p2, FC, BC, p2, (k2 tog, yo) 3 times, k1, p3, RT, p2.

Row 17—P2, k2, p3, k2, (yo, ssk) 3 times, p3, FKC, p3, (k2 tog, yo) 3 times, k2, p3, k2, p2.

Row 19—P2, RT, p3, k1, (yo, ssk) 4 times, BC, FC, (k2 tog, yo) 4 times, k1, p3, RT, p2.

Row 21—P2, k2, p3, k2, (yo, ssk) twice, k1, BC, p4, FC, k1, (k2 tog, yo) twice, k2, p3, k2, p2.

Row 22—K2, p2, (k3, p9, k3, p2) twice, k2.

Row 23—P2, RT, p3, k1, (yo, ssk) twice, BC, p2, k2 tog, (yo) twice, ssk, p2, FC, (k2 tog, yo) twice, k1, p3, RT, p2.

Row 24—K2, p2, k3, p7, k4, p1, (k1, p1) into the double yo, p1, k4, p7, k3, p2, k2.

Row 25—P2, k2, p3, k3, BC, p3, k2 tog, yo, k2, yo, ssk, p3, FC, k3, p3, k2, p2.

Row 26—K2, p2, k3, p5, k5, p6, k5, p5, k3, p2, k2.

Row 27—P2, RT, p3, k1, BC, p4, (k2 tog, yo) twice, (yo, ssk) twice [note: this makes a double yo at center], p4, FC, k1, p3, RT, p2.

Row 28—K2, p2, k3, p3, k6, p3, (k1, p1) into the double yo, p3, k6, p3, k3, p2, k2.

Row 29—P2, k2, p2, BC, p6, (k1-b, p1) twice, (p1, k1-b) twice, p6, FC, p2, k2, p2.

Row 30—K2, p2, k12, (p1-b, k1) twice, (k1, p1-b) twice, k12, p2, k2.

Row 31—P2, RT, p12, (k1-b, p1) twice, (p1, k1-b) twice, p12, RT, p2.

Row 32—Repeat Row 30.

Repeat Rows 1–32.

Cabled Feather Pattern

Contributed by Leona Hughes, Sarasota, Florida

Nearly all the best innovations in knitting are brought about by a simple association of ideas—like this one. Who, other than Mrs. Hughes, ever thought of putting a cable into Feather and Fan Stitch before? The idea is a thoroughly happy one, and the result is beautiful. The cables deepen the scallops, and emphasize the lace.

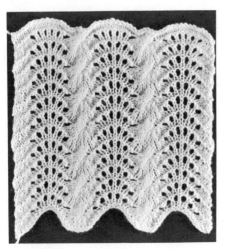

Cabled Feather Pattern

Wave cables could be used as well as simple cables, by crossing the stitches in front on every alternate cable row. For the larger version of Feather and Fan Stitch that is worked on multiples of 24 (8 decreases, 8 yo's), simply cross 4 stitches over 4. For a test swatch of this pattern, cast on a *minimum* of 36 stitches.

Multiple of 18 sts.

Row 1 (Wrong side)—Purl.
Row 2—* (K2 tog) 3 times, (yo, k1) 6 times, (k2 tog) 3 times; rep from *.
Row 3—K15, * p6, k12; rep from *, end k3.
Row 4—K15, * sl next 3 sts to dpn and hold in back, k3, then k3 from dpn; k12; rep from *, end k3.
Rows 5, 6, and 7—Repeat Rows 1, 2, and 3.
Row 8—Knit.

Repeat Rows 1–8.

Lace Lozenges

Lace Lozenges

An interesting "twist" of the cable needle is employed in this pattern to make an eight-stitch cross—or rather, to cross the two outside stitches in front of the intervening six. The rows are repetitive, and so are not given in consecutive order; but it is easy to see that there are four central yo's and three lateral ones, alternately, in each lozenge.

Multiple of 18 sts plus 1.

Rows 1, 5, 9, and 13 (Wrong side)—K1, * p1, k1, p4, k1, p1, k1; rep from *.
Rows 2, 6, 10, and 14—P1, * k1, p1, k2 tog, (yo) twice, ssk, p1, k1, p1; rep from *.
Rows 3, 7, 11, and 15—K1, * p1, k1, p1, (k1, p1) into the double yo of previous row, (p1, k1) twice; rep from *.
Rows 4 and 12—P1, * k1, p1, yo, k2 tog, ssk, yo, p1, k1, p1; rep from *.
Row 8—P1, * cross next 8 sts as follows: sl next st to dpn and hold in front, sl next 6 sts to right-hand needle, sl next st to dpn and hold in front, sl the same 6 sts back to left-hand needle; then twist dpn a half-turn counterclockwise, thus reversing positions of the 2 sts on it; then k1 from dpn; then p1, k4, p1; then knit the last st from dpn (8 sts crossed); p1, k1, p1, yo, k2 tog, ssk, yo, p1, k1, p1; rep from *.
Row 16—* P1, k1, p1, yo, k2 tog, ssk, yo, p1, k1, p1, cross next 8 sts as in Row 8; rep from *, end p1.

Repeat Rows 1–16.

Barrel Stitch

Contributed by Dorothy M. Singer, Concord, Vermont

This pattern comes from France, and makes a fabric that is pretty on both sides. It can be either a close fabric or one that is quite "open", depending on the weight of the yarn used and the degree to which it is stretched.

Barrel Stitch

Multiple of 10 sts plus 8.

Rows 1, 3, and 5 (Wrong side)—K1, * k6, p4; rep from *, end k7.

Row 2—K1, * p6, sl next 2 sts to dpn and hold in back, k2, then k2 from dpn; rep from *, end p6, k1.

Row 4—K1, * p6, yo, k2 tog-b, k2 tog, yo; rep from *, end p6, k1.

Row 6—Repeat Row 2.

Row 7—K1, * k3 tog-b, k3 tog, pass the first of these 2 sts over the second; p4; rep from *, end last repeat k1 instead of p4.

Row 8—K1, * (k1, p1) 3 times in the next st, making 6 sts from one; yo, k2 tog-b, k2 tog, yo; rep from *, end (k1, p1) 3 times in next st, k1.

Repeat Rows 1–8.

The Enchanted Cottage

Lace and cable stitches combine with simple knit-purl textures to make this pretty "picture". The ground on which the cottage stands is a simple block stitch, its walls and chimney are "shingled" with Dot Stitch (*A Treasury of Knitting Patterns,* p. 12), and its door, window, and loft are made of lace. Make an enchanting sweater for a child with the Enchanted Cottage at its center, or work this pattern into an afghan square.

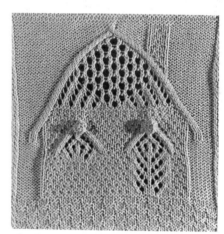

The Enchanted Cottage

Panel of 54 sts.

NOTES: Front Cross (FC)—sl 2 sts to dpn and hold in front, p1, then k2 from dpn.

Front Knit Cross (FKC)—sl 2 sts to dpn and hold in front, k1, then k2 from dpn.

Double Front Cross (DFC)—sl 2 sts to dpn and hold in front, p2, then k2 from dpn.

Back Cross (BC)—sl 1 st to dpn and hold in back, k2, then p1 from dpn.

Back Knit Cross (BKC)—sl 1 st to dpn and hold in back, k2, then k1 from dpn.

Double Back Cross (DBC)—sl 2 sts to dpn and hold in back, k2, then p2 from dpn.

Yo2—double yarn-over. Odd-numbered rows are right-side rows.

Rows 1 and 2—* K3, p3; rep from *.

Rows 3 and 4—* P3, k3; rep from *.

Rows 5 through 12—Repeat Rows 1 through 4 twice more.

Row 13—Purl.

Rows 14, 16, 18, 20, 22, 24, 26, 28, 30, 32, and 34—K7, p40, k7.

Row 15—P7, k2, p1, k1, p1, k2, k2 tog, yo, k3, yo, ssk, k2, (p1, k1) 12 times, p7.

Row 17—P7, (k1, p1) twice, k2, (k2 tog, yo) twice, k1, (yo, ssk) twice, k2, (p1, k1) 11 times, k1, p7.

Rows 19, 21, and 23—Repeat Rows 15, 17, and 15 again.

Row 25—P7, (k1, p1) twice, k2, (k2 tog, yo) twice, k1, (yo, ssk) twice, k2, (p1, k1) 4 times, p9, (k1, p1) twice, k2, p7.

Row 27—P7, k2, p1, k1, p1, k2, * k2 tog, yo, k3, yo, ssk *, k2, (p1, k1) 5 times, rep from * to *, (k1, p1) 3 times, k1, p7.

Row 29—P7, (k1, p1) twice, k2, * (k2 tog, yo) twice, k1, (yo, ssk) twice *, k2, (p1, k1) 4 times, rep from * to *, (k1, p1) twice, k2, p7.

Row 31—P7, k2, p1, * FKC, k1, yo, ssk, yo, sl 2—k1—p2sso, yo, k2 tog, yo, k1, BKC *, (p1, k1) twice, rep from * to *, k1, p1, k1, p7.

Row 33—P7, (k1, p1) twice, * FKC, k1, yo, ssk, k1, k2 tog, yo, k1, BKC *, (p1, k1) 3 times, rep from * to *, k1, p1, k2, p7.

Row 35—P3, k2, p2, k2, p1, k1, p1, * FKC, k1, yo, sl 1—k2 tog—psso, yo, k1, BKC *, (p1, k1) 4 times, rep from * to *, (k1, p1) twice, k1, p2, k2, p3.

Rows 36 and 38—K3, p2, k2, p40, k2, p2, k3.

Row 37—P3, k2, p2, (k1, p1) 3 times, * FKC, k3, BKC *, (p1, k1) 5 times, rep from * to *, (k1, p1) twice, k2, p2, k2, p3.

Row 39—P3, FC, p1, k2, (k1, p1) twice, p1, * FKC, k1, BKC *, (p1, k1) 6 times, rep from * to *, (k1, p1) 4 times, BC, p3.

Row 40—K4, p2, k1, p40, k1, p2, k4.

Row 41—P4, FC, (k1, p1) 5 times, * (k1, yo, k1, yo, k1, yo, k1) in next st, making 7 sts from one; turn and k7, turn and p7, turn and k2, sl 1—k2 tog—psso, k2; turn and p5, turn and k1, sl 1—k2 tog—psso, k1; turn and p3 tog *; (p1, k1) 9 times, rep from * to *, (k1, p1) 4 times, k2, BC, p4.

Row 42—K5, p12, p1-b, p18, p1-b, p12, k5.

Row 43—P5, FC, (k1, p1) 19 times, BC, p5.

Row 44—K6, p42, k6.

Row 45—P6, FC, (k1, p1) 18 times, BC, p6.

Row 46—K7, p40, k7.

Row 47—P7, FC, p34, BC, p7.

Row 48—K8, p38, k8.

Row 49—P8, FC, (k1, yo, ssk) 4 times, k2, k2 tog, yo2, ssk, k2, (k2 tog, yo, k1) 4 times, BC, p8.

Row 50 and all subsequent wrong-side rows through Row 74—Knit all knit sts and purl all purl sts, always working (k1, p1) into every double yo of a preceding row.

NOTE: after formation of Chimney on Rows 57–66, purl all sts on wrong side of Chimney even though some are purled on right-side rows, as in texture stitch for Cottage.

Row 51—P9, FC, (k1, yo, ssk) 3 times, k1, yo, k3 tog, yo2, ssk, k2 tog, yo2, sl 1—k2 tog—psso, yo, k1, (k2 tog, yo, k1) 3 times, BC, p9.

Row 53—P10, FC, (k1, yo, ssk) twice, k1, yo, k3 tog, (yo2, ssk, k2 tog) twice, yo2, sl 1—k2 tog—psso, yo, k1, (k2 tog, yo, k1) twice, BC, p10.

Row 55—P11, FC, k1, yo, ssk, k1, yo, k3 tog, (yo2, ssk, k2 tog) 3 times, yo2, sl 1—k2 tog—psso, yo, k1, k2 tog, yo, k1, BC, p11.

Row 57—P12, FKC, k1, yo, k3 tog, (yo2, ssk, k2 tog) 4 times, yo2, sl 1—k2 tog—psso, yo, k1, BC, p12.

Row 59—P12, k1, FKC, k1, yo, ssk, (k2 tog, yo2, ssk) 4 times, k2 tog, yo, k1, BC, p13.

Row 61—P12, k1, p1, FKC, (k2 tog, yo2, ssk) 5 times, BC, p14.

Row 63—P12, k2, p1, FKC, k1, (k2 tog, yo2, ssk) 4 times, k1, BC, p15.

Row 65—P12, (k1, p1) twice, FKC, k2, (k2 tog, yo2, ssk) 3 times, k2, BC, p16.

Row 67—P12, k2, p1, k2, DFC, k2, (k2 tog, yo2, ssk) twice, k2, DBC, p17.

Row 69—P12, (k1, p1) twice, k1, p2, DFC, k2, k2 tog, yo2, ssk, k2, DBC, p19.

Row 71—P12, k2, p1, k2, p4, DFC, k4, DBC, p21.

Row 73—P12, (k1, p1) twice, k1, p6, DFC, DBC, p23.

Row 75—P12, k2, p1, k2, p8, DFC, p25.

Row 76—K37, p5, k12.

Finish with 6 rows reverse stockinette or garter stitch.

CHAPTER TEN

Yarn-Over Patterns

Classification of patterns in the yarn-over category is difficult. Some of them look like lace; some look like eyelets; and some are solid fabrics. Generally, the reason for grouping them here in a separate chapter is some novelty in texture that gives a different quality to the pattern's allover effect. Every pattern in this group makes use of yarn-over stitches, but the manner of using them varies widely.

The yarn-over is by far the simplest, and by far the most adaptable, of all knitting operations. One little strand placed over the needle between stitches: that's all there is to it. Yet there are literally hundreds of things that can be done with this little strand. The patterns in this group do many different things with it, and thus constitute a suitable introduction to more stylized patterns such as the laces, in which the working of yarn-overs is as disciplined and orderly as the movements of classical ballet.

You *could* make almost any kind of knitted article, from the heaviest to the most delicate, from the patterns in this chapter alone. There are dainty lace-like patterns for fine work such as blouses, baby clothes, table mats and curtains; and there are patterns for more solid articles such as sweaters, coats, and afghans. Different weights of yarn, too, will give different effects. Sometimes the same pattern will look lacy in fine yarn, solid in heavy yarn. Try them out in various ways, and combine them for original and interesting knitting. It is fun to learn a variety of yarn-over patterns; and just learning them will do much to improve your knitting skills in general.

Fascine Braid

As a variation, this pattern can be made with a background of garter stitch (by purling every wrong-side row throughout) or with only 2 or 3 ground stitches between braids instead of 4. A single Braid can be used quite successfully in place of an ordinary cable.

Multiple of 8 sts plus 4.

Rows 1 and 3 (Wrong side)—K4, * p4, k4; rep from *.
Row 2—P4, * (sl 1 wyib, k1, yo, pass sl-st over the knit st and the yo st) twice, p4; rep from *.
Row 4—P4, * k1, sl 1 wyib, k1, yo, pass sl-st over the knit st and the yo st, k1, p4; rep from *.

Repeat Rows 1–4.

Fascine Braid

Star Cluster

This is a pretty mesh-like pattern of the Star Stitch type, with "cluster" strands to add texture interest. It is a rather tight fabric, and must be worked with large needles, in proportion to the weight of the yarn, so that the open mesh-like effect is not lost.

Multiple of 4 sts plus 2.

Row 1 (Right side)—K1, * k2 tog, (yo) twice, k2 tog-b; rep from *, end k1.
Row 2—P2, * p1 (the first yo), p1-b (the second yo); Cluster the next 2 sts as follows: sl 2 wyib, bring yarn to front between needles, sl the same 2 sts back to left-hand needle, pass yarn to back between needles, sl the same 2 sts wyib again; rep from *, end p1, p1-b, p2.
Row 3—K3, * k2 tog, (yo) twice, k2 tog-b; rep from *, end k3.
Row 4—P2, * Cluster 2, p1, p1-b; rep from *, end Cluster 2, p2.

Repeat Rows 1–4.

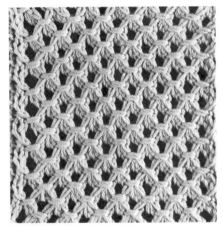

Star Cluster

Ladder Lace Rib

Contributed by Berniece Hampson, San Clemente, California

This delicate rib pattern is very highly embossed. The "ladder" is half hidden; it can be seen only when the fabric is looked at from an angle at the side. Under this condition, the lace becomes so evident that the ribbing almost resembles a mesh.

Multiple of 5 sts plus 2.

Row 1 (Wrong side)—K2, * p3 tog, k2; rep from *.
Row 2—P2, * yo, p1, yo, p2; rep from *.

Repeat Rows 1 and 2.

Ladder Lace Rib

Seafoam Pattern

Seafoam Pattern

This simple stitch, when worked in fine yarn, makes the most delicate and lacy fabric imaginable. It is ideal for cobwebby stoles, scarves, bedjackets, peignoirs, fancy baby clothes, and overskirts for evening wear. It can also be worked in fine cotton for lovely tablecloths, luncheon cloths and place mats. Actually it is nothing but garter stitch—plain knitting—but it is certainly a garter stitch with an aristocratic air.

Multiple of 10 sts plus 6.

Rows 1 and 2—Knit.
Row 3 (Right side)—K6, * (yo) twice, k1, (yo) 3 times, k1, (yo) 4 times, k1, (yo) 3 times, k1, (yo) twice, k6; rep from *.
Row 4—Knit, dropping all yo's off needle.
Rows 5 and 6—Knit.
Row 7—K1, rep from * of Row 3, end last repeat k1 instead of k6.
Row 8—As Row 4.

Repeat Rows 1–8.

Open Bobble

Contributed by Georgia Berry, Chicago, Illinois

This is a very highly embossed purl fabric, easy to work and suitable for novelty items such as hats and handbags. The cast-on edge will scallop, and the bound-off edge will show some of the yo's, most of which are concealed in the rest of the fabric by the projecting clusters.

Multiple of 12 sts plus 1.

Rows 1, 3, and 5 (Wrong side)—K1, * yo, k4, p3 tog, k4, yo, k1; rep from *.
Rows 2, 4, and 6—K1, * yo, p4, p3 tog, p4, yo, k1; rep from *.
Rows 7, 9, and 11—P2 tog, * k4, yo, k1, yo, k4, p3 tog; rep from *, end last repeat p2 tog instead of p3 tog.
Rows 8, 10, and 12—P2 tog, * p4, yo, k1, yo, p4, p3 tog; rep from *, end last repeat p2 tog instead of p3 tog.

Repeat Rows 1–12.

Open Bobble

Roman Stripe

Here is a charming lacy pattern that is very easy to work. The fabric is reversible, of course, since there are 7 rows (an odd number). But it can be given a right and a wrong side by omitting Row 7 and doing the pattern with only 6 rows.

This pattern makes very lovely scarves, shawls, stoles, baby blankets (summer weight), light throws for sofas and chairs, etc. A few repeats of the 7 pattern rows will form a very pleasing border for skirts, sleeves, or lacy blouses.

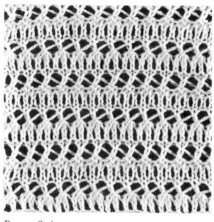

Even number of sts.

Row 1—K1, * yo, k1; rep from * across to last st, end k1.

Row 2—K1, purl across to last st, end k1.

Row 3—K1, * k2 tog; rep from * across to last st, end k1.

Rows 4 and 5—K1, * yo, k2 tog; rep from * across to last st, end k1.

Rows 6 and 7—Knit.

Repeat Rows 1–7.

Roman Stripe

Vertical Drop-Stitch

Contributed by Hildegard M. Elsner, Aldan, Pennsylvania

This pattern is pretty on both sides of the fabric, and also can be used horizontally, as in a sweater worked from one side to the other. To finish, work Row 6 or Row 12 omitting the yo's, then bind off—the original number of stitches will be thus restored.

Multiple of 8 sts plus 4.

Preparation row, right side—K1, * p2, k1, yo, k1, p2, k2; rep from *, end p2, k1.

Rows 1, 3, and 5 (Wrong side)—P1, * k2, p2, k2, p3; rep from *, end k2, p1.

Rows 2 and 4—K1, * p2, k3, p2, k2; rep from *, end p2, k1.

Row 6—K1, * p2, k1, drop next st off needle and unravel down to the yo six rows below; k1, p2, k1, yo, k1; rep from *, end p2, k1.

Rows 7, 9, and 11—P1, * k2, p3, k2, p2; rep from *, end k2, p1.

Rows 8 and 10—K1, * p2, k2, p2, k3; rep from *, end p2, k1.

Row 12—K1, * p2, k1, yo, k1, p2, k1, drop next st off needle and unravel six rows down as before, k1; rep from *, end p2, k1.

Repeat Rows 1–12.

Vertical Drop-Stitch

Fluffy Brioche

Fluffy Brioche

All Brioche patterns are fluffy and loose, but this one is particularly so. It makes a beautiful, soft, honeycomb-like texture that is perfect for summer sweaters, baby blankets, shawls, etc. It should be worked with a light hand, on needles that are not too small. When casting on, use two needles held together, so that the cast-on stitches will be large enough to spread to the width of the fabric. Bind off *very* loosely, preferably with larger needles, on one of the right-side rows.

Even number of sts.

Row 1 (Wrong side)—* Yo, sl 1 wyib, k1; rep from *.
Row 2—* K1, k2 tog (the yo and sl-st of previous row); rep from *.
Row 3—K1, * yo, sl 1 wyib, k1; rep from *, end k1.
Row 4—K2, * k2 tog, k1; rep from *.

Repeat Rows 1–4.

Diagonal Brioche

Diagonal Brioche

One never ceases to be amazed by the variety displayed by different small alterations in the Brioche technique. The wrong side of this fluffy fabric is perhaps even more charming than the right side; it shows a graceful Brioche Knot Stitch. Still another variation can be obtained by the tiniest of substitutions: slip all the yo's purlwise instead of knitwise in Rows 1 and 3. Try the pattern both ways, and see which you like better.

Note: all slip-stitches are slipped with yarn in back. The Preparation Row is not to be repeated.

Odd number of sts.

Preparation Row (Wrong side)—P2, * sl 1, yo, p1; rep from *, end p1.
Row 1—Sl 1, p1, * sl the yo knitwise, p2; rep from *, end p1.
Row 2—P1, * sl 1, yo, p2 tog; rep from *, end sl 1, yo, p1.
Row 3—P1, * sl the yo knitwise, p2; rep from *.
Row 4—Sl 1, p2 tog, * sl 1, yo, p2 tog; rep from *, end p1.

Repeat Rows 1–4.

Wildflower Knot Stitch

This dainty texture pattern is easy to work, and pretty in children's wear or casual sweaters. The technique is similar to Daisy Stitch.

Wildflower Knot Stitch

Multiple of 8 sts plus 5.

Rows 1 and 3 (Wrong side)—Purl.
Row 2—Knit.
Row 4—K5, * p3 tog, leave on needle; yo, purl same 3 sts tog again, k5; rep from *.
Rows 5, 6, and 7—Repeat Rows 1, 2, and 3.
Row 8—K1, * p3 tog, leave on needle; yo, purl same 3 sts tog again, k5; rep from *, end last repeat k1.

Repeat Rows 1–8.

Berry Stitch

Both Berry Stitch and its variation, Clove Stitch, are often confused with Trinity Stitch. All three are worked in a similar way, but their appearance is very different. Berry Stitch really does resemble rows of little blackberries or strawberries, complete with stems. The fabric has an extraordinarily beautiful wrong side, and so is appropriate for scarves and such articles, where both sides will be seen.

Berry Stitch

Multiple of 4 sts.

Row 1 (Wrong side)—* (K1, yo, k1) in same st, p3 tog; rep from *.
Row 2—* K1, p3; rep from *.
Row 3—* K3, p1; rep from *.
Row 4—* P1, k3; rep from *.
Row 5—* P3 tog, (k1, yo, k1) in same st; rep from *.
Row 6—* P3, k1; rep from *.
Row 7—* P1, k3; rep from *.
Row 8—* K3, p1; rep from *.

Repeat Rows 1–8.

VARIATION: *CLOVE STITCH*

Clove Stitch

Multiple of 4 sts.

Row 1 (Wrong side)—* (K1, yo, k1) in same st, p3 tog; rep from *.
Row 2—* P1, k3; rep from *.
Row 3—* P3 tog, (k1, yo, k1) in same st; rep from *.
Row 4—* K3, p1; rep from *.

Repeat Rows 1–4.

Berry-in-a-Box

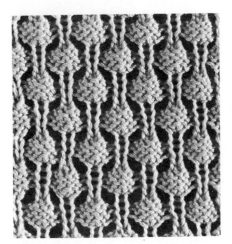

Berry-in-a-Box

Contributed by Leona Hughes, Sarasota, Florida

This perfectly charming openwork fabric consists of purled "berries" enclosed by little square frames of lace and set off by small ribs. Berry-in-a-Box is delightful in stoles and evening sweaters. Try it with a fancy yarn—slubbed, crinkled, ombre, or a sparkling metallic.

Multiple of 6 sts plus 1.

Row 1 (Right side)—P3, * k1, p5; rep from *, end k1, p3.

Row 2—K3 tog, * yo, (k1, yo, k1) in next st, yo, Decrease 5 as follows: k2 tog-b, k3 tog, pass the k2-tog-b st over the k3-tog st; rep from *, end yo, (k1, yo, k1) in next st, yo, k3 tog-b.

Rows 3 and 5—K1, * p5, k1; rep from *.

Row 4—P1, * k5, p1; rep from *.

Row 6—Inc in first st, * yo, Decrease 5 as in Row 2, yo, (k1, yo, k1) in next st; rep from *, end yo, Decrease 5, yo, inc in last st.

Row 7—Repeat Row 1.

Row 8—K3, * p1, k5; rep from *, end p1, k3.

Repeat Rows 1–8.

Gooseberry Stitch

Gooseberry Stitch

This is a splendid "knobbly" pattern for hats, jacket panels, pockets, collars and cuffs, handbags, afghans, and extra-chunky sweaters. The gooseberries are bigger and bolder than any other "berry" motifs, and have more firmness and body than bobbles. The wrong side of the fabric is perfectly flat; this pattern requires no blocking.

Odd number of sts.

Row 1 (Right side)—Knit.

Row 2—K1, * (p1, yo, p1, yo, p1) in next st, making 5 sts from one; k1; rep from *.

Row 3—Purl.

Row 4—K1, * sl 2 wyif, p3 tog, p2sso, k1; rep from *.

Row 5—Knit.

Row 6—K2, * (p1, yo, p1, yo, p1) in next st, k1; rep from *, end k1.

Row 7—Purl.

Row 8—K2, * sl 2 wyif, p3 tog, p2sso, k1; rep from *, end k1.

Repeat Rows 1–8.

Crochet-Knit Mesh Pattern

Contributed by Berniece Hampson, San Clemente, California

This pattern stretches enormously, and must be cast on and bound off with needles much larger than those used for the knitting, or else with two needles held together. The knitting action is similar to a "psso", in that the stitch, and the 3 subsequent yo's, are drawn over the yo loop and off the needle. This forms a small crochet-like "chain" in every other stitch. The last stitch of the row is treated the same way, using the now empty left-hand needle to work the chain of yo's.

The fabric may be worked in fine or heavy yarn; in both cases it will be loose, soft, fluffy, and very elastic, which makes it appropriate for stoles, scarves, shrugs, bedjackets and the like.

Even number of sts.

* K2, (yo, pull the last st over the yo) 4 times; rep from *.

Repeat this same row.

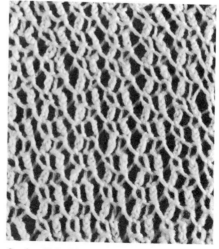

Crochet-Knit Mesh Pattern

Pine Burr Pattern

This fascinating fabric is like an expanded Trinity Stitch. The wrong side is not unattractive, so the pattern is suitable for scarves and other articles that show both sides. NOTE: A needle 3 or 4 sizes larger than the other needles should be used to work Rows 3 and 7, so that the stitches are enlarged enough to make the pattern rows (4 and 8) easier to work.

Multiple of 6 sts plus 2.

Row 1 (Right side)—Knit.

Row 2—Knit.

Row 3—With larger needle, k1, purl to last st, k1.

Row 4—K1, * (k1, yo, k1, yo, k1) in one st, k5 tog-b; rep from *, end k1.

Rows 5, 6, and 7—Repeat Rows 1, 2, and 3.

Row 8—K1, * k5 tog-b, (k1, yo, k1, yo, k1) in one st; rep from *, end k1.

Repeat Rows 1–8.

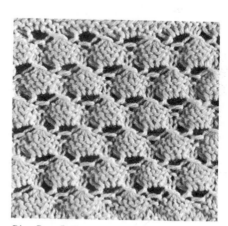

Pine Burr Pattern

Purl Shell Pattern

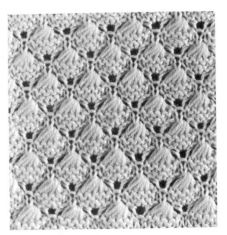

Purl Shell Pattern

This pretty fabric is similar to Pine Burr in its construction, and closely resembles the classic crocheted Shell Stitch. It is a dressy fabric, suitable for blouses, evening sweaters and baby wear.

Multiple of 6 sts plus 3.

Rows 1 and 2—Knit.

Row 3 (Right side)—K1, (k1, yo, k1) in next st, * k5 wrapping yarn twice for each st, (k1, yo, k1, yo, k1) in next st; rep from *, end k5 wrapping yarn twice for each st, (k1, yo, k1) in next st, k1.

Row 4—K4, * sl 5 wyif dropping extra wraps, then insert left-hand needle back into these 5 long sts and p5 tog; k5; rep from *, end last repeat k4.

Rows 5 and 6—Knit.

Row 7—K1, k3 wrapping yarn twice for each st, * (k1, yo, k1, yo, k1) in next st, k5 wrapping yarn twice for each st; rep from *, end (k1, yo, k1, yo, k1) in next st, k3 wrapping yarn twice for each st, k1.

Row 8—K1, sl 3 wyif dropping extra wraps, insert left-hand needle into these 3 sts and p3 tog; * k5, sl 5 wyif dropping extra wraps, insert left-hand needle into these 5 sts and p5 tog; rep from *, end k5, sl 3 wyif dropping extra wraps, insert needle into these 3 sts and p3 tog, k1.

Repeat Rows 1–8.

Portcullis Stitch

ABOVE: *Portcullis Stitch*
BELOW: *Portcullis Stitch in two colors*

In a single color, this pattern makes a handsome, symmetrical ribbed fabric resembling crochet. In two colors, it makes a stunningly textured stripe. The two-color version is just as simple as the original version: Rows 1 and 2 in the first color, then Rows 1 and 2 again in the second color, and so on alternating colors. Note that for the best effect, the colors should be changed before the *purl* row (Row 1), so that the strands will be carried up the left-hand edge instead of the right-hand edge, as is more usual.

The fabric is free of curl, sturdy, and easy to block; it keeps its shape well.

Multiple of 4 sts plus 1.

Row 1 (Wrong side)—Purl.

Row 2—K2 tog, * (k1, yo, k1) in the same st, sl 1—k2 tog—psso; rep from *, end (k1, yo, k1) in the same st, ssk.

Repeat Rows 1 and 2.

Raisin Stitch

Here, the "crochet-knit" technique of making a yo chain is used to make a solid, nubby fabric similar to Peppercorn Stitch, but looser and more elastic. The strands are passed over subsequent strands in the manner of a "psso". The first st to be passed over is an actual stitch; the other 3 are yo's.

Odd number of sts.

Rows 1 and 3 (Wrong side)—Purl.

Row 2—* K2, (yo, pull the last st over the yo) 4 times; rep from *, end k1.

Row 4—K1, rep from * of Row 2 across to last 2 sts, end k2.

Repeat Rows 1–4.

Raisin Stitch

Bear Track

Contributed by Hildegard M. Elsner, Aldan, Pennsylvania

This is a beautiful Bavarian version of the Umbrella Pattern, very useful for stoles, capes, soft lacy blouses and crib blankets, and very easy to work.

Multiple of 16 sts plus 1.

Row 1 (Right side)—K1, * yo, (k1, p1) 7 times, k1, yo, k1; rep from *.

Row 2—K1, * p2, (k1, p1) 7 times, p1, k1; rep from *.

Row 3—K2, * yo, (k1, p1) 7 times, k1, yo, k3; rep from *, end last repeat k2.

Row 4—K2, * p2, (k1, p1) 7 times, p1, k3; rep from *, end last repeat k2.

Row 5—K3, * yo, (k1, p1) 7 times, k1, yo, k5; rep from *, end last repeat k3.

Row 6—K3, * p2, (k1, p1) 7 times, p1, k5; rep from *, end last repeat k3.

Row 7—K4, * yo, (k1, p1) 7 times, k1, yo, k7; rep from *, end last repeat k4.

Row 8—K4, * p2, (k1, p1) 7 times, p1, k7; rep from *, end last repeat k4.

Row 9—K5, * (ssk) 3 times, sl 1—k2 tog—psso, (k2 tog) 3 times, k9; rep from *, end last repeat k5.

Row 10—Purl.

Repeat Rows 1–10.

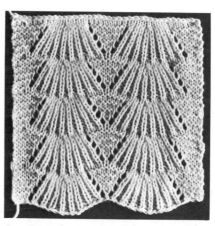

Bear Track

Lucina Shell Pattern

Lucina Shell Pattern

Contributed by Georgia Berry, Chicago, Illinois

This pattern makes a beautiful and delicate fabric for shawls, scarves, blouses, and fancy sweaters. It is easy to work, being made on the same gradual-increase and sudden-decrease principle that is exemplified by "Bear Track".

Multiple of 9 sts plus 3.

Row 1 (Right side)—K2, * yo, k8, yo, k1; rep from *, end k1.
Row 2—K3, * p8, k3; rep from *.
Row 3—K3, * yo, k8, yo, k3, rep from *.
Row 4—K4, * p8, k5; rep from *, end last repeat k4.
Row 5—K4, * yo, k8, yo, k5; rep from *, end last repeat k4.
Row 6—K5, * p8, k7; rep from *, end last repeat k5.
Row 7—K5, * k4 tog-b, k4 tog, k7; rep from *, end last repeat k5.
Row 8—Knit.

Repeat Rows 1–8.

Lily of the Valley

Lily of the Valley

Contributed by Billie Booth, Pompano Beach, Florida

This pattern, related to Vine Lace Zigzag with popcorn-like knots added, is really upside down; the illusion of the "lily" is more realistic when the pattern is used in a garment made from the top down. But whether is it made to look truly flower-like or not, the pattern is an extremely pretty one with a dainty, ladylike air.

Panel of 27 sts.

NOTE: Make Knot (MK) as follows: (k1, p1, k1, p1, k1) all in the same st, making 5 sts from one; then pass the 4th, 3rd, 2nd, and 1st of the new sts separately over the last st made.

Row 1 (Wrong side) and all other wrong-side rows—K2, p23, k2.
Row 2—P2, ssk, k6, (yo, k1) twice, sl 1—k2 tog—psso, (k1, yo) twice, k6, k2 tog, p2.
Row 4—P2, ssk, k5, yo, k1, yo, k2, sl 1—k2 tog—psso, k2, yo, k1, yo, k5, k2 tog, p2.
Row 6—P2, ssk, k4, yo, k1, yo, MK, k2, sl 1—k2 tog—psso, k2, MK, yo, k1, yo, k4, k2 tog, p2.
Row 8—P2, ssk, k3, yo, k1, yo, MK, k3, sl 1—k2 tog—psso, k3, MK, yo, k1, yo, k3, k2 tog, p2.
Row 10—P2, ssk, k2, yo, k1, yo, MK, k4, sl 1—k2 tog—psso, k4, MK, yo, k1, yo, k2, k2 tog, p2.

Row 12—P2, ssk, (k1, yo) twice, MK, k5, sl 1—k2 tog—psso, k5, MK, (yo, k1) twice, k2 tog, p2.

Row 14—P2, ssk, yo, k1, yo, MK, k6, sl 1—k2 tog—psso, k6, MK, yo, k1, yo, k2 tog, p2.

Repeat Rows 1–14.

Flying Chevron

Contributed by Hildegard M. Elsner, Aldan, Pennsylvania

Multiple of 13 sts plus 3.

Row 1 (Wrong side)—K1, purl to last st, k1.

Row 2—P3, * k2 tog, k3, yo, k3, ssk, p3; rep from *.

Row 3—K3, * p4, (k1, p1) into the yo of previous row, p4, k3; rep from *.

Row 4—P3, * k2 tog, (k2, yo) twice, k2, ssk, p3; rep from *.

Rows 5, 7, and 9—K3, * p10, k3; rep from *.

Row 6—P3, * k2 tog, k1, yo, k4, yo, k1, ssk, p3; rep from *.

Row 8—P3, * k2 tog, yo, k6, yo, ssk, p3; rep from *.

Row 10—P2, * k2 tog, yo, k8, yo, ssk, p1; rep from *, end p1.

Row 11—K2, * p12, k1; rep from *, end k1.

Row 12—P1, k2 tog, * yo, k10, yo, sl 1—k2 tog—psso; rep from *, end yo, k10, yo, ssk, p1.

Repeat Rows 1–12.

Flying Chevron

Fancy Rib Patterns

These eight patterns should be studied with great care, because they have much to teach. The knitter who comprehends precisely why and how these patterns do what they do will never be confused about the manipulation of decreases at a distance from their corresponding yo's, or about the arrangement of any curvilinear pattern.

Comb Stitch and Folded-Ribbon Stitch are a pair, one the opposite of the other. In Comb Stitch, the *decreases* are aligned directly over each other, first at one side of the rib and then at the other side, while the yo's travel diagonally across the rib. In Folded-Ribbon Stitch, the yo's remain in alternate vertical alignment while the decreases travel diagonally. Notice, though, that in both cases the stationary units look—in the finished knitting—as if they are *not* in vertical alignment. They are drawn slightly left and right by the bias pull of the other stitches.

In the #2 versions of both of these patterns, the rib is worked on both sides of the fabric instead of the right side only. This condenses the pattern so that there are fewer rows to each repeat. Pay close attention to the relationship of the four different types of decreases used in these second versions, and you will understand how to work any other decrease series from the wrong side, so that it slants left or right as desired.

Track of the Turtle and Waved-Ribbon Stitch are another pair, again opposite in technique. In the first, *both* decreases and yo's travel diagonally; in the second, *both* are stationary, except that they switch from one side of the rib to the other. The #2 versions, again, have shorter motifs because they are worked from both sides.

Every knitter should try out all eight of these patterns and give them a good long think. They are not only pretty, but as a series they present a short but thorough lesson in pattern construction.

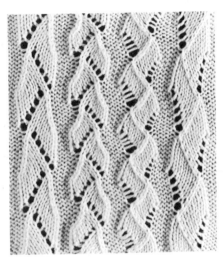

Fancy Rib Patterns I

LEFT TO RIGHT:
1. *Comb Stitch, Version I*
2. *Comb Stitch, Version II*
3. *Folded-Ribbon Stitch, Version II*
4. *Folded-Ribbon Stitch, Version I*

1. COMB STITCH, VERSION I

Panel of 12 sts.

Row 1 (Wrong side) and all other wrong-side rows—K3, p6, k3.
Row 2—P3, yo, k4, k2 tog, p3.
Row 4—P3, k1, yo, k3, k2 tog, p3.
Row 6—P3, k2, yo, k2, k2 tog, p3.
Row 8—P3, k3, yo, k1, k2 tog, p3.
Row 10—P3, k4, yo, k2 tog, p3.
Row 12—P3, ssk, k4, yo, p3.
Row 14—P3, ssk, k3, yo, k1, p3.
Row 16—P3, ssk, k2, yo, k2, p3.
Row 18—P3, ssk, k1, yo, k3, p3.
Row 20—P3, ssk, yo, k4, p3.

Repeat Rows 1–20.

2. COMB STITCH, VERSION II

Panel of 12 sts.

Row 1 (Wrong side)—K3, p6, k3.
Row 2—P3, ssk, k4, yo, p3.
Row 3—K3, p1, yo, p3, p2 tog-b, k3.
Row 4—P3, ssk, k2, yo, k2, p3.
Row 5—K3, p3, yo, p1, p2 tog-b, k3.
Row 6—P3, ssk, yo, k4, p3.
Row 7—Repeat Row 1.
Row 8—P3, yo, k4, k2 tog, p3.
Row 9—K3, p2 tog, p3, yo, p1, k3.
Row 10—P3, k2, yo, k2, k2 tog, p3.
Row 11—K3, p2 tog, p1, yo, p3, k3.
Row 12—P3, k4, yo, k2 tog, p3.

Repeat Rows 1–12.

3. FOLDED-RIBBON STITCH, VERSION I

Panel of 12 sts.

Row 1 (Wrong side) and all other wrong-side rows—K3, p6, k3.
Row 2—P3, yo, ssk, k4, p3.
Row 4—P3, yo, k1, ssk, k3, p3.
Row 6—P3, yo, k2, ssk, k2, p3.
Row 8—P3, yo, k3, ssk, k1, p3.
Row 10—P3, yo, k4, ssk, p3.
Row 12—P3, k4, k2 tog, yo, p3.
Row 14—P3, k3, k2 tog, k1, yo, p3.
Row 16—P3, k2, k2 tog, k2, yo, p3.
Row 18—P3, k1, k2 tog, k3, yo, p3.
Row 20—P3, k2 tog, k4, yo, p3.

Repeat Rows 1–20.

4. FOLDED-RIBBON STITCH, VERSION II

Panel of 12 sts.

Row 1 (Wrong side)—K3, p6, k3.
Row 2—P3, k4, k2 tog, yo, p3.
Row 3—K3, yo, p1, p2 tog, p3, k3.
Row 4—P3, k2, k2 tog, k2, yo, p3.
Row 5—K3, yo, p3, p2 tog, p1, k3.
Row 6—P3, k2 tog, k4, yo, p3.
Row 7—Repeat Row 1.
Row 8—P3, yo, ssk, k4, p3.
Row 9—K3, p3, p2 tog-b, p1, yo, k3.
Row 10—P3, yo, k2, ssk, k2, p3.
Row 11—K3, p1, p2 tog-b, p3, yo, k3.
Row 12—P3, yo, k4, ssk, p3.

Repeat Rows 1–12.

5. TRACK OF THE TURTLE, VERSION I

Panel of 15 sts.

Row 1 (Wrong side) and all other wrong-side rows—K3, p9, k3.
Row 2—P3, yo, k4, ssk, k3, p3.
Row 4—P3, k1, yo, k4, ssk, k2, p3.
Row 6—P3, k2, yo, k4, ssk, k1, p3.
Row 8—P3, k3, yo, k4, ssk, p3.
Row 10—P3, k3, k2 tog, k4, yo, p3.
Row 12—P3, k2, k2 tog, k4, yo, k1, p3.
Row 14—P3, k1, k2 tog, k4, yo, k2, p3.
Row 16—P3, k2 tog, k4, yo, k3, p3.

Repeat Rows 1–16.

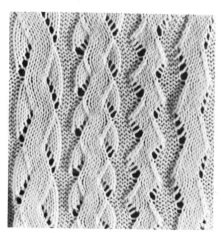

Fancy Rib Patterns II

LEFT TO RIGHT:
1. Track of the Turtle, Version I
2. Track of the Turtle, Version II
3. Waved-Ribbon Stitch, Version II
4. Waved-Ribbon Stitch, Version I

6. TRACK OF THE TURTLE, VERSION II

Panel of 15 sts.

Row 1 (Wrong side)—K3, p9, k3.
Row 2—P3, yo, k4, ssk, k3, p3.
Row 3—K3, p2, p2 tog-b, p4, yo, p1, k3.
Row 4—P3, k2, yo, k4, ssk, k1, p3.
Row 5—K3, p2 tog-b, p4, yo, p3, k3.
Row 6—P3, k9, p3.
Row 7—K3, yo, p4, p2 tog, p3, k3.
Row 8—P3, k2, k2 tog, k4, yo, k1, p3.
Row 9—K3, p2, yo, p4, p2 tog, p1, k3.
Row 10—P3, k2 tog, k4, yo, k3, p3.

Repeat Rows 1–10.

7. WAVED-RIBBON STITCH, VERSION I

Panel of 12 sts.

Row 1 (Wrong side) and all other wrong-side rows—K3, p6, k3.
Rows 2, 4, 6, and 8—P3, yo, k4, k2 tog, p3.
Rows 10, 12, 14, and 16—P3, ssk, k4, yo, p3.

Repeat Rows 1–16.

8. WAVED-RIBBON STITCH, VERSION II

Panel of 12 sts.

Row 1 (Wrong side)—K3, p6, k3.
Rows 2 and 4—P3, yo, k4, k2 tog, p3.
Rows 3 and 5—K3, p2 tog, p4, yo, k3.
Row 6—P3, k6, p3.
Rows 7 and 9—K3, yo, p4, p2 tog-b, k3.
Rows 8 and 10—P3, ssk, k4, yo, p3.

Repeat Rows 1–10.

Pilsener Pleating

Contributed by Hildegard M. Elsner, Aldan, Pennsylvania

The city of Plzen, in Bohemia (honored in this country by the lovers of good beer), is the source of this openwork variation on the old Triangular Stitch. Version I makes pleats that fold to the right, and Version II makes pleats that fold to the left. Notice that larger holes are created by Version I, because the purl stitches follow the yo's and thus cause the yarn to travel a greater distance around the needle, to the front. The two versions could be combined in a zigzag, as shown in the center of the swatch, simply by alternating them: Rows 1–14 of I, followed by Rows 1–14 of II, etc. In this case the pleats disappear, and the result is a form of Block Stitch.

Multiple of 8 sts plus 1.

VERSION I

Row 1 (Right side)—* K6, k2 tog, yo; rep from *, end k1.
Row 2—P1, * k1, p7; rep from *.
Row 3—* K5, k2 tog, yo, p1; rep from *, end k1.
Row 4—P1, * k2, p6; rep from *.
Row 5—* K4, k2 tog, yo, p2; rep from *, end k1.
Row 6—P1, * k3, p5; rep from *.
Row 7—* K3, k2 tog, yo, p3; rep from *, end k1.
Row 8—P1, * k4, p4; rep from *.
Row 9—* K2, k2 tog, yo, p4; rep from *, end k1.
Row 10—P1, * k5, p3; rep from *.
Row 11—* K1, k2 tog, yo, p5; rep from *, end k1.
Row 12—P1, * k6, p2; rep from *.
Row 13—* K2 tog, yo, p6; rep from *, end k1.
Row 14—P1, * k7, p1; rep from *.

Repeat Rows 1–14.

Pilsener Pleating
ABOVE: *Version I*
BELOW: *Version II*

VERSION II

Row 1 (Right side)—K1, * yo, ssk, k6; rep from *.
Row 2—* P7, k1; rep from *, end p1.
Row 3—K1, * p1, yo, ssk, k5; rep from *.
Row 4—* P6, k2; rep from *, end p1.
Row 5—K1, * p2, yo, ssk, k4; rep from *.
Row 6—* P5, k3; rep from *, end p1.
Row 7—K1, * p3, yo, ssk, k3; rep from *.
Row 8—* P4, k4; rep from *, end p1.
Row 9—K1, * p4, yo, ssk, k2; rep from *.
Row 10—* P3, k5; rep from *, end p1.
Row 11—K1, * p5, yo, ssk, k1; rep from *.
Row 12—* P2, k6; rep from *, end p1.
Row 13—K1, * p6, yo, ssk; rep from *.
Row 14—* P1, k7; rep from *, end p1.

Repeat Rows 1–14.

Gate Pattern

Contributed by Leona Hughes, Sarasota, Florida

Like Pilsener Pleating, this pattern combines purl blocks with knit blocks that are traversed by diagonal yo's. But the arrangement is reversed, to form a flat (non-pleating) fabric with a checked effect, and the motifs are square rather than triangular. The pattern is easy to work, and attractive in sweaters, blouses, baby blankets, or dresses.

Multiple of 10 sts plus 2.

Row 1 (Right side)—K1, * yo, ssk, k3, p5; rep from *, end k1.
Rows 2, 4, 6, and 8—K1, * k5, p5; rep from *, end k1.
Row 3—K1, * k1, yo, ssk, k2, p5; rep from *, end k1.
Row 5—K1, * k2, yo, ssk, k1, p5; rep from *, end k1.
Row 7—K1, * k3, yo, ssk, p5; rep from *, end k1.
Row 9—K1, * p5, k3, k2 tog, yo; rep from *, end k1.
Rows 10, 12, 14, and 16—K1, * p5, k5; rep from *, end k1.
Row 11—K1, * p5, k2, k2 tog, yo, k1; rep from *, end k1.
Row 13—K1, * p5, k1, k2 tog, yo, k2; rep from *, end k1.
Row 15—K1, * p5, k2 tog, yo, k3; rep from *, end k1.

Repeat Rows 1–16.

Gate Pattern

Moorish Lattice

Double increases and double decreases alone, with no other special knitting operations, make this attractively textured fabric. The purled background stitches are compressed at some points and stretched at others because of the reduction of stitch number on Rows 4 and 14.

Multiple of 6 sts plus 5.

Rows 1 and 3 (Wrong side)—K4, * p3, k3; rep from *, end k1.
Row 2—K1, * p3, k3; rep from *, end p3, k1.
Row 4—K1, * p3, sl 2—k1—p2sso; rep from *, end p3, k1.
Row 5—K4, * p1, k3; rep from *, end k1.
Row 6—K1, * p3, (k1, yo, k1) in next st; rep from *, end p3, k1.
Rows 7, 8, and 9—Repeat Rows 1, 2, and 3.
Row 10—K2, p2 tog, * k1, (k1, yo, k1) in next st, k1, p3 tog; rep from *, end last repeat p2 tog, k2 instead of p3 tog.
Rows 11 and 13—Repeat Row 2.
Row 12—Repeat Row 1.
Row 14—K1, * sl 2—k1—p2sso, p3; rep from *, end sl 2—k1—p2sso, k1.

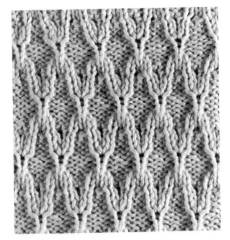

Moorish Lattice

Row 15—K1, * p1, k3; rep from *, end p1, k1.

Row 16—K1, * (k1, yo, k1) in next st, p3; rep from *, end (k1, yo, k1) in next st, k1.

Rows 17, 18, and 19—Repeat Rows 11, 12, and 13.

Row 20—K2, knit into front and back of next st, * k1, p3 tog, k1, (k1, yo, k1) in next st; rep from *, end k1, p3 tog, k1, knit into front and back of next st, k2.

Repeat Rows 1–20.

Mist Drops

Contributed by Hildegard M. Elsner, Aldan, Pennsylvania

Mist Drops

The wrong side of this fabric is often seen as the right side, and very lovely it is, too. The side edge is wavy, so when working two flat pieces that will be sewn together, it is a good idea to begin one piece with Row 1 and the other with Row 9. In this way, the waves will be made to fit into each other like the parts of a jigsaw puzzle. To begin with Row 9, it is necessary to cast on a multiple of 14 stitches *plus 11*, because the edge stitches increase on Rows 1, 3, and 5, and decrease on Rows 9, 11, and 13, each row adding or subtracting 2.

Multiple of 14 sts plus 5.

Row 1 (Right side)—P1, k1, (yo, k1) twice, p1, * k3, sl 2 knitwise—k1—p2sso, k3, p1, k1, (yo, k1) twice, p1; rep from *.

Row 2—K1, p5, k1, * p7, k1, p5, k1; rep from *.

Row 3—P1, k2, yo, k1, yo, k2, p1, * k2, sl 2 knitwise—k1—p2sso, k2, p1, k2, yo, k1, yo, k2, p1; rep from *.

Row 4—K1, p7, k1, * p5, k1, p7, k1; rep from *.

Row 5—P1, k3, yo, k1, yo, k3, p1, * k1, sl 2 knitwise—k1—p2sso, k1, p1, k3, yo, k1, yo, k3, p1; rep from *.

Row 6—K1, p4, (k1, yo, k1, yo, k1) in next st, p4, k1, * p3, k1, p4, (k1, yo, k1, yo, k1) in next st, p4, k1; rep from *.

Row 7—P1, k4, p5, k4, p1, * k3, p1, k4, p5, k4, p1; rep from *.

Row 8—K1, p4, p5 tog, p4, k1, * p3, k1, p4, p5 tog, p4, k1; rep from *.

Row 9—P1, k3, sl 2 knitwise—k1—p2sso, k3, p1, * k1, (yo, k1) twice, p1, k3, sl 2 knitwise—k1—p2sso, k3, p1; rep from *.

Row 10—Repeat Row 4.

Row 11—P1, k2, sl 2 knitwise—k1—p2sso, k2, p1, * k2, yo, k1, yo, k2, p1, k2, sl 2 knitwise—k1—p2sso, k2, p1; rep from *.

Row 12—Repeat Row 2.

Row 13—P1, k1, sl 2 knitwise—k1—p2sso, k1, p1, * k3, yo, k1, yo, k3, p1, k1, sl 2 knitwise—k1—p2sso, k1, p1; rep from *.

Row 14—K1, p3, k1, * p4, (k1, yo, k1, yo, k1) in next st, p4, k1, p3, k1; rep from *.

Row 15—P1, k3, p1, * k4, p5, k4, p1, k3, p1; rep from *.

Row 16—K1, p3, k1, * p4, p5 tog, p4, k1, p3, k1; rep from *.

Repeat Rows 1–16.

Cable-Framed Leaf Pattern

Cable-Framed Leaf Pattern

Used in a panel of 30, 58, or 86 stitches, this pattern makes a beautiful decoration for a fabric of reverse stockinette stitch.

Multiple of 28 sts plus 2.

Rows 1 and 3 (Wrong side)—P2, * k3, p11, k3, p2, k3, p1, k3, p2; rep from *.

Row 2—RT, * p3, k1-b, p3, RT, p3, k3, ssk, yo, k1, yo, k2 tog, k3, p3, RT; rep from *.

Row 4—K2, * p3, (k1, yo, k1) in next st, p3, k2, p3, ssk, k1, ssk, yo, k1, yo, k2 tog, k1, k2 tog, p3, k2; rep from *.

Row 5—P2, * k3, p9, k3, p2, k3, p3, k3, p2; rep from *.

Row 6—RT, * p3, (k1, yo) twice, k1, p3, RT, p3, ssk, k5, k2 tog, p3, RT; rep from *.

Row 7—P2, * k3, p7, k3, p2, k3, p5, k3, p2; rep from *.

Row 8—K2, * p3, k2, yo, k1, yo, (k2, p3) twice, ssk, k3, k2 tog, p3, k2; rep from *.

Row 9—P2, * k3, p5, k3, p2, k3, p7, k3, p2; rep from *.

Row 10—RT, * p3, k3, yo, k1, yo, k3, p3, RT, p3, ssk, k1, k2 tog, p3, RT; rep from *.

Row 11—P2, * k3, p3, k3, p2, k3, p9, k3, p2; rep from *.

Row 12—K2, * p3, k4, yo, k1, yo, k4, p3, k2, p3, sl 1—k2 tog—psso, p3, k2; rep from *.

Rows 13 and 15—P2, * k3, p1, k3, p2, k3, p11, k3, p2; rep from *.

Row 14—RT, * p3, k3, ssk, yo, k1, yo, k2 tog, k3, p3, RT, p3, k1-b, p3, RT; rep from *.

Row 16—K2, * p3, ssk, k1, ssk, yo, k1, yo, k2 tog, k1, k2 tog, p3, k2, p3, (k1, yo, k1) in next st, p3, k2; rep from *.

Rows 17, 19, 21, and 23—Repeat Rows 11, 9, 7, and 5.

Row 18—RT, * p3, ssk, k5, k2 tog, p3, RT, p3, (k1, yo) twice, k1, p3, RT; rep from *.

Row 20—K2, * p3, ssk, k3, k2 tog, (p3, k2) twice, yo, k1, yo, k2, p3, k2; rep from *.

Row 22—RT, * p3, ssk, k1, k2 tog, p3, RT, p3, k3, yo, k1, yo, k3, p3, RT; rep from *.

Row 24—K2, * p3, sl 1—k2 tog—psso, p3, k2, p3, k4, yo, k1, yo, k4, p3, k2; rep from *.

Repeat Rows 1–24.

The Cloisters

This is an easy pattern to work, but richly textured and full of dignity. A lace chevron breaks the pillar-like ribs, and the little purled "archways" are attractively shadowed by the decreases. This pattern adapts very well to horizontal bands and borders, and also makes lovely vertical panels.

Multiple of 10 sts plus 3.

Rows 1, 3, and 5 (Right side)—K3, * p7, k3; rep from *.

Rows 2, 4, and 6—P3, * k7, p3; rep from *.

Row 7—K2, * yo, ssk, p5, k2 tog, yo, k1; rep from *, end k1.

Row 8—P4, * k5, p5; rep from *, end last repeat p4.

Row 9—K3, * yo, ssk, p3, k2 tog, yo, k3; rep from *.

Row 10—P5, * k3, p7; rep from *, end last repeat p5.

Row 11—K2, * (yo, ssk) twice, p1, (k2 tog, yo) twice, k1; rep from *, end k1.

Row 12—P6, * k1, p9; rep fron *, end last repeat p6.

Row 13—K3, * yo, ssk, yo, sl 1—k2 tog—psso, yo, k2 tog, yo, k3; rep from *.

Rows 14, 16, and 18—Purl.

Row 15—K4, * yo, ssk, k1, k2 tog, yo, k5; rep from *, end last repeat k4.

Row 17—K5, * yo, sl 1—k2 tog—psso, yo, k7; rep from *, end last repeat k5.

Row 19—K3, * p3, (k1, p1, k1, p1, k1) in next st, then pass the 2nd, 3rd, 4th, and 5th sts on right-hand needle separately over the last st made; p3, k3; rep from *.

Row 20—P3, * k7, p3; rep from *.

Repeat Rows 1–20.

The Cloisters

Twin Leaf Panel

Here is a very graceful, lacy pattern related to Twin Leaf Lace, and rich in texture, line, and openwork. It is easy to work, and makes a beautiful asset to any sort of garment. It is shown with 2 purl stitches added at each side of the panel.

Panel of 22 sts.

Row 1 (Wrong side) and all other wrong-side rows—P10, k2, p10.

Row 2—K6, ssk, return the resulting stitch to left-hand needle and with point of right-hand needle pass the *next* stitch over it and off needle; then sl the stitch back to right-hand needle (this is "ssk and pass"); yo, k1, yo, p2, yo, k1, yo, sl 1—k2 tog—psso, k6.

Row 4—K4, ssk and pass, k1, (yo, k1) twice, p2, k1, (yo, k1) twice, sl 1—k2 tog—psso, k4.

Row 6—K2, ssk and pass, k2, yo, k1, yo, k2, p2, k2, yo, k1, yo, k2, sl 1—k2 tog—psso, k2.

Row 8—Ssk and pass, k3, yo, k1, yo, k3, p2, k3, yo, k1, yo, k3, sl 1—k2 tog—psso.

Repeat Rows 1–8.

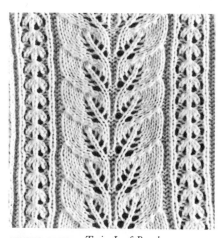

CENTER PANEL: *Twin Leaf Panel*
SIDE PANELS: *Fancy Shell Rib*

Fancy Shell Rib

This is a beautiful little openwork rib suitable for panel treatment or for use all over the fabric. It can set off other openwork designs very well.

Multiple of 7 sts plus 2. (Or, panel of 9 sts.)

Row 1 (Right side)—P2, * k1, (yo, k1) 4 times, p2; rep from *.
Row 2—K2, * p1, (k1, p1) 4 times, k2; rep from *.
Row 3—P2, * k1, p1, ssk, k1, k2 tog, p1, k1, p2; rep from *.
Row 4—K2, * p1, k1, p3 tog, k1, p1, k2; rep from *.

Repeat Rows 1–4.

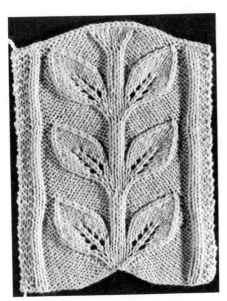

Embossed Double Leaf Panel

Embossed Double Leaf Panel

Two of the classic "leaf" motifs are combined here, slanting outward from a central "stem". It is a pretty arrangement to be used singly or in combination with other embossed patterns. This is an increase pattern; the original 29 stitches can be counted only on the first and last rows.

Panel of 29 sts.

NOTE: M1 (Make One): lift running thread between the st just worked and the next st, and knit into the back of this thread.

Row 1 (Wrong side)—K10, p9, k10.
Row 2—P8, p2 tog, (k1, yo) twice, knit into front and back of next st, k2, knit into front and back of next st, (k1, yo) twice, k1, p2 tog, p8.
Row 3—K9, p5, k1, p3, k1, p5, k9.
Row 4—P7, p2 tog, k2, yo, k1, yo, k2, purl into front and back of next st (purl inc), k3, purl inc, k2, yo, k1, yo, k2, p2 tog, p7.
Row 5—K8, p7, k2, p3, k2, p7, k8.
Row 6—P6, p2 tog, k3, yo, k1, yo, k3, purl inc, p1, k3, p1, purl inc, k3, yo, k1, yo, k3, p2 tog, p6.
Row 7—K7, p9, k3, p3, k3, p9, k7.
Row 8—P5, p2 tog, k4, yo, k1, yo, k4, purl inc, p2, k3, p2, purl inc, k4, yo, k1, yo, k4, p2 tog, p5.
Row 9—K6, p11, k4, p3, k4, p11, k6.
Row 10—P4, p2 tog, ssk, k7, k2 tog, purl inc, p3, k3, p3, purl inc, ssk, k7, k2 tog, p2 tog, p4.
Row 11—K5, p9, k5, p3, k5, p9, k5.
Row 12—P3, p2 tog, ssk, k5, k2 tog, purl inc, p4, k3, p4, purl inc, ssk, k5, k2 tog, p2 tog, p3.

Row 13—K4, p7, k6, p3, k6, p7, k4.

Row 14—P2, p2 tog, ssk, k3, k2 tog, purl inc, p5, (k1, M1) twice, k1, p5, purl inc, ssk, k3, k2 tog, p2 tog, p2.

Row 15—K3, (p5, k7) twice, p5, k3.

Row 16—P1, p2 tog, ssk, k1, k2 tog, purl inc, p6, k1, M1, k3, M1, k1, p6, purl inc, ssk, k1, k2 tog, p2 tog, p1.

Row 17—K2, p3, k8, p7, k8, p3, k2.

Row 18—P2, sl 1—k2 tog—psso, p6, p2 tog, k1, M1, k5, M1, k1, p2 tog, p6, sl 1—k2 tog—psso, p2.

Repeat Rows 1–18.

Ornamental Rib Pattern

Multiple of 22 sts plus 7.

NOTE: Bind 3 as follows—sl 1 wyib, k1, yo, k1, then pass sl-st over the 3 subsequent sts (i.e., 2 knit sts with the yo in the middle).

Row 1 (Right side)—P2, k3, p2, * k1, (k1, yo, k1) in next st, k1, p2, k3, p2, k1, sl 2—k1—p2sso, k1, p2, k3, p2; rep from *.

Row 2—* (K2, p3) 3 times, k2, p5; rep from *, end k2, p3, k2.

Row 3—P2, bind 3, p2, * k2, (k1, yo, k1) in next st, k2, p2, bind 3, p2, sl 3 wyif, p2, bind 3, p2; rep from *.

Row 4—K2, p3, k2, * sl 3 wyib, k2, p3, k2, p7, k2, p3, k2; rep from *.

Row 5—P2, k3, p2, * k7, p2, k3, p2, sl 3 wyif, p2, k3, p2; rep from *.

Row 6—Repeat Row 4.

Row 7—P2, bind 3, p2, * k2, sl 2—k1—p2sso, k2, p2, bind 3, p2, sl 3 wyif, p2, bind 3, p2; rep from *.

Row 8—Repeat Row 2.

Row 9—P2, k3, p2, * k1, sl 2—k1—p2sso, k1, p2, k3, p2, k1, (k1, yo, k1) in next st, k1, p2, k3, p2; rep from *.

Row 10—K2, p3, k2, * p5, k2, (p3, k2) 3 times; rep from *.

Row 11—P2, bind 3, p2, * sl 3 wyif, p2, bind 3, p2, k2, (k1, yo, k1) in next st, k2, p2, bind 3, p2; rep from *.

Row 12—K2, p3, k2, * p7, k2, p3, k2, sl 3 wyib, k2, p3, k2; rep from *.

Row 13—P2, k3, p2, * sl 3 wyif, p2, k3, p2, k7, p2, k3, p2; rep from *.

Row 14—Repeat Row 12.

Row 15—P2, bind 3, p2, * sl 3 wyif, p2, bind 3, p2, k2, sl 2—k1—p2sso, k2, p2, bind 3, p2; rep from *.

Row 16—Repeat Row 10.

Repeat Rows 1–16.

Ornamental Rib Pattern

Embossed Twining Vine Leaf

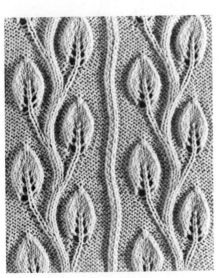

Embossed Twining Vine Leaf

This is perhaps the most graceful of all the embossed-leaf patterns. It gives a lovely effect either in a single panel or all over the fabric. When a rib of one or two knit stitches is inserted between panels of Embossed Twining Vine Leaf, as shown, the knit rib receives a slight but definite wave that adds to the beauty of the pattern in general. Sweaters are delightful when done with this pattern, and matching skirts can be made by placing plain knit panels between pattern panels, and working all decreases within the knit panels so that they narrow toward the waist.

Panel of 26 sts.

Row 1 (Wrong side)—K5, p5, k4, p3, k9.

Row 2—P7, p2 tog, knit into front and back of next st, k2, p4, k2, yo, k1, yo, k2, p5.

Row 3—K5, p7, k4, p2, k1, p1, k8.

Row 4—P6, p2 tog, k1, purl into front and back of next st (purl inc), k2, p4, k3, yo, k1, yo, k3, p5.

Row 5—K5, p9, k4, p2, k2, p1, k7.

Row 6—P5, p2 tog, k1, purl inc, p1, k2, p4, ssk, k5, k2 tog, p5.

Row 7—K5, p7, k4, p2, k3, p1, k6.

Row 8—P4, p2 tog, k1, purl inc, p2, k2, p4, ssk, k3, k2 tog, p5.

Row 9—K5, p5, k4, p2, k4, p1, k5.

Row 10—P5, yo, k1, yo, p4, k2, p4, ssk, k1, k2 tog, p5.

Row 11—K5, p3, k4, p2, k4, p3, k5.

Row 12—P5, (k1, yo) twice, k1, p4, k1, lift running thread between the st just worked and the next st, and knit into the *back* of this thread (Make One, M1), k1, p2 tog, p2, sl 2 knitwise—k1—p2sso, p5.

Row 13—K9, p3, k4, p5, k5.

Row 14—P5, k2, yo, k1, yo, k2, p4, k1, knit into front and back of next st, k1, p2 tog, p7.

Row 15—K8, p1, k1, p2, k4, p7, k5.

Row 16—P5, k3, yo, k1, yo, k3, p4, k2, purl inc, k1, p2 tog, p6.

Row 17—K7, p1, k2, p2, k4, p9, k5.

Row 18—P5, ssk, k5, k2 tog, p4, k2, p1, purl inc, k1, p2 tog, p5.

Row 19—K6, p1, k3, p2, k4, p7, k5.

Row 20—P5, ssk, k3, k2 tog, p4, k2, p2, purl inc, k1, p2 tog, p4.

Row 21—K5, p1, k4, p2, k4, p5, k5.

Row 22—P5, ssk, k1, k2 tog, p4, k2, p4, yo, k1, yo, p5.

Row 23—K5, p3, k4, p2, k4, p3, k5.

Row 24—P5, sl 2 knitwise—k1—p2sso, p2, p2 tog, k1, M1, k1, p4, (k1, yo) twice, k1, p5.

Repeat Rows 1–24.

Lucky Leaf Pattern

This pattern is repetitious, and easy to learn in the first repeat of the pattern rows; therefore it cannot be called difficult, in spite of its length. It makes a very prettily embossed purl fabric with sprays of leaves arranged in fleur-de-lis fashion. It is a "hybrid" pattern, containing a little of everything—twist stitches, increased stitches, yarn-over stitches, crossed knit stitches, decreases. Lucky Leaf makes lovely afghans and bedspreads as well as garments. A single motif can be used as an isolated ornament on any purl background. A horizontal row of them makes an attractive border.

Lucky Leaf Pattern

Multiple of 18 sts plus 6.

NOTE: Increase (inc) by *purling* into the front and back of one stitch.

PREPARATION ROWS

Row 1 (Right side)—P7, * k1-b, p17; rep from *, end last repeat p16.

Row 2—K16, * p1, k17; rep from *, end last repeat k7.

Row 3—P6, * k1, k1-b, k1, p15; rep from *.

Row 4—* K15, p3; rep from *, end k6.

Row 5—P5, * RT, k1-b, LT, p13; rep from *, end p1.

End of preparation rows.

Row 6—K14, * (p1, k1) twice, p1, k13; rep from *, end last repeat k5.

Row 7—P4, * RT, p1, k1-b, p1, LT, p11; rep from *, end p2.

Row 8—K13, * (p1, k2) twice, p1, k11; rep from *, end last repeat k4.

Row 9—P2, * p2 tog, (k1, yo, k1) in next st, inc, p1, k1-b, p1, inc, (k1, yo, k1) in next st, p2 tog, p7; rep from *, end p4.

Row 10—K12, * p3, k3, p1, k3, p3, k9; rep from *, end last repeat k3.

Row 11—P1, * p2 tog, (k1, yo) twice, k1, inc, p2, k1-b, p2, inc, (k1, yo) twice, k1, p2 tog, p5; rep from *, end p5.

Row 12—K11, * p5, k4, p1, k4, p5, k7; rep from *, end last repeat k2.

Row 13—* P2 tog, k2, yo, k1, yo, k2, inc, p3, k1-b, p3, inc, k2, yo, k1, yo, k2, p2 tog, p3; rep from *, end p6.

Row 14—K10, * p7, k5, p1, k5, p7, k5; rep from *, end last repeat k1.

Row 15—P1, * ssk, k3, k2 tog, p5, (k1, yo, k1) in next st, p5, ssk, k3, k2 tog, p5; rep from *, end p5.

Row 16—K10, * p5, k5, p3, k5, p5, k5; rep from *, end last repeat k1.

Row 17—P1, * ssk, k1, k2 tog, p5, (k1, yo) twice, k1, p5, ssk, k1, k2 tog, p5; rep from *, end p5.

Row 18—K10, * p3, k5, p5, k5, p3, k5; rep from *, end last repeat k1.

Row 19—P1, * sl 1—k2 tog—psso, p5, k2, yo, k1, yo, k2, p5, sl 1—k2 tog—psso, p5; rep from *, end p5.

Row 20—K16, * p7, k17; rep from *, end last repeat k7.

Row 21—P7, * ssk, k3, k2 tog, p8, k1-b, p8; rep from *, end last repeat p7.

Row 22—K7, * p1, k8, p5, k8; rep from *, end last repeat k7.

Row 23—* P7, ssk, k1, k2 tog, p7, k1, k1-b, k1; rep from *, end p6.

Row 24—K6, * p3, k7; rep from *.

Row 25—P7, * sl 1—k2 tog—psso, p6, RT, k1-b, LT, p6; rep from *, end last repeat p5.

Row 26—K5, rep from * of Row 6, end k1.

Row 27—P13, rep from * of Row 7, end last repeat p4.

Row 28—K4, rep from * of Row 8, end k2.

Row 29—P11, rep from * of Row 9, end last repeat p2.

Row 30—K3, rep from * of Row 10, end k3.

Row 31—P10, rep from * of Row 11, end last repeat p1.

Row 32—K2, rep from * of Row 12, end k4.

Row 33—P9, rep from * of Row 13, omit final "p3" from last repeat.

Row 34—K1, rep from * of Row 14, end k5.

Row 35—P10, rep from * of Row 15, end last repeat p1.

Row 36—K1, rep from * of Row 16, end k5.

Row 37—P10, rep from * of Row 17, end last repeat p1.

Row 38—K1, rep from * of Row 18, end k5.

Row 39—P10, rep from * of Row 19, end last repeat p1.

Row 40—K7, rep from * of Row 20, end last repeat k16.

Row 41—P7, * k1-b, p8, ssk, k3, k2 tog, p8; rep from *, end last repeat p7.

Row 42—K7, * p5, k8, p1, k8; rep from *, end last repeat k7.

Row 43—P6, * k1, k1-b, k1, p7, ssk, k1, k2 tog, p7; rep from *.

Row 44—* K7, p3; rep from *, end k6.

Row 45—P5, * RT, k1-b, LT, p6, sl 1—k2 tog—psso, p6; rep from *, end p1.

Omitting preparation rows, repeat Rows 6–45.

Fireworks

Fireworks

Here is an unabashedly "fancy" pattern, richly decorated with little bobbles, openwork, and embossed ribs. It is beautiful as a wide central panel in a dress or overblouse, or repeated all over a garment. The pattern requires the knitter's attention, because one stitch out of place would be glaringly obvious; but it is so interesting as to be well worth some care. In a single panel of 35 stitches it can combine nicely with other patterns.

Multiple of 30 sts plus 5.

NOTE: Make Bobble (MB) as follows: (k1, yo, k1, yo, k1) all in one st, turn, p5, turn, k2 tog-b, k3 tog, then pass 1st st over 2nd, completing bobble.

Row 1 (Wrong side)—K2, * p1, k1, p1, k3, p2, k15, p2, k3, p1, k1; rep from *, end p1, k2.

Row 2—K3, * k2 tog, p3, k1, yo, p8, MB, p8, yo, k1, p3, ssk, k1; rep from *, end k2.

Row 3—K2, p2, * k3, p2, k8, p1-b, k8, p2, k3, p3; rep from *, end last repeat p2, k2 instead of p3.

Row 4—K4, * p2 tog, p1, k1, yo, p5, MB, p3, k1, p3, MB, p5, yo, k1, p1, p2 tog, k3; rep from *, end k1.

Row 5—K2, p2, * k2, p2, k5, p1-b, k3, p1, k3, p1-b, k5, p2, k2, p3; rep from *, end last repeat p2, k2 instead of p3.

Row 6—K4, * p2 tog, k1, yo, p2, MB, (p3, k1) 3 times, p3, MB, p2, yo, k1, p2 tog, k3; rep from *, end k1.

Row 7—K2, p2, * k1, p2, k2, p1-b, (k3, p1) 3 times, k3, p1-b, k2, p2, k1, p3; rep from *, end last repeat p2, k2 instead of p3.

Row 8—K4, * k2 tog, yo, (p3, k1) 5 times, p3, yo, ssk, k3; rep from *, end k1.

Row 9—K2, p4, * (k3, p1) 5 times, k3, p7; rep from *, end last repeat p4, k2 instead of p7.

Row 10—K3, * k2 tog, yo, p4, yo, k1, p3, k1, p1, p2 tog, k1, p2 tog, p1, k1, p3, k1, yo, p4, yo, ssk, k1; rep from *, end k2.

Row 11—K2, p3, * k4, p2, k3, (p1, k2) twice, p1, k3, p2, k4, p5; rep from *, end last repeat p3, k2 instead of p5.

Row 12—K2, k2 tog, * yo, p6, yo, k1, p3, (k1, p2 tog) twice, k1, p3, k1, yo, p6, yo, sl 1—k2 tog—psso; rep from *, end last repeat ssk, k2 instead of sl 1—k2 tog—psso.

Row 13—K10, * p2, k3, (p1, k1) twice, p1, k3, p2, k15; rep from *, end last repeat k10.

Row 14—K2, * MB, p8, yo, k1, p3, ssk, k1, k2 tog, p3, k1, yo, p8; rep from *, end MB, k2.

Row 15—K2, * p1-b, k8, p2, k3, p3, k3, p2, k8; rep from *, end p1-b, k2.

Row 16—K3, * p3, MB, p5, yo, k1, p1, p2 tog, k3, p2 tog, p1, k1, yo, p5, MB, p3, k1; rep from *, end k2.

Row 17—K2, * p1, k3, p1-b, k5, p2, k2, p3, k2, p2, k5, p1-b, k3; rep from *, end p1, k2.

Row 18—K3, * p3, k1, p3, MB, p2, yo, k1, p2 tog, k3, p2 tog, k1, yo, p2, MB, (p3, k1) twice; rep from *, end k2.

Row 19—K2, * (p1, k3) twice, p1-b, k2, p2, k1, p3, k1, p2, k2, p1-b, k3, p1, k3; rep from *, end p1, k2.

Row 20—K3, * (p3, k1) twice, p3, yo, ssk, k3, k2 tog, yo, (p3, k1) 3 times; rep from *, end k2.

Row 21—K2, * (p1, k3) 3 times, p7, (k3, p1) twice, k3; rep from *, end p1, k2.

Row 22—K3, * p2 tog, p1, k1, p3, k1, yo, p4, yo, ssk, k1, k2 tog, yo, p4, yo, k1, p3, k1, p1, p2 tog, k1; rep from *, end k2.

Row 23—K2, * p1, k2, p1, k3, p2, k4, p5, k4, p2, k3, p1, k2; rep from *, end p1, k2.

Row 24—K3, * p2 tog, k1, p3, k1, yo, p6, yo, sl 1—k2 tog—psso, yo, p6, yo, k1, p3, k1, p2 tog, k1; rep from *, end k2.

Repeat Rows 1–24.

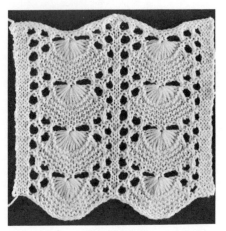

Grand Shell, or Hoopskirt Pattern

Grand Shell, or Hoopskirt Pattern

Raw beginners should stay away from this one. But a moderately experienced knitter can make exquisite stoles, scarves, evening wraps and baby things with this lovely openwork and its large shell- or fan-shaped motifs. Notice that throughout the pattern all the double yo's (with the exception of those worked in Row 10) are treated as *two stitches* on the return row, one of them being knitted, the other being purled; but the purl may come either before or after the knit.

Multiple of 19 sts plus 2.

NOTE: *All* yo's in this pattern are *double,* and are written "00".

Row 1 (Wrong side)—Knit.

Row 2—Knit.

Row 3—K1, * k1, 00, p2 tog-b, k13, p2 tog, 00, k1; rep from *, end k1.

Row 4—K1, * k2, p1, k15, p1, k2; rep from *, end k1.

Rows 5 and 6—Knit.

Row 7—K1, * k1, (00, p2 tog-b) twice, k11, (p2 tog, 00) twice, k1; rep from *, end k1.

Row 8—K1, * k2, p1, k1, p1, k14, (p1, k2) twice; rep from *, end k1.

Row 9—Knit.

Row 10—K1, * k6, (00, k1) 14 times, k5; rep from *, end k1.

Row 11—K1, * k1, (00, p2 tog-b) twice, 00, s1 next 15 sts dropping extra yo's to make 15 long sts; insert left-hand needle into the backs of these 15 long sts and purl them all together as 1 st; (00, p2 tog) twice, 00, k1; rep from *, end k1. (On this row, be careful not to lose the double yo that is worked immediately before the 15 sts are slipped; hold yarn in *front,* ready to purl, as the sts are slipped.)

Row 12—K1, * k1, p1, (k2, p1) twice, k3, (p1, k2) twice, p1, k1; rep from *, end k1.

Repeat Rows 1–12.

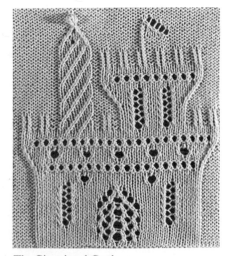

The Gingerbread Castle

The Gingerbread Castle

To delight a child, work this bit of fairy-tale architecture on the front of his or her sweater! The Castle is made of a combination of easy knitting techniques. There is a lace door, there are windows of faggoting and picot eyelets, ribbed battlements with an openwork banner floating above them, and a twist-stitch tower topped with a bobble. The entire pattern is a good example of "picture knitting": much less complicated than its lengthy directions seem to indicate, and great fun to work.

Panel of 50 sts.

NOTE: (K1, p1) in parentheses indicates that these two stitches are worked into a double yo of a preceding row.

Foundation: 5 rows of garter stitch.

Row 1 (Wrong side)—K7, p36, k7.

Row 2—P7, k14, ssk, yo, ssk, (yo) twice, k2 tog, yo, k2 tog, k14, p7.

Row 3—K7, p17, (k1, p1), p17, k7.

Row 4—P7, k14, (yo, ssk) twice, (k2 tog, yo) twice, k14, p7.

Rows 5 and 6—Repeat Rows 1 and 2.

Row 7—K7, p5, p2 tog, yo, p10, (k1, p1), p8, p2 tog, yo, p7, k7.

Row 8—P7, k5, ssk, yo, k7, (yo, ssk) twice, (k2 tog, yo) twice, k5, ssk, yo, k7, p7.

Row 9—K7, p5, p2 tog, yo, p20, p2 tog, yo, p7, k7.

Row 10—P7, k5, ssk, yo, k7, ssk, yo, ssk, (yo) twice, k2 tog, yo, k2 tog, k5, ssk, yo, k7, p7.

Rows 11, 12, and 13—Repeat Rows 7, 8, and 9.

Row 14—P7, k5, ssk, yo, k8, yo, sl 1—k2 tog—psso, (yo) twice, k3 tog, yo, k6, ssk, yo, k7, p7.

Rows 15, 17, and 19—Repeat Rows 7, 9, and 1.

Row 16—P7, k5, ssk, yo, k9, yo, ssk, k2 tog, yo, k7, ssk, yo, k7, p7.

Row 18—P7, k5, ssk, yo, k10, LT, k8, ssk, yo, k7, p7.

Row 20—P7, k9, k2 tog, (yo) twice, ssk, k10, k2 tog, (yo) twice, ssk, k9, p7.

Row 21—K7, p10, (k1, p1), p12, (k1, p1), p10, k7.

Row 22—P7, k36, p7.

Row 23—K7, p2, k32, p2, k7.

Row 24—P6, RT, k1, (yo, k2 tog) 16 times, k1, LT, p6.

Row 25—K6, p3, k32, p3, k6.

Row 26—P5, RT, k36, LT, p5.

Row 27—K5, p40, k5.

Row 28—P4, RT, [k3, k2 tog, (yo) twice, ssk] 5 times, k3, LT, p4.

Row 29—K4, p6, [(k1, p1), p5] 5 times, p1, k4.

Row 30—P3, RT, k40, LT, p3.

Rows 31 and 33—K3, p2, k40, p2, k3.

Row 32—P3, k2, (yo, k2 tog) 20 times, k2, p3.

Row 34—P3, k44, p3.

Row 35—K3, p44, k3.

Row 36—P3, k30, RT, k1, RT, k9, p3.

Rows 37, 39, and 41—K3, (p2-b, k2) twice, p8, k2, p2-b, k2, p2, (p2 tog, yo, p4) twice, (k2, p2-b) twice, k3.

Row 38—P3, (k2-b, p2) twice, k2, (ssk, yo, k4) twice, p2, k2-b, p2, (k1, RT) twice, k2, (p2, k2-b) twice, p3.

Row 40—P3, (k2-b, p2) twice, k2, (ssk, yo, k4) twice, p2, k2-b, p2, (RT, k1) twice, RT, (p2, k2-b) twice, p3.

Row 42—P11, k2, (ssk, yo, k4) twice, p6, k2, (RT, k1) twice, p11.

Row 43—K11, p8, k6, p2, (p2 tog, yo, p4) twice, k11.

Row 44—P10, RT, k1, ssk, yo, k4, ssk, yo, k3, LT, p5, (k1, RT) twice, k2, p11.

Row 45—K11, p8, k5, p3, (p2 tog, yo, p4) twice, p1, k10.

Row 46—P9, RT, k2, (ssk, yo, k4) twice, LT, p4, (RT, k1) twice, RT, p11.

Row 47—K11, p8, k4, (p4, p2 tog, yo) twice, p6, k9.

Row 48—P8, RT, k3, ssk, yo, k4, ssk, yo, k5, LT, p3, k2, (RT, k1) twice, p11.

Row 49—K11, p8, k3, p20, k8.

Row 50—P7, RT, k18, LT, p2, (k1, RT) twice, k2, p11.

Rows 51 and 53—K11, p8, k2, p2, k18, p2, k7.

Row 52—P7, k2, (yo, k2 tog) 9 times, k2, p2, (RT, k1) twice, RT, p11.

Row 54—P7, k22, p2, k2, (RT, k1) twice, p11.

Row 55—K11, p8, k2, p22, k7.

Row 56—P7, k22, p2, (k1, RT) twice, k2, p11.

Rows 57, 59, and 61—K11, p8, (k2, p2-b) 6 times, k7.

Row 58—P7, (k2-b, p2) 6 times, (RT, k1) twice, RT, p11.

Row 60—P7, (k2-b, p2) 6 times, k2, (RT, k1) twice, p11.

Row 62—P19, k1-b, p11, (k1, RT) twice, k2, p11.

Row 63—K11, p8, k11, p1-b, k19.

Row 64—P19, k1-b, p11, LT, k1, k2 tog, yo, k1, RT, p11.

Row 65—K12, p6, k12, p1-b, k19.

Row 66—P14, yo, ssk, k3, k1-b, p12, LT, k2, RT, p12.

Row 67—K13, p4, k13, p1-b, p2, p2 tog-b, yo, p1, k14.

Row 68—P16, yo, ssk, k1, k1-b, p13, LT, RT, p13.

Row 69—K14, p2, k14, p1-b, p2 tog-b, yo, p1, k16.

Row 70—P18, yo, ssk, p14, LT, p14.

Row 71—K14, p1, k15, p2, k18.

Row 72—P35, (k1, yo, k1, yo, k1) in next st, turn and p5, turn and k5, turn and p2 tog, p1, p2 tog, turn and sl 1—k2 tog—psso, p14.

Row 73—K14, p1-b, k35.

Row 74—Purl.

Finish with 4 rows of garter stitch.

CHAPTER ELEVEN

Eyelets

Technically, an eyelet in knitting is an opening that is separated from neighboring openings by more than two strands of yarn. The holes in a lace pattern, on the other hand, are separated from each other by a single strand or by two strands twisted together. But this rule is flexible. Sometimes an eyelet pattern is a "grouping" of lace holes, which are placed at intervals in the solid fabric. Generally, eyelet patterns are less open than laces; but there is a good deal of overlapping between the two types of pattern, so this rule is flexible too.

Most eyelet patterns are very dainty, lending themselves especially well to fine-yarn sweaters, baby clothes, dressy aprons, scarves, and "party" dresses. Like lace, these patterns should be well stretched when blocked, so that the openings are widened as much as possible; and the needles should not be too small in proportion to the weight of the yarn. An eyelet worked in heavy yarn on too-small needles is always a failure; it comes out looking like a sort of dimple instead of an eyelet. Neither should the needles be too large, for then the holes will be limp and gaping. Try different needle sizes on different weights of yarn, to see how your eyelets look best.

Allover Cabled Eyelet

Here is the popular Yarn-Over Cable worked as an allover pattern, which turns out to be quite interesting. The eyelets are vertically aligned, whereas the passed slip-stitches lend a diagonal quality to the fabric. This dainty pattern is ideal for baby clothes, summer-weight stoles, and shells.

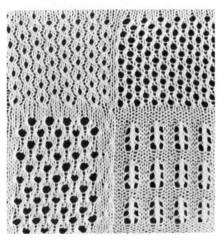

ABOVE, LEFT: *Allover Cabled Eyelet*
ABOVE, RIGHT: *Cellular Stitch*
BELOW, LEFT: *German Honeycomb Stitch*
BELOW, RIGHT: *Spanish Window*

Multiple of 6 sts.

Row 1 (Right side)—* Sl 1, k2, pass slipped st over 2 knit sts, k3; rep from *.
Row 2—P4, * yo, p5; rep from *, end yo, p1.
Row 3—* K3, sl 1, k2, pass slipped st over 2 knit sts; rep from *.
Row 4—P1, * yo, p5; rep from *, end yo, p4.

Repeat Rows 1–4.

Cellular Stitch

This is a pretty little eyelet mesh, as simple as a pattern can be. With it, the beginner can make a dainty mesh blouse, a delicate scarf, or a summer sweater. It can be used also in blocks, bands, or insertion panels. For a quick beginner project, try it in a baby's coat-and-booties set, or work rectangles of it in a fancy metallic yarn, line them with silk or satin of a contrasting color, and sew them together to make an elegant evening purse.

Multiple of 3 sts.

Rows 1 and 3 (Wrong side)—Purl.
Row 2—K2, * k2 tog, yo, k1; rep from *, end k1.
Row 4—K2, * yo, k1, k2 tog; rep from *, end k1.

Repeat Rows 1–4.

German Honeycomb Stitch

Contributed by Hildegard M. Elsner, Aldan, Pennsylvania

Here is a pretty eyelet fabric that is a little different, by reason of its being worked from the right and wrong sides alternately. The pattern makes graceful shawls, overblouses or head scarves. A few repeats (12 to 20 sts) will make an attractive openwork panel.

Multiple of 4 sts.

Row 1 (Right side)—Knit.
Row 2—P2, * p2 tog-b, yo, p2 tog; rep from *, end p2.
Row 3—K3, * (k1, p1) into the yo of previous row, k2; rep from *, end k1.
Row 4—Purl.
Row 5—* K2 tog, yo, ssk; rep from *.
Row 6—P1, * (k1, p1) into the yo of previous row, p2; rep from *, end last repeat p1.

Repeat Rows 1–6.

Spanish Window

Contributed by Margaret Sheppard, Houston, Texas

Multiple of 4 sts plus 3.

Rows 1 and 3 (Wrong side)—Knit.
Row 2—Purl.
Row 4—P3, * yo, k1, yo, p3; rep from *.
Rows 5, 7, and 9—K3, * p3, k3; rep from *.
Rows 6 and 8—P3, * yo, k3 tog, yo, p3; rep from *.
Row 10—P3, * k3 tog, p3; rep from *.

Repeat Rows 1–10.

Flower Eyelet

This is an ancient pattern, and one of the nicest arrangements of eyelets in formation. It is beautiful in skirts, shells, summer dresses, carriage-blankets and sweaters for infants. The "flowers" can be placed anywhere on a fabric, or combined with other types of eyelets.

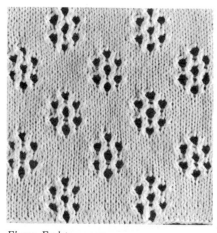

Flower Eyelet

Multiple of 16 sts plus 8.

NOTE: All yo's are double ones, written "yo2" instead of the usual "(yo) twice".

Row 1 (Right side)—K10, * k2 tog, yo2, ssk, k12; rep from *, end last repeat k10.
Row 2 and all other wrong-side rows—Purl, working (k1, p1) into every double yo.
Row 3—K8, * (k2 tog, yo2, ssk) twice, k8; rep from *.
Row 5—Repeat Row 1.
Row 7—Repeat Row 3.
Row 9—Repeat Row 1.
Row 11—K2, * k2 tog, yo2, ssk, k12; rep from *, end last repeat k2.
Row 13—* (K2 tog, yo2, ssk) twice, k8; rep from *, end (k2 tog; yo2, ssk) twice.
Row 15—Repeat Row 11.
Row 17—Repeat Row 13.
Row 19—Repeat Row 11.
Row 20—See Row 2.

Repeat Rows 1–20.

Snowflake Eyelet

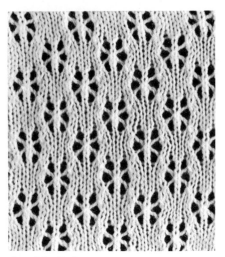

Snowflake Eyelet

This is a truly beautiful pattern, simple yet striking—perfection itself for a dainty blouse, an evening sweater, or a child's dress. And it is so easy to work that even a beginner can master it very quickly.

Multiple of 8 sts plus 5.

Row 1 (Wrong side) and all other wrong-side rows—Purl.
Row 2—K4, * ssk, yo, k1, yo, k2 tog, k3; rep from *, end k1.
Row 4—K5, * yo, sl 2—k1—p2sso, yo, k5; rep from *.
Row 6—Repeat Row 2.
Row 8—Ssk, yo, k1, yo, k2 tog, * k3, ssk, yo, k1, yo, k2 tog; rep from *.
Row 10—K1, * yo, sl 2—k1—p2sso, yo, k5; rep from *, end last repeat k1.
Row 12—Repeat Row 8.

Repeat Rows 1–12.

Purl-Fabric Eyelets: Eiffel Tower Eyelet, Stirrup Eyelet, and Tunnel Eyelet

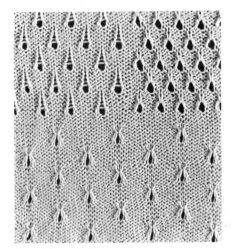

Purl-Fabric Eyelets
ABOVE, LEFT: *Eiffel Tower Eyelet*
ABOVE, RIGHT: *Stirrup Eyelet*
BELOW: *Tunnel Eyelet*

All three of these patterns give pretty ways of decorating a plain purl fabric. Eiffel Tower is the simplest, and is recommended for beginners. The Stirrup is a wide, bold eyelet, with strands arched above the opening by slip-stitches. The Tunnel is similar, but is made by dipping downward into the opening from four rows above.

I. EIFFEL TOWER EYELET

Multiple of 6 sts.

Row 1 (Right side)—* P4, yo, p2 tog; rep from *.
Rows 2, 4, and 6—K1, * p1, k5; rep from *, end p1, k4.
Rows 3 and 5—P4, * k1, p5; rep from *, end k1, p1.
Row 7—P1, * yo, p2 tog, p4; rep from *, end yo, p2 tog, p3.
Rows 8, 10, and 12—K4, * p1, k5; rep from *, end p1, k1.
Rows 9 and 11—P1, * k1, p5; rep from *, end k1, p4.

Repeat Rows 1–12.

II. STIRRUP EYELET

Multiple of 4 sts plus 3.

Row 1 (Right side)—P1, * yo, p2 tog, p2; rep from *, end yo, p2 tog.
Row 2—K1, * holding yarn in front, sl the yo; k3; rep from *, end sl the yo, k1.
Row 3—P1, * holding yarn in back, insert needle from behind into the yo space, and sl *both* of the strands that lie above this space (i.e., one on the left-hand needle, and one beneath it) as one st; p3; rep from *, end last repeat p1.
Row 4—K1, * insert right-hand needle from behind into the yo space and purl the 3 loose strands tog (i.e., the 2 on needle, and the 1 beneath needle); k3; rep from *, end last repeat k1.
Row 5—P1, * sl 1 wyib, p3; rep from *, end sl 1, p1.
Row 6—K1, * p1, k3; rep from *, end p1, k1.
Row 7—P3, * yo, p2 tog, p2; rep from *.
Row 8—K3, rep from * of Row 2.
Row 9—P3, rep from * of Row 3.
Row 10—K3, rep from * of Row 4.
Row 11—P3, * sl 1 wyib, p3; rep from *.
Row 12—K3, * p1, k3; rep from *.

Repeat Rows 1–12.

III. TUNNEL EYELET

Multiple of 12 sts plus 7.

NOTE: When picking up the yo loops in Rows 8 and 14, be sure to hold the yarn in front and pass the right-hand needle down behind it; then the yarn is in the right position to purl the loops tog when they are on the left-hand needle.

Row 1 (Preparation row—wrong side)—Knit.
Row 2 (Preparation row—right side)—Purl.
Row 3—K3, * yo, k2 tog, k10; rep from *, end yo, k2 tog, k2.
Rows 4, 5, 6, and 7—Repeat Row 2, Row 1, Row 2, Row 1.
Row 8—P3, * insert right-hand needle downward along front of fabric into the top and bottom loops of the yo 4 rows below; lift up these 2 loops, place them on the left-hand needle, and purl them tog; then purl the next 2 sts tog; p10; rep from *, end last repeat p2.
Row 9—K9, * yo, k2 tog, k10; rep from *, end yo, k2 tog, k8.
Rows 10, 11, 12, and 13—As 4, 5, 6, and 7.
Row 14—P9, rep from * of Row 8; end last repeat p8 instead of p10.

Omitting preparation rows, repeat Rows 3–14.

Corona

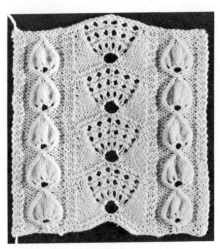

CENTER PANEL: *Corona*
SIDE PANELS: *Crown-Embossed Rosebud*

This beautiful old pattern was popular in the United States in the late 19th and early 20th century. Basically it is an enlargement of the Shetland Crown of Glory pattern. It is very striking as an insertion, or as a central panel in an article knitted in lace or eyelets. When worked continuously across the fabric, instead of in a single panel, it makes an attractively scalloped edge.

Panel of 20 sts.

Rows 1, 2, and 3—Knit.
Row 4 (Right side)—K10, (yo) twice, k10.
Row 5—K3, p7, make 5 new sts out of the double yo loop by working (k1, p1, k1, p1, k1) into this loop; p7, k3.
Row 6—K2, ssk, k17, k2 tog, k2.
Row 7—K3, p17, k3.
Row 8—K2, ssk, k5, (yo, k1) 5 times, yo, k5, k2 tog, k2.
Row 9—K3, p5, k11, p5, k3.
Row 10—K2, ssk, k19, k2 tog, k2.
Row 11—K3, p4, k11, p4, k3.
Row 12—K2, ssk, k2, (ssk, yo) 3 times, k1, (yo, k2 tog) 3 times, k2, k2 tog, k2.
Row 13—K3, p3, k11, p3, k3.
Row 14—K2, ssk, k15, k2 tog, k2.
Row 15—K3, p2, k11, p2, k3.
Row 16—K2, (ssk) twice, (yo, ssk) twice, yo, k1, (yo, k2 tog) 3 times, k4.

Repeat Rows 1–16.

Crown-Embossed Rosebud

An adaptation of the eyelet "crown" type of increase is utilized in this pattern to make an attractive column of highly embossed bud motifs. A single cable cross in Row 2 defines the motifs. Some knitters may find it difficult to knit five times into the *backs* of the five yo loops that are wound around the needle in Row 3, though this is easily accomplished by taking the *front* of each loop purlwise onto the right-hand needle, and sliding the needle *under the loop* over the left-hand needle, where it is in position to knit in the back. However, if this should seem troublesome, working "k1, p1, k1, p1, k1" into the 5-yo loop will serve just as well. The result is not quite so tidy, but the difference is so small as to be hardly noticeable.

Panel of 8 sts.

Row 1 (Wrong side)—K3, p2, k3.
Row 2—P3, sl next st to dpn and hold in front, k1, (yo) 5 times, then knit the st from dpn; p3.
Row 3—K3, p1, (k1-b) 5 times into the yo loops, p1, k3.
Row 4—P3, (k1, yo) 6 times, k1, p3.
Row 5—K3, p13, k3.
Row 6—P3, k13, p3.
Row 7—K3, p2 tog, p9, p2 tog-b, k3.
Row 8—P3, ssk, k7, k2 tog, p3.
Row 9—K3, p2 tog, p5, p2 tog-b, k3.
Row 10—P3, ssk, k3, k2 tog, p3.
Row 11—K3, p2 tog, p1, p2 tog-b, k3.
Row 12—P3, ssk, k1, p3.

Repeat Rows 1–12.

Fish Hooks

This delightful pattern can be used all over a fabric, as shown, or in panels (9 stitches each), or in isolated bands (Rows 1 through 14) such as border bands. Worked into a garment from the top down, the upside-down "hooks" become "candy canes" —does this give you an idea for a child's Christmas-party dress? Another idea: if your initial happens to be J, work Rows 15 through 28 for a series of lace "monograms".

Fish Hooks

Multiple of 8 sts plus 1.

Row 1 (Wrong side) and all other wrong-side rows—Purl.
Row 2—Knit.
Row 4—K2, * ssk, yo, k1, yo, k2 tog, k3; rep from *, end last repeat k2.
Row 6—K1, * ssk, yo, k3, yo, k2 tog, k1; rep from *.
Row 8—K4, * ssk, yo, k6; rep from *, end last repeat k3.
Row 10—K3, * ssk, yo, k6; rep from *, end last repeat k4.
Row 12—K2, * ssk, yo, k6; rep from *, end last repeat k5.
Row 14—K1, * ssk, yo, k6; rep from *.
Rows 16, 18, and 20—Repeat Rows 2, 4, and 6.
Row 22—K3, * yo, k2 tog, k6; rep from *, end last repeat k4.
Row 24—K4, * yo, k2 tog, k6; rep from *, end last repeat k3.
Row 26—K5, * yo, k2 tog, k6; rep from *, end last repeat k2.
Row 28—* K6, yo, k2 tog; rep from *, end k1.

Repeat Rows 1–28.

Garland Pattern

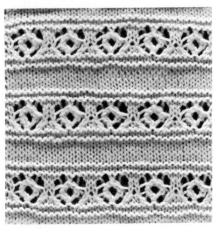
Garland Pattern

This dainty eyelet band is good for infants' wear and girls' party clothes. A single repeat makes a pleasing border for lace sleeves, collars, etc.

Multiple of 7 sts.

Row 1 (Wrong side)—Purl.
Rows 2, 3, 4 and 5—Knit.
Row 6—* K1, k2 tog, yo, k1, yo, ssk, k1; rep from *.
Row 7—* P2 tog-b, yo, p3, yo, p2 tog; rep from *.
Row 8—* K1, yo, k2 tog, yo, sl 1—k2 tog—psso, yo, k1; rep from *.
Row 9—* P1, yo, p2 tog, p1, p2 tog-b, yo, p1; rep from *.
Row 10—* K2, yo, sl 1—k2 tog—psso, yo, k2; rep from *.
Rows 11, 12, 13, and 14—Knit.
Row 15—Purl.
Row 16—Knit.

Repeat Rows 1–16.

Sequin Eyelet

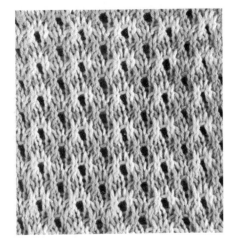
Sequin Eyelet

Contributed by Bernice Haedike, Oak Park, Illinois

This pretty pattern is worked in two colors—though it may be worked in a single color if desired, and is attractive also in three colors. For the latter, simply use A, B, C, A, B, C, etc., changing colors after each group of 4 rows. The pattern makes a dainty, dressy checked fabric with an eyelet in the center of each check. To show these eyelets, the fabric must be stretched. If left unstretched, it closes up into a soft, fluffy texture.

Multiple of 6 sts plus 5. Colors A and B.

Row 1 (Wrong side)—With A, k2, * p1, k1; rep from *, end k1.
Row 2—With B, k4, * sl 3 wyib, k3; rep from *, end k1.
Row 3—With B, k1, * p3, sl 3 wyif; rep from *, end p3, k1.
Row 4—With B, k2, * yo, k2 tog, k1, sl 1 wyib, k2; rep from *, end yo, k2 tog, k1.
Row 5—With B, k1, * p1, k1; rep from *.
Row 6—With A, k1, * sl 3 wyib, k3; rep from *, end sl 3, k1.
Row 7—With A, k1, * sl 3 wyif, p3; rep from *, end sl 3, k1.
Row 8—With A, k2, * sl 1 wyib, k2, yo, k2 tog, k1; rep from *, end sl 1, k2.

Repeat Rows 1–8.

Alternating Leaf Stitch

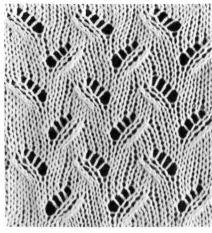

Multiple of 9 sts plus 3.

Row 1 (Right side)—Knit.
Row 2—Purl.
Row 3—K3, * k2 tog, k1, yo, k6; rep from *.
Row 4—P1, * p6, yo, p1, p2 tog; rep from *, end p2.
Row 5—K1, * k2 tog, k1, yo, k6; rep from *, end k2.
Row 6—P3, * p6, yo, p1, p2 tog; rep from *.
Rows 7 and 8—Repeat Rows 1 and 2.
Row 9—* K6, yo, k1, ssk; rep from *, end k3.
Row 10—P2, * p2 tog-b, p1, yo, p6; rep from *, end p1.
Row 11—K2, * k6, yo, k1, ssk; rep from *, end k1.
Row 12—* P2 tog-b, p1, yo, p6; rep from *, end p3.

Repeat Rows 1–12.

Alternating Leaf Stitch

Faun's Eyes

Contributed by Hildegard M. Elsner, Aldan, Pennsylvania

This pattern achieves its effect by "straining" stitches, which causes some of the yo's to open wide and others to compress. The fabric may be stretched into a very lacy openwork, or it may be left unpressed. In the latter case it will develop a very interesting bumpy texture as the solid clusters of stitches lift forward.

Multiple of 12 sts plus 1.

Row 1 (Right side)—K1, * ssk, k3, yo, k1, yo, k3, k2 tog, k1; rep from *.
Row 2—P1, * p2 tog, p2, yo, p3, yo, p2, p2 tog-b, p1; rep from *.
Row 3—K1, * ssk, k1, yo, k5, yo, k1, k2 tog, k1; rep from *.
Row 4—P1, * yo, p2 tog, p7, p2 tog-b, yo, p1; rep from *.
Row 5—K1, * yo, k3, k2 tog, k1, ssk, k3, yo, k1; rep from *.
Row 6—P2, * yo, p2, p2 tog-b, p1, p2 tog, p2, yo, p3; rep from *, end last repeat p2.
Row 7—K3, * yo, k1, k2 tog, k1, ssk, k1, yo, k5; rep from *, end last repeat k3.
Row 8—P4, * p2 tog-b, yo, p1, yo, p2 tog, p7; rep from *, end last repeat p4.

Repeat Rows 1–8.

Faun's Eyes

Three "Repeatable" Panels: Totem Pole, Ears of Grass, and Eyelet-Waved Rib

Of course, *any* panels are repeatable—they can be worked as many times as you like across the width of your piece. But these three are particularly effective as allover patterns, even though each is given in panel form. They are simple, uncluttered, graceful patterns that will blend well with other patterns too.

I. TOTEM POLE

Panel of 16 sts.

Rows 1, 3, and 5 (Wrong side)—K1, p14, k1.
Row 2—P1, k3, k2 tog, yo, k4, yo, ssk, k3, p1.
Row 4—P1, k2, k2 tog, yo, k6, yo, ssk, k2, p1.
Row 6—P1, k1, k2 tog, yo, k2, p4, k2, yo, ssk, k1, p1.
Row 7—K1, p5, k4, p5, k1.
Row 8—P1, k2 tog, yo, k3, p4, k3, yo, ssk, p1.

Repeat Rows 1–8.

II. EARS OF GRASS

Panel of 15 sts.

Rows 1 and 3 (Wrong side)—Purl.
Row 2—Ssk, k4, yo, k3, yo, k4, k2 tog.
Row 4—Ssk, k5, yo, k1, yo, k5, k2 tog.
Rows 5, 7, 9, 11, 13, 15, 17, and 19—P7, k1, p7.
Row 6—Ssk, k3, yo, k2, p1, k2, yo, k3, k2 tog.
Row 8—Ssk, k4, yo, k1, p1, k1, yo, k4, k2 tog.
Row 10—Ssk, k2, yo, k3, p1, k3, yo, k2, k2 tog.
Row 12—Repeat Row 6.
Row 14—Ssk, k1, yo, k4, p1, k4, yo, k1, k2 tog.
Row 16—Repeat Row 10.
Row 18—Ssk, yo, k5, p1, k5, yo, k2 tog.
Row 20—Repeat Row 14.

Repeat Rows 1–20.

III. EYELET-WAVED RIB

Panel of 15 sts.

Row 1 (Wrong side)—K3, (p3, k3) twice.
Row 2—P3, k3, yo, sl 2—k1—p2sso, k3, p3.
Rows 3, 5, 7, and 9—K3, p9, k3.

LEFT: *Totem Pole*
CENTER: *Ears of Grass*
RIGHT: *Eyelet-Waved Rib*

Row 4—P3, k1, ssk, yo, k3, yo, k2 tog, k1, p3.
Row 6—Repeat Row 2.
Row 8—Repeat Row 4.
Row 10—Repeat Row 2.
Row 11—Repeat Row 1.
Row 12—P1, ssk, yo, k3, p3, k3, yo, k2 tog, p1.
Rows 13, 15, and 17—K2, p4, k3, p4, k2.
Row 14—P2, k1, yo, k2 tog, k1, p3, k1, ssk, yo, k1, p2.
Row 16—Repeat Row 12.
Row 18—Repeat Row 14.
Row 19—Repeat Row 1.
Row 20—Repeat Row 12.

Repeat Rows 1–20.

Jack-In-The-Pulpit

Contributed by Hildegard M. Elsner, Aldan, Pennsylvania

"Jack" is an elongated slip-stitch, and each "pulpit" is a window-like eyelet hooded over with bundled strands. This is an old German pattern that has been copied frequently in machine knitting. The wrong side has a beautiful puff-texture effect.

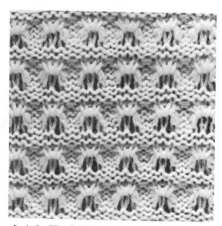

Jack-In-The-Pulpit

Multiple of 4 sts plus 3.

NOTE: Slip all sl-sts with yarn in back.

Row 1 (Right side)—K2, p1, * yo, p4; rep from *, end yo, p2, k2.

Row 2—K3, * yo, sl 1, drop the yo of preceding row off needle, k3; rep from *.

Row 3—K2, p1, * yo, sl both the yo and sl-st of preceding row, p3; rep from *, end last repeat p1, k2.

Row 4—K3, * yo, sl the 2 yo's and sl-st of preceding rows, k3; rep from *.

Row 5—K2, p1, * yo, sl the 3 yo's and sl-st of preceding rows, p3; rep from *, end last repeat p1, k2.

Row 6—K3, * insert right-hand needle from behind under the bundle of 4 yo strands (but *not* the sl-st) and purl these strands all together, removing them from left-hand needle but leaving the sl-st behind; then knit the sl-st; then insert left-hand needle from front under the 4 yo strands and purl them together again; k3; rep from *.

Row 7—K2, * k2 tog, p1, ssk, p1; rep from *, end last repeat k2 instead of p1.

Row 8—Knit.

Repeat Rows 1–8.

Candle of Glory

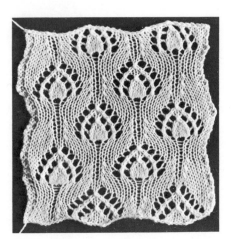

Candle of Glory

This is a very "lacy" pattern although, like most other eyelets, it consists of openwork motifs in a solid fabric. The background fabric itself, however, is gracefully waved and curved by the decreases. Notice that there are two stitches removed from each repeat on Rows 2, 4, 6, 14, 16, and 18. The original number of stitches is restored only on Rows 12 and 24.

Multiple of 20 sts plus 5.

Row 1 (Wrong side) and all other wrong-side rows—Purl.
Row 2— * K2, (yo, ssk) twice, k3, (k2 tog, yo) twice, k2, ssk, k1, k2 tog; rep from *, end k5.
Row 4—K3, * (yo, ssk) twice, k1, (k2 tog, yo) twice, k2, ssk, k1, k2 tog, k2; rep from *, end k2.
Row 6—K4, * yo, ssk, yo, sl 1—k2 tog—psso, yo, k2 tog, yo, k2, ssk, k1, k2 tog, k2; rep from *, end k1.
Row 8—K5, * yo, ssk, k1, k2 tog, yo, k9; rep from *.
Row 10—K6, * yo, sl 1—k2 tog—psso, yo, k11; rep from *, end last repeat k10.
Row 12—K14, * (k1, yo, k1, yo, k1, yo, k1) in next st, making 7 sts from 1; k13; rep from *, end last repeat k4.
Row 14—K5, * ssk, k1, k2 tog, k2, (yo, ssk) twice, k3, (k2 tog, yo) twice, k2; rep from *.
Row 16—K4, * ssk, k1, k2 tog, k2, (yo, ssk) twice, k1, (k2 tog, yo) twice, k2; rep from *, end k1.
Row 18—K3, * ssk, k1, k2 tog, k2, yo, ssk, yo, sl 1—k2 tog—psso, yo, k2 tog, yo, k2; rep from *, end k2.
Row 20— * K9, yo, ssk, k1, k2 tog, yo; rep from *, end k5.
Row 22—K10, * yo, sl 1—k2 tog—psso, yo, k11; rep from *, end last repeat k6.
Row 24—K4, * (k1, yo, k1, yo, k1, yo, k1) in next st, k13; rep from *, end k1.

Repeat Rows 1–24.

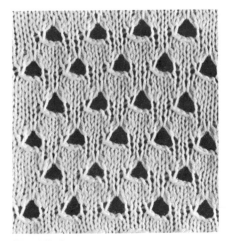

Bound Eyelet

Bound Eyelet

This interesting pattern makes large triangular eyelets bound off at the base. "Pass 2nd st over" in the second and eighth rows refers to the usual operation in binding off—i.e., inserting the left-hand needle into the 2nd stitch on right-hand needle and passing it over the first stitch. "Bind off 3, k3" also describes the action in these rows, but here is it written more precisely, so there can be no mistaking *which* stitches are to be bound.

Though its directions may sound complex, this pattern works very easily and makes a strikingly unusual fabric. The large eyelets can be left open for unlined articles such as stoles, scarves, over-skirts, and evening jackets. For dresses, a contrast-colored lining may be used; or, alternatively, a lovely effect can be obtained by threading a fairly broad ribbon diagonally through the eyelets on the finished piece.

Multiple of 6 sts plus 1.

Row 1 (Wrong side)—Purl.

Row 2—* K4, (pass 2nd st over, k1) twice, pass 2nd st over; rep from *, end k1.

Row 3—P2, * yo, p3; rep from *, end yo, p2.

Row 4—K1, * knit into the back of the st in the row below next st (inserting needle from the top down into the head of st), then knit the st on needle; yo, drop the yo of preceding row, knit into the front of st in the row below the next st, then knit the st on needle; k1; rep from *.

Row 5—P3, * yo, drop the yo of preceding row, p5; rep from *, end last repeat p3.

Row 6—K3, * drop the yo of preceding row, then insert needle from front under all 3 loose yo strands and knit, catching all 3 strands tog in st; k5; rep from *, end last repeat k3.

Row 7—Purl.

Row 8—K3, rep from * of Row 2; end k4.

Row 9—P5, * yo, p3; rep from *, end p2.

Row 10—K4, rep from * of Row 4; end k3.

Row 11—P6, rep from * of Row 5; end p1.

Row 12—K6, rep from * of Row 6; end k1.

Repeat Rows 1–12.

CHAPTER TWELVE

 Lace

Knit two together, yarn-over. It makes a little hole. Like the mighty oak growing from the acorn, during hundreds of years a tremendous and dazzling structure of knitting art has grown from just that little hole. Though its basic unit is the simplest of all, lace is by far the most varied and variable form of knitting. For centuries, the world's best knitters have been arranging and re-arranging those little holes to make beautiful designs. These designs are the precious heritage of a unique art.

The incredible variety of knitted lace encompasses every degree of skill; there are patterns for the beginner, patterns for the intermediate, and patterns for the expert. Many of the loveliest ones are also the easiest to work. Sometimes, novice knitters are frightened away from lace because it *looks* so intricate. But in a large number of cases the intricacy is an illusion. There are lace patterns so easy that a child could work them.

Lace knitting has been well known in Europe since the 15th century, when silk yarns first became popular. These yarns inspired knitters to create dainty openwork designs suitable to the medium. The well-appointed wardrobe then demanded knitted lace stockings, gloves, and scarves. Invention and innovation in this field continued to gather force, and attained great heights early in the 18th century, when cotton and muslin threads began to be imported from the East. All of Europe participated in the subsequent craze for "white knitting"—that is, fine lace knitting in white cotton yarn. During this period, masterpieces of knitting art were produced by the thousands and hundreds of thousands. Shawls, fichus, doilies, medallions, collars, ball gowns, draperies, edgings for linens, and similar articles were knitted with gossamer-like thread on the thinnest possible needles, which were called "wires". Aristocratic ladies spent much time on this delicate work. Still in existence are lace samplers made in this period by women who copied many different patterns in order to develop their knowledge and skill.

Fine wool lace attained a peak of development in the Shetland Islands, where a special breed of sheep produced delicate wool that was spun into hair-thin yarns. The famous Shetland shawls were the pride of Great Britain, examples of them being worn by the royal family since the time of Queen Victoria. So cobwebby in texture were these shawls that, it was said, they could be drawn through a wedding-ring. The patterns used in making them are now a cherished part of knitting tradition.

Modern knitters usually do not devote themselves to work so dainty; nor is it necessary for them to do so. Today's cotton and fingering yarns are heavier, but they can display the beauty of lace patterns just as well as the threadlike yarns of the "white knitting" era. Wool, synthetics, and metallics can be worked in lace patterns to make high-fashion dresses, blouses, stoles, stockings, gloves, and dozens of other wearables. Cotton lace is delightful not only for clothes, but also for table settings, curtains, bedspreads and other household articles. Crochet cotton is inexpensive, and very good for trying out lace patterns on size 1 or 2 needles. "Practice swatches" made in this way, with some simple border such as garter stitch or seed stitch, can be starched and stretched and used as beautiful, durable place mats. Lace samplers can be made in long strips—in wool fingering yarn, for instance—and used as scarves.

Lace knitting is an essential part of every knitter's education. There are some who say that you are not a real knitter until you can work with lace. But this implies that an expert's knowledge is needed before you can start—which is not the case at all. Anyone can work the simpler lace patterns. As in any other kind of knitting, you don't learn first and then start doing; you learn *by* doing. So even if you have never worked lace before, you can start right now—today. Get some fingering yarn and a pair of needles (size 3 is about standard for the average knitter) and try out some of these patterns. You will find them exciting to learn, and highly satisfying to use. Just one hint: never cast on too many stitches for the width measurement you want. *Lace requires stretching.* All its beauty is lost if it is allowed to contract and close up the holes. Start with only three-quarters of the number of stitches you think you might need for a given measurement, and *stretch* your swatch to that measurement when you block it. You'll be surprised to see how far it will go, and how handsomely the pattern shows when the fabric is treated in this way. Then you can take a revised stitch gauge from the blocked piece of lace.

Once you have an accurate stitch gauge for any particular lace pattern in a particular yarn on a particular size of needle, you can go ahead and multiply that gauge by the number of inches desired in any part of a garment, and make yourself a lace original. Some knitters prefer to use a "repeat gauge" instead of a stitch gauge. This means: so many repeats of the pattern to so many inches. For instance, if you make a swatch 6 inches wide by working 3 pattern repeats, then you know that a piece 18 inches wide will require 9 pattern repeats. Shaping takes place at the edges, just as in solid-fabric knitting. Shaping lace in such a way as to keep the pattern correct is not difficult, if you remember one simple rule: every time a yarn-over (that is, a hole) is eliminated from the pattern, its corresponding decrease must also be eliminated. Conversely, when adding more stitches to make the piece wider, you do not work a new yarn-over until you have room to work its corresponding decrease also.

Among the laces there are patterns old and new, simple and complex; so many of them that any knitter can find patterns to please, challenge, or inspire her. This is the most creative category in a highly creative craft. Use it to the best of your present ability, and your future ability will flourish a hundredfold.

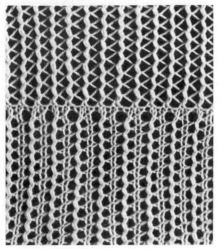

ABOVE: *Rick Rib*
BELOW: *Rickrack Faggoting Stitch*

Rick Rib

Contributed by Gretchen Cranz, Gettysburg, Pennsylvania

Here is a beautiful and unusual kind of faggoting that is very easy to work. In fine yarn, it makes an attractive mesh or a lace insertion; in heavier yarn, it makes a handsome ribbing that is soft and elastic. This pattern differs from most other types of faggoting in having a right and a wrong side, both of them quite pretty.

Even number of sts.

Row 1 (Right side)—K1, * yo, sl 1 wyib, k1, psso; rep from *, end k1.
Row 2—P1, * yo, sl 1 wyif, p1, psso; rep from *, end p1.

Repeat Rows 1 and 2.

Rickrack Faggoting Stitch

Like Rick Rib, this faggoting pattern makes small zigzag or "plaited" columns of knit stitches. An extra stitch is added between the columns, which changes the herringbone strands that are typical of faggoting into fairly straight ones, extending to each side alternately in a ladder-like design. This pattern is pretty as an allover lace stitch, or in panels, yoke bands, stocking insertions, etc.

Multiple of 3 sts plus 1.

Row 1 (Right side)—K1, * yo, ssk, k1; rep from *.
Row 2—K1, * yo, p2 tog, k1; rep from *.

Repeat Rows 1 and 2.

Stripe with Twisted Bars

Contributed by Leona Hughes, Sarasota, Florida

Here is a simple two-row pattern with a neat, ladder-like effect. The broader ribs are given texture interest by being knitted on the wrong side. This pattern is suitable for insertions or bands, sleeves, scarves, and blouses. Several repeats may be used in combination with other lace panels.

Multiple of 6 sts plus 1.

Row 1 (Right side)—K1, * yo, k1, k3 tog, k1, yo, k1; rep from *.
Row 2—P1, * k5, p1; rep from *.

Repeat Rows 1 and 2.

Stripe with Twisted Bars

Ribbon Rib

Notice the subtle widening and narrowing of the lace ribs here, as the decreases are switched from one edge to the other. The "grained" effect of the curved stitches is very pretty, and lends an interesting touch to a simple pattern that might seem too pedestrian without it.

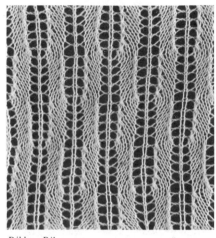

Ribbon Rib

Multiple of 14 sts plus 1.

Row 1 (Wrong side) and all other wrong-side rows—Purl.

Rows 2, 4, 6, 8, and 10—K1, * yo, k3, sl 1—k2 tog—psso, yo, k1, yo, k3 tog, k3, yo, k1; rep from *.

Rows 12, 14, 16, 18, and 20—K1, * yo, k3 tog, k3, yo, k1, yo, k3, sl 1—k2 tog—psso, yo, k1; rep from *.

Repeat Rows 1–20.

Sunray Pattern

NOTE: The yo at the beginning and the yo at the end of each line combine as a double yo when two or more pattern repeats are being worked at once.

Sunray Pattern

Multiple of 24 sts plus 2.

Row 1 (Wrong side) and all other wrong-side rows—Purl, always working (k1, p1) into each double yo of a previous row.

Row 2—K1, * yo, (k2 tog) twice, yo, k2, k2 tog, yo, k2, ssk, (yo) twice, k2 tog, k2, yo, ssk, k2, yo, (ssk) twice, yo; rep from *, end k1.

Row 4—K1, * yo, k3 tog, yo, (k2, k2 tog, yo) twice, k2, (yo, ssk, k2) twice, yo, sl 1—k2 tog—psso, yo; rep from *, end k1.

Row 6—K1, * yo, k2 tog, (k2, k2 tog, yo) twice, ssk, (yo) twice, k2 tog, (yo, ssk, k2) twice, ssk, yo; rep from *, end k1.

Row 8—K1, * yo, k2 tog, k1, k2 tog, yo, k2, k2 tog, yo, k1, ssk, (yo) twice, k2 tog, k1, yo, ssk, k2, yo, ssk, k1, ssk, yo; rep from *, end k1.

Repeat Rows 1–8.

Harebell Lace

This is a beautiful "little lace" with a rather interesting zigzag design. Since it is very easy to work, it is recommended for the beginner who wants a blouse or sweater in some delicate allover openwork.

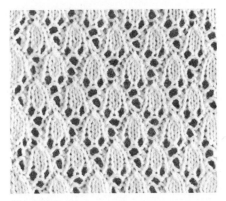

Harebell Lace

Multiple of 6 sts plus 3.

Rows 1, 3, and 5 (Wrong side)—P3, * k3, p3; rep from *.
Row 2—K3, * p2 tog, yo, p1, k3; rep from *.
Row 4—K3, * p1, yo, p2 tog, k3; rep from *.
Row 6—K1, k2 tog, * (p1, yo) twice, p1, sl 1—k2 tog—psso; rep from *, end last repeat ssk, k1 instead of sl 1—k2 tog—psso.
Rows 7, 9, and 11—K3, * p3, k3; rep from *.
Row 8—P1, yo, p2 tog, * k3, p1, yo, p2 tog; rep from *.
Row 10—P2 tog, yo, p1, * k3, p2 tog, yo, p1; rep from *.
Row 12—P2, yo, p1, * sl 1—k2 tog—psso, (p1, yo) twice, p1; rep from *, end sl 1—k2 tog—psso, p1, yo, p2.

Repeat Rows 1–12.

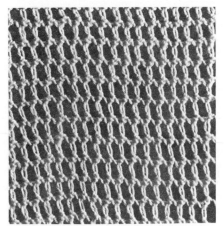

Knot-Stitch Mesh

Knot-Stitch Mesh

Contributed by Hildegard M. Elsner, Aldan, Pennsylvania

This intriguing mesh pattern does very well as a horizontal insertion when combined with several rows of Garter Stitch. At least six rows of Knot-Stitch Mesh should be used for each open-work band.

When used as an allover lace fabric, the mesh should be cast on and bound off very loosely, because it will spread. For binding off (after Row 2), the following method is recommended: K1, * yo, bind off the yo st, k1, bind off the knit st; repeat from * across.

Any number of sts.

Row 1—* (Yo) twice, k1; rep from *.
Row 2—* K2 (that is, knit the first st and the first yo loop), p1 (the second yo loop); then pass the 2 knit sts over the purl st; rep from *.

Repeat Rows 1 and 2.

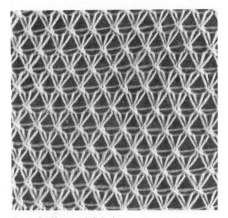

Lace Background Stitch

Lace Background Stitch

Contributed by Dorothy Reade, Eugene, Oregon

Odd number of sts.

Row 1 (Right side)—K1, * yo, sl 1, k1, yo, psso the knit st and the following yo; rep from *.
Row 2—* P2, drop the yo of preceding row; rep from *, end p1.
Row 3—K2, rep from * of Row 1, end k1.
Row 4—P3, * drop the yo of preceding row, p2; rep from *.

Repeat Rows 1–4.

Grand Trefoil

This simple little three-row mesh has a surprisingly sophisticated structure. For a real challenge, try to figure out from the picture alone how it is made, without reading the directions. If you can do it, you qualify as a Master Knitter!

Grand Trefoil is easy to work when you know how, and makes a reversible, noncurling, graceful fabric for scarves, shawls, insertions, etc. This fabric spreads, and so must be cast on and bound off very loosely. When binding off, leave both loops of the double yo on the needle and bind off each loop separately; this will help to loosen the final selvage.

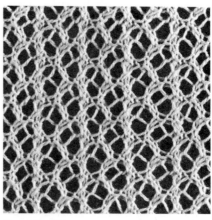

Grand Trefoil

Multiple of 5 sts plus 3.

Note: Drop Loop (DL): drop the second loop of the double yo of previous row off the needle. The first loop is already knitted.

Preparation Row—K3, * (yo) twice, k2 tog, k3; rep from *.
Row 1—K5, * DL, (yo) twice, k2 tog, k3; rep from *, end last repeat k1.
Row 2—K3, * DL, k2, (yo) twice, k2 tog, k1; rep from *.
Row 3—K3, * DL, (yo) twice, k2 tog, k3; rep from *.

Repeat Rows 1–3.

Tilting Block Pattern

Here is an easy-to-work lace check with an absolutely fascinating appearance. The garter-stitch blocks which seem to be tipped at precarious angles are not *worked* that way at all; they are simply worked straight across. Small areas of bias lace trellis pull them this way and that, to create a most unusual pattern.

If a smooth-surfaced fabric is desired, instead of the garter-stitch ridges as contrast to the trellis, then all wrong-side rows may be simply purled across. The shapes of the pattern will not change, but the "blocks" will appear in stockinette stitch.

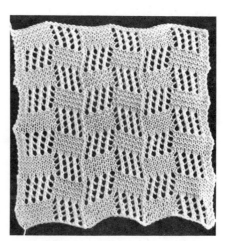

Tilting Block Pattern

Multiple of 16 sts plus 1.

Rows 1, 3, 5, and 7 (Right side)—* (Ssk, yo) 4 times, k8; rep from *, end k1.
Rows 2, 4, 6, and 8—* K9, p7; rep from *, end k1.
Rows 9, 11, 13, and 15—K1, * k8, (yo, k2 tog) 4 times; rep from *.
Rows 10, 12, 14, and 16—K1, * p7, k9; rep from *.

Repeat Rows 1–16.

Pyramidal Lace Check

Here is a pretty, easy-to-work pattern with triangular lace motifs in which the decreases run alternately left and right. Any fine-yarn blouse or sweater pattern calling for stockinette stitch can be beautifully varied by this lace, which would turn it into a "creation" instead of just another piece of knitting.

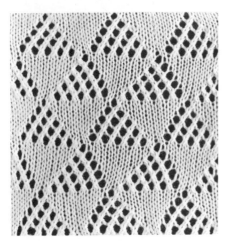

Pyramidal Lace Check

Multiple of 12 sts plus 1.

Row 1 (Wrong side) and all other wrong-side rows—Purl.
Row 2—K1, * (k2 tog, yo) 5 times, k2; rep from *.
Row 4—K2, * (k2 tog, yo) 4 times, k4; rep from *, end last repeat k3.
Row 6—K3, * (k2 tog, yo) 3 times, k6; rep from *, end last repeat k4.
Row 8—K4, * (k2 tog, yo) twice, k8; rep from *, end last repeat k5.
Row 10—K5, * k2 tog, yo, k10; rep from *, end last repeat k6.
Row 12—K2, (yo, ssk) twice, * k2, (yo, ssk) 5 times; rep from *, end k2, (yo, ssk) twice, k1.
Row 14—K1, (yo, ssk) twice, * k4, (yo, ssk) 4 times; rep from *, end k4, (yo, ssk) twice.
Row 16—K2, yo, ssk, * k6, (yo, ssk) 3 times; rep from *, end k6, yo, ssk, k1.
Row 18—K1, yo, ssk, * k8, (yo, ssk) twice; rep from *, end k8, yo, ssk.
Row 20—K12, * yo, ssk, k10; rep from *, end k1.

Repeat Rows 1–20.

Swing Stitch

Here is a charming pattern with quarter-diamonds interestingly placed in a solid stockinette fabric. Notice that the decreases are worked in opposition to the slant of the stitches, which gives a "soft" effect.

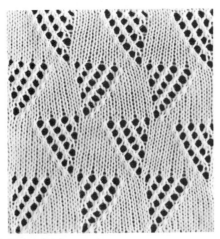

Swing Stitch

Multiple of 12 sts plus 1.

Row 1 (Wrong side) and all other wrong-side rows—Purl.
Row 2—* K10, ssk, yo; rep from *, end k1.
Row 4—K9, * ssk, yo, k10; rep from *, end last repeat k2.
Row 6—* K8, (ssk, yo) twice; rep from *, end k1.
Row 8—K7, * (ssk, yo) twice, k8; rep from *, end last repeat k2.
Row 10—* K6, (ssk, yo) 3 times; rep from *, end k1.

Row 12—K5, * (ssk, yo) 3 times, k6; rep from *, end last repeat k2.

Row 14—* K4, (ssk, yo) 4 times; rep from *, end k1.

Row 16—K1, * yo, k2 tog, k10; rep from *.

Row 18—K2, * yo, k2 tog, k10; rep from *, end last repeat k9.

Row 20—K1, * (yo, k2 tog) twice, k8; rep from *.

Row 22—K2, * (yo, k2 tog) twice, k8; rep from *, end last repeat k7.

Row 24—K1, * (yo, k2 tog) 3 times, k6; rep from *.

Row 26—K2, * (yo, k2 tog) 3 times, k6; rep from *, end last repeat k5.

Row 28—K1, * (yo, k2 tog) 4 times, k4; rep from *.

Repeat Rows 1–28.

Arbor Pattern

Multiple of 16 sts plus 1.

Row 1 (Right side)—K1, * yo, k2, ssk, p7, k2 tog, k2, yo, k1; rep from *.

Row 2—P5, * k7, p9; rep from *, end last repeat p5.

Row 3—K2, * yo, k2, ssk, p5, k2 tog, k2, yo, k2 tog, yo, k1; rep from *, end yo, k2, ssk, p5, k2 tog, k2, yo, k2.

Row 4—P6, * k5, p11; rep from *, end last repeat p6.

Row 5—* K2 tog, yo, k1, yo, k2, ssk, p3, k2 tog, k2, yo, k2 tog, yo; rep from *, end k1.

Row 6—P7, * k3, p13; rep from *, end last repeat p7.

Row 7—K1, * k2 tog, yo, k1, yo, k2, ssk, p1, k2 tog, k2, yo, (k2 tog, yo) twice; rep from *, end k2 tog, yo, k1, yo, k2, ssk, p1, k2 tog, k2, yo, k2 tog, yo, k2.

Row 8—P8, * k1, p15; rep from *, end last repeat p8.

Row 9—P4, * k2 tog, k2, yo, k1, yo, k2, ssk, p7; rep from *, end last repeat p4.

Row 10—K4, * p9, k7; rep from *, end last repeat k4.

Row 11—P3, * k2 tog, k2, yo, k2 tog, yo, k1, yo, k2, ssk, p5; rep from *, end last repeat p3.

Row 12—K3, * p11, k5; rep from *, end last repeat k3.

Row 13—P2, * k2 tog, k2, yo, (k2 tog, yo) twice, k1, yo, k2, ssk, p3; rep from *, end last repeat p2.

Row 14—K2, * p13, k3; rep from *, end last repeat k2.

Row 15—P1, * k2 tog, k2, yo, (k2 tog, yo) 3 times, k1, yo, k2, ssk, p1; rep from *.

Row 16—K1, * p15, k1; rep from *.

Repeat Rows 1–16.

Arbor Pattern

Crystal Pattern

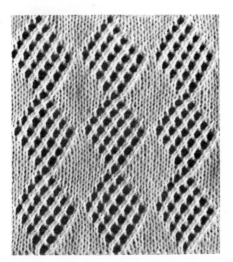

Crystal Pattern

This simple but wonderfully effective lace is most instructive. It is likely to be a surprise to the novice lace knitter. Having learned from trying various kinds of Lace Trellis that a series of similar decreases creates a bias fabric, she now encounters a pattern in which the decreases *are* all the same, and yet there are all the stitches going ruler-straight—up! Why?

The answer is that the bias effect is overcome by moving the pattern on the diagonal, one stitch at a time. A Lace Trellis cannot be inserted successfully into a solid fabric in the shape of a square, but it can be so inserted when the square is tipped to make a diamond. The decreases only *seem* to fall in vertical alignment; actually they are staggered. The pattern is lovely, easy to work, and suitable for panel treatment or for use as an allover fabric.

Multiple of 11 sts plus 1.

Row 1 (Wrong side) and all other wrong-side rows—Purl.
Row 2—K5, * k2 tog, yo, k9; rep from *, end last repeat k5.
Row 4—K4, * (k2 tog, yo) twice, k7; rep from *, end last repeat k4.
Row 6—K3, * (k2 tog, yo) 3 times, k5; rep from *, end last repeat k3.
Row 8—K2, * (k2 tog, yo) 4 times, k3; rep from *, end last repeat k2.
Row 10—K1, * (k2 tog, yo) 5 times, k1; rep from *.
Row 12—Repeat Row 8.
Row 14—Repeat Row 6.
Row 16—Repeat Row 4.

Repeat Rows 1–16.

SPECIAL NOTE: This pattern may be reversed, so that it runs to the left instead of to the right, simply by working a "yo, ssk" in place of every "k2 tog, yo".

Crystal and Pearl

Crystal and Pearl

This is an exceedingly simple pattern, which may be varied by slanting the trellis in the opposite direction, as in Crystal Pattern, by working "k2 tog, yo" in place of every "yo, ssk". Thus the design can be balanced when worked in bisymmetrical panels. The dainty "pearl" (purl) ridges add texture interest, and make the pattern a lovely choice for fine-yarn delicacies like baby clothes, bedjackets, etc.

Multiple of 8 sts.

Rows 1 and 2—Purl.
Row 3 (Wrong side)—Knit.
Row 4—* K1, (yo, ssk) 3 times, k1; rep from *.
Row 5 and all subsequent wrong-side rows—Purl.
Row 6—* K2, (yo, ssk) twice, k2; rep from *.
Row 8—* K3, yo, ssk, k3; rep from *.
Rows 10 and 12—Repeat Rows 6 and 4.

Repeat Rows 1–12.

Checkerboard Mesh

This beautiful lace is simple to work. Try it in a place mat knitted in fine cotton, or in a formal blouse with fine wool. It can be worked with heavier yarn, too, to make a lovely stole or scarf.

Multiple of 10 sts plus 4.

Row 1 (Wrong side) and all other wrong-side rows—Purl.
Row 2—K4, * yo, ssk, k1, (k2 tog, yo) twice, k3; rep from *.
Row 4—* K3, (yo, ssk) twice, k1, k2 tog, yo; rep from *, end k4.
Row 6—K2, * (yo, ssk) 3 times, k4; rep from *, end yo, ssk.
Row 8—K1, * (yo, ssk) 4 times, k2; rep from *, end yo, ssk, k1.
Rows 10, 12, and 14—Repeat Rows 6, 4, and 2.
Row 16—K2 tog, yo, * k4, (k2 tog, yo) 3 times; rep from *, end k2.
Row 18—K1, k2 tog, yo, * k2, (k2 tog, yo) 4 times; rep from *, end k1.
Row 20—Repeat Row 16.

Repeat Rows 1–20.

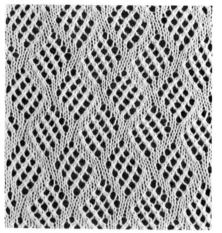

Checkerboard Mesh

Mermaid's Mesh

This dazzling mesh pattern has all the best qualities of knitted lace: it is delicate, graceful, and very open; it appears intricate when finished, but is not difficult to make. Worked in a glittering metallic yarn, and lined with satin or silk, it would make a high-fashion formal dress or blouse that could rival anything from a top designer. Worked in cotton, it makes beautiful curtains, or square or rectangular doilies.

Multiple of 9 sts plus 4.

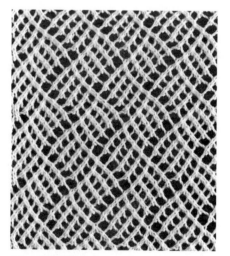

Mermaid's Mesh

Row 1 (Wrong side) and all other wrong-side rows—Purl. NOTE: Throughout pattern, work (k1, p1) into every *double* yo.

Row 2—K1, yo, * (ssk, yo) 3 times, k3 tog, (yo) twice; rep from *, end ssk, k1.

Row 4—* K2 tog, (yo) twice, (ssk, yo) twice, k3 tog, yo; rep from *, end k2 tog, yo, k2.

Row 6—K1, * k2 tog, (yo) twice, ssk, yo, k3 tog, yo, k2 tog, yo; rep from *, end k2 tog, yo, k1.

Row 8—K2 tog, yo, * k2 tog, (yo) twice, sl 1—k2 tog—psso, (yo, k2 tog) twice, yo; rep from *, end k2.

Row 10—K1, k2 tog, yo, * k2 tog, (yo) twice, sl 1—k2 tog—psso, (yo, k2 tog) twice, yo; rep from *, end k1.

Row 12—K2 tog, yo, * k2 tog, (yo) twice, ssk, yo, sl 1—k2 tog—psso, yo, k2 tog, yo; rep from *, end k2.

Row 14—K1, k2 tog, * (yo) twice, (ssk, yo) twice, sl 1—k2 tog—psso, yo, k2 tog; rep from *, end yo, k1.

Row 16—K2 tog, * (yo) twice, (ssk, yo) 3 times, k3 tog; rep from *, end (yo) twice, ssk.

Repeat Rows 1–16.

Spider Stitch

This very old pattern is of the utmost simplicity—a real "beginner's lace"—but quite charming. In structure it is just one of the miniature leaf patterns with alternate motifs elongated by repeating the same row three times. It would be lovely with beads knitted in: three of them, say, in the central stitch of each of the elongated motifs (on Rows 2, 4, and 6) and one in each of the small diamonds (on Row 10). It is attractive as an insertion, either vertical or horizontal.

Multiple of 6 sts plus 1.

Row 1 (Wrong side) and all other wrong-side rows—Purl.

Rows 2, 4, and 6—K1, * yo, ssk, k1, k2 tog, yo, k1; rep from *.

Row 8—K2, * yo, sl 1—k2 tog—psso, yo, k3; rep from *, end last repeat k2.

Row 10—K1, * k2 tog, yo, k1, yo, ssk, k1; rep from *.

Row 12—K2 tog, * yo, k3, yo, sl 1—k2 tog—psso; rep from *, end yo, k3, yo, ssk.

Repeat Rows 1–12.

Spider Stitch

Pierced Diamond Pattern

In this version of the Diamond, the leftward-slanting decreases are cleverly arranged to give a diagonal line, as in some of the Madeira laces. This method gives a beautiful small-patterned lace that is novel, yet just as easy to work as the more common types.

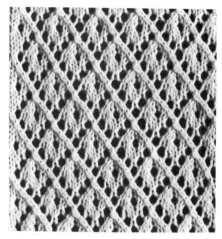

Pierced Diamond Pattern

Multiple of 6 sts plus 3.

Row 1 (Wrong side) and all other wrong-side rows—Purl.

Row 2—K1, * yo, ssk, k1, yo, k2 tog, k1; rep from *, end yo, ssk.

Row 4—K2, * yo, ssk, k1, k2 tog, yo, k1; rep from *, end k1.

Row 6—K3, * yo, sl 1—k2 tog—psso, yo, k3; rep from *.

Row 8—K1, * yo, k2 tog, k1, yo, ssk, k1; rep from *, end yo, k2 tog.

Row 10—K2, * k2 tog, yo, k1, yo, ssk, k1; rep from *, end k1.

Row 12—K1, k2 tog, yo, * k3, yo, sl 1—k2 tog—psso, yo; rep from *, end k3, yo, ssk, k1.

Repeat Rows 1–12.

Coral Pattern

Contributed by Leona Hughes, Sarasota, Florida

In this charming old version of the classic Diamonds, a single knit stitch is inserted between each yo and its corresponding decrease. This gives the unusual effect of "framing" the diamonds within wavy borders. The pattern is simple to work, and very attractive for any kind of lace garment.

Coral Pattern

Multiple of 10 sts plus 1.

Row 1 (Wrong side) and all other wrong-side rows—Purl.

Row 2—K2, * k2 tog, (k1, yo) twice, k1, ssk, k3; rep from *, end last repeat k2.

Row 4—K1, * k2 tog, k1, yo, k3, yo, k1, ssk, k1; rep from *.

Row 6—K2 tog, * k1, yo, k5, yo, k1, sl 1—k2 tog—psso; rep from *, end last repeat ssk instead of sl 1—k2 tog—psso.

Row 8—K1, * yo, k1, ssk, k3, k2 tog, k1, yo, k1; rep from *.

Row 10—K2, * yo, k1, ssk, k1, k2 tog, k1, yo, k3; rep from *, end last repeat k2.

Row 12—K3, * yo, k1, sl 1—k2 tog—psso, k1, yo, k5; rep from *, end last repeat k3.

Repeat Rows 1–12.

Flemish Block Lace

Flemish Block Lace

Here is an easy-to-work and interesting lace based on the classic Openwork Diamonds. In this case the diamonds are elongated into rectangular blocks laid diagonally like fancy Flemish brickwork.

Multiple of 14 sts plus 3.

Row 1 (Wrong side) and all other wrong-side rows—Purl.

Row 2—K2, * k2 tog, yo, k1, yo, ssk, k3, k2 tog, yo, k4; rep from *, end k1.

Row 4—K1, * k2 tog, yo, k3, yo, ssk, k1, k2 tog, yo, k4; rep from *, end k2.

Row 6—K2 tog, yo, * k5, yo, sl 1—k2 tog—psso, yo, k4, k2 tog, yo; rep from *, end k1.

Row 8—K2, * yo, ssk, k4, yo, ssk, k3, k2 tog, yo, k1; rep from *, end k1.

Row 10—K3, * yo, ssk, k4, yo, ssk, k1, k2 tog, yo, k3; rep from *.

Row 12—K4, * yo, ssk, k4, yo, k3 tog, yo, k5; rep from *, end last repeat k4.

Repeat Rows 1–12.

Cameo Lattice

Cameo Lattice

For an interesting variation of this pattern, see Morning Glory.

Multiple of 13 sts plus 2.

Row 1 (Wrong side) and all other wrong-side rows—Purl. NOTE: On Rows 11, 13, 23, and repeats of Row 1, work (k1, p1) into every *double* yo.

Row 2—K2, * yo, k2, ssk, k3, k2 tog, k2, yo, k2; rep from *.

Row 4—K3, * yo, k2, ssk, k1, k2 tog, k2, yo, k4; rep from *, end last repeat k3.

Row 6—K4, * yo, k2, sl 1—k2 tog—psso, k2, yo, k6; rep from *, end last repeat k4.

Row 8—K5, * yo, k2, sl 1—k2 tog—psso, yo, k2, k2 tog, yo, k4; rep from *, end last repeat k1.

Row 10—K4, * k2 tog, (yo) twice, k2, ssk, k1, k2 tog, (yo) twice, ssk, k2; rep from *, on last repeat omit final "k2".

Row 12—K3, * k2 tog, k2, (yo) twice, k2, ssk, k5; rep from *, end last repeat k4.

Row 14—K2, * k2 tog, k2, (yo, k2) twice, ssk, k3; rep from *.

Row 16—K1, * k2 tog, k2, yo, k4, yo, k2, ssk, k1; rep from *, end k1.

Row 18—K2 tog, * k2, yo, k6, yo, k2, k3 tog; rep from *, end last repeat k2 tog, k1 instead of k3 tog.

Row 20—K7, * yo, ssk, k2, yo, k3 tog, k2, yo, k4; rep from *,
end yo, ssk, k2, yo, k2 tog, k2.

Row 22—K6, * k2 tog, (yo) twice, ssk, k1, k2 tog, k2, (yo) twice,
ssk, k2; rep from *, end k2 tog, (yo) twice, ssk, k5.

Row 24—K1, yo, * k2, ssk, k5, k2 tog, k2, (yo) twice; rep from
*, end last repeat yo, k1 instead of (yo) twice.

Repeat Rows 1–24.

Morning Glory

Who would believe from their appearance that this pattern and
Cameo Lattice are really the same? But they are. The only difference is that Morning Glory is squeezed down to half the number
of rows, so that every alternate pattern row is transposed to the
wrong side—and the eyelets, of course, are omitted. This is a
notable example of the flexibility of knitting patterns; a relatively
minor change in technique produces radically different shapes on
the fabric. Little discoveries like this are what make knitting so
eternally fascinating, and reward the experimental knitter with
innumerable pleasant surprises.

Morning Glory

Multiple of 13 sts plus 2.

Row 1 (Preparation row—right side)—K2, * yo, k2, ssk, k3, k2
tog, k2, yo, k2; rep from *.

Row 2—P3, * yo, p2, p2 tog, p1, p2 tog-b, p2, yo, p4; rep from
*, end last repeat p3.

Row 3—K4, * yo, k2, sl 1—k2 tog—psso, k2, yo, k6; rep from *, end last repeat
k4.

Row 4—P5, * yo, p2 tog and return resulting st to left-hand needle; keeping yarn
in front, pass next st over p2-tog st and off left-hand needle; then sl the st back
to right-hand needle; p2, yo, p8; rep from *, end last repeat p5.

Row 5—K4, * k2 tog, (yo) twice, k2, ssk, k7; rep from *, end last repeat k5.

Row 6—P4, * p2 tog-b, p2, (yo) twice, (k1, p1) into the double yo of previous row,
p2 tog, p5; rep from *, end last repeat p3.

Row 7—K2, * k2 tog, k2, yo, (k1, p1) into the double yo of previous row, yo, k2,
ssk, k3; rep from *.

Row 8—P2, * p2 tog-b, p2, yo, p4, yo, p2, p2 tog, p1; rep from *.

Row 9—K2 tog, * k2, yo, k6, yo, k2, k3 tog; rep from *, end last repeat k2 tog,
k1 instead of k3 tog.

Row 10—P2, p2 tog, yo, * p8, yo, p2, p3 tog, yo; rep from *, end p11.

Row 11—K11, * k2 tog, k2, (yo) twice, ssk, k7; rep from *, end k4.

Row 12—P1, yo, * p2, p2 tog, p5, p2 tog-b, (k1, p1) into the double yo of previous
row, (yo) twice; rep from *, end p2, p2 tog, p5, p2 tog-b, p2, yo, p1.

Row 13—K2, * yo, k2, ssk, k3, k2 tog, k2, yo, (k1, p1) into the double yo of previous
row; rep from *, end yo, k2, ssk, k3, k2 tog, k2, yo, k2.

Omitting Row 1 from subsequent repeats, repeat Rows 2–13.

Vine Stripe Pattern

Contributed by Hildegard M. Elsner, Aldan, Pennsylvania

Multiple of 15 sts plus 2.

Row 1 (Wrong side) and all other wrong-side rows—Purl.

Row 2—P2, * k3, (yo, k1) twice, ssk, k3, k2 tog, k1, p2; rep from *.

Row 4—P2, * (k3, yo) twice, k1, ssk, k1, k2 tog, k1, p2; rep from *.

Row 6—P2, * k3, yo, k5, yo, k1, sl 1—k2 tog—psso, k1, p2; rep from *.

Row 8—P2, * k1, ssk, k3, k2 tog, (k1, yo) twice, k3, p2; rep from *.

Row 10—P2, * k1, ssk, k1, k2 tog, k1, (yo, k3) twice, p2; rep from *.

Row 12—P2, * k1, k3 tog, k1, yo, k5, yo, k3, p2; rep from *.

Repeat Rows 1–12.

Vine Stripe Pattern

Fountain Lace

Only four pattern rows, yet what a beautiful lace design this is! It is stunning as an allover pattern, but also lends itself very nicely to panel treatment—one panel 17 stitches wide, or two panels together as shown, on 33 stitches. Knowledgeable knitters will see an element of the Shetland Horseshoe Pattern in the arches formed by adjoining panels; but the main motif is quite unique.

Multiple of 16 sts plus 1.

Row 1 (Wrong side) and all other wrong-side rows—Purl.

Row 2—Ssk, * yo, k2, k2 tog, yo, k1, yo, sl 1—k2 tog—psso, yo, k1, yo, ssk, k2, yo, sl 1—k2 tog—psso; rep from *, end last repeat k2 tog instead of sl 1—k2 tog—psso.

Row 4—Ssk, * k3, yo, k2 tog, yo, k3, yo, ssk, yo, k3, sl 1—k2 tog—psso; rep from *, end last repeat k2 tog instead of sl 1—k2 tog—psso.

Row 6—Ssk, * (k2, yo) twice, k2 tog, k1, ssk, (yo, k2) twice, sl 1—k2 tog—psso; rep from *, end last repeat k2 tog instead of sl 1—k2 tog—psso.

Row 8—Ssk, * k1, yo, k3, yo, k2 tog, k1, ssk, yo, k3, yo, k1, sl 1—k2 tog—psso; rep from *, end last repeat k2 tog instead of sl 1—k2 tog—psso.

Repeat Rows 1–8.

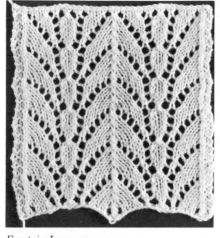

Fountain Lace

Honeybee Pattern with Faggoting

Contributed by Hildegard M. Elsner, Aldan, Pennsylvania

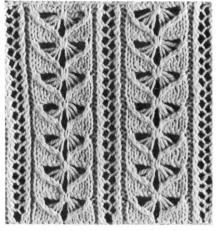

Patterns like this one are used by peasant women of Bohemia, Moravia, Silesia and Slovakia to make the fancy stockings that are part of the traditional regional costume worn on festive occasions. Such stockings usually are knitted in red or white cotton and often are richly embroidered in contrasting colors.

Multiple of 18 sts plus 6.

"A" portion of pattern (6 sts): P1, k2, yo, ssk, p1.
"B" portion of pattern (6 sts): K1, p2, yo, p2 tog, k1.

NOTE: A and B form the panels of faggoting between Honeybee motifs.

Row 1(Right side)—A, * k4, k2 tog, yo, ssk, k4, A; rep from *.
Row 2—B, * p3, p2 tog-b, drop the yo of previous row off needle, (yo) twice, p2 tog, p3, B; rep from *.
Row 3—A, * k2, k2 tog, drop the yo's of previous row off needle, (yo) 3 times, ssk, k2, A; rep from *.
Row 4—B, * p1, p2 tog-b, drop the yo's of previous row off needle, (yo) 4 times, p2 tog, p1, B; rep from *.
Row 5—A, * k2 tog, drop the yo's of previous row off needle, cast on 4 sts on right-hand needle, k1 *under* and 4 loose strands of the dropped yo's; then yo and k1 again under the 4 loose strands; cast on 4 sts on right-hand needle, ssk, A; rep from *.
Row 6—B, * p5, p2 tog (st and following yo), p6, B; rep from *.

Repeat Rows 1–6.

Honeybee Pattern with Faggoting

Arrow Pattern

Contributed by Hildegard M. Elsner, Aldan, Pennsylvania

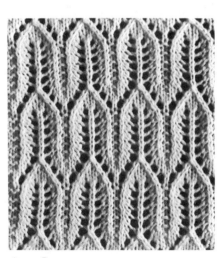

Multiple of 8 sts plus 1.

Row 1 (Wrong side) and all other wrong-side rows—Purl.
Row 2—K1, * yo, ssk, k3, k2 tog, yo, k1; rep from *.
Row 4—K2, * yo, ssk, k1, k2 tog, yo, k3; rep from *, end last repeat k2.
Row 6—P1, * k2, yo, sl 1—k2 tog—psso, yo, k2, p1; rep from *.
Rows 8, 10, 12, 14, and 16—P1, * ssk, (k1, yo) twice, k1, k2 tog, p1; rep from *.

Repeat Rows 1–16.

Arrow Pattern

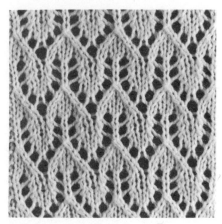

Small Arrow Pattern

VARIATION: *SMALL ARROW PATTERN*

Multiple of 6 sts plus 1.

Row 1 (Wrong side) and all other wrong-side rows—Purl.
Row 2—K3, * yo, ssk, k4; rep from *, end yo, ssk, k2.
Row 4—K1, * k2 tog, yo, k1, yo, ssk, k1; rep from *.
Row 6—K2 tog, yo, * k3, yo, sl 1—k2 tog—psso, yo; rep from *, end k3, yo, ssk.
Rows 8 and 10—K1, * yo, ssk, k1, k2 tog, yo, k1; rep from *.

Repeat Rows 1–10.

Chevron and Berry Stripe Pattern

Contributed by Hildegard M. Elsner, Aldan, Pennsylvania

In each repeat of this pattern there is one stitch decreased on Row 2; the original number of stitches is restored on Row 9.

Multiple of 17 sts plus 1.

Row 1 (Wrong side)—Purl.
Row 2—K1, * (yo, ssk, k4, k2 tog) twice, yo, k1; rep from *.
Row 3—P8, * k1, p15; rep from *, end k1, p8.
Row 4—K1, * yo, ssk, k3, k2 tog, yo, p1, yo, ssk, k3, k2 tog, yo, k1; rep from *.
Row 5—P7, * k3, p13; rep from *, end k3, p7.
Row 6—K1, * yo, ssk, k2, k2 tog, yo, p3, yo, ssk, k2, k2 tog, yo, k1; rep from *.
Row 7—P6, * k5, p11; rep from *, end k5, p6.
Row 8—K1, * yo, ssk, k1, k2 tog, yo, k1, yo, p3 tog, yo, k1, yo, ssk, k1, k2 tog, yo, k1; rep from *.
Row 9—P8, * knit into front and back of next st, p15; rep from *, end last repeat p8.
Row 10—K1, * yo, ssk, k2 tog, yo, k8, yo, ssk, k2 tog, yo, k1; rep from *.
Row 11—Purl.
Row 12—K1, * yo, sl 1—k2 tog—psso, yo, k10, yo, k3 tog, yo, k1; rep from *.

Repeat Rows 1–12.

Chevron and Berry Stripe Pattern

Dainty Chevron

This is an abbreviated Arrow Pattern without right-side purl stitches, and with only 2 "stationary rows" instead of 5. An even smaller version is done on a multiple of 6 sts plus 1, without the 6th row and with 2 less stitches on each of the other rows. It is a classic pattern with numerous variations—the most interesting of which is given as Daintier Chevron, below.

ABOVE: *Dainty Chevron*
BELOW: *Daintier Chevron*

Multiple of 8 sts plus 1.

Row 1 (Wrong side) and all other wrong-side rows—Purl.

Rows 2 and 4—K1, * ssk, (k1, yo) twice, k1, k2 tog, k1; rep from *.

Row 6—K1, * yo, ssk, k3, k2 tog, yo, k1; rep from *.

Row 8—K2, * yo, ssk, k1, k2 tog, yo, k3; rep from *, end last repeat k2.

Row 10—K3, * yo, sl 2—k1—p2sso, yo, k5; rep from *, end last repeat k3.

Repeat Rows 1–10.

VARIATION: *DAINTIER CHEVRON*

This beautiful mesh-like pattern shows how Dainty Chevron looks when it is done on circular needles, omitting all the wrong-side "plain" rows and working only the 5 pattern rows. It is an exceedingly delicate single-strand lace that is easy in round knitting. But to convert it to flat knitting necessitates doubling the pattern rows to make an even number of them, and working several wrong-side decreases, including the perhaps unfamiliar "sl 2—p1—p2sso" (see Glossary). This version of the pattern is instructive, however, and should be tried in flat knitting so that the knitter may better comprehend its construction, and that of similar patterns.

Multiple of 8 sts plus 1.

Row 1 (Right side)—K1, * ssk, (k1, yo) twice, k1, k2 tog, k1; rep from *.

Row 2—P1, * p2 tog, (p1, yo) twice, p1, p2 tog-b, p1; rep from *.

Row 3—K1, * yo, ssk, k3, k2 tog, yo, k1; rep from *.

Row 4—P2, * yo, p2 tog, p1, p2 tog-b, yo, p3; rep from *, end last repeat p2.

Row 5—K3, * yo, sl 2—k1—p2sso, yo, k5; rep from *, end last repeat k3.

Row 6—Repeat Row 2.

Row 7—Repeat Row 1.

Row 8—P1, * yo, p2 tog, p3, p2 tog-b, yo, p1; rep from *.

Row 9—K2, * yo, ssk, k1, k2 tog, yo, k3; rep from *, end last repeat k2.

Row 10—P3, * yo, sl 2—p1—p2sso, yo, p5; rep from *, end last repeat p3.

Repeat Rows 1–10.

Flame Chevron

This pattern, which comes from Mexico, is a variation of the Scroll Pattern. The curving lines of stitches form its chief adornment; the openwork is rather incidental. The same pattern will make a fascinatingly textured solid fabric if a closed "M1" is worked in place of each "yo".

Flame Chevron

Multiple of 7 sts plus 4.

Row 1 (Wrong side) and all other wrong-side rows—Purl.
Row 2—K3, * ssk, k5, yo; rep from *, end k1.
Row 4—K3, * ssk, k4, yo, k1; rep from *, end k1.
Row 6—K3, * ssk, k3, yo, k2; rep from *, end k1.
Row 8—K3, * ssk, k2, yo, k3; rep from *, end k1.
Row 10—K3, * ssk, k1, yo, k4; rep from *, end k1.
Row 12—K3, * ssk, yo, k5; rep from *, end k1.
Row 14—K1, * yo, k5, k2 tog; rep from *, end k3.
Row 16—K2, * yo, k4, k2 tog, k1; rep from *, end k2.
Row 18—K3, * yo, k3, k2 tog, k2; rep from *, end k1.
Row 20—K4, * yo, k2, k2 tog, k3; rep from *.
Row 22—K5, * yo, k1, k2 tog, k4; rep from *, end last repeat k3.
Row 24—K6, * yo, k2 tog, k5; rep from *, end last repeat k3.

Repeat Rows 1–24.

Pointed Chevron

Contributed by Lena Menegus, Belvidere, New Jersey

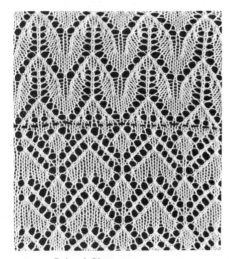

ABOVE: *Pointed Chevron*
BELOW: *Palm-Leaf Chevron*

Multiple of 10 sts plus 1.

Row 1 (Wrong side) and all other wrong-side rows—Purl.
Row 2—K1, * yo, ssk, k2 tog, yo, k1; rep from *.
Row 4—K2, * yo, ssk, k3, k2 tog, yo, k3; rep from *, end last repeat k2.
Row 6—K3, * yo, ssk, k1, k2 tog, yo, k5; rep from *, end last repeat k3.
Row 8—K4, * yo, sl 1—k2 tog—psso, yo, k7; rep from *, end last repeat k4.
Rows 10; 12, and 14—K1, * ssk, k2, yo, k1, yo, k2, k2 tog, k1; rep from *.

Repeat Rows 1–14.

Palm-Leaf Chevron

Contributed by Hildegard M. Elsner, Aldan, Pennsylvania

Multiple of 12 sts plus 1.

Row 1 (Wrong side) and all other wrong-side rows—Purl.
Row 2—K4, * k2 tog, yo, k1, yo, ssk, k7; rep from *, end last repeat k4.
Row 4—K3, * k2 tog, yo, k3, yo, ssk, k5; rep from *, end last repeat k3.
Row 6—K2, * (k2 tog, yo) twice, k1, (yo, ssk) twice, k3; rep from *, end last repeat k2.
Row 8—K1, * (k2 tog, yo) twice, k3, (yo, ssk) twice, k1; rep from *.
Row 10—K2 tog, * yo, k2 tog, yo, k5, yo, ssk, yo, sl 1—k2 tog—psso; rep from *, end last repeat ssk instead of sl 1—k2 tog—psso.
Row 12—K1, * k2 tog, yo, k1, yo, ssk, k1; rep from *.
Row 14—K2 tog, * yo, k3, yo, sl 1—k2 tog—psso; rep from *, end last repeat ssk instead of sl 1—k2 tog—psso.

Repeat Rows 1–14.

Pendants

Contributed by Dorothy Reade, Eugene, Oregon

Multiple of 14 sts plus 1.

Row 1 (Wrong side) and all other wrong-side rows—Purl.
Row 2 (Preparation row)—K1, * k2 tog, yo, k1-b, k1, k2 tog, yo, (k1-b, yo, ssk, k1) twice; rep from *.
Row 4—K1, * k2 tog, yo, k1, k2 tog, yo, k1-b, k1, k1-b, (yo, ssk, k1) twice; rep from *.
Row 6—K2 tog, * yo, k1-b, k2 tog, yo, k1-b, k3, k1-b, yo, ssk, k1-b, yo, sl 1—k2 tog—psso; rep from *, end last repeat ssk instead of sl 1—k2 tog—psso.
Row 8—K1, * (k1-b, k2 tog, yo) twice, (k1-b, yo, ssk) twice, k1-b, k1; rep from *.
Row 10—K1, * (k2 tog, yo, k1-b) twice, k1, (k1-b, yo, ssk) twice, k1; rep from *.
Row 12—K2 tog, * yo, k1-b, k2, yo, ssk, k1, k2 tog, yo, k2, k1-b, yo, sl 1—k2 tog—psso; rep from *, end last repeat ssk instead of sl 1—k2 tog—psso.
Row 14—K1, * k1-b, (yo, ssk, k1) twice, k2 tog, yo, k1, k2 tog, yo, k1-b, k1; rep from *.
Row 16—K1, * k2 tog, yo, k2, k1-b, yo, sl 1—k2 tog—psso, yo, k1-b, k2, yo, ssk, k1; rep from *.

Omitting preparation row, repeat Rows 3–16.

Pendants

Field of Wheat

In this beautiful fabric the "fern" motifs are gently waved left and right, each one being topped with a bobble. Grace, delicacy, and an intriguing texture are combined here in an easy-to work pattern.

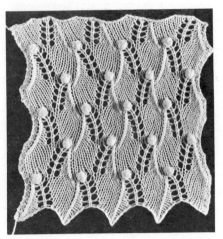

Field of Wheat

Multiple of 11 sts.

NOTE: Make Bobble (MB) as follows: (k1, yo, k1, yo, k1) in one stitch, making 5 sts from one; turn and k5, turn and p5, turn and k1, sl 1—k2 tog—psso, k1; turn and p3 tog, completing bobble. On the return row, purl into the *back* of each bobble stitch.

Row 1 (Right side)—* K1, MB, k2, yo, k1, yo, k4, k2 tog; rep from *.
Rows 2, 4, 6, 8, and 10—* P2 tog, p10; rep from *.
Row 3—* K5, yo, k1, yo, k3, k2 tog; rep from *.
Row 5—* K6, yo, k1, yo, k2, k2 tog; rep from *.
Row 7—* K7, (yo, k1) twice, k2 tog; rep from *.
Row 9—* K8, yo, k1, yo, k2 tog; rep from *.
Row 11—* Ssk, k4, yo, k1, yo, k2, MB, k1; rep from *.
Rows 12, 14, 16, 18, and 20—* P10, p2 tog-b; rep from *.
Row 13—* Ssk, k3, yo, k1, yo, k5; rep from *.
Row 15—* Ssk, k2, yo, k1, yo, k6; rep from *.
Row 17—* Ssk, (k1, yo) twice, k7; rep from *.
Row 19—* Ssk, yo, k1, yo, k8; rep from *.

Repeat Rows 1–20.

Ostrich Plumes

This interesting fabric is a Feather and Fan Stitch varied by a half-drop. The pattern has a rather complicated appearance because the stitch lines wave and curl into each other in a very graceful manner; but it is quite repetitive, and simple to work.

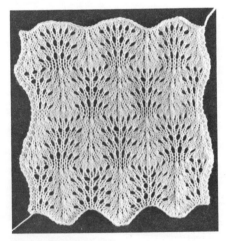

Ostrich Plumes

Multiple of 16 sts plus 1.

Row 1 (Wrong side) and all other wrong-side rows—Purl.
Rows 2, 6, 10, 14, 18, 22, 26, and 30—Knit.
Rows 4, 8, 12, and 16—(K1, yo) 3 times, * (ssk) twice, sl 2 knitwise—k1—p2sso, (k2 tog) twice, (yo, k1) 5 times, yo; rep from *, end (ssk) twice, sl 2 knitwise—k1—p2sso, (k2 tog) twice, (yo, k1) 3 times.
Rows 20, 24, 28, and 32—(K2 tog) 3 times, * (yo, k1) 5 times, yo, (ssk) twice, sl 2 knitwise—k1—p2sso, (k2 tog) twice; rep from *, end (yo, k1) 5 times, yo, (ssk) 3 times.

Repeat Rows 1–32.

Double Vine

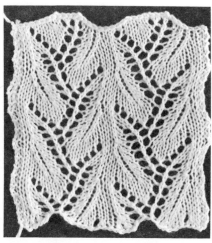

Multiple of 16 sts plus 1.

Row 1(Wrong side) and all other wrong-side rows—Purl.

Row 2—K1, * k3 tog, k1, (yo, k1-b) 3 times, yo, k1, (ssk) twice, k4; rep from *.

Row 4—K1, * ssk, k2, yo, k3, yo, k1-b, yo, k1, (ssk) twice, k3; rep from *.

Row 6—K1, * ssk, k1, yo, k5, yo, k1-b, yo, k1, (ssk) twice, k2; rep from *.

Row 8—K1, * ssk, yo, k3, k2 tog, k1, (yo, k1-b) twice, yo, k1, (ssk) twice, k1; rep from *.

Row 10—* K4, (k2 tog) twice, k1, (yo, k1-b) 3 times, yo, k1, sl 1—k2 tog—psso; rep from *, end k1.

Row 12—* K3, (k2 tog) twice, k1, yo, k1-b, yo, k3, yo, k2, k2 tog; rep from *, end k1.

Row 14—* K2, (k2 tog) twice, k1, yo, k1-b, yo, k5, yo, k1, k2 tog; rep from *, end k1.

Row 16—K1, * (k2 tog) twice, k1, (yo, k1-b) twice, yo, k1, ssk, k3, yo, k2 tog, k1; rep from *.

Repeat Rows 1–16.

Double Vine

Candlelight Pattern

The Candlelight Pattern has become confused, over the course of many decades, with the much simpler Fern Lace, which somewhat resembles it. Here is the original Candlelight, a unique pattern that deserves to retain its ancient form. One of its unusual qualities is the beauty of its reverse side, where the embossed "candle-flame" motifs appear in knit stitches against a background of purled openwork. If this side (given here in the even-numbered rows) is utilized as the right side, then the pattern can be said to be worked from its "wrong" side—a novel proceeding, indeed. In fact either side is lovely, and any knitter who enjoys working lace will find this pattern highly rewarding. In spite of its many rows, it cannot be called complicated, because its formation is easy to see and to learn.

Candlelight Pattern

Multiple of 20 sts plus 1.

Row 1 (Right side)—P6, * k2, ssk, yo, k1, yo, k2 tog, k2, p11; rep from *, end last repeat p6.

Row 2—K6, * p9, k11; rep from *, end last repeat k6.

Row 3—P6, * k1, k2 tog, yo, k3, yo, ssk, k1, p11; rep from *, end last repeat p6.

Row 4—Repeat Row 2.

Row 5—P2 tog, * p4, k2, yo, k2 tog, yo, k1, yo, ssk, yo, k2, p4, p3 tog; rep from *, end last repeat p2 tog.

Row 6—K5, * p11, k9; rep from *, end last repeat k5.

Row 7—P2 tog, * p3, k2, yo, k2 tog, (k1, yo) twice, k1, ssk, yo, k2, p3, p3 tog; rep from *, end last repeat p2 tog.

Row 8—K4, * p13, k7; rep from *, end last repeat k4.

Row 9—P2 tog, * p2, k2, yo, k2 tog, k2, yo, k1, yo, k2, ssk, yo, k2, p2, p3 tog; rep from *, end last repeat p2 tog.

Row 10—K3, * p15, k5; rep from *, end last repeat k3.

Row 11—P2 tog, * p1, k2, yo, k2 tog, k2, p1, yo, k1, yo, p1, k2, ssk, yo, k2, p1, p3 tog; rep from *, end last repeat p2 tog.

Row 12—K2, * p6, k1, p3, k1, p6, k3; rep from *, end last repeat k2.

Row 13—P2 tog, * k2, yo, k2 tog, k2, p2, yo, k1, yo, p2, k2, ssk, yo, k2, p3 tog; rep from *, end last repeat p2 tog.

Row 14—K1, * p6, k2, p3, k2, p6, k1; rep from *.

Row 15—K2 tog, * k1, yo, k2 tog, k2, p3, yo, k1, yo, p3, k2, ssk, yo, k1, sl 1—k2 tog—psso; rep from *, end last repeat ssk.

Row 16—P6, * k3, p3, k3, p11; rep from *, end last repeat p6.

Row 17—Ssk, * yo, k2 tog, k2, p4, yo, k1, yo, p4, k2, ssk, yo, sl 1—k2 tog—psso; rep from *, end last repeat k2 tog.

Row 18—P5, * k4, p3, k4, p9; rep from *, end last repeat p5.

Row 19—K1, * yo, k2 tog, k2, p11, k2, ssk, yo, k1; rep from *.

Row 20—P5, * k11, p9; rep from *, end last repeat p5.

Row 21—K2, * yo, ssk, k1, p11, k1, k2 tog, yo, k3; rep from *, end last repeat k2.

Row 22—Repeat Row 20.

Row 23—K1, * yo, ssk, yo, k2, p4, p3 tog, p4, k2, yo, k2 tog, yo, k1; rep from *.

Row 24—P6, * k9, p11; rep from *, end last repeat p6.

Row 25—K1, * yo, k1, ssk, yo, k2, p3, p3 tog, p3, k2, yo, k2 tog, k1, yo, k1; rep from *.

Row 26—P7, * k7, p13; rep from *, end last repeat p7.

Row 27—K1, * yo, k2, ssk, yo, k2, p2, p3 tog, p2, k2, yo, k2 tog, k2, yo, k1; rep from *.

Row 28—P8, * k5, p15; rep from *, end last repeat p8.

Row 29—K1, * yo, p1, k2, ssk, yo, k2, p1, p3 tog, p1, k2, yo, k2 tog, k2, p1, yo, k1; rep from *.

Row 30—P2, * k1, p6, k3, p6, k1, p3; rep from *, end last repeat p2.

Row 31—K1, * yo, p2, k2, ssk, yo, k2, p3 tog, k2, yo, k2 tog, k2, p2, yo, k1; rep from *.

Row 32—P2, * k2, p6, k1, p6, k2, p3; rep from *, end last repeat p2.

Row 33—K1, * yo, p3, k2, ssk, yo, k1, sl 1—k2 tog—psso, k1, yo, k2 tog, k2, p3, yo, k1; rep from *.

Row 34—P2, * k3, p11, k3, p3; rep from *, end last repeat p2.

Row 35—K1, * yo, p4, k2, ssk, yo, sl 1—k2 tog—psso, yo, k2 tog, k2, p4, yo, k1; rep from *.

Row 36—P2, * k4, p9, k4, p3; rep from *, end last repeat p2.

Repeat Rows 1–36.

Candlelight #2

A pattern as beautiful and popular as the old Candlelight is bound to have several variations. This one is perhaps even more lovely than the original. The unique touch here is that all the decreases are worked in opposition to the slant of the stitches—that is, in the reverse of the usual way—which gives softness to all the outlines, as real candlelight does too!

Candlelight # 2

Multiple of 20 sts plus 1.

Row 1 (Wrong side) and all other wrong-side rows—Purl.

Row 2—K1, * yo, k2 tog, k2, yo, k2 tog, k7, ssk, yo, k2, ssk, yo, k1; rep from *.

Row 4—K1, * yo, k1, k2 tog, k2, yo, k2 tog, k5, ssk, yo, k2, ssk, k1, yo, k1; rep from *.

Row 6—K1, * yo, k2, k2 tog, k2, yo, k2 tog, k3, ssk, yo, k2, ssk, k2, yo, k1; rep from *.

Row 8—K1, * yo, k3, k2 tog, k2, yo, k2 tog, k1, ssk, yo, k2, ssk, k3, yo, k1; rep from *.

Row 10—K1, * yo, k4, k2 tog, k2, yo, sl 1—k2 tog—psso, yo, k2, ssk, k4, yo, k1; rep from *.

Row 12—K1, * yo, k1, yo, ssk, k2, k2 tog, k5, ssk, k2, k2 tog, (yo, k1) twice; rep from *.

Row 14—K1, * yo, k1, k2 tog, yo, k3, k2 tog, k3, ssk, k3, yo, ssk, k1, yo, k1; rep from *.

Row 16—K1, * yo, k2, k2 tog, yo, k3, k2 tog, k1, ssk, k3, yo, ssk, k2, yo, k1; rep from *.

Row 18—K1, * yo, k3, k2 tog, yo, k3, sl 1—k2 tog—psso, k3, yo, ssk, k3, yo, k1; rep from *.

Row 20—K4, * ssk, yo, k2, ssk, yo, k1, yo, k2 tog, k2, yo, k2 tog, k7; rep from *, end last repeat k4.

Row 22—K3, * ssk, yo, k2, ssk, (k1, yo) twice, k1, k2 tog, k2, yo, k2 tog, k5; rep from *, end last repeat k3.

Row 24—K2, * ssk, yo, k2, ssk, k2, yo, k1, yo, k2, k2 tog, k2, yo, k2 tog, k3; rep from *, end last repeat k2.

Row 26—K1, * ssk, yo, k2, ssk, k3, yo, k1, yo, k3, k2 tog, k2, yo, k2 tog, k1; rep from *.

Row 28—Ssk, * yo, k2, ssk, k4, yo, k1, yo, k4, k2 tog, k2, yo, sl 1—k2 tog—psso; rep from *, end last repeat k2 tog instead of sl 1—k2 tog—psso.

Row 30—K3, * ssk, k2, k2 tog, (yo, k1) 3 times, yo, ssk, k2, k2 tog, k5; rep from *, end last repeat k3.

Row 32—K2, * ssk, k3, yo, ssk, (k1, yo) twice, k1, k2 tog, yo, k3, k2 tog, k3; rep from *, end last repeat k2.

Row 34—K1, * ssk, k3, yo, ssk, k2, yo, k1, yo, k2, k2 tog, yo, k3, k2 tog, k1; rep from *.

Row 36—Ssk, * k3, yo, ssk, k3, yo, k1, yo, k3, k2 tog, yo, k3, sl 1—k2 tog—psso; rep from *, end last repeat k2 tog instead of sl 1—k2 tog—psso.

Repeat Rows 1–36.

Porcupine Stitch

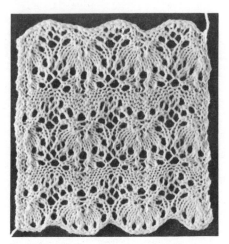

Porcupine Stitch

This unusual pattern is mid-Victorian or earlier, and was used for shawls, scarves, and those unique articles of headgear that our grandmothers called "clouds". Having an odd number of rows, the pattern is therefore reversible. The arrangement of openwork seems rather haphazard during the first few repeats, but a definite design appears after the 9 rows have been worked several times over.

Multiple of 12 sts plus 4.

Row 1—K2, * yo, k2 tog; rep from * to last 2 sts, end k2.

Rows 2 and 4—K2, purl to last 2 sts, end k2.

Row 3—Knit.

Rows 5 and 8—K2, * sl 1—k2 tog—psso, k4, yo, k1, yo, k4; rep from *, end k2.

Rows 6, 7, and 9—K2, * p3 tog, p4, yo, p1, yo, p4; rep from *, end k2.

Repeat Rows 1–9.

Strawberry Pattern

Strawberry Pattern

Unless it is well stretched, this fabric will close up into a scale-like texture, with the openwork largely hidden. In this form it is useful for garments where a not-too-lacy look is wanted. The knitter should experiment with it, because it will give different kinds of effects with different yarns and needle sizes.

Multiple of 12 sts plus 1.

Row 1 (Right side)—Ssk, * k4, yo, k1, yo, k4, sl 1—k2 tog—psso; rep from *, end last repeat ssk instead of sl 1—k2 tog—psso.

Row 2—P2 tog, * (p3, yo) twice, p3, p3 tog; rep from *, end last repeat p2 tog instead of p3 tog.

Row 3—Ssk, * k2, yo, k5, yo, k2, sl 1—k2 tog—psso; rep from *, end last repeat ssk instead of sl 1—k2 tog—psso.

Row 4—P2 tog, * p1, yo, p7, yo, p1, p3 tog; rep from *, end last repeat p2 tog instead of p3 tog.

Row 5—Ssk, * yo, k9, yo, sl 1—k2 tog—psso; rep from *, end last repeat ssk instead of sl 1—k2 tog—psso.

Row 6—P1, * yo, p4, p3 tog, p4, yo, p1; rep from *.

Row 7—K2, * yo, k3, sl 1—k2 tog—psso, k3, yo, k3; rep from *, end last repeat k2.

Row 8—P3, * yo, p2, p3 tog, p2, yo, p5; rep from *, end last repeat p3.

Row 9—K4, * yo, k1, sl 1—k2 tog—psso, k1, yo, k7; rep from *, end last repeat k4.

Row 10—P5, * yo, p3 tog, yo, p9; rep from *, end last repeat p5.

Repeat Rows 1–10.

Lace Puff

Contributed by Lena Menegus, Belvidere, New Jersey

Though very similar to the Strawberry Pattern in structure, this pattern benefits by being left *un*stretched. Then the purled puffs at the base of each motif will lift forward to make a deep, soft, "pebbly" texture that is attractive in fancy blouses, sweaters and stoles.

Multiple of 12 sts plus 2.

Row 1 (Right side)—K1, * ssk, k3, yo, p2, yo, k3, k2 tog; rep from *, end k1.

Row 2—K1, * p2 tog, p2, yo, k4, yo, p2, p2 tog-b; rep from *, end k1.

Row 3—K1, * ssk, k1, yo, p6, yo, k1, k2 tog; rep from *, end k1.

Row 4—K1, * p2 tog, yo, k8, yo, p2 tog-b; rep from *, end k1.

Row 5—K1, * p1, yo, k3, k2 tog, ssk, k3, yo, p1; rep from *, end k1.

Row 6—K1, * k2, yo, p2, p2 tog-b, p2 tog, p2, yo, k2; rep from *, end k1.

Row 7—K1, * p3, yo, k1, k2 tog, ssk, k1, yo, p3; rep from *, end k1.

Row 8—K1, * k4, yo, p2 tog-b, p2 tog, yo, k4; rep from *, end k1.

Repeat Rows 1–8.

Lace Puff

Milanese Lace

While this lovely lace is not exclusively Italian, this particular version does come from Milan. It is both graceful and interesting. From the strongly diagonal "lie" of the stitches, one would think that the pattern might form a bias fabric; yet it does not. It is appropriate for circular knitting, where the diagonals will form unbroken spirals.

Milanese Lace

Multiple of 6 sts plus 2.

Row 1 (Right side)—K1, * k4, k2 tog, yo; rep from *, end k1.
Row 2—P1, * yo, p1, p2 tog, p3; rep from *, end p1.
Row 3—K1, * k2, k2 tog, k2, yo; rep from *, end k1.
Row 4—P1, * yo, p3, p2 tog, p1; rep from *, end p1.
Row 5—K1, * k2 tog, k4, yo; rep from *, end k1.
Row 6—P2, * p4, yo, p2 tog; rep from *.
Row 7—K1, * k1, yo, k3, k2 tog; rep from *, end k1.
Row 8—P1, * p2 tog, p2, yo, p2; rep from *, end p1.
Row 9—K1, * k3, yo, k1, k2 tog; rep from *, end k1.
Row 10—P1, * p2 tog, yo, p4; rep from *, end p1.

Repeat Rows 1–10.

Lace Ribbon Stitch

Lace Ribbon Stitch

Contributed by Pauline Balbes, Hollywood, California

Multiple of 10 sts plus 5.

Row 1 (Right side)—K1, * ssk, yo, k5, k2 tog, yo, k1; rep from *, end ssk, yo, k2.
Row 2—P1, * p2 tog, yo, p2, yo, p1, p2 tog, p3; rep from *, end p2 tog, yo, p2.
Row 3—K1, * ssk, yo, k3, k2 tog, k2, yo, k1; rep from *, end ssk, yo, k2.
Row 4—P1, * p2 tog, yo, p2, yo, p3, p2 tog, p1; rep from *, end p2 tog, yo, p2.
Row 5—K1, * ssk, yo, k2, ssk, k3, yo, k1; rep from *, end ssk, yo, k2.
Row 6—P1, * p2 tog, yo, p2, yo, p3, p2 tog-b, p1; rep from *, end p2 tog, yo, p2.
Row 7—K1, * ssk, yo, k2, yo, ssk, k4; rep from *, end ssk, yo, k2.
Row 8—P1, * p2 tog, yo, p4, p2 tog-b, p1, yo, p1; rep from *, end p2 tog, yo, p2.
Row 9—K1, * ssk, (yo, k2) twice, ssk, k2; rep from *, end ssk, yo, k2.
Row 10—P1, * p2 tog, yo, p2, p2 tog-b, p3, yo, p1; rep from *, end p2 tog, yo, p2.
Row 11—K1, * ssk, yo, k2, yo, k3, k2 tog, k1; rep from *, end ssk, yo, k2.
Row 12—P1, * p2 tog, yo, p2, p2 tog, p3, yo, p1; rep from *, end p2 tog, yo, p2.

Repeat Rows 1–12.

Chinese Lace

Contributed by Marjorie B. Bialkowski, Richmond, Virginia

Multiple of 16 sts plus 7.

NOTES: "A" portion of pattern (7 sts)—P2, yo, sl 1—k2 tog—psso, yo, p2.

"B" portion of pattern (same 7 sts, wrong side)—K2, p3, k2.

"C" portion of pattern (same 7 sts)—P2, yo, k3 tog, yo, p2.

Row 1 (Right side)—A, * ssk, k7, yo, A; rep from *.
Row 2—B, * p1, yo, p6, p2 tog-b, B; rep from *.
Row 3—C, * ssk, k5, yo, k2, C; rep from *.
Row 4—B, * p3, yo, p4, p2 tog-b, B; rep from *.
Row 5—A, * k3, k2 tog, k4, yo, A; rep from *.
Row 6—B, * p1, yo, p4, p2 tog, p2, B; rep from *.
Row 7—C, * k1, k2 tog, k4, yo, k2, C; rep from *.
Row 8—B, * p3, yo, p4, p2 tog, B; rep from *.
Row 9—A, * yo, k3, k2 tog, k4, A; rep from *.
Row 10—B, * p4, p2 tog, p2, yo, p1, B; rep from *.
Row 11—C, * k2, yo, k1, k2 tog, k4, C; rep from *.
Row 12—B, * p4, p2 tog, yo, p3, B; rep from *.
Row 13—A, * yo, k7, k2 tog, A; rep from *.
Row 14—B, * p2 tog, p6, yo, p1, B; rep from *.
Row 15—C, * k2, yo, k5, k2 tog, C; rep from *.
Row 16—B, * p2 tog, p4, yo, p3, B; rep from *.
Row 17—A, * yo, k4, ssk, k3, A; rep from *.
Row 18—B, * p2, p2 tog-b, p4, yo, p1, B; rep from *.
Row 19—C, * k2, yo, k4, ssk, k1, C; rep from *.
Row 20—B, * p2 tog-b, p4, yo, p3, B; rep from *.
Row 21—A, * k4, ssk, k3, yo, A; rep from *.
Row 22—B, * p1, yo, p2, p2 tog-b, p4, B; rep from *.
Row 23—C, * k4, ssk, k1, yo, k2, C; rep from *.
Row 24—B, * p3, yo, p2 tog-b, p4, B; rep from *.

Repeat Rows 1–24.

Chinese Lace

Japanese Feather

Another pretty pattern from the Far East showing a side-to-side wave that pulls stitches right and left. The side edges are gracefully scalloped, which will create wavy front bands if the pattern is used for a jacket or cardigan. This effect is attractive; buttonholes can be worked into each scallop if desired. If front and back pieces of the garment are worked separately, the scallops will fit into each other to make a wavy side seam. The pattern is ideal for circular knitting; in this case there are no side edges showing.

Japanese Feather

Multiple of 11 sts plus 1.

Row 1 (Wrong side) and all other wrong-side rows—K1, * p10, k1; rep from *.

Rows 2 and 4—P1, * k10, p1; rep from *.

Rows 6, 10, and 14—P1, * k1, (yo, k1) 3 times, (ssk) 3 times, p1; rep from *.

Rows 8 and 12—P1, * k1, (k1, yo) 3 times, (ssk) 3 times, p1; rep from *.

Rows 16 and 18—Repeat Rows 2 and 4.

Rows 20, 24, and 28—P1, * (k2 tog) 3 times, (k1, yo) 3 times, k1, p1; rep from *.

Rows 22 and 26—P1, * (k2 tog) 3 times, (yo, k1) 3 times, k1, p1; rep from *.

Repeat Rows 1–28.

Trellis and Pear

Very often this pattern is given with the decreases worked in opposition to the pattern lines, so that the trellis is "wrapped" and fuzzy-looking rather than sharp. Often, too, it is worked in a single panel; but the half-drop arrangement here is preferable because the six-stitch increase will spread out and destroy the beauty of the trellis unless the slack is taken up by an adjoining panel. This version is the most graceful and striking, therefore, of several possible ones. It makes a lovely mesh for fancy sweaters, blouses, lace mats, luncheon cloths and stockings.

Trellis and Pear

Multiple of 22 sts plus 1.

Row 1 (Wrong side) and all other wrong-side rows—Purl.

Row 2—Ssk, * (yo, ssk) twice, k3, (k2 tog, yo) twice, sl 2—k1—p2sso, yo, ssk, yo, (k1, yo, k1, yo, k1, yo, k1) in next st, making 7 sts from 1; yo, k2 tog, yo, sl 2—k1—p2sso; rep from *, end last repeat k2 tog.

Row 4—Ssk, * (yo, ssk) twice, k1, (k2 tog, yo) twice, sl 2—k1—p2sso, yo, ssk, yo, k1, p5, k1, yo, k2 tog, yo, sl 2—k1—p2sso; rep from *, end last repeat k2 tog.

Row 6—Ssk, * yo, ssk, yo, sl 1—k2 tog—psso, yo, k2 tog, yo, sl 2—k1—p2sso, yo, ssk, yo, k1, p5, k1, yo, k2 tog, yo, sl 2—k1—p2sso; rep from *, end last repeat k2 tog.

Row 8—Ssk, * yo, ssk, yo, (k1, yo, k1, yo, k1, yo, k1) in next st, yo, k2 tog, yo, sl 2—k1—p2sso, (yo, ssk) twice, k3, (k2 tog, yo) twice, sl 2—k1—p2sso; rep from *, end last repeat k2 tog.

Row 10—Ssk, * yo, ssk, yo, k1, p5, k1, yo, k2 tog, yo, sl 2—k1—p2sso, (yo, ssk) twice, k1, (k2 tog, yo) twice, sl 2—k1—p2sso; rep from *, end last repeat k2 tog.

Row 12—Ssk, * yo, ssk, yo, k1, p5, k1, yo, k2 tog, yo, sl 2—k1—p2sso, yo, ssk, yo, sl 1—k2 tog—psso, yo, k2 tog, yo, sl 2—k1—p2sso; rep from *, end last repeat k2 tog.

Repeat Rows 1–12.

English Lace

Contributed by Georgia Berry, Chicago, Illinois

Multiple of 8 sts plus 3.

Row 1 (Wrong side)—Purl.

Row 2—K4, * yo, sl 1—k2 tog—psso, yo, k5; rep from *, end last repeat k4.

Row 3—P3, * yo, p2 tog, p1, p2 tog-b, yo, p3; rep from *.

Row 4—K2, * yo, ssk, yo, sl 1—k2 tog—psso, yo, k2 tog, yo, k1; rep from *, end k1.

Rows 5, 6, and 7—Repeat Rows 3, 2, and 1.

Row 8—K1, k2 tog, * yo, k5, yo, sl 1—k2 tog—psso; rep from *, end yo, k5, yo, ssk, k1.

Row 9—P2, * p2 tog-b, yo, p3, yo, p2 tog, p1; rep from *, end p1.

Row 10—K1, k2 tog, * yo, k2 tog, yo, k1, yo, ssk, yo, sl 1—k2 tog—psso; rep from *, end yo, k2 tog, yo, k1, (yo, ssk) twice, k1.

Rows 11 and 12—Repeat Rows 9 and 8.

Repeat Rows 1–12.

English Lace

Rosebud Mesh

This pattern does not maintain the same stitch count on every row; but Rows 6 and 8 will have the original number.

Multiple of 10 sts plus 1.

Row 1 (Wrong side) and all other wrong-side rows—Purl.

Row 2—K2 tog, * yo, k3, yo, knit into front and back of next st, yo, k3, yo, sl 1—k2 tog—psso; rep from *, end last repeat ssk instead of sl 1—k2 tog—psso.

Row 4—Ssk, * yo, sl 2—k1—p2sso, yo, k2 tog, yo, ssk, (yo, sl 2—k1—p2sso) twice; rep from *, end last repeat k2 tog instead of the second sl 2—k1—p2sso.

Row 6—K2, * k2 tog, yo, k3, yo, ssk, k3; rep from *, end last repeat k2.

Row 8—K1, * k2 tog, yo, k1-b, yo, sl 1—k2 tog—psso, yo, k1-b, yo, ssk, k1; rep from *.

Repeat Rows 1–8.

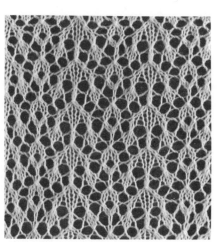

Rosebud Mesh

Starlight Lace

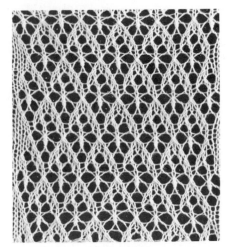

Starlight Lace

This deceptively simple-looking lace is very cleverly made. Two different kinds of double decrease on Rows 6 and 14 sharply reduce the number of stitches, thus widening the motifs at these points to enhance the starlike shapes in the openwork. The original number of stitches is restored on Rows 8 and 16. Notice, also, the crossed knit stitches, which help to sharpen the pattern. It is a very fine lace indeed, extremely delicate and graceful.

Multiple of 6 sts plus 5.

Row 1 (Wrong side) and all other wrong-side rows—Purl.
Row 2—K2, * yo, ssk, k1, yo, ssk, k1-b; rep from *, end yo, ssk, k1.
Row 4—K3, * k2 tog, yo, k1-b, yo, ssk, k1-b; rep from *, end k2.
Row 6—K2, k2 tog, * yo, sl 2—k1—p2sso, yo, sl 1—k2 tog—psso; rep from *, end yo, sl 2—k1—p2sso, yo, ssk, k2.
Row 8—K3, * k1-b, yo, k1, yo, k1-b, k1; rep from *, end k2.
Row 10—K2, * yo, ssk, k1-b, yo, ssk, k1; rep from *, end yo, ssk, k1.
Row 12—* K2 tog, yo, k1-b, yo, ssk, k1-b; rep from *, end k2 tog, yo, k1-b, yo, ssk.
Row 14—K1, * yo, sl 2—k1—p2sso, yo, sl 1—k2 tog—psso; rep from *, end yo, sl 2—k1—p2sso, yo, k1.
Row 16—K1, k1-b, * k1, yo, k1-b, k1, k1-b, yo; rep from *, end k1, k1-b, k1.

Repeat Rows 1–16.

Gothic Leaf Pattern

Gothic Leaf Pattern

This is a very beautiful wide-motif lace dating from the early 19th century. In it can be traced the various "leaf" and "diamond" themes combined with lace trellis, but the arrangement here is definitely unusual.

Multiple of 16 sts plus 1.

Row 1(Wrong side) and all other wrong-side rows—Purl.
Row 2—K1, * ssk, k3, yo, k2 tog, yo, k1, yo, ssk, yo, k3, k2 tog, k1; rep from *.
Row 4—K1, * ssk, k2, yo, k2 tog, yo, k3, yo, ssk, yo, k2, k2 tog, k1; rep from *.
Row 6—K1, * ssk, k1, yo, k2 tog, yo, k5, yo, ssk, yo, k1, k2 tog, k1; rep from *.
Row 8—K1, * ssk, yo, k2 tog, yo, k7, yo, ssk, yo, k2 tog, k1; rep from *.

Row 10—K1, * (ssk, yo) twice, k7, (yo, k2 tog) twice, k1; rep from *.

Row 12—K1, * yo, ssk, yo, k3, k2 tog, k1, ssk, k3, yo, k2 tog, yo, k1; rep from *.

Row 14—K2, * yo, ssk, yo, k2, k2 tog, k1, ssk, k2, yo, k2 tog, yo, k3; rep from * , end last repeat k2.

Row 16—K3, * yo, ssk, yo, k1, k2 tog, k1, ssk, k1, yo, k2 tog, yo, k5; rep from *, end last repeat k3.

Row 18—K4, * yo, ssk, yo, k2 tog, k1, ssk, yo, k2 tog, yo, k7; rep from *, end last repeat k4.

Row 20—K4, * (yo, k2 tog) twice, k1, (ssk, yo) twice, k7; rep from *, end last repeat k4.

Repeat Rows 1–20.

Oriel Pattern

Here is another of the very old and exquisitely beautiful lace patterns that have been unjustly forgotten within the past six or seven decades. This one is never seen today, because hardly anyone knows it. But it is very lovely, and easy to work as well, and therefore richly deserves to be resurrected from the yellowed old page upon which it was found.

Oriel Pattern

Multiple of 12 sts plus 1.

Rows 1, 3, and 5 (Right side)—P1, * ssk, k3, yo, p1, yo, k3, k2 tog, p1; rep from *.

Rows 2, 4, 6, and 8—K1, * p5, k1; rep from *.

Row 7—P1, * yo, k3, k2 tog, p1, ssk, k3, yo, p1; rep from *.

Row 9—P2, * yo, k2, k2 tog, p1, ssk, k2, yo, p3; rep from *, end last repeat p2.

Row 10—K2, * p4, k1, p4, k3; rep from *, end last repeat k2.

Row 11—P3, * yo, k1, k2 tog, p1, ssk, k1, yo, p5; rep from *, end last repeat p3.

Row 12—K3, * p3, k1, p3, k5; rep from *, end last repeat k3.

Row 13—P4, * yo, k2 tog, p1, ssk, yo, p7; rep from *, end last repeat p4.

Row 14—K4, * p2, k1, p2, k7; rep from *, end last repeat k4.

Rows 15, 17, and 19—Repeat Row 7.

Rows 16, 18, 20, and 22—Repeat second row.

Row 21—Repeat first row.

Row 23—P1, * ssk, k2, yo, p3, yo, k2, k2 tog, p1; rep from *.

Row 24—K1, * p4, k3, p4, k1; rep from *.

Row 25—P1, * ssk, k1, yo, p5, yo, k1, k2 tog, p1; rep from *.

Row 26—K1, * p3, k5, p3, k1; rep from *.

Row 27—P1, * ssk, yo, p7, yo, k2 tog, p1; rep from *.

Row 28—K1, * p2, k7, p2, k1; rep from *.

Repeat Rows 1–28.

Thistle Leaf Pattern

This is a very beautiful Victorian lace.

Multiple of 10 sts plus 1.

Row 1 (Wrong side) and all other wrong-side rows—Purl.

Row 2—(Ssk) twice, * (yo, k1) 3 times, yo, k2 tog, sl 1—k2 tog—psso, ssk; rep from *, end (yo, k1) 3 times yo, (k2 tog) twice.

Row 4—Ssk, * k3, yo, k1, yo, k3, sl 1—k2 tog—psso; rep from *, end k3, yo, k1, yo, k3, k2 tog.

Row 6—Ssk, * k2, yo, k3, yo, k2, sl 1—k2 tog—psso; rep from *, end k2, yo, k3, yo, k2, k2 tog.

Row 8—Ssk, * k1, yo, k5, yo, k1, sl 1—k2 tog—psso; rep from *, end k1, yo, k5, yo, k1, k2 tog.

Row 10—Ssk, * yo, k1, yo, ssk, k1, k2 tog, yo, k1, yo, sl 1—k2 tog—psso; rep from *, end last repeat k2 tog instead of sl 1—k2 tog—psso.

Row 12—Ssk, * yo, k2, yo, sl 1—k2 tog—psso; rep from *, end yo, k2, yo, k2 tog.

Row 14—K1, * yo, k3, sl 1—k2 tog—psso, k3, yo, k1; rep from *.

Row 16—K1, * yo, k1, yo, k2 tog, sl 1—k2 tog—psso, ssk, (yo, k1) twice; rep from *.

Row 18—Repeat Row 14.

Row 20—K2, * yo, k2, sl 1—k2 tog—psso, k2, yo, k3; rep from *, end last repeat k2.

Row 22—K3, * yo, k1, sl 1—k2 tog—psso, k1, yo, k5; rep from *, end last repeat k3.

Row 24—K1, * k2 tog, yo, k1, yo, sl 1—k2 tog—psso, yo, k1, yo, ssk, k1; rep from *.

Row 26—Repeat Row 12.

Row 28—Repeat Row 4.

Repeat Rows 1–28.

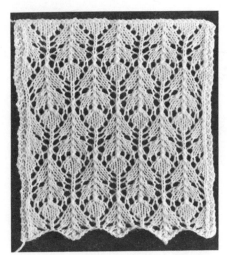

Thistle Leaf Pattern

Viennese Horseshoe

This lovely pattern is part of the great Viennese tradition of lace knitting. Its lines are crisp and clear, suitable for any type of lace work.

Multiple of 20 sts plus 2.

Row 1 (Wrong side) and all other wrong-side rows—Purl, always working (k1, p1) into each double yo of a previous row.

Row 2—K1, yo, * ssk, k2, yo, ssk, k1, yo, k2 tog, p2, ssk, yo, k1, k2 tog, yo, k2, k2 tog, (yo) twice; rep from *, end last repeat yo, k1 instead of (yo) twice.

Viennese Horseshoe

Row 4—P2, * (yo, ssk, k2) twice, p2, (k2, k2 tog, yo) twice, p2; rep from *.

Row 6—P2, * k1, yo, ssk, k2, yo, ssk, k1, p2, k1, k2 tog, yo, k2, k2 tog, yo, k1, p2; rep from *.

Row 8—P2, * ssk, (yo) twice, ssk, k2, yo, ssk, p2, k2 tog, yo, k2, k2 tog, (yo) twice, k2 tog, p2; rep from *.

Row 10—P2, * ssk, (yo) twice, k2 tog, k3, yo, ssk, k2 tog, yo, k3, ssk, (yo) twice, k2 tog, p2; rep from *.

Row 12—P2, * ssk, (yo) twice, k2 tog, k1, k2 tog, yo, k4, yo, ssk, k1, ssk, (yo) twice, k2 tog, p2; rep from *.

Row 14—P2, * ssk, (yo) twice, (k2 tog) twice, yo, k6, yo, (ssk) twice, (yo) twice, k2 tog, p2; rep from *.

Row 16—P2, * ssk, yo, k1, k2 tog, yo, k2, k2 tog, (yo) twice, ssk, k2, yo, ssk, k1, yo, k2 tog, p2; rep from *.

Row 18—P2, * (k2, k2 tog, yo) twice, p2, (yo, ssk, k2) twice, p2; rep from *.

Row 20—P2, * k1, k2 tog, yo, k2, k2 tog, yo, k1, p2, k1, yo, ssk, k2, yo, ssk, k1, p2; rep from *.

Row 22—P2, * k2 tog, yo, k2, k2 tog, (yo) twice, k2 tog, p2, ssk, (yo) twice, ssk, k2, yo, ssk, p2; rep from *.

Row 24—K1, * k2 tog, yo, k3, ssk, (yo) twice, k2 tog, p2, ssk, (yo) twice, k2 tog, k3, yo, ssk; rep from *, end k1.

Row 26—K3, * yo, ssk, k1, ssk, (yo) twice, k2 tog, p2, ssk, (yo) twice, k2 tog, k1, k2 tog, yo, k4; rep from *, end last repeat k3.

Row 28—K4, * yo, (ssk) twice, (yo) twice, k2 tog, p2, ssk, (yo) twice, (k2 tog) twice, yo, k6; rep from *, end last repeat k4.

Repeat Rows 1–28.

Bell Lace

Contributed by Bernice Haedike, Oak Park, Illinois

Turn-of-the-century elegance distinguishes this handsome lace, which is ornate yet easy to work. The pattern alternates with a precise half-drop, each portion consisting of 14 rows. The number of stitches does not remain the same on every row, but an accurate count may be taken on Rows 12, 14, 26, or 28.

Multiple of 18 sts plus 1.

Row 1 (Right side)—K1, * (p2, k1) twice, yo, k2 tog, yo, k1, yo, ssk, yo, (k1, p2) twice, k1; rep from *.

Row 2—* (P1, k2) twice, p9, k2, p1, k2; rep from *, end p1.

Row 3—K1, * (p2, k1) twice, yo, k2 tog, yo, k3, yo, ssk, yo, (k1, p2) twice, k1; rep from *.

Row 4—* (P1, k2) twice, p11, k2, p1, k2; rep from *, end p1.

Row 5—K1, * (p2 tog, k1) twice, yo, k2 tog, yo, ssk, k1, k2 tog, yo, ssk, yo, (k1, p2 tog) twice, k1; rep from *.

Row 6—* (P1, k1) twice, p11, k1, p1, k1; rep from *, end p1.

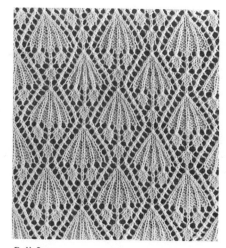

Bell Lace

Row 7—K1, * (p1, k1) twice, yo, k2 tog, yo, k1-b, yo, sl 1—k2 tog—psso, yo, k1-b, yo, ssk, yo, (k1, p1) twice, k1; rep from *.

Row 8—* (P1, k1) twice, p13, k1, p1, k1; rep from *, end p1.

Row 9—K1, * (k2 tog) twice, yo, k2 tog, yo, k3, yo, k1, yo, k3, yo, ssk, yo, (ssk) twice, k1; rep from *.

Rows 10, 12, and 14—Purl.

Row 11—K1, * (k2 tog, yo) twice, ssk, k1, k2 tog, yo, k1, yo, ssk, k1, k2 tog, (yo, ssk) twice, k1; rep from *.

Row 13—K2 tog, * yo, k2 tog, yo, k1-b, yo, sl 1—k2 tog—psso, yo, k3, yo, sl 1—k2 tog—psso, yo, k1-b, yo, ssk, yo, sl 1—k2 tog—psso; rep from *, end last repeat ssk instead of sl 1—k2 tog—psso.

Row 15—K1, * yo, ssk, yo, (k1, p2) 4 times, k1, yo, k2 tog, yo, k1; rep from *.

Row 16—P5, * (k2, p1) 3 times, k2, p9; rep from *, end last repeat p5.

Row 17—K2, * yo, ssk, yo, (k1, p2) 4 times, k1, yo, k2 tog, yo, k3; rep from *, end last repeat k2.

Row 18—P6, * (k2, p1) 3 times, k2, p11; rep from *, end last repeat p6.

Row 19—K1, * k2 tog, yo, ssk, yo, (k1, p2 tog) 4 times, k1, yo, k2 tog, yo, ssk, k1; rep from *.

Row 20—P6, *(k1, p1) 3 times, k1, p11; rep from *, end last repeat p6.

Row 21—K2 tog, * yo, k1-b, yo, ssk, yo, (k1, p1) 4 times, k1, yo, k2 tog, yo, k1-b, yo, sl 1—k2 tog—psso; rep from *, end last repeat ssk instead of sl 1—k2 tog—psso.

Row 22—P7, * (k1, p1) 3 times, k1, p13; rep from *, end last repeat p7.

Row 23—K1, * yo, k3, yo, ssk, yo, (ssk) twice, k1, (k2 tog) twice, yo, k2 tog, yo, k3, yo, k1; rep from *.

Rows 24 and 26—Purl.

Row 25—K1, * yo, ssk, k1, k2 tog, (yo, ssk) twice, k1, (k2 tog, yo) twice, ssk, k1, k2 tog, yo, k1; rep from *.

Row 27—K2, * yo, sl 1—k2 tog—psso, yo, k1-b, yo, ssk, yo, sl 1—k2 tog—psso, yo, k2 tog, yo, k1-b, yo, sl 1—k2 tog—psso, yo, k3; rep from *, end last repeat k2.

Row 28—Purl.

Repeat Rows 1–28.

Spade Pattern

Spade Pattern

This lovely 19th-century lace is worked with a slightly un-usual twist; 4 increases are made on each right-side row in each repeat, but only 2 decreases. The two extra stitches are removed by each subsequent wrong-side row.

Multiple of 18 sts plus 1.

Row 1 (Right side)—K2, * yo, k1, yo, ssk, k9, k2 tog, yo, k1, yo, k3; rep from *, end last repeat k2.

Row 2—P5, * p2 tog, p7, p2 tog-b, p9; rep from *, end last repeat p5.

Row 3—K2, * yo, k3, yo, ssk, k5, k2 tog, (yo, k3) twice; rep from *, end last repeat k2.

Row 4—P7, * p2 tog, p3, p2 tog-b, p13; rep from *, end last repeat p7.

Row 5—K2, * yo, k5, yo, ssk, k1, k2 tog, yo, k5, yo, k3; rep from *, end last repeat k2.

Row 6—P9, * p3 tog, p17; rep from *, end last repeat p9.

Row 7—K5, * k2 tog, yo, k1, yo, k3, yo, k1, yo, ssk, k9; rep from *, end last repeat k5.

Row 8—P4, * p2 tog-b, p9, p2 tog, p7; rep from *, end last repeat p4.

Row 9—K3, * k2 tog, (yo, k3) 3 times, yo, ssk, k5; rep from *, end last repeat k3.

Row 10—P2, * p2 tog-b, p13, p2 tog, p3; rep from *, end last repeat p2.

Row 11—K1, * k2 tog, yo, k5, yo, k3, yo, k5, yo, ssk, k1; rep from *.

Row 12—P2 tog, * p17, p3 tog; rep from *, end last repeat p2 tog instead of p3 tog.

Repeat Rows 1–12.

Lotus Pattern

This lovely lace comes from Japan, and lends itself to several different treatments. Rows 1 through 5 can be worked in a contrasting color, to emphasize the graceful garter-stitch scallops. A single repeat of the pattern rows will yield a nicely scalloped border; two or three repeats will make a wider band of lace at the lower edge of a blouse or sleeve. Caution! Before trying this pattern, *read* the explanation of the double decrease "sl 2—p1—p2sso" in the Glossary.

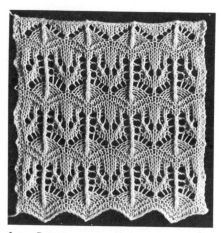

Lotus Pattern

Multiple of 10 sts plus 1.

Rows 1, 2, 3, 4, and 5—Knit.

Row 6 (Wrong side)—P1, * yo, p3, sl 2—p1—p2sso, p3, yo, p1; rep from *.

Row 7—K2, * yo, k2, sl 2—k1—p2sso, k2, yo, k3; rep from *, end last repeat k2.

Row 8—P3, * yo, p1, sl 2—p1—p2sso, p1, yo, p5; rep from *, end last repeat p3.

Row 9—K4, * yo, sl 2—k1—p2sso, yo, k7; rep from *, end last repeat k4.

Row 10—P2, * k2, p3; rep from *, end last repeat p2.

Row 11—K1, * yo, ssk, p1, yo, sl 2—k1—p2sso, yo, p1, k2 tog, yo, k1; rep from *.

Row 12—P3, * k1, p3, k1, p5; rep from *, end last repeat p3.

Row 13—K2, * yo, ssk, yo, sl 2—k1—p2sso, yo, k2 tog, yo, k3; rep from *, end last repeat k2.

Row 14—P2, * k1, p5, k1, p3; rep from *, end last repeat p2.

Row 15—K2, * p1, k1, yo, sl 2—k1—p2sso, yo, k1, p1, k3; rep from *, end last repeat k2.

Row 16—Repeat Row 14.

Repeat Rows 1–16.

Peri's Parasol

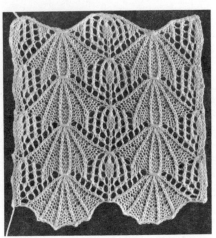

Peri's Parasol

This lovely pattern is of ancient lineage, and has many relatives (see Grand Shell and Bear Track). These directions are a modern adaptation of one of the oldest versions. The lower edge forms scallops, so the pattern makes its own border for a garment such as a lace blouse, skirt or apron. The stitch count varies from row to row; Row 13 restores the original number.

Multiple of 22 sts plus 1.

NOTE: Cluster—sl the given number of sts wyib, pass yarn to front, sl the same number of sts back to left-hand needle, pass yarn to back, sl the same sts again wyib.

Row 1 (Right side)—K1, * yo, (k1-b, p3) 5 times, k1-b, yo, k1; rep from *.

Row 2—P3, * (k3, p1) 4 times, k3, p5; rep from *, end last repeat p3.

Row 3—K1, * yo, k1-b, yo, (k1-b, p3) 5 times, (k1-b, yo) twice, k1; rep from *.

Row 4—P5, * (k3, p1) 4 times, k3, p9; rep from *, end last repeat p5.

Row 5—K1, * yo, k1-b, yo, ssk, yo, (k1-b, p2 tog, p1) 5 times, k1-b, yo, k2 tog, yo, k1-b, yo, k1; rep from *.

Row 6—P7, * (k2, p1) 4 times, k2, p13; rep from *, end last repeat p7.

Row 7—K1, * k1-b, (yo, ssk) twice, yo, (k1-b, p2) 5 times, k1-b, yo, (k2 tog, yo) twice, k1-b, k1; rep from *.

Row 8—P8, * (k2, p1) 4 times, k2, p15; rep from *, end last repeat p8.

Row 9—K2, * (yo, k2 tog) twice, yo, k1-b, yo, (k1-b, p2 tog) 5 times, (k1-b, yo) twice, (ssk, yo) twice, k3; rep from *, end last repeat k2.

Rows 10 and 12—P10, * (k1, p1) 4 times, k1, p19; rep from *, end last repeat p10.

Row 11—Ssk, * (yo, k2 tog) 3 times, k1-b, yo, (k1-b, p1) 5 times, k1-b, yo, k1-b, (ssk, yo) 3 times, sl 2—k1—p2sso; rep from *, end last repeat k2 tog instead of sl 2—k1—p2sso.

Row 13—K1, * (k2 tog, yo) twice, k2 tog, k1, k1-b, yo, (ssk) twice, sl 1—k2 tog—psso, (k2 tog) twice, yo, k1-b, k1, ssk, (yo, ssk) twice, k1; rep from *.

Row 14—Cluster 2, * p7, Cluster 5, p7, Cluster 3; rep from *, end last repeat Cluster 2 instead of Cluster 3.

Repeat Rows 1–14.

Chinoiserie

Multiple of 16 sts plus 3.

Row 1 (Wrong side)—Purl.

Row 2—K2, * yo, ssk, k5, yo, ssk, k4, k2 tog, yo, k1; rep from *, end k1.

Row 3—P7, * p2 tog-b, yo, p1, yo, p2 tog, p11; rep from *, end last repeat p7.

Row 4—K2, * yo, ssk, k2, k2 tog, yo, k1, (yo, ssk) twice, k2, k2 tog, yo, k1; rep from *, end k1.

Row 5—P5, * (p2 tog-b, yo) twice, p1, (yo, p2 tog) twice, p7; rep from *, end last repeat p5.

Row 6—K2, * yo, ssk, (k2 tog, yo) twice, k3, (yo, ssk) twice, k2 tog, yo, k1; rep from *, end k1.

Row 7, 9, 11, 13, and 15—Purl.

Row 8—K3, * (k2 tog, yo) twice, k5, (yo, ssk) twice, k3; rep from *.

Rows 10 and 12—K2, * (k2 tog, yo) twice, k1, k2 tog, yo, k1, yo, ssk, k1, (yo, ssk) twice, k1; rep from *, end k1.

Row 14—K1, k2 tog, * yo, k2 tog, yo, k2, k2 tog, yo, k1, yo, ssk, k2, yo, ssk, yo, sl 1—k2 tog—psso; rep from *, end last repeat ssk, k1 instead of sl 1—k2 tog—psso.

Row 16—K1, * yo, ssk, k4, k2 tog, yo, k1, yo, ssk, k5; rep from *, end yo, ssk.

Row 17—P2, * yo, p2 tog, p11, p2 tog-b, yo, p1; rep from *, end p1.

Row 18—K1, * (yo, ssk) twice, k2, k2 tog, yo, k1, yo, ssk, k2, k2 tog, yo, k1; rep from *, end k2.

Row 19—P2, * (yo, p2 tog) twice, p7, (p2 tog-b, yo) twice, p1; rep from *, end p1.

Row 20—K3, * (yo, ssk) twice, k2 tog, yo, k1, yo, ssk, (k2 tog, yo) twice, k3; rep from *.

Rows 21, 23, 25, and 27—Purl.

Row 22—K4, * (yo, ssk) twice, k3, (k2 tog, yo) twice, k5; rep from *, end last repeat k4.

Rows 24 and 26—K2, * yo, ssk, k1, (yo, ssk) twice, k1, (k2 tog, yo) twice, k1, k2 tog, yo, k1; rep from *, end k1.

Row 28—K2, * yo, ssk, k2, yo, ssk, yo, sl 1—k2 tog—psso, yo, k2 tog, yo, k2, k2 tog, yo, k1; rep from *, end k1.

Repeat Rows 1–28.

Chinoiserie

Pyrenees Pattern

This beautiful old pattern features double diamonds worked in delicate single-strand lace. Like all patterns of this type, it must be well stretched.

Multiple of 18 sts plus 1.

Row 1 (Wrong side)—Purl.

Row 2—K2 tog, * yo, k1, k2 tog, yo, k2, k2 tog, yo, k1, yo, ssk, k2, yo, ssk, k1, yo, sl 1—k2 tog—psso; rep from *, end last repeat ssk.

Row 3—P2, * p2 tog-b, yo, p2, p2 tog-b, yo, p3, yo, p2 tog, p2, yo, p2 tog, p3; rep from *, end last repeat p2.

Row 4—K1, * k2 tog, yo, k2, k2 tog, yo, k5, yo, ssk, k2, yo, ssk, k1; rep from *.

Row 5—P2 tog-b, * yo, p2, p2 tog-b, yo, p7, yo, p2 tog, p2, yo, p3 tog; rep from *, end last repeat p2 tog.

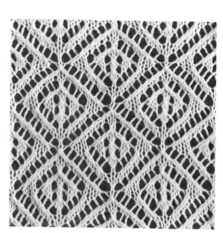

Pyrenees Pattern

Row 6—K3, * k2 tog, yo, k2, k2 tog, yo, k1, yo, ssk, k2, yo, ssk, k5; rep from *, end last repeat k3.

Rows 7 and 8—Repeat Rows 3 and 4.

Row 9—P2 tog-b, * yo, p2, p2 tog-b, yo, p2, yo, p3 tog, yo, p2, yo, p2 tog, p2, yo, p3 tog; rep from *, end last repeat p2 tog.

Row 10—Knit.

Row 11—P1, * yo, p2 tog, p2, yo, p2 tog, p1, yo, p3 tog, yo, p1, p2 tog-b, yo, p2, p2 tog-b, yo, p1; rep from *.

Row 12—K2, * yo, ssk, k2, yo, ssk, k3, k2 tog, yo, k2, k2 tog, yo, k3; rep from *, end last repeat k2.

Row 13—P3, * yo, p2 tog, p2, yo, p2 tog, p1, p2 tog-b, yo, p2, p2 tog-b, yo, p5; rep from *, end last repeat p3.

Row 14—K4, * yo, ssk, k2, yo, sl 1—k2 tog—psso, yo, k2, k2 tog, yo, k7; rep from *, end last repeat k4.

Row 15—P1, * yo, p2 tog, p2, yo, p2 tog, p5, p2 tog-b, yo, p2, p2 tog-b, yo, p1; rep from *.

Rows 16 and 17—Repeat Rows 12 and 13.

Row 18—K2 tog, * yo, k2, yo, ssk, k2, yo, sl 1—k2 tog—psso, yo, k2, k2 tog, yo, k2, yo, sl 1—k2 tog—psso; rep from *, end last repeat ssk.

Repeat Rows 1–18.

Closed Bud

Contributed by Dorothy Reade, Eugene, Oregon

Multiple of 22 sts plus 1.

Row 1 (Wrong side) and all other wrong-side rows—Purl.

Row 2—K3, * k2 tog, yo, k1-b, k2, k2 tog, k1-b, yo, k1, yo, k1-b, ssk, k2, k1-b, yo, ssk, k5; rep from *, end last repeat k3.

Row 4—K2, * k2 tog, yo, k1-b, k2, k2 tog, k1, k1-b, yo, k1, yo, k1-b, k1, ssk, k2, k1-b, yo, ssk, k3; rep from *, end last repeat k2.

Row 6—K1, * k2 tog, yo, k1-b, k2, k2 tog, k2, yo, k1-b, k1, k1-b, yo, k2, ssk, k2, k1-b, yo, ssk, k1; rep from *.

Row 8—K2 tog, * yo, k1-b, k2, k2 tog, k2, yo, k1-b, k3, k1-b, yo, k2, ssk, k2, k1-b, yo, sl 1—k2 tog—psso; rep from *, end last repeat ssk instead of sl 1—k2 tog—psso.

Row 10—K1, * yo, k3, k2 tog, k2, yo, ssk, k3, k2 tog, yo, k2, ssk, k3, yo, k1; rep from *.

Row 12—K1, * yo, k3, ssk, k2, yo, ssk, k3, k2 tog, yo, k2, k2 tog, k3, yo, k1; rep from *.

Row 14—K1, * k1-b, yo, k3, ssk, k1, k1-b, yo, ssk, k1, k2 tog, yo, k1-b, k1, k2 tog, k3, yo, k1-b, k1; rep from *.

Closed Bud

Row 16—K2, * k1-b, yo, k3, ssk, k1, k1-b, yo, sl 1—k2 tog—psso, yo, k1-b, k1, k2 tog, k3, yo, k1-b, k3; rep from *, end last repeat k2.

Row 18—K1, * k2 tog, yo, k1-b, yo, k3, k3 tog, yo, k1-b, k1, k1-b, yo, sl 1—k2 tog—psso, k3, yo, k1-b, yo, ssk, k1; rep from *.

Row 20—K2 tog, * yo, k1-b, k1, k1-b, k2, (k2 tog, yo) twice, k1, (yo, ssk) twice, k2, k1-b, k1, k1-b, yo, sl 1—k2 tog—psso; rep from *, end last repeat ssk instead of sl 1—k2 tog—psso.

Row 22—K1, * yo, ssk, k3, k2 tog, yo, k1-b, k2 tog, yo, k1, yo, ssk, k1-b, yo, ssk, k3, k2 tog, yo, k1; rep from *.

Row 24—K1, * k1-b, yo, ssk, k1, k2 tog, yo, k1-b, k1, k2 tog, yo, k1, yo, ssk, k1, k1-b, yo, ssk, k1, k2 tog, yo, k1-b, k1; rep from *.

Row 26—K2, * k1-b, yo, k3 tog, yo, k1-b, k2, k2 tog, yo, k1, yo, ssk, k2, k1-b, yo, sl 1—k2 tog—psso, yo, k1-b, k3; rep from *, end last repeat k2.

Repeat Rows 1–26.

Ring Medallion

This delicate lace requires careful knitting. Consult the Glossary, under Decreases, for explanations of "sl 2—k1—p2sso" and "sl 2—p1—p2sso".

Multiple of 12 sts plus 1.

Row 1 (Wrong side)—Purl.

Row 2—K4, * k2 tog, yo, k1, yo, ssk, k7; rep from *, end last repeat k4.

Row 3—P3, * p2 tog-b, yo, p3, yo, p2 tog, p5; rep from *, end last repeat p3.

Row 4—K2, * k2 tog, yo, k5, yo, ssk, k3; rep from *, end last repeat k2.

Row 5—P1, * p2 tog-b, yo, p7, yo, p2 tog, p1; rep from *

Rows 6, 8, and 10—Ssk, yo, * k3, yo, sl 2—k1—p2sso, yo; rep from *, end k3, yo, k2 tog.

Rows 7 and 9—P2 tog, * yo, p1, p2 tog, yo, p3, yo, p2 tog-b, p1, yo, sl 2—p1—p2sso; rep from *, end last repeat p2 tog-b instead of sl 2—p1—p2sso.

Row 11—P2, * yo, p2 tog, p5, p2 tog-b, yo, p3; rep from *, end last repeat p2.

Row 12—K3, * yo, ssk, k3, k2 tog, yo, k5; rep from *, end last repeat k3.

Row 13—P4, * yo, p2 tog, p1, p2 tog-b, yo, p7; rep from *, end last repeat p4.

Row 14—K5, * yo, sl 2—k1—p2sso, yo, k9; rep from *, end last repeat k5.

Repeat Rows 1–14.

Ring Medallion

Ivy Leaf

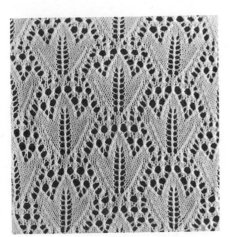

Ivy Leaf

Contributed by Hildegard M. Elsner, Aldan, Pennsylvania

Here is a somewhat revised version of an old German lace of much beauty. It is recommended for extra-fancy baby things, evening blouses, or stoles; anything worked in this pattern is bound to be a showpiece. The stitch count is constant in each row.

Multiple of 34 sts plus 1.

NOTE: All double yo's are written "yo2".

Row 1 (Wrong side) and all other wrong-side rows—Purl, working (k1, p1) into every double yo of a preceding row.

Row 2—K1-b, * yo, k6, ssk, k1, k2 tog, yo, k1, yo, sl 1—k2 tog—psso, yo, k3, yo, sl 1—k2 tog—psso, yo, k1, yo, ssk, k1, k2 tog, k6, yo, k1-b; rep from *.

Row 4—K1-b, * yo, k2, k2 tog, yo, ssk, k6, yo, ssk, k2 tog, yo, k1-b, yo, ssk, k2 tog, yo, k6, k2 tog, yo, ssk, k2, yo, k1-b; rep from *.

Row 6—K3, * k2 tog, yo, k1, yo, ssk, k1, k2 tog, yo2, ssk, k1, k2 tog, k1, yo, k1-b, yo, k1, ssk, k1, k2 tog, yo2, ssk, k1, k2 tog, yo, k1, yo, ssk, k5; rep from *, end last repeat k3.

Row 8—K2, * k2 tog, (yo2, sl 1—k2 tog—psso) twice, yo2, ssk, k1, k2 tog, k2, yo, k1-b, yo, k2, ssk, k1, k2 tog, yo2, (sl 1—k2 tog—psso, yo2) twice, ssk, k3; rep from *, end last repeat k2.

Row 10—K1, * k2 tog, yo, k6, yo, ssk, k1, k2 tog, k3, yo, k1-b, yo, k3, ssk, k1, k2 tog, yo, k6, yo, ssk, k1; rep from *.

Row 12—K2 tog, * (yo2, sl 1—k2 tog—psso) twice, yo2, ssk, k1, k2 tog, k4, yo, k1-b, yo, k4, ssk, k1, k2 tog, yo2, (sl 1—k2 tog—psso, yo2) twice, sl 1—k2 tog—psso; rep from *, end last repeat ssk instead of sl 1—k2 tog—psso.

Row 14—K7, * yo, ssk, k1, k2 tog, k5, yo, k1-b, yo, k5, ssk, k1, k2 tog, yo, k13; rep from *, end last repeat k7.

Row 16—K2, * yo, sl 1—k2 tog—psso, yo, k1, yo, ssk, k1, k2 tog, k6, yo, k1-b, yo, k6, ssk, k1, k2 tog, yo, k1, yo, sl 1—k2 tog—psso, yo, k3; rep from *, end last repeat k2.

Row 18—K1-b, * yo, ssk, k2 tog, yo, k6, k2 tog, yo, ssk, k2, yo, k1-b, yo, k2, k2 tog, yo, ssk, k6, yo, ssk, k2 tog, yo, k1-b; rep from *.

Row 20—K1-b, * yo, k1, ssk, k1, k2 tog, yo2, ssk, k1, k2 tog, yo, k1, yo, ssk, k5, k2 tog, yo, k1, yo, ssk, k1, k2 tog, yo2, ssk, k1, k2 tog, k1, yo, k1-b; rep from *.

Row 22—K1-b, * yo, k2, ssk, k1, k2 tog, (yo2, sl 1—k2 tog—psso) twice, yo2, ssk, k3, k2 tog, yo2, (sl 1—k2 tog—psso, yo2) twice, ssk, k1, k2 tog, k2, yo, k1-b; rep from *.

Row 24—K1-b, * yo, k3, (ssk, k1, k2 tog, yo, k6, yo) twice, ssk, k1, k2 tog, k3, yo, k1-b; rep from *.

Row 26—K1-b, * yo, k4, ssk, k1, k2 tog, (yo2, sl 1—k2 tog—psso) 5 times, yo2, ssk, k1, k2 tog, k4, yo, k1-b; rep from *.

Row 28—K1-b, * yo, k5, ssk, k1, k2 tog, yo, k13, yo, ssk, k1, k2 tog, k5, yo, k1-b; rep from *.

Repeat Rows 1–28.

Queen's Lace

This is an exquisite lace with crisp, interesting geometry. Each motif is four-fifths of a pentagon, with radiant lines flaring outward into the next motif; sub-patterns within the pattern are created by openwork ribs and deep triangles of knit stitches. The working of the pattern is straightforward and conventional, with the number of stitches remaining always the same on every row.

Queen's Lace

Multiple of 24 sts plus 1.

Row 1 (Right side)—K1, * yo, k2 tog, k3, (k2 tog, yo) twice, ssk, yo, k1, yo, k2 tog, (yo, ssk) twice, k3, ssk, yo, k1; rep from *.

Row 2—P5, * p2 tog-b, yo, p11, yo, p2 tog, p9; rep from *, end last repeat p5.

Row 3—K1, * yo, k2 tog, k1, (k2 tog, yo, k1) twice, ssk, yo, k1, yo, k2 tog, (k1, yo, ssk) twice, k1, ssk, yo, k1; rep from *.

Row 4—P3, * p2 tog-b, yo, p15, yo, p2 tog, p5; rep from *, end last repeat p3.

Row 5—K2, * (k2 tog, yo, k2) twice, ssk, yo, k1, yo, k2 tog, (k2, yo, ssk) twice, k3; rep from *, end last repeat k2.

Row 6—P1, * p2 tog-b, yo, p19, yo, p2 tog, p1; rep from *.

Row 7—K2 tog, * yo, k3, k2 tog, yo, k3, ssk, yo, k1, yo, k2 tog, k3, yo, ssk, k3, yo, sl 1—k2 tog—psso; rep from *, end last repeat ssk instead of sl 1—k2 tog—psso.

Row 8—Purl.

Row 9—K1, * yo, k2 tog, (yo, ssk) twice, k3, ssk, yo, k1, yo, k2 tog, k3, (k2 tog, yo) twice, ssk, yo, k1; rep from *.

Row 10—P6, * yo, p2 tog, p9, p2 tog-b, yo, p11; rep from *, end last repeat p6.

Row 11—K1, * yo, k2 tog, (k1, yo, ssk) twice, k1, ssk, yo, k1, yo, k2 tog, k1, (k2 tog, yo, k1) twice, ssk, yo, k1; rep from *.

Row 12—P8, * yo, p2 tog, p5, p2 tog-b, yo, p15; rep from *, end last repeat p8.

Row 13—K1, * yo, k2 tog, (k2, yo, ssk) twice, k3, (k2 tog, yo, k2) twice, ssk, yo, k1; rep from *.

Row 14—P10, * yo, p2 tog, p1, p2 tog-b, yo, p19; rep from *, end last repeat p10.

Row 15—K1, * yo, k2 tog, k3, yo, ssk, k3, yo, sl 1—k2 tog—psso, yo, k3, k2 tog, yo, k3, ssk, yo, k1; rep from *.

Row 16—Purl.

Repeat Rows 1–16.

CHAPTER THIRTEEN

Lace Panels and Insertions

This section contains some of the most useful patterns known to lace knitting. Panels and insertions are wonderfully adaptable, because they can be placed and combined at will, just like cables. Even a novice knitter can enrich a plain garment without any complicated re-figuring of stitches, by putting a lace panel or two into the center where the pattern will not be affected by shaping.

For example, let's say you want to run an insertion of lace up the front of a sweater. Your garment pattern calls for 100 stitches and you have chosen a panel 20 stitches wide. This leaves 40 stitches on each side to be worked plain. So to start the panel, work 40 stitches, place a marker on the needle, work the panel pattern on the next 20 stitches, place another marker on the needle, and proceed across to the other side. Then as the work progresses, the panel rows are continued between the markers—so there is no need to worry about where to begin and end them.

Should you choose a panel that has an odd number of stitches, while the garment pattern calls for an even number, simply cast on one extra stitch or omit one, so that the panel can be exactly centered. Usually, any lace pattern will "open up" the knitting a little, because it can be so readily stretched. Therefore it is better to use fewer stitches rather than more.

The most exciting kind of lace knitting is the kind that uses many different patterns in the same piece, just as a fisherman sweater combines many different cables. Lace panels or insertions can be placed side by side in gorgeous variety, to make exquisite blouses, sweaters, place mats, table runners, curtains, stoles, or dresses. Choose several that you like; put a particularly effective one in the center, then a second one on the right side and on the left side of it, then a third one on each side of that, and so on, adding up the total number of stitches as you go until you have the number required for the whole width, or a few less. Leftover stitches can always be worked plain at the side edges. As you knit, it is a good idea to keep a written row count of each separate pattern, so you will not "lose your place" in any one of them.

Of course, there is nothing to prevent the knitter from converting a panel into an allover pattern, simply by repeating it all the way across. By the same token, an allover lace pattern can be converted into a panel. This is done by using just one or two pattern repeats on a limited number of stitches, the remainder of the stitches being worked plain or in a different pattern.

Lace panels and insertions can be combined with cables, knit-purl patterns, texture patterns, or anything else that strikes your fancy. Actually there is no difference between a "panel" and an "insertion" except that the latter term is applied to lace that is set into an otherwise solid fabric. These patterns can be used as spot-patterns, too, just by working the pattern rows once in one section of the garment and then once again in another section.

Be creative: mix and match, play one pattern against another, work only part of a pattern if this gives the effect you want. In knitting, anything is possible. The variety of fabrics that you can achieve is limited only by your imagination and skill—and both of these can be greatly extended by constantly trying out new patterns.

Double Herringbone Mesh

In this handsome pattern, the trick is in the center. The converging lines of lace trellis are "invisibly" worked into each other so that a small zigzag is formed where ordinarily there would be a rib of decrease stitches.

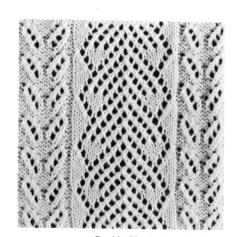

CENTER PANEL: *Double Herringbone Mesh*
SIDE PANELS: *Wasp Wings*

Panel of 21 sts.

Row 1 (Wrong side) and all other wrong-side rows—Purl.

Row 2—K2, (yo, ssk) 3 times, yo, sl 1—k2 tog—psso, (yo, k2 tog) 4 times, yo, k2.

Row 4—K3, (yo, ssk) 3 times, yo, sl 1—k2 tog—psso, (yo, k2 tog) 3 times, yo, k3.

Row 6—K4, (yo, ssk) twice, yo, sl 1—k2 tog—psso, (yo, k2 tog) 3 times, yo, k4.

Row 8—K2, k2 tog, yo, k1, (yo, ssk) twice, yo, sl 1—k2 tog—psso, (yo, k2 tog) twice, yo, k1, yo, ssk, k2.

Row 10—K1, k2 tog, yo, k3, yo, ssk, yo, sl 1—k2 tog—psso, (yo, k2 tog) twice, yo, k3, yo, ssk, k1.

Row 12—K2 tog, yo, k5, yo, ssk, yo, sl 1—k2 tog—psso, yo, k2 tog, yo, k5, yo, ssk.

Repeat Rows 1–12.

Wasp Wings

Here is a pretty little panel of openwork on a purled background. Use it with other lace patterns for texture interest, or combine it with alternate panels of stockinette stitch, seed stitch, ribbing, etc.

Panel of 13 sts.

Row 1 (Right side)—P3, k2 tog, yo, k1, p1, k1, yo, ssk, p3.
Row 2—K3, p3, k1, p3, k3.
Row 3—P2, (k2 tog, yo) twice, p1, (yo, ssk) twice, p2.
Row 4—K2, p3, k1-b, k1, k1-b, p3, k2.
Row 5—P1, (k2 tog, yo) twice, p3, (yo, ssk) twice, p1.
Row 6—K1, p3, k1-b, k3, k1-b, p3, k1.
Row 7—P1, yo, sl 1—k2 tog—psso, yo, p5, yo, ssk, slip ssk st back to left-hand needle and pass next st over it, then return it to right-hand needle; yo, p1.
Row 8—K1, (k1-b, p1) twice, k3, (p1, k1-b) twice, k1.

Repeat Rows 1–8.

Triple Leaf Pattern

Here is a beautiful old-fashioned lace insertion that is agelessly graceful in any modern article of lace knitting. The stitches are increased by 2 on Row 6 and again on Row 8, and are decreased to the original number on Rows 10 and 12.

Panel of 15 sts.

Row 1 (Wrong side) and all other wrong-side rows—Purl.
Row 2—K1, yo, k2 tog, k3 tog, (yo, k1) 3 times, yo, k3 tog-b, ssk, yo, k1.
Row 4—K1, yo, k3 tog, yo, k7, yo, k3 tog-b, yo, k1.
Row 6—K1, yo, k2 tog, yo, k1, yo, k2, sl 2 knitwise—k1—p2sso, k2, yo, k1, yo, ssk, yo, k1.
Row 8—K1, yo, k2 tog, yo, k3, yo, k1, sl 2 knitwise—k1—p2sso, k1, yo, k3, yo, ssk, yo, k1.
Row 10—K1, yo, (k2 tog) twice, k3, yo, sl 2 knitwise—k1—p2sso, yo, k3, (ssk) twice, yo, k1.
Row 12—K1, yo, (k2 tog) 3 times, (k1, yo) twice, k1, (ssk) 3 times, yo, k1.

Repeat Rows 1–12.

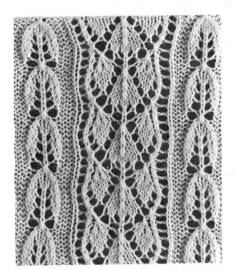

CENTER PANEL: *Triple Leaf Pattern*
SIDE PANELS: *Veined Leaf Panel*

Veined Leaf Panel

This variation on the embossed-leaf theme is a little different from the usual ones. It is very handsome as a single panel, or as an allover pattern on a multiple of 6 stitches plus 3.

Panel of 9 sts.

Row 1 (Right side)—P3, (k1, yo) twice, k1, p3.
Row 2—K3, p5, k3.
Row 3—P3, k2, yo, k1, yo, k2, p3.
Row 4—K3, p7, k3.
Row 5—P3, ssk, k1, (yo, k1) twice, k2 tog, p3.
Row 6—Repeat Row 4.
Row 7—P3, ssk, k3, k2 tog, p3.
Row 8—Repeat Row 2.
Row 9—P3, ssk, k1, k2 tog, p3.
Row 10—K3, p3, k3.
Row 11—P3, yo, sl 2 knitwise—k1—p2sso, yo, p3.
Row 12—Repeat Row 10.

Repeat Rows 1–12.

Lyre Pattern

Contributed by Hildegard M. Elsner, Aldan, Pennsylvania

Panel of 21 sts.

Row 1 (Wrong side) and all other wrong-side rows—Purl.
Row 2—K1, yo, k2 tog, k5, k2 tog, yo, k1, yo, ssk, k5, ssk, yo, k1.
Row 4—K1, yo, k2 tog, k4, k2 tog, yo, k3, yo, ssk, k4, ssk, yo, k1.
Row 6—K1, yo, k2 tog, k3, k2 tog, yo, k5, yo, ssk, k3, ssk, yo, k1.
Row 8—K1, yo, k2 tog, k2, (k2 tog, yo) twice, k3, (yo, ssk) twice, k2, ssk, yo, k1.
Rows 10, 12, 14, 16, and 18—K1, yo, k2 tog, k3, yo, k2 tog, yo, ssk, k1, k2 tog, yo, ssk, yo, k3, ssk, yo, k1.
Row 20—K1, yo, k2 tog, k1, k2 tog, yo, k9, yo, ssk, k1, ssk, yo, k1.

Repeat Rows 1–20.

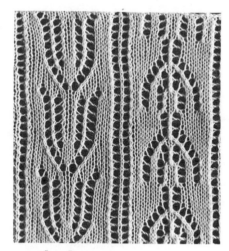

LEFT: *Lyre Pattern*
RIGHT: *Arch Pattern*

LACE PANELS AND INSERTIONS   303

Arch Pattern

Panel of 21 sts.

Row 1 (Wrong side) and all other wrong-side rows—Purl.
Rows 2, 4, and 6—K1, (yo, k2 tog, k1, ssk, yo, k2) twice, yo, k2 tog, k1, ssk, yo, k1.
Row 8—K1, yo, k2 tog, k3, yo, ssk, k1, yo, sl 2—k1—p2sso, yo, k1, k2 tog, yo, k3, ssk, yo, k1.
Row 10—K1, yo, k2 tog, k4, yo, ssk, yo, sl 2—k1—p2sso, yo, k2 tog, yo, k4, ssk, yo, k1.
Row 12—K1, yo, k2 tog, k5, yo, ssk, k1, k2 tog, yo, k5, ssk, yo, k1.
Rows 14, 16, and 18—K1, yo, k2 tog, k6, yo, sl 2—k1—p2sso, yo, k6, ssk, yo, k1.

Repeat Rows 1–18.

Flemish Braid

Here is a panel of enlarged Flemish Block, the single yarn-overs converted into double ones and the whole constituting a wide "feature" pattern for lace mats, runners, curtains or garments.

Panel of 25 sts.

Row 1 (Wrong side) and all other wrong-side rows—Purl.
Row 2—K5, (yo, ssk) twice, k3, (k2 tog, yo) twice, k4, (k2 tog, yo) twice, k1.
Row 4—K3, k2 tog, yo, k1, (yo, ssk) twice, k1, (k2 tog, yo) twice, k4, (k2 tog, yo) twice, k2.
Row 6—K2, (k2 tog, yo) twice, k1, yo, ssk, yo, sl 1—k2 tog—psso, yo, k2 tog, yo, k4, (k2 tog, yo) twice, k3.
Row 8—K1, (k2 tog, yo) twice, k3, yo, ssk, yo, sl 1—k2 tog—psso, yo, k4, (k2 tog, yo) twice, k4.
Row 10—K1, (yo, ssk) twice, k4, (yo, ssk) twice, k3, (k2 tog, yo) twice, k5.
Row 12—K2, (yo, ssk) twice, k4, (yo, ssk) twice, k1, (k2 tog, yo) twice, k1, yo, ssk, k3.
Row 14—K3, (yo, ssk) twice, k4, yo, ssk, yo, k3 tog, yo, k2 tog, yo, k1, (yo, ssk) twice, k2.
Row 16—K4, (yo, ssk) twice, k4, yo, k3 tog, yo, k2 tog, yo, k3, (yo, ssk) twice, k1.

Repeat Rows 1–16.

CENTER PANEL: *Flemish Braid*
LEFT SIDE PANEL: *Miniature Openwork Cable, right twist*
RIGHT SIDE PANEL: *Miniature Openwork Cable, left twist*

Miniature Openwork Cable

These "cables" look like standard Diamonds at first, but a closer inspection shows that they are off-center, which gives them a twisted appearance. This jog in the pattern can be created either to the left or to the right.

Panel of 7 sts.

I. LEFT-TWIST "CABLE"

Row 1 (Wrong side) and all other wrong-side rows—Purl.
Row 2—K2, k2 tog, yo, k3.
Row 4—K1, k2 tog, yo, k1, yo, ssk, k1.
Row 6—K2 tog, yo, k3, yo, ssk.
Row 8—K2 tog, yo, k2, k2 tog, yo, k1.
Row 10—K2, yo, k3 tog, yo, k2.

Repeat Rows 1–10.

II. RIGHT-TWIST "CABLE"

Rows 4 and 6 are the same as in Version I, above. The other 3 pattern rows are worked as follows:
Row 2—K3, yo, ssk, k2.
Row 8—K1, yo, ssk, k2, yo, ssk.
Row 10—K2, yo, sl 1—k2 tog—psso, yo, k2.

Grace Note

Panel of 15 sts.

Row 1 (Wrong side) and all other wrong-side rows—Purl.
Row 2—K4, k2 tog, yo, k2, k2 tog, yo, k3, yo, ssk.
Row 4—K3, k2 tog, yo, (k1, yo, ssk) twice, k1, k2 tog, yo, k1.
Row 6—K2, k2 tog, yo, k3, yo, ssk, k1, yo, k3 tog, yo, k2.
Row 8—K1, k2 tog, yo, k1, yo, ssk, k2, yo, ssk, k2 tog, yo, k3.
Row 10—K2 tog, yo, k3, yo, ssk, k2, yo, ssk, k4.
Row 12—K1, yo, ssk, (k1, k2 tog, yo) twice, k1, yo, ssk, k3.
Row 14—K2, yo, sl 1—k2 tog—psso, yo, k1, k2 tog, yo, k3, yo, ssk, k2.
Row 16—K3, yo, ssk, k2 tog, yo, k2, k2 tog, yo, k1, yo, ssk, k1.

Repeat Rows 1–16.

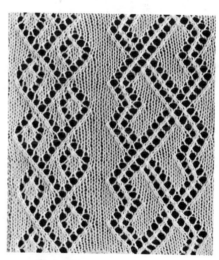

LEFT: *Grace Note*
RIGHT: *Butterfly Braid*

LACE PANELS AND INSERTIONS   305

Butterfly Braid

Panel of 22 sts.

Row 1 (Wrong side) and all other wrong-side rows—Purl.
Row 2—K5, (yo, ssk) twice, k3, (k2 tog, yo) twice, k6.
Row 4—K3, (k2 tog, yo) twice, k4, (k2 tog, yo) twice, k1, yo, ssk, k4.
Row 6—K2, (k2 tog, yo) twice, k4, (k2 tog, yo) twice, k1, (yo, ssk) twice, k3.
Row 8—K1, (k2 tog, yo) twice, k4, (k2 tog, yo) twice, k3, (yo, ssk) twice, k2.
Row 10—K3, (yo, ssk) twice, k1, (k2 tog, yo) twice, k5, (yo, ssk) twice, k1.
Row 12—K4, yo, ssk, yo, sl 1—k2 tog—psso, yo, k2 tog, yo, k4, (k2 tog, yo) twice, k3.
Row 14—K5, yo, ssk, yo, sl 1—k2 tog—psso, yo, k4, (k2 tog, yo) twice, k4.
Row 16—K6, (yo, ssk) twice, k3, (k2 tog, yo) twice, k5.
Row 18—K4, k2 tog, yo, k1, (yo, ssk) twice, k4, (yo, ssk) twice, k3.
Row 20—K3, (k2 tog, yo) twice, k1, (yo, ssk) twice, k4, (yo, ssk) twice, k2.
Row 22—K2, (k2 tog, yo) twice, k3, (yo, ssk) twice, k4, (yo, ssk) twice, k1.
Row 24—K1, (k2 tog, yo) twice, k5, (yo, ssk) twice, k1, (k2 tog, yo) twice, k3.
Row 26—K3, (yo, ssk) twice, k4, yo, ssk, yo, k3 tog, yo, k2 tog, yo, k4.
Row 28—K4, (yo, ssk) twice, k4, yo, k3 tog, yo, k2 tog, yo, k5.

Repeat Rows 1–28.

Wings of the Swan

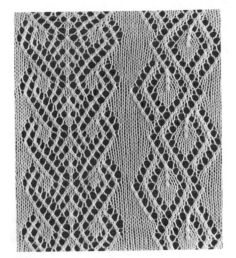

LEFT: *Wings of the Swan*
RIGHT: *Vandyke Leaf Pattern*

Here is an intricate and beautiful lace panel of the double cable-twist type, set off by open trellis work in the center, which creates a sort of mesh. It would be lovely as a center for any lace article, in combination with panels of other laces.

Panel of 23 sts.

Row 1 (Wrong side) and all other wrong-side rows—Purl.
Row 2—K4, (k2 tog, yo) twice, k1, yo, ssk, k1, k2 tog, yo, k1, (yo, ssk) twice, k4.
Row 4—K3, (k2 tog, yo) twice, k1, yo, ssk, yo, sl 1—k2 tog—psso, yo, k2 tog, yo, k1, (yo, ssk) twice, k3.
Row 6—K2, * (k2 tog, yo) twice, k1, (yo, ssk) twice, k1; rep from * once, end k1.
Row 8—K1, (k2 tog, yo) twice, k3, yo, ssk, yo, sl 1—k2 tog—psso, yo, k2 tog, yo, k3, (yo, ssk) twice, k1.
Row 10—* K1, (yo, ssk) twice, k2, (k2 tog, yo) twice; rep from * once, end k1.
Row 12—K2, * (yo, ssk) twice, (k2 tog, yo) twice, k3; rep from * once, ending k2 instead of k3.
Row 14—K3, yo, ssk, (k2 tog, yo) twice, k1, yo, sl 1—k2 tog—psso, yo, k1, (yo, ssk) twice, k2 tog, yo, k3.

Repeat Rows 1–14.

Vandyke Leaf Pattern

Panel of 23 sts.

Row 1 (Wrong side) and all other wrong-side rows—Purl.
Row 2—K3, k2 tog, yo, k1, k2 tog, yo, k3, yo, ssk, k1, yo, ssk, k7.
Row 4—K2, k2 tog, yo, k1, k2 tog, yo, k5, yo, ssk, k1, yo, ssk, k6.
Row 6—(K1, k2 tog, yo) twice, k7, yo, ssk, k1, yo, ssk, k5.
Row 8—K3, yo, ssk, k1, yo, k2, sl 2—k1—p2sso, k2, yo, k1, k2 tog, yo, k7.
Row 10—K4, yo, ssk, k1, yo, k1, sl 2—k1—p2sso, k1, yo, k1, k2 tog, yo, k8.
Row 12—K5, yo, ssk, k1, yo, sl 2—k1—p2sso, yo, k1, k2 tog, yo, k2, yo, ssk, k5.
Row 14—K6, yo, ssk, (k2 tog, yo, k1) twice, yo, ssk, k1, yo, ssk, k4.
Row 16—K7, k2 tog, yo, k1, k2 tog, yo, k3, yo, ssk, k1, yo, ssk, k3.
Row 18—K6, k2 tog, yo, k1, k2 tog, yo, k5, yo, ssk, k1, yo, ssk, k2.
Row 20—K5, k2 tog, yo, k1, k2 tog, yo, k7, (yo, ssk, k1) twice.
Row 22—K7, yo, ssk, k1, yo, k2, sl 2—k1—p2sso, k2, yo, k1, k2 tog, yo, k3.
Row 24—K8, yo, ssk, k1, yo, kl, sl 2—k1—p2sso, k1, yo, k1, k2 tog, yo, k4.
Row 26—K5, k2 tog, yo, k2, yo, ssk, k1, yo, sl 2—k1—p2sso, yo, k1, k2 tog, yo, k5.
Row 28—K4, (k2 tog, yo, k1) twice, yo, ssk, k1, yo, ssk, k2 tog, yo, k6.

Repeat Rows 1–28.

Two Victorian "Leaf" Patterns: Double Rose Leaf and Tracery Pattern

Contributed by Leona Hughes, Sarasota, Florida

Both of these patterns are relatives of the classic Beech Leaf, with the Double Rose Leaf bearing the nearest resemblance. Neither pattern maintains the same number of stitches throughout. In Double Rose Leaf, the stitches are immediately reduced to 15 in Row 2, and not restored to 17 until Row 8. In Tracery Pattern, 2 stitches are increased in Row 4, and removed in Row 6.

DOUBLE ROSE LEAF

Panel of 17 sts.

Row 1 (Wrong side)—Purl.
Row 2—K1, yo, k1, ssk, p1, k2 tog, k1, p1, k1, ssk, p1, k2 tog, k1, yo, k1.
Row 3—P4, (k1, p2) twice, k1, p4.
Row 4—(K1, yo) twice, ssk, p1, k2 tog, p1, ssk, p1, k2 tog, (yo, k1) twice.
Row 5—P5, (k1, p1) twice, k1, p5.

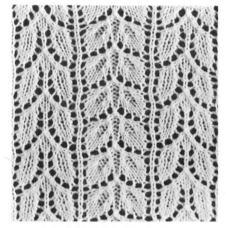

CENTER PANEL: *Double Rose Leaf*
SIDE PANELS: *Tracery Pattern*

Row 6—K1, yo, k3, yo, sl 1—k2 tog—psso, p1, k3 tog, yo, k3, yo, k1.

Row 7—P7, k1, p7.

Row 8—K1, yo, k5, yo, sl 1—k2 tog—psso, yo, k5, yo, k1.

Repeat Rows 1–8.

TRACERY PATTERN

Panel of 13 sts.

Row 1 (Wrong side) and all other wrong-side rows—Purl.

Row 2—(K1, yo) twice, sl 1—k2 tog—psso, k3, k3 tog, (yo, k1) twice.

Row 4—K1, yo, k3, yo, ssk, k1, k2 tog, yo, k3, yo, k1.

Row 6—K1, yo, ssk, k1, k2 tog, yo, sl 1—k2 tog—psso, yo, ssk, k1, k2 tog, yo, k1.

Rows 8 and 10—K1, (yo, ssk, k1, k2 tog, yo, k1) twice.

Repeat Rows 1–10.

Palm Leaf with Mesh

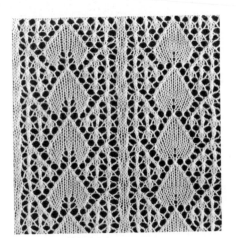

LEFT: *Palm Leaf With Mesh*
RIGHT: *Variation*

Here the classic Palm Leaf is placed on an openwork background, making a charming design for a wide insertion or for combination with other panels. The difference between the original pattern and its variation is slight (just a "yo, k1, yo" opposed to a "k1, yo, k1") but it determines whether the Leaf is open or closed at the center of its base.

Panel of 23 sts.

Row 1 (Wrong side) and all other wrong-side rows—Purl.

Row 2—Ssk, yo, sl 2—k1—p2sso, yo, k1-b, yo, ssk, k7, k2 tog, yo, k1-b, yo, sl 2—k1—p2sso, yo, k2 tog.

Row 4—Ssk, yo, k1, yo, k3, yo, ssk, k5, k2 tog, yo, k3, yo, k1, yo, k2 tog.

Row 6—K1, (yo, sl 2—k1—p2sso) twice, yo, k1-b, yo, ssk, k3, k2 tog, yo, k1-b, (yo, sl 2—k1—p2sso) twice, yo, k1.

Row 8—(K1, yo, k3, yo) twice, ssk, k1, k2 tog, (yo, k3, yo, k1) twice.

Row 10—Ssk, (yo, sl 2—k1—p2sso) 3 times, yo, k1-b, yo, sl 1—k2 tog—psso, yo, k1-b, (yo, sl 2—k1—p2sso) 3 times, yo, k2 tog.

Row 12—Ssk, yo, k1, yo, k2, k2 tog, yo, k3, yo, k1, yo, k3, yo, ssk, k2, yo, k1, yo, k2 tog.

Row 14—K1, (yo, sl 2—k1—p2sso) twice, yo, k2 tog, k3, yo, k1, yo, k3, ssk, (yo, sl 2—k1—p2sso) twice, yo, k1.

Row 16—K1, yo, k2, k2 tog, yo, k2 tog, k9, ssk, yo, ssk, k2, yo, k1.

Repeat Rows 1–16.

VARIATION

Work the same as above, except for Rows 12 and 14:

Row 12—Ssk, yo, k1, yo, k2, k2 tog, yo, k3, (k1, yo, k1) in next st, k3, yo, ssk, k2, yo, k1, yo, k2 tog.

Row 14—K1, (yo, sl 2—k1—p2sso) twice, yo, k2 tog, k3, (k1, yo, k1) in next st, k3, ssk, (yo, sl 2—k1—p2sso) twice, yo, k1.

Offset Diamonds

Panel of 22 sts.

Row 1 (Wrong side) and all other wrong-side rows—Purl.

Row 2—K3, yo, ssk, k1, k2 tog, yo, k1, yo, ssk, k11.

Row 4—K4, yo, sl 1—k2 tog—psso, yo, k3, yo, ssk, k3, k2 tog, yo, k5.

Row 6—K5, yo, ssk, k4, yo, ssk, k1, k2 tog, yo, k1, yo, ssk, k3.

Row 8—K12, yo, k3 tog, yo, k3, yo, ssk, k2.

Row 10—K12, k2 tog, yo, k5, yo, ssk, k1.

Row 12—K11, k2 tog, yo, k1, yo, ssk, k1, k2 tog, yo, k3.

Row 14—K5, yo, ssk, k3, k2 tog, yo, k3, yo, k3 tog, yo, k4.

Row 16—K3, k2 tog, yo, k1, yo, ssk, k1, k2 tog, yo, k4, k2 tog, yo, k5.

Row 18—K2, k2 tog, yo, k3, yo, sl 1—k2 tog—psso, yo, k12.

Row 20—K1, k2 tog, yo, k5, yo, ssk, k12.

Repeat Rows 1–20.

LEFT: *Offset Diamonds*
RIGHT: *Orchid Pattern*

Orchid Pattern

Panel of 19 sts.

Row 1 (Wrong side) and all other wrong-side rows—Purl.

Row 2—K2, yo, k4, k2 tog, yo, sl 2—k1—p2sso, yo, ssk, k4, yo, k2.

Row 4—K3, yo, k2, k3 tog, yo, k3, yo, sl 1—k2 tog—psso, k2, yo, k3.

Row 6—K4, yo, k1, k2 tog, yo, k1, sl 2—k1—p2sso, k1, yo, ssk, k1, yo, k4.

Row 8—K5, yo, k2 tog, yo, k1, sl 2—k1—p2sso, k1, yo, ssk, yo, k5.

Row 10—K3, k2 tog, yo, k1, yo, k2, sl 2—k1—p2sso, k2, yo, k1, yo, ssk, k3.

Row 12—K2, k2 tog, yo, k3, yo, k1, sl 2—k1—p2sso, k1, yo, k3, yo, ssk, k2.

Row 14—K1, k2 tog, yo, k5, yo, sl 2—k1—p2sso, yo, k5, yo, ssk, k1.

Repeat Rows 1–14.

Janus Pattern

Like the old Roman god of the gateway, this beautiful pattern "looks both ways" as the laterally-elongated diamonds alternate. For two panels symmetrically opposed, begin one with Row 1 and the other with Row 15.

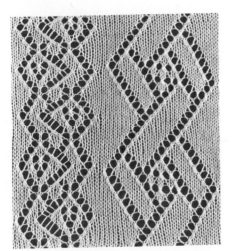

LEFT: *Janus Pattern*
RIGHT: *Embedded Diamond*

Panel of 17 sts.

Rows 1, 3, and 5 (Wrong side)—Purl.

Row 2—K4, yo, sl 1—k2 tog—psso, yo, k3, yo, sl 1—k2 tog—psso, yo, k4.

Row 4—K3, (k2 tog, yo, k1, yo, ssk, k1) twice, k2.

Row 6—K2, k2 tog, yo, k3, yo, sl 1—k2 tog—psso, yo, k3, yo, ssk, k2.

Row 7—P7, p2 tog-b, yo, p8.

Row 8—K1, k2 tog, yo, (k2, yo, ssk) twice, k3, yo, ssk, k1.

Row 9—P5, p2 tog-b, yo, p10.

Row 10—(K2 tog, yo, k1) twice, yo, ssk, k3, yo, ssk, k2, yo, ssk.

Row 11—P6, yo, p2 tog, p9.

Row 12—K2, yo, ssk, yo, sl 1—k2 tog—psso, yo, k1, k2 tog, yo, k3, k2 tog, yo, k2.

Row 13—P8, yo, p2 tog, p7.

Row 14—K3, (yo, ssk, k1, k2 tog, yo, k1) twice, k2.

Rows 15 through 19—Repeat Rows 1 through 5.

Row 20—K2, k2 tog, yo, k3, yo, k3 tog, yo, k3, yo, ssk, k2.

Row 21—Repeat Row 13.

Row 22—K1, k2 tog, yo, k3, (k2 tog, yo, k2) twice, yo, ssk, k1.

Row 23—P10, yo, p2 tog, p5.

Row 24—K2 tog, yo, k2, k2 tog, yo, k3, k2 tog, yo, (k1, yo, ssk) twice.

Row 25—P9, p2 tog-b, yo, p6.

Row 26—K2, yo, ssk, k3, yo, ssk, k1, yo, sl 1—k2 tog—psso, yo, k2 tog, yo, k2.

Row 27—Repeat Row 7.

Row 28—Repeat Row 14.

Repeat Rows 1–28.

Embedded Diamond

Contributed by Arlene M. Haines, Whippany, New Jersey

Panel of 25 sts.

Row 1 (Wrong side) and all other wrong-side rows—Purl.

Row 2—K8, k2 tog, yo, k6, k2 tog, yo, k7.

Row 4—K7, k2 tog, yo, k6, k2 tog, yo, k8.

Row 6—(K6, k2 tog, yo) twice, k9.

Row 8—K5, k2 tog, yo, k6, k2 tog, yo, k1-b, yo, ssk, k7.

Row 10—K4, k2 tog, yo, k6, k2 tog, yo, k3, yo, ssk, k6.
Row 12—K3, k2 tog, yo, k6, k2 tog, yo, k5, yo, ssk, k5.
Row 14—K2, (k2 tog, yo, k1-b, yo, ssk, k3) twice, k1, yo, ssk, k4.
Row 16—(K1, k2 tog, yo, k3, yo, ssk) twice, k4, yo, ssk, k3.
Row 18—K2 tog, yo, k5, (yo, sl 1—k2 tog—psso, yo, k1-b) twice, yo, ssk, k4, yo, ssk, k2.
Row 20—K2, yo, ssk, k4, yo, ssk, k6, yo, ssk, k4, yo, ssk, k1.
Row 22—K3, yo, ssk, k4, yo, ssk, yo, sl 1—k2 tog—psso, yo, k2 tog, yo, k1-b, yo, ssk, k4, yo, ssk.
Row 24—(K4, yo, ssk) twice, k1, k2 tog, yo, k3, yo, ssk, k1, k2 tog, yo, k2.
Row 26—K5, yo, ssk, k4, yo, k3 tog, yo, k5, yo, k3 tog, yo, k3.
Row 28—K6, yo, ssk, k3, k2 tog, yo, k6, k2 tog, yo, k4.
Row 30—K7, yo, ssk, k1, k2 tog, yo, k6, k2 tog, yo, k5.
Row 32—K8, yo, k3 tog, yo, k6, k2 tog, yo, k6.

Repeat Rows 1–32.

Dayflower

The old-time knitters were not *always* right. Here is a revised version of a lovely 19th-century pattern which was so badly botched in its original form that its graceful lines were scarcely discernible. Probably one reason for its having lain so long in obscurity was the disappointing result given by the original directions. These new directions, however, are guaranteed to please. Two panels are shown side by side, sharing the same two edge stitches between them (a total of 36 sts). Notice that these edge stitches are drawn into gentle waves by the bias pull of the pattern. Any number of Dayflower panels can be set together like this, to make an extremely pretty allover lace.

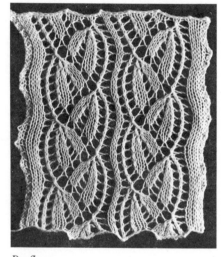

Dayflower

Panel of 19 sts (or, multiple of 17 sts plus 2).

Row 1 (Wrong side) and all other wrong-side rows *except* Rows 5 and 13—Purl.
Row 2—K2, yo, k2 tog, yo, (k2 tog) 3 times, k2, yo, k3, yo, ssk, yo, k2. (19 sts)
Row 4—K2, yo, k2 tog, (k3 tog) twice, yo, k1, yo, k2, (ssk, yo) twice, k2. (17 sts)
Row 5—P11, p2 tog, p4. (16 sts)
Row 6—K2, yo, k3 tog, yo, k3, yo, k2, (ssk, yo) twice, k2. (17 sts)
Row 8—K2, yo, k2 tog, yo, k1, (yo, k2, ssk) twice, yo, ssk, yo, k2. (19 sts)
Row 10—K2, yo, k2 tog, yo, k3, yo, k2, (ssk) 3 times, yo, ssk, yo, k2. (19 sts)
Row 12—K2, (yo, k2 tog) twice, k2, yo, k1, yo, (sl 1—k2 tog—psso) twice, ssk, yo, k2. (17 sts)
Row 13—P4, p2 tog-b, p11. (16 sts)
Row 14—K2, (yo, k2 tog) twice, k2, yo, k3, yo, sl 1—k2 tog—psso, yo, k2. (17 sts)
Row 16—K2, yo, k2 tog, yo, (k2 tog, k2, yo) twice, k1, yo, ssk, yo, k2. (19 sts)

Repeat Rows 1–16.

Leaf Shadows

On the second pattern row, this panel is increased to 25 stitches and remains at that number until Row 8 brings it down to 21 stitches. Row 10 restores the original 19.

Panel of 19 sts.

Row 1 (Wrong side) and all other wrong-side rows—Purl.
Row 2—Ssk, yo, k5, (yo, k1) 5 times, yo, k5, yo, k2 tog.
Row 4—Ssk, yo, ssk, k1, (k2 tog, yo) twice, k3, yo, k1, yo, k3, (yo, ssk) twice, k1, k2 tog, yo, k2 tog.
Row 6—Ssk, yo, sl 2—k1—p2sso, yo, k2 tog, yo, k5, yo, k1, yo, k5, yo, ssk, yo, sl 2—k1—p2sso, yo, k2 tog.
Row 8—Sl 1—k2 tog—psso, yo, k2 tog, yo, k1, yo, ssk, k1, k2 tog, yo, sl 2—k1—p2sso, yo, ssk, k1, k2 tog, yo, k1, yo, ssk, yo, k3 tog.
Row 10—K1, k2 tog, yo, k3, (yo, sl 2—k1—p2sso) 3 times, yo, k3, yo, ssk, k1.

Repeat Rows 1–10.

LEFT: *Leaf Shadows*
RIGHT: *Tiger Eye Pattern*

Tiger Eye Pattern

Panel of 25 sts.

Rows 1, 5, 7, 9, 11, 13, and 15 (Wrong side)—Purl.
Row 2—K2, (yo, k2 tog) twice, k1, (yo) 4 times, k1, (k2 tog, yo) twice, k1, (yo, ssk) twice, k1, (yo) 4 times, k1, (ssk, yo) twice, k2.
Row 3—P7, (k1, p1) twice into the 4-yo loop, p11, (k1, p1) twice into the 4-yo loop, p7.
Row 4—K2, (yo, k2 tog) twice, k4, k3 tog, yo, k2 tog, yo, k3, yo, ssk, yo, sl 1—k2 tog—psso, k4, (ssk, yo) twice, k2.
Row 6—K2, (yo, k2 tog) twice, k2, k3 tog, yo, k2 tog, yo, k5, yo, ssk, yo, sl 1—k2 tog—psso, k2, (ssk, yo) twice, k2.
Row 8—K2, (yo, k2 tog) twice, k3 tog, yo, k2 tog, yo, k3, yo, ssk, k2, yo, ssk, yo, sl 1—k2 tog—psso, (ssk, yo) twice, k2.
Row 10—K2, yo, k2 tog, k3 tog, yo, k2 tog, yo, k2, k2 tog, yo, k1, yo, ssk, k2, yo, ssk, yo, sl 1—k2 tog—psso, ssk, yo, k2.
Row 12—K3, (k2 tog, yo) twice, k2, k2 tog, yo, k3, yo, ssk, k2, (yo, ssk) twice, k3.
Row 14—K2, (k2 tog, yo) twice, k2, k2 tog, yo, k1, yo, sl 1—k2 tog—psso, yo, k1, yo, ssk, k2, (yo, ssk) twice, k2.
Row 16—K1, (k2 tog, yo) twice, k4, yo, sl 1—k2 tog—psso, yo, k1, yo, k3 tog, yo, k4, (yo, ssk) twice, k1.

Repeat Rows 1–16.

Pinwheel Pattern

This unusual and pretty design is completed in 30 rows, so it can be used as a spot-pattern as well as a panel. A single repeat of the pattern rows will make a square.

CENTER PANEL: *Pinwheel Pattern*
SIDE PANELS: *Wineglass Lace*

Panel of 21 sts.

Row 1 (Wrong side) and all other wrong-side rows—Purl.
Row 2—K12, k2 tog, yo, k7.
Row 4—K11, k2 tog, yo, k8.
Row 6—K10, (k2 tog, yo) twice, k7.
Row 8—K9, (k2 tog, yo) twice, k8.
Row 10—K8, (k2 tog, yo) 3 times, k7.
Row 12—K2, (yo, ssk) twice, yo, sl 1—k2 tog—psso, yo, (k2 tog, yo) twice, k1, yo, ssk, k5.
Row 14—K3, (yo, ssk) twice, k1, (k2 tog, yo) twice, k3, yo, ssk, k4.
Row 16—K4, yo, ssk, yo, sl 1—k2 tog—psso, yo, (k2 tog, yo) twice, k1, (yo, ssk) twice, k3.
Row 18—K5, yo, ssk, k1, (k2 tog, yo) twice, k3, (yo, ssk) twice, k2.
Row 20—K6, yo, sl 1—k2 tog—psso, yo, (k2 tog, yo) twice, k1, (yo, ssk) 3 times, k1.
Row 22—K6, (k2 tog, yo) 3 times, k9.
Row 24—K7, (k2 tog, yo) twice, k10.
Row 26—K6, (k2 tog, yo) twice, k11.
Row 28—K7, k2 tog, yo, k12.
Row 30—K6, k2 tog, yo, k13.

Repeat Rows 1–30.

Wineglass Lace

Contributed by Hildegard M. Elsner, Aldan, Pennsylvania

This pattern calls for a panel of 5 stitches, but in fact it is considerably wider than that, because the 5-stitch minimum is retained for only one row. Also it requires stretching in order to show the pattern, so the actual width is nearly twice that of a 5-stitch gauge.

Panel of 5 sts.

Row 1 (Wrong side)—P1, (yo, p1) 4 times. (9 sts.)
Row 2—Ssk, yo, k1, yo, k3, yo, k1, yo, k2 tog. (11 sts.)
Row 3—P3, yo, p5, yo, p3. (13 sts.)
Row 4—Ssk, (yo, k1) twice, k2 tog, k1, ssk, (k1, yo) twice, k2 tog. (13 sts.)
Row 5—P4, p2 tog-b, p1, p2 tog, p4. (11 sts.)
Row 6—Ssk, yo, k1, k2 tog, k1, ssk, k1, yo, k2 tog. (9 sts.)
Row 7—P9.
Row 8—(Ssk) twice, k1, (k2 tog) twice. (5 sts.)

Repeat Rows 1–8.

CENTER PANEL: *Blossoming Branch*
SIDE PANELS: *Branched Fern*

Blossoming Branch

This beautiful lace panel is fancy enough to stand by itself in an otherwise plain fabric, or it may be combined with different lace panels.

NOTE: "Ssk and pass next st" in Rows 8 and 12 is the opposite of "sl 1—k2 tog—psso", and is worked as follows: ssk, then return the resulting st to left-hand needle and with the point of right-hand needle pass the *next* st over the ssk st and off needle; then slip the st back to right-hand needle and proceed. (See Glossary on Double Decreases.)

Panel of 17 sts.

Row 1 (Wrong side) and all other wrong-side rows—Purl.
Row 2—K5, yo, ssk, k2, k2 tog, yo, k1, yo, ssk, k3.
Row 4—K3, k2 tog, yo, k1, yo, ssk, (k2 tog, yo) twice, k1, yo, ssk, k2.
Row 6—K2, (k2 tog, yo) twice, k1, yo, ssk, k2 tog, yo, k1, (yo, ssk) twice, k1.
Row 8—K1, (k2 tog, yo) twice, k3, yo, ssk, yo, ssk and pass next st, yo, k2 tog, yo, k2.
Row 10—(K2 tog, yo) twice, k5, yo, ssk, k1, k2 tog, yo, k3.
Row 12—K1, k2 tog, yo, k2, yo, ssk, k3, yo, ssk and pass next st, yo, k4.
Row 14—K3, k2 tog, yo, k1, yo, ssk, k2, k2 tog, yo, k5.
Row 16—K2, k2 tog, yo, k1, (yo, ssk) twice, k2 tog, yo, k1, yo, ssk, k3.
Row 18—K1, (k2 tog, yo) twice, k1, yo, ssk, k2 tog, yo, k1, (yo, ssk) twice, k2.
Row 20—K2, yo, ssk, yo, sl 1—k2 tog—psso, yo, k2 tog, yo, k3, (yo, ssk) twice, k1.
Row 22—K3, yo, ssk, k1, k2 tog, yo, k5, (yo, ssk) twice.
Row 24—K4, yo, sl 1—k2 tog—psso, yo, k3, k2 tog, yo, k2, yo, ssk, k1.

Repeat Rows 1–24.

Branched Fern

Here is a highly decorative lace panel that is quite easy to work, and looks very nice when used as a "trimming" for wider panels of a different type.

Panel of 17 sts.

Row 1 (Wrong side) and all other wrong-side rows—K1, p15, k1.
Row 2—P1, k1, (k2 tog) twice, (yo, k1) 3 times, yo, (ssk) twice, k3, p1.

Row 4—P1, (k2 tog) twice, yo, k1, yo, k3, yo, k1, yo, (ssk) twice, k2, p1.

Row 6—P1, k3, (k2 tog) twice, (yo, k1) 3 times, yo, (ssk) twice, k1, p1.

Row 8—P1, k2, (k2 tog) twice, yo, k1, yo, k3, yo, k1, yo, (ssk) twice, p1.

Repeat Rows 1–8.

Imperial Branch

This is a larger and slightly fancier version of Blossoming Branch, and employs the same "opposite" double decrease, which occurs here in Rows 8 and 16. For the explanation of "ssk and pass next st", see Blossoming Branch.

Panel of 29 sts.

Row 1 (Wrong side) and all other wrong-side rows—Purl.

Row 2—K1, k2 tog, yo, k3, (yo, ssk) twice, k4, k2 tog, yo, k3, yo, ssk, k1, k2 tog, yo, k5.

Row 4—K2 tog, yo, k2, yo, ssk, k1, (yo, ssk) twice, k2, k2 tog, yo, k5, yo, sl 1—k2 tog—psso, yo, k6.

Row 6—K1, yo, ssk, k2, yo, ssk, k1, k2 tog, yo, k2, k2 tog, yo, k1, yo, ssk, k12.

Row 8—K2, yo, ssk, k2, yo, ssk and pass next st, yo, k2, k2 tog, yo, k1, (yo, ssk) twice, k5, yo, ssk, k4.

Row 10—K3, yo, ssk, k5, k2 tog, yo, k1, (yo, ssk) 3 times, k2, k2 tog, yo, k1, yo, ssk, k3.

Row 12—K4, yo, ssk, k3, k2 tog, yo, k1, (yo, ssk) 4 times, (k2 tog, yo) twice, k1, yo, ssk, k2.

Row 14—K5, yo, ssk, k1, k2 tog, yo, k3, yo, ssk, k4, (k2 tog, yo) twice, k3, yo, ssk, k1.

Row 16—K6, yo, ssk and pass next st, yo, k5, yo, ssk, k2, (k2 tog, yo) twice, k1, k2 tog, yo, k2, yo, ssk.

Row 18—K12, k2 tog, yo, k1, yo, ssk, k2, yo, ssk, k1, k2 tog, yo, k2, k2 tog, yo, k1.

Row 20—K4, k2 tog, yo, k5, (k2 tog, yo) twice, k1, yo, ssk, k2, yo, sl 1—k2 tog—psso, yo, k2, k2 tog, yo, k2.

Row 22—K3, k2 tog, yo, k1, yo, ssk, k2, (k2 tog, yo) 3 times, k1, yo, ssk, k5, k2 tog, yo, k3.

Row 24—K2, k2 tog, yo, k1, (yo, ssk) twice, (k2 tog, yo) 4 times, k1, yo, ssk, k3, k2 tog, yo, k4.

Repeat Rows 1–24.

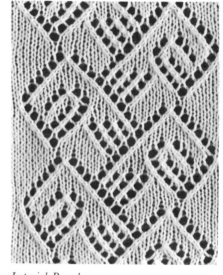

Imperial Branch

Three "Floral" Motifs: Broad-Leaved Flower, Floral Panel II, and Four-Leaved Flower

I. BROAD-LEAVED FLOWER

This pattern, a variation on a Japanese design, displays wide knit-stitch "leaves" on a purled background. The "flower" is a simple lace medallion. Charming borders can be made out of this pattern on a multiple of 18 stitches plus 1, the "p2 tog" rows being converted into "p3 tog" between the motifs.

Panel of 19 sts.

Three "Floral" Motifs
LEFT: *Broad-Leaved Flower*
CENTER: *Floral Panel II*
RIGHT: *Four-Leaved Flower*

Rows 1 and 3 (Wrong side)—Knit.
Rows 2 and 4—Purl.
Rows 5 and 7—K8, p3, k8.
Row 6—P8, k3, p8.
Row 8—P2 tog, p6, (k1, yo) twice, k1, p6, p2 tog.
Row 9—K7, p5, k7.
Row 10—P2 tog, p5, k2, yo, k1, yo, k2, p5, p2 tog.
Row 11—K6, p7, k6.
Row 12—P2 tog, p4, k3, yo, k1, yo, k3, p4, p2 tog.
Row 13—K5, p9, k5.
Row 14—P2 tog, p3, k4, yo, k1, yo, k4, p3, p2 tog.
Row 15—K4, p11, k4.
Row 16—P2 tog, p2, k5, yo, k1, yo, k5, p2, p2 tog.
Rows 17, 19, 21, 23, and 25—K3, p13, k3.
Row 18—P3, ssk, k4, yo, k1, yo, k4, k2 tog, p3.
Row 20—P3, ssk, (k3, yo) twice, k3, k2 tog, p3.
Row 22—P3, ssk, k2, yo, k2 tog, yo, k1, yo, ssk, yo, k2, k2 tog, p3.
Row 24—P3, ssk, k1, yo, k2 tog, yo, k3, yo, ssk, yo, k1, k2 tog, p3.
Row 26—P3, ssk, k1, yo, ssk, yo, k3, yo, k2 tog, yo, k1, k2 tog, p3.
Rows 27, 29, and 31—Repeat Rows 13, 11, and 9.
Row 28—P5, k1, yo, ssk, yo, sl 1—k2 tog—psso, yo, k2 tog, yo, k1, p.
Row 30—P6, k1, yo, ssk, k1, k2 tog, yo, k1, p6.
Row 32—P7, k1, yo, sl 1—k2 tog—psso, yo, k1, p7.

Repeat Rows 1–32.

II. FLORAL PANEL II

Contributed by Dorothy Reade, Eugene, Oregon

Mrs. Reade's original design includes two narrow panels of Miniature Leaf Pattern (*A Treasury of Knitting Patterns*, p. 215) on either side of the large flower motif. These have been omitted here, for better comparison of this pattern with the other two; but the knitter may restore them, or use some other narrow panel to enhance the "flower".

Panel of 19 sts.

Row 1 (Wrong side) and all other wrong-side rows—Purl.
Row 2—K5, (k2 tog, yo) twice, k1, (yo, ssk) twice, k5.

Row 4—K4, k2 tog, yo, k2 tog, k1-b, yo, k1, yo, k1-b, ssk, yo, ssk, k4.

Row 6—K3, k2 tog, yo, k2 tog, k1, k1-b, yo, k1, yo, k1-b, k1, ssk, yo, ssk, k3.

Row 8—K2, k2 tog, yo, k2 tog, k2, k1-b, yo, k1, yo, k1-b, k2, ssk, yo, ssk, k2.

Row 10—K1, k2 tog, yo, k2 tog, k3, k1-b, yo, k1, yo, k1-b, k3, ssk, yo, ssk, k1.

Row 12—K2 tog, yo, k2 tog, k4, k1-b, yo, k1, yo, k1-b, k4, ssk, yo, ssk.

Row 14—K1, yo, ssk, k3, k2 tog, yo, k1-b, k1, k1-b, yo, ssk, k3, k2 tog, yo, k1.

Row 16—K1, yo, ssk, k2, (k2 tog, yo) twice, k1, (yo, ssk) twice, k2, k2 tog, yo, k1.

Row 18—K1, yo, ssk, k1, k2 tog, yo, k2 tog, k1-b, yo, k1, yo, k1-b, ssk, yo, ssk, k1, k2 tog, yo, k1.

Row 20—K1, yo, ssk, k2 tog, yo, k2 tog, k1, k1-b, yo, k1, yo, k1-b, k1, ssk, yo, ssk, k2 tog, yo, k1.

Row 22—K1, yo, sl 1—k2 tog—psso, yo, k2 tog, k2, k1-b, yo, k1, yo, k1-b, k2, ssk, yo, sl 1—k2 tog—psso, yo, k1.

Row 24—K1, k1-b, k1, yo, ssk, k1, k2 tog, yo, k1-b, k1, k1-b, yo, ssk, k1, k2 tog, yo, k1, k1-b, k1.

Row 26—K3, yo, ssk, (k2 tog, yo) twice, k1-b, (yo, ssk) twice, k2 tog, yo, k3.

Row 28—K3, yo, sl 1—k2 tog—psso, yo, k2 tog, yo, k1-b, k1, k1-b, yo, ssk, yo, sl 1—k2 tog—psso, yo, k3.

Row 30—K3, k1-b, k1, (yo, ssk) twice, k1, (k2 tog, yo) twice, k1, k1-b, k3.

Row 32—K5, k1-b, yo, ssk, yo, sl 1—k2 tog—psso, yo, k2 tog, yo, k1-b, k5.

Row 34—K6, k1-b, yo, ssk, k1, k2 tog, yo, k1-b, k6.

Row 36—K7, k1-b, yo, sl 1—k2 tog—psso, yo, k1-b, k7.

Repeat Rows 1–36.

III. FOUR-LEAVED FLOWER

Here again is a medallion-shaped "flower", a little flatter than the others because the lace is formed on both sides of the fabric instead of the right side only.

Panel of 15 sts.

Row 1 (Wrong side)—Purl.

Row 2—K4, k2 tog, (k1, yo) twice, k1, ssk, k4.

Row 3—P3, p2 tog-b, p1, yo, p3, yo, p1, p2 tog, p3.

Row 4—K2, k2 tog, (k1, yo) twice, sl 2—k1—p2sso, (yo, k1) twice, ssk, k2.

Row 5—P1, p2 tog-b, p1, yo, p7, yo, p1, p2 tog, p1.

Row 6—K2 tog, k1, yo, k3, yo, sl 2—k1—p2sso, yo, k3, yo, k1, ssk.

Rows 7 through 13—Repeat Rows 1 through 6, then Row 1 again.

Row 14—K5, k2 tog, yo, k1, yo, ssk, k5.

Row 15—P4, p2 tog-b, yo, p3, yo, p2 tog, p4.

Row 16—K3, (k2 tog, yo) twice, k1, (yo, ssk) twice, k3.

Row 17—P2, p2 tog-b, yo, p7, yo, p2 tog, p2.

Row 18—(K1, k2 tog, yo) twice, k3, (yo, ssk, k1) twice.

Rows 19 and 21—Purl.

Row 20—K3, (yo, ssk) twice, k1, (k2 tog, yo) twice, k3.

Row 22—K4, yo, ssk, yo, sl 1—k2 tog—psso, yo, k2 tog, yo, k4.

Row 23—P5, yo, p2 tog, p1, p2 tog-b, yo, p5.

Row 24—K6, yo, sl 1—k2 tog—psso, yo, k6.

Repeat Rows 1–24.

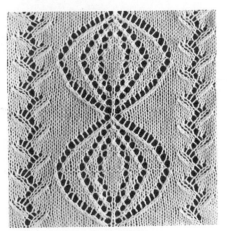

CENTER PANEL: *Jewel Medallion*
SIDE PANELS: *Little Vine*

Jewel Medallion

Like Grand Medallion, this pattern is very handsome as a central and dominating motif in any lace article. The delicate single-strand openwork that surrounds the medallion is well set off by a lining of contrasting color. Evening bags in metallic yarn, small cushions, and place mats are enhanced by a central Jewel Medallion.

Panel of 27 sts.

Row 1 (Wrong side)—Purl.
Row 2—K11, k2 tog, yo, k1, yo, ssk, k11.
Row 3—P10, p2 tog-b, yo, p3, yo, p2 tog, p10.
Row 4—K9, (k2 tog, yo) twice, k1, (yo, ssk) twice, k9.
Row 5—P8, p2 tog-b, yo, k7, yo, p2 tog, p8.
Row 6—K7, k2 tog, yo, k1, k2 tog, yo, k3, yo, ssk, k1, yo, ssk, k7.
Row 7—P6, p2 tog-b, yo, p11, yo, p2 tog, p6.
Row 8—K5, k2 tog, yo, k2, (k2 tog, yo) twice, k1, (yo, ssk) twice, k2, yo, ssk, k5.
Row 9—P4, p2 tog-b, yo, p15, yo, p2 tog, p4.
Row 10—K3, k2 tog, yo, k3, (k2 tog, yo) twice, k3, (yo, ssk) twice, k3, yo, ssk, k3.
Row 11—P4, k19, p4.
Row 12—K2, k2 tog, yo, k3, k2 tog, yo, k1, k2 tog, yo, k3, yo, ssk, k1, yo, ssk, k3, yo, ssk, k2.
Row 13—Purl.
Row 14—K1, k2 tog, yo, k3, k2 tog, yo, k1, k2 tog, yo, k5, yo, ssk, k1, yo, ssk, k3, yo, ssk, k1.
Row 15—Purl.
Row 16—K2 tog, yo, k3, k2 tog, yo, k2, k2 tog, yo, k5, yo, ssk, k2, yo, ssk, k3, yo, ssk.
Row 17—P1, k25, p1.
Row 18—K1, yo, ssk, k3, yo, ssk, k2, yo, ssk, k3, k2 tog, yo, k2, k2 tog, yo, k3, k2 tog, yo, k1.
Row 19—Purl.
Row 20—K2, yo, ssk, k3, yo, ssk, k1, yo, ssk, k3, k2 tog, yo, k1, k2 tog, yo, k3, k2 tog, yo, k2.
Row 21—Purl.
Row 22—K3, yo, ssk, k3, (yo, ssk, k1) twice, k2 tog, yo, k1, (k2 tog, yo, k3) twice.
Row 23—Repeat Row 11.
Row 24—K4, yo, ssk, k3, (yo, ssk) twice, k1, (k2 tog, yo) twice, k3, k2 tog, yo, k4.
Row 25—P5, yo, p2 tog, p13, p2 tog-b, yo, p5.
Row 26—K6, yo, ssk, k2, yo, ssk, yo, sl 1—k2 tog—psso, yo, k2 tog, yo, k2, k2 tog, yo, k6.
Row 27—P7, yo, p2 tog, p9, p2 tog-b, yo, p7.
Row 28—K8, (yo, ssk, k1) twice, k2 tog, yo, k1, k2 tog, yo, k8.
Row 29—P9, yo, p2 tog, k5, p2 tog-b, yo, p9.
Row 30—K10, yo, ssk, yo, sl 1—k2 tog—psso, yo, k2 tog, yo, k10.
Row 31—P11, yo, p2 tog, p1, p2 tog-b, yo, p11.
Row 32—K12, yo, sl 1—k2 tog—psso, yo, k12.

Repeat Rows 1–32 for vertical panel.

Little Vine

This dainty insertion is a variation on the "Vandyke" theme, since it forms a small zigzag; but the decreases are removed one stitch away from the yarn-overs, which adds texture interest to the fabric.

Panel of 10 sts.

Row 1 (Right side)—K4, yo, k1, ssk, k3.
Row 2—P2, p2 tog-b, p1, yo, p5.
Row 3—K6, yo, k1, ssk, k1.
Row 4—P2 tog-b, p1, yo, p7.
Row 5—K3, k2 tog, k1, yo, k4.
Row 6—P5, yo, p1, p2 tog, p2.
Row 7—K1, k2 tog, k1, yo, k6.
Row 8—P7, yo, p1, p2 tog.

Repeat Rows 1–8.

Grand Medallion

Panel of 41 sts.

Row 1 (Right side)—Knit.
Row 2—P20, yo, p2 tog, p19.
Row 3—K18, k2 tog, yo, k1, yo, ssk, k18.
Row 4—P17, p2 tog-b, yo, p3, yo, p2 tog, p17.
Row 5—K16, (k2 tog, yo) twice, k1, (yo, ssk) twice, k16.
Row 6—P15, p2 tog-b, yo, p7, yo, p2 tog, p15.
Row 7—K14, k2 tog, yo, k1, k2 tog, yo, k3, yo, ssk, k1, yo, ssk, k14.
Row 8—P13, p2 tog-b, yo, p11, yo, p2 tog, p13.
Row 9—K12, k2 tog, yo, k2, k2 tog, yo, k5, yo, ssk, k2, yo, ssk, k12.
Row 10—P11, p2 tog-b, yo, p15, yo, p2 tog, p11.
Row 11—K10, k2 tog, yo, k3, k2 tog, yo, k7, yo, ssk, k3, yo, ssk, k10.

Grand Medallion

Row 12—P9, p2 tog-b, yo, p19, yo, p2 tog, p9.
Row 13—K8, k2 tog, yo, k4, k2 tog, yo, k9, yo, ssk, k4, yo, ssk, k8.
Row 14—P7, p2 tog-b, yo, p23, yo, p2 tog, p7.
Row 15—K6, (k2 tog, yo, k5) twice, yo, ssk, k4, yo, ssk, k5, yo, ssk, k6.

Row 16—Purl.

Row 17—(K5, k2 tog, yo) twice, k4, k2 tog, yo, k1, yo, ssk, k4, (yo, ssk, k5) twice.

Row 18—Repeat Row 10.

Row 19—(K4, k2 tog, yo) twice, k5, k2 tog, yo, k3, yo, ssk, k5, (yo, ssk, k4) twice.

Row 20—Repeat Row 12.

Row 21—(K3, k2 tog, yo) twice, k6, k2 tog, yo, k5, yo, ssk, k6, (yo, ssk, k3) twice.

Row 22—Repeat Row 14.

Row 23—(K2, k2 tog, yo) twice, k7, k2 tog, yo, k2, yo, sl 1—k2 tog—psso, yo, k2, yo, ssk, k7, (yo, ssk, k2) twice.

Row 24—P5, p2 tog-b, yo, p27, yo, p2 tog, p5.

Row 25—(K1, k2 tog, yo) twice, k8, k2 tog, yo, k1, ssk, yo, k3, yo, k2 tog, k1, yo, ssk, k8, (yo, ssk, k1) twice.

Row 26—P3, p2 tog-b, yo, p31, yo, p2 tog, p3.

Row 27—(K2 tog, yo) twice, k11, yo, k2 tog, k2, yo, sl 1—k2 tog—psso, yo, k2, ssk, yo, k11, (yo, ssk) twice.

Row 28—Purl.

Row 29—K1, (yo, ssk) twice, k10, yo, k2 tog, ssk, yo, k3, yo, k2 tog, ssk, yo, k10, (k2 tog, yo) twice, k1.

Row 30—P4, yo, p2 tog, p29, p2 tog-b, yo, p4.

Row 31—K2, yo, ssk, k1, yo, ssk, k8, yo, k2 tog, k2, yo, sl 1—k2 tog—psso, yo, k2, ssk, yo, k8, k2 tog, yo, k1, k2 tog, yo, k2.

Row 32—P6, yo, p2 tog, p25, p2 tog-b, yo, p6.

Row 33—K3, yo, ssk, k2, yo, ssk, k7, yo, ssk, k2, yo, ssk, k1, k2 tog, yo, k7, k2 tog, yo, k2, k2 tog, yo, k3.

Row 34—P8, yo, p2 tog, p21, p2 tog-b, yo, p8.

Row 35—K4, yo, ssk, k3, yo, ssk, k6, yo, ssk, k3, k2 tog, yo, k6, k2 tog, yo, k3, k2 tog, yo, k4.

Row 36—P10, yo, p2 tog, p17, p2 tog-b, yo, p10.

Row 37—K5, yo, ssk, k4, yo, ssk, k5, yo, ssk, k1, k2 tog, yo, k5, k2 tog, yo, k4, k2 tog, yo, k5.

Row 38—P12, yo, p2 tog, p13, p2 tog-b, yo, p12.

Row 39—K6, yo, ssk, k5, yo, ssk, k4, yo, sl 1—k2 tog—psso, yo, k4, k2 tog, yo, k5, k2 tog, yo, k6.

Row 40—Purl.

Row 41—K7, yo, ssk, k5, yo, ssk, k4, yo, ssk, k3, k2 tog, yo, k5, k2 tog, yo, k7.

Row 42—Repeat Row 34.

Row 43—K9, yo, ssk, k4, yo, ssk, k7, k2 tog, yo, k4, k2 tog, yo, k9.

Row 44—Repeat Row 36.

Row 45—K11, yo, ssk, k3, yo, ssk, k5, k2 tog, yo, k3, k2 tog, yo, k11.

Row 46—Repeat Row 38.

Row 47—K13, yo, ssk, k2, yo, ssk, k3, k2 tog, yo, k2, k2 tog, yo, k13.

Row 48—P14, yo, p2 tog, p9, p2 tog-b, yo, p14.

Row 49—K15, (yo, ssk, k1) twice, k2 tog, yo, k1, k2 tog, yo, k15.

Row 50—P16, yo, p2 tog, p5, p2 tog-b, yo, p16.

Row 51—K17, yo, ssk, yo, sl 1—k2 tog—psso, yo, k2 tog, yo, k17.

Row 52—P18, yo, p2 tog, p1, p2 tog-b, yo, p18.

Row 53—K19, yo, sl 1—k2 tog—psso, yo, k19.

Row 54—P19, p2 tog-b, yo, p20.

Repeat Rows 1–54.

Scrolls

Contributed by Dorothy Reade, Eugene, Oregon

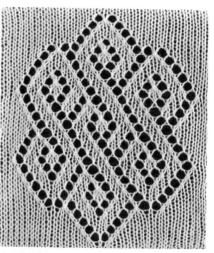

Scrolls

Panel of 31 sts.

Row 1 (Wrong side) and all other wrong-side rows—Purl.

Row 2—K13, k2 tog, yo, k1-b, yo, ssk, k13.

Row 4—K12, k2 tog, yo, k1-b, k1, k1-b, yo, ssk, k12.

Row 6—K11, k2 tog, yo, k1-b, k3, k1-b, yo, ssk, k11.

Row 8—K10, k2 tog, yo, k1-b, k1, k2 tog, yo, k2, k1-b, yo, ssk, k10.

Row 10—K5, k2 tog, yo, k1-b, yo, sl 1—k2 tog—psso, yo, k1-b, k1, k2 tog, yo, k1-b, yo, ssk, k1, k1-b, yo, k3 tog, yo, k1-b, yo, ssk, k5.

Row 12—K4, (k2 tog, yo, k1-b, k1, k1-b, yo, ssk, k1) 3 times, k3.

Row 14—K3, * k2 tog, yo, k1-b, k3, k1-b, yo, ssk, * k1, k1-b, yo, sl 1—k2 tog—psso, yo, k1-b, k1, rep from * to *, k3.

Row 16—K2, * k2 tog, yo, k1-b, k1, k2 tog, yo, k2, k1-b, yo, ssk, * k1, k1-b, yo, ssk, k1, rep from * to *, k2.

Row 18—K1, k2 tog, * yo, k1-b, k1, k2 tog, yo, (k1-b, yo, ssk, k1) twice, * k1-b, yo, sl 1—k2 tog—psso, rep from * to *.

Row 20—K2 tog, yo, k1-b, * k1, k2 tog, yo, k1-b, k1, k1-b, yo, ssk, k1, k1-b, yo, ssk, * k1, k1-b, yo, ssk, rep from * to *.

Row 22—* K1, k1-b, yo, ssk, k1, k1-b, yo, sl 1—k2 tog—psso, yo, k1-b, k1, k2 tog, yo, k1-b, * yo, ssk, rep from * to *, k1.

Row 24—K2, (k1-b, yo, ssk, k1) twice, * k2 tog, yo, k1-b, k1, * (k1-b, yo, ssk, k1) 3 times, rep from * to *, k1.

Row 26—K3, * k1-b, yo, ssk, k1, k1-b, yo, sl 1—k2 tog—psso, yo, k1-b, * k1, k2 tog, yo, k1-b, yo, ssk, k1, rep from * to *, k3.

Row 28—K4, (k1-b, yo, ssk, k1) twice, k2 tog, yo, k1-b, k1, (k1-b, yo, ssk, k1) 3 times, k3.

Row 30—K3, * k2 tog, yo, k1-b, yo, ssk, k1, k1-b, yo, ssk, * k1, k1-b, yo, sl 1—k2 tog—psso, yo, k1-b, k1, rep from * to *, k3.

Row 32—K2, * k2 tog, yo, k1-b, k1, * (k1-b, yo, ssk, k1) 3 times, rep from * to *, (k1-b, yo, ssk, k1) twice, k1.

Rows 34, 36, 38, and 40—Repeat Rows 18, 20, 22, and 24.

Row 42—K3, * k1-b, yo, ssk, k1, k1-b, k1, k2 tog, yo, k1-b, * k1, k2 tog, yo, k1-b, yo, ssk, k1, rep from * to *, k3.

Row 44—K4, * k1-b, yo, ssk, k1, k2 tog, yo, k1-b, * k1, k2 tog, yo, k1-b, k1, k1-b, yo, ssk, k1, rep from * to *, k4.

Row 46—K5, * k1-b, yo, sl 1—k2 tog—psso, yo, k1-b, * yo, ssk, k1, rep from * to *, k1, k2 tog, yo, rep from * to *, k5.

Row 48—K6, (k1-b, k1) twice, (k1-b, yo, ssk, k1) twice, k2 tog, yo, (k1-b, k1) twice, k1-b, k6.

Row 50—K11, k1-b, yo, ssk, k1, k1-b, k1, k2 tog, yo, k1-b, k11.

Row 52—K12, k1-b, yo, ssk, k1, k2 tog, yo, k1-b, k12.

Row 54—K13, k1-b, yo, sl 1—k2 tog—psso, yo, k1-b, k13.

Row 56—K14, k1-b, k1, k1-b, k14.

Repeat Rows 1–56.

The Windmill

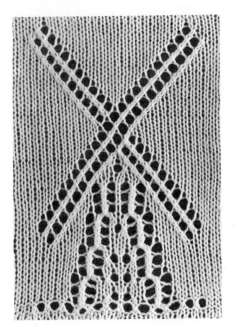

The Windmill

Here is a quaint and charming pattern for children's wear, casual clothes, and items of home decoration. 64 rows complete the pattern, but it may be continued from Row 1 in vertical arrangement if desired. A band of Windmill panels side by side would make a delightful border for a little girl's skirt or petticoat.

Careful attention must be paid to the double decreases in the Windmill. Three different kinds are used: k3 tog, sl 1—k2 tog—psso, and sl 2—k1—p2sso. Remember that in the third type of decrease the two stitches are always slipped *knitwise*, and *both together*, not one at a time.

Panel of 25 sts.

Row 1 (Wrong side)—Purl.

Rows 2 and 3—Knit.

Row 4—K1, * yo, k2 tog; rep from * across.

Row 5—Knit.

Row 6—K6, yo, sl 2—k1—p2sso, yo, k1, k2 tog, yo, k1, yo, ssk, k1, yo, sl 2—k1—p2sso, yo, k6.

Row 7 and all subsequent wrong-side rows—Purl.

Row 8—K6, yo, sl 2—k1—p2sso, yo, k7, yo, sl 2—k1—p2sso, yo, k6.

Row 10—Repeat Row 6.

Row 12—K7, yo, sl 1—k2 tog—psso, yo, k5, yo, k3 tog, yo, k7.

Row 14—K7, yo, sl 2—k1—p2sso, yo, k2 tog, yo, k1, yo, ssk, yo, sl 2—k1—p2sso, yo, k7.

Row 16—K7, yo, sl 2—k1—p2sso, yo, k5, yo, sl 2—k1—p2sso, yo, k7.

Row 18—K2, yo, ssk, k4, yo, sl 1—k2 tog—psso, yo, k3, yo, k3 tog, yo, k4, k2 tog, yo, k2.

Row 20—K1, (yo, ssk) twice, k3, yo, sl 2—k1—p2sso, yo, k2 tog, yo, k1, yo, sl 2—k1—p2sso, yo, k3, (k2 tog, yo) twice, k1.

Row 22—K2, (yo, ssk) twice, k2, yo, sl 2—k1—p2sso, yo, k3, yo, sl 2—k1—p2sso, yo, k2, (k2 tog, yo) twice, k2.

Row 24—K3, (yo, ssk) twice, k2, yo, sl 1—k2 tog—psso, yo, k1, yo, k3 tog, yo, k2, (k2 tog, yo) twice, k3.

Row 26—K4, (yo, ssk) twice, (k1, yo, sl 2—k1—p2sso, yo) twice, k1, (k2 tog, yo) twice, k4.

Row 28—K5, (yo, ssk) twice, yo, sl 2—k1—p2sso, yo, k1, yo, sl 2—k1—p2sso, yo, (k2 tog, yo) twice, k5.

Row 30—K6, (yo, ssk) twice, k5, (k2 tog, yo) twice, k6.

Row 32—K7, (yo, ssk) twice, k2 tog, yo, k1, (k2 tog, yo) twice, k7.

Row 34—K8, (yo, ssk) twice, k1, (k2 tog, yo) twice, k8.

Row 36—K9, yo, ssk, yo, sl 1—k2 tog—psso, yo, k2 tog, yo, k9.

Row 38—K10, yo, sl 1—k2 tog—psso, yo, k2 tog, yo, k10.

Row 40—K10, (k2 tog, yo) twice, k11.

Row 42—K9, (k2 tog, yo) twice, k1, yo, ssk, k9.

Row 44—K8, (k2 tog, yo) twice, k1, (yo, ssk) twice, k8.

Row 46—K7, (k2 tog, yo) twice, k3, (yo, ssk) twice, k7.

Row 48—K6, (k2 tog, yo) twice, k5, (yo, ssk) twice, k6.

Row 50—K5, (k2 tog, yo) twice, k7, (yo, ssk) twice, k5.
Row 52—K4, (k2 tog, yo) twice, k9, (yo, ssk) twice, k4.
Row 54—K3, (k2 tog, yo) twice, k11, (yo, ssk) twice, k3.
Row 56—K2, (k2 tog, yo) twice, k13, (yo, ssk) twice, k2.
Row 58—K1, (k2 tog, yo) twice, k15, (yo, ssk) twice, k1.
Row 60—(K2 tog, yo) twice, k17, (yo, ssk) twice.
Row 62—K1, k2 tog, yo, k19, yo, ssk, k1.
Row 64—Knit.

The Crown

Panel of 31 sts.

NOTE: Make Bobble (MB) as follows: (k1, yo, k1, yo, k1) in one st, making 5 sts from one; turn and k5, turn and p5, turn and k1, sl 1—k2 tog—psso, k1, turn and p3 tog, completing bobble.

CENTER PANEL: *The Crown*
SIDE PANELS: *Swiss Fan*

Rows 1 and 3 (Wrong side)—Purl.
Rows 2 and 4—Knit.
Rows 5 and 7—P8, k15, p8.
Row 6—K8, p15, k8.
Row 8—K9, (p1, k1) 6 times, p1, k9.
Rows 9 and 11—P8, (k1, p1) 7 times, k1, p8.
Row 10—K9, (MB, k1, p1, MB, p1, k1) twice, MB, k9.
Row 12—Repeat Row 8.
Row 13—P14, k1, p1, k1, p14.
Row 14—K7, (k2 tog, yo) 3 times, k2, MB, k2, (yo, ssk) 3 times, k7.
Row 15—P6, (p2 tog-b, yo) twice, p4, k1, p1, k1, p4, (yo, p2 tog) twice, p6.
Row 16—K5, [(k2 tog, yo) twice, k1] twice, p1, [k1, (yo, ssk) twice] twice, k5.
Row 17—P4, (p2 tog-b, yo) twice, p15, (yo, p2 tog) twice, p4.
Row 18—K3, (k2 tog, yo) twice, k2, (k2 tog, yo) twice, k1, yo, sl 2—k1—p2sso, yo, k1, (yo, ssk) twice, k2, (yo, ssk) twice, k3.
Row 19—P2, (p2 tog-b, yo) twice, p19, (yo, p2 tog) twice, p2.
Row 20—K1, (k2 tog, yo) twice, k3, (k2 tog, yo) twice, k2, yo, sl 2—k1—p2sso, yo, k2, (yo, ssk) twice, k3, (yo, ssk) twice, k1.
Row 21 and all subsequent wrong-side rows—Purl.
Row 22—K2, yo, sl 2—k1—p2sso, yo, k2, (k2 tog, yo) twice, k3, yo, sl 2—k1—p2sso, yo, k3, (yo, ssk) twice, k2, yo, sl 2—k1—p2sso, yo, k2.
Row 24—K2, (yo, sl 2—k1—p2sso, yo, k3) 5 times ending last repeat k2 instead of k3.
Row 26—K3, MB, k4, (yo, sl 2—k1—p2sso, yo, k3) 3 times, k1, MB, k3.
Row 28—K9, MB, k4, yo, sl 2—k1—p2sso, yo, k4, MB, k9.
Row 30—K15, MB, k15.

Repeat Rows 1–30.

Swiss Fan

Here is a Feather-and-Fan variation from Switzerland, which is both pretty and simple to work. It may be used as shown to set off wider and fancier panels, or it may be worked all over the fabric on a multiple of 8 sts plus 1.

Panel of 9 sts.

Row 1 (Right side)—P1, ssk, (yo, k1) 3 times, yo, k2 tog, p1.
Row 2—K1, p9, k1.
Row 3—P1, ssk, k5, k2 tog, p1.
Row 4—K1, p7, k1.

Repeat Rows 1–4.

The Star

The Star

Panel of 51 sts.

Row 1 (Right side)—Knit.
Row 2—Purl.
Row 3—K23, k2 tog, yo, k1, yo, ssk, k23.
Row 4—P5, yo, p2 tog, p37, p2 tog-b, yo, p5.
Row 5—K6, yo, ssk, k14, k2 tog, yo, k3, yo, ssk, k14, k2 tog, yo, k6.
Row 6—P7, yo, p2 tog, p33, p2 tog-b, yo, p7.
Row 7—K6, (yo, ssk) twice, k11, k2 tog, yo, k5, yo, ssk, k11, (k2 tog, yo) twice, k6.
Row 8—P9, yo, p2 tog, p29, p2 tog-b, yo, p9.
Row 9—K7, yo, ssk, k1, yo, ssk, k8, k2 tog, yo, k7, yo, ssk, k8, k2 tog, yo, k1, k2 tog, yo, k7.
Row 10—P11, yo, p2 tog, p25, p2 tog-b, yo, p11.
Row 11—K8, yo, ssk, k2, yo, ssk, k5, k2 tog, yo, k9, yo, ssk, k5, k2 tog, yo, k2, k2 tog, yo, k8.
Row 12—P13, yo, p2 tog, p21, p2 tog-b, yo, p13.
Row 13—K9, yo, ssk, k3, yo, ssk, k2, k2 tog, yo, k3, k2 tog, yo, k1, yo, ssk, k3, yo, ssk, k2, k2 tog, yo, k3, k2 tog, yo, k9.
Row 14—P15, yo, p2 tog, p17, p2 tog-b, yo, p15.
Row 15—K10, yo, ssk, k4, yo, sl 1—k2 tog—psso, yo, k3, k2 tog, yo, k3, yo, ssk, k3, yo, k3 tog, yo, k4, k2 tog, yo, k10.
Row 16—P17, yo, p2 tog, p13, p2 tog-b, yo, p17.
Row 17—K11, yo, ssk, k5, yo, ssk, k4, yo, sl 1—k2 tog—psso, yo, k4, k2 tog, yo, k5, k2 tog, yo, k11.

Row 18—P19, yo, p2 tog, p9, p2 tog-b, yo, p19.

Row 19—K12, yo, ssk, k6, yo, ssk, k7, k2 tog, yo, k6, k2 tog, yo, k12.

Row 20—P21, yo, p2 tog, p5, p2 tog-b, yo, p21.

Row 21—K13, yo, ssk, k7, yo, ssk, k3, k2 tog, yo, k7, k2 tog, yo, k13.

Row 22—P23, yo, p2 tog, p1, p2 tog-b, yo, p23.

Row 23—K11, k2 tog, yo, k1, yo, ssk, k8, yo, sl 1—k2 tog—psso, yo, k8, k2 tog, yo, k1, yo, ssk, k11.

Row 24—P10, p2 tog-b, yo, p27, yo, p2 tog, p10.

Row 25—K9, k2 tog, yo, (k4, yo, ssk) twice, k5, (k2 tog, yo, k4) twice, yo, ssk, k9.

Row 26—P8, p2 tog-b, yo, p31, yo, p2 tog, p8.

Row 27—K7, k2 tog, yo, k7, yo, ssk, k4, yo, ssk, k3, k2 tog, yo, k4, k2 tog, yo, k7, yo, ssk, k7.

Row 28—P6, p2 tog-b, yo, p35, yo, p2 tog, p6.

Row 29—K5, k2 tog, yo, k10, yo, ssk, k4, yo, ssk, k1, k2 tog, yo, k4, k2 tog, yo, k10, yo, ssk, k5.

Row 30—P4, p2 tog-b, yo, p39, yo, p2 tog, p4.

Row 31—K3, k2 tog, yo, k5, k2 tog, (yo) twice, ssk, k4, yo, ssk, k4, yo, sl 1—k2 tog—psso, yo, k4, k2 tog, yo, k4, k2 tog, (yo) twice, ssk, k5, yo, ssk, k3.

Row 32—P2, p2 tog-b, yo, p7, (k1, p1) into the double yo of previous row, p25, (k1, p1) into the double yo of previous row, p7, yo, p2 tog, p2.

Row 33—K1, k2 tog, yo, k5, (k2 tog, yo twice, ssk) twice, k3, yo, ssk, k2, k2 tog, yo, k1, yo, ssk, k2, k2 tog, yo, k3, (k2 tog, yo twice, ssk) twice, k5, yo, ssk, k1.

Row 34—P3, yo, p2 tog, p4, (k1, p1) into the double yo, p2, (k1, p1) into the double yo, p21, (k1, p1) into the double yo, p2, (k1, p1) into the double yo, p4, p2 tog-b, yo, p3.

Row 35—K4, yo, ssk, k4, k2 tog, (yo) twice, ssk, (k3, k2 tog, yo) twice, (k3, yo, ssk) twice, k3, k2 tog, (yo) twice, ssk, k4, k2 tog, yo, k4.

Row 36—P5, yo, p2 tog, p4, (k1, p1) into the double yo, p25, (k1, p1) into the double yo, p4, p2 tog-b, yo, p5.

Row 37—K6, yo, ssk, k8, k2 tog, yo, k3, k2 tog, yo, k5, yo, ssk, k3, yo, ssk, k8, k2 tog, yo, k6.

Row 38—Repeat Row 6.

Row 39—K8, yo, ssk, k5, k2 tog, yo, k3, k2 tog, yo, k7, yo, ssk, k3, yo, ssk, k5, k2 tog, yo, k8.

Row 40—Repeat Row 8.

Row 41—K10, yo, ssk, k2, k2 tog, yo, k19, yo, ssk, k2, k2 tog, yo, k10.

Row 42—P11, yo, p2 tog, p10, p2 tog-b, yo, p1, yo, p2 tog, p10, p2 tog-b, yo, p11.

Row 43—K12, yo, k3 tog, yo, k7, k2 tog, yo, k3, yo, ssk, k7, yo, sl 1—k2 tog—psso, yo, k12.

Row 44—P21, p2 tog-b, yo, p5, yo, p2 tog, p21.

Row 45—K12, k2 tog, yo, k6, k2 tog, yo, k7, yo, ssk, k6, yo, ssk, k12.

Row 46—P19, p2 tog-b, yo, p9, yo, p2 tog, p19.

Row 47—K11, k2 tog, yo, k5, k2 tog, yo, k3, k2 tog, yo, k1, yo, ssk, k3, yo, ssk, k5, yo, ssk, k11.

Row 48—P17, p2 tog-b, yo, p13, yo, p2 tog, p17.

Row 49—K10, k2 tog, yo, k4, k2 tog, (yo) twice, ssk, k2, k2 tog, yo, k3, yo, ssk, k2, k2 tog, (yo) twice, ssk, k4, yo, ssk, k10.

Row 50—P15, p2 tog-b, yo, (k1, p1) into the double yo of previous row, p13, (k1, p1) into the double yo of previous row, yo, p2 tog, p15.

Row 51—K9, (k2 tog, yo, k3) twice, yo, ssk, k3, yo, sl 1—k2 tog—psso, yo, k3, k2 tog, yo, (k3, yo, ssk) twice, k9.

Row 52—P13, p2 tog-b, yo, p21, yo, p2 tog, p13.

Row 53—K8, k2 tog, yo, k2, k2 tog, yo, k6, yo, ssk, k7, k2 tog, yo, k6, yo, ssk, k2, yo, ssk, k8.

Row 54—P11, p2 tog-b, yo, p25, yo, p2 tog, p11.

Row 55—K7, k2 tog, yo, k1, k2 tog, yo, k9, yo, ssk, k5, k2 tog, yo, k9, yo, ssk, k1, yo, ssk, k7.

Row 56—P9, p2 tog-b, yo, p29, yo, p2 tog, p9.

Row 57—K6, (k2 tog, yo) twice, k12, yo, ssk, k3, k2 tog, yo, k12, (yo, ssk) twice, k6.

Row 58—P7, p2 tog-b, yo, p33, yo, p2 tog, p7.

Row 59—K6, k2 tog, yo, k15, yo, ssk, k1, k2 tog, yo, k15, yo, ssk, k6.

Row 60—P5, p2 tog-b, yo, p37, yo, p2 tog, p5.

Row 61—K24, yo, sl 1—k2 tog—psso, yo, k24.

Row 62—Purl.

Repeat Rows 1–62.

CHAPTER FOURTEEN

Borders

Borders are horizontal patterns generally placed at or near an edge to add decoration and interest. Borders differ from Edgings in their direction of knitting. An edging is worked in a strip, and sewn onto the finished article by one of its sides; but a border is worked in the same direction as the article itself, and usually is integral with it. Thus a border is worked on the same number of stitches as the article it embellishes, or on a "close" number. In many border patterns, the number of stitches is easily varied to match the number required for the article, so the stitch counts given for these must be considered samples only. Once you understand how to make a pattern of this type, you can make it larger or smaller as desired. In other border patterns, the stitch count is invariable, so the article must be worked on the same number as the border, or else a row of evenly-spaced increases or decreases must follow (or precede) the border to make the numbers come out right.

Most of the time, a border is not made more than once during the progress of the work. But like all other forms of knitting, border patterns can be adapted to many purposes. There is no rule that says a border *can't* be repeated all the way up a knitted piece; nor is there any objection to *combining* different border patterns to make a "horizontal sampler"—just as a fisherman sweater is a "vertical sampler" of cables.

Neither are the patterns in this section to be considered the only possible patterns for borders. By no means! Hundreds of other patterns can serve the purpose very well, just by being worked through only one or two repeats. Most lace or eyelet patterns can be used in this way. Slip-stitch color patterns and Mosaic Patterns make charming borders wherever a touch of contrasting color is wanted. Knit-purl combinations are often good as borders too. Any kind of pattern that is basically a horizontal design is ideal.

The "straight" border patterns—that is, the ones that do not form a fancy edge— can be used in any way at all. They need not be placed near an upper or lower edge; they can sail right across the middle if you want them to! What's more, it isn't even necessary to work the border all the way across. You can enclose just two or three repeats of it within vertical frames—such as a cable at either side—and work it in the form of a panel. Or, you can work just a little of it, to make a square or rectangular motif placed somewhere on the fabric. "Straight" border patterns make very exciting diagonal designs, too, when placed in a bias-knit garment. This kind of knitting is easy to do, by continually increasing at one edge and decreasing at the other as the work progresses. Usually the increase and its corresponding decrease are made on either end of every right-side row. There are technicalities, of course, in regard to the proper shaping of the garment; but they are not complicated. The knitter can learn to deal with them by following just one commercial garment pattern for a bias-knit garment.

Borders, then, are "fun" patterns that can be thrown into your knitting just about anywhere. All sorts of knitting techniques are represented among them, so that you can easily find a border for any type of knitting that you may have in hand. But try other patterns from other sections of this book as borders too. There is no limit to the original touches that can be given to your hand-knits by horizontal designs.

ABOVE: *Round-Edge Ribbing*
CENTER: *Picot Ribbing*
BELOW: *Ruffled Bell Border*

Round-Edge Ribbing

Contributed by Barbara N. Rankin, Cleveland Heights, Ohio

This is a method of casting on for knit-one purl-one ribbing, which makes a lovely rounded edge that is identical on both sides of the fabric. It is useful not only for the lower edge of a sweater or the cuff of a sleeve, but also for collars and button bands; in the latter cases, the border piece would be cast on at the outer edge, worked for the desired width, and then woven or sewn into the garment edges without casting off. Use an even number of stitches, because the original number cast on must be exactly half of the desired number. If an odd number is wanted, you can always increase one stitch later.

Step 1. With a loose piece of contrasting colored yarn (CC), cast on *half* of the desired number of stitches.

Step 2. Take up main color (MC—the yarn to be used for the actual ribbing) and purl one row, knit one row, purl one row, knit one row: 4 rows stockinette stitch. Do *not* tie MC strand into the cast-on row; leave the end hanging loose.

Step 3. * Purl the first st on needle, then insert right-hand needle upward into the first (upside-down) MC loop connecting 2 CC loops from the cast-on row below, and knit this MC loop; rep from * across. The last full MC loop below will be picked up and knitted after the next-to-last st on needle has been purled. Then purl the *last* st on needle, then pick up and knit the half-loop of MC yarn on the very edge. There are now twice the original number of stitches on needle.

Step 4. Begin ribbing—next row—* P1, k1; rep from *. Repeat this row for desired width.

Step 5. Remove the cast-on sts of CC yarn, leaving the edge in MC only. It will be a firm yet elastic edge that looks as though it was never cast on at all!

Picot Ribbing

The detailed instructions for this method of casting on a knit-one purl-one ribbing sound formidable indeed. But they are only the thousand words than which one picture is said to be better; a split-second of action is dragged out into five paragraphs for clarity's sake. Those who are accustomed to casting on with one needle in the right hand, and yarn held only in the left hand, will soon see that this kind of casting on is exactly the same thing, with just one small added twist.

This method makes a very pretty edge to the ribbing. It is elastic and "invisible"—showing no perceptible cast-on row—and is definitely recommended for beginning the lower edge of a sweater or a ribbed cuff.

Step 1. Take a long end of yarn sufficient for the required number of stitches, and hold yarn in the left hand, passing from the skein between little finger and ring finger from front (palm) to back of hand, then up the back of fingers and over the forefinger from back to front; then down under thumb from back to front and over thumb from front to back. The loose end of the yarn crosses *above* the strand between thumb and forefinger, and runs down the palm, to be held lightly against the palm by the little finger.

Step 2. Holding needle in right hand, insert needle point upward under the strand on the front of thumb, then from right to left under the strand that runs between thumb and forefinger, then out forward under the same thumb strand, carrying the thumb-forefinger strand on needle as when knitting a stitch. Drop loop off thumb, and pull up the loop on needle to tighten. This makes the first stitch.

Step 3. Insert thumb from left to right *behind* the free-end strand (which is still held against the palm by the little finger), and bring thumb back to original position, carrying yarn on thumb ready to cast on the next stitch. This is like the position in Step 1, *except* that the *front* thumb strand, under which the needle will be inserted, now runs directly down the palm to the free end, instead of back to the forefinger as before.

Step 4. Before casting on the next stitch, insert the needle from front to back *under* the strand between thumb and needle (i.e., the back thumb strand), then *over* the strand between needle and forefinger. Bring this last strand on the needle through to front, under the thumb-needle strand. This makes a loop passing over the needle from front to back, which will be the second stitch.

Step 5. Insert needle from front to back *under* the front thumb strand and *over* the needle-forefinger strand, bringing another loop on needle through to the front as in Step 2 and dropping loop off thumb to make the third stitch. Pull loop up firmly on needle.

Repeat Steps 3, 4, and 5 to make each subsequent pair of stitches, ending with Step 5 as the last stitch is cast on. There will be an *odd* number of stitches, since the first cast-on stitch is an extra one.

When the desired number of stitches has been cast on, turn and work in k1, p1 ribbing, beginning and ending with a *knit* stitch on the first and all other odd-numbered rows, and with a *purl* stitch on all even-numbered rows. The odd-numbered rows will be the right side of the ribbing.

Ruffled Bell Border

This particular ruffle is a sample only, since obviously it can be made in many different ways. The garter-stitch foundation may be omitted, or the "bells" may be longer or shorter (more or fewer rows worked), or spaced farther apart or closer together; or the increases can be done by some solid-stitch method instead of by yo's; or the pattern can be worked from the bottom of the ruffle upward, using decreases instead of increases. Any piece of knitting can be finished off (or started) with a ruffle by applying the basic principles of this pattern.

Cast on a multiple of 6 sts plus 1.

Knit 5 rows (garter stitch)

Row 6 (Wrong side)—K3, * p1, k5; rep from *, end last repeat k3.
Row 7—P3, * yo, k1, yo, p5; rep from *, end last repeat p3.
Row 8—K3, * p3, k5; rep from *, end last repeat k3.
Row 9—P3, * yo, k3, yo, p5; rep from *, end last repeat p3.
Row 10—K3, * p5, k5; rep from *, end last repeat k3.
Row 11—P3, * yo, k5, yo, p5; rep from *, end last repeat p3.
Row 12—K3, * p7, k5; rep from *, end last repeat k3.
Row 13—P3, * yo, k7, yo, p5; rep from *, end last repeat p3.
Row 14—K3, * p9, k5; rep from *, end last repeat k3.
Row 15—P3, * yo, k9, yo, p5; rep from *, end last repeat p3.
Row 16—K3, * p11, k5; rep from *, end last repeat k3.
Row 17—P3, * yo, k11, yo, p5; rep from *, end last repeat p3.
Row 18—K3, * p13, k5; rep from *, end last repeat k3.
Row 19—P3, * yo, k13, yo, p5; rep from *, end last repeat p3.
Row 20—K3, * p15, k5; rep from *, end last repeat k3.

Bind off, knitting all knit sts and purling all purl sts.

ABOVE: *Little Trees*
BELOW: *Skyscraper*

Two Knit-Purl Borders: Little Trees and Skyscraper

Both of these borders look lovely when started off with the Picot Rib Cast-on.

I. LITTLE TREES

Multiple of 12 sts plus 1.

Row 1 (Right side)—K1, * p1, k1; rep from *.
Row 2 and all other wrong-side rows—Knit all knit sts and purl all purl sts.

Rows 3, 5, and 7—P6, * k1, p11; rep from *, end k1, p6.

Row 9—P2, * k1, p3; rep from *, end k1, p2.

Row 11—P2, * k2, p2, k1, p2, k2, p3; rep from *, end last repeat p2.

Row 13—P2, * k3, p3; rep from *, end k3, p2.

Row 15—P2, * k4, p1, k4, p3; rep from *, end last repeat p2.

Row 17—P3, * k7, p5; rep from *, end k7, p3.

Row 19—P4, * k5, p7; rep from *, end k5, p4.

Row 21—P5, * k3, p9; rep from *, end k3, p5.

Row 23—P6, * k1, p11; rep from *, end k1, p6.

Row 25—Purl.

II. SKYSCRAPER

Multiple of 14 sts plus 3.

Rows 1 and 3 (Right side)—K1, * p1, k1; rep from *.

Row 2 and all other wrong-side rows—Knit all knit sts and purl all purl sts.

Rows 5, 7, and 9—P3, * (k1, p1) 5 times, k1, p3; rep from *

Row 11—P4, * (k1, p1) 4 times, k1, p5; rep from *, end last repeat p4.

Rows 13, 15, and 17—P5, * (k1, p1) 3 times, k1, p7; rep from *, end last repeat p5.

Row 19—P6, * (k1, p1) twice, k1, p9; rep from *, end last repeat p6.

Rows 21, 23, and 25—P7, * k1, p1, k1, p11; rep from *, end last repeat p7.

Row 27—P8, * k1, p13; rep from *, end k1, p8.

Row 29—Purl.

Borders for Color Contrast

All of these "borders" are portions of simple color patterns, as indicated by the repeat lines following the pattern rows. In each case, only one repeat is shown. This will give the knitter a good idea of how to use *any* color pattern as a contrasting border.

Since these patterns are not shown in their entirety, the reader is advised to try each one in a swatch of 3 or 4 repeats, to see how it looks as a continuous design. Then, try a favorite Slip-Stitch, Mosaic, or Fancy Color Pattern in a single repeat, to see how it might look as a border. Most of them will be just as pleasing as the selection of patterns given here. NOTE: CC (contrasting color) is the actual border color.

1. GREEK STRIPE

Multiple of 6 sts plus 4.

Row 1 (Right side)—With MC, knit.

Row 2—With MC, purl.

Row 3—With CC, k4, * sl 2 wyib, k4; rep from *.
Row 4—With CC, k4, * sl 2 wyif, k4; rep from *.
Row 5—With MC, k3, * sl 1 wyib, k2; rep from *, end k1.
Row 6—With MC, p3, * sl 1 wyif, p2; rep from *, end p1.
Row 7—With CC, k1, * sl 2 wyib, k4; rep from *, end sl 2, k1.
Row 8—With CC, k1, * sl 2 wyif, k4; rep from *, end sl 2, k1.

Repeat Rows 1–8.

Borders for Color Contrast I
ABOVE: *Greek Stripe*
SECOND BAND: *Hammerhead Stripe*
THIRD BAND: *Dotted Box*
FOURTH BAND: *Alternating Chain*
FIFTH BAND: *Crested Chain*
BELOW: *Pointed Stripe*

2. HAMMERHEAD STRIPE

Multiple of 4 sts plus 3.

Row 1 (Right side)—With MC, knit.
Row 2—With MC, purl.
Row 3—With CC, k3, * sl 1 wyib, k3; rep from *.
Row 4—With CC, k3, * sl 1 wyif, k3; rep from *.
Row 5—With MC, k1, * sl 1 wyib, k3; rep from *, end sl 1, k1.
Row 6—With MC, p1, * sl 1 wyif, p3; rep from *, end sl 1, p1.
Rows 7 and 8—With CC, knit.
Rows 9 and 10—With MC, repeat Rows 5 and 6.
Rows 11 and 12—With CC, repeat Rows 3 and 4.

Repeat Rows 1–12.

3. DOTTED BOX

Multiple of 8 sts plus 3.

Row 1 (Right side)—With MC, knit.
Row 2—With MC, purl.
Row 3—With CC, k2, * sl 1 wyib, k5, sl 1 wyib, k1; rep from *, end k1.
Row 4—With CC, k2, * sl 1 wyif, k5, sl 1 wyif, k1; rep from *, end k1.
Row 5—With MC, k3, * sl 1 wyib, k3; rep from *.
Row 6—With MC, p3, * sl 1 wyif, p3; rep from *.
Row 7—With CC, k4, * sl 1 wyib, k1, sl 1 wyib, k5; rep from *, end last repeat k4.
Row 8—With CC, k4, * sl 1 wyif, k1, sl 1 wyif, k5; rep from *, end last repeat k4.
Rows 9 and 10—With MC, repeat Rows 5 and 6.
Rows 11 and 12—With CC, repeat Rows 3 and 4.

Repeat Rows 1–12.

4. ALTERNATING CHAIN

Multiple of 4 sts plus 3.

Row 1 (Right side)—With MC, knit.
Row 2—With MC, purl.
Row 3—With CC, k3, * sl 1 wyib, k3; rep from *.

Row 4—With CC, k3, * sl 1 wyif, k3; rep from *.
Row 5—With MC, k2, * sl 1 wyib, k1; rep from *, end k1.
Row 6—With MC, k2, * sl 1 wyif, p1, sl 1 wyif, k1; rep from *, end k1.
Rows 7 and 8—With CC, knit.
Row 9—With MC, repeat Row 5.
Row 10—With MC, p2, * sl 1 wyif, k1, sl 1 wyif, p1; rep from *, end p1.
Row 11—With CC, k1, * sl 1 wyib, k3; rep from *, end sl 1, k1.
Row 12—With CC, k1, * sl 1 wyif, k3; rep from *, end sl 1, k1.

Repeat Rows 1–12.

5. CRESTED CHAIN

Multiple of 4 sts plus 3.

Row 1 (Right side)—With MC, knit.
Row 2—With MC, purl.
Row 3—With CC, k3, * sl 1 wyib, k3; rep from *.
Row 4—With CC, k3, * sl 1 wyif, k3; rep from *.
Row 5—With MC, k2, * sl 1 wyib, k1; rep from *, end k1.
Row 6—With MC, k2, * sl 1 wyif, p1, sl 1 wyif, k1; rep from *, end k1.
Rows 7 and 8—With CC, knit.
Rows 9 and 10—With MC, repeat Rows 5 and 6.
Rows 11 and 12—With CC, repeat Rows 3 and 4.
Row 13—With MC, k1, * sl 1 wyib, k3; rep from *, end sl 1, k1.
Row 14—With MC, p1, * sl 1 wyif, p3; rep from *, end sl 1, p1.

Repeat Rows 1–14.

6. POINTED STRIPE

Multiple of 4 sts plus 3.

Row 1 (Right side)—With MC, knit.
Row 2—With MC, purl.
Row 3—With CC, k2, * sl 1 wyib, k1; rep from *, end k1.
Row 4—With CC, k2, * sl 1 wyif, p1, sl 1 wyif, k1; rep from *, end k1.
Row 5—With MC, k3, * sl 1 wyib, k3; rep from *.
Row 6—With MC, p3, * sl 1 wyif, p3; rep from *.
Row 7—With CC, k1, * sl 1 wyib, k3; rep from *, end sl 1, k1.
Row 8—With CC, k1, * sl 1 wyif, k3; rep from *, end sl 1, k1.
Row 9—With MC, repeat Row 3.
Row 10—With MC, p2, * sl 1 wyif, k1, sl 1 wyif, p1; rep from *, end p1.
Rows 11 and 12—With CC, knit.
Row 13—With MC, repeat Row 7.
Row 14—With MC, p1, * sl 1 wyif, p3; rep from *, end sl 1, p1.

Repeat Rows 1–14.

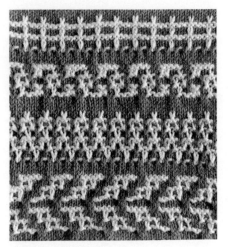

Borders for Color Contrast II

ABOVE: *Picket Fence*
SECOND BAND: *Double Hook*
THIRD BAND: *Paper Dolls*
BELOW: *Broken Arrow*

7. PICKET FENCE

Multiple of 4 sts plus 3.

Row 1 (Right side)—With MC, knit.
Row 2—With MC, purl.
Row 3—With CC, k2, * sl 1 wyib, k1; rep from *, end k1.
Row 4—With CC, p2, * sl 1 wyif, k1, sl 1 wyif, p1; rep from *, end p1.
Row 5—With MC, k1, * sl 1 wyib, k3; rep from *, end sl 1, k1.
Row 6—With MC, p1, * sl 1 wyif, p3; rep from *, end sl 1, p1.
Rows 7 and 8—With CC, knit.
Rows 9 through 14—Repeat Rows 5, 6, 7, and 8, then Rows 5 and 6 again.

Repeat Rows 1–14.

8. DOUBLE HOOK

Multiple of 7 sts plus 2.

Row 1 (Right side)—With MC, knit.
Row 2—With MC, purl.
Row 3—With CC, * k5, sl 2 wyib; rep from *, end k2.
Row 4—With CC, k2, * sl 2 wyif, k5; rep from *.
Row 5—With MC, k1, sl 1 wyib, * k2, sl 1 wyib, k2, sl 2 wyib; rep from *, end (k2, sl 1 wyib) twice, k1.
Row 6—With MC, p1, sl 1 wyif, * p2, sl 1 wyif, p2, sl 2 wyif; rep from *, end (p2, sl 1 wyif) twice, p1.
Row 7—With CC, k2, * sl 1 wyib, k3, sl 1 wyib, k2; rep from *.
Row 8—With CC, k2, * sl 1 wyif, k3, sl 1 wyif, k2; rep from *.
Row 9—With MC, k3, * sl 1 wyib, k1, sl 1 wyib, k4; rep from *, end last repeat k3.
Row 10—With MC, p3, * sl 1 wyif, k1, sl 1 wyif, p4; rep from *, end last repeat p3.
Rows 11 and 12—With CC, repeat Rows 7 and 8.
Rows 13 and 14—With MC, repeat Rows 5 and 6.
Row 15—With CC, k2, * sl 2 wyib, k5; rep from *.
Row 16—With CC, * k5, sl 2 wyif; rep from *, end k2.

Repeat Rows 1–16.

9. PAPER DOLLS

Multiple of 4 sts plus 3.

Row 1 (Right side)—With MC, knit.
Row 2—With MC, purl.
Row 3—With CC, k2, * sl 1 wyib, k1; rep from *, end k1.
Row 4—With CC, k2, * sl 1 wyif, p1, sl 1 wyif, k1; rep from *, end k1.
Row 5—With MC, k3, * sl 1 wyib, k3; rep from *.

Row 6—With MC, p3, * sl 1 wyif, p3; rep from *.
Row 7—With CC, k1, * sl 1 wyib, k3; rep from *, end sl 1, k1.
Row 8—With CC, k1, * sl 1 wyif, k3; rep from *, end sl 1, k1.
Row 9—With MC, repeat Row 3.
Row 10—With MC, p2, * sl 1 wyif, p1; rep from *, end p1.
Row 11—With CC, repeat Row 5.
Row 12—With CC, k3, * sl 1 wyif, k3; rep from *.
Row 13—With MC, repeat Row 7.
Row 14—With MC, p1, * sl 1 wyif, p3; rep from *, end sl 1, p1.
Rows 15 and 16—With CC, repeat Rows 11 and 12.
Rows 17 and 18—With MC, repeat Rows 3 and 4.
Rows 19 and 20—With CC, repeat Rows 11 and 12.
Rows 21 and 22—With MC, repeat Rows 13 and 14.

Repeat Rows 1–22.

10. BROKEN ARROW

Multiple of 7 sts plus 2.

Row 1 (Right side)—With MC, knit.
Row 2—With MC, purl.
Row 3—With CC, * k5, sl 2 wyib; rep from *, end k2.
Row 4—With CC, k2, * sl 2 wyif, k5; rep from *.
Row 5—With MC, k2, * sl 1 wyib, k1, sl 1 wyib, k4; rep from *.
Row 6—With MC, * p4, sl 1 wyif, k1, sl 1 wyif; rep from *, end p2.
Row 7—With CC, k1, sl 1 wyib, * k5, sl 2 wyib; rep from *, end k5, sl 1, k1.
Row 8—With CC, k1, sl 1 wyif, * k5, sl 2 wyif; rep from *, end k5, sl 1, k1.
Row 9—With MC, * k4, sl 1 wyib, k1, sl 1 wyib; rep from *, end k2.
Row 10—With MC, p2, * sl 1 wyif, k1, sl 1 wyif, p4; rep from *.
Row 11—With CC, k2, * sl 2 wyib, k5; rep from *.
Row 12—With CC, * k5, sl 2 wyif; rep from *, end k2.
Rows 13 and 14—With MC, repeat Rows 1 and 2.
Rows 15 and 16—With CC, repeat Rows 11 and 12.
Rows 17 and 18—With MC, repeat Rows 9 and 10.
Rows 19 and 20—With CC, repeat Rows 7 and 8.
Rows 21 and 22—With MC, repeat Rows 5 and 6.
Rows 23 and 24—With CC, repeat Rows 3 and 4.

Repeat Rows 1–24.

11. DANCING CROSS

Multiple of 10 sts plus 3.

Row 1 (Right side)—With MC, knit.
Row 2—With MC, purl.
Row 3—With CC, k6, * sl 2 wyib, k1, sl 2 wyib, k5; rep from *, end last repeat k2.
Row 4—With CC, k2, * sl 2 wyif, k1, sl 2 wyif, k5; rep from *, end k1.

Borders for Color Contrast III
ABOVE: *Dancing Cross*
SECOND BAND: *Alternating Block*
THIRD BAND: *Spot and Square*
BELOW: *Broken Chain*

Row 5—With MC, k8, * sl 1 wyib, k9; rep from *, end last repeat k4.

Row 6—With MC, p4, * sl 1 wyif, p9; rep from *, end last repeat p8.

Row 7—With CC, k1, * (sl 1 wyib, k3) twice, sl 1 wyib, k1; rep from *, end sl 1, k1.

Row 8—With CC, k1, sl 1 wyif, * k1, (sl 1 wyif, k3) twice, sl 1 wyif; rep from *, end k1.

Row 9—With MC, k4, * sl 1 wyib, k1, sl 1 wyib, k7; rep from *, end last repeat k6.

Row 10—With MC, p6, * sl 1 wyif, p1, sl 1 wyif, p7; rep from *, end last repeat p4.

Row 11—With CC, k2, * sl 2 wyib, k5, sl 2 wyib, k1; rep from *, end k1.

Row 12—With CC, k2, * sl 2 wyif, k5, sl 2 wyif, k1; rep from *, end k1.

Row 13—With MC, k6, * sl 1 wyib, k1, sl 1 wyib, k7; rep from *, end last repeat k4.

Row 14—With MC, p4, * sl 1 wyif, p1, sl 1 wyif, p7; rep from *, end last repeat p6.

Row 15—With CC, k1, * sl 1 wyib, k1, (sl 1 wyib, k3) twice; rep from *, end sl 1, k1.

Row 16—With CC, k1, sl 1 wyif, * (k3, sl 1 wyif) twice, k1, sl 1 wyif; rep from *, end k1.

Row 17—With MC, k4, * sl 1 wyib, k9; rep from *, end last repeat k8.

Row 18—With MC, p8, * sl 1 wyif, p9; rep from *, end last repeat p4.

Row 19—With CC, k2, * sl 2 wyib, k1, sl 2 wyib, k5; rep from *, end k1.

Row 20—With CC, k6, * sl 2 wyif, k1, sl 2 wyif, k5; rep from *, end last repeat k2.

Repeat Rows 1–20.

12. ALTERNATING BLOCK

Multiple of 10 sts plus 4.

Row 1 (Right side)—With MC, knit.

Row 2—With MC, purl.

Row 3—With CC, k7, * sl 2 wyib, k1, sl 2 wyib, k5; rep from *, end last repeat k2.

Row 4—With CC, k2, * sl 2 wyif, k1, sl 2 wyif, k5; rep from *, end k2.

Row 5—With MC, k2, * (sl 1 wyib, k1) twice, sl 1 wyib, k5; rep from *, end k2.

Row 6—With MC, k1, sl 1 wyif, * p5, (sl 1 wyif, k1) twice, sl 1 wyif; rep from *, end p2.

Rows 7 and 8—With CC, knit.

Row 9—With MC, k1, sl 1 wyib, * k5, (sl 1 wyib, k1) twice, sl 1 wyib; rep from *, end k2.

Row 10—With MC, p2, * (sl 1 wyif, k1) twice, sl 1 wyif, p5; rep from *, end sl 1, k1.

Row 11—With CC, k2, * sl 2 wyib, k1, sl 2 wyib, k5; rep from *, end k2.
Row 12—With CC, k7, * sl 2 wyif, k1, sl 2 wyif, k5; rep from *, end last repeat
  k2.

Repeat Rows 1–12.

13. SPOT AND SQUARE

Multiple of 7 sts plus 4.

Row 1 (Right side)—With MC, knit.
Row 2—With MC, purl.
Row 3—With CC, k3, * sl 2 wyib, k1, sl 2 wyib, k2; rep from *, end k1.
Row 4—With CC, p3, * sl 2 wyif, k1, sl 2 wyif, p2; rep from *, end p1.
Row 5—With MC, k1, * sl 2 wyib, k2, sl 1 wyib, k2; rep from *, end sl 2, k1.
Row 6—With MC, p1, * sl 2 wyif, p2, sl 1 wyif, p2; rep from *, end sl 2, p1.
Row 7—With CC, k3, * sl 1 wyib, k3, sl 1 wyib, k2; rep from *, end k1.
Row 8—With CC, p3, * sl 1 wyif, k3, sl 1 wyif, p2; rep from *, end p1.
Row 9—With MC, k4, * sl 1 wyib, k1, sl 1 wyib, k4; rep from *.
Row 10—With MC, p4, * sl 1 wyif, k1, sl 1 wyif, p4; rep from *.
Rows 11 and 12—With CC, repeat Rows 7 and 8.
Rows 13 and 14—With MC, repeat Rows 5 and 6.
Rows 15 and 16—With CC, repeat Rows 3 and 4.

Repeat Rows 1–16.

14. BROKEN CHAIN

Multiple of 11 sts plus 3.

Row 1 (Right side)—With MC, knit.
Row 2—With MC, purl.
Rows 3 and 4—With CC, knit.
Row 5—With MC, k1, * sl 1 wyib, k10; rep from *, end sl 1, k1.
Row 6—With MC, p1, * sl 1 wyif, p10; rep from *, end sl 1, p1.
Row 7—With CC, k2, * sl 1 wyib, k3, sl 2 wyib, k3, sl 1 wyib, k1; rep from *, end
  k1.
Row 8—With CC, p2, * sl 1 wyif, k3, sl 2 wyif, k3, sl 1 wyif, p1; rep from *, end
  p1.
Row 9—With MC, k1, * sl 1 wyib, k1, sl 1 wyib, k6, sl 1 wyib, k1; rep from *, end
  sl 1, k1.
Row 10—With MC, p1, * sl 1 wyif, p1, sl 1 wyif, p6, sl 1 wyif, p1; rep from *, end
  sl 1, p1.
Row 11—With CC, k4, * sl 1 wyib, k4, sl 1 wyib, k5; rep from *, end last repeat
  k4.
Row 12—With CC, k1, * p1, k2, sl 1 wyif, k4, sl 1 wyif, k2; rep from *, end p1,
  k1.
Rows 13 and 14—With MC, repeat Rows 9 and 10.
Rows 15 and 16—With CC, repeat Rows 7 and 8.
Rows 17 and 18—With MC, repeat Rows 5 and 6.
Rows 19 and 20—With CC, repeat Rows 3 and 4.

Repeat Rows 1–20.

Tassel Border

Little knit-in tassels like these are wonderfully effective as a decorative edge to any garment. Being worked in a single stitch, they can be placed anywhere, in combination with any pattern; but they make a particularly striking finish to the twisted chevron given here. In this pattern, purl stitches are worked below the chevron, knit stitches above; the knitting can continue in plain stockinette over the border. These two background textures could be reversed, or changed. A tassel border with similar chevrons works just as well over ribbing, garter stitch, seed stitch, etc. If the loops of each tassel are made a good length (wrap them around two or more fingers) and very firmly knit together in Row 7, they can be cut and trimmed if desired.

Multiple of 10 sts.

Rows 1, 3, and 5 (Right side)—Purl.

Rows 2 and 4—Knit.

Row 6—K5, * make Tassel in next st as follows: insert needle into st as if to knit, lay forefinger along needle point and wind yarn 5 times around finger and needle; then knit the st drawing all 5 loops through together; k9; rep from *, end last repeat k4.

Row 7—P4, * k5 tog-b (the 5 tassel strands), p9; rep from *, end last repeat p5.

Row 8—K5, * p1, k9; rep from *, end p1, k4.

Row 9—P4, * LT, p8; rep from *, end LT, p4.

Row 10—K4, * p2, k8; rep from *, end p2, k4.

Row 11—P3, * RT, LT, p6; rep from *, end RT, LT, p3.

Row 12—K3, * p4, k6; rep from *, end p4, k3.

Row 13—P2, * RT, k2, LT, p4; rep from *, end last repeat p2.

Row 14—K2, * p6, k4; rep from *, end p6, k2.

Row 15—P1, * RT, k4, LT, p2; rep from *, end last repeat p1.

Row 16—K1, * p8, k2; rep from *, end p8, k1.

Row 17—* RT, k6, LT; rep from *.

Row 18—Purl.

Row 19—K9, * RT, k8; rep from *, end k1.

Row 20—Purl.

Chandelier Pattern

This is a very fancy slip-stitch pattern that does well as a border, though it may be placed in any other context the knitter pleases. Rows 31 and 32 can be repeated indefinitely, to continue the rib lines all the way up to the top of a garment after the border is completed; or, these ribs can lead into another pattern that is worked on a multiple of 9 sts plus 5. Before working this pattern, be sure you understand "sl 2—k1—p2sso" and "sl 2—p1—p2sso" (see Glossary). A simple "k3 tog" and "p3 tog" can be substituted for these central decreases if you prefer, though in this pattern the central decreases are a little more elegant.

Multiple of 18 sts plus 5.

NOTES: Left Slip (LS): drop sl-st off needle to front of work, p1, then pick up dropped st and knit it. (If sl-st shortens up too much, use dpn to hold it.)

Right Slip (RS): slip 1 purl st, drop next st off needle to front of work, sl the same purl st back to left-hand needle, pick up dropped st and knit it, p1.

All sl-sts on all wrong-side rows are slipped with yarn in *front*.

Row 1 (Right side)—Purl.
Row 2—Knit.
Row 3—P11, * (k1, yo, k1, yo, k1) in next st, making 5 sts from one; p17; rep from *, end last repeat p11.
Row 4—K11, * p5, k17; rep from *, end p5, k11.
Row 5—P11, * k1, sl 2—k1—p2sso, k1, p17; rep from *, end last repeat p11.
Row 6—K11, * sl 2—p1—p2sso, k17; rep from *, end last repeat k11.
Row 7—P8, * (k1, yo, k1, yo, k1) in next st, p2, k1, p2, (k1, yo, k1, yo, k1) in next st, p11; rep from *, end last repeat p8.
Row 8—K8, * p5, k2, sl 1, k2, p5, k11; rep from *, end last repeat k8.
Row 9—P8, * k1, sl 2—k1—p2sso, k1, (p2, k1) twice, sl 2—k1—p2sso, k1, p11; rep from *, end last repeat p8.
Row 10—K8, * sl 2—p1—p2sso, k2, sl 1, k2, sl 2—p1—p2sso, k11; rep from *, end last repeat k8.
Row 11—P5, * (k1, yo, k1, yo, k1) in next st, (p2, k1) 3 times, p2, (k1, yo, k1, yo, k1) in next st, p5; rep from *.
Row 12—K5, * p5, (k2, sl 1) 3 times, k2, p5, k5; rep from *.
Row 13—P5, * k1, sl 2—k1—p2sso, k1, (p2, k1) 4 times, sl 2—k1—p2sso, k1, p5; rep from *.
Row 14—K5, * sl 2—p1—p2sso, (k2, sl 1) 3 times, k2, sl 2—p1—p2sso, k5; rep from *.
Row 15—* P2, (k1, yo, k1, yo, k1) in next st, (p2, k1) 5 times; rep from *, end p2, (k1, yo, k1, yo, k1) in next st, p2.
Row 16—* K2, p5, (k2, sl 1) 5 times; rep from *, end k2, p5, k2.
Row 17—P2, * k1, sl 2—k1—p2sso, (k1, p2) 6 times; rep from *, end k1, sl 2—k1—p2sso, k1, p2.
Row 18—* K2, sl 2—p1—p2sso, (k2, sl 1) 5 times; rep from *, end k2, sl 2—p1—p2sso, k2.
Row 19—P2, * k1, p2; rep from *.
Row 20—K2, * sl 1, k2; rep from *.
Row 21—P2, k1, p2, * (LS, p1) twice, k1, (p1, RS) twice, p2, k1, p2; rep from *.
Row 22—K2, * sl 1, k3, sl 1, k2, (sl 1, k1) twice, sl 1, k2, sl 1, k3; rep from *, end sl 1, k2.
Row 23—P2, * k1, p3, LS, p1, LS, k1, RS, p1, RS, p3; rep from *, end k1, p2.
Row 24—K2, * sl 1, k4, sl 1, k2, sl 3, k2, sl 1, k4; rep from *, end sl 1, k2.
Row 25—P2, * k1, p4, LS, p2, k1, p2, RS, p4; rep from *, end k1, p2.
Row 26—K2, * sl 1, k5, (sl 1, k2) twice, sl 1, k5; rep from *, end sl 1, k2.
Row 27—P2, * k1, p5, LS, p1, k1, p1, RS, p5; rep from *, end k1, p2.

Row 28—K2, * sl 1, k6, (sl 1, k1) twice, sl 1, k6; rep from *, end sl 1, k2.
Row 29—P2, * k1, p6, LS, k1, RS, p6; rep from *, end k1, p2.
Row 30—K2, * sl 1, k7, sl 3, k7; rep from *, end sl 1, k2.
Row 31—P2, * k1, p8; rep from *, end k1, p2.
Row 32—K2, * sl 1, k8; rep from *, end sl 1, k2.
Rows 33 and 34—Repeat Rows 1 and 2.

Swiss Ribbing

This is a simple and pretty ribbing that finishes with a slip-stitch chain and leads into a purl fabric. The next time you are making anything with a purled background, try this ribbing at the lower edge.

Multiple of 6 sts plus 3.

Rows 1 and 3 (Right side)—P3, * k3, p3; rep from *.
Rows 2 and 4—K3, * p3, k3; rep from *.
Row 5—P3, * k1, sl 1 wyib, k1, p3; rep from *.
Row 6—K3, * p1, sl 1 wyif, p1, k3; rep from *.
Row 7—P4, * k1-b, p5; rep from *, end k1-b, p4.
Row 8—K4, * p1, k5; rep from *, end p1, k4.
Row 9—P4, * sl 1 wyib, p5; rep from *, end sl 1, p4.
Row 10—K4, * sl 1 wyif, k5; rep from *, end sl 1, k4.
Row 11—Repeat Row 7.
Row 12—Knit.

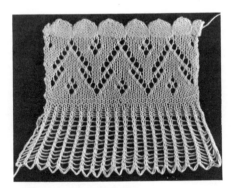

ABOVE: *Scalloped Purl Trim*
CENTER: *Christmas Chevron*
BELOW: *Cobweb Frill*

Scalloped Purl Trim

This is an easy and pretty way to finish a neckline, a sleeve, a pocket top, or the front edges of a jacket; try it in place of the usual crocheted edge or plain garter-stitch border worked on picked-up stitches. For further embellishment, a bead or a pearl can be sewn on each scallop. Buttonholes or button loops also can be used with this trim, but if buttonholes are knitted in, be careful to place the binding-strands exactly between them when sewing the stitches off the needle.

Step 1. Foundation—knit 2 rows.
Step 2. Work in reverse stockinette stitch (knit on the wrong side, purl on the right side) for *twice* the desired width of border. Do not bind off.
Step 3. Fold border in half with the purl side out. Break yarn, leaving a long end.
Step 4. On the wrong side of work, sew stitches off needle one by one, attaching each stitch to the corresponding stitch in

foundation row. At even intervals (i.e., every 8th stitch or every 10th stitch) pass sewing strand over the top of border and pull tight to form scallop.

Christmas Chevron

Multiple of 14 sts plus 1.

Row 1 (Wrong side) and all other wrong-side rows—Purl.
Row 2—K6, * k2 tog, yo, k5; rep from *, end k2.
Row 4—K1, * yo, ssk, k2, k2 tog, yo, k1; rep from *.
Row 6—K2, * yo, ssk, k3, yo, ssk, k2, k2 tog, yo, k3; rep from *, end last repeat k2.
Row 8—K3, * yo, ssk, k5, k2 tog, yo, k5; rep from *, end last repeat k3.
Row 10—K2, * (yo, ssk) twice, k3, (k2 tog, yo) twice, k3; rep from *, end last repeat k2.
Row 12—Repeat Row 8.
Row 14—K4, * yo, ssk, k3, k2 tog, yo, k7; rep from *, end last repeat k4.
Row 16—K5, * yo, ssk, k1, k2 tog, yo, k3, k2 tog, yo, k4; rep from *, end yo, ssk, k1, k2 tog, yo, k5.
Row 18—K1, * yo, ssk, k3, yo, sl 1—k2 tog—psso, yo, k3, k2 tog, yo, k1; rep from *.
Row 20—K7, * yo, ssk, k5; rep from *, end k1.

Cobweb Frill

This simple "trick" design makes a beautiful lacy ruffle that will decorate sleeves, bedjackets, peignoirs, evening stoles, fancy aprons, or the neckline and lower edges of a soft feminine blouse. When worked at the beginning of a piece, it can proceed right into the garment if you remember that one-third of the stitches are going to be dropped, and so cast on an extra third for this purpose. Or the frill can be worked separately, bound off, and then sewn to side or upper edges of the garment.

Multiple of 3 sts plus 1.

Row 1—K1-b, * p2, k1-b; rep from *.
Row 2—P1, * k1-b, k1, p1; rep from *.
Repeat Rows 1 and 2 for desired length of border, ending with Row 2.
Next row—K1-b, * drop next st off needle, p1, k1-b; rep from *.
Now work in ribbing as follows:
Row 1—P1, * k1-b, p1; rep from *.
Row 2—K1-b, * p1, k1-b; rep from *.
Repeat these last 2 rows twice more, then either bind off (if frill is to be made as a separate piece) or continue knitting on the remaining sts. Unravel the dropped stitches all the way down to the cast-on row.

Picot Hem

This kind of border can be placed either at the beginning or at the end of the knitting, but is most commonly used at the end for a pretty finish to collars, cuffs, and the front edges of cardigans, coats, and jackets (where the stitches for the border are picked up vertically from the garment pieces). Since the border stitches need not be bound off, but can be sewn in right from the needle, there is no bulky bind-off row and hence no unsightly lumpiness such as frequently disfigures the hems in knitted garments. The next time you make a dress or skirt from the top down, and want to finish it off with a hem, try this one!

Odd number of sts.

Step 1. Work in stockinette stitch to the desired width of border, ending with a wrong-side (purl) row.

Step 2. Picot row: K1, * yo, k2 tog; rep from *.

Step 3. Continue in stockinette stitch for the same number of rows as before, to form the hem facing. Do not bind off. Break yarn, leaving a long end for sewing.

Step 4. Turn facing to the inside at the row of holes, thus forming the picot points. Sew the stitches off the needle one by one, attaching each stitch to the corresponding stitch below in the first row of border, with an overcast seam.

NOTE: To work a Picot Hem at the beginning of a piece, cast on, work the facing portion first and the picot row as given. Later the facing can be turned under, and the cast-on edge sewn to the wrong side of the work, matching corresponding stitches.

ABOVE: *Picot Hem*
SECOND BAND: *Wide Leaf Border*
THIRD BAND: *Diamond Twist Border*
BELOW: *Shell and Eyelet Border*

Wide Leaf Border

Multiple of 14 sts plus 1.

Rows 1 and 2—Purl.

Row 3 (Right side)—K5, * k2 tog, (k1, yo, k1) in next st, ssk, k9; rep from *, end last repeat k5.

Row 4—K5, * p5, k9; rep from *, end last repeat k5.

Row 5—K4, * k2 tog, (k1, yo) twice, k1, ssk, k7; rep from *, end last repeat k4.

Row 6—K4, * p7, k7; rep from *, end last repeat k4.

Row 7—K3, * k2 tog, k2, yo, k1, yo, k2, ssk, k5; rep from *, end last repeat k3.

Row 8—K3, * p9, k5; rep from *, end last repeat k3.

Row 9—K2, * k2 tog, k3, yo, k1, yo, k3, ssk, k3; rep from *, end last repeat k2.

Row 10—K2, * p11, k3; rep from *, end last repeat k2.

Row 11—K1, * k2 tog, k4, yo, k1, yo, k4, ssk, k1; rep from *.

Rows 12 and 14—K1, * p13, k1; rep from *.

Row 13—K1, * ssk, (k3, yo) twice, k3, k2 tog, k1; rep from *.

Row 15—K1, * yo, ssk, k3, yo, sl 1—k2 tog—psso, yo, k3, k2 tog, yo, k1; rep from *.

Rows 16, 18, 20, and 22—Repeat Rows 10, 8, 6, and 4.

Row 17—K2, * yo, ssk, k7, k2 tog, yo, k3; rep from *, end last repeat k2.

Row 19—K3, * yo, ssk, k5, k2 tog, yo, k5; rep from *, end last repeat k3.

Row 21—K4, * yo, ssk, k3, k2 tog, yo, k7; rep from *, end last repeat k4.

Row 23—K5, * yo, ssk, k1, k2 tog, yo, k9; rep from *, end last repeat k5.

Row 24—K6, * p3, k11; rep from *, end last repeat k6.

Row 25—K6, * yo, sl 2—k1—p2sso, yo, k11; rep from *, end last repeat k6.

Row 26—Purl.

Rows 27 and 28—Knit.

Diamond Twist Border

Multiple of 17 sts plus 2.

Row 1 (Wrong side)—Knit.

Rows 2, 3, and all subsequent odd-numbered rows except the last—Purl.

Row 4—K2, * yo, ssk, k11, k2 tog, yo, k2; rep from *.

Row 6—K3, * yo, ssk, k9, k2 tog, yo, k4; rep from *, end last repeat k3.

Row 8—K4, * yo, ssk, k7, k2 tog, yo, k6; rep from *, end last repeat k4.

Row 10—K1, * LT, (k2, yo, ssk) twice, k1, k2 tog, yo, k2, RT; rep from *, end k1.

Row 12—K2, * LT, k2, yo, k3 tog, yo, k1-b, yo, sl 1—k2 tog—psso, yo, k2, RT, k2; rep from *.

Row 14—K2, * RT, k2, k2 tog, yo, k3, yo, ssk, k2, LT, k2; rep from *.

Row 16—K1, * RT, k2, k2 tog, yo, k5, yo, ssk, k2, LT; rep from *, end k1.

Row 18—RT, * k2, k2 tog, yo, k7, yo, ssk, k2, RT; rep from *.

Row 20—K1, * LT, k3, yo, ssk, k3, k2 tog, yo, k3, RT; rep from *, end k1.

Row 22—K2, * LT, k3, yo, ssk, k1, k2 tog, yo, k3, RT, k2; rep from *.

Row 24—K2, * RT, k1, k2 tog, yo, k1-b, yo, sl 1—k2 tog—psso, yo, k1-b, yo, ssk, k1, LT, k2; rep from *.

Row 26—K1, * RT, k1, k2 tog, yo, k3, yo, ssk, k2, yo, ssk, k1, LT; rep from *, end k1.

Row 28—RT, * k1, k2 tog, yo, k4, k1-b, k4, yo, ssk, k1, RT; rep from *.

Row 30—K2, * k2 tog, yo, k11, yo, ssk, k2; rep from *.

Row 32—K1, * k2 tog, yo, k13, yo, ssk; rep from *, end k1.

Row 34—Purl.

Row 35—Knit.

Shell and Eyelet Border

This is a narrow border arranged in small downward-pointing "picots" with a straight edge between them. The eyelet row (Row 7) may be omitted if an even narrower border is desired. Be sure you understand "sl 2—k1—p2sso" and "sl 2—p1—p2sso" (see Glossary).

Multiple of 14 sts plus 5.

Rows 1 and 2—Knit.
Row 3 (Right side)—K5, * yo, k3, sl 2—k1—p2sso, k3, yo, k5; rep from *.
Row 4—P6, * yo, p2, sl 2—p1—p2sso, p2, yo, p7; rep from *, end last repeat p6.
Row 5—K7, * yo, k1, sl 2—k1—p2sso, k1, yo, k9; rep from *, end last repeat k7.
Row 6—P8, * yo, sl 2—p1—p2sso, yo, p11; rep from *, end last repeat p8.
Row 7—K1, * yo, sl 2—k1—p2sso, yo, k11; rep from *, end last repeat k1.
Row 8—Purl.

Picot Point Border

ABOVE: *Picot Point Border*
BELOW: *Geometric Wave Border*

This adaptable pattern, in which each point is worked separately, can be used to create any desired number of stitches. I.e., for 10 points of 13 sts each (130 sts), work each point through Row 12 (yo, k12, which makes 13 sts) and repeat the process 10 times. For 6 points of 10 sts each (60 sts), work each point through Row 9 (yo, k9, making 10 sts) and repeat 6 times. If an *even* number of rows are used to make each point, then the next point should be cast on the same needle as given. If an *uneven* number of rows are used, then the next point should be cast *on the free needle* so that all points will finish on the same needle.

This is a beautiful pattern for collars, cuffs, scarf-ends, or the lower edge of a skirt. It may be completed in a separate piece and sewn to side or top edges as well as knitted in straight from the bottom. It need not be worked in simple garter stitch; a decorative pattern can be used, such as an eyelet or bobble in the center of each point, etc.

Cast on 2 sts.

Row 1—K2.	Row 5—Yo, k5.	Row 9—Yo, k9.	Row 13—Yo, k13.
Row 2—Yo, k2.	Row 6—Yo, k6.	Row 10—Yo, k10.	Row 14—Yo, k14.
Row 3—Yo, k3.	Row 7—Yo, k7.	Row 11—Yo, k11.	Etc.
Row 4—Yo, k4.	Row 8—Yo, k8.	Row 12—Yo, k12.	

Break yarn and leave the finished point at the non-working end of the needle. On the same needle (if an even number of rows were used), cast on 2 sts and work another point the same as the first. Continue until there are as many points as desired; do not break yarn upon completing the last one. Turn and knit across all sts on needle, joining all points together; then work a few more rows of garter stitch to complete border. To finish, weave all loose ends of yarn through border.

A tassel or a bead or some other ornament may be tied to the yarn end left at each cast-on point.

Geometric Wave Border

Multiple of 18 sts plus 2.

Preparation (if desired)—4 or 5 rows of garter stitch.

Row 1 (Wrong side) and all other wrong-side rows—Purl.
Row 2—K5, * yo, ssk, k16; rep from *, end last repeat k13.
Row 4—K3, * k2 tog, yo, k1, yo, ssk, k13; rep from *, end last repeat k12.
Row 6—K2, * (k2 tog, yo) twice, k1, yo, ssk, k11; rep from *.
Row 8—K1, * (k2 tog, yo) twice, k1, (yo, ssk) twice, k9; rep from *, end k1.
Row 10—* (K2 tog, yo) twice, k3, (yo, ssk) twice, k7; rep from *, end k2.
Row 12—K1, k2 tog, yo, * k5, (yo, ssk) twice, k5, (k2 tog, yo) twice; rep from *, end last repeat k2 tog, yo, k1 instead of (k2 tog, yo) twice.
Row 14—* K2 tog, yo, k2, k2 tog, yo, k3, (yo, ssk) twice, k3, k2 tog, yo; rep from *, end k2.
Row 16—K3, * (k2 tog, yo) twice, k2; rep from *, end last repeat k1.
Row 18—K2, * (k2 tog, yo) twice, k2; rep from *.
Row 20—K1, * (k2 tog, yo) twice, k2; rep from *, end k1.
Row 22—K1, * (yo, ssk) twice, k1, (k2 tog, yo) twice, k2, (k2 tog, yo) twice, k3; rep from *, end k1.
Row 24—K2, * (yo, ssk) twice, k1, k2 tog, yo, k2, (k2 tog, yo) twice, k5; rep from *.
Row 26—K3, * (yo, ssk) twice, k3, (k2 tog, yo) twice, k7; rep from *, end last repeat k6.
Row 28—K4, * (yo, ssk) twice, k1, (k2 tog, yo) twice, k9; rep from *, end last repeat k7.
Row 30—K5, * yo, ssk, yo, sl 1—k2 tog—psso, yo, k2 tog, yo, k11; rep from *, end last repeat k8.
Row 32—K6, * yo, ssk, k1, k2 tog, yo, k13; rep from *, end last repeat k9.
Row 34—K7, * yo, sl 1—k2 tog—psso, yo, k15; rep from *, end last repeat k10.
Row 36—K8, * yo, ssk, k16; rep from *, end last repeat k10.

This completes pattern rows. If desired, work 4 or 5 rows of garter stitch to finish; or, pattern may be continued above for a double or triple border.

Snow Forest Border

A deep border for either lace or plain fine-yarn knits. The last three pattern rows (44, 46, and 48) make pretty little eyelets that could be continued as a spot-pattern over the remainder of the knitting.

Multiple of 14 sts plus 1.

Row 1 (Wrong side) and all other wrong-side rows—Purl.
Row 2—K1, * yo, ssk, k9, k2 tog, yo, k1; rep from *.
Row 4—K2, * yo, ssk, k7, k2 tog, yo, k3; rep from *, end last repeat k2.

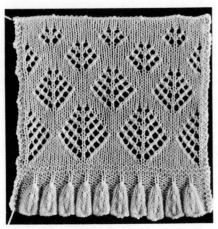

Row 6—K1, * (yo, ssk) twice, k5, (k2 tog, yo) twice, k1; rep from *.

Row 8—K2, * (yo, ssk) twice, k3, (k2 tog, yo) twice, k3; rep from *, end last repeat k2.

Row 10—K1, * (yo, ssk) 3 times, k1, (k2 tog, yo) 3 times, k1; rep from *.

Rows 12, 14, 16, and 18—Repeat Rows 8, 6, 4, and 2.

Row 20—K5, * k2 tog, yo, k1, yo, ssk, k9; rep from *, end last repeat k5.

Row 22—K4, * k2 tog, yo, k3, yo, ssk, k7; rep from *, end last repeat k4.

Row 24—K3, * (k2 tog, yo) twice, k1, (yo, ssk) twice, k5; rep from *, end last repeat k3.

Row 26—K2, * (k2 tog, yo) twice, k3, (yo, ssk) twice, k3; rep from *, end last repeat k2.

Rows 28, 30, and 32—Repeat Rows 24, 22, and 20.

Rows 34, 36, 38, 40, and 42—Repeat Rows 2, 4, 6, 4, and 2.

Rows 44, 46, and 48—Repeat Rows 20, 22, and 20.

Row 50—Knit.

Dinner-Bell Ruffle

This is another "basic" ruffle made from the bottom up. It can be varied in dozens of ways, according to the number of stitches, the type of yarn, the length of ruffle desired, etc. 12, 14, or 16 stitches can be cast on for every 4, to make a fuller ruffle; the decreases can be worked on every right-side row instead of every other one, to make it shorter. The ruffle need not be worked on a bottom edge; it can be made separately, or sewn on some distance *above* the edge, as a flounce.

Cast on 10 sts for every 4 sts required at finish of the ruffle, plus 3 edge sts.

Rows 1 and 3 (Wrong side)—K3, * p7, k3; rep from *.

Row 2—P3, * k7, p3; rep from *.

Row 4—P3, * k2, sl 2—k1—p2sso, k2, p3; rep from *.

Rows 5 and 7—K3, * p5, k3; rep from *.

Row 6—P3, * k5, p3; rep from *.

Row 8—P3, * k1, sl 2—k1—p2sso, k1, p3; rep from *.

Rows 9 and 11—K3, * p3, k3; rep from *.

Row 10—P3, * k3, p3; rep from *.

Row 12—P3, * sl 2—k1—p2sso, p3; rep from *.

Rows 13 and 15—K3, * p1, k3; rep from *.

Rows 14 and 16—P3, * k1, p3; rep from *.

Finish with several rows of garter stitch.

Lace Window Border

Here is a good example of a regular lace pattern used in a couple of repeats to make a border. The pattern is obviously made for vertical-panel arrangement, but as a border it is chopped off after two repeats (three repeats of the first pattern row) and the result is quite delightful, resembling nearly-square traceried windows.

Multiple of 20 sts plus 3.

Row 1 (Wrong side) and all other wrong-side rows—Purl.
Rows 2 and 4—Knit.
Row 6—K3, * ssk, yo, (k1, yo, sl 2—k1—p2sso, yo) 3 times, k1, yo, k2 tog, k3; rep from *.
Rows 8 and 10—K3, * ssk, yo, k5, yo, sl 2—k1—p2sso, yo, k5, yo, k2 tog, k3; rep from *.
Row 12—K5, * yo, ssk, k1, k2 tog, yo, k3, yo, ssk, k1, k2 tog, yo, k7; rep from *, end last repeat k5.
Rows 14, 16, 18, 20, and 22—Repeat Rows 6, 8, 10, and 12, then Row 6 again.

Finish with 5 rows of stockinette stitch, as at beginning.

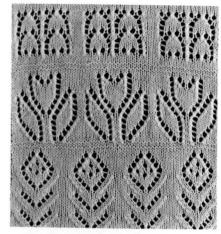

ABOVE: *Lace Window Border*
CENTER: *Tulip Border*
BELOW: *Stylized Flower Border*

Tulip Border

Multiple of 20 sts plus 1.

Row 1 (Wrong side) and all other wrong-side rows—Purl.
Row 2—K5, * k2 tog, yo, k1, yo, k2 tog, k1, ssk, yo, k1, yo, ssk, k9; rep from *, end last repeat k5.
Row 4—K4, * k2 tog, yo, k2, yo, k2 tog, k1, ssk, yo, k2, yo, ssk, k7; rep from *, end last repeat k4.
Row 6—K3, * k2 tog, yo, k3, yo, k2 tog, k1, ssk, yo, k3, yo, ssk, k5; rep from *, end last repeat k3.
Row 8—K2, * k2 tog, yo, k4, yo, k2 tog, k1, ssk, yo, k4, yo, ssk, k3; rep from *, end last repeat k2.
Row 10—K1, * k2 tog, yo, k5, yo, k2 tog, k1, ssk, yo, k5, yo, ssk, k1; rep from *.
Row 12—K2, * yo, k2 tog, k2, (k2 tog, yo) twice, k1, (yo, ssk) twice, k2, ssk, yo, k3; rep from *, end last repeat k2.
Row 14—K2, * yo, k2 tog, k1, (k2 tog, yo) twice, k3, (yo, ssk) twice, k1, ssk, yo, k3; rep from *, end last repeat k2.
Row 16—K2, * yo, (k2 tog) twice, yo, k2 tog, yo, k5, yo, ssk, yo, (ssk) twice, yo, k3; rep from *, end last repeat k2.
Row 18—K2, * yo, sl 2—k1—p2sso, yo, k2 tog, yo, k7, yo, ssk, yo, sl 2—k1—p2sso, yo, k3; rep from *, end last repeat k2.
Row 20—K2, * k2 tog, yo, k2, yo, k2 tog, k5, ssk, yo, k2, yo, ssk, k3; rep from *, end last repeat k2.
Row 22—K6, * yo, k2 tog, k5, ssk, yo, k11; rep from *, end last repeat k6.

Row 24—K6, * yo, (k2 tog) twice, yo, k1, yo, (ssk) twice, yo, k11; rep from *, end last repeat k6.
Row 26—K6, * yo, sl 2—k1—p2sso, yo, k3, yo, sl 2—k1—p2sso, yo, k11; rep from *, end last repeat k6.
Row 28—Knit.

Stylized Flower Border

Contributed by Hildegard M. Elsner, Aldan, Pennsylvania

Multiple of 15 sts.

Row 1 (Wrong side) and all other wrong-side rows—Purl.
Row 2—K4, * k2 tog, (k1, yo) twice, k1, ssk, k8; rep from *, end last repeat k4.
Row 4—K3, * k2 tog, k1, yo, k3, yo, k1, ssk, k6; rep from *, end last repeat k3.
Row 6—K2, * k2 tog, k1, yo, k5, yo, k1, ssk, k4; rep from *, end last repeat k2.
Row 8—K1, * k2 tog, k1, yo, k7, yo, k1, ssk, k2; rep from *, end last repeat k1.
Rows 10 through 22—Repeat Rows 2 through 8, then Rows 2 through 6 again.
Row 24—K1, * k2 tog, k1, yo, k2, k2 tog, yo, k3, yo, k1, ssk, k2; rep from *, end last repeat k1.
Row 26—K3, * yo, sl 1—k2 tog—psso, yo, k3, yo, k3 tog, yo, k6; rep from *, end last repeat k3.
Row 28—K4, * yo, ssk, k1, yo, k1, k3 tog, yo, k8; rep from *, end last repeat k4.
Row 30—K5, * yo, ssk, k1, k2 tog, yo, k10; rep from *, end last repeat k5.
Row 32—K6, * yo, sl 1—k2 tog—psso, yo, k12; rep from *, end last repeat k6.

Snake Border

Contributed by Hildegard M. Elsner, Aldan, Pennsylvania

This pattern is pretty when worked all over the fabric, as well as when used as a border. This is done by repeating Rows 1 through 18 continuously. The border can be applied horizontally, by casting on the same number of stitches required for the knitted article, or it can be sewn in as a vertical insertion, by casting on the number of stitches required to reach from the top to the bottom edge. Or use it in a garment worked from side to side, by placing it in the center for a "vertical" panel.

Multiple of 12 sts plus 1

Foundation (if desired): 6 or 7 rows of garter stitch.

Row 1 (Wrong side) and all other wrong-side rows—Purl.
Row 2—K1, * yo, ssk, k7, k2 tog, yo, k1; rep from *.
Row 4—K2, * yo, ssk, k5, k2 tog, yo, k3; rep from *, end last repeat k2.

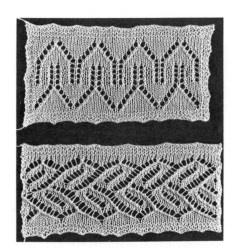

ABOVE: *Snake Border*
BELOW: *Versailles Border*

Row 6—K3, * yo, ssk, k3, k2 tog, yo, k5; rep from *, end last repeat k3.

Row 8—K4, * yo, ssk, k1, k2 tog, yo, k7; rep from *, end last repeat k4.

Row 10—K5, * yo, sl 1—k2 tog—psso, yo, k9; rep from *, end last repeat k5.

Rows 12, 14, 16, and 18—K1, * yo, ssk, k1, k2 tog, yo, k1; rep from *.

Rows 20 through 28—Repeat Rows 2 through 10.

Finish with several rows of garter stitch if desired.

Versailles Border

This exquisite old French pattern can be used as an allover lace as well as a border. To work the pattern continuously, do Rows 3 through 22 inclusive. These 20 rows will make Versailles Lace.

Multiple of 10 sts plus 4.

Foundation (if desired)—5 or 6 rows of garter stitch.

Row 1 (Wrong side)—Purl.

Row 2—K2, * yo, ssk, k8; rep from *, end k2.

Row 3—K2, * yo, p2 tog, p5, p2 tog-b, yo, p1; rep from *, end k2.

Row 4—K4, * yo, ssk, k3, k2 tog, yo, k3; rep from *.

Row 5—K2, p2, * yo, p2 tog, p1, p2 tog-b, yo, p5; rep from *, end last repeat p3, k2.

Row 6—K6, * yo, sl 1—k2 tog—psso, yo, k7; rep from *, end last repeat k5.

Row 7—K2, * p3, p2 tog-b, yo; rep from *, end k2.

Row 8—K3, * yo, ssk, k3; rep from *, end k1.

Row 9—K2, p1, * p2 tog-b, yo, p3; rep from *, end last repeat p2, k2.

Row 10—K5, * yo, ssk, k3; rep from *, end last repeat k2.

Row 11—K1, * p2 tog-b, yo, p3; rep from *, end p1, k2.

Row 12—K2, * yo, ssk, k3; rep from *, end k2.

Rows 13, 14, 15, and 16—Repeat Rows 3, 4, 5, and 6.

Row 17—K2, p1, * p3, yo, p2 tog; rep from *, end k1.

Row 18—K5, * k2 tog, yo, k3; rep from *, end last repeat k2.

Row 19—K2, p1, * yo, p2 tog, p3; rep from *, end last repeat p2, k2.

Row 20—K3, * k2 tog, yo, k3; rep from *, end k1.

Row 21—K2, * p3, yo, p2 tog; rep from *, end k2.

Row 22—K1, * k2 tog, yo, k3; rep from *, end k3.

Rows 23, 24, 25, and 26—Repeat Rows 3, 4, 5, and 6.

Row 27—Purl.

Finish with 5 or 6 rows of garter stitch.

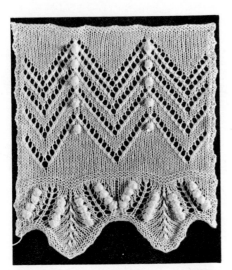

Graduated-Chevron Border with Bobbles

This design of diminishing chevrons can be used once as a border, or it can be repeated indefinitely as an allover lace. Although its 50 rows make the directions long, it is uncomplicated to work. The clear, straight diagonal lines make it easy for the knitter to see what comes next as the work proceeds.

Multiple of 20 sts plus 3.

NOTE: Make Bobble (MB) as follows: (k1, yo, k1, yo, k1) in one stitch, making 5 sts from one; turn and k5, turn and p5, turn and k1, sl 1—k2 tog—psso, k1; turn and p3 tog, completing bobble. On the return row, purl into the *back* of each bobble stitch.

Row 1 (Wrong side) and all other wrong-side rows—Purl.
Row 2—K1, * yo, ssk, k18; rep from *, end yo, ssk.
Row 4—K2, * yo, ssk, k15, k2 tog, yo, k1; rep from *, end k1.
Row 6—K3, * yo, ssk, k13, k2 tog, yo, k3; rep from *.
Row 8—K4, * yo, ssk, k11, k2 tog, yo, k5; rep from *, end last repeat k4.
Row 10—K5, * yo, ssk, k9, k2 tog, yo, k7; rep from *, end last repeat k5.
Row 12—K1, * yo, ssk, k3, yo, ssk, k7, k2 tog, yo, k4; rep from *, end yo, ssk.
Row 14—K2, * yo, ssk, k3, yo, ssk, k5, k2 tog, yo, k3, k2 tog, yo, k1; rep from *, end k1.
Row 16—K3, * yo, ssk, k3, yo, ssk, k1, MB, k1, (k2 tog, yo, k3) twice; rep from *.
Row 18—K4, * yo, ssk, k3, yo, ssk, k1, k2 tog, yo, k3, k2 tog, yo, k5; rep from *, end last repeat k4.
Row 20—K1, * yo, ssk, k2, yo, ssk, k3, yo, sl 1—k2 tog—psso, yo, k3, k2 tog, yo, k3; rep from *, end yo, ssk.
Row 22—K2, * yo, ssk, k2, yo, ssk, k7, k2 tog, yo, k2, k2 tog, yo, k1; rep from *, end k1.
Row 24—K3, * yo, ssk, k2, yo, ssk, k5, k2 tog, yo, k2, k2 tog, yo, k3; rep from *.
Row 26—K1, * yo, ssk, k1, yo, ssk, k2, yo, ssk, k1, MB, k1, (k2 tog, yo, k2) twice; rep from *, end yo, ssk.
Row 28—K2, * yo, ssk, k1, yo, ssk, k2, yo, ssk, k1, k2 tog, yo, k2, (k2 tog, yo, k1) twice; rep from *, end k1.
Row 30—K1, * (yo, ssk) twice, k1, yo, ssk, k2, yo, sl 1—k2 tog—psso, yo, k2, (k2 tog, yo, k1) twice; rep from *, end yo, ssk.
Row 32—K2, * (yo, ssk) twice, k1, yo, ssk, k5, k2 tog, yo, k1, (k2 tog, yo) twice, k1; rep from *, end k1.
Row 34—K3, * (yo, ssk) twice, k1, yo, ssk, k1, MB, k1, k2 tog, yo, k1, (k2 tog, yo) twice, k3; rep from *.
Row 36—K4, * (yo, ssk) twice, k1, yo, ssk, k1, k2 tog, yo, k1, (k2 tog, yo) twice, k5; rep from *, end last repeat k4.
Row 38—K5, * (yo, ssk) twice, k1, yo, sl 1—k2 tog—psso, yo, k1, (k2 tog, yo) twice, k7; rep from *, end last repeat k5.
Row 40—K6, * (yo, ssk) twice, k1, MB, k1, (k2 tog, yo) twice, k9; rep from *, end last repeat k6.

Row 42—K7, * (yo, ssk) twice, k1, (k2 tog, yo) twice, k11; rep from *, end last repeat k7.

Row 44—K8, * yo, ssk, yo, sl 1—k2 tog—psso, yo, k2 tog, yo, k13; rep from *, end last repeat k8.

Row 46—K9, * yo, ssk, MB, k2 tog, yo, k15; rep from *, end last repeat k9.

Row 48—K10, * yo, sl 1—k2 tog—psso, yo, k17; rep from *, end last repeat k10.

Row 50—Knit.

Mimosa Border

Clustered bobbles and lace combine to make a deeply scalloped traditional border that is a strong fashion accent. To work this pattern, you have to *like* making bobbles—there are so many of them! But if you don't like making bobbles, you can omit them; the border is still lovely without them.

Multiple of 26 sts plus 1.

NOTE: Make Bobble (MB) the same as for Graduated-Chevron Border with Bobbles.

Rows 1 and 3 (Wrong side)—Knit.

Row 2—Purl.

Row 4—P1, * k25, p1; rep from *.

Rows 5, 7, 9, 11, 13, 15, and 17—K1, * p25, k1; rep from *.

Row 6—P1, * (k1, yo) twice, k7, ssk, sl 1—k2 tog—psso, k2 tog, k7, (yo, k1) twice, p1; rep from *.

Row 8—P1, * k2, yo, k1, yo, k2, MB, k3, ssk, sl 1—k2 tog—psso, k2 tog, k3, MB, k2, yo, k1, yo, k2, p1; rep from *.

Row 10—P1, * MB, k2, yo, k1, yo, k2, MB, k2, ssk, sl 1—k2 tog—psso, k2 tog, k2, MB, k2, yo, k1, yo, k2, MB, p1; rep from *.

Row 12—P1, * k1, MB, k2, yo, k1, yo, k2, MB, k1, ssk, sl 1—k2 tog—psso, k2 tog, k1, MB, k2, yo, k1, yo, k2, MB, k1, p1; rep from *.

Row 14—P1, * k2, MB, k2, yo, k1, yo, k2, MB, ssk, sl 1—k2 tog—psso, k2 tog, MB, k2, yo, k1, yo, k2, MB, k2, p1; rep from *.

Row 16—P1, * k3, MB, k2, yo, k1, yo, k2, ssk, sl 1—k2 tog—psso, k2 tog, k2, yo, k1, yo, k2, MB, k3, p1; rep from *.

Row 18—Repeat Row 4.

Rows 19, 20, and 21—Repeat Rows 1, 2, and 3.

Row 22—Knit.

CHAPTER FIFTEEN

Edgings

Among the edgings are some of the oldest and finest lace patterns. Many edgings were invented in the era of "white knitting", to embellish the great knitted bedspreads, tablecloths, scarves, shawls, doilies and fancy underclothing of that era. These beautiful old patterns will enhance modern garments or household articles just as well. They can be applied to blouses, place mats, curtains, stoles, skirts, pillow covers, cuffs, collars, baby jackets, and dozens of other things.

An edging usually has one straight side edge, by which it is attached to the article. The other edge is scalloped, wavy, indented, pointed, or looped. The width of an edging pattern is set—wide, medium or narrow, depending on the pattern—but the length depends on the number of rows worked, and so is indefinitely variable. The knitter has only to repeat the pattern rows a sufficient number of times to span the edge of the garment or whatever.

Most edgings look best when worked in thin cotton yarn, which can be starched and pinned out to hold its shape. But wool or synthetic yarns can be used too; these can be pinned to shape, then steamed or lightly pressed. Metallic-yarn edgings add a lot of glitter to fancy collars and cuffs, evening stoles or cocktail dresses; these too can be blocked into shape, and will retain it. Garter stitch is almost always the basis of an edging pattern, because it does not curl. Great use is made, too, of various kinds of faggoting—because this also produces the flat fabric required in an edging.

If you want to make a large article—tablecloth, curtain or bedspread—in cotton or linen "straight-knit" strips, it is almost mandatory to add an edging, because this is the only thing that will finish off the sides in an appropriate fashion. It is easy to work an edging on both sides at once of a straight-knit piece as the work progresses; this saves the trouble of sewing the edging on separately. For this purpose, choose a reversible edging—that is, one without any specified right or wrong side—and work the odd-numbered rows of the edging pattern at one side of the piece, the even numbered rows of the edging pattern at the other side *on the same row*. In this way the fancy edge is made to face outward on both sides, while the straight edge is knitted right into the piece as if it were a panel.

Some edgings go bias, which means that the cast-on row is concave and the bound-off row is convex, or vice versa. This kind of edging is intended to go *all the way around* something, like a skirt hem or a cuff. When the cast-on row and the bound-off row are sewn together, they will fit nicely into each other and make a diagonal seam.

Here are a few points on general knitting technique, which apply to many of the patterns in this section. You will see double or even triple yarn-overs frequently used. Extra yarn-overs are *always* treated as separate, new stitches, and must *not* be dropped off the needle on the return row unless the directions so state. Usually a double yarn-over is worked on the return row with a "k1, p1" or "p1, k1"—each of the two loose loops being worked as a separate stitch. In these pattern directions, the extra yarn-over is not mentioned specifically on the return row, but an extra stitch will be provided for it. So count stitches carefully when trying out an edging, and don't "lose" any of the extra loops.

When working edgings that are formed by binding off groups of stitches at intervals, remember to start counting the bound-off stitches as the *second* stitch is worked. That is, slip the first stitch, knit the second, then pass the first stitch over the second, meanwhile counting bound-off stitch Number One. When you have passed the last stitch over (Number Five, say, if there are to be five stitches bound off), then the binding-off is finished and one stitch still remains on the right-hand needle. Ignore that stitch and proceed to work the stitches on the left-hand needle according to subsequent directions. Of course this is a basic bit of knowledge that comes to most knitters with their first lesson, but since the stitch count is particularly important in edging patterns, it might bear repeating here for the benefit of a few who are uncertain about it.

Edgings cover a wide range of knitting skill. Some are very simple beginner's patterns; others are exceedingly fancy. In between these two extremes there is a whole spectrum of intermediate patterns. They are wonderful to try out and practice, even if you have no immediate use for an edging as such. From them, any knitter can learn much about the use of lace in unusual and interesting forms. To work with edgings is to understand shaping in new ways. Increases, decreases, slanting stitches this way and that—all are thoroughly demonstrated by a selection of edgings. Since an edging has a rather small number of stitches to it, it works quickly. The knitter can see how it is going to "come out" after one or two repeats. And best of all, edging patterns are extremely attractive. They can add a real "designer touch" to a plain dress—a touch that the designer perhaps never dreamed of! So next time, try an edging instead of a hem. Or sew cotton lace edgings to your best guest-pillowcases. Or decorate a fancy apron with a knit edging. Or trim the lower edge of a summer blouse. The article to which a knitted edging is attached does *not* have to be knitted also. These edgings look lovely on linen tablecloths, cotton or silk petticoats, collars, sleeves, woven curtains and bedspreads. Just knit the edging to the proper length and sew it on—by machine, if you wish.

A few of these patterns are modern inventions, but most of them are old—at least a century old. Still, their beauty is timeless. Frills, ruffles and laces have come back again to the fashion leadership that they enjoyed in the 1860's and 1870's. Thus, fancy touches like knitted lace edgings are as much in style today as then. So why not make use of the same delightful patterns that were developed more than a century ago? Here they are, at your fingertips. If you are one of the knitters who think only in terms of socks and sweaters, this is your opportunity to branch out and try a little "dainty work"!

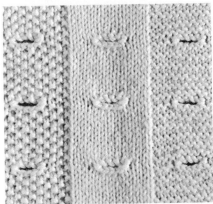

A Self-Reinforcing One-Row Buttonhole

LEFT: *On Seed Stitch*
CENTER: *On Stockinette Stitch*
RIGHT: *On Garter Stitch*

A Self-Reinforcing One-Row Buttonhole

Contributed by Berniece L. Hampson, San Clemente, California

This is a finishing detail, and does not really belong in a book about patterns. But it is well worth knowing, so it is included here for the benefit of those who may not know it.

Methods of making buttonholes are many and various. Nearly every knitter has a different favorite. But for neatness and durability combined with ease of working, your author has never seen a buttonhole to beat this one. There are "bound" stitches all the way around it, with no loose strands in the corners. It can be worked from the right or wrong side of the fabric, as desired, for both sides of the buttonhole are very trim; in fact, the second or "wrong" side is perhaps even tidier than the side on which the buttonhole is started. On a purl fabric (reverse stockinette) or garter stitch it is well-nigh invisible. It stretches readily to let the button through, yet keeps straight and does not gap open. And it is all finished on the same row.

Worked in reasonably sturdy yarn, this buttonhole requires no extra reinforcing or ribbon backing. With loose, soft, or fuzzy yarns you can still make self-reinforcing buttonholes by this method, by knitting a thin cotton thread (or two) along with the yarn across the buttonhole stitches *on the row before* the buttonhole; then on the next row the entire buttonhole is made with the yarn and cotton thread(s) held together. The cotton is dropped after completion of the buttonhole. Its free ends remain at the left-hand side of the buttonhole, where they can be knotted together on the wrong side. This will create a strong buttonhole even on a very soft or limp fabric.

The buttonhole is shown on seed stitch, stockinette stitch, and garter stitch, three popularly used button-band fabrics. It can be worked also on double seed stitch, moss stitch, reverse stockinette, ribbing, or any other fabric that your button-band happens to be made of.

Step 1. Work desired number of stitches before starting buttonhole.

Step 2. Bring yarn to front of work, sl 1 st from left-hand needle to right-hand needle, pass yarn to back of work and *drop* it there. (The yarn is left hanging, and is *not* used during Steps 3 and 4.)

Step 3. Slip another st from left-hand needle to right-hand needle, and pass the first st over it—1 st bound off. Repeat Step 3 until the desired number of sts for buttonhole have been bound off.

Step 4. Slip the last bound-off st back to left-hand needle, and turn work.

Step 5. Pick up hanging yarn and pass it between needles to back. Now cast on the same number of stitches that were bound off for the buttonhole, *plus one more,* using the Cable Cast-on as follows: * insert right-hand needle *between* the 1st and 2nd sts on left-hand needle, draw through a loop, and sl this loop onto left-hand needle to serve as a new first st; rep from * until the desired number of sts have been cast on. Before placing the *last* loop on left-hand needle, bring yarn through to the front, to form a dividing strand between the last st and the next-to-last one. Turn work again.

Step 6. Slip the first st from left-hand needle to right-hand needle, then pass the last, extra cast-on st over it. Buttonhole completed—work to end of row.

NOTE: Step 6 may be worked also as a plain "k2 tog"—i.e., the first 2 sts on left-hand needle. This is an alternative way of decreasing the extra stitch.

Bias Band for Necklines

A new type of increase occurs here, which is useful in making a two-sided bias binding for an inside curve such as a neckline. Most increases will show small holes when worked continuously on every other row, but this one is fairly tight and solid. The bias band will draw up to an inside curve and fold naturally down its center. The edges can be stitched to the front and back of the neckline just like a piece of bias tape. Make the band as wide as you wish. Use smallish needles, in proportion to the weight of the yarn.

This kind of increase can be used also for raglan shapings in a garment worked from the top down. But because it is naturally tight, the raglan seam will require a little stretching.

Cast on 14 sts.

Purl one row, knit one row, purl one row.

Row 1 (Right side)—K6, then * insert left-hand needle from the left under the *left side loop* of the stitch 2 rows below the first stitch on right-hand needle (i.e., in the row below the row now on left-hand needle); draw this loop slightly up, * and knit into the *back* of it; k2, rep from * to * and this time knit into the *front* of the loop (which will twist it); k6.
Row 2—P2 tog, p12, p2 tog.

Repeat Rows 1 and 2.

ABOVE: *Bias Band for Necklines*
CENTER: *Plain Scalloped Edging*
BELOW: *Welted Ruffle*

Plain Scalloped Edging

This is the basic edging—a simple construction of increases and decreases, which can be worked in any kind of yarn and applied to anything. Shallower scallops can be made by increasing and decreasing on every other row instead of every row. Also, the number of stitches is optional, and so is the number of rows used to complete a scallop. The only rule here is that the number of increase rows must be equal to the number of decrease rows. Further decoration can be added by working a bobble into the center of each scallop, or coloring the scallops with embroidery, or tying on a fringe.

Cast on 7 sts and knit one row.

Row 1—K5, inc in next st (by knitting into front and back of it), k1.
Row 2—K1, inc in next st, k6.
Row 3—K7, inc in next st, k1.
Row 4—K1, inc in next st, k8.
Row 5—K9, inc in next st, k1.
Row 6—K1, inc in next st, k10.
Row 7—K11, inc in next st, k1.
Row 8—K1, inc in next st, k12.
Row 9—K12, k2 tog, k1.
Row 10—K1, k2 tog, k11.
Row 11—K10, k2 tog, k1.
Row 12—K1, k2 tog, k9.
Row 13—K8, k2 tog, k1.
Row 14—K1, k2 tog, k7.
Row 15—K6, k2 tog, k1.
Row 16—K1, k2 tog, k5.

Repeat Rows 1–16.

Welted Ruffle

Any "beginner's baby sweater" would be beautifully finished off by this firm, handsome ruffle, which is made in the easiest possible way and runs lengthwise like an edging. It is an exceedingly simple construction of purled welts fluffed out by short rows, with a little border of garter stitch for attaching the ruffle. If you *are* a beginner, and *do* want to work this ruffle for your first baby sweater (or anything else), remember one hint about turning short rows: the yarn should be looped around the next stitch before turning, in order to avoid leaving a hole. For example, in working Row 2 of this pattern: purl 10, sl 1 wyib, turn, slip the same stitch again wyib, k10. Thus the yarn of the short row is looped around an unworked stitch.

Cast on 13 sts.

Row 1—Knit.
Row 2—P10, turn, k10.
Row 3—P10, k3.
Row 4—K3, p10.
Row 5—K10, turn, p10.
Row 6—Knit.

Repeat Rows 1–6.

Tulip-Bud Edging

This is a beautiful little edging for a bedspread or baby blanket knitted in the Tulip-Bud Pattern, or for any garment worked in Candle Flames, Embossed Leaf, The Candle Tree, or any of the other variations on this type of design.*

Cast on 8 sts.

Row 1 (Right side)—K5, yo, k1, yo, k2.
Row 2—P6, knit into front and back of next st (inc), k3.
Row 3—K4, p1, k2, yo, k1, yo, k3.
Row 4—P8, inc in next st, k4.
Row 5—K4, p2, k3, yo, k1, yo, k4.
Row 6—P10, inc in next st, k5.
Row 7—K4, p3, k4, yo, k1, yo, k5.
Row 8—P12, inc in next st, k6.
Row 9—K4, p4, ssk, k7, k2 tog, k1.
Row 10—P10, inc in next st, k7.
Row 11—K4, p5, ssk, k5, k2 tog, k1.
Row 12—P8, inc in next st, k2, p1, k5.
Row 13—K4, p1, k1, p4, ssk, k3, k2 tog, k1.
Row 14—P6, inc in next st, k3, p1, k5.
Row 15—K4, p1, k1, p5, ssk, k1, k2 tog, k1.
Row 16—P4, inc in next st, k4, p1, k5.
Row 17—K4, p1, k1, p6, sl 1—k2 tog—psso, k1.
Row 18—P2 tog, bind off next 5 sts using p2-tog st to bind off first st; p3, k4.

Repeat Rows 1–18.

*A Treasury of Knitting Patterns, pp. 227, 160, 152, 290.

ABOVE: *Tulip-Bud Edging*
BELOW: *Faggoted Fringe*

Faggoted Fringe

Directions as given will make a long loop fringe. A thicker fringe can be made by using three or four strands of yarn instead of two; a shorter fringe can be made by reducing the 6 stitches at the end of Row 1 to 3 or 4, and of course the 5 stitches at the beginning of Row 2 to 2 or 3. Conversely, a longer fringe is made simply by adding more stitches. In any case the stitches to be unraveled for the fringe are worked in plain stockinette stitch, while the edging stitches are done in faggoting. If a straight fringe is wanted instead of a loop fringe, each loop may be cut at the bottom.

Using a double strand of yarn, cast on 13 sts.

Row 1—K2, yo, k2 tog, k1, yo, k2 tog, k6.
Row 2—P5, k2, (yo, k2 tog, k1) twice.

Repeat these 2 rows for desired length, ending with Row 2. On next row sl the first st, bind off next 7 sts, draw yarn through and finish. Drop remaining 5 sts off needle and unravel them all the way down to the beginning to make fringe loops.

Corded Edging

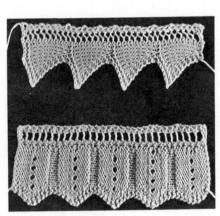

ABOVE: *Corded Edging*
BELOW: *Pleated Edging*

This is a tidy little edging for those who particularly enjoy working into the backs of stitches to make twisted knitting. But the stitches need not be twisted, if you prefer plain knits and purls. Or, the stitches may be worked through the backs on the right-side rows only, to make a Crossed stockinette fabric. "Inc" in this pattern can be "Make One", but the recommended method is the side-loop increase used in the Bias Band for Necklines.

Cast on 9 sts.

Knit one row, purl one row.

Row 1 (Right side)—Sl 1, k2, yo, k2 tog-b, k2-b, inc, k2-b.
Row 2—K2-b, p1, p2-b, k2, yo, k2 tog-b, p1.
Row 3—Sl 1, k2, yo, k2 tog-b, k3-b, inc, k2-b.
Row 4—K2-b, p1, p3-b, k2, yo, k2 tog-b, p1.
Row 5—Sl 1, k2, yo, k2 tog-b, k4-b, inc, k2-b.
Row 6—K2-b, p1, p4-b, k2, yo, k2 tog-b, p1.
Row 7—Sl 1, k2, yo, k2 tog-b, k5-b, inc, k2-b.
Row 8—K2-b, p1, p5-b, k2, yo, k2 tog-b, p1.
Row 9—Sl 1, k2, yo, k2 tog-b, k6-b, inc, k2-b.
Row 10—K2-b, p1, p6-b, k2, yo, k2 tog-b, p1.
Row 11—Sl 1, k2, yo, k2 tog-b, k7-b, inc, k2-b.
Row 12—K2-b, p1, p7-b, k2, yo, k2 tog-b, p1.
Rows 13 and 15—Sl 1, k2, yo, k2 tog-b, k10-b.
Row 14—K10-b, k2, yo, k2 tog-b, p1.
Row 16—Bind off 6 sts, k1-b, p1, p1-b, k2, yo, k2 tog-b, p1.

Repeat Rows 1–16.

Pleated Edging

The recommended increase for this pattern is: purl into the front, then into the back, of one stitch. When "turning" for the short rows, remember to hook the yarn around the first unworked stitch so as not to leave a hole. This is done by slipping the stitch, passing the yarn around it, then slipping it back again to the needle that is in the right hand after the work is turned.

Cast on 16 sts and purl one row.

Row 1 (Right side)—K1, ssk, (yo) twice, k2 tog, p8, inc in next st, k2.
Row 2—K14, p1, k2.
Row 3—K1, ssk, (yo) twice, k2 tog, p9, inc in next st, k2.
Row 4—K12, turn, p9, inc in next st, k2.
Row 5—K16, p1, k2.
Row 6—K1, ssk, (yo) twice, k2 tog, p1, (yo, p2 tog) 5 times, p1, k2.
Row 7—K13, turn, p9, p2 tog, k2.
Row 8—K15, p1, k2.
Row 9—K1, ssk, (yo) twice, k2 tog, p9, p2 tog, k2.
Row 10—Repeat Row 2.
Row 11—K1, ssk, (yo) twice, k2 tog, p8, p2 tog, k2.
Row 12—K13, p1, k2.
Row 13—K1, ssk, (yo) twice, k2 tog, k11.
Row 14—K2, p8, turn, k10.
Row 15—Repeat Row 14.
Row 16—K2, p9, k2, p1, k2.

Repeat Rows 1–16.

Bold-Faggoted Edging

This is a simple but striking pattern consisting of grand eyelets, small points, and extra-large faggoting. Row 2 calls for working (k1, p1) into each of the double yo's of Row 1.

Cast on 11 sts and work a Preparation Row, as follows:
K9, yo, k2 (making 12 sts).

Row 1—K2, (k1, p1, k1) in the yo of previous row, yo, p4 tog, k1, (yo) twice, k2 tog, (yo) twice, k2. (15 sts)
Row 2—Sl 1, (k2, p1) twice, k2, (k1, p1, k1) in the yo of previous row, yo, p4 tog, k1. (15 sts)
Row 3—K2, (k1, p1, k1) in the yo of previous row, yo, p4 tog, k8. (15 sts)
Row 4—Bind off 3, k5, (k1, p1, k1) in the yo of previous row, yo, p4 tog, k1. (12 sts)

Repeat Rows 1–4.

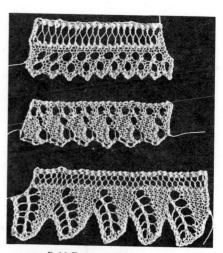

ABOVE: *Bold-Faggoted Edging*
CENTER: *Sickle Edging*
BELOW: *Oak-Leaf Edging*

Sickle Edging

Cast on 8 sts.

Row 1—Knit.
Row 2—K2, (yo) twice, k2 tog, k3, yo, k1. (10 sts)
Row 3—K7, p1, k2.
Row 4—K9, yo, k1. (11 sts)
Row 5—Knit.
Row 6—K2, [(yo) twice, k2 tog] twice, k4, yo, k1. (14 sts)
Row 7—K8, (p1, k2) twice.
Row 8—K9, pass 8th st over 9th st, then bind off remaining 5 sts, leaving 8 sts on needle—7 sts separated from the last bound-off st by a space. On the following Row 1 this last st is drawn up to the others.

Repeat Rows 1–8.

Oak-Leaf Edging

Several versions of this handsome antique pattern exist. In the Victorian era it was popularly used for collars, cuffs, bed linens, curtains, and the hems of dressing-gowns or petticoats.

Cast on 10 sts and knit one row.

"A" portion of pattern: (Yo) twice, k2 tog, (yo) twice, k2 tog, k1.
"B" portion of pattern: Sl 1, (k2, p1) twice. (The purl stitches are made in the second loop of the double yo.)

Row 1—Sl 1, k2, yo, k2 tog, A.
Row 2—B, k2, yo, k2 tog, k1.
Row 3—Sl 1, k2, yo, k2 tog, k2, A.
Row 4—B, k4, yo, k2 tog, k1.
Row 5—Sl 1, k2, yo, k2 tog, k4, A.
Row 6—B, k6, yo, k2 tog, k1.
Row 7—Sl 1, k2, yo, k2 tog, k6, A.
Row 8—B, k8, yo, k2 tog, k1.
Row 9—Sl 1, k2, yo, k2 tog, k8, A.
Row 10—B, k10, yo, k2 tog, k1.
Row 11—Sl 1, k2, yo, k2 tog, k15.
Row 12—Bind off 10, k6, yo, k2 tog, k1.

Repeat Rows 1–12.

Godmother's Edging

This simple but very beautiful pattern was designed in the 1890's for "the hems of infants' christening-dresses and matching lace cushions". It was recommended also as an edging for "fine linen pillow-cases and counterpanes". Modern godmothers, or anyone else, might use it on the hems of nightgowns, robes, shifts, lace overskirts, shawls, head scarves, or tablecloths. It is a graceful, uncluttered pattern, especially lovely when worked in fine cotton yarn.

Cast on 20 sts and knit one row.

Row 1—Sl 1, k3, (yo, k2 tog) 7 times, yo, k2.
Rows 2, 4, 6, and 8—Knit.
Row 3—Sl 1, k6, (yo, k2 tog) 6 times, yo, k2.
Row 5—Sl 1, k9, (yo, k2 tog) 5 times, yo, k2.
Row 7—Sl 1, k12, (yo, k2 tog) 4 times, yo, k2.
Row 9—Sl 1, k23.
Row 10—Bind off 4, k19.

Repeat Rows 1–10.

ABOVE: *Godmother's Edging*
BELOW: *Turret Edging*

Turret Edging

This is the plain "cast-on-and-cast-off" edging that is so useful as a finish to a bedspread or slip—anything that hangs downward. It also makes a beautiful and unusual finish for a sleeve or a turned-down collar.

Cast on 6 sts.

Rows 1, 2, and 3—Knit.
Row 4—Cast on 3 sts, knit.
Rows 5, 6, and 7—Knit.
Row 8—Cast on 3 sts, knit.
Rows 9, 11, 13, 14, and 15—Knit.
Rows 10 and 12—Purl.
Row 16—Bind off 3 sts, knit.
Rows 17, 18, and 19—Knit.
Row 20—Bind off 3 sts, knit.

Repeat Rows 1–20.

Two Edgings with an Insertion: Beech Leaf Edging, Bird's-Eye Edging, and Moorish Diamonds

These patterns are worked together in one piece to give the knitter an idea of how any edging can be combined with any lace panel or panels to make attractive lace mats, hangings, or scarves. With the same edging on both sides, you can work any number of insertions in the center to make an article of any width. The left-hand edging and the right-hand edging are worked on opposite sides of the fabric alternately, of course, so that the scalloped portion faces outward both ways.

I. BEECH LEAF EDGING

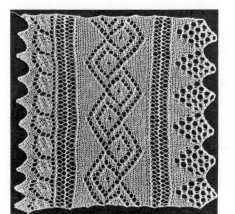

LEFT: *Beech Leaf Edging*
RIGHT: *Bird's-Eye Edging*
CENTER: *Moorish Diamonds* (*insertion*)

Cast on 17 sts and knit one row.

Rows 1 and 3 (Right side)—K3, (yo, p2 tog) twice, yo, k1-b, k2 tog, p1, ssk, k1-b, yo, k3.

Rows 2 and 4—K3, p3, k1, p3, k2, (yo, p2 tog) twice, k1.

Row 5—K3, (yo, p2 tog) twice, yo, k1-b, yo, k2 tog, p1, ssk, yo, k4.

Row 6—K4, p2, k1, p4, k2, (yo, p2 tog) twice, k1.

Row 7—K3, (yo, p2 tog) twice, yo, k1-b, k1, k1-b, yo, sl 1—k2 tog—psso, yo, k5.

Row 8—K5, p7, k2, (yo, p2 tog) twice, k1.

Row 9—K3, (yo, p2 tog) twice, yo, k1-b, k3, k1-b, yo, k7.

Row 10—Bind off 4 sts, k2, p7, k2, (yo, p2 tog) twice, k1.

Repeat Rows 1–10.

II. BIRD'S-EYE EDGING

Contributed by Nan Ward, Farmerville, Louisiana

Cast on 17 sts.

NOTE: Yo2 = a double yo. All single purl sts on even-numbered rows go into the *second* loop of a double yo made on a preceding row.

Row 1—K3, (yo, p2 tog) twice, k10.

Row 2—K12, (yo, p2 tog) twice, k1.

Row 3—K3, (yo, p2 tog) twice, k6, k2 tog, yo2, k1, inc in last st.

Row 4—K4, p1, k9, (yo, p2 tog) twice, k1.

Row 5—K3, (yo, p2 tog) twice, k4, k2 tog, yo2, (k2 tog) twice, yo2, k1, inc in last st.

Row 6—K4, p1, k3, p1, k7, (yo, p2 tog) twice, k1.

Row 7—K3, (yo, p2 tog) twice, k2, k2 tog, [yo2, (k2 tog) twice] twice, yo2, k1, inc in last st.

Row 8—K4, (p1, k3) twice, p1, k5, (yo, p2 tog) twice, k1.
Row 9—K3, (yo, p2 tog) twice, k2 tog, [yo2, (k2 tog) twice] 3 times, yo2, k2 tog.
Row 10—K2, (p1, k3) 4 times, (yo, p2 tog) twice, k1.
Row 11—K3, (yo, p2 tog) twice, k2, k2 tog, [yo2, (k2 tog) twice] 3 times.
Row 12—K2 tog, k1, (p1, k3) twice, p1, k5, (yo, p2 tog) twice, k1.
Row 13—K3, (yo, p2 tog) twice, k4, k2 tog, [yo2, (k2 tog) twice] twice.
Row 14—K2 tog, k1, p1, k3, p1, k7, (yo, p2 tog) twice, k1.
Row 15—K3, (yo, p2 tog) twice, k6, k2 tog, yo2, (k2 tog) twice.
Row 16—K2 tog, k1, p1, k9, (yo, p2 tog) twice, k1.

Repeat Rows 1–16.

III. MOORISH DIAMONDS (INSERTION)

Panel of 21 sts.

Row 1 (Wrong side) and all other wrong-side rows—Purl.
Row 2—K2, yo, ssk, k1, yo, ssk, k3, k2 tog, yo, k1, yo, ssk, k6.
Row 4—K3, (yo, ssk, k1) twice, k2 tog, yo, k3, yo, ssk, k5.
Row 6—K4, yo, ssk, k1, yo, k3 tog, yo, k2, yo, ssk, k1, yo, ssk, k4.
Row 8—K5, yo, ssk, (k2 tog, yo, k1) twice, yo, ssk, k1, yo, ssk, k3.
Row 10—K6, yo, ssk, k1, k2 tog, yo, k3, yo, ssk, k1, yo, ssk, k2.
Row 12—K7, yo, k3 tog, yo, k5, (yo, ssk, k1) twice.
Row 14—K7, k2 tog, yo, k3, yo, ssk, k2, yo, ssk, k1, yo, ssk.
Row 16—K6, k2 tog, yo, k1, yo, ssk, k3, k2 tog, yo, k1, k2 tog, yo, k2.
Row 18—K5, k2 tog, yo, k3, yo, ssk, (k1, k2 tog, yo) twice, k3.
Row 20—K4, k2 tog, yo, k1, k2 tog, yo, k2, yo, sl 1—k2 tog—psso, yo, k1, k2 tog, yo, k4.
Row 22—K3, (k2 tog, yo, k1) twice, yo, ssk, k1, yo, ssk, k2 tog, yo, k5.
Row 24—K2, k2 tog, yo, k1, k2 tog, yo, k3, yo, ssk, k1, k2 tog, yo, k6.
Row 26—(K1, k2 tog, yo) twice, k5, yo, sl 1—k2 tog—psso, yo, k7.
Row 28—K2 tog, yo, k1, k2 tog, yo, k2, k2 tog, yo, k3, yo, ssk, k7.

Repeat rows 1–28.

Grand Eyelet Edging

This striking pattern makes deep loops attached to an eyelet mesh. There is a preparation row (Row 1) which is not repeated. At the last pattern repeat, when the edging has reached the desired length, bind off after-Row 8.

Try this one in thin cotton, stiffly starched, as a novel trim for a lamp shade!

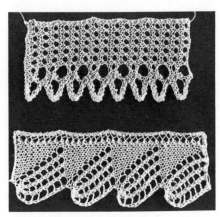

Cast on 15 sts and knit one row.

Row 1 (Preparation row)—K2, (yo) 4 times, k2 tog, (yo, k2 tog) 5 times, k1.

Row 2—K12, (k1, p1) twice into the 4-yo loop, k2.

Rows 3 and 4—Knit.

Row 5—K2, (yo) 5 times, k2 tog, k1, (yo, k2 tog) 6 times, k1.

Row 6—K15, (k1, p1) twice and k1 into the 5-yo loop, k2.

Rows 7 and 8—Knit.

Row 9—Bind off 7, k1, (yo) 4 times, k2 tog, (yo, k2 tog) 5 times, k1.

Repeat Rows 2–9.

Open Shell Edging

In this pretty pattern the head of each 8-stitch scallop is gathered up all at once on Row 15—an interesting and novel method of formation. It is an excellent edging for the bottom of fancy skirts or aprons. In very fine crochet cotton it makes a delicate border for formal table mats.

Cast on 13 sts and purl one row.

"A" portion of pattern: Sl 1, k1, yo, p2 tog.

"B" portion of pattern: (Yo, ssk) 3 times, (yo) twice, k2 tog.

Row 1 (Right side)—A, k1, B.

Row 2—Yo, k2 tog, p9, yo, p2 tog, k1. (The "k2 tog" here includes the first loop of the double yo; the second loop constitutes the first purl st.)

Row 3—A, k2, B.

Row 4—Yo, k2 tog, p10, yo, p2 tog, k1.

Row 5—A, k3, B.

Row 6—Yo, k2 tog, p11, yo, p2 tog, k1.

Row 7—A, k4, B.

Row 8—Yo, k2 tog, p12, yo, p2 tog, k1.

Row 9—A, k5, B.

Row 10—Yo, k2 tog, p13, yo, p2 tog, k1.

Row 11—A, k6, B.

Row 12—Yo, k2 tog, p14, yo, p2 tog, k1.

Row 13—A, k7, B.

Row 14—Yo, k2 tog, p15, yo, p2 tog, k1.

Row 15—A, k8, yo, k1, return last knit st to left-hand needle and with point of right-hand needle pass the last 7 sts one at a time over this st and off needle; then sl the st back to right-hand needle.

Row 16—P2 tog, p9, yo, p2 tog, k1.

Repeat Rows 1–16.

Crystal Edging

Here, a miniature Crystal Pattern makes a beautiful edging with the addition of garter-stitch points and three bands of faggoting.

Cast on 18 sts.

Preparation Row (Wrong side)—K6, p7, k5.
Row 1—Sl 1, k2, yo, k2 tog, k2, k2 tog, yo, k5, yo, k2 tog, (yo, k1) twice.
Row 2—K6, yo, k2 tog, p7, k2, yo, k2 tog, k1.
Row 3—Sl 1, k2, yo, k2 tog, k1, (k2 tog, yo) twice, k4, yo, k2 tog, (yo, k1) twice, k2.
Row 4—K8, yo, k2 tog, p7, k2, yo, k2 tog, k1.
Row 5—Sl 1, k2, yo, k2 tog, (k2 tog, yo) 3 times, k3, yo, k2 tog, (yo, k1) twice, k4.
Row 6—K10, yo, k2 tog, p7, k2, yo, k2 tog, k1.
Row 7—Sl 1, k2, yo, k2 tog, k1, (k2 tog, yo) twice, k4, yo, k2 tog, (yo, k1) twice, k6.
Row 8—Bind off 8, k3, yo, k2 tog, p7, k2, yo, k2 tog, k1.

Repeat Rows 1–8.

ABOVE: *Crystal Edging*
BELOW: *Double Fern Edging*

Double Fern Edging

In this pattern the "Oak-Leaf" is scaled down and doubled for a most attractive edging with interesting lines.

Cast on 17 sts and knit one row.

"A" portion of pattern (on 4 sts): * (yo) twice, k2 tog; rep from * once.

Row 1—K2, yo, p2 tog, (k2, A) twice, k1. (21 sts)
Row 2—K3, (p1, k2) twice, (k2 tog, p1) twice, k2, yo, p2 tog, k2. (19 sts)
Row 3—K2, yo, p2 tog, (k3, A) twice, k1. (23 sts)
Row 4—K3, p1, k2, p1, k3, (k2 tog, p1) twice, k3, yo, p2 tog, k2. (21 sts)
Row 5—K2, yo, p2 tog, (k4, A) twice, k1. (25 sts)
Row 6—K3, p1, k2, p1, k4, (k2 tog, p1) twice, k4, yo, p2 tog, k2. (23 sts)
Row 7—K2, yo, p2 tog, k5, (yo) twice, k2 tog, k12. (24 sts)
Row 8—K12, k2 tog, p1, k5, yo, p2 tog, k2. (23 sts)
Row 9—K2, yo, p2 tog, k17, k2 tog. (22 sts)
Row 10—Bind off 5, k12, yo, p2 tog, k2. (17 sts)

Repeat Rows 1–10.

Double-Faggoted Edging

Cast on 16 sts and knit one row.

Row 1—Sl 1, k2, yo, k1-b, (yo, ssk) twice, (k1, yo, k2 tog) twice, k2.
Row 2—Sl 1, k3, (yo, k2 tog, k1) twice, k7.
Row 3—Sl 1, k2, yo, k1-b, (yo, ssk) twice, k2, (yo, k2 tog, k1) twice, k1.
Row 4—Sl 1, k3, (yo, k2 tog, k1) twice, k8.
Row 5—Sl 1, k2, yo, k1-b, (yo, ssk) 3 times, (k1, yo, k2 tog) twice, k2.
Row 6—Sl 1, k3, (yo, k2 tog, k1) twice, k9.
Row 7—Sl 1, k2, yo, k1-b, (yo, ssk) 3 times, k2, (yo, k2 tog, k1) twice, k1.
Row 8—Sl 1, k3, (yo, k2 tog, k1) twice, k10.
Row 9—Sl 1, k1, psso, k2, (yo, ssk) 4 times, (k1, yo, k2 tog) twice, k2.
Row 10—Sl 1, k3, (yo, k2 tog, k1) twice, k9.
Row 11—Sl 1, k1, psso, k2, (yo, ssk) 3 times, k2, (yo, k2 tog, k1) twice, k1.
Row 12—Sl 1, k3, (yo, k2 tog, k1) twice, k8.
Row 13—Sl 1, k1, psso, k2, (yo, ssk) 3 times, (k1, yo, k2 tog) twice, k2.
Row 14—Sl 1, k3, (yo, k2 tog, k1) twice, k7.
Row 15—Sl 1, k1, psso, k2, (yo, ssk) twice, k2, (yo, k2 tog, k1) twice, k1.
Row 16—Sl 1, k3, (yo, k2 tog, k1) twice, k6.

Repeat Rows 1–16.

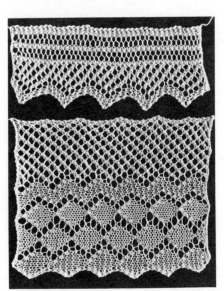

ABOVE: *Double-Faggoted Edging*
BELOW: *Torchon Lace Edging*

Torchon Lace Edging

Contributed by Pauline Balbes, Hollywood, California

Cast on 34 sts and knit one row.

Row 1—Sl 1, k3, yo, ssk, k3, k2 tog, yo, p3, yo, ssk, k3, yo, ssk, (yo, k2 tog) 6 times, k1.
Row 2—Sl 1, k23, p5, k3, (k1, p1) in next st, k1.
Row 3—Sl 1, k5, yo, ssk, k1, k2 tog, yo, p5, yo, ssk, k3, (yo, k2 tog) 6 times, k2.
Row 4—Sl 1, k24, p3, k5, (k1, p1) in next st, k1.
Row 5—Sl 1, k7, yo, sl 1—k2 tog—psso, yo, p7, yo, ssk, k3, (yo, k2 tog) 6 times, k1.
Row 6—Sl 1, k25, p1, k7, (k1, p1) in next st, k1.
Row 7—Sl 1, k6, k2 tog, yo, k3, yo, p2 tog, p3, p2 tog-b, yo, k3, k2 tog, yo, k1-b, (yo, k2 tog) 5 times, k2.
Row 8—Sl 1, k24, p3, k6, k2 tog, k1.

Row 9—Sl 1, k4, k2 tog, yo, k5, yo, p2 tog, p1, p2 tog-b, yo, k3, k2 tog, yo, k1-b, (yo, k2 tog) 6 times, k1.
Row 10—Sl 1, k23, p5, k4, k2 tog, k1.
Row 11—Sl 1, k2, k2 tog, yo, k7, yo, p3 tog, yo, k3, k2 tog, yo, k1-b, (yo, k2 tog) 6 times, k2.
Row 12—Sl 1, k21, p7, k2, k2 tog, k2.

Repeat Rows 1–12.

Loop Edging

This charming old pattern with its prominent picot loops would decorate the lower edge of a lace blouse very nicely, or would decorate a fancy pillow-slip equally well. It would also look handsome as a gauntlet for a cotton lace glove.

Cast on 11 sts and knit one row.

Row 1—K3, (yo, ssk, k1) twice, (yo) twice, k1, (yo) twice, k1.
Row 2—(K2, p1) 4 times, k3. (On this row each double yo is treated as 2 sts, the first being knitted, the second purled.)
Row 3—K3, yo, ssk, k1, yo, ssk, k7.
Row 4—Bind off 4 sts, k3, p1, k2, p1, k3.

Repeat Rows 1–4.

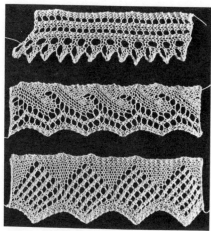

ABOVE: *Loop Edging*
CENTER: *Wave Edging*
BELOW: *Openwork Edging*

Wave Edging

Making a subtle, gently scalloped edge, this pattern is excellent for curtains and stoles.

Cast on 13 sts.

Row 1 and all other odd-numbered rows—K2, purl to last 2 sts, k2. (Number of purl sts will vary on different rows.)
Row 2—Sl 1, k3, yo, k5, yo, k2 tog, yo, k2.
Row 4—Sl 1, k4, sl 1—k2 tog—psso, k2, (yo, k2 tog) twice, k1.
Row 6—Sl 1, k3, ssk, k2, (yo, k2 tog) twice, k1.
Row 8—Sl 1, k2, ssk, k2, (yo, k2 tog) twice, k1.
Row 10—Sl 1, k1, ssk, k2, (yo, k2 tog) twice, k1.
Row 12—K1, ssk, k2, yo, k1, yo, k2 tog, yo, k2.
Row 14—Sl 1, (k3, yo) twice, k2 tog, yo, k2.

Repeat Rows 1–14.

Openwork Edging

Here is a simple but very pretty edging in which the bias inclination of the lace helps to form the scallops.

Cast on 13 sts.

Row 1 (Wrong side) and all other wrong-side rows—K2, purl to last 2 sts, k2.
Row 2—K7, yo, ssk, yo, k4.
Row 4—K6, (yo, ssk) twice, yo, k4.
Row 6—K5, (yo, ssk) 3 times, yo, k4.
Row 8—K4, (yo, ssk) 4 times, yo, k4.
Row 10—K3, (yo, ssk) 5 times, yo, k4.
Row 12—K4, (yo, ssk) 5 times, k2 tog, k2.
Row 14—K5, (yo, ssk) 4 times, k2 tog, k2.
Row 16—K6, (yo, ssk) 3 times, k2 tog, k2.
Row 18—K7, (yo, ssk) twice, k2 tog, k2.
Row 20—K8, yo, ssk, k2 tog, k2.

Repeat Rows 1–20.

Narrow Dice Edging

Cast on 6 sts and knit one row.

Row 1—K2, yo, k2 tog, yo, k2.
Row 2—K2, (yo, k1) twice, yo, k2 tog, k1.
Row 3—K2, yo, k2 tog, yo, k3, yo, k2.
Row 4—K2, yo, k5, yo, k1, yo, k2 tog, k1.
Row 5—K2, yo, k2 tog, yo, ssk, k3, k2 tog, yo, k2.
Row 6—K3, yo, ssk, k1, k2 tog, yo, k2, yo, k2 tog, k1.
Row 7—K2, yo, k2 tog, k2, yo, sl 1—k2 tog—psso, yo, k4.
Row 8—Bind off 7 sts, k2, yo, k2 tog, k1.

Repeat Rows 1–8.

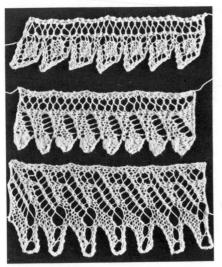

ABOVE: *Narrow Dice Edging*
CENTER: *Paddle Edging*
BELOW: *Quill Edging*

Paddle Edging

Although the edging is flat, this delightful little pattern gives the impression of a ball fringe. The "cable cast-on" recommended for this pattern is worked as follows: * insert right-hand needle from the front between the first and second sts on left-hand needle, draw through a loop, and slip this loop on left-hand needle to make a new first st; rep from * until the desired number of sts have been cast on. (It is a good idea to bring the yarn through to the front before placing the last st on the left-hand needle; this forms a separating strand between the last and next-to-last sts and makes them easier to work.)

To finish a strip of Paddle Edging, work Row 6 through the final "k1"; turn, omit the cast-on, and bind off all sts on the wrong side.

Cast on 13 sts and knit one row.

Row 1 (Wrong side)—K2, yo, p1, yo, p2 tog, k5, yo, k2 tog, k1.
Row 2—K3, yo, k2 tog, k2, k2 tog, yo, k3, yo, k2.
Row 3—K2, yo, p1, k3, p1, yo, p2 tog, k3, yo, k2 tog, k1.
Row 4—K3, yo, (k2 tog) twice, yo, k7, yo, k2.
Row 5—K2, yo, p1, k7, p1, yo, p2 tog, k1, yo, k2 tog, k1.
Row 6—K3, yo, k2 tog, k4, then with point of right-hand needle (pass the 2nd st on left-hand needle over the first st) 8 times; k1. (The last knit st is the single st remaining on left-hand needle with all 8 sts passed over it.) Turn. Cast on 3 sts, using the cable cast-on—13 sts now on needle. With wrong side still facing, begin again at Row 1.

Quill Edging

Cast on 10 sts and knit one row.

Row 1 (Right side)—K3, yo, k5, yo, k2.
Row 2—K2, (yo) twice, p1, yo, p2 tog, k4, yo, k2 tog, k1.
Row 3—K3, yo, k2 tog, k1, (k2 tog, yo) twice, k1, p1, k2.
Row 4—K2, (yo) twice, k3, (yo, p2 tog) twice, k2, yo, k2 tog, k1.
Row 5—K4, (k2 tog, yo) twice, k5, p1, k2.
Row 6—K2, (yo) twice, k7, (yo, p2 tog) twice, k3.
Row 7—K2, (k2 tog, yo) twice, k9, p1, k2.
Row 8—Bind off 8 sts, k4, (yo, p2 tog) twice, k1.

Repeat Rows 1–8.

Grape Edging

This is a very old pattern forming a graceful, lightly scalloped border of small "picot faggoting" points: these are the single loops left by the yo's on the outside edge. When an edging like this is washed and pinned out, a pin should be inserted into each single loop to draw it away from the next stitch, thus forming the picot.

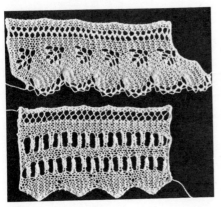

Cast on 20 sts and knit one row.

Row 1—K3, yo, p2 tog, k3, yo, k10, yo, p2 tog.

Row 2—Yo, p2 tog, k14, yo, p2 tog, k3.

Row 3—K3, yo, p2 tog, k3, yo, k1, yo, k10, yo, p2 tog.

Row 4—Yo, p2 tog, k16, yo, p2 tog, k3.

Row 5—K3, yo, p2 tog, k3, (yo, k1) 3 times, yo, k10, yo, p2 tog.

Row 6—Yo, p2 tog, k20, yo, p2 tog, k3.

Row 7—K3, yo, p2 tog, k6, yo, k1, yo, k13, yo, p2 tog.

Row 8—Yo, p2 tog, k22, yo, p2 tog, k3.

Row 9—K3, yo, p2 tog, k13, then with point of right-hand needle (pass the 2nd st on left-hand needle over the first st and off needle) 9 times—2 sts now remain on left-hand needle—yo, p2 tog.

Row 10—Yo, p2 tog, k13, yo, p2 tog, k3.

Repeat Rows 1–10.

Louvered Edging

The "louvers" are made like buttonholes, except that the stitches are not cast on, but increased in a yo. This ladder-like pattern can be used in other ways, to decorate any portion of a knitted piece.

Cast on 15 sts loosely.

Row 1 (Preparation row—right side)—K3, yo, k2 tog, k6, yo, k4.

Row 2—K1, inc in next st, * p2, (k1, p1) twice into the yo loop of previous row, p1, k1, p1, yo, p2, k3, yo, k2 tog, k1. *

Row 3—* K3, yo, k2 tog, k3, (k1, p1) twice into the yo loop of previous row, k3, bind off 4 sts in knit, * k2, inc in next st, k1.

Row 4—K1, inc in next st, k2, * p2, yo, p1, k1, p1, bind off 4 sts in purl, p1, k3, yo, k2 tog, k1. *

Row 5—* K3, yo, k2 tog, k3, yo, k3, (k1, p1) twice into the yo loop of previous row, * k5, inc in next st, k1.

Row 6—K1, inc in next st, k4, * p2, bind off 4 sts in purl, k1, p1, (k1, p1) twice into the yo loop of previous row, p2, k3, yo, k2 tog, k1. *

Row 7—* K3, yo, k2 tog, k3, bind off 4 sts in knit, k2, yo, * k7, inc in next st, k1.

Row 8—K1, k2 tog, k5, rep from * to * of Row 2.

Row 9—Rep from * to * of Row 3, k5, k2 tog, k1.

Row 10—K1, k2 tog, k3, rep from * to * of Row 4.

Row 11—Rep from * to * of Row 5, k4, k2 tog, k1.

Row 12—K1, k2 tog, k1, rep from * to * of Row 6.

Row 13—Rep from * to * of Row 7, k2, k2 tog, k1.

Omitting preparation row, repeat Rows 2–13.

Primrose Edging

This edging is particularly nice on a wide, elbow-length or three-quarter sleeve. The blouse, dress, lounge coat or peignoir to which the sleeve is attached need not be knitted—edgings like these can be sewn to cloth as well as to knitted fabrics.

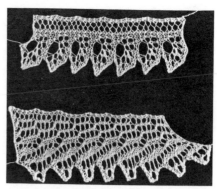

ABOVE: *Primrose Edging*
BELOW: *Grecian Lace Edging*

Cast on 11 sts and knit one row.

Row 1—K3, yo, k2 tog, k1, ssk, cast on 4 sts, k2 tog, k1. (13 sts)
Row 2—K10, yo, k2 tog, k1.
Row 3—K3, yo, k2 tog, ssk, (yo, k1) 4 times, yo, k2 tog. (16 sts)
Row 4—K13, yo, k2 tog, k1.
Row 5—K3, yo, k2 tog, ssk, (yo, k1) twice, yo, sl 1—k2 tog—psso, (yo, k1) twice, yo, k2 tog. (18 sts)
Row 6—K15, yo, k2 tog, k1.
Row 7—K3, yo, k2 tog, k11, k2 tog. (17 sts)
Row 8—Bind off 6 sts, k7, yo, k2 tog, k1. (11 sts)

Repeat Rows 1–8.

Grecian Lace Edging

Every line in this handsome bias pattern slopes gently "downhill" from right to left, terminating at the bound-off scallop. Six repeats of the pattern rows are required to move one series of openings all the way down from the straight edge to the scallop.

Being strongly bias, this pattern is not suitable for a straight edge, such as the side of a table mat or curtain, but must go *around* something—a sleeve, a skirt, or a round doily, for instance. The first row and the last row can be sewn together invisibly, matching the pattern lines.

Cast on 15 sts and purl one row.

Row 1 (Right side)—Sl 1, k1, (yo, k2 tog) 3 times, (k1, yo) twice, k1, k2 tog, (yo) twice, k2 tog.
Row 2—K2, p13, k2.
Row 3—Sl 1, k1, (yo, k2 tog) 3 times, k1, yo, k2, yo, k1, k2 tog, (yo) twice, k2 tog, k1.
Row 4—K3, p14, k2.
Row 5—Sl 1, k1, (yo, k2 tog) 3 times, k1, yo, k3, yo, k1, k2 tog, [(yo) twice, k2 tog] twice.
Row 6—K2, p1, k2, p15, k2.
Row 7—Sl 1, (k1, yo) twice, (ssk, yo) twice, k2 tog, yo, (k2 tog) twice, yo, k3 tog, k6.
Row 8—Bind off 6 sts, p12, k2.

Repeat Rows 1–8.

Shark's Tooth Edging

Here is a beautiful bold pattern with long points supported by two rows of simple faggoting. It is very good for novelty blouses and sweaters, lace mats, lace aprons, or slip hems.

Cast on 8 sts and knit one row.

Row 1—Sl 1, k1, (yo, k2 tog) twice, yo, k2.
Row 2—K2, yo, k2, (yo, k2 tog) twice, k1.
Row 3—Sl 1, k1, (yo, k2 tog) twice, k2, yo, k2.
Row 4—K2, yo, k4, (yo, k2 tog) twice, k1.
Row 5—Sl 1, k1, (yo, k2 tog) twice, k4, yo, k2.
Row 6—K2, yo, k6, (yo, k2 tog) twice, k1.
Row 7—Sl 1, k1, (yo, k2 tog) twice, k6, yo, k2.
Row 8—K2, yo, k8, (yo, k2 tog) twice, k1.
Row 9—Sl 1, k1, (yo, k2 tog) twice, k8, yo, k2.
Row 10—K2, yo, k10, (yo, k2 tog) twice, k1.
Row 11—Sl 1, k1, (yo, k2 tog) twice, k10, yo, k2.
Row 12—Bind off 11 sts, k2, (yo, k2 tog) twice, k1.

Repeat Rows 1–12.

ABOVE: *Shark's Tooth Edging*
BELOW: *Cockleshell Edging*

Cockleshell Edging

Uncluttered and easy to work, this broad edging is in the grand Victorian tradition of lace knitting. Characteristic of its period are the garter-stitch basis and the single plain decrease (k2 tog) used throughout. A hundred years ago, knitters liked to put edgings like this on knitted cotton petticoats, tablecloths, and curtains.

Cast on 16 sts and knit one row.

Row 1—Yo, k2 tog, k1, yo, k10, yo, k2 tog, k1.
Row 2—K2, yo, k2 tog, k12, p1.
Row 3—Yo, k2 tog, k1, yo, k2 tog, yo, k9, yo, k2 tog, k1.
Row 4—K2, yo, k2 tog, k13, p1.
Row 5—Yo, k2 tog, k1, (yo, k2 tog) twice, yo, k8, yo, k2 tog, k1.
Row 6—K2, yo, k2 tog, k14, p1.
Row 7—Yo, k2 tog, k1, (yo, k2 tog) 3 times, yo, k7, yo, k2 tog, k1.
Row 8—K2, yo, k2 tog, k15, p1.
Row 9—Yo, k2 tog, k1, (yo, k2 tog) 4 times, yo, k6, yo, k2 tog, k1.
Row 10—K2, yo, k2 tog, k16, p1.
Row 11—Yo, k2 tog, k1, (yo, k2 tog) 5 times, yo, k5, yo, k2 tog, k1.
Row 12—K2, yo, k2 tog, k17, p1.
Row 13—Yo, k2 tog, k1, (yo, k2 tog) 6 times, yo, k4, yo, k2 tog, k1.
Row 14—K2, yo, k2 tog, k18, p1.
Row 15—Yo, k2 tog, k1, (yo, k2 tog) 7 times, yo, k3, yo, k2 tog, k1.
Row 16—K2, yo, k2 tog, k19, p1.
Row 17—Yo, (k2 tog) twice, (yo, k2 tog) 7 times, k3, yo, k2 tog, k1.

Rows 18, 20, 22, 24, 26, 28, and 30—Repeat Rows 14, 12, 10, 8, 6, 4, and 2.
Row 19—Yo, (k2 tog) twice, (yo, k2 tog) 6 times, k4, yo, k2 tog, k1.
Row 21—Yo, (k2 tog) twice, (yo, k2 tog) 5 times, k5, yo, k2 tog, k1.
Row 23—Yo, (k2 tog) twice, (yo, k2 tog) 4 times, k6, yo, k2 tog, k1.
Row 25—Yo, (k2 tog) twice, (yo, k2 tog) 3 times, k7, yo, k2 tog, k1.
Row 27—Yo, (k2 tog) twice, (yo, k2 tog) twice, k8, yo, k2 tog, k1.
Row 29—Yo, (k2 tog) twice, yo, k2 tog, k9, yo, k2 tog, k1.
Row 31—Yo, (k2 tog) twice, k10, yo, k2 tog, k1.
Row 32—K2, yo, k2 tog, k11, p1.

Repeat Rows 1–32.

The Queen's Edging

The dainty fan-shaped motifs of this lovely old pattern have a tendency to puff outward, which can give an unusual embossed effect. The edging is very attractive when worked in fine cotton and applied to linens, such as pillowcases, fancy hand towels, bedspreads and tablecloths. It also makes a beautiful border for a stole or evening scarf.

Cast on 13 sts and knit one row.

Row 1—Sl 1, k12.
Row 2—Sl 1, k1, k2 tog, (yo) twice, k2 tog, k7.
Row 3—Sl 1, k8, p1, k3.
Rows 4 and 5—Sl 1, k12.
Row 6—Sl 1, k1, k2 tog, (yo) twice, k2 tog, k2, (yo) twice, [k1, (yo) twice] 3 times, k2.
Row 7—Sl 1, (k2, p1) 4 times, k4, p1, k3.
Rows 8 and 9—Sl 1, k20.
Row 10—Sl 1, k1, k2 tog, (yo) twice, k2 tog, k15.
Row 11—K12 wrapping yarn 3 times for each st, (yo) 3 times, k5, p1, k3.
Row 12—Sl 1, k9, p1, k1; sl the remaining 12 sts to right-hand needle dropping extra wraps to make 12 long loops; sl these 12 long loops back to left-hand needle and knit them all together as one st.

Repeat Rows 1–12.

ABOVE: *The Queen's Edging*
BELOW: *Purl-Gathered Edging*

Purl-Gathered Edging

Starching is important for this pattern, because the scallops are worked in stockinette stitch instead of the more usual garter stitch, and so they will curl unless stiffened.

Cast on 16 sts and purl one row.

Row 1 (Right side)—Sl 1, k2, yo, k2 tog, k2, (yo) twice, k2 tog, k7.

Row 2—Sl 1, p8, k1, p3, k1, yo, k2 tog, k1.

Row 3—Sl 1, k2, yo, k2 tog, k12.

Row 4—Sl 1, p12, k1, yo, k2 tog, k1.

Row 5—Sl 1, k2, yo, k2 tog, k2, [(yo) twice, k2 tog] twice, k6.

Row 6—Sl 1, p7, k1, p2, k1, p3, k1, yo, k2 tog, k1.

Row 7—Sl 1, k2, yo, k2 tog, k14.

Row 8—Sl 1, p14, k1, yo, k2 tog, k1.

Row 9—Sl 1, k2, yo, k2 tog, k2, [(yo) twice, k2 tog] 3 times, k6.

Row 10—Sl 1, p7, (k1, p2) twice, k1, p3, k1, yo, k2 tog, k1.

Row 11—Sl 1, k2, yo, k2 tog, k17.

Row 12—P6 tog, p1, pass the p6-tog st over the last st made, p11, k1, yo, k2 tog, k1.

Repeat Rows 1–12.

Square Filet Edging

In this simple but ingenious pattern, small diamonds are given a quarter-turn by the natural bias of the knitting; thus they are converted into squares. The rows run diagonally across these squares, showing that they are in fact worked at an angle. All yo's in the pattern are double ones, written "yo2". The purl stitches on the return rows are placed in the second loop of each double yo. Caution: the 7th row has a single "k*3* tog", the only double decrease in the pattern.

Cast on 15 sts and knit one row.

Row 1—K1, k2 tog, yo2, k2 tog, k1, yo2, k7, yo2, k2.

Row 2—K3, p1, k8, p1, k3, p1, k2.

Row 3—K1, k2 tog, yo2, k2 tog, k1, (yo2, k2 tog) twice, k3, k2 tog, yo2, k4.

Row 4—K5, p1, k6, p1, k2, p1, k3, p1, k2.

Row 5—K1, k2 tog, yo2, k2 tog, k1, yo2, (k2 tog, k1, k2 tog, yo2) twice, k6.

Row 6—K7, (p1, k4) twice, p1, k3, p1, k2.

Row 7—K1, k2 tog, yo2, k2 tog, k1, yo2, k2 tog, k3, k2 tog, yo2, k3 tog, yo2, k8.

Row 8—K9, p1, k2, p1, k6, p1, k3, p1, k2.

Row 9—K1, k2 tog, yo2, k2 tog, k21.

Row 10—Bind off 10 sts, k8, k2 tog, k2, p1, k2.

Repeat Rows 1–10.

ABOVE: *Square Filet Edging*
BELOW: *Double Edging*

Double Edging

Here is a real old-fashioned pattern done in the real old-fashioned way—that is, all in simple garter stitch with all decreases worked "k2 tog"; or, as it was written at the turn of the century, "narrow". The isolated purl stitches in Rows 2, 8, 14, 20, and 26 go into the second of the two consecutive yo's in the preceding row.

This pattern is more than a single edging. It is a collar, a cuff, an appliqué, or a finish for fancy aprons, baby clothes, or lingerie. The eyelet band in the center of the pattern is meant to take a threaded ribbon of satin or velvet; behind this ribbon the edging is tacked on to the garment, so that both of the edge motifs are displayed. The edging can be drawn around a curve, such as the neckline of a peignoir, nightgown, or evening blouse. If it is to be used for such a purpose, care must be taken to bind off the stitches in Row 30 very loosely. When binding off, remember that the first stitch is slipped, and the *second* stitch is bound-off stitch no. 1; so that in Row 30 the last bound-off stitch is already on the right-hand needle when there are 16 remaining.

Cast on 17 sts and knit one row.

Row 1—Sl 1, k1, yo, k2 tog, yo, k1, yo, (k2 tog) twice, (yo) twice, (k2 tog) twice, yo, k1, yo, k3.

Row 2—Sl 1, k8, p1, k9.

Row 3—Sl 1, k1, yo, k2 tog, yo, k2, yo, k2 tog, k4, k2 tog, yo, k2, yo, k3.

Row 4—Sl 1, k20.

Row 5—Sl 1, k1, yo, k2 tog, yo, k3, yo, k2 tog, k4, k2 tog, (yo, k3) twice.

Row 6—Sl 1, k22.

Row 7—Sl 1, k7, yo, (k2 tog) twice, (yo) twice, (k2 tog) twice, yo, k1, yo, k2 tog, k1, yo, k3.

Row 8—Sl 1, k11, p1, k11.

Row 9—Bind off 3, k4, yo, k2 tog, k4, k2 tog, yo, k2, yo, k2 tog, k1, yo, k3.

Row 10—Sl 1, k21.

Row 11—Sl 1, k1, yo, k2 tog, yo, k1, yo, k2 tog, k4, k2 tog, yo, k3, yo, k2 tog, k1, yo, k3.

Row 12—Sl 1, k23.

Row 13—Sl 1, k1, yo, k2 tog, yo, k2, yo, (k2 tog) twice, (yo) twice, (k2 tog) twice, yo, k1, (yo, k2 tog, k1) twice, yo, k3.

Row 14—Sl 1, k14, p1, k10.

Row 15—Sl 1, k1, yo, k2 tog, yo, k3, yo, k2 tog, k4, k2 tog, yo, k2, (yo, k2 tog, k1) twice, yo, k3.

Row 16—Sl 1, k27.

Row 17—Sl 1, k7, yo, k2 tog, k4, k2 tog, yo, k3, (yo, k2 tog, k1) twice, yo, k3.

Row 18—Sl 1, k28.

Row 19—Bind off 3, k4, yo, (k2 tog) twice, (yo) twice, (k2 tog) twice, yo, k1, (yo, k2 tog, k1) 3 times, yo, k3.

Row 20—Sl 1, k17, p1, k8.

Row 21—Sl 1, k1, yo, k2 tog, yo, k1, yo, k2 tog, k4, k2 tog, yo, k2, (yo, k2 tog, k1) 3 times, yo, k3.

Row 22—Sl 1, k28.

Row 23—Sl 1, k1, yo, k2 tog, yo, k2, yo, k2 tog, k4, k2 tog, yo, k3, (yo, k2 tog, k1) 3 times, yo, k3.

Row 24—Sl 1, k30.

Row 25—Sl 1, k1, yo, k2 tog, yo, k3, yo, (k2 tog) twice, (yo) twice, (k2 tog) twice, yo, k1, (yo, k2 tog, k1) 4 times, yo, k3.

Row 26—Sl 1, k20, p1, k11.

Row 27—Sl 1, k7, yo, k2 tog, k4, k2 tog, yo, k2, (yo, k2 tog, k1) 4 times, yo, k3.

Row 28—Sl 1, k33.

Row 29—Bind off 3, k4, yo, k2 tog, k4, k2 tog, yo, k18.

Row 30—Bind off 14 (loosely), k16.

Repeat Rows 1–30.

Domino Edging

ABOVE: *Domino Edging*
BELOW: *Buttercup Edging*

Need a fancy mask for a costume party? Two repeats of this pattern, plus the first 4 rows again, will make a most unusual one! Knit it in black cotton, lightly starched, or a glistening metallic yarn, and add ribbon or elastic at the sides, planning the gauge so the eyelets will fit your eyes. The eyelets may be widened and reinforced with buttonhole stitch in a contrasting color.

Or—use it in the conventional way as an edging. It makes a very handsome one.

Cast on 14 sts and knit one row.

NOTE: Throughout pattern, increase (inc) by knitting into front and back of the same stitch.

Rows 1 and 3—Sl 1, (k3, yo, k2 tog) twice, k3.

Rows 2 and 4—Sl 1, k4, yo, k2 tog, k3, yo, k2 tog, k2.

Row 5—Sl 1, k3, yo, k2 tog, inc, k2, yo, k2 tog, inc in each of the last 3 sts.

Row 6—Bind off 3, (k4, yo, k2 tog) twice, k2.

Row 7—Sl 1, k3, yo, k2 tog, k1, inc, k2, yo, k2 tog, k3.

Row 8—Sl 1, k4, yo, k2 tog, k5, yo, k2 tog, k2.

Row 9—Sl 1, k3, yo, k2 tog, k2, inc, k2, yo, k2 tog, k3.

Row 10—Sl 1, k4, yo, k2 tog, k6, yo, k2 tog, k2.

Row 11—Sl 1, k3, yo, k2 tog, k3, inc, k2, yo, k2 tog, inc in each of the last 3 sts.

Row 12—Bind off 3, k4, yo, k2 tog, k7, yo, k2 tog, k2.

Row 13—Sl 1, k3, yo, k2 tog, k4, inc, k2, yo, k2 tog, k3.

Row 14—Sl 1, k4, yo, k2 tog, k8, yo, k2 tog, k2.

Row 15—Sl 1, k3, yo, k2 tog, k5, inc, k2, yo, k2 tog, k3.

Row 16—Sl 1, k4, yo, k2 tog, k9, yo, k2 tog, k2.

Row 17—Sl 1, k3, yo, k2 tog, sl 2—k2 tog—p2sso, (yo) 5 times, sl 1—k2 tog—psso, k2, yo, k2 tog, inc in each of the last 3 sts.

Row 18—Bind off 3, k4, yo, k2 tog, k1, (k1, p1, k1, p1, k1) into the 5-yo loop, k3, yo, k2 tog, k2.

Row 19—Sl 1, k3, yo, k2 tog, k5, k2 tog, k2, yo, k2 tog, k3.

Row 20—Repeat Row 14.

Row 21—Sl 1, k3, yo, k2 tog, k4, k2 tog, k2, yo, k2 tog, k3.

Row 22—Sl 1, k4, yo, k2 tog, k7, yo, k2 tog, k2.

Row 23—Sl 1, k3, yo, k2 tog, k3, k2 tog, k2, yo, k2 tog, inc in each of the last 3 sts.

Row 24—Bind off 3, k4, yo, k2 tog, k6, yo, k2 tog, k2.

Row 25—Sl 1, k3, yo, (k2 tog, k2) twice, yo, k2 tog, k3.

Row 26—Repeat Row 8.

Row 27—Sl 1, k3, yo, k2 tog, k1, k2 tog, k2, yo, k2 tog, k3.

Row 28—Sl 1, (k4, yo, k2 tog) twice, k2.

Row 29—Sl 1, k3, yo, (k2 tog) twice, k2, yo, k2 tog, inc in each of the last 3 sts.

Row 30—Bind off 3, k4, yo, k2 tog, k3, yo, k2 tog, k2.

Repeat Rows 1–30.

Buttercup Edging

This is a classic pattern that was probably used by the grand-mothers of today's knitters. Yet today's knitters may also use it to good effect, for dress and sleeve hems, shawls, curtains and table mats.

The "p2 tog-b" in Row 6 may occasion some difficulty, since the second stitch is a yo and is sometimes—depending on the elasticity of the yarn—hard to catch. But this can be worked easily by purling one stitch, returning it to the left-hand needle, passing the *next* stitch (the yo) over it, and then slipping it back to the right-hand needle. Note that the first 7 stitches are worked the same on every right-side row.

Cast on 14 sts and purl one row.

Row 1 (Right side)—* Sl 1, k2 tog, yo, k1, yo, ssk, k1, * yo, k1, yo, (k1, yo, k1) in the next st, (yo, k1) twice, (yo) twice, k2 tog, k1.

Row 2—K3, p1, k1, p9, k1, p5, k1.

Row 3—Rep from * to *, (yo, k3) 3 times, yo, [k1, (yo) twice] twice, k2 tog, k1.

Row 4—K3, p1, k2, p1, k1, p5, p3 tog, (p5, k1) twice.

Row 5—Rep from * to *, (yo, ssk, k1, k2 tog, yo, k1) twice, [(yo) twice, k2 tog] 3 times, k1.

Row 6—K3, p1, (k2, p1) twice, k1, p2 tog, p1, p2 tog-b, p1, p2 tog, p1, p2 tog-b, k1, p5, k1.

Row 7—Rep from * to *, yo, k3 tog-b, k1, k3 tog, yo, k11.

Row 8—Bind off 7, k4, p3 tog, k2, p5, k1.

Repeat Rows 1–8.

Snail Shell Edging

Cast on 19 sts and knit one row.

Row 1 (Wrong side)—K5, p1, yo, p2 tog, k8, yo, k2 tog, k1.

Row 2—K3, yo, k2 tog, k5, k2 tog, yo, k1, yo, ssk, k2, (yo) twice, k2.

Row 3—K3, p1, k1, p2 tog-b, yo, p3, yo, p2 tog, k6, yo, k2 tog, k1.

Row 4—K3, yo, k2 tog, k3, k2 tog, yo, k2, k2 tog, yo, k1, yo, ssk, k2, (yo) twice, k2.

Row 5—K3, p1, k1, p2 tog-b, yo, p3, yo, p2 tog, p2, yo, p2 tog, k4, yo, k2 tog, k1.

Row 6—K3, yo, k2 tog, k1, (k2 tog, yo, k2) twice, yo, ssk, k1, yo, ssk, k2, (yo) twice, k2.

Row 7—K3, p1, k1, (p2 tog-b, yo, p1) twice, yo, p2 tog, p1, yo, p2 tog, p2, yo, p2 tog, k2, yo, k2 tog, k1.

Row 8—K3, yo, k3 tog, yo, k2, k2 tog, yo, k1, k2 tog, yo, k3, yo, ssk, k1, yo, ssk, k2 tog, (yo) twice, k2 tog.

Row 9—K2, p1, k1, p2, yo, p2 tog, p1, yo, p3 tog, yo, p1, p2 tog-b, yo, p2, p2 tog-b, yo, k3, yo, k2 tog, k1.

Row 10—K3, yo, k2 tog, (k2, yo, ssk) twice, k3, k2 tog, yo, k2, sl 1—k2 tog—psso, (yo) twice, k2 tog.

Row 11—K2, p5, yo, p2 tog, p1, p2 tog-b, yo, p2, p2 tog-b, yo, k5, yo, k2 tog, k1.

Row 12—K3, yo, k2 tog, k4, yo, ssk, k2, yo, k3 tog, yo, k2, k3 tog, yo, k2 tog, k1.

Row 13—K3, p1, k3, yo, p2 tog, p1, p2 tog-b, yo, k7, yo, k2 tog, k1.

Row 14—K3, yo, k2 tog, k6, yo, k3 tog, yo, k2, k3 tog, yo, k3 tog.

Repeat Rows 1–14.

Vandyke Medallion Edging

Here is a very elegant lace edging in the ornate Victorian tradition.

Cast on 26 sts and knit one row.

Row 1—K2 tog, k1, yo, k2 tog, k5, k2 tog, yo, k2 tog, k9, yo, k2 tog, k1. (24 sts)

Row 2—Sl 1, k2, yo, k2 tog, k1, k2 tog, (yo, k2 tog) twice, k2, yo, k2 tog, k3, k2 tog, yo, k3. (23 sts)

Row 3—Yo, k4, yo, k2 tog, k1, k2 tog, yo, k11, yo, k2 tog, k1. (24 sts)

Row 4—Sl 1, k2, yo, k2 tog, k3, (yo, k2 tog) twice, k3, yo, sl 1—k2 tog—psso, yo, k6. (24 sts)

Row 5—Yo, k1, k2 tog, (yo) twice, k18, yo, k2 tog, k1. (26 sts)

Row 6—Sl 1, k2, yo, k2 tog, k4, (yo, k2 tog) twice, k8, (k1, p1) into the double yo, k3. (26 sts)

Row 7—K1, k2 tog, (yo) twice, k2 tog, (yo) twice, k2 tog, k16, yo, k2 tog, k1. (27 sts)

Row 8—Sl 1, k2, yo, k2 tog, k5, (yo, k2 tog) twice, k6, (k1, p1) into the double yo, k1, (k1, p1) into the double yo, k2. (27 sts)

Row 9—K2 tog, k1, k2 tog, (yo) twice, k2 tog, k3, yo, k1, yo, k2 tog, k11, yo, k2 tog, k1. (27 sts)

Row 10—Sl 1, k2, yo, k2 tog, k3, k2 tog, yo, k2 tog, (yo, k3) twice, yo, k2 tog, k2, (k1, p1) into the double yo, k2 tog, k1. (27 sts)

Row 11—K2 tog, k3, k2 tog, yo, k5, yo, k2 tog, k10, yo, k2 tog, k1. (26 sts)

Row 12—Sl 1, k2, yo, k2 tog, k2, (k2 tog, yo) twice, k3, yo, k7, yo, k2 tog, k1, k2 tog. (26 sts)

Repeat Rows 1–12.

Classic Bead Edging

An old favorite of lace knitters, this pattern has dozens of variations. This version is a "basic" without additional frills or enlargements.

Cast on 17 sts and knit one row.

Row 1 (Right side)—K4, (yo, k1, k2 tog) twice, yo, k3, yo, k4.

Row 2—K4, yo, k5, (yo, p2 tog, k1) twice, yo, k4.

Row 3—K4, (yo, k1, k2 tog) twice, yo, k1, yo, ssk, k1, k2 tog, yo, k1, yo, k4.

Row 4—K4, yo, k3, yo, p3 tog, yo, k3, (yo, p2 tog, k1) twice, yo, k4.

Row 5—K5, k2 tog, yo, k1, k2 tog, yo, k11, yo, k4.

Row 6—K2 tog, k3, yo, p2 tog, k1, p2 tog-b, yo, k1, yo, p2 tog, k1, p2 tog-b, (yo, k1, p2 tog) twice, k4.

Row 7—K4, (yo, ssk, k1) twice, yo, sl 1—k2 tog—psso, yo, k3, yo, k3 tog, yo, k3, k2 tog.

Row 8—K2 tog, k3, yo, p2 tog, k3, p2 tog-b, (yo, k1, p2 tog-b) twice, yo, k2 tog, k3.

Row 9—K3, k2 tog, yo, ssk, (k1, yo, ssk) twice, k1, k2 tog, yo, k3, k2 tog.

Row 10—K2 tog, k3, yo, p3 tog, (yo, k1, p2 tog-b) twice, yo, k2 tog, k3.

Row 11—K3, k2 tog, yo, ssk, k1, yo, ssk, k2, yo, k3, k2 tog.

Row 12—K2 tog, k3, yo, k1, (yo, p2 tog, k1) twice, yo, k4.

Repeat Rows 1–12.

ABOVE: *Classic Bead Edging*
BELOW: *Alpine Edging*

Alpine Edging

Here is an exquisite old French pattern, made up of single-strand lace with the usual flattened diamonds, plus a "vandyke" or zigzag band of large eyelets. Most of the decreases are purled, which slightly lengthens the yo's and makes the lace more open.

Cast on 17 sts and knit one row.

"A" portion of pattern: K2, k1-b, yo, k1, p2 tog, (yo) twice, (p2 tog) twice, yo. (10 stitches increased to 11)

"B" portion of pattern: K2, p2 tog, yo, (p2 tog) twice, (yo) twice, p2 tog, yo, p2 tog. (12 stitches decreased to 11)

Row 1 (Right side)—K4, yo, p2 tog, k2, yo, k2, p1, k3, yo, k1-b, k2.

Row 2—A, k5, yo, p2 tog, k2.

Row 3—(K4, yo, p2 tog) twice, k1, p1, k3, yo, k1-b, k2.

Row 4—A, k7, yo, p2 tog, k2.

Row 5—K4, yo, p2 tog, k6, yo, p2 tog, k1, p1, k3, yo, k1-b, k2.

Row 6—A, k9, yo, p2 tog, k2.

Row 7—K4, yo, p2 tog, k5, k2 tog, yo, k1, yo, p2 tog, k1, p1, k3, yo, k1-b, k2.

Row 8—A, k3, yo, p2 tog, k6, yo, p2 tog, k2.

Row 9—K4, yo, p2 tog, k3, k2 tog, yo, k5, yo, p2 tog, k1, p1, k3, yo, k1-b, k2.

Row 10—A, k7, yo, p2 tog, k4, yo, p2 tog, k2.

Row 11—K4, yo, p2 tog, k1, k2 tog, yo, k9, yo, k3, p1, k3, yo, k1-b, k2.

Row 12—K2, k1-b, yo, k1, p2 tog, (yo) twice, p2 tog, p3 tog, yo, k11, (yo, p2 tog, k2) twice.

Row 13—K4, yo, p2 tog, k2, yo, ssk, k7, k2 tog, yo, k4, p1, p2 tog, yo, p2 tog, k2.

Row 14—K2, p2 tog, yo, (p2 tog) twice, (yo) twice, p2 tog, k1, yo, p2 tog, k5, p2 tog-b, yo, k5, yo, p2 tog, k2.

Row 15—K4, yo, p2 tog, k4, yo, ssk, k3, k2 tog, yo, k1, p2 tog, k1, p1, p2 tog, yo, p2 tog, k2.

Row 16—B, k1, p2 tog-b, yo, k7, yo, p2 tog, k2.

Row 17—K4, yo, p2 tog, k6, yo, k3 tog, yo, k3, p1, p2 tog, yo, p2 tog, k2.

Row 18—B, k8, yo, p2 tog, k2.

Row 19—K4, yo, p2 tog, k5, k2 tog, yo, k3, p1, p2 tog, yo, p2 tog, k2.

Row 20—B, k6, yo, p2 tog, k2.

Row 21—K4, yo, p2 tog, k3, k2 tog, yo, k3, p1, p2 tog, yo, p2 tog, k2.

Row 22—B, k4, yo, p2 tog, k2.

Row 23—K4, yo, p2 tog, k1, k2 tog, yo, k3, p1, p2 tog, yo, p2 tog, k2.

Row 24—B, k2, yo, p2 tog, k2.

Repeat Rows 1–24.

Eye-Spot Edging

Another name for this old pattern was Wagon Wheel—although a wagon with wheels shaped like these motifs would be a hard-riding vehicle indeed. An enlarged version of the motif appears as the "Candle-Flame Scallop" in Bead Medallion Edging.

Cast on 10 sts and knit one row.

Row 1—Sl 1, k1, (yo, k2 tog) twice, (yo) 4 times, k2 tog, yo, p2 tog.

Row 2—Yo, p2 tog, k1, (k1, p1) twice into the large yo loop, (k1, p1) twice, k2.

Row 3—Sl 1, (k1, yo, k2 tog) twice, k4, yo, p2 tog.

Row 4—Yo, p2 tog, k5, (p1, k2) twice.

Row 5—Sl 1, k1, yo, k2 tog, k2, yo, k2 tog, k3, yo, p2 tog.

Row 6—Yo, p2 tog, k4, p1, k3, p1, k2.

Row 7—Sl 1, k1, yo, k2 tog, k3, yo, k2 tog, k2, yo, p2 tog.

Row 8—Yo, p2 tog, k3, p1, k4, p1, k2.

Row 9—Sl 1, k1, yo, k2 tog, k4, yo, k2 tog, k1, yo, p2 tog.

Row 10—Yo, p2 tog, k2, p1, k5, p1, k2.

Row 11—Sl 1, k1, yo, k2 tog, k5, yo, k2 tog, yo, p2 tog.

Row 12—Bind off 3 sts, then slip the st from right-hand needle back to left-hand needle; yo, p2 tog, k5, p1, k2.

Repeat Rows 1–12.

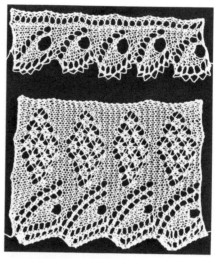

ABOVE: *Eye-Spot Edging*
BELOW: *Bead Medallion Edging with Candle-Flame Scallop*

Bead Medallion Edging with Candle-Flame Scallop

This is a beautiful 19th century edging that was applied to all kinds of lace work. Concerning the Bead Medallion, one word of warning: be sure that each "p3 tog" includes 3 *stitches,* and *not* a yo. Because of the nature of the pattern, especially when it is worked in very fine yarn, the yo following these 3 stitches sometimes becomes crossed over the 3rd stitch on the needle, and must be kept out of the decrease.

Cast on 30 sts and knit one row.

Row 1 (Right side)—Sl 1, k18, (yo, k2 tog) twice, k1, (yo) twice, k1, (yo, k2 tog) twice, k1.

Row 2—Sl 1, k5, in the double yo loop (k1, p1) twice, making 4 sts from this loop; k24.

Row 3—Sl 1, k8, k2 tog, yo, k1, yo, ssk, k6, (yo, k2 tog) twice, k5, (yo, k2 tog) twice, k1.

Row 4—Sl 1, k18, p2 tog-b, yo, p3, yo, p2 tog, k8.

Row 5—Sl 1, k5, (k2 tog, yo, k1, yo, ssk, k1) twice, k3, (yo, k2 tog) twice, k4, (yo, k2 tog) twice, k1.

Row 6—Sl 1, k15, p2 tog-b, yo, p3, yo, p3 tog, yo, p3, yo, p2 tog, k5.

Row 7—Sl 1, k2, (k2 tog, yo, k1, yo, ssk, k1) 3 times, k1, (yo, k2 tog) twice, k3, (yo, k2 tog) twice, k1.

Row 8—Sl 1, k12, p2 tog-b, (yo, p3, yo, p3 tog) twice, yo, p3, yo, p2 tog, k2.

Row 9—Sl 1, k2, (yo, ssk, k1, k2 tog, yo, k1) 3 times, [k2, (yo, k2 tog) twice] twice, k1.

Row 10—Sl 1, k14, (yo, p3 tog, yo, p3) twice, yo, p3 tog, yo, k4.

Row 11—Sl 1, k5, (yo, ssk, k1, k2 tog, yo, k1) twice, k6, [(yo, k2 tog) twice, k1] twice.

Row 12—Sl 1, k17, yo, p3 tog, yo, p3, yo, p3 tog, yo, k7.

Row 13—Sl 1, k8, yo, ssk, k1, k2 tog, yo, k11, (yo, k2 tog) 4 times, k1.

Row 14—Sl 1, k20, yo, p3 tog, yo, k10.

Row 15—Sl 1, k25, (yo, k2 tog) twice, k4.

Row 16—Sl 1, k4, pass the 1st 4 sts on right-hand needle over the last st worked, k29.

Repeat Rows 1–16.

Palm Leaf or Heart Edging

ABOVE: *Palm Leaf or Heart Edging*
BELOW: *Portuguese Edging*

This is an antique pattern of extraordinary beauty. It is not a simple edging, but it is so unusually graceful that to take care in working it is well worth while. Whether the motif resembles a palm leaf or a heart depends upon whether it is looked at upside down or right side up; if the edging is used horizontally, this is only a matter of choice.

Cast on 15 sts and knit one row.

Row 1 (Right side)—K2, yo, p2 tog, k2, (yo) twice, k2 tog, yo, k1, yo, k2 tog-b, (yo) twice, k2, (yo) twice, k2. (21 sts)

Row 2—K3, p1, k3, p7, k4, yo, p2 tog, k1. (21 sts)

Row 3—K2, yo, p2 tog, k2, (yo) twice, k2 tog, k2, yo, k1, yo, k2, k2 tog-b, (yo) twice, k4, (yo) twice, k2. (27 sts)

Row 4—K3, p1, k5, p11, k4, yo, p2 tog, k1. (27 sts)

Row 5—K2, yo, p2 tog, k2, (yo) twice, k2 tog, k4, yo, k1, yo, k4, k2 tog-b, (yo) twice, k6, (yo) twice, k2. (33 sts)

Row 6—K3, p1, k7, p15, k4, yo, p2 tog, k1. (33 sts)

Row 7—K2, yo, p2 tog, k3, (yo) twice, k3 tog-b, k9, k3 tog, (yo) twice, k11. (33 sts)

Row 8—Bind off 8, k3, p13, k5, yo, p2 tog, k1. (25 sts)

Row 9—K2, yo, p2 tog, k4, (yo) twice, k3 tog-b, k7, k3 tog, (yo) twice, k2, (yo) twice, k2. (27 sts)

Row 10—K3, p1, k3, p11, k6, yo, p2 tog, k1. (27 sts)

Row 11—K2, yo, p2 tog, k5, (yo) twice, k3 tog-b, k5, k3 tog, (yo) twice, k5, (yo) twice, k2. (29 sts)

Row 12—K3, p1, k6, p9, k7, yo, p2 tog, k1. (29 sts)

Row 13—K2, yo, p2 tog, k6, (yo) twice, k3 tog-b, k3, k3 tog, (yo) twice, k8, (yo) twice, k2. (31 sts)

Row 14—K3, p1, k9, p7, k8, yo, p2 tog, k1. (31 sts)

Row 15—K2, yo, p2 tog, k7, k3 tog-b, k4 tog, pass the k3 tog-b st over the k4 tog st, k13. (25 sts)

Row 16—Bind off 10, k2, p1, k8, yo, p2 tog, k1. (15 sts)

Repeat Rows 1–16.

Portuguese Edging

This beautiful old pattern shows a dainty faggoted cable with picot points. It is appropriate for any article worked with cables, faggoting, or a combination of cables and lace.

NOTES: DL—Drop Loop; drop the yo of previous row off needle.

Inc—increase; knit into front and back of the same st (in this pattern it will be a yo of previous row).

Cast on 2 and bind off 2—Knit first st, leaving it on needle, and place new st on left-hand needle; then knit this st and place next new st on left-hand needle. Then k2 (the 2 new sts) and pass the first st over the second; then knit the third st (the original first st) and pass the second st over it. This completes one picot point.

Cast on 18 sts and knit one row.

PREPARATION ROW—K5, k2 tog, k2, yo, k1, k2 tog, yo, k2 tog, k1, yo, k3.

Row 1—Sl 1, k2, yo, slip the yo of previous row, k2, inc, k3, sl next 2 sts to dpn and hold in front, k3, then k2 from dpn, yo, k2 tog, k1.

Row 2—Cast on 2 and bind off 2, k6, k2 tog, yo, k2 tog, k4, (k1, p1) into both yo loops together, as if they were a single loop, k3.

Row 3—Sl 1, k1, k2 tog, yo, k2 tog, k10, yo, k2 tog, k1.

Row 4—K5, (yo, k1) twice, k2 tog, yo, k2 tog, k3, yo, DL, k3.

Row 5—Sl 1, k2, (k1, p1) into the yo of previous row, k7, inc, k1, inc, k2, yo, k2 tog, k1.

Row 6—Cast on 2 and bind off 2, k4, yo, k2, yo, k2 tog, k1, yo, (k1, k2 tog, yo, k2 tog) twice, k2.

Row 7—Sl 1, k2, yo, DL, k6, (yo, k2 tog, k1) 4 times.

Row 8—K5, (yo, k2 tog, k1) 3 times, yo, k2 tog, k2, (k1, p1) into the yo of previous row, k3.

Row 9—Sl 1, k1, k2 tog, yo, k2 tog, k5, (yo, k2 tog, k1) 4 times.

Row 10—Cast on 2 and bind off 2, k4, (yo, k2 tog, k1) 3 times, yo, k2 tog, k2, yo, DL, k3.

Row 11—Sl 1, k2, (k1, p1) into the yo of previous row, k6, (yo, k2 tog, k1) 4 times.

Row 12—K5, (yo, k2 tog, k1) 4 times, k2 tog, yo, k2 tog, k2.

Rows 13 and 15—Repeat Rows 7 and 9.

Row 14—Cast on 2 and bind off 2, k4, (yo, k2 tog, k1) 3 times, yo, k2 tog, k2, (k1, p1) into the yo of previous row, k3.

Row 16—K5, (yo, k2 tog, k1) 3 times, yo, k2 tog, k2, yo, DL, k3.

Row 17—Sl 1, k2, (k1, p1) into the yo of previous row, k6, yo, (k2 tog, k1) twice, (yo, k2 tog, k1) twice.

Row 18—Cast on 2 and bind off 2, k4, yo, k2 tog, k1, k2 tog, yo, k2 tog, k1, yo, k3, k2 tog, yo, k2 tog, k2.

Row 19—Sl 1, k2, yo, DL, k7, yo, k2 tog, k2, (yo, k2 tog, k1) twice.

Row 20—K5, yo, (k2 tog) twice, yo, k2 tog, k1, yo, k5, (k1, p1) into the yo of previous row, k3.

Row 21—Sl 1, k1, k2 tog, yo, k2 tog, k7, (k2 tog, k1) twice, yo, k2 tog, k1.

Row 22—K5, k2 tog, k2, yo, k1, k2 tog, yo, k2 tog, k1, yo, DL, k3.

Repeat Rows 1–22.

Mexican Edging

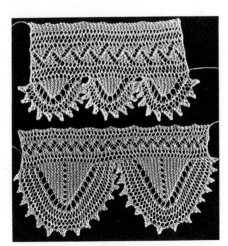

ABOVE: *Mexican Edging*
BELOW: *Chinese Edging*

Patterned with the same intricacy and boldness of design that can be seen in the finest Mexican silver, this beautiful edging adds a touch of elegance to any knitted article, plain or fancy. The concept is unusual, and the knitting is complex but can be followed by anyone with moderate experience in lace knitting and careful attention to the directions. See Special Note at the end of pattern rows.

Cast on 19 sts and knit one row.

"A" portion of pattern—worked on the first 8 sts of every odd-numbered row: Sl 1, k3, (yo, p2 tog) twice.

Row 1 (Right side)—A, k4, yo, ssk, (yo, p2 tog) twice, k1.

Row 2—K1, (yo, p2 tog) 3 times, k4, (yo, p2 tog) twice, k4.

Row 3—A, k3, k2 tog, yo, k1, (yo, p2 tog) twice, yo, (p1, k1) in last st.

Row 4—K1, yo, k2, (yo, p2 tog) twice, k2, yo, p2 tog, k2, (yo, p2 tog) twice, k4.

Row 5—A, k1, k2 tog, yo, k3, (yo, p2 tog) twice, yo, k3, (p1, k1) in last st. Turn. K1, yo, k2, yo, p2 tog. Turn. Yo, p2 tog, yo, k3, (p1, k1) in last st.

Row 6—Bind off 5, yo, p2 tog, k1, (yo, p2 tog) twice, k4, (yo, p2 tog) 3 times, k4.

Row 7—A, yo, ssk, k4, (yo, p2 tog) twice, (p1, k1) in next st, yo, p2 tog, yo, (p1, k1) in last st. * Turn. K3, yo, p2 tog. Turn. Yo, p2 tog, yo, k2, yo, (p1, k1) in last st. * (NOTE: The directions between * and * in this row make the second and the next 8 of the 10 picot points, and are repeated at the end of every subsequent odd-numbered row through Row 23, hereafter written "rep * — * ".)

Row 8—Bind off 5, yo, p2 tog, yo, k2, (yo, p2 tog) twice, k3, p2 tog-b, yo, k1, (yo, p2 tog) twice, k4.

Row 9—A, k2, yo, ssk, k2, (yo, p2 tog) twice, k2, (p1, k1) in next st, yo, p2 tog, yo (p1, k1) in last st. Rep * — *.

Row 10—Bind off 5, yo, p2 tog, yo, k4, (yo, p2 tog) twice, k1, p2 tog-b, yo, k3, (yo, p2 tog) twice, k4.

Row 11—A, k4, yo, ssk, (yo, p2 tog) twice, k4, (p1, k1) in next st, yo, p2 tog, yo, (p1, k1) in last st. Rep * — *.

Row 12—Bind off 5, yo, p2 tog, yo, k6, (yo, p2 tog) 3 times, k4, (yo, p2 tog) twice, k4.

Row 13—A, k3, k2 tog, yo, k1, (yo, p2 tog) twice, k6, (p1, k1) in next st, yo, p2 tog, yo, (p1, k1) in last st. Rep * — *.

Row 14—Bind off 5, yo, p2 tog, yo, k8, (yo, p2 tog) twice, k2, yo, p2 tog, k2, (yo, p2 tog) twice, k4.

Row 15—A, k1, k2 tog, yo, k3, (yo, p2 tog) twice, k8, (p1, k1) in next st, yo, p2 tog, yo, (p1, k1) in last st. Rep * — *.

Row 16—Bind off 5, yo, p2 tog, yo, p3 tog, k7, (yo, p2 tog) twice, k4, (yo, p2 tog) 3 times, k4.

Row 17—A, yo, ssk, k4, (yo, p2 tog) twice, k6, k2 tog, k1, yo, p2 tog, yo, (p1, k1) in last st. Rep * — *.

Row 18—Bind off 5, yo, p2 tog, yo, p3 tog, k5, (yo, p2 tog) twice, k3, p2 tog-b, yo, k1, (yo, p2 tog) twice, k4.

Row 19—A, k2, yo, ssk, k2, (yo, p2 tog) twice, k4, k2 tog, k1, yo, p2 tog, yo, (p1, k1) in last st. Rep * — *.

Row 20—Bind off 5, yo, p2 tog, yo, p3 tog, k3, (yo, p2 tog) twice, k1, p2 tog-b, yo, k3, (yo, p2 tog) twice, k4.

Row 21—A, k4, yo, ssk, (yo, p2 tog) twice, k2, k2 tog, k1, yo, p2 tog, yo, (p1, k1) in last st. Rep * — *.

Row 22—Bind off 5, yo, p2 tog, yo, p3 tog, k1, (yo, p2 tog) 3 times, k4, (yo, p2 tog) twice, k4.

Row 23—A, k3, k2 tog, yo, k1, (yo, p2 tog) twice, k2 tog, k1, yo, p2 tog, yo, (p1, k1) in last st. Rep * — *.

Row 24—Bind off 5, yo, (p2 tog) twice, (yo, p2 tog) twice, k2, yo, p2 tog, k2, (yo, p2 tog) twice, k4.

Row 25—A, k1, k2 tog, yo, k3, (yo, p2 tog) twice, sl 1—k2 tog—psso, k1.

Row 26—K2 tog, (yo, p2 tog) twice, k4, (yo, p2 tog) 3 times, k4.

Row 27—A, yo, ssk, k4, (yo, p2 tog) twice, k1.

Row 28—K1, (yo, p2 tog) twice, k3, p2 tog-b, yo, k1, (yo, p2 tog) twice, k4.

Row 29—A, k2, yo, ssk, k2, (yo, p2 tog) twice, k1.

Row 30—K1, (yo, p2 tog) twice, k1, p2 tog-b, yo, k3, (yo, p2 tog) twice, k4.

Repeat Rows 1–30.

Special Note on possible "mistake points": Rows 16, 18, 20, and 22 have a "p3 tog" in place of the second "p2 tog". Row 24 has a double "p2 tog" with no yo in between. When making the picot points as in Row 7, be sure to place a yo on the needle immediately after the *second* turning.

Chinese Edging

Whether this elaborate and beautiful pattern really originated in China is perhaps doubtful. But it was known as Chinese Edging to the European and American knitters of the 19th century, and so its name remains. Because the directions are long, each row is broken down here into various component parts, to prevent the knitter's getting "lost" in the middle of an interminable row. The Border, given separately, is worked on the first 12 sts of each odd-numbered row and the last 12 sts of each even-numbered row; the Border itself is a simple 6-row construction that is repeated 9 times throughout a single pattern repeat. The faggoted edge with its picot points incorporates three different "turning rows", which first appear in Rows 10, 12, and 14. The material between the asterisks of Row 10 is repeated in Rows 16, 22, 32, 38; the material between the asterisks of Row 12 is repeated in Rows 18, 24, 34, 40; the material between the asterisks of Row 14 is repeated in Rows 20, 26, 28, 30, 36, 42. It is important to notice that in the first two cases (Rows 10 and 12) this material *finishes with a yo;* in the third case (Row 14) it does not.

Note also that the direction (k1, p1), in parentheses, always means (k1, p1) into the same single stitch, which will be sometimes a regular knit stitch and sometimes a yo.

Border—worked on 12 sts.

Border Row 1—K2, yo, p2 tog, k1, k2 tog, yo, k3, yo, p2 tog.
Border Row 2—Yo, p2 tog, k4, yo, k2 tog, yo, p2 tog, k2.
Border Row 3—K2, yo, p2 tog, k2, yo, k2 tog, k2, yo, p2 tog.
Border Row 4—Yo, p2 tog, k1, k2 tog, yo, k3, yo, p2 tog, k2.
Border Row 5—K2, yo, p2 tog, k4, yo, k2 tog, yo, p2 tog.
Border Row 6—Yo, p2 tog, k2, yo, k2 tog, k2, yo, p2 tog, k2.

Cast on 14 sts and knit one row.

Row 1—Border Row 1, (k1, p1) into each of the last 2 sts.
Row 2—K4, Border Row 2.
Row 3—Border Row 3, (k1, p1), k2, (k1, p1).
Row 4—K3, yo, p2 tog, yo, k1, Border Row 4.
Row 5—Border Row 5, (k1, p1), k1, yo, p2 tog, k2, (k1, p1).
Row 6—Bind off 3, (yo, p2 tog) twice, yo, k1, Border Row 6.
Row 7—Border Row 1, (k1, p1), k1, (yo, p2 tog) twice, (k1, p1).
Row 8—K2, (yo, p2 tog) 3 times, yo, k1, Border Row 2.
Row 9—Border Row 3, k1, (k1, p1), (yo, p2 tog) 3 times, k1, (k1, p1).
Row 10—* K3, (yo, p2 tog) 3 times; turn; (yo, p2 tog) 3 times, k2, (k1, p1); turn;
    bind off 3, (yo, p2 tog) 3 times, yo, * k3, Border Row 4.
Row 11—Border Row 5, k3, (k1, p1), (yo, p2 tog) 3 times, (k1, p1).
Row 12—* K2, (yo, p2 tog) 3 times; turn; (yo, p2 tog) 3 times, k1, (k1, p1); turn;
    k3, (yo, p2 tog) 3 times, yo, * k5, Border Row 6.
Row 13—Border Row 1, k5, (k1, p1), (yo, p2 tog) 3 times, k2, (k1, p1).
Row 14—* Bind off 3, (yo, p2 tog) 3 times; turn; (yo, p2 tog) 3 times, (k1, p1);
    turn; k2, (yo, p2 tog) 3 times, * yo, k7, Border Row 2.
Row 15—Border Row 3, k7, (k1, p1), (yo, p2 tog) 3 times, k1, (k1, p1).
Row 16—Repeat * — * of *Row 10;* k9, Border Row 4.
Row 17—Border Row 5, k9, (k1, p1), (yo, p2 tog) 3 times, (k1, p1).
Row 18—Repeat * — * of *Row 12;* k11, Border Row 6.
Row 19—Border Row 1, k11, (k1, p1), (yo, p2 tog) 3 times, k2, (k1, p1).
Row 20—Repeat * — * of *Row 14;* yo, k13, Border Row 2.
Row 21—Border Row 3, k13, (k1, p1), (yo, p2 tog) 3 times, k1, (k1, p1).
Row 22—Repeat * — * of *Row 10;* k15, Border Row 4.
Row 23—Border Row 5, k15, (k1, p1), (yo, p2 tog) 3 times, (k1, p1).
Row 24—Repeat * — * of *Row 12;* k17, Border Row 6.
Row 25—Border Row 1, k1, (yo, k2 tog) 8 times, yo, (k1, p1) (yo, p2 tog) 3 times,
    k2, (k1, p1).
Row 26—[Repeat * — * of *Row 14;* turn; (yo, p2 tog) 3 times, k1, (k1, p1); turn;
    k3, (yo, p2 tog) 3 times, yo, sl 1—k2 tog—psso,] k17, Border Row 2.
Row 27—Border Row 3, k16, k2 tog, k1, (yo, p2 tog) 3 times, k2, (k1, p1).
Row 28—Repeat [to] of *Row 26;* k15, Border Row 4.
Row 29—Border Row 5, k14, k2 tog, k1, (yo, p2 tog) 3 times, k2, (k1, p1).
Row 30—Repeat * — * of *Row 14;* yo, sl 1—k2 tog—psso, k13, Border Row 6.
Row 31—Border Row 1, k12, k2 tog, k1, (yo, p2 tog) 3 times, k1, (k1, p1).
Row 32—Repeat * — * of *Row 10;* sl 1—k2 tog—psso, k11, Border Row 2.
Row 33—Border Row 3, k10, k2 tog, k1, (yo, p2 tog) 3 times, (k1, p1).
Row 34—Repeat * — * of *Row 12;* sl 1—k2 tog—psso, k9, Border Row 4.

Row 35—Border Row 5, k8, k2 tog, k1, (yo, p2 tog) 3 times, k2, (k1, p1).

Row 36—Repeat * — * of *Row 14;* yo, sl 1—k2 tog—psso, k7, Border Row 6.

Row 37—Border Row 1, k6, k2 tog, k1, (yo, p2 tog) 3 times, k1, (k1, p1).

Row 38—Repeat * — * of *Row 10;* sl 1—k2 tog—psso, k5, Border Row 2.

Row 39—Border Row 3, k4, k2 tog, k1, (yo, p2 tog) 3 times, (k1, p1).

Row 40—Repeat * — * of *Row 12;* sl 1—k2 tog—psso, k3, Border Row 4.

Row 41—Border Row 5, k2, k2 tog, k1, (yo, p2 tog) 3 times, k2, (k1, p1).

Row 42—Repeat * — * of *Row 14;* yo, sl 1—k2 tog—psso, k1, Border Row 6.

Row 43—Border Row 1, k2 tog, k1, (yo, p2 tog) 3 times, k1, (k1, p1).

Row 44—K3, (yo, p2 tog) 3 times, yo, k2 tog, Border Row 2.

Row 45—Border Row 3, k2 tog, (yo, p2 tog) 3 times, k2, (k1, p1).

Row 46—Bind off 3, (yo, p2 tog) 3 times, k1, Border Row 4.

Row 47—Border Row 5, sl 1—k2 tog—psso, (yo, p2 tog) twice, (k1, p1).

Row 48—K2, (yo, p2 tog) twice, k1, Border Row 6.

Row 49—Border Row 1, sl 1—k2 tog—psso, yo, p2 tog, k1, (k1, p1).

Row 50—K3, yo, p2 tog, k1, Border Row 2.

Row 51—Border Row 3, sl 1—k2 tog—psso, k2, (k1, p1).

Row 52—Bind off 3, k1, Border Row 4.

Row 53—Border Row 5, k2.

Row 54—K2, Border Row 6.

Repeat Rows 1–54.

Great-Grandmother's Edging

This is the edging that goes with the famous antique bedspread pattern called Great-Grandmother's Bedspread, otherwise known as The Garden-Plot Square. The bedspread is knitted in squares, each square being worked diagonally from one corner to the opposite corner, with a single embossed leaf at the start and a row of embossed leaves across the widest diagonal. The squares are sewn or crocheted together with four of the single leaves adjoining, and thus can be made any size, depending on the number of squares worked. This beautiful bedspread was very popular around the turn of the century, and many American families still treasure one that came from the hands of a real great-grandmother.

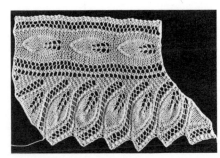

Great-Grandmother's Edging

Cast on 45 sts and knit one row.

Row 1 (Right side)—Sl 1, k3, yo, k2 tog, p8, k1, yo, k2 tog, yo, k3, yo, k2 tog, p1, yo, p1, k2, yo, k2 tog, p1, ssk, k5, k2 tog, p1, k2, yo, k2 tog, k2. (45 sts)

Row 2—Sl 1, k3, yo, k2 tog, k1, p7, k3, yo, k2 tog, k1, p1, k3, yo, k2 tog, k4, yo, k2 tog, k9, yo, k2 tog, k2. (45 sts)

Row 3—Sl 1, k3, yo, k2 tog, p3, yo, k1, yo, p4, k1, yo, k2 tog, yo, k4, yo, k2 tog, p1, yo, k1, yo, p1, k2, yo, k2 tog, p1, k7, p1, k2, yo, k2 tog, k2. (50 sts)

Row 4—Sl 1, k3, yo, k2 tog, k1, p7, k3, yo, k2 tog, k1, p3, k3, yo, k2 tog, k5, yo, k2 tog, k3, p3, k5, yo, k2 tog, k2. (50 sts)

Row 5—Sl 1, k3, yo, k2 tog, p3, (k1, yo) twice, k1, p4, k1, yo, k2 tog, yo, k5, yo, k2 tog, p1, (k1, yo) twice, k1, p1, k2, yo, k2 tog, p1, ssk, k3, k2 tog, p1, k2, yo, k2 tog, k2. (53 sts)

Row 6—Sl 1, k3, yo, k2 tog, (k1, p5, k3, yo, k2 tog) twice, k6, yo, k2 tog, k3, p5, k5, yo, k2 tog, k2. (53 sts)

Row 7—Sl 1, k3, yo, k2 tog, p3, k2, yo, k1, yo, k2, p4, k1, yo, k2 tog, yo, k6, yo, k2 tog, p1, k2, yo, k1, yo, k2, p1, k2, yo, k2 tog, p1, ssk, k1, k2 tog, p1, k2, yo, k2 tog, k2. (56 sts)

Row 8—Sl 1, k3, yo, k2 tog, k1, p3, k3, yo, k2 tog, k1, p7, k3, yo, k2 tog, k7, yo, k2 tog, k3, p7, k5, yo, k2 tog, k2. (56 sts)

Row 9—Sl 1, k3, yo, k2 tog, p3, k3, yo, k1, yo, k3, p4, k1, yo, k2 tog, yo, k7, yo, k2 tog, p1, k3, yo, k1, yo, k3, p1, k2, yo, k2 tog, p1, sl 1—k2 tog—psso, p1, k2, yo, k2 tog, k2. (59 sts)

Row 10—Sl 1, k3, yo, k2 tog, k1, p1, k3, yo, k2 tog, k1, p9, k3, yo, k2 tog, k8, yo, k2 tog, k3, p9, k5, yo, k2 tog, k2. (59 sts)

Row 11—Sl 1, k3, yo, k2 tog, p3, k9, p4, k1, yo, k2 tog, yo, k2, yo, k2 tog, p2, k2, yo, k2 tog, p1, k9, p1, k2, yo, k2 tog, p1, k8. (60 sts)

Row 12—Sl first st and bind off 3 sts, k4, pass 4 sts over the last st worked, k3, yo, k2 tog, k1, p9, k3, yo, k2 tog, k4, (yo, k2 tog, k3) twice, p9, k5, yo, k2 tog, k2. (53 sts)

Row 13—Sl 1, k3, yo, k2 tog, p3, ssk, k5, k2 tog, p4, k1, yo, k2 tog, yo, k3, yo, k2 tog, p1, yo, p1, k2, yo, k2 tog, p1, ssk, k5, k2 tog, p1, k2, yo, k2 tog, k2. (51 sts)

Row 14—Sl 1, k3, yo, k2 tog, k1, p7, k3, yo, k2 tog, k1, p1, k3, yo, k2 tog, k4, yo, k2 tog, k3, p7, k5, yo, k2 tog, k2. (51 sts)

Row 15—Sl 1, k3, yo, k2 tog, p3, k7, p4, k1, yo, k2 tog, yo, k4, yo, k2 tog, p1, yo, k1, yo, p1, k2, yo, k2 tog, p1, k7, p1, k2, yo, k2 tog, k2. (54 sts)

Row 16—Sl 1, k3, yo, k2 tog, k1, p7, k3, yo, k2 tog, k1, p3, k3, yo, k2 tog, k5, yo, k2 tog, k3, p7, k5, yo, k2 tog, k2. (54 sts)

Row 17—Sl 1, k3, yo, k2 tog, p3, ssk, k3, k2 tog, p4, k1, yo, k2 tog, yo, k5, yo, k2 tog, p1, (k1, yo) twice, k1, p1, k2, yo, k2 tog, p1, ssk, k3, k2 tog, p1, k2, yo, k2 tog, k2. (53 sts)

Row 18—Sl 1, k3, yo, k2 tog, (k1, p5, k3, yo, k2 tog) twice, k6, yo, k2 tog, k3, p5, k5, yo, k2 tog, k2. (53 sts)

Row 19—Sl 1, k3, yo, k2 tog, p3, ssk, k1, k2 tog, p4, k1, yo, k2 tog, yo, k6, yo, k2 tog, p1, k2, yo, k1, yo, k2, p1, k2, yo, k2 tog, p1, ssk, k1, k2 tog, p1, k2, yo, k2 tog, k2. (52 sts)

Row 20—Sl 1, k3, yo, k2 tog, k1, p3, k3, yo, k2 tog, k1, p7, k3, yo, k2 tog, k7, yo, k2 tog, k3, p3, k5, yo, k2 tog, k2. (52 sts)

Row 21—Sl 1, k3, yo, k2 tog, p3, sl 1—k2 tog—psso, p4, k1, yo, k2 tog, yo, k7, yo, k2 tog, p1, k3, yo, k1, yo, k3, p1, k2, yo, k2 tog, p1, sl 1—k2 tog—psso, p1, k2, yo, k2 tog, k2. (51 sts)

Row 22—Sl 1, k3, yo, k2 tog, k1, p1, k3, yo, k2 tog, k1, p9, k3, yo, k2 tog, k8, yo, k2 tog, k3, p1, k5, yo, k2 tog, k2. (51 sts)

Row 23—Sl 1, k3, yo, k2 tog, p8, k1, yo, k2 tog, yo, k2, yo, k2 tog, p2, k2, yo, k2 tog, p1, k9, p1, k2, yo, k2 tog, p1, k8. (52 sts)

Row 24—Sl first st and bind off 3 sts, k4, pass 4 sts over the last st worked, k3, yo, k2 tog, k1, p9, k3, yo, k2 tog, k4, yo, k2 tog, k3, yo, k2 tog, k9, yo, k2 tog, k2. (45 sts)

Repeat Rows 1–24.

BIBLIOGRAPHY

Arnold, Eleanor. *Book of Crocheting and Knitting.* Glasco Lace Thread Co., Glasco, Conn. 1889

Art of Knitting, The. Butterick Publishing Co., London & New York, 1897

Barnes, Sarah. *Manual of Knitting and Crocheting.* Wm. H. Horstmann Co., Philadelphia, 1936

Caulfeild, S. F. A., and Saward, Blanche. *Dictionary of Needlework.* A. W. Cowan, England

Croly, Jane. *Knitting and Crochet.* A. L. Burt, New York, 1885

de Dillmont, Thérèse. *Encyclopedia of Needlework.* DMC Library, Mulhouse, France, 1924

Fleisher's Knitting and Crocheting Manual. Fleisher Yarns, Philadelphia, 1910

Hall, Mary E. *The Starlight Manual of Knitting and Crocheting.* Nonantum Worsted Co., Boston, 1887

Kerzman, Marie Louise. *Knitting: How to Knit and What to Knit.* Henry Bistow, Brooklyn, N.Y., 1884

Knitting, IIIrd Series. DMC Library, Mulhouse, France

Lambert, Miss. *The Hand-Book of Needlework.* Wiley & Putnam, New York, 1842

Mee, Cornelia. *A Manual of Knitting, Netting, and Crochet.* David Bogue, London, 1844

Merryman, Effie N. *Home Decorative Work.* Buckeye Publishing Co., Minneapolis, 1891

Mrs. Leach's Fancy Work Basket, Vols. I–VI. P. S. Cartwright, London, 1887

Niles, Eva M. *The Ladies' Guide to Elegant Lace Patterns, etc., Done With Common Steel Needles.* Proctor Bros., Gloucester, Mass. 1884

Norbury, James, and Agutter, Margaret. *Odhams Encyclopedia of Knitting.* Odhams Books Ltd., London

Nuova Enciclopedia dei Lavori Femminili. Edizioni Mani di Fata, Milan, 1955

Orr, Anne. *Decorative Bedspreads—Knitting.* Nashville, Tenn. 1941

Patterns for Knitting, 4 vols. Japan-Vogue, Tokyo

Reade, Dorothy. *25 Original Knitting Designs.* Eugene, Oregon, 1968

Robinson, Belle. *The Priscilla Cotton Knitting Book.* Priscilla Publishing Co., Boston, 1918

Schachenmayr. *Das Neue Strick- und Häkelbuch.* Otto Maier Verlag, Ravensburg, 1968

Schumacker, Anna. *The Columbia Book of Yarns.* Columbia Yarns, Philadelphia, 1918

Seligman & Hughes. *Domestic Needlework.* Country Life, England, 1926

Stevens, Mrs. Ann S. *The Ladies' Complete Guide to Crochet, Fancy Knitting, and Needlework.* Garrett & Co., New York, 1854

Tillotson, Marjory. *The Complete Knitting Book.* Sir Isaac Pitman & Sons Ltd., London, 1947

Weldon's Practical Needlework. Weldon's Ltd., London

INDEX